Choices

Your feedback is welcome. Please take the time to send comments and suggestions to the author:

E-mail: b_shebib@douglas.bc.ca

Bob Shebib
P.O. Box 2503
New Westminster, BC
Canada
V3L 5B2
Phone (604) 527-5139

Customized workshops and seminars based on this book are available. Please contact the author at the above E-mail or mailing addresses.

Choices

Counseling Skills for Social Workers and Other Professionals

Bob Shebib

Douglas College

Allyn and Bacon

Boston   New York   San Francisco
Mexico City   Montreal   Toronto   London   Madrid   Munich   Paris
Hong Kong   Singapore   Tokyo   Cape Town   Sydney

Vice President, Editorial Director: *Karen Hanson*
Series Editor: *Patricia Quinlin*
Editorial Assistant: *AnneMarie Kennedy*
Marketing Manager: *Megan St. Peter*
Production Editor: *Christine Tridente*
Composition Buyer: *Linda Cox*
Editorial Production Service: *Chestnut Hill Enterprises, Inc.*
Electronic Composition: *Peggy Cabot, Cabot Computer Services*
Manufacturing Buyer: *JoAnne Sweeney*
Cover Administrator: *Kristina Mose-Libon*

For related titles and support materials, visit our online catalog at
www.ablongman.com.

Library of Congress Cataloging-in-Publication Data
Shebib, Bob.
    Choices : counseling skills for social workers / Bob Shebib.
      p. cm.
    Includes bibliographical references and index.
    ISBN 0-205-34247-7
      1. Social case work. 2. Interviewing in social service. 3. Counseling.
    4. Helping behavior. 5. Confidential communications—Social case work.
    6. Social workers—Professional ethics. I. Title.
    HV40.35 .S54 2002
    361'.06—dc21   2002018343

Printed in the United States of America

10 9 8 7 6 5 4 3   07 06 05

To Joyce

CONTENTS

Preface   xi

Acknowledgments   xxi

1 An Introduction to the Skills and Process of Counseling   1

An Overview of Counseling   1
The Scope of Counseling   2
The Need for Versatility   5
Values and Ethics   8
Skill Clusters   8
Failure in Counseling   14
The Phases of Counseling   20
Summary   31
Exercises   32

2 Ethics, Values, and Self-Awareness   35

Professional Behavior   35
Working with Competence   51
Self-Awareness   54
Summary   62
Exercises   63

3 Relationship: The Foundation for Change   69

What Is a Counseling Relationship?   69
Creating a Counseling Relationship   70
The Contract   75
Immediacy   79
Ending the Counseling Relationship   89
Summary   91
Exercises   93

4 **Listening: The Basis for Understanding   97**

    The Challenge of Listening   97

    Active Listening   102

    Summary   122

    Exercises   123

5 **Interviewing Skills: The Search for Meaning   126**

    Questioning   126

    Concreteness   138

    Key Questions for Every Interview   145

    Interview Transitions   150

    Summary   154

    Exercises   157

6 **The Pursuit of Empathic Understanding   160**

    Emotions   160

    Empathy   169

    Summary   185

    Exercises   187

7 **Empowerment: The Purpose of Counseling   193**

    Empowerment and Change   193

    Motivating Clients   195

    Confronting Clients   200

    Helping Clients Think Differently   205

    Goal Setting   211

    Action Planning   216

    Summary   223

    Exercises   224

8 **Difficult Situations   227**

    Resistance   227

    Potentially Dangerous Clients   239

    Summary   255

    Exercises   256

9 **Variations with Selected Target Groups**   257

    Employment Counseling   257

    Counseling People with Mental Disorders   263

    Suicide Counseling   276

    Counseling HIV-Positive Clients and Clients with AIDS   280

    Brief Counseling   284

    Summary   289

    Exercises   290

10 **Cultural Diversity: The Future of Counseling**   292

    Context for Counseling Culturally Diverse Clients   292

    Cross-Cultural Understanding   295

    Key Elements of Cross-Cultural Understanding   301

    Counseling Immigrants and Multicultural Clients   308

    Spirituality and Counseling   311

    Cross-Cultural Competency   314

    Summary   320

    Exercises   321

APPENDIX 1   Code of Ethics of the National Association of Social Workers   323

    Preamble   325

    Purpose of the NASW Code of Ethics   325

    Ethical Principles   327

    Ethical Standards   329

APPENDIX 2   ACA Code of Ethics and Standards of Practice   345

    Code of Ethics   345

    Standards of Practice   365

APPENDIX 3   Glossary   371

References   379

Index   387

PREFACE

> *It is not for him to pride himself who loveth his own country, but rather for him who loveth the whole world. The earth is but one country, and mankind its citizens.*
>
> (Bahá'u'lláh)

Purpose

Choices: Counseling Skills for Social Workers and Other Professionals is a snapshot of my lifetime work in the fascinating and complex field of counseling. My intention is to provide a practical guide that assists professionals in the helping disciplines to develop knowledge, skills, and attitudes for effective interviewing and counseling. Although the book is intended primarily as a textbook for introductory counseling and interviewing courses, it is also designed as a reference text for more advanced practitioners. *Choices* is intended for students of counseling and professionals in disciplines such as social work and youth counseling. It may also be of interest to people in allied disciplines such as psychology, criminology, teaching, and nursing who wish to develop their interviewing and counseling skills.

Choices contributes to the development of professional competence in four ways:

1. It introduces basic concepts and models to help learners understand the theory and reasoning behind the use of skills.
2. It provides a range of realistic examples that illustrate concepts in action.
3. It contains challenging exercises that promote skill development, conceptual understanding, and self-awareness.
4. It emphasizes the notion of a range of skill choices for interviewing, rather than rules and recipes.

I believe in the importance of intelligent choice in the use of skills and strategies, which requires social workers and other professionals to develop a wide range of practice skills that are used based on the unique needs of clients and situations as well as supported theory (science) and proven practice. *Choices* emphasizes cultural competence by encouraging workers to consider culture as a major component of rational choice. Clearly, this is true when working with clients who are culturally different, but because everyone is unique, with his or her own mix of values and beliefs, culture is a variable for work with all clients.

When working with clients from visible minorities and those who are marginalized by poverty or discrimination, examination of the sociopolitical realities that frame their circumstances becomes crucial. Social workers need to develop sufficient self-awareness to escape or manage any tendency to be culture-bound, for example, assuming that all clients share their values, perspectives, and ambitions, or, worse still, that their clients' differences represent deficiencies. By sustaining a multicultural perspective that recognizes and prizes diversity, social workers can avoid the pitfalls of ethnocentrism (the belief that one's one views and culture are superior).

There is substantial research that documents the fact that traditional counseling approaches and techniques are ineffective or limited when used with racial and ethnic minority populations (Sue, 1992). Commitment to a multicultural perspective will engage social workers in cooperative efforts with clients to mobilize strategies that more closely meet their clients' needs and worldview. It reminds them that their clients' communication styles, comfort with eye contact, or emotional disclosure, for example, are influenced by their culture. Clients do not always respond in the manner preferred by their counselors, nor do they necessarily need to do so. In fact, culturally competent workers will view cultural differences as opportunities to widen their horizons and deepen their versatility. They remember to be humble enough to learn from their clients.

Central Values and Assumptions

Choices and Respect for Diversity

Diversity includes differences in such major variables as race, religion, age, sex, sexual orientation, physical and mental ability, economic capacity, language, culture, values, beliefs, preferences, and ways of thinking and behaving. This diversity of today's counseling caseloads requires that social workers and other professionals develop a range of interviewing and counseling skills. Competent workers are able to vary their style depending on the unique needs of different clients and situations. In simplest terms, the more choices workers have, the greater they are able to match their work to the needs and wants of their clients and the less they need to repeatedly use the same skill. Effective social workers can use particular skills, but they are wise enough to know when not to use them. Similarly, the goal of counseling is to help clients achieve versatility in their capacity to solve problems and achieve goals. Effective clients are also able to vary their responses based on the differing needs of situations.

All workers need to be aware of their own personal and cultural values and how they might affect their dealings with clients from different cultures, members of minority groups, and disempowered groups. They must be sensitive to ensure that they do not abuse their power when relating to marginalized groups who may have suffered economic, social, and political disadvantage.

Self-Awareness

Knowledge of self, including consciousness of one's values and beliefs and the impact of one's behavior on others, is a prerequisite for effective counseling. When workers lack self-awareness they may confuse their clients' feelings with their own, or they may assume that clients will feel as they do. When workers are unaware of their own needs, including those that are unmet, they risk unconsciously using their counseling relationships to meet personal goals instead of client goals. Without self-awareness, they will be ignorant of those areas of practice in which they are competent and those in which it will be difficult for them to work with objectivity.

Everyone, including professional social workers, has personal values and beliefs. Competent professionals know themselves, and they ensure that their values do not become a burden to their clients. They accept that exploring and reflecting on one's competence and the limits of one's role and expertise are fundamental to professional practice. For professional counselors, this process of self-examination continues throughout their careers.

Self-Determination

Whenever possible, counseling should draw on the expertise of clients to participate in decisions related to the goals and process of counseling. To facilitate this involvement, workers will need to develop comfort and ability to openly discuss their work and methodology with clients. By so doing, the work of counseling is demystified. Moreover, commitment to client self-determination restrains workers from unhelpful behaviors, such as advice giving and abuse of power or control.

By promoting client self-determination, social workers use a strengths approach that empowers clients by assuming their capacity to cope and change. In practice this means

> believing that people are capable of making their own choices and decisions. It means not only that human beings possess the strengths and potential to resolve their own difficult life situations, but also that they increase their strength and contribute to society by doing so. The role of the social worker in clinical practice is to nourish, encourage, assist, enable, support, stimulate, and unleash the strengths within people, to illuminate the strengths available to people in their own environments, and to promote equity and justice at all levels of society. To do that, the social worker helps clients articulate the nature of their situations, identify what they want, explore alternatives for achieving those wants, and achieve them (Cowger, 1994:264).

Although it is beyond the scope of this book to fully explore the necessity of social advocacy, social workers should consider their responsibility to extend beyond their role as counselors to social and political action. As advocates for social justice, social workers strive to reduce gender, cultural, and other bases for discrimination. They promote changes in social policy as well as modification in the functioning of formal organizations and institutions to better meet the needs of clients.

The Nature of Counseling and Interviewing

Interviewing is an information-gathering process that is free from any conscious attempt to influence the subject. Interviewing is the foundation of counseling, a process that goes beyond interviewing to enable clients to cope with the problems of daily living. Social workers negotiate a working relationship with clients to accomplish some agreed-on purpose, such as assisting clients to make decisions, deal with painful feelings, solve problems, or learn new skills.

Counseling is a complex blend of skill, attitude, and art. Although core skills can be learned and practiced, they are not recipes. The ideas in this book are presented as a starting point with the hope that they will be customized and adapted to fit individual worker–client interactions. Skill and technique can be impressive, sometimes even appearing to be magical, but alone they are insufficient. Workers need to be genuine, they need to have warm and caring regard for their clients, and they need to recognize the inherent worth of people. To some extent these beliefs and values can be shaped by professional training, but to a greater extent they must come from the hearts and souls of workers. Kadushin discusses the important mix of skill and feeling:

> Many might say that if they had to choose between feeling and technique they would choose feeling as the more important prerequisite. Perhaps so, but if one has to make a choice between these qualifications, an injustice has already been done to the client. It should be possible to offer the client an interviewer who is both attitudinally correct and technically proficient (1990:xii).

The counseling model featured in *Choices* rests on the assumption that counseling and interviewing are most effective when:

- Interviews and counseling relationships have a clear contract and purpose.
- Working relationships with a clear understanding of roles are established.
- A climate of trust and safety in taking risks is established.
- Workers' responses are genuine, i.e., based on real feelings and attitudes.
- Workers respect their clients' independence and their right to self-determination.

The Four Phases of Counseling

In this book, counseling relationships and interviews are described as evolving through four phases: preliminary, beginning, action, and ending. Each phase involves common as well as unique tasks and skills. For example, the beginning phase usually focuses on relationship development and problem exploration. Predictably, skills in developing relationships such as active listening will be favored, whereas skills such as confrontation are not recommended. In contrast, the action phase focuses on helping clients develop new perspectives, set goals, and implement change strategies; thus, skills such as reframing and confronting may be used more extensively in this phase. In Chapter 1 the model will be described in more detail and elements of the preliminary and ending phases will be discussed.

The four phases are developmental, with success at one phase dependent in part on success at previous phases. Thus, clients are more willing to accept confrontation if a solid relationship or trust is present. In general, reference to the four-phase model allows workers to make some predictions about the climate of the interview and what skills and tasks will be in the foreground at different points. However, practitioners must be cautious in applying the model to individual counseling interviews, in which the sequence of events may differ sharply from the model.

Structure of the Book

The book is divided into ten chapters.

Chapter 1 explores the basic nature of counseling skills and strategies. In this chapter four major skill clusters are introduced: relationship building, exploring/probing, empowering, and challenging. A four-phase model of counseling (preliminary, beginning, action, and ending) is proposed as a model for understanding the evolution of the counseling relationship.

Chapter 2 introduces readers to the basic concepts of ethics, values, and self-awareness.

Chapter 3 examines the helping relationship and considers the core conditions necessary for counseling to be effective.

Chapter 4, Chapter 5, and **Chapter 6** explore the active listening skills of attending, silence, paraphrasing and summarizing (Chapter 4), questioning (Chapter 5), and empathy (Chapter 6).

Chapter 7 is concerned with action phase skills that motivate clients to think differently and to make changes in their lives.

Chapter 8 presents information for working in difficult situations, such as when clients are resistant or potentially violent.

Chapter 9 looks at strategies for working with various populations, including those who are seeking work, dealing with mental disorders, contemplating suicide, and coping with an HIV-positive diagnosis or AIDS.

Chapter 10 explores important concepts and issues related to counseling clients from different cultures. The inclusion of spirituality as a topic in this chapter reflects growing interest and acceptance of the importance of spiritual issues in counseling.

Appendix 1 is the National Association of Social Workers' Code of Ethics.

Appendix 2 is the American Counseling Association's Code of Ethics and Standards of Practice.

Features

People learn in different ways, so this book includes a range of features designed to assist learners to understand at cognitive, emotional, and behavioral levels. Each chapter contains the following elements:

Chapter Preview: key concepts that will be addressed in the chapter

Summary: a short review at the end of each chapter that highlights important ideas

Conversations: a unique addition, offering debate or opinions on frequently asked questions

Sample Interviews: annotated interview excerpts that illustrate and explain chapter concepts

Exercises: end-of-chapter reflective questions that are designed to give readers practice in the development of skills, or questions framed to promote self-awareness and creative thinking

Note to Students

If you are studying this book as part of a course on counseling skills, you will probably have the opportunity to develop skill competence in a number of different ways, including:

- watching instructor demonstrations
- conducting practice interviews using role-played or (preferably) real-life scenarios
- completing the chapter exercises
- receiving feedback and evaluation from instructors and student colleagues who observe your work
- using audio and video recordings to understand and assess your verbal and nonverbal responses
- working with clients

In most counseling skills courses, learning groups are used to practice skills. Usually, these learning groups use classroom simulations and practice interviews, in which you assume the roles of client, counselor, and observer. Each of these roles offers unique challenges and opportunities for learning.

Being a Client

The client's role offers a powerful opportunity for you to understand the feelings and expectations that clients may bring to the session. You may find that your reactions are similar to those that clients experience, including:

- ambivalence about sharing feelings or details about personal issues
- feelings of vulnerability, including fear of being judged, embarrassed, or ridiculed

As a client, it will be up to you to control how much you wish to disclose; however, by taking reasonable risks, your learning opportunities and insights are enhanced.

Being a Counselor

When you are asked to practice your newly learned skills as a counselor you may feel clumsy and insecure. As a counselor you will be encouraged to change established communication patterns or to experiment with new skills and strategies, and this can be unsettling. As a student with limited training, you may be reluctant to ask questions that seem to invade the privacy of your colleagues. When dealing with sensitive issues, you may fear that your lack of experience may damage your clients. You may fear that your colleagues will judge you as inept. When you are observed by others, the intense focus on your work can be unsettling and anxiety provoking. These reactions are common, and you will probably find that your colleagues feel the same way. For most professionals it takes many years of practice and study to become competent and comfortable using a full range of skills. What is important is that you persist and avoid the natural temptation to stick with familiar patterns of communicating. Skills that seem awkward at first may, with practice, become part of your natural and preferred style.

Minuchin and Fishman (1981) offer this interesting conclusion: "Only a person who has mastered technique and then contrived to forget it can become an expert . . ." (p. 1). Elsewhere, they observe that:

> Unfortunately, the teaching of new skills often disorganizes the beginning student. As in any learning or relearning process, the student finds himself concentrating so much on the trees that he misses the forest. . . . As in the training of the samurai, the student needs a number of years to achieve expertise and many more to achieve spontaneity (Minuchin & Fishman, 1981:10).

Being an Observer

Student observers are responsible for watching the interview and for providing feedback to other student colleagues who are practicing their counseling skills. You may be reluctant to offer feedback, perhaps worrying that your remarks will generate anger or hurt feelings. The observer's role gives you an excellent opportunity to develop and practice giving feedback.

Helpful feedback is energizing and does not detract from another person's self-esteem. As people learn and practice interviewing and counseling skills they may feel vulnerable and awkward, hence the importance of remaining sensitive to their emotional and psychological needs while balancing their needs for information and correction. Feedback may be of two types: supportive or corrective.

Supportive feedback reinforces or acknowledges achievements. "Catch them doing something right." However obvious this idea seems, many people are problem oriented and they fail to recognize strengths. Consider how you respond differently when your strengths are acknowledged than when your weaknesses are targeted. Supportive feedback, to be effective, must be genuine (true), and delivered without rescuing or patronizing. If you lie to others in order to avoid hurting them, your credibility as a source of feedback will diminish.

Corrective feedback challenges others to examine or change behavior. Before giving corrective feedback, consider your relationship with the other person. If your relationship is based on trust and caring, corrective feedback has the potential to be effective. However, if your relationship is stressed, for example, in situations where there is unresolved conflict, corrective feedback is more likely to be perceived as an attack. If people think your feedback is harsh, demanding or controlling, there is a higher probability of their resisting.

Don't use corrective feedback as a means to control, impress, or to punish. Pay attention to your voice tone and other nonverbal behavior. Make sure that you avoid lecturing and pointing fingers. Timing and pacing are important. Supportive feedback is more useful when self-esteem is low. It's best to give feedback as soon as possible, but ensure that personal privacy is protected. Avoid overwhelming others by remembering that you do not have to accomplish everything at once. As a general rule, ask people to self-evaluate before offering your opinions. You may be surprised to find that they already have insight into the problem areas. Then, the number of areas for which you have to provide direct feedback is reduced.

Feedback has the most potential for success if it is invited and/or targeted to perceived areas of need. Contract with others to receive feedback. Ask questions such as: "Would you like me to offer my ideas on what happened?" or "Are there specific issues that you are concerned about?" When you work with others (clients or colleagues), don't forget individual differences. Some people prefer feedback to be direct and to the point. Others may prefer it "sandwiched" between positives. Some need time to reflect before responding or they may profit from visual and written illustrations.

People may have an immediate reaction to your feedback that differs from their reaction once they have had time to ponder what you have said. Thus, a person who responds defensively, or even with anger, may on reflection come to accept your input. The opposite can also be true: People who react favorably may develop other feelings such as resentment or confusion. Checking back during future encounters is one strategy for keeping abreast of others' reactions.

Finally, remember that giving helpful and caring feedback is one way of developing and strengthening relationships. If you are honest and supportive with others, you greatly increase the probability they will be honest and supportive with you when you ask for their helpful feedback.

Developing an Effective Learning Group

When you work with student colleagues in each of the three roles, it is helpful to candidly discuss your fears as well as your expectations of one another. You will need to work to develop a contract or agreement on how you will work together.

Practice interviews will be more powerful learning opportunities if they are based on real rather than role-played feelings and issues. Consequently, it will be important to establish a climate of safety, in which confidentiality will be respected. Some important principles to remember:

- Colleagues who are in the client's role are disclosing personal issues and feelings, so it is essential that their dignity and right to privacy are respected.
- Everyone has different capacities for intimacy. Don't expect that all members of a learning group will disclose at the same level. Accept individual differences.
- Learning the skills of counseling requires a certain willingness to give up familiar patterns of communication and to attempt new approaches. Expand your limits by taking appropriate risks to try new skills and be tolerant of colleagues who are engaged in similar risk taking.
- Expect that the process of learning and experimenting with new skills will result in a period of awkwardness and self-consciousness. For a time it may seem as though

your capacity to counsel others is regressing.

■ Feedback for others is an important part of learning. Therefore, try to make it easy for others to give you feedback and respond in a nondefensive manner. Help others give specific feedback by asking targeted questions.

Keeping a Personal Journal

A personal "for your eyes only" journal can be a significant adjunct to your learning. The journal is a tool for introspection that provides a private means for documenting and exploring your thoughts and feelings related to the development of your counseling skills. There are no rules for journal writing, other than the need to make entries on a regular basis and to try to avoid self-censorship.

Using This Book

If you are using *Choices* as part of a course on counseling, your teacher will propose a suggested reading schedule that structures your reading over the semester and he or she will assign or adapt the chapter exercises to fit your learning needs. Another way to use the book is on an "as you need it" basis and to use the index or chapter headings to research content that fits your needs. As well, you are encouraged to use other books, journals, and tools, such as Internet research, to supplement your learning. However, you should read this book (or any book) critically and seek to understand and explore the ideas and try them out, but don't forget that there is room for other perspectives.

Counseling Skills as a Way of Life

You may be surprised to discover that the skills of counseling are also the skills of effective everyday communication and that the process of developing your counseling competence begins to influence your personal relationships. As counseling skills become part of your style, you may find yourself becoming a little more inquisitive and more sensitive to the feelings of others. However, you may find that others in your life do not welcome the changes in your manner and style. When you change, others around you have to accommodate your changes. If you become more probing in your questions, they must be forthcoming with their answers. When you become more empathic, their feelings become more transparent. These changes move the relationship to a deeper level of intimacy, which may be frightening for some, particularly if the pace is too fast for their comfort level.

ACKNOWLEDGMENTS

Sincere thanks to the many people who assisted me to bring my ideas to publication. I am especially grateful to the talented people at Allyn and Bacon for their support and creative input including: Patricia Quinlin, Acquisitions Editor; Annemarie Kennedy, Editorial Assistant; Christine Tridente, Production Editor; Joel Gendron, Cover Designer have provided terrific assistance in the long process of bringing my ideas to publication. Special thanks to Myrna Breskin, Packager at Chestnut Hill Enterprises, for her meticulous handling of the final manuscript.

My colleagues Bob Martel, John Fox, and Sharon Smith assisted me by reviewing selected sections. I want to express special appreciation for their many helpful comments. I also appreciate the support and suggestions of other colleagues at Douglas College, Doug Estergaard, Julie Roper, Nancy Newman, and especially Dave Burgess who contributes ongoing thoughtful criticism. Thanks also to Ellen Edwards at NETWERRC and Roberta Neault for their support.

I have been aided by many reviewers who critically evaluated pre-publication drafts. I want them to know that their input was extremely useful and much appreciated. I want to acknowledge the contributions of the following reviewers: Kia J. Bentley, Virginia Commonwealth University; Joan DiGuilio, Youngstown State University; Jan Wrenn, Andrews University; Jeff Arbus, Sault College; Marilyn Jeske, Grant MacEwan College; and Lourdes A. D. de la Cruz, Sheridan College. I also wish to thank the faculty at Vancouver Community College, Joanne Rykers, Lee McLeod, Susan Runytu, and Sara Menzel, who have given me many helpful suggestions that have been incorporated in this book.

The students of the Community Social Service Worker program at Douglas College offered candid and helpful recommendations to me when I field-tested the ideas in this book. Similarly, Jim Edwards and the great team at Covenant House in Vancouver, BC, Canada offered insightful comments and suggestions.

This book is dedicated to Joyce Shebib, to whom I owe an enormous debt of gratitude. Her constant support, encouragement, and painstaking review of every chapter through many rewrites made the final product much better than it would have been otherwise.

1

An Introduction to the Skills and Process of Counseling

Preview

After reading this chapter you should be able to

- define the range of counseling activities
- list the people who provide counseling services
- explain why it is important for social workers to be versatile
- describe the necessary range of skill versatility
- classify the four skill clusters of counseling
- describe why counseling fails
- list the four phases of counseling
- summarize the developmental objectives of the four phases of counseling

An Overview of Counseling

Training as a Counselor

A large number of people at various levels of training are counselors, including social workers, psychologists, psychiatrists, and psychiatric nurses. Many counselors are members of professional associations such as the Canadian Association of Social Workers (CASW), the American Counseling Assocation (ACA), the National Association of Social Workers (NASW), and the American Psychological Association (APA). As members, they are subject to codes of ethics governing acceptable professional behavior. Membership in these associations usually requires a master's degree or a Ph.D.

Social workers generally have university training with a bachelor's degree in social work (B.S.W.) or a master's degree in social work (M.S.W.) In addition, they may have specialized training in specialty areas such as family therapy or group work. Social workers might work in private practice or be employed in hospitals, prisons, schools, or community social service agencies, for example, working with people who have drug addictions. Many social workers work for government agencies investigating incidents of child abuse and neglect.

In the United States, the National Association of Social Workers (NASW) recognizes and certifies social workers in a number of different areas including:

- NASW Specialty Certifications Program
- Academy of Certified Social Workers (ACSW)
- Qualified Clinical Social Worker (QCSW)
- Diplomate in Clinical Social Work (DCSW)

For these specialty certifications, a master's degree and several years of supervised practice experience are required. Further information can be obtained on-line at the NASW Web site, <http://www.naswdc.org>.

Counseling psychologists are usually qualified at the Ph.D. level, but some jurisdictions allow registration for those with a master's degree. Psychologists may work as counselors, or they may specialize in other areas such as in administering and interpreting psychological tests. Psychologists are often employed in private practice, but they also may work in settings such as prisons, hospitals, schools, and private industry.

Psychiatrists are medical doctors with advanced training in psychiatry. They are specialists in the treatment of people with mental disorders. Psychiatrists are the only counseling professionals who are licensed to prescribe medication. Psychiatric nurses generally have two to four years of training. Historically, they worked in psychiatric hospitals and wards, but, increasingly, they are working in community-based mental health settings.

Volunteers and paraprofessional counselors who have one to two years of university or college training also may provide counseling services. In addition, the professional counseling community is often supported or replaced by an array of self-help support groups. Frequently, counselors work with clients who are attending a self-help group such as Alcoholics Anonymous (AA) or Narcotics Anonymous (NA).

The Scope of Counseling

Counseling involves a time-limited relationship in which the worker helps clients increase their ability to deal with the demands of life. Typically, people seek or are referred for counseling because of some unmanageable crisis, such as the loss of a job, relationship problems, or feelings of distress. The immediate goal of counseling is to provide assistance so that people seeking help (clients) can gain some control over their problems. The long-term goal of counseling is to work with clients to restore or develop their ability to cope with the changing demands of their lives.

The focus of counseling depends on three variables: the needs and wants of the client, the mandate of the counseling setting, and the expertise or competence of the worker. Professional counselors know when their competence limits are exceeded and when they need to make an appropriate referral. They are also aware of their own needs and unresolved issues, and they refer clients to other professionals when they cannot work with reasonable objectivity. They accept that no one is qualified to work with all clients. Table 1.1 summarizes how counseling knowledge and skills evolve from beginning to advanced levels.

TABLE 1.1   Beginning to Advanced Level Social Workers

Beginning Level Social Workers	Advanced Level Social Workers
Basic use of core listening and responding skills	Exemplary use of broad range of listening and counseling skills and strategies; capacity to be creative to meet unique needs of individual clients
Sensitivity to overt nonverbal cues	Responsive to subtle nonverbal cues and themes
Basic content knowledge of field of practice	In-depth knowledge of current science and practice in the field; ability to analyze and adapt published material
Rudimentary understanding of self	Sophisticated knowledge of self, one's impact on others, and the ability to selectively use aspects of self to influence others
Struggle to manage biases and personal reactions	"Second nature" capacity to stay appropriately detached and in control of self
Tendency to "mimic" mentors and textbook responses	Capacity to customize approach; development of individual styles
Self-consciousness	Focus on clients
Tendency to want to fix, rescue, or solve client problems	Recognition of the need to empower clients to problem-solve

CONVERSATION **1.1**
Counseling and Psychotherapy

STUDENT: What's the difference between counseling and psychotherapy?

TEACHER: The terms *psychotherapy* and *counseling* are often used interchangeably to describe the application of specific skills to assist clients in a process of change. Both counseling and psychotherapy strive to help clients to learn skills, deal with feelings, and manage problems. In counseling and psychotherapy, appropriate relationships with clients are the medium for promoting change. In both psychotherapy and counseling, these relationships with clients are crucial to success. They provide an important foundation of safety and security for clients to undertake the change process.

Although there is no clear dividing line between the two terms, the major difference between counseling and psychotherapy is that psychotherapy tends to be more long-term than counseling, with an emphasis on severe emotional and behavioral difficulties or disorders. On the other hand, counseling is targeted toward assisting clients in managing situational problems.

The work of counseling may entail a broad range of activities, including:

- helping clients cope with painful feelings
- teaching clients new skills
- helping clients develop problem-solving skills
- mediating relationship communication difficulties
- aiding clients in identifying and accessing resources
- helping clients make decisions and implement action plans
- supporting or motivating clients

Interviewing skills are indispensable to effective counseling. The goal of **interviewing** is to acquire and organize relevant information through timely listening and responding skills. When the interview is used as an information-gathering process, interviewers do not try to promote change. However, clients may feel relief from sharing, and organizing their thoughts in response to a systematic interview may allow them to grow.

Good interviewers are comfortable with silence and know when to listen without interrupting. Workers who listen to clients give them a chance to air their feelings, and this step can be therapeutic in itself. Patient listening shows clients that workers are willing to accept them without judgment and without burdening them with quick-fix solutions to complex problems and feelings.

At the beginning of counseling sessions or interviews, silent listening may give workers valuable clues about the potential focus of the interview. Listening helps them understand something about their clients' priorities. It reveals which methods clients may have used and not used to try to solve their problems.

Good listeners also know when and how to respond. A range of skills, including paraphrasing, summarizing, questioning, and showing empathy, complete the foundation of effective listening. These skills enable helpers to focus and deepen the interview. Questions may be used to clarify meaning and to seek detail and example, whereas paraphrasing and summarizing responses are useful for confirming understanding and for sorting out important from less important information. A good interview involves methodical questioning and exploration of issues, a process that can help clients to clarify and organize their thoughts. Workers use empathy skills to confirm their understanding of the client's feelings.

Social Work and Counseling

One special feature that distinguishes social work counseling from that performed by other professionals is its dual focus on working with the individual as well as the environment. Social workers assume that individuals can only be understood in the context of their environment and they pay particular attention to the interaction of people and their environment. Like other professionals in the helping field, social workers may counsel clients to help them develop insight, problem-solve, deal with emotional pain, or enhance relationships. They may support clients by providing information, social skills training, or resources. Unique to social work is the important responsibility that the profession gives social workers to promote change or adaptation in social and political systems so that they can respond more effectively to the needs of clients. Specht (1990) emphasizes that one defining feature of social work must be its continuing mission to build better systems and communities that are structured to provide social support and helping networks to its clientele.

> It is a mission to deal with the enormous social problems under which our society staggers: the social isolation of our aged, the anomie experienced by our youth, the neglect and abuse of children, homelessness, drug addiction, and AIDS (p. 354).

Counseling, while an important component of helping individuals cope, is insufficient in dealing with these great challenges. Thus, while the intent of this book is to explore the counseling component of social work practice, practitioners are cautioned to approach this task with the broader mission of social work in mind. The Code of Ethics of the National Association of Social Workers (1996) outlines the obligations of social workers to the broader society.

> Social workers should promote the general welfare of society, from local to global levels, and the development of people, their communities, and their environments. Social workers should advocate for living conditions conducive to the fulfillment of basic human needs and should promote social, economic, political, and cultural values and institutions that are compatible with the realization of social justice (Standard 6.01).

> Social workers should facilitate informed participation by the public in shaping social policies and institutions (Standard 6.02).

> Social workers should engage in social and political action that seeks to ensure that all people have equal access to the resources, employment, services, and opportunities they require to meet their basic human needs and to develop fully. Social workers should be aware of the impact of the political arena on practice and should advocate for changes in policy and legislation to improve social conditions in order to meet basic human needs and promote social justice (Standard 6.04a).

> Social workers should act to expand choice and opportunity for all people, with special regard for vulnerable, disadvantaged, oppressed, and exploited people and groups (Standard 6.04b).

The Need for Versatility

The typical counseling caseload is characterized by **diversity.** Culture, gender, age, religion, sexual orientation, language, education, economic ability, and intellectual capacity, as well as beliefs, values, preferences, and personal style, make every client different. Therefore, a "one-size-fits-all" model of counseling is precluded. Respect for client diversity requires workers to be versatile in adapting their methods to fit the needs of each client or context. Social workers and other professionals who persist in using the same strategy for all clients, without regard to individual differences, will be ineffective. As Haley observes, skilled workers expect that they "will approach each new person with the idea that a unique procedure might be necessary for this particular person and social situation" (1987:7).

Expert social workers draw on research theory and experience as guides in determining which skills and procedures will best meet their clients' needs. They work from a model or process for exploring problems and helping clients build solutions, but they adapt that model to each client situation. Every client and problem circumstance will favor different skills, and each situation requires workers to know how to use skills, as well as when to use them. Many workers consider themselves eclectic, and they use concepts and skills from four hundred or more varieties of psychotherapy (Lazarus and Beutler, 1993). In the process, they may use an assortment of counseling tools, including drama, role play, toys, music, art, films, visual charts such as genealogical diagrams, personality tests, and audio or visual recordings. Lazarus and Beutler remind us that no one theoretical orientation has all the answers, but they caution against selecting skills and procedures haphazardly, arguing that helpers must act based on "a logical decisional process that takes into account the client, setting, problem, and the nature of the counselor's skills" (1993:384).

At the same time, this need for **versatility** does not mean that workers have to suppress their basic personality. It does not require them to compromise their professional ethics nor to ignore the core conditions or values of clients. Successful helpers model a high level of congruence between who they are and how they act. They are sincere and real in the way they relate to clients.

Competence Using a Wide Range of Skills

The element of versatility requires that workers understand and perfect new skills. Only then will they have choices. With choices, workers have freedom to relate to each client differently. When one strategy fails, counselors can use others. They have the ability to use a skill, but they also have the ability to refrain from applying it compulsively.

Skill versatility enables social workers to customize their approach. For example, although most clients respond favorably to empathy, some clients may see empathy as intrusive and respond with defensiveness, preferring to keep their feelings private. Effective workers are alert to such reactions and have the ability to use skills other than empathy with such clients.

Knowing how to use a skill is not the same as knowing when it is wise to use it. Being able to predict an outcome is an important part of timing. Although workers can make some generalizations about when a particular skill is appropriate, they need to apply these generalizations with caution and consideration for individual differences. For example, at the start of a counseling relationship, the social worker usually wants to use skills that promote the development of the working alliance and, thus, avoids more demanding strategies, such as confrontation. Conversely, once they have established a firm working relationship, they will want to use skills that help clients gain new perspectives, so confrontation may be warranted. As another example, empathy often encourages clients to share deeper feelings. Therefore, social workers who use empathy should be willing to invest the time that this sharing requires. If the interview is near an end, the worker might decide to avoid empathic responses that stimulate emotions that cannot be dealt with in the time available.

Matching the Language of Clients

Careful listening tells workers about the language and metaphors that characterize their clients' communication styles. In turn, this knowledge helps guide them to modify their language to fit that of their clients. Skillful workers are alert to their clients' use of humor and metaphor. They also need to pay attention to such variables as voice tone, volume, and tempo, then respond appropriately. To a depressed client, a high-energy, fast-talking worker might be annoying. Similarly, the worker who responds in a monotone to a client who is ecstatic about finding a job might come across as cold and indifferent.

Grinder and Bandler (1976) suggest that everyone has a different way of using language to represent experiences. According to their theory, people process ideas in one of three major modalities: in the visual mode through pictures and images; in the auditory mode with sounds; and in the kinesthetic or feeling mode. A person who thinks visually will be more likely to say, "I see what you mean," whereas a person who processes in the auditory mode might say, "I hear you." Someone else might say, "I have a handle on my problem" or "I feel in touch with . . ."; these responses suggest that they process in the kinesthetic mode. Workers may find it easier to establish rapport and build trust when they match their clients' words with similar language (see Table 1.2).

Other Versatility Variables

Counselor adaptability also includes the need to be flexible regarding such variables as where the interview takes place, how long the interview lasts, the pace of the interview, the fees, and the people who are involved. Although some social workers still work in office settings with scheduled 45-minute or hour-long interviews, many work in settings where counseling interviews are less structured. Process versatility gives counselors choices regarding the sequence and pace of counseling activities. With most clients, the beginning phase is concerned with exploring problems and feelings, but with other clients workers may move immediately to action and problem solving. With some clients, social workers spend a great deal of time helping them explore their feelings, but with others they spend little or no time in this activity.

The need for versatility also extends to other factors, such as the amount of eye contact that is expected or desired, seating arrangements, and physical distance. Some clients are comfortable in an office setting, but others prefer to work in their own home or to meet in a neutral setting. Adolescent boys, for example, might prove more approachable if counseling interventions are combined with some activity. Some clients favor an open seating arrangement with no desk or obstacle between them and their workers. Others prefer to work over the corner of a desk (Kadushin, 1990).

TABLE 1.2   Matching Clients' Language Styles

Style	Client Statement	Sample Worker Response
Visual	My view of the problem is . . .	If I get the picture correctly, the way you see it is . . .
Auditory	When I listen to myself I know what I have to do.	Tell me more about what you are saying to yourself.
Kinesthetic	I can't seem to get a handle on my problem.	What prevents you from grasping the solution?

Values and Ethics

Ethics are principles of acceptable conduct. Professional codes of ethics, such as those of the National Association of Social Workers (1996) and the American Counseling Association (1995), are formal statements that define the responsibilities of its members. **Values** are what individuals and groups consider important or worthwhile. The behavior of professionals in their interviews is influenced to a great extent by their values, including their philosophical view of people and of how they are motivated. Thus, social workers who see people as basically good and goal directed will behave very differently than those who believe people are evil and must be monitored or controlled. In social work, two values are of particular importance:

1. belief in the dignity and worth of people
2. respect for clients' rights to self-determination, i.e., freedom of choice and control of their own lives

These professional values are at the root of the counseling model described in this book. By respecting the dignity of people, social workers try to be nonjudgmental in their work and to treat all clients with respect and caring. The self-determination principle values the right of clients to be involved in decision making and to control decisions that affect their lives. Chapter 2 considers these concepts in greater depth.

Skill Clusters

There is no standardized method for classifying counseling skills. Nevertheless, it is useful to think about skills in terms of their function or intended purpose. In this book four major **skill clusters,** based on their intended purpose, are used: (1) relationship building, (2) exploring or probing, (3) empowering, and (4) challenging. Each major skill is further categorized into subclusters of related skills (see Table 1.3).

Significantly, some skills achieve multiple purposes. Sensitive active listening, for example, contributes to the development of the relationship because it communicates acceptance and the sincere desire to understand. At the same time, active listening is essential for getting information, so these skills are also classified as exploring/probing. Building on the need for versatility, practitioners need to be versatile in seeking to build competence based on knowledge of (1) what particular skills involve, including their intended purpose, (2) when and how to use individual skills, and (3) their own skill strengths and limitations.

Relationship-Building Skills

Relationship-building skills are the basic tools for engaging clients, developing trust, and defining the purpose of the counseling. They are of central importance during the beginning phase of helping, but effective counseling requires that the relationship be sustained and deepened through all phases of helping. Listening is at the heart of this cluster of skills. When clients feel heard, they respond with further disclosure. Unless helpers listen, there

TABLE 1.3   Skill Clusters

Relationship Building	Exploring or Probing	Empowering	Challenging
Active listening	*Active listening*	*Searching for Strengths*	*Confronting*
▪ Attending	▪ Attending	▪ Defining client capacities and rights	▪ Providing critical feedback
▪ Using silence	▪ Using silence	▪ Defining problems as opportunities	▪ Promoting strengths
▪ Paraphrasing	▪ Paraphrasing	▪ Identifying resources	▪ Encouraging
▪ Summarizing	▪ Summarizing		▪ Correcting distortions
▪ Questioning	▪ Questioning		▪ Reframing
▪ Showing empathy	▪ Showing empathy		▪ Asking clients to take responsibility
Promoting core conditions	*Other interviewing skills*	*Teaching*	
▪ Showing congruence or genuineness	▪ Using directives	▪ Providing skills training	*Action planning*
▪ Showing empathy	▪ Providing simple encouragers	▪ Modeling	▪ Defining clear and measurable targets for change
▪ Revealing positive regard	▪ Using counselor self-disclosure	▪ Role playing	▪ Helping clients identify and evaluate alternatives for reaching goals
	▪ Using humor	*Information giving*	
Defining the relationship		▪ Offering advice and information	▪ Helping clients choose, develop, and carry out change strategies
▪ Contracting		▪ Referring	
▪ Using immediacy			▪ Use of authority and power
▪ Using counselor self-disclosure		*Supporting*	▪ Limit setting
		▪ Reassuring	▪ Praise
		▪ Fostering optimism	
		▪ Reinforcing	
		▪ Advocating	
		▪ Providing direct aid	
		▪ Praise	

is no way for them to understand the complexities and uniqueness of their clients' situations. Other relationship-building skills involve conveying interest, warmth, and willingness to become involved.

Active Listening.   **Active listening** involves six separate skills: attending, using silence, paraphrasing, summarizing, questioning, and showing empathy. **Attending** is the manner in which workers communicate that they are physically and psychologically interested in what their clients are saying or doing. Appropriate **silence** gives clients time to think and respond. Effective workers understand the multiple meanings of silence. Is the client confused? Have we reached the end of the topic? Is the client thinking? Skilled helpers know when to interrupt a silence and when to allow it to continue. **Paraphrasing** involves restating (usually in shortened form) the client's thoughts to clarify the essence of what he or she has said. **Summarizing** is an interviewing tool used to condense the essential content and to identify essential themes and ideas. **Questioning** involves probing for information to confirm understanding and seek clarification, such as by saying, "Do you mean that. . . ?" **Empathy** is "the process of accurately understanding the emotional perspective of another person and the communication of this understanding" (Shebib, 1997:177).

Active listening skills provide psychological incentive for clients to open up. When clients experience a deep sense of having been heard, they are motivated to open up. They learn to trust the listener when their ideas are not judged or rejected and when their feelings are validated. This trust results in a climate of safety, and clients begin to reveal more. Furthermore, active listening skills provide a structure for exploring thoughts and feelings. Paraphrasing and summarizing, for example, help clients to organize ideas, identify key points, and recognize priorities. Questions provide a systematic way of exploring ideas for detail, definition, and example. Empathy opens opportunities for understanding and accepting feelings.

Active listening says to the client, "I have heard you," "I am willing to understand your problems and feelings without judgment," and "I accept you." Consequently, active listening is a powerful tool for establishing rapport and understanding, the basis for a strong working relationship. The skills of active listening will be discussed in depth in Chapters 4, 5, and 6.

Promoting Core Conditions.   The values of this model are inspired by the views of Carl Rogers (1961, 1980) and his belief that people are essentially good, self-deterministic (able to make their own decisions), and goal directed. Rogers identified three factors that are essential for helpers: congruence, empathy, and positive regard. In Chapter 3, these core conditions will be explored further.

Congruence, or **genuineness,** is the capacity to be real and consistent with clients. Congruent workers are open with their reactions and feelings and demonstrate consistency in what they believe, say, and do. Congruency requires workers to be "transparent," or without hidden agendas or false demeanors. Rogers believed that the more helpers are aware of their feelings and the more they genuinely express these feelings in the counseling relationship, the more effective the counseling will be.

Empathy as a core condition means being able to see the world through the eyes of the clients. Essential to empathic understanding is the ability to understand feelings without imposing one's own feelings or reactions. "Empathy becomes judgmental when the counselor not only reflects the client's feeling state but also applies his or her own emotional yardstick in measuring its appropriateness for the client" (Gilliland and James, 1998:117–18).

Positive regard, or respect for clients, is the ability to recognize the inherent worth of people, regardless of their behavior. As Gilliland and James conclude, "At any given time, the counselor needs to be willing to accept the confusion, fear, anger, resentment, courage, sorrow, and multiplicity of other feelings the client may have. Such caring is total and nonpossessive and lacks prior conditions of rightness or appropriateness of the client's feelings" (1998:117).

Defining the Relationship.   Rogers emphasized the importance of avoiding moral judgment of clients in order to develop an effective helping relationship. He vividly captured the significance of nonjudgmental exploration to the development of the relationship: "It is only as I understand the feelings and thoughts which seem so horrible to you, or so weak, or so sentimental, or so bizarre—it is only as I see them as you see them, and accept them and you, that you feel really free to explore all the hidden nooks and frightening crannies of your inner and often buried experience" (1961:34).

Three major skills are associated with defining the relationship: contracting, immediacy, and self-disclosure. Contracting involves negotiating the intended purpose of the counseling relationship, including agreeing on the expected roles of both worker and client. The counseling contract is an agenda of the activities and tasks that counseling will address, but the contract may change, sometimes frequently, as the work proceeds. Contracting defines a plan for the work that is individualized to meet the needs of each client. Consider, for example, three women who seek counseling with an identical problem, a relationship breakdown. As a result of contracting, client one may identify her need as help in managing her stress and pain. Client two may want to focus on developing her assertive communication skills for dealing with an abusive spouse. Client three, on the other hand, might want help with decision making in choosing between leaving the relationship or remaining in hopes of solving the relationship problems.

Immediacy (Egan, 1998) is a tool for examining and deepening the counseling relationship. It involves a process of evaluation that addresses the quality of the relationship in terms of its contracted objectives. Thus, the skill of immediacy means prompting candid discussion regarding how the relationship might be changed in order to better serve its objectives. Worker self-disclosure can be an important component of immediacy, or it can be used as a skill that reduces a client's sense that "I'm the only one who thinks and feels this way."

Exploring/Probing Skills

Exploring/probing skills are the basic tools of interviewing that workers use to gather information, clarify definitions, seek examples, and obtain necessary detail. These skills enable workers to avoid making assumptions. Questions are central to probing, but other skills also have the effect of encouraging clients to tell their stories.

Other Interviewing Skills.   **Directives** such as "Tell me more" or "Please expand on your feelings" are statements that are used to control the direction and pace of the interview. As well, directives can be used to focus the client on relevant priorities. Directives are the road signs of the interview.

Simple encouragers are short verbal and nonverbal cues that motivate clients to continue. Verbal statements such as "Uh huh" or "Yes" and short directives such as "Please continue," along with nonverbal signals such as head nods and an attentive posture, are the essence of this skill set.

Worker self-disclosure, used sparingly, can be a useful tool that models appropriate sharing of feelings. Worker self-disclosure may reduce the clients' sense that their experiences or feelings are strange or abnormal. Subsequently, when experiences are "normalized" clients are more apt to open up and share. In this way, worker self-disclosure acts as an exploring/probing skill.

Humor, if it is timely, can be used as a way to reduce tension or to encourage clients to take a lighter view of their situation. Humor must be used cautiously so that it does not offend clients or trivialize their problems.

Empowering Skills

Empowering skills are used to help clients develop confidence, self-esteem, and control over their lives. Five skill subclusters are the essence of empowering: searching for strengths, teaching, supporting, giving information, and managing anxiety.

Searching for strengths moves counseling from a process of identifying deficits and problems to one in which clients' strengths, capacities, and resources are recognized. Strengths are the resources that enable clients to overcome problems, so they cannot be ignored. Helping clients realize their strengths empowers them with the belief that they are capable of change. Sometimes reframing how clients think about problems can help them to see their problems as opportunities.

Teaching may be used in counseling as a way to assist clients in developing strengths. Skills training, role playing, and other tools can be used as ways to help clients develop their capacities and expand their range of choices.

Information giving empowers clients with knowledge of alternative courses of action, including resources that might assist them in dealing with their problems. Workers may also offer suggestions and advice regarding problem management, but they should do this is a way that does not disempower clients.

Supporting is used to help bolster clients' energy and optimism. To some extent, all counseling skills are supportive. Supporting reduces clients' feelings of isolation and provides the incentive for clients to address their problems, express their feelings, and begin a process of change. Supporting can be used to tell clients that they are on the right track and to inform clients that their feelings and reactions are normal. Supporting helps clients manage anxiety and stress, thus increasing their energy, self-confidence, and capacity for problem solving.

Cowger (1994) offers this important reminder that the role of social workers is not to change, treat, or empower people:

> To assume a social worker can empower someone else is naive and condescending and has little basis in reality. Power is not something that social workers possess for distribution at will. Clients, not social workers, own the power that brings significant change in clinical practice. A clinical social worker is merely a resource person with professional training on the use of resources who is committed to people empowerment and willing to share his or her knowledge in a manner that helps people realize their own power, take control of their own lives, and solve their own problems (p. 264).

By using a strengths approach social workers identify and reinforce client competence. In this sense, client assessment moves beyond identifying obstacles and problems to discussion of personal and environmental resources. Such an approach reduces some of the power differential that comes when client vulnerabilities and deficits are given priority.

Challenging Skills

Challenging skills are used to encourage clients to critically evaluate their behavior and ideas. They push clients toward change and growth and in this way fulfill the fundamental reason for the counseling relationship. Excessive or premature reliance on challenging skills may strain the counseling relationship. As Young puts it, "when challenging skills are used, the aura of safety and support, so carefully constructed by the helper, is at risk. There is a fundamental shift from relationship building to a focus on the goals set by the client and helper, conveying to the client that the helping relationship is not a friendship but a business partnership" (1998:100).

Two subclusters are contained within this skill set: confronting and action planning. **Confrontation** prods clients to critically examine their actions and/or consider other viewpoints. This process may involve workers in providing critical or corrective feedback, identifying overlooked strengths, correcting distortions, suggesting other viewpoints (reframing), and requesting that clients assume responsibility. Confrontation skills are most effective when there is a strong relationship of trust and when clients understand and accept the value of their use. Brill offers this perspective on the challenging skill of confrontation:

> Misuse of confrontation can be devastating, destroying all previous efforts. Workers must assess the amount and quality of confrontation the client is willing or able to use, and they must be able to give support if the reality is overwhelming. Workers must not use confrontation to express their own anger and frustration, although these are certainly a part of the reality with which both workers and clients must deal (1998:166).

Ideally, confrontation skills will increase clients' motivation for change. Social workers and other professionals develop the credibility necessary for successful confronting when they have listened to clients and have persuaded them that they are accepted and understood. With this base, clients may be appropriately confronted when they

- are working from false assumptions or incomplete information
- misread the actions of others
- lack self-awareness regarding the impact of their actions, for example, when they blame others for their problems rather than examine their own responsibility
- demonstrate contradictions in their behavior, thoughts, and feelings
- deny or do not recognize their personal strengths, capacities, or resources

Action planning is a way of helping clients bring about changes in their lives. These changes may include finding new ways of managing feelings, forming strategies for modifying ways of thinking, or developing new skills or behaviors. Action planning helps clients to define clear and measurable targets for change (goals), to identify and evaluate alternative strategies, and to select and develop plans for reaching these goals.

Use of Power and Authority.   Social workers derive or are given power by virtue of their position. Such power comes from many sources: competence, knowledge, education, control of resources, position in the agency/status in the community, or simply the fact that the client is the one who is in the position of needing or seeking help. Social workers are representatives of agencies that wield power. They have the right and responsibility to make decisions and judgments that impact clients' lives. Notwithstanding the personal style of the social worker, however gentle and caring, from the perspective of clients, social workers are perceived as persons with power and influence, and often as people to be feared. As such, social workers should heed Compton and Galaway's (1999) caution to accept and use power wisely.

> Questions of power and authority are particularly relevant when we are required to enter a situation by court order or agency decision. Prior experiences of the misuse of professional authority may underlie the family's negative expectations, lack of trust and fear of commitment. When we intervene in people's lives at the request of others, we must be prepared to explain very clearly—many times, if necessary—what authority and power we carry, what the limits of our authority and power are, and how we will use it. This is often difficult because of our own feelings about authority (1999:181).

Failure in Counseling

It is inevitable that counseling will sometimes fail, so social workers need to develop their capacity to systematically investigate and review failure. They need to be able to distinguish between failures that are beyond their control and those that originate from their own mistakes. Failure may originate with the client; it may arise from personal issues associated with the worker, such as faulty technique or lack of skill; or it may come from factors that are beyond the client's and worker's control.

Client Variables

Client variables that could lead to failure include unrealistic expectations, poor motivation, unconscious self-sabotage, destructive personality, organic factors, and poor capacity for insight (Kottler, 1993:18). For example, substance abuse or mental disorders may make it difficult or impossible for clients to engage with the work of counseling. Clients may resist or undermine counseling because of secondary gain, when the payoffs from maintaining the problem outweigh the benefits of change. Or clients may resist change because of unconscious fear of success, because they expect to fail, or because the risks of change are too frightening to face.

Kottler suggests using caution to ensure that workers are not too quick to blame failure on clients. "Many of us avoid dealing with our failures by blaming clients for not cooperating. If only they were more motivated and less ambivalent, if only they were willing to work harder and take greater risks, if only they did what we asked of them, if only they would act more like we would prefer, then counseling could work out quite nicely" (1993:17).

Counselor Variables

Intellectually and emotionally secure professionals are willing to examine their methods and attitudes, and they are willing to take their share of responsibility for poor counseling outcomes. Worker variables include such factors as mental attitudes, moods, and behaviors, which can dramatically affect how they relate to and assess their clients. Worker variables that can affect counseling outcomes may arise from burnout, personal problems, or loss of objectivity.

Burnout.   A career working with people in crisis may be intensely satisfying, but it can also be emotionally stressful and draining. Workers may experience unrelenting pressure in workplace demands, including high caseloads, limited resources, and crushing paperwork. They can become depleted from trying to respond to the needs of their clients and the organization. In addition, they are subject to their own family and economic stress and trauma. Workers may be resilient, but even the most sturdy person can become debilitated by stress.

Burnout is a state of emotional, mental, and physical exhaustion that hinders or prevents people from performing their jobs. Burnout may affect people in different ways, but certain symptoms are typical. The stress of burnout may show itself as a general state of physical exhaustion, including signs of diminished health such as headaches, sleep disruptions, and digestive upset. Emotional and mental burnout may be revealed as increased anxiety, inability to cope with the normal demands of work, depression, excessive worry, discouragement, pessimism toward clients, loss of a sense of purpose, general irritability, and inability to find joy in one's career or life.

Social workers who suspect that they suffer from burnout should first consult a physician to rule out any medical condition that might be a factor. The best way to deal with burnout is to prevent it from happening. For social workers, this means balancing the demands of their work life by taking care of themselves. They need to develop personal wellness plans that address their own emotional, physical, and spiritual needs. An essential part of this plan is time away from the job. They need to avoid becoming overinvolved such as by working unreasonably long hours and weekends or by skipping vacations. They need to make intelligent decisions about the limits of what they can do.

Workers can also prevent burnout by setting up and using a support system of family, friends, supervisors, and colleagues. By doing so, they ensure that they have people to whom they can turn for assistance and emotional support. Work colleagues and supervisors are essential for helping workers manage their emotional reactions toward clients, such as fear and anger. Workers need to recognize that being able to accept help from others is a sign of strength and that they should model this belief in their own behavior. Talking to others reduces isolation and allows for team participation and support with difficult decisions or situations. It is particularly important for workers to have someone to debrief with after stressful interviews, such as those with angry or assaultive clients (see Chapter 8).

Continued professional development is another important strategy for preventing burnout. Attending seminars, courses, and conferences exposes workers to new ideas and the latest research and can help them renew their enthusiasm and creativity.

Personal Problems.   Social workers are subject to the same stresses in life as other people. They can become depressed, their children can become ill, their marriages can fail, or they can become responsible for caring for ailing and elderly parents. Responsible workers accept that there may be times when they need help. They recognize the importance of having people in their lives to whom they can turn for assistance. When workers have healthy reciprocal relationships with others, they are less likely to subconsciously use their clients to meet these needs.

During acute periods of stress, social workers recognize their vulnerability and take steps to protect their clients. These steps might include taking a temporary reduction in workload, shifting to a less demanding caseload, taking a "mental health" break, and seeking increased supervision or consultation to monitor their work. In extreme circumstances, they may choose to take extended leave or switch careers.

Loss of Objectivity.   **Objectivity** is a measure of workers' capacity to relate to clients without allowing their own feelings and biases to distort their judgment (see Chapter 2 for a detailed discussion). A number of factors can lead to a loss of objectivity, including unresolved personal problems, difficulty dealing with particular emotions or topics, attraction or revulsion to clients, overidentification with clients, and excessive or unrealistic fear of particular clients.

Workers who are not self-aware of their values, their beliefs, and the impact of their behavior on others are limited in their ability to monitor their level of objectivity. Those who seek to increase their objectivity make themselves available for feedback or supervision. Moreover, they recognize their personal limitations and the fact that they may be unable to work with objectivity with every client. They know when to refer clients to other professionals.

Process or Technique Variables

Process variables that can lead to failure include pseudocounseling, inappropriate advice giving, rescuing, and miscellaneous problems with technique or procedure.

Pseudocounseling.   The goal of every counseling relationship is to improve the quality of life for the client. Achieving this goal may involve problem resolution, assistance with decision making, or management of painful feelings. Social workers need to screen their responses and activities to ensure that their work supports the objectives of counseling.

Pseudocounseling involves what Shulman (1992) describes as the **illusion of work**—counseling sessions are animated and active, but they are essentially empty and without real meaning. The illusion of work can be created through:

- interesting but irrelevant exploration of issues that do not contribute to problem solving, including an excessive focus on finding the root causes of problems
- use of clichés and patronizing platitudes
- overly intellectual exploration of issues
- avoidance of subjects or feelings that involve pain in favor of safe topics (of course, it is sometimes appropriate to shift the focus to safe areas of discussion, for example,

if the interview is almost over or if clients are clearly unable to handle additional stress)

Inappropriate Advice Giving. Society conditions us to seek advice from experts, so it's not surprising that many clients come to counselors expecting "expert advice" on how to manage their lives and solve their problems. Students and beginning counselors often believe that counseling requires them to listen patiently to their clients' problems, then offer advice on what they should do. However, they need to learn that this approach is rarely helpful and is sometimes harmful for clients, particularly when such advice is based on values that are inconsistent with the client's lifestyle or culture.

Clients often seek advice even when they know what to do to manage their problems. Seeking advice can be a way of expressing dependency or transferring responsibility for decisions and outcomes to someone else. This dependency inhibits the right of clients to make choices, and it may leave clients feeling resentful or frustrated, particularly if the advice was unsolicited.

Advice giving may increase workers' self-esteem by underscoring their ability to be resourceful and helpful, but it may undermine clients' self-esteem, leaving them feeling inadequate because they have been unable to figure out their problems for themselves or because they lack the will or resources to act on the "good advice." Workers who tend to give advice can become overly concerned about whether clients follow their advice, and, if so, whether the advice is successful. They can become disappointed when clients do not follow advice.

As Compton and Galaway conclude, wisdom "lies less in the substantive areas of knowing what is best for the client and more in the process area of assisting clients to develop alternatives for themselves, make decisions among the alternatives, and implement decisions" (1984:73). This is the essence of empowering and self-determination: instead of giving advice, workers can encourage clients to generate their own ideas. Some questions they might ask to accomplish this goal are:

- What are your thoughts about what to do?
- What ideas have you considered but rejected?
- What advice could you give yourself?
- What alternatives have you considered?
- What would your friends or family encourage you to do?
- What advice do you think I will give you?
- What do you see as your choices? (Shebib, 1997:31)

The injunction against advice giving does not mean that workers should withhold information or ideas that might benefit their clients. Examples of information or advice that they might provide are listed below.

- tentative suggestions regarding alternative courses of action that the client has overlooked. However, "when counsellors are unwilling or unable to present and explore all viable alternatives neutrally, they have an ethical responsibility to refer the client to another counsellor, or at the very least, to make their biases or limitations explicit" (Shebib, 1997:33).

- expert information based on research or knowledge (e.g., job search techniques, child-rearing principles)
- ideas for improving communication or problem solving
- suggestions regarding the process of problem resolution
- opinions and information that will help clients avoid unforeseen consequences (dangers) to themselves or impulsive or poorly considered action

Where there is a range of individual choices such as decisions related to marriage or career, advice giving is inappropriate. In such circumstances the role of workers is to assist clients in identifying alternative courses of action, then to help them weigh the advantages and disadvantages of each alternative. They may suggest alternatives, but they should do this in such a way that clients feel free to reject their suggestions.

Rescuing.   **Rescuing,** or band-aiding, involves actions that prevent or protect clients from dealing with issues or feelings. Rescuing arises from the worker's need to avoid tension and keep the session cheerful, but it is misguided because rescuing diverts clients from addressing important though difficult issues in their lives. Rescuing is a misuse of the support function of helping. Workers may become so preoccupied with avoiding or reducing tension that they interfere with their clients' ability to cope or problem-solve. If problem situations are to be worked through successfully, clients must be allowed to experience and express painful emotions and, when necessary, confront reality (Shebib, 1997).

There are three major types of rescue behavior:

1. responses that minimize tension, such as avoiding tough but otherwise timely and important topics and feelings by changing the subject, using humor to cut off discussion, or suggesting a coffee break

   Rodney was finally willing to address his sadness over the death of his father. As he began to talk, he cried softly. As he did so, his worker reached out and put her hands on his shoulders, reassuring him that his grief would pass.

   Par hesitated for a moment as he struggled to collect his thoughts. Sensing that this might be a painful moment for him, his worker suggested that he might prefer to talk about something else.

   Worker responses such as these impede the work of counseling by preventing or discouraging clients from dealing with their feelings. For clients to learn how to manage emotions, they must be allowed to experience their pain. If workers communicate discomfort or disapproval with expressed emotions, important opportunities for work may be lost.

2. placating by withholding potentially helpful but critical confrontation or by offering false feedback and empty reassurance

   Tara expressed fear about contacting her father, with whom she had not had contact for five years. Her counselor offered support: "Everything is going to work out well. I'm sure your father will be ecstatic to see you."

Shirley decided not to confront her client over an obvious hygiene problem. She concluded that it would be best not to upset her client and jeopardize a strong relationship.

3. behaviors that impede independence, such as speaking for clients and doing for clients what they are able to do for themselves

Jessie's counselor wanted to be seen as helpful and resourceful. She offered to rewrite her client's résumé and pick up application forms from local employers.

José was having trouble understanding a school assignment. His child-care counselor phoned his teacher to ask for clarification, even though José was capable of talking to the teacher himself

For clients to become independent, they need to develop the skills and strength to deal with their lives. This may be a difficult process for clients, requiring workers to be supportive without stifling their clients' growth. Workers must avoid unduly protecting their clients by interfering with their opportunities and capacity to face their difficulties. This requires them to be fully aware of their own need for power and control and to accept that successful counseling requires clients to be their own problem solvers. Furthermore, workers must rid themselves of any fantasy that their clients can be saved only by them.

CONVERSATION **1.2**
Rescuing and Supporting

STUDENT: What is the difference between supporting clients and rescuing them?

TEACHER: Rescuing robs clients of legitimate opportunities for growth. Supporting promotes self-determination by providing encouragement or resources to motivate clients toward growth and change. Timing is also a factor. Rescuing occurs when clients have the strength to deal with difficult areas or feelings, but their workers avoid the work or pain that this would entail. On the other hand, if clients are overwhelmed, some direct assistance to lessen their burden is supportive. It may be wise to avoid excessive intimacy in the beginning of a relationship, and it may be hazardous to explore highly emotional topics near the end of an interview. An important question for workers to consider is "Whose needs are being met, mine or the client's?" Rescuing behavior meets workers' needs under the guise of helping clients, but supportive behavior helps clients to realize their objectives. In the long run, there are times when it is more supportive to allow clients to face their struggles and experience their pain. Effective workers are courageous enough to allow clients to express their pain and accept the reality that they cannot provide solutions to all problems.

Faulty Technique. Some of the problems that arise in counseling can be attributed to workers' inept use of skills. Poor technique can lead to missed opportunities and, in extreme cases, can be harmful to clients. For example, workers might fail to respond to individual differences (e.g., gender and culture), or they may cling to a rigid "one style fits all" approach to counseling. They may be poor listeners, or they may lack empathy. They might push clients too quickly, or they might allow them to stagnate by neglecting to motivate them to make changes.

Uncontrollable Variables.   Large caseloads may preclude social workers from spending sufficient time with their clients. Resources may not be available to support clients in the change process, such as detox facilities for a client who wants treatment for heroin addiction. Unexpected events and crises, such as illness, death, or job loss, may frustrate progress. In some cases, client changes may be subverted by family and friends who are unprepared to support change.

The Phases of Counseling

This book is based on a model of four **phases of counseling:** (1) preliminary, (2) beginning, (3) action, and (4) ending (Shebib, 1997). This organization builds on similar models presented by others such as Egan (1998), Shulman (1992), and Young (1998). Each phase of counseling is characterized by common as well as unique objectives and skills.

One common objective of each phase is forming and sustaining a working relationship. This counseling relationship is the vehicle for change and provides a base of safety and security for clients to explore and understand their emotions and difficulties. The counseling contract, an agreement on the goals and roles of the participants, is the reference point for the relationship. It is continually reviewed and revised as the work progresses.

A second common objective of all phases is to establish open, honest, and productive communication. Effective communication enables workers to learn about their clients' needs and feelings. As well, it empowers clients to learn new ways of handling old problems.

The third common objective of all phases is evaluation. Ongoing evaluation can be targeted to the essential elements of the counseling plan, the working relationship, its goals and methods, and the overall satisfaction of all participants with the pace of the work and its results. By using a problem-solving approach, workers workers and clients can explore ways to ensure that the work is relevant and efficient.

Each phase is distinguished by its focus on different activities. The preliminary phase is essentially for planning. Proper planning increases the likelihood that clients will perceive that their needs can be met through counseling. The beginning phase is a time of engagement, when both the client and the worker make decisions about whether they will work together and, if so, under what structure. The beginning phase is also a time for exploring problems and feelings. Although clients may begin to change their behavior or manage their feelings more effectively during the beginning phase, the action phase is more concerned with initiating change. During the ending phase, the working relationship is brought to a close, perhaps with a referral to another resource or counselor.

Skill clusters were introduced as a way to organize skills based on function. Because each phase of counseling supports different activities, it seems logical that each phase would also favor different skills. For example, during the beginning phase of counseling, relationship-building skills are the priority, whereas challenging skills are usually avoided, at least until a foundation of trust and safety is established. Exploration/probing skills are also vital during the beginning phase. They enable workers to acquire information for understanding and to avoid any tendency to make assumptions. Challenging and directing/teaching skills tend to be more effective in the action phase, when a strong relationship and a solid base of understanding have been established. Table 1.4 summarizes the principal activities and priority skills of each phase.

Counseling tends to move through the phases sequentially, with success at each phase depending, in part, on the success of preceding phases. For example, the preliminary phase is designed to support the work of the beginning phase. It allows the worker to complete the preparations that will help welcome clients to the agency. As well, it works as a kind of warm-up, so workers can be ready and sensitive to the needs of their clients. Weak planning results in weak beginnings. Similarly, effective work in the action phase is easier when the beginning phase has been successful. A solid base of understanding will permit workers and clients to set more pertinent goals, and a foundation of trust allows workers to be more challenging in their approach. In contrast, workers who attempt to challenge clients from a thin base of trust are likely to meet with resistance or rejection. In the action phase, it is important to try to sequence the steps. If clients try to develop action plans before they have set clear goals, their action plans are more likely to be vague and directionless.

Although counseling work tends to evolve sequentially through the four phases, flexibility in applying the model is necessary, because counseling does not always advance in a linear fashion. Workers cannot insist that clients move through the phases in a neat and orderly manner.

TABLE 1.4   Counseling Activities and Skills

Phase	Principal Activities	Priority Skills
Preliminary	• Interview preplanning • Preparing the interview setting	• Planning • Establishing self-awareness
Beginning	• Establishing a working relationship • Interviewing for understanding • Evaluation	• Active listening • Promoting core conditions • Defining the relationship • Searching for strengths
Action	• Goal setting • Action planning • Helping clients change behavior, manage feelings, change perception • Revising the contract, deepening the relationship, managing communication difficulties • Evaluation	• Teaching • Information giving • Supporting • Confronting • Action planning
Ending	• Ending the helping relationship • Referring to other resources • Evaluation	• Information giving • Supporting

The phases of counselling provide a systematic and useful way of organizing our thoughts and actions. Acting as a kind of checklist, the phases remind counsellors of the essential activities and logical steps that are part of any process of change or problem solving. The model can act as a reference point to plan our actions, to predict what might come next, and to understand the reactions of our clients. Practical experience shows, however, that each counselling encounter is different, each relationship is uniquely complex, and the work may evolve in unpredictable ways (Shebib, 1997:71).

By referring to the phases of counseling, workers and clients can remain clear on where they are in the counseling process, what has been done, what remains to be accomplished, and what options remain open. Sometimes clear divisions between the phases of counseling are apparent. More frequently, there will be overlap between the phases and shifts forward and back between one phase or another, and in some cases phases may be skipped. Some typical counseling scenarios are provided below.

Jessica, a very private person, was distraught over the breakup of her marriage. Aware of her inability to cope and not knowing what to do, she attended several sessions with a counselor. Her counselor proceeded slowly, gently encouraging Jessica to talk about her feelings. Jessica was surprised that during the second counseling session she began to weep. Afterward, she remarked that she felt as if a great weight had been lifted from her shoulders. She never felt the need to return for a third session.

Clint was not interested in exploring his problem beyond a superficial level. Anxious to effect change in his life, he wanted to brainstorm ideas for dealing with his problems. Counseling work focused on helping him set goals. As this work progressed, Clint became more trusting, and the sessions began to focus on exploring his feelings.

As Fernando talked about his problem, he suddenly realized that his situation was not as hopeless as he thought. Discovering another way to look at his problem, he identified several new ways to solve it.

After a single session, Bob remarked to his worker, "My problem is the same as when I came in here, but somehow it doesn't seem to bother me as much."

Effective workers are comfortable discussing feelings, and they don't tell clients how they should feel. Good workers are excellent listeners, and they invest time to make sure they accurately understand clients' feelings and concerns. They know how to systematically explore problems, set goals, and develop plans for action. They assist clients in identifying and evaluating alternatives, while recognizing that the clients must choose for themselves. Therefore, they do not impose advice or try to rescue clients by taking on their problems. Unlike friendships, counseling relationships are directed to meet the needs of one person only—the client.

CONVERSATION **1.3**
Why Counseling Works

STUDENT: What is the difference between a conversation with a helpful friend and a counseling interview?

TEACHER: The goal of a friendship is to meet the needs of both people. Friends (and family) are important. If they are understanding, caring, and supportive, they can be an effective source of help. Much like a counseling relationship, just talking to a friend can be cathartic to the individual, but there may be limits to what friends can offer. Sometimes friends and families don't have specialized knowledge, or they may not know what resources or services are available to deal with specific problems. Friends and family may be so emotionally involved with you that it is hard for them to be objective. They may have a great deal of difficulty separating their feelings from the situation, and when this happens they may resort to giving well-intentioned but not very helpful advice.

The Preliminary Phase

The preliminary phase is essentially a time of planning. The planning targets two important areas: First, the agency setting is made attractive for clients so they are motivated to engage and remain with the agency. Second, workers prepare themselves for the interview.

The Agency Setting. Ideally, the agency is set up to appeal to the client groups that it serves. A drop-in counseling center for teens would be very different from a day program for seniors. Dim lighting and beanbag chairs meet the needs of teens but present a safety hazard for seniors. Tea is appropriate for seniors, but soda pop makes more sense when the clients are teens. Ideally, the agency should:

- have uncrowded waiting rooms
- allow for reception and interview space that is private and confidential
- have procedures so that clients are greeted in a warm and friendly manner
- provide for the needs of children (by supplying a play area, appropriate toys)
- allow for wheelchair access
- have posters and other art that do not violate the values, religion, or culture of the agency's clients (generally, they should be politically neutral)
- have up-to-date reading material for clients who are waiting

Workers should take precautions to ensure that the interview time is protected from phone calls and other interruptions that will impede the flow of conversation. When workers allow their interviews to be interrupted, the message to clients may be "I have other concerns that are more important than you. Hurry up and finish."

The office should be structured to favor flexibility. Some clients and many workers prefer an unobstructed arrangement without a desk between the participants, but others favor working over the desk. The office needs to be arranged with careful consideration to the messages that the design communicates. Chairs and desks should be arranged so that no psychological advantage or power is given to the worker. Seating arrangements should allow for adequate personal space between counselors and clients. A comfort zone of about 1 to 2 m (4 to 7 feet) is adequate for most clients, but other factors might result in a need for more or less distance. Workers need to be careful in choosing personal items to display. Pictures and memorabilia that punctuate differences between themselves and their clients ought to be avoided. Of course, clients may have different reactions. For example, some clients expect and appreciate seeing their worker's degrees or diplomas hung on the wall. For these clients, knowing something about the training and credentials of their workers helps to establish confidence and credibility. Other clients, however, may react negatively to such a display. For them, the display sets up social and intellectual barriers. Generally, counselors should structure their offices with the needs and background of their clients in mind. In this respect, clients can be an invaluable source of consultation. Their opinions on office decor and layout should be solicited.

Client Files.   Some clients will have a history with the agency, and workers may have access to considerable information about these clients before their first contact. Depending on the agency, various kinds of useful information can be obtained from client files, including age, place of birth, address, marital status, work history, educational background, prior experiences with counseling, and assessments of personality, values, past problems, ability to handle stress, communication patterns, and so on. Client files can also alert workers to any past incidents of violence and point out any need to take special precautions in dealing with a particular client.

Ideally, professionals should give clients reasonable access to the records concerning them. In many jurisdictions, legislation gives clients the right to access information held by organizations. Usually, the onus is on the agency or government department to provide a reason for withholding information. Workers need to be familiar with the regulations in their area.

A review of client files can greatly speed the intake process, but it is important to maintain an open mind and avoid prejudgment, particularly with respect to the assessments other workers have made regarding such variables as manner and personality. Client reactions are influenced in part (and occasionally to a great extent) by the personality and behavior of their workers, as shown in the following example.

> *Russ waited for his worker, who was half an hour late for the scheduled interview. Russ was stressed because of personal problems and was anxious to get home to care for his sick children. Estelle, his worker, was also stressed owing to a difficult week of work. She was also aware that her next appointment was already waiting for her to finish with Russ. Determined to catch up, she moved quickly with questions to complete her assessment of Russ's situation. Russ, taken aback by Estelle's abrupt style, proceeded cautiously, hesitating to share personal information too quickly. Later, when completing her file notes on the interview, Estelle wrote: "Client was defensive and guarded. He appeared unusually resistant to exploring his feelings.*

CONVERSATION **1.4**
Should I Read the File?

STUDENT: If there's already a file on the client, should I read it before seeing the client for the first time?

TEACHER: There are reasons for reading and not reading files. It's important to be aware of the risks of either route. Some workers prefer to conduct their first interviews without reading their clients' files. They argue that, by not reading the files, they are prevented from being unduly influenced (biased) by prior information. After a first interview, they feel more able to objectively evaluate the validity of previous records. In addition, they argue that clients can change, and approaching the interview with a fresh perspective makes it easier to relate to the client's present condition. Remember that you may be biased against some workers, even to the point of rejecting what would otherwise be valid assessments.

STUDENT: But suppose the client has a history of violence that is reported in the file. How would I be able to get that information in order to protect myself, but still keep an open mind? Is there a way of getting only the pertinent information from the file that would allow me to identify those problems?

TEACHER: That's one of the drawbacks of not reading the file. I like your idea of setting up some kind of process for identifying clients who might be dangerous. Clients who present safety concerns could be "red flagged" in some way.

STUDENT: I think another drawback is that if you don't look at the file, you will miss out on knowing what's been done, what worked, what issues are key, and so forth. Is there a way of reading a file without being influenced by other writers?

TEACHER: Being aware of the potential for influence is crucial. It is important to remind our selves that opinions in files are not those of the clients, but of the person writing the record. Ideally, records should be shared with clients and the conclusions jointly supported. Of course, this is not always possible.

STUDENT: Could I share the file with the client to get his or her reactions?

TEACHER: Probably not, at least not without the permission of the person who wrote the record. Depending on where you live, legislation regarding freedom of access to information may give clients the right to petition for access to the file.

Interview Preparation.   Workers can anticipate in the preliminary phase how the interview time will be utilized and consider decisions related to the time, place, and structure of the interview. As well, they might begin thinking about specific questions and responses for working with particular clients and then map out a tentative structure for the interview; however, they should avoid using this structure as a script or rigid agenda. This is also a time when workers can seek any facts that will help them understand their client's problem. For example, a worker may have advance knowledge that the client has a child who has been diagnosed with Tourette's syndrome. The worker's credibility will be greatly increased in the client's eyes if the worker grasps the essential nature and implications of this condition. Knowing something about Tourette's syndrome provides an important starting point for exploration.

Shulman (1992) suggests that for a variety of reasons clients often do not share feelings and concerns directly. They may be ambivalent about sharing, or they may hold back because of societal and cultural taboos about talking about sex, authority, and money. As a result, clients may raise these concerns indirectly, and workers must be alert to recognize clues about their clients' concerns. For example, a single parent who asks her welfare worker if he has ever been on welfare may be indirectly expressing her fear that the worker will be insensitive to the stress she faces in trying to cope with a limited budget. Sometimes, questions regarding personal background or circumstances may be indirect ways clients have of exploring concerns about trust.

Shulman introduces the preliminary phase skill of tuning in as a tool for anticipating the feelings and concerns that clients might bring to the interview. By tuning in, workers can think about what clients might express and how they will do so. The preliminary phase is also a time when workers examine their own readiness. For example, they can take a few moments prior to each interview to self-examine through questions such as the following:

- Am I dealing with personal stress or problems that might make me less effective or more vulnerable?
- Am I sufficiently disengaged from my last client to be open and objective?
- What personal biases do I need to manage in order to work effectively with this client?
- What reservations do I have about meeting this client?
- Do I have unfinished business with this client that I have not addressed?
- What feelings do I have toward this client that might impede my objectivity?

The Beginning Phase

When it is successful, the preliminary phase establishes a base for developing a helping relationship. Counseling relationships are formed to provide a safe and trusting vehicle for clients to work toward their goals. The relationship between counselors and their clients influences whether clients will be willing to risk disclosure and is a significant variable that determines whether clients will continue with counseling. The objective at this stage is to negotiate a working relationship that is goal directed and based on trust and mutual understanding of expectations. This relationship is time limited and based on a contract that outlines the objectives and terms of the relationship.

Some clients come willingly to counseling, perhaps as a result of an unresolved crisis or because they have been persuaded by others to seek help. Other clients are involuntary. They may also be coming as a result of a crisis, or they may have been pressured by others. An employer, for example, may insist that a staff member seek counseling to address attitudinal or addiction problems.

Many clients are under considerable stress, and this stress is intensified if the clients perceive workers negatively. To some extent, this view is under the control of the worker. However, clients' past experiences with other agencies and counselors also shape their perceptions and expectations. Clients who have had bad experiences with counselors will understandably be guarded against further disappointment. Because social workers are often in a position of authority, or clients see them in such a position, clients' past experiences with others in authority will come into play. Most clients, however strongly they may be motivated, will have some degree of resistance or ambivalence to change. Involuntary clients, in particular, may be especially resistant and, in some cases, hostile. They may perceive any initiative by their workers, however well meaning, as a hostile act.

The relationship between workers and clients is fundamental to counseling success. Even in short, one-session encounters, when a high level of intimacy is not crucial, clients will be more apt to engage and share when the worker gives some attention to developing the relationship. Chapter 2 more fully explores the importance of the helping relationship and specific skills for developing and maintaining it.

A second major task of the beginning phase is to acquire and deepen understanding of the client's situation or problem. Simply put, clients are asked to tell their stories, describe their feelings, and explore their problems and dilemmas. For their part, workers must be prepared to listen, and this means being prepared to learn. Preliminary phase work may help workers predict possible themes, and experience may teach them a great deal about common needs and issues. However, in the beginning phase, they need to put aside any assumptions as they attempt to appreciate the unique nature of each client. Active listening skills of attending, using silence, summarizing, paraphrasing, questioning, and showing empathy are the basic tools for this exploration. These skills tend to motivate clients to gradually open up, organize their thoughts, and identify their feelings. They move the relationship beyond superficiality and help both the worker and the client achieve shared understanding. Active listening enables workers to probe for details, definitions, and examples—information that is essential for preventing assumptions. Active listening skills will be explored in depth in Chapters 3 to 5.

The Therapeutic Value of the Beginning Phase.   Even though the beginning phase focuses on developing the counseling relationship and on exploration, clients often deepen their understanding and become empowered by the process. The therapeutic value of workers listening without judgment can be enormous. Because intense listening is rare in everyday encounters, clients may be visibly moved when they feel heard. When workers accept clients without judgment, clients become better able to accept themselves.

Effective workers probe for detail by asking questions systematically. They identify feelings and mirror them with empathic statements. This work enables clients to better organize their thinking and to explore and accept their feelings. When clients are confused or indecisive, orderly questioning helps them to categorize information and to pinpoint details or issues that they may have overlooked.

Effective workers encourage clients to explore the emotional components of their lives. When clients share emotions, workers need to be careful not to sabotage this sharing by rescuing, telling clients not to feel as they do, changing the subject, or conveying discomfort or judgment. As clients talk, they may release a flood of emotions. A client might remark, "I've told you things that no one else knows." As clients open up, they may begin to feel unburdened, a process that is known as **catharsis,** which Barker defines as a "verbalization and other expression of ideas, fears, past significant events, and associations, the expected result of which is a release of anxiety or tension, resulting in improved functioning; also called **ventilation**" (1995:49).

A Caution.   Some clients don't return for the next scheduled interview. Sometimes they decide not to return because they feel they don't need to. A single session may be sufficient to meet their needs. The cathartic release of emotions in a single session empowers them enough to deal with their problems.

Other clients may quickly respond to the power of the counseling relationship and disclose at a level they would not have predicted. Later, they may feel embarrassed, fearing that they have gone too far, or they may resent their workers for probing into areas they would have preferred to keep private. In response, clients may cut off the counseling relationship prematurely, or they may come to the next session but remain distant and guarded in order to protect themselves from overdisclosing.

One way to prevent problems is to be sensitive to individual pacing needs. Clients may give clues that the session is moving too quickly. The worker should watch for indicators such as hesitation, questioning why the worker wants to know something, or statements that the client would rather not discuss particular issues.

Another strategy is to candidly discuss with clients how they feel about the session. The following exchange illustrates this technique.

> **SOCIAL WORKER:** *Later tonight, when you think about our time together, how do you think you will feel?*
>
> **CLIENT:** *I think I'll have mixed feelings. It was really good to talk, but I wonder if I told you too much. I hope you won't think less of me.*
>
> **SOCIAL WORKER:** *You took a real risk with me in sharing your private thoughts and feelings. I think it's reasonable to worry about how I reacted. Would you like to know?*
>
> **CLIENT:** *Yes, very much.*
>
> **SOCIAL WORKER:** *Do you trust me enough to believe that I won't lie to you or tell you something just to make you feel better?*

If client says yes, the worker can candidly share reaction to the client disclosure:

I admire your courage to face such painful issues. As a result, I feel closer to you and better able to understand your struggle. No, I don't think less of you.

If client says no, the worker can initiate discussion of what work needs to be done to establish trust:

Perhaps we could talk a bit about what needs to happen between you and me in order for you to trust me.

In the above example, the worker helps the client anticipate feelings that might arise after the session. By doing so, the worker can help prevent the client from reaching false conclusions or making erroneous assumptions about what happened. In order for workers to have such discussions with clients, a high level of **self-awareness** is crucial. Workers need to be willing to examine how they are relating to their clients. They should be adept at identifying any personal biases (positive and negative) that they need to manage in order to work effectively with their client.

The Action Phase

The action phase is a time of change, a time when clients set goals, explore alternatives, and develop strategies for reaching their objectives. In the beginning phase, workers work to understand their clients' perspectives. Now, in the action phase, they look for opportunities to assist clients in identifying other ways of looking at or dealing with their situation. This can happen or be facilitated in two ways.

First, clients may make discoveries or reach insight spontaneously from exploring issues, feelings, and problems. Skilled helpers ask questions systematically, probing for detail as appropriate. This process alone helps clients organize their thoughts on complex issues. As well, summary, paraphrase, and empathy responses provide an important mirror for reflecting clients' feelings and ideas. As a result, clients may see their problems in a different light, or they may discover choices for action that they had overlooked.

Second, workers may play a key role by providing new information, ideas, or perspectives. This role could involve challenging distortions in the way clients think about problems or encouraging them to consider overlooked aspects. As well, they need to encourage the work of change by ensuring that clients set clear and specific goals, which form the basis for the development of realistic action plans. Subsequently, they may assist clients in implementing their plans. This assistance includes helping them to anticipate and address potential problems, as well as supporting them through the struggles of the change process. Workers also help clients develop new strategies for coping through a variety of skill acquisition strategies, such as role playing, or by teaching techniques for managing self-defeating thought patterns.

When clients experience (from their workers) core conditions of congruence, empathy, and positive regard, they become better able to accept themselves, less defensive, and more open to experiencing and accepting their feelings. Client attitudes and feelings change as counseling progresses successfully. Some of the important signals that clients are changing and growing include the following:

- cues that they feel less apprehensive about counseling and the counseling relationship
- increased acceptance of feelings and more honest expression of previously denied feelings
- diminished negativism, self-doubt, and blaming of others and increased optimism and self-acceptance
- increased acceptance of responsibility for behaviors or choices
- reduced sense of responsibility for the actions and choices of others
- increased empathy for others (Gilliland and James, 1998:115)

Frequently, beginning and action phase activities happen simultaneously. Shifts between beginning and action phase work are also common. Clients may explore a problem in depth, begin a change program, then revert to beginning phase work to tackle another problem area. Some common scenarios are the following:

Angelo's worker encouraged him to describe his situation. As he talked, he discovered aspects of his problem that he had overlooked and that suggested new possibilities for immediate action.

Pari tended to keep her feelings so well hidden that she was unaware of their effect or intensity. With gentle encouragement from her worker, she began to open up. Talking about her feelings represented a dramatic shift in her behavior. The therapeutic value of this change was enormous, as she unburdened herself from a lifetime of pent-up emotions.

Chapter 7 will explore how to assist clients through the work of the action phase.

The Ending Phase

Successful termination starts in the beginning phase, when the nature and limits of the counseling contract are defined. When workers and clients agree on the activities and goals of counseling, the point of termination is defined. This point of termination becomes a target of all counseling work, and though it may change as client needs and progress are reevaluated, workers should reinforce termination as one reality of the relationship.

Although evaluation is a component of all phases of counseling, the ending phase is a major opportunity to assess what was accomplished and what remains to be done. It is a time to help clients make the step to independence, and it is a time for clients to consider new directions and goals. It may be a point of transition as workers refer clients to other services. The ending phase is also a time to evaluate the counseling relationship. This evaluation may involve addressing any unresolved feelings or concerns and expressing feelings about the ending of the relationship.

Workers need to be able to make intelligent decisions about when to terminate the relationship. Termination of counseling relationships may be warranted for a number of reasons. First, the relationship may be ended when the goals of counseling have been reached. Counseling relationships are time–limited, and when clients have developed a sufficient capacity to work on their own, it is time to end the relationship. Second, workers may end the relationship if they do not have the time or competence to fulfill their clients' needs. In such cases, the ending will include referral to other counselors or agencies. Third, workers may determine that they are unable to work with sufficient objectivity. Here, again, referral is the preferred alternative. Finally, if evidence shows that counseling has not worked and that there is little potential that it will become successful, it is time to terminate or refer.

Counseling relationships can be exceptionally intimate, and the termination of the relationship may evoke painful feelings of loss for both workers and clients. This sense of loss may be especially pronounced in long-term relationships, but even short-term relationships that have dealt with crises or intimate matters may rouse feelings of sadness 'as the relationship ends. Clients who have difficulty with transitions and who have become dependent on their workers may experience the ending as a crisis.

Young suggests that "a helper's feelings of loss at termination may also be due to a reliance on helping relationships to meet needs for intimacy (friendship) as well as a conscious or unconscious sexual attraction" (1998:286). The termination may also remind workers of other losses in their lives. When these losses remain unresolved, there is a risk that workers may be unable to appropriately handle termination with the client. They may feel guilty for leaving the client, and they might delay or avoid termination in order to elude their own feelings of pain.

The ending phase can be a time of continuing growth for clients. As Hess and McCartt Hess conclude:

> Clients should be empowered through the termination process to embark upon a self-directed course of action based upon realistic assessment of their problem-solving strengths. Mastery of termination issues supports client self-esteem and reinforces the client's hopes that ongoing progress can be achieved. The work of the ending also frees the client to reinvest energy in appropriate life tasks and ongoing relationships which support problem solving (1984:562).

Termination of the counseling relationship will be considered in more detail in Chapter 3.

Summary

Counseling involves a time-limited relationship designed to help clients increase their capacity to deal with the demands of life. Counseling work may include many activities, such as helping clients deal with feelings, learn new skills, make decisions, and access resources.

Counseling is conducted by a wide range of people at various levels of education. Interviewing skills are imperative for effective counseling. Interviewing is essentially an information-gathering process; however, clients may experience some therapeutic relief from sharing their stories.

Counseling caseloads are characterized by diversity in culture, gender, age, religion, sexual orientation, language, education, economic ability, and so on. Working with diversity requires workers to be adaptive. Expert workers use research theory and experience as guides to determine which skills and procedures best meet the needs of their clients. Competent workers use a wide range of skills; they know when to use skills; they match the language of their clients; and they adapt other variables, such as the time and place of the interview.

Four major skill clusters define the range of necessary skills: (1) relationship-building, (2) exploring/probing, (3) empowering, and (4) challenging skills. Workers use relationship-building skills for engaging clients and developing trust. They use exploring/probing skills in order to gather information, clarify definitions, seek examples, and obtain necessary detail. They use empowering skills to help clients develop confidence, self-esteem, and control over their lives. As well, they help clients manage anxiety and stress and use challenging skills to encourage clients to critically evaluate their behavior and ideas.

Many variables can lead to poor outcomes in counseling. Client variables include unrealistic expectations and poor motivation. Worker factors such as burnout, personal problems, and loss of objectivity can also lead to failure. Process or faulty techniques, including pseudocounseling, advice giving, and rescuing, can contribute to failure. Finally, failure may arise from factors outside the control of workers and clients.

The four counseling phases are: (1) preliminary, (2) beginning, (3) action, and (4) ending. Each phase is characterized by unique tasks and skills. The preliminary phase focuses on preparing for the interview and setting up the right environment for counseling. The beginning phase is concerned with establishing the counseling relationship and with exploring for understanding. In the action phase, the focus shifts to goal setting and implementing change. In the ending phase, the relationship is concluded. During different phases of the relationship different skill clusters assume priority.

EXERCISES

1. Assess the following statements as "true" or "false." Be prepared to defend your answers.

   a. It is important for social workers to develop a personal style so that all clients are treated in the same way.

   b. The counseling process has a lot in common with the process used by other professionals, such as doctors and lawyers; thus, competent social workers gather information, diagnose the problem, and offer solutions or advice to their clients on the best resolution.

   c. Usually clients who seek help are in crisis, and their ability to make decisions is significantly impaired. Therefore, it is important that workers are comfortable with making important decisions on behalf of their clients.

   d. Application of skills or techniques detracts from spontaneity.

   e. Professional counselors are free from biases.

   f. Personal experience with the same problem or issues as clients is necessary for workers.

   g. The counseling process evolves sequentially through a number of phases, with each phase having defined skills and tasks.

   h. Effective workers are consistent, and they use the same skills in the same way throughout the counseling process.

   i. If the principles of counseling are applied effectively, all clients will be helped.

   j. Everything that happens in the counseling interview must be treated as confidential and must be shared with no one.

   k. Effective counseling involves blending the client's needs with those of the worker so that everyone involved is satisfied.

   l. The skills of counseling are also the skills of effective everyday communication.

2. Write a short essay supporting the following argument: The capacity to accept help from another person is a sign of strength.

3. Imagine that you are responding to the following client questions: What is counseling? How does it work?

4. Explore the extent to which you tend to give advice or rescue. Seek feedback from others who know you to see if their perceptions agree with your self-evaluation.

5. In what ways might advice giving disempower clients?

6. Think of a recent or current problem that you are facing. Describe the ways that counseling might be used to assist you in addressing this problem. Using concepts from this chapter, identify what might be the major activities for each phase of counseling.

7. Review the tasks of each of the phases of helping. With which phase do you feel most comfortable? Least comfortable?

8. What do you think are the advantages and disadvantages of working from a four-phase model of counseling?

9. Reflect on your competence across the broad range of counseling skills listed in this chapter. Rate yourself on a scale of 1 to 5 for each of the following counseling skills.

5 = very strong
4 = strong
3 = satisfactory
2 = needs development
1 = needs considerable development

a. Active listening

____ attending

____ allowing appropriate silence

____ paraphrasing

____ summarizing

____ questioning

____ showing empathy

b. Promoting core conditions

____ communicating with genuineness

____ showing positive regard

c. Defining the relationship

____ contracting (defining roles and the purpose of counseling)

____ promoting immediacy (open discussion and evaluation of the relationship)

____ allowing self-disclosure and admitting feelings

d. Other interviewing skills

____ using directives

____ using small encouragers ("Yes," "Tell me more," head nods)

____ using humor

e. Searching for strengths

____ defining client capacities, skills, and abilities

____ redefining problems as challenges and opportunities for learning identifying resources

f. Teaching

____ training in skills

____ modeling behaviors, skills, or attitudes

____ role playing/rehearsing behaviors

g. Information giving

____ offering opinions or advice

____ making referrals

h. Supporting

___ reassuring

___ expressing optimism

___ reinforcing (rewarding, praising)

___ acting as an advocate for the client

i. Confrontation

___ providing feedback to help clients recognize inappropriate reactions

___ confronting strengths (pointing out client capacities and strengths)

___ encouraging or urging

___ correcting distortions/testing reality

___ asking the client to take responsibility

j. Action planning

___ assisting and motivating clients in defining clear and measurable targets for change

___ helping clients identify and evaluate alternatives

___ helping clients choose, develop, and carry out change strategies

k. Use of power and authority

___ limit setting

___ enforcement

10. Based on your ratings identify:

a. three main skill strengths

b. the skills you are more likely to use

c. the skills that you typically have difficulty using

d. three priority areas for development/goal setting

11. Identify and explore clients' legal rights to access file information (in your jurisdiction).

2 Ethics, Values, and Self-Awareness

Preview

After reading this chapter you should be able to:

- explain the importance of ethics
- list core standards of ethical behavior, including principles governing confidentiality
- identify principles for resolving ethical dilemmas
- explain the principle of self-determination
- describe how counselors can understand and work with diversity
- understand the importance of counselor objectivity and self-awareness. Know how to increase self-awareness
- understand and manage personal needs and values in counseling

Professional Behavior

Ethics

Ethics are the principles and rules of acceptable or proper conduct. All professions have ethical guidelines that define the limits of permissible behavior and the sanctions or remedies that might be applied if members violate ethical standards. Codes of ethics protect social workers and other professionals as well as their clients.

Professionals can use their codes to assist them with decision making and as reference for their practice. Clients are offered some shelter from incompetent practice. Ethical codes also provide guidance on how counselors can deal fairly with colleagues. The codes detail expectations and procedures for protecting clients from unethical conduct by other members of the profession. Unethical behavior typically arises from issues related to the following: breaking confidentiality, misrepresenting or working beyond one's level of expertise, conducting improper relationships, including sexual activity with clients, and causing conflicts of interest, such as entering into business or other dual relationships with clients.

Professional associations are responsible for monitoring their own policies and for investigating and resolving violations of ethical conduct. The National Association of Social Workers (NASW), the American Counseling Association (ACA), and the Canadian Association of Social Workers (CASW) are examples of professional bodies that may formally discipline members who violate their codes of ethics. Alternatively, counselors who are not members of professional associations may work with agencies that provide guidelines for ethical behavior and decision making.

Legislation may define and restrict the use of certain titles, such as social worker, psychologist, and psychiatrist, to those who have completed the appropriate degree or training. The clients of these professionals can report misconduct or concerns to the appropriate professional association. However, there may be no legislation preventing people from offering counseling services under a wide range of other titles, such as counselor, personal therapist, family and marital counselor, and personal growth consultant. These practitioners may not have had formal preparation or training, and clients should be cautious when they seek their services.

Since its inception in 1955, the National Association of Social Workers (NASW) has become the primary organization representing the needs and governing the actions of social workers in the United States. NASW, like all professional associations, has attempted to assist its members by adopting guidelines for correct professional behavior. The NASW code of ethics, first adopted in 1960, has now evolved into 155 ethical standards organized under six ethical principles. The current code, ratified in 1996 by the NASW Delegate Assembly, affirms the central mission of the profession of social work "to enhance human well-being and help meet the basic human needs of all people, with particular attention to the needs and empowerment of people who are vulnerable, oppressed, and living in poverty" (NASW, 1996:preamble). In addition, the code articulates the core values that define the social work profession as follows:

> The mission of the social work profession is rooted in a set of core values. These core values, embraced by social workers throughout the profession's history, are the foundation of social work's unique purpose and perspective:
>
> - service
> - social justice
> - dignity and worth of the person
> - importance of human relationships
> - integrity
> - competence (NASW, 1996:preamble).

The complete National Association of Social Workers Code of Ethics is included in this book as Appendix 1.

The American Counseling Association Code of Ethics and Standards of Practice (ACA, 1995) is included in this book as Appendix 2. Ethical guidelines such as the ACA and NASW codes are designed to protect and respect clients' needs and interests. Ethical codes recognize that clients may be vulnerable and subject to manipulation and abuse of power by professionals, so they constrain professionals from taking advantage of them. As well, codes of ethics contain standards of behavior for dealing with colleagues, other professionals, and society in general. Codes outline the responsibility of its members to address the unethical conduct of colleagues.

The NASW code recognizes that, whereas it provides values, principles, and standards to guide practice, it cannot offer precise guidelines for action in all situations. Social workers are reminded that there may be no simple answers to complex ethical problems. Consequently, the code recommends that social workers use a variety of information sources to make decisions.

> Social workers should consider ethical theory and principles generally, social work theory and research, laws, regulations, agency policies, and other relevant codes of ethics, recognizing that among codes of ethics social workers should consider the *NASW Code of Ethics* as their primary source. Social workers also should be aware of the impact on ethical decision making of their clients' and their own personal values and cultural and religious beliefs and practices. They should be aware of any conflicts between personal and professional values and deal with them responsibly. For additional guidance social workers should consult the relevant literature on professional ethics and ethical decision making and seek appropriate consultation when faced with ethical dilemmas. This may involve consultation with an agency-based or social work organization's ethics committee, a regulatory body, knowledgeable colleagues, supervisors, or legal counsel (1996:3).

Core Standards of Ethical Behavior

Ethics are derived from values. Values are principles or qualities that individuals and groups consider important or worthwhile. Values represent beliefs about what is desirable and good. Personal values describe what individuals consider desirable and what they believe is right and wrong. Professional values describe fundamental beliefs that the profession holds about people and how the work of the profession ought to be conducted. Clearly, professional values (as reflected in ethical codes of conduct) and personal values have a major impact in shaping the practice of counseling professionals. The key values of social work and counseling are discussed below.

The Belief in the Dignity and Worth of People. Belief in the dignity and worth of people is a core value of social work and counseling. This value has a number of implications for practice. Central to this value is the commitment to ensuring that clients are treated with regard for their rights. It obligates social workers to demonstrate acceptance of the individual and to uphold confidentiality. Social workers who value the dignity of their clients appreciate diversity and reject stereotyping, labeling, and other dehumanizing practices. This means that they must treat clients fairly, regardless of their personal feelings toward them. For example, they must resist the natural temptation to spend more time with clients they favor and less time with those whom they find difficult. Any discriminatory practice is strictly prohibited: "Counselors do not condone or engage in discrimination based on age, color, culture, disability, ethnic group, gender, race, religion, sexual orientation, marital status, or socioeconomic status" (ACA, 1995:A.2.a). The NASW Code of Ethics (1996) articulates this ethical standard for social workers regarding cultural competence and social diversity:

(a) Social workers should understand culture and its function in human behavior and society, recognizing the strengths that exist in all cultures.

(b) Social workers should have a knowledge base of their clients' cultures and be able to demonstrate competence in the provision of services that are sensitive to clients' cultures and to differences among people and cultural groups.

(c) Social workers should obtain education about and seek to understand the nature of social diversity and oppression with respect to race, ethnicity, national origin, color, sex, sexual orientation, age, marital status, political belief, religion, and mental or physical disability (Standard 1.05).

This expectation is also explicit in the ACA code of ethics:

> Respecting Differences. Counselors will actively attempt to understand the diverse cultural backgrounds of the clients with whom they work. This includes, but is not limited to, learning how the counselor's own cultural/ethnic/racial identity impacts her or his values and beliefs about the counseling process (1995:A.2.b).

These ethical guidelines underscore the need for social workers to actively engage in learning about other cultures. They need to increase their sensitivity regarding how their values and beliefs have affected their behaviour, worldview, and the way they relate to others. This topic will be explored in more depth in Chapter 10.

Social workers are expected to apply their skills and knowledge at an optimum level for each client, regardless of their personal reaction toward any individual. Clients may have behaved in ways that social workers perceive to be offensive, but this belief does not give them license to be disrespectful or to withhold service.

Compton and Galaway (1984:70) suggest five guidelines for putting this value into practice:

1. Be sensitive and aware of what we are communicating regarding client dignity by the way we organize and administer our services.
2. Avoid stereotyping clients.
3. Help clients to discover and use their strengths.
4. Expect client participation in problem solving.
5. Focus on clients' wants rather than on clients' needs.

Social workers who work with high-risk clients, such as those with chronic addiction problems, need to be careful that their view of and attitudes toward clients do not become jaded. Jaded social workers have abandoned any optimistic view of human nature, including the belief that people are generally goal directed and capable of change. In place of this view they have developed, sometimes gradually over a period of years, a more cynical and pessimistic perspective of the willingness and capacity of their clients to change and grow. Social workers who believe that clients are incapable of growth are likely to invest less energy in supporting change. Moreover, they may be more prone to use controlling responses because of their expectation that the "clients cannot do it on their own." What would you predict to be the likely outcome of a counseling session when the counselor labels the client as "a hopeless alcoholic?"

The Importance of Avoiding Dual Relationships.   The essential purpose of the counseling relationship is to meet the needs of clients while respecting their individuality and rights. This goal has a number of implications for ethical practice. Social workers must not misuse professional relationships for personal gain. A **dual** (or **multiple**) **relationship** is, one that involves both a professional relationship and another type of relationship (e.g., friendship, sexual, business, supervisory). Dual relationships "are problematic because they reduce the counselor's objectivity, confuse the issue, and often put the client in a position of diminished consent" (Cormier and Cormier, 1985:19). In dual relationships, the professional has a personal interest that may conflict with the client's interest. This may lead to intended or unintended exploitation, harm, manipulation, or coercion of clients. To prevent these problems and any conflict of interest, dual relationships should be avoided, particularly when they could potentially harm the client. Professionals who are emotionally stable will not want or need to involve themselves in dual relationships to meet their own needs.

Not surprisingly, the codes of ethics for the various counseling professions strictly prohibit certain types of dual relationships, especially sexual involvement. The ACA code, for example, is explicit in prohibiting this relationship, stating that "counselors do not have any type of sexual intimacies with clients and do not counsel persons with whom they have had a sexual relationship" (1995:A.7.a). In addition, the ACA code discourages sexual intimacy with former clients:

> Counselors do not engage in sexual intimacies with former clients within a minimum of 2 years after terminating the counseling relationship. Counselors who engage in such relationship after 2 years following termination have the responsibility to examine and document thoroughly that such relations did not have an exploitative nature, based on factors such as duration of counseling, amount of time since counseling, termination circumstances, client's personal history and mental status, adverse impact on the client, and actions by the counselor suggesting a plan to initiate a sexual relationship with the client after termination (A.7.b).

The ACA position is echoed in the NASW code, which prohibits social workers from having sexual relations with current clients, clients' relatives, or from accepting as clients individuals with whom they have had a prior sexual relationship (1996:1.09). The NASW code highlights the risk of client exploitation and potential harm as well as the difficulty for the social worker to keep appropriate professional boundaries. As the code makes explicit:

> Social workers should not engage in sexual activities or sexual contact with former clients because of the potential for harm to the client. If social workers engage in conduct contrary to this prohibition or claim that an exception to this prohibition is warranted because of extraordinary circumstances, it is social workers—not their clients—who assume the full burden of demonstrating that the former client has not been exploited, coerced, or manipulated, intentionally or unintentionally (Standard 1.09:c).

It is notable that the NASW code explicitly states that dual or multiple relationships can occur simultaneously or consecutively. Thus, the fact that a social worker/client relationship has ended does not mean that the social worker can enter into other links with his or her client.

Notwithstanding these injunctions, abuses continue to occur. Reviewing the available research, Thoreson et al. (1993) found that the incidence of sexual contact between counselors and clients ranges from 3.6 to 12.1 percent, with as many as 80 percent of counselors who had sexual contact with clients engaging in it with more than one client. Conducting their own study, the researchers found, after surveying 1,000 randomly selected male members of the ACA, that 1.7 percent of the respondents reported engaging in sexual contact with a client during a professional relationship, and 7 percent reported engaging in sexual contact after a professional relationship (Thoreson et al., 1993).

The NASW code cautions social workers to avoid physical contact with clients, including cradling or caressing them. However, the code acknowledges that there may be circumstances when physical contact is reasonable as long as social workers set "clear, appropriate, and culturally sensitive boundaries that govern such contact" (Standard 1.10). Although the code does not give examples of when physical contact might be acceptable, one of the authors of the code suggests elsewhere that, "comforting a distraught child who has been removed from his home because of parental neglect or holding the hand of a nursing home resident whose spouse has died" (Reamer, 1998:18) may be permissible.

The Need to Promote Client Self-Determination.

The principle of client **self-determination** promotes the rights of clients to have autonomy and freedom of choice. Adherence to the principle does not prevent counselors from helping clients understand how their actions might violate the rights of others, nor does it prevent counselors from helping clients appreciate the potential consequences of their actions. Some clients, such as people with mental disabilities and young children, may be unable to make competent choices. The NASW code provides this guideline:

> Social workers may limit clients' right to self-determination when, in the social workers' professional judgment, clients' actions or potential actions pose a serious, foreseeable, and imminent risk to themselves or others (Standard 1.02).

Thus, social workers may prevent clients from acting in ways that are potentially harmful to themselves or others, but, as Cottone and Tarvydas (1998) warn, expert knowledge does not give counselors the moral authority to act on behalf of their clients with the assumption that only they know what is best for them.

Choice is an integral part of client self-determination. When clients have no choices or feel that they have none, self-determination is not possible. Social workers can assist clients in self-determination through a number of strategies. First, they can help clients identify their choices. Sometimes clients have overlooked alternatives or need concrete information regarding their options. Social workers can also provide information to help clients make informed choices. Second, social workers can use advocacy skills to help clients access resources or remove barriers to existing options.

The principle of self-determination obligates social workers to avoid behaviors that control and manipulate clients and, instead, to employ strategies that empower clients. **Empowerment** is the process of assisting clients to discover personal strengths and capacities. Empowerment seeks to help clients take control of their lives and realize that they can improve their situation through their actions. As much as possible, clients should be encouraged to make independent decisions.

Sometimes, beginning social workers are misinformed about the nature of counseling. They believe that their role is to listen to their clients' problems, then offer helpful advice or solutions. This gives rise to what Dumont describes as the rescue fantasy, a belief that the counselor's role is save people and put happiness back into their lives. He concludes that when this notion is communicated to clients, "they have no choice other than to rebel and leave or become even more helpless, dependent and sick" (1968:6).

When social workers understand the principle of self-determination, they avoid advice giving by helping clients identify and explore options, then encouraging them to make their own decisions. This puts clients clearly in the position of being the major decision makers and problem solvers. For their part, social workers play a major role in orchestrating the process.

Effective social workers accept that clients have a right to be involved in counseling decision making. They have the right to be treated as active partners in the counseling process and to participate in decisions affecting their lives. This right is underscored in the ACA code of ethics:

> Disclosure to Clients. When counseling is initiated, and throughout the counseling process as necessary, counselors inform clients of the purposes, goals, techniques, procedures, limitations, potential risks, and benefits of services to be performed, and other pertinent information. Counselors take steps to ensure that clients understand the implications of diagnosis, the intended use of tests and reports, fees, and billing arrangements (1995:A.3.a).

The NASW code emphasizes the importance of informed consent and offers this guideline for social workers:

> Social workers should use clear and understandable language to inform clients of the purpose of the services, risks related to the services, limits to services because of the requirements of a third-party payer, relevant costs, reasonable alternatives, clients' right to refuse or withdraw consent, and the time frame covered by the consent. Social workers should provide clients with an opportunity to ask questions (Standard 1.03).

Thus, social workers should promote client awareness of the issues affecting counseling. They should encourage clients to ask questions about their counseling techniques and strategies. They should welcome client involvement in evaluating the progress of counseling and the counseling relationship itself. Finally, when dealing with clients who are receiving services involuntarily, such as those under court order, social workers should provide information to clients regarding the limits of their right to decline service, as well as the consequences of such denial.

The Need for Professional Development. Professional counselors and social workers need a core knowledge base, which typically requires two or more years of academic training, including supervised clinical experience in a recognized counseling or social service setting. Moreover, throughout their careers, professionals should expect to spend time reading books and journals to increase their knowledge. As well, regular attendance of courses, seminars, and conferences should be a part of everyone's professional career.

By keeping their knowledge base current, social workers are better able to be empathic because they are more aware of the issues and feelings that their clients face.

Moreover, keeping up-to-date will help social workers avoid any judgmental responses that might occur if they reacted from only their own frames of reference. The range of knowledge that social workers need to pursue includes the following:

- Specific issues, problems, and challenges that their clients are facing. For example, professionals working in corrections need to know something about finding a job if one has a criminal record and coping with the stigma of a criminal record. Many clients are dealing with poverty, and their counselors need to be aware of its social and psychological effects.
- Relevant medical and psychiatric conditions (e.g., attention deficit disorder, multiple sclerosis, schizophrenia, bipolar disorder). Counselors' credibility and competence is greatly enhanced if their knowledge of these conditions is current.
- Lifestyle variation (e.g., same-sex relationships, single parents, extended families, and blended families).
- Cultural wisdom about the values, beliefs, and customs of others.
- Lifespan development (i.e., developmental changes and milestones from birth to death).

Life experience can greatly increase a social worker's capacity for empathy and understanding. Of course, life experience may also cloud judgment and objectivity, so it is important that they seek training and consultation to increase their understanding of others' experiences.

Confidentiality

The rules regarding confidentiality are integral to every code of ethics. Ethical guidelines stress that the confidentiality of clients must be protected. Indeed, most clients enter counseling with an expectation that what they say will be kept private. For the most part, social workers can assure clients that they will keep their disclosures confidential. However, it is often not so simple. **Absolute confidentiality** means that client disclosures are not shared with anyone. **Relative confidentiality** means that information is shared within the agency with supervisors or colleagues, outside the agency with the client's permission, or in courts of law owing to legal requirements, such as child-abuse legislation. Usually, clients can be assured only of relative confidentiality.

In order to provide optimum service to clients, information about them must be shared within the agency. To monitor the quality of work and help social workers improve their skills, supervisors need to review client files, or they may consult with social workers by reviewing audio and video recordings of their interviews. Other social workers within the agency also have access to files.

Many people believe that social workers and other professionals enjoy "privileged communication," i.e., that they are legally protected from having to share information that they have obtained while exercising their professional duties. However, the courts may subpoena counselors' records. A recent U.S. Supreme Court decision (*Jafee v. Redmond*, cited in Remley, Herlihy, and Herlihy, 1997) held that communication between licensed psychotherapists (those with master's degrees) and their clients does not have to be disclosed in federal court. However, protection for unlicensed psychotherapists has not been established.

There are valid reasons, including some legal requirements, for sharing information. For example, all jurisdictions in North America have legislation that requires everyone, including social workers and other professionals, to report suspicions of child abuse and neglect to the appropriate authorities. Similarly, professionals might have to break confidentiality when they believe that clients might harm themselves or others. It is vital that social workers acquaint themselves with the precise wording of relevant statutes because laws may vary significantly in different parts of the country (Glosoff, Herlihy, and Spence, 2000).

One often quoted legal precedent is the Tarasoff case, in which the client had told his counselor of his intent to kill his girlfriend. The counselor told the campus police of the threat, but he did not warn his client's girlfriend or her family. The client, a student at the school, subsequently carried out his threat and killed the young woman. A successful lawsuit was brought by the girl's parents against the counselor and the university. This litigation established that, when counselors believe that a client represents "a serious danger of violence to another," they have a duty to warn potential victims (*Tarasoff v. Regents of the University of California* [1976], cited in Woodside and McClam, 1990:267). Since the Tarasoff decision, there have been numerous state laws and legal precedents that address the duty-to-warn issue. Reamer (1998) concluded that, although some court rulings have been contradictory, trends suggest that four conditions warrant disclosure of confidential information without a client's permission:

1. There must be evidence that the client is a threat to another person.
2. Based on a client's behavior, there should be evidence that the violent act is likely to occur.
3. There should be evidence suggesting that the violent act is imminent.
4. Social workers and other professionals should be able to identify the potential victim.

The ACA code permits counselors to notify persons who are at risk of contracting a communicable and fatal disease from a client, providing that the counselors are certain that the client has not informed the person and does not intend to. "A counselor who receives information confirming that a client has a disease commonly known to be both communicable and fatal is justified in disclosing information to an identifiable third party, who by his or her relationship with the client is at a high risk of contracting the disease" (1995:B.1.d). The NASW code permits social workers to divulge confidential information for "compelling professional reasons . . . when disclosure is necessary to prevent serious, foreseeable, and imminent harm to a client or other identifiable person" (Standard 1.07c). The NASW code does not list specific examples when client consent is not required, so social work practitioners should consult relevant state and federal laws as well as their professional literature for guidance.

Zastrow (1990:64) notes that breaking confidentiality may be warranted or required when:

- a client formally authorizes the release
- a professional is called to testify in a criminal case
- a client files a lawsuit against a professional
- a client threatens suicide
- a client threatens to harm his or her therapist
- a professional becomes aware that a minor has committed a crime, that a minor is being used by adults as an accessory in a crime, or that a minor is a victim of criminal actions
- there is evidence of child abuse or neglect
- a client's emotional or physical condition makes his or her employment a clear danger, such as when an airline pilot has a serious drinking problem

Clients have a right to be fully informed regarding the limits of confidentiality, including any legal and ethical responsibilities that require social workers to share information. Through discussions regarding confidentiality, social workers can reassure clients that computer and file records are not shared indiscriminately. Table 2.1 provides guidelines for protecting oneself and one's clients.

There are a number of steps that counselors can take to protect client confidentiality. They should discipline themselves not to discuss clients in public places and at parties or other social events. Counseling work is demanding, and an important part of dealing with the stress of the job is to unwind by talking about difficult cases and personal reactions with colleagues and supervisors. This is a healthy and necessary component of professional wellness. Unfortunately, time pressures and large caseloads may leave little or no time for this process during the working day, so it is easy to fall into the trap of discussing clients over lunch or in other settings where confidentiality cannot be ensured. The obvious risk is that the conversation will be overheard. Even when names are not used, accidental listeners may think that they know the person being discussed. In addition, they may decide that they would never go for counseling because what they say will soon be all over town.

Although it is tempting for counselors to discuss clients with family and friends because they are available as supportive listeners, they should avoid doing so. Family and

---

TABLE 2.1   Confidentiality Guidelines

- Involve clients. Keep them informed and seek their permission to release information. Remember that freedom of information statutes may give clients the right to access your files.
- Become familiar with relevant legal statutes (e.g., child-abuse or mental health legislation) that define and limit confidentiality. Disclose only that information that is required.
- Review professional guidelines such as the NASW Code of Ethics and ACA Code of Ethics.
- Protect client records with secure filing systems. Do not leave files, notes, or phone messages about clients where they may be read by others. Insure that electronically stored data is protected.
- Insure that consultations with others concerning clients are legitimate and conducted in a private and professional manner. This precludes conversations about clients at social gatherings or in a public place such as a restaurant.
- Ensure that interviews are private and free from interruptions.

friends are not bound by the same ethics as counseling professionals and could accidentally disclose what they have heard, perhaps with a seemingly innocent observation or comment.

Sometimes social workers breach confidentiality by failing to take simple precautions. For example, taking phone calls during a counseling session can lead to careless breaches of confidentiality and suggests to clients that their worker treats their private matters casually. In addition, social workers should remove all case records, phone messages, and notes from their desk. This prevents clients from seeing the names of other clients and reinforces the fact that private records will not be left in public places.

When social workers leave phone messages for clients, they should leave only their first name and say nothing about their title or the nature of their call. Clients may not have informed roommates or family members that they are seeing a social worker.

The interview itself should be conducted in private, not in the waiting room or where other staff or clients may overhear. When greeting a client in the waiting room, social workers should refrain from using surnames. However, they need to be sensitive to the fact that many seniors and people from some cultures are insulted by the casual use of their first names.

Sometimes social workers meet clients by chance in public places. When this happens, social workers should ensure that they maintain confidentiality, even when the client appears unconcerned. They should gently shift the conversation to a neutral topic or suggest a private time and place to continue the discussion. At that time, they can explain why they avoided public discussion.

CONVERSATION **2.1**
Black Humor

STUDENT: I've just started my field placement and I'm disturbed by what's happening. When we go for coffee, everyone jokes and makes fun of the clients. If they knew the way their workers talked about them, they would never come back. I didn't know that professionals could be so coldhearted. Isn't their behavior unethical?

TEACHER: Many professionals deal with the enormous stress of their lobs through "black humor" (also known as "gallows humor") by making jokes about tragic events or clients' misfortunes. It's one way that they sustain their emotional well-being. It doesn't mean that they've become hardened or uncaring toward their clients; rather, it's a way of unwinding and relieving constant pressure. As you've discovered, one of the dangers of black humor is that others will overhear it and draw conclusions about the person's attitudes. Is it unethical? What do you think?

Ethical Dilemmas

Ethical codes attempt to define acceptable behavior, and, although they cannot provide precise guidelines for resolving all dilemmas, they provide an important reference for decision making. Ethics have their origin in the values of the profession, but "because people interpret abstract imperatives differently, they often disagree about what constitutes ethical behavior or 'appropriate actions.'"(DuBois and Miley, 1996:123).

Codes of ethics provide guidelines for making ethical decisions, but they usually do not offer answers to specific situations that arise for counseling professionals. An **ethical dilemma** exists when a choice must be made between competing values. A common example is the potential conflict between a client's right to confidentiality and the rights of society, for example, when a client discloses an intention to harm someone else. Such a dilemma might be resolved with the conclusion that the rights of an intended victim supersede the rights of the client. Other examples of ethical dilemmas include:

- A 15-year-old girl discloses that her father has been abusive, but in recent weeks he seems to have changed. She asks that you do not make a report to the authorities. She says she knows her father will retaliate if he finds out that she told anyone.
- A 17-year-old girl asks for your help to obtain an abortion without involving her parents.
- Your client informs you that he has tested positive for HIV, but he hasn't informed his partner.
- A 16-year-old boy tells you that he is working as a prostitute.
- Your client casually mentions that he robbed a bank several months ago but was not caught.

Cottone and Tarvydas (1998:135) identify five ethical rules or principles that can be used to help resolve ethical dilemmas: autonomy, beneficence, nonmaleficence, justice, and fidelity. They describe the obligations of each principle as follows:

1. *autonomy:* honoring the right to individual decisions
2. *beneficence:* doing good to others
3. *nonmaleficence:* doing no harm to others
4. *justice:* being fair; giving equally to others
5. *fidelity:* being loyal, honest, and keeping promises

Under ideal conditions, counselors can honor all five principles, but ethical dilemmas by nature represent competing principles, and different choices involve unique consequences. Ethical decision making involves identifying and weighing which of the five principles ought to have priority in any given situation. As well, professional judgment for resolving ethical dilemmas can be enhanced by consulting legislation and codes of ethics and by consulting with supervisors or colleagues.

A 50-year-old man confides that he often thinks of killing himself, but he pleads with you not to tell his spouse or anyone else. Here the principle of autonomy, which respects the client's right to self-determination, appears to be in conflict with the beneficence principle. The counselor must decide whether to sacrifice the client's right to make his own decision or to interfere with his autonomy because of a belief that intervention will be better for him in the long term. In addition, if the counselor keeps his client's secret (fidelity principle) and the client subsequently commits suicide, the counselor might be held responsible for not acting to prevent his actions (nonmaleficence). What would you do?

In its Code of Ethics, the Canadian Counselling Association (CCA) attempted to integrate various models of ethical decision making, and suggested a six-step sequence for ethical decision making and for resolving ethical dilemmas.

Step One—What are the key ethical issues in this situation?

Step Two—What ethical guidelines are relevant to this situation? This step consists of referring to the CCA Code of Ethics to see if the situation is dealt with under one or more of the articles in the Code.

Step Three—What ethical principles are of major importance in this situation?

    a. respect for the dignity of persons
    b. not willfully harming others
    c. integrity in relationships
    d. responsible caring
    e. responsibility to society
    f. respect for self-determination

Step Four—What are the most important principles, and what are the risks and benefits if these principles are acted upon? The fourth step consists of choosing the most important principles and relevant ethical articles and beginning to implement some possible action by:

    a. generating alternatives and examining the risks and benefits of each
    b. securing additional information, including possible discussion with the client
    c. consulting with knowledgeable colleagues, with provincial or CCA ethics committees, or with other appropriate sources, and
    d. examining the probable outcomes of various courses of action

Step Five—Will I feel the same about this situation if I think about it a little longer? Until this point, this decision-making process has concentrated on fairly cognitive, rational steps, so at the fifth step counselors should acknowledge and include in their decision-making process the feelings and intuitions evoked by the ethical challenge. In so doing, they could use such techniques as:

    a. Quest—take a solitary walk in the woods or park where your emotions evoked by the ethical challenge are brought into full awareness
    b. Incubation—"sleep on it"
    c. Time projection—project the ethical situation into the future and think about the various probable scenarios

Step Six—What plan of action will be most helpful in this situation? This step consists of taking some action. Counselors should follow a concrete action plan, evaluate the plan, and be prepared to correct any negative consequences that might occur from the action taken (CCA, 1999:iv–2).[1]

Shulz (2000) presents an example demonstrating the six steps in action. A high school counselor developed a strong relationship with John, a Grade 11 student, who confided that he was making extra money by stealing from his employer. The counselor struggled with what to do because he had assured John that their conversations would be confidential. Key ethical issues in this situation (step one) play off the promise of confidentiality with the illegal nature of the students' actions. As well, the potential that the student might be caught, with serious consequences, must be considered. The key ethical articles (step two) include those related to confidentiality with an exception for circumstances when there is a danger to others. Ethics also require counselors to remember that their first responsibility is to help the client. As well, counselors must inform clients regarding potential exceptions to confidentiality at the onset of counseling. Step three involves identification of the most important ethical principles. Of the six principles listed in the CCA code (see step three) Shulz suggests that five are significant in this case: integrity in relationships, responsible caring, not willfully harming others, responsibility to society, and respect for self-determination. Step four considers the risks and benefits of various courses of action such as reporting the theft and not reporting the theft and continuing to work with the client. In this particular situation, the counselor concluded (after consultation with a colleague) that "responsible caring" and "responsibility to society" should be the priorities. After "sleeping on it" (step five) the counselor took action (step six) by informing his client that he had concluded that he would not be acting responsibly by allowing the stealing to continue and that confidentiality must be broken. However, he worked with his client to identify several options, including the client reporting the theft himself, or the counselor going with the client to inform the employer of his illegal actions. Shulz proposes that decision making can be organized using charts such as the one provided in Table 2.2.

Application of the CCA model (or any other model) for ethicial decision making does not mean that resolution of ethical dilemmas will be easy. When values and ethics compete, the decision as to which one should have priority can be painfully difficult. Hepworth, Rooney, and Larsen (1997) propose the following four principles as guidelines:

1. The right to life, health, well-being, and necessities of life takes precedence over rights to confidentiality. . . .
2. An individual's basic right to well-being takes precedence over another person's right to privacy, freedom, or self-determination.
3. People's right to self-determination takes precedence over their right to basic well-being.
4. A person's right to well-being may override laws, policies, and arrangements of organizations (pp. 85–86).

Intimate knowledge of ethical principles and legal guidelines can make the decision-making process clearer, albeit no less difficult. For example, a client's right to confidentiality and self-determination must be given up when he or she discloses child abuse, and the **"duty to warn"** principle means that professionals must warn potential victims. However, it is not always clear the extent to which a client's behavior constitutes danger to others. Another example: Hepworth, Rooney, and Larsen (1997) assert that people have a right "to carry out actions that appear contrary to their best interests, providing they are competent to make an informed and relevant decision" (p. 85). This would protect the rights of people to make errors and carry out actions that others might consider wrong. However, counselors must consider when application of this principle must be abandoned because the individual's behavior might result in death, such as when clients threaten suicide. While counselors have a clear legal and ethical responsibility to intervene to prevent suicide,

TABLE 2.2   Making Decisions during Counseling

Action Choices	Benefits	Risks	Potential Outcomes
Choice 1 Avoid confronting the issue in counseling	May be the easiest	The problem behavior continues; Avoidance may implicitly condone the client's behavior	Counsellor could lose his job. Unchecked, the client's illegal activity might escalate with potential serious consequences.
Choice 2 Keep counseling the client; Encourage him to change his behavior and make restitution.	Maintains counseling relationship	Client may continue to come for counseling but not alter his behavior	If stealing continues, client's employer is further victimized; Client's behavior may escalate.
Choice 3 After telling client, report the activities to the appropriate authorities	In the long run, this may help the client to act more responsibly; Respects rights of employer	Lose John as a client; Possibly lose other clients	Initially, client may be angry, but this action would clearly communicate to him that the stealing must stop.

Adapted from Shulz, 2000:13.

other challenges are not so easy to resolve. For example, homeless persons' lifestyles may reach the point at which their hygiene and living and eating habits become dangerous for them. The point at which their right to self-determination should yield to their right to health and well-being is not easy to establish.

Objectivity

Effective social workers may become intimately familiar with the lives of their clients. Objectivity is defined as the capacity to understand situations and people without bias or distortion. When social workers are objective, they understand their clients' feelings, thoughts, and behaviors without allowing their personal values, beliefs, and biases to contaminate their understanding. When they are objective, they do not directly or subtly try to impose their preferred solutions on clients.

There are a number of ways that social workers can fail to be objective. The first is to make assumptions. **Assumptions** are distortions or false conclusions based on simplistic reasoning, incomplete information, or bias. Social workers who have had experiences similar to their clients' may assume that their clients' problems and feelings are the same. Consequently, they do not take the time to investigate the distinctive viewpoints of their clients. They also may make assumptions about the meaning of words. This danger can be avoided if they remain alert to the need to probe for individual client definition and meaning, as in the following example:

> **CLIENT (SPEAKING TO A FIRST NATIONS COUNSELOR):** *I moved here about five years ago. I guess you know how tough it is for an Indian in this city.*
>
> **SOCIAL WORKER (CHOICE 1):** *I sure do. Prejudice is everywhere.*
>
> **SOCIAL WORKER (CHOICE 2):** *Like you say, it's not easy. But it's different for everyone. I need your help to understand better what it's been like for you.*

CONVERSATION **2.2**
Personal Involvement with Clients

STUDENT: Is it ever okay to be sexually intimate with clients?

TEACHER: No! Universally, ethical codes of behavior prohibit sexual intimacies with clients. For example, the APA succinctly states that "psychologists do not engage in sexual intimacies with current patients or clients" (Cottone and Tarvydas, 1998:57). Their code also prohibits counselors from accepting patients with whom they have had past sexual intimacy. Similarly, the NASW code states, "The social worker should under no circumstances engage in sexual activities or sexual contact with current clients whether such contact is consensual or forced" (Standard 1.099).

STUDENT: That seems straightforward. What about becoming involved with former clients?

TEACHER: That's a more difficult question. My opinion is that you never should, but you should consult individual codes of ethics for specific guidelines. For example, the APA requires a minimum of two years between the end of the counseling relationship and the beginning of a sexual relationship, but they prefer that psychologists do not become sexually involved "even after a two-year interval except in the most unusual circumstances" (Cottone and Tarvydas, 1998:57). Similarly, The NASW code strongly discourages sexual involvement with former clients except in the case of extraordinary circumstances. A recent review of the literature concluded that harm to clients does occur when professionals have sexual contact with clients including "denial, guilt, shame, isolation, anger, depression, impaired ability to trust, loss of self-esteem, difficulty expressing anger, emotional lability, psychosomatic disorders, sexual confusion, and increased risk of suicide" (Beckman, Turner, Cooper, Polnerow, & Swartz, 2000:2).

STUDENT: What about other types of involvement? If you are a counselor in a small town, it's impossible to avoid social contact with clients. Your client might be the owner of the only grocery store in town.

TEACHER: Codes of ethics for the various counseling professions (e.g., psychology or social work) frown on dual relationships when there is a possibility of counselors losing objectivity or when there is potential for client exploitation. In large cities, it's usually easy to refer clients in order to avoid the conflict of interest of dual relationships. As you point out, it's much more difficult in a small town, and some dual relationship arrangements may be inevitable, but these relationships should never include sexual intimacy with current clients.

Choice 1 may cut off discussion and the social worker will lose a valuable opportunity to appreciate his client's experience. Choice 2, on the other hand, offers gentle empathy then probes for more detail. This response reduces the risk that the social worker will make errors of assumption.

A second way that social workers can lose objectivity is by overidentifying with clients. When overidentification occurs, they lose their capacity to keep sufficient emotional distance from their clients. Their own feelings and reactions become mixed up with those of their clients, clouding their judgment. Counselors who find themselves in this position may find that personal counseling or consultation with a supervisor is sufficient to help them regain objectivity, or they may conclude that referral to another worker is necessary.

A third way that social workers can lose objectivity is by becoming overly involved with clients. This overinvolvement includes dual relationships prohibited by ethical codes, as well as relationships in which social workers rely on clients to meet their social and psychological needs. To prevent this from happening, social workers need to make sure that they are meeting their personal needs in other ways. As well, they should be alert to signs that they may be overinvolved with particular clients.

Table 2.3 summarizes protective strategies social workers can use to avoid loss of objectivity.

Working with Competence

High self-awareness enables social workers to make important decisions regarding areas in which they are competent and those in which referral to other professionals is warranted. Counselors must practice only within the range of their competence, and they should not misrepresent their training or experience. This helps to ensure that they do no harm to clients. As Mehr succinctly put it: "Do your best, do what you know how to do, do not get in—or stay in—over your head, and do not take advantage of a client for your own needs" (1998:190). The ACA code provides specific reference on practicing within the boundaries of competence, including working in specialty areas and accepting employment only for positions for which one is qualified (1995:C.2). As well, it states that counselors must represent their professional credentials accurately (C.4).

Social workers should monitor their work and seek supervision, training, or consultation in order to evaluate their effectiveness. They should be involved in continual professional development to increase their competence and to keep their knowledge current. Until they have received the necessary training, they should not work in specialized areas of practice, such as interviewing children in abuse situations or administering or interpreting psychological tests. Untrained social workers and other professionals should not attempt to make psychiatric diagnoses. Competent workers know that the support and assistance of other professionals is necessary for issues that exceed their expertise.

The NASW code offers these explicit guidelines for working with competence:

(a) Social workers should accept responsibility or employment only on the basis of existing competence or the intention to acquire the necessary competence.

TABLE 2.3 Maintaining Objectivity

Loss of Objectivity	Protective Strategies for Social Workers
Making assumptions	Attempt to understand your prejudices and preferences.
	Listen to, but don't be controlled by the opinions of others.
	Develop self-awareness regarding personal needs and values.
	Be inquisitive, and explore each client's situation to discover his or her unique perspective.
	Brainstorm other points of view or seek other opinions.
	Check your conclusions with clients to see if they match theirs—seek definition, detail, and example.
	Monitor cultural and gender bias.
Overidentification	Monitor reactions to discover areas of vulnerability; be alert to strong negative or positive reactions to clients.
	Refer clients when you cannot be impartial.
	Know why you want to be a counselor—understand your needs.
	Use colleagues to critique your reactions and to give you feedback.
	Use tools such as video recordings to review interviews for inappropriate attempts to influence or control.
Overinvolvement	Avoid promoting client dependency.
	Develop a wellness program to ensure that you are not relying on your clients to meet your needs for social and psychological involvement and acceptance.
	Recognize warning signs (e.g., interviews that consistently run overtime, relief when a client does not show up for an interview, excessive worry about clients, reluctance to end a counseling relationship that has reached a point of termination).

(b) Social workers should strive to become and remain proficient in professional practice and the performance of professional functions. Social workers should critically examine and keep current with emerging knowledge relevant to social work. Social workers should routinely review the professional literature and participate in continuing education relevant to social work practice and social work ethics.

(c) Social workers should base practice on recognized knowledge, including empirically based knowledge, relevant to social work and social work ethics (Standard 4.01).

When access to other professionals is limited or unavailable, such as in rural settings or urban areas where there are long waiting lists, social workers and other professionals must not conclude that "the provision of well-intentioned but unskilled service [is] . . . better than no service at all" (Daniluk and Haverkamp, 1993:18).

Clients have a right to expect that their workers are able to be objective about the issues being discussed and that their judgment is not impaired by bias or unresolved personal problems. The ACA code offers this guideline:

> Impairment. Counselors refrain from offering or accepting professional services when their physical, mental, or emotional problems are likely to harm a client or others. They are alert to the signs of impairment, seek assistance for problems, and, if necessary, limit, suspend, or terminate their professional responsibilities (1995:C.2.g).

Social workers need to know when particular topics or problems are sensitive for clients, and aware of when their clients' problems parallel unresolved issues in their own lives. This knowledge is important to help them to know when to seek consultation or supervision, when to refer clients to other workes, and when to enter counseling to address their own needs. The NASW code offers this guidance to professional social workers:

> Social workers whose personal problems, psychosocial distress, legal problems, substance abuse, or mental health difficulties interfere with their professional judgment and performance should immediately seek consultation and take appropriate remedial action by seeking professional help, making adjustments in workload, terminating practice, or taking any other steps necessary to protect clients and others (Standard 4.05b).

Interviewing

Interviewing is a process of gathering information without any expectation of influencing or changing clients. Competent interviewing requires an ability to explore and understand clients' attitudes, feelings, and perspectives. The basis for this competence is a nonjudgmental attitude and intelligent application of the active listening skills of attending, using silence, paraphrasing, summarizing, and asking questions (see Chapters 4 to 6). Although the principal goal of interviewing is information gathering, the process of interviewing may lead clients to unexpectedly release painful or forgotten feelings. Thus, adept interviewers are capable of dealing with unpredictable reactions that the interview may promote or of referring clients to appropriate alternative resources. Moreover, they know when and how to probe effectively.

Counseling requires skilled interviewing but includes the additional goal of helping clients with such activities as problem solving, dealing with painful feelings, and developing new skills. Psychotherapy involves intensive counseling with emphasis on personality change or the treatment of more severe mental disorders. Working within the limits of one's ability requires counselors to use only those techniques and strategies that they have been adequately trained to apply. For example, attendance at a short seminar on hypnosis would not qualify counselors to use hypnosis in their work. As well, it is expected that counselors will use methods that have a reasonable chance of success, supported by experience and research evidence.

Large caseloads and the emotional demands of counseling may result in emotional and physical fatigue, thereby weakening competent performance. "Counsellors must be cognizant of their own limits and must act to protect themselves and their clients from the consequences of burnout" (Daniluk and Haverkamp, 1993:18). Competent professionals know how to set limits on the amount of work they can provide. They know when to seek consultation and when to seek support or personal counseling.

CONVERSATION 2.3
I'm Just a Beginner

STUDENT: I'm just a beginner, so, if I'm supposed to work within the limits of my competence, I shouldn't do anything.

TEACHER: Like a lot of social workers who are just starting, you may feel a bit overwhelmed.

STUDENT: I don't want to say or do the wrong thing. What if I don't know the right answers or if I don't say the right thing to clients?

TEACHER: First, there's rarely a single right way to respond. Most often, there is a range of choices of things to say or do in any situation. Second, no one knows all the right answers. Be honest with clients about the fact that you are still a student, and don't be afraid to admit your limitations, as this provides great modeling for clients. One goal of training is for you to expand your range of choices so that you can respond based on the needs of your clients and their situations. Remember, learning to be an effective social worker is a lifelong process. At this stage, your professional responsibility is to make effective use of supervisors to monitor your work. Use them to develop your skills. Make it easy for them to give you feedback. Seek it out, then try to be nondefensive. Look for opportunities to apply your developing knowledge base by taking some risks to learn new skills.

Self-Awareness

We live in a house of mirrors and think we're looking out.

—Fritz Perls

The Importance of Self-Awareness

Competent social workers need to acquire a high level of awareness of who they are. Until social workers develop self-awareness of their own needs, feelings, thoughts, and behaviors, including their personal problems and their areas of vulnerability, they will be unable to respond to their clients with objectivity.

Table 2.4 contrasts the characteristics of social workers who have high levels of self-awareness with those who have low levels of self-awareness.

Social workers who lack self-awareness and those who are not motivated to pursue it are destined to remain unaware of the ways they influence clients. They may, for example, be unaware of how their nonverbal reactions to controversial topics betray their biases and discomfort. They may avoid particular topics, or they may behave in certain ways to mask their insecurities or to unconsciously meet their personal needs. For example, social workers who have personal needs for control may meet this need through excessive and inappropriate advice giving.

Increasing Self-Awareness

Social workers who are serious about developing their self-awareness are secure enough to risk exploring their strengths and limitations. Self-awareness involves becoming alert and knowledgeable about their ways of thinking, acting, and feeling. This means that they are strong enough to be open to discovering aspects of themselves that they might prefer to keep hidden. For social workers, this is a continuing process throughout their careers. It requires them to honestly look at themselves and how they relate to others, but as Harris

TABLE 2.4   Self-Awareness

Social Workers with Self-Awareness	Social Workers without Self-Awareness
Identify and label their personal feelings	Avoid or are unaware of their feelings
Know where their feelings end and those of their clients begin	Project personal feelings onto clients
Recognize and accept areas of vulnerability and unresolved issues	Respond inappropriately because unresolved problems interfere with their capacity to be objective
Understand personal values and their influence on the counseling relationship	React emotionally to their clients but don't understand why or how
Recognize and manage internal dialogue	Behave nonassertively (using excessive caution, placating behavior, etc.) because they are unaware of the limiting effects of self-defeating thought
Understand and control personal defense mechanisms	Remain blind to their own defensive reactions
Know when and how clients are reacting to their style	Are unconsciously influenced in their relationships by personal values and do not manage the effects of their values
Realize how they influence outcomes	Remain unaware how their behavior influences others
Modify behavior based on reactions of clients	Behave based on personal needs and style rather than in response to the needs and reactions of clients
Set professional goals based on knowledge of personal and skill strengths and limitations	Avoid or limit goal setting because they are unaware of personal and professional needs

and Maloney (1996) suggest, some behaviors, including racism, sexism, ageism, and heterosexism, operate unconsciously. Consequently, they must overcome any natural tendency to be defensive. They can do this by asking others for feedback.

Colleagues, supervisors, and clients can be extremely helpful sources of information, but their feedback needs to be cultivated. Generally, people are reluctant to deliver critical feedback, however helpful it may be. Thus, the onus is on social workers to create the conditions to encourage feedback. They can invite input from others through a number of strategies.

The first strategy is to create a safe climate. People balk at giving feedback to others because they fear how it will be received. One concern is the risk of retaliation. "If I say something, will I be attacked or made to feel guilty?" Another common worry is that feedback will damage the relationship. The major concern also might be that feedback will cripple the other person's self-esteem.

Therefore, it is important for social workers to demonstrate that they are ready, willing, and able to respond nondefensively to feedback. Social workers have a responsibility to consider feedback and, when appropriate, to act on it. This means that they do not have to unconditionally agree with what has been said to them. It does mean that they listen with responses that are nonaggressive, in other words, without blaming or making excuses. Sometimes, such control can be difficult to sustain, particularly if feedback is delivered in an uncaring and hostile manner. A general rule when dealing with clients is, no matter what clients say or do, social workers must maintain a professional role. Of course, this does not preclude setting appropriate limits, nor does it mean that they have to tolerate personal or physical abuse. It means staying calm, being nondefensive, and refraining from retaliatory responses such as name-calling or punishing statements.

The second strategy is to use active listening skills to ensure that feedback is concrete or specific. To promote this, social workers can ask for details, definitions, examples, and clarification. Summarizing and paraphrasing can be used to confirm understanding.

Who Am I?

The essence of self-awareness is the answer to the question "Who am I?" This question needs to be explored in a number of different dimensions, including understanding personal feelings, thoughts, and behavior; personal needs; one's impact on clients; the limits of competence; personal and cultural values; and areas of vulnerability.

Feelings, Thoughts, and Behavior.   Social workers need to know and understand their feelings, thoughts, and behaviors, including the defense mechanisms that they use to protect themselves from stress. Effective social workers are comfortable discussing a wide range of emotions. They don't avoid feelings; in fact, they recognize that, for many clients, understanding and managing painful emotions is the greatest outcome from counseling. To understand clients' emotions, social workers must be in tune with their own emotional reactions. Empathy, the basic tool for understanding the feelings of others, will be contaminated unless social workers are fully in touch with their own feelings. This includes knowing where their feelings end and those of their clients begin.

Self-Defeating Thought. Social workers need to be aware of their own internal dialogue—the inner voices that evaluate their actions. Social workers with low self-worth typically find that the inner voice is critical, issuing messages such as "I'm no good." Negative self-talk can lead to emotional distress and interfere with counseling performance in a number of ways.

- Social workers may be reluctant to be assertive with clients and may be excessively gentle or nonconfrontational.
- General feelings of incompetence may lead to structuring "the counseling process to meet our own self-image problems or to confirm our negative self-pictures" (Cormier and Cormier, 1985:13).
- Social workers may be unable to objectively assess counseling relationship outcomes, because they tend to interpret problems as personal failures and to discount positive feedback or outcomes.

Significant research has been conducted regarding the ways that personal beliefs can influence performance and lead to maladaptive emotions and behavior (Cormier and Cormier, 1985; Ellis, 1984). Social workers need to become aware of negative self-talk as a crucial first step in developing a program to combat its effects. Subsequently, systematic techniques such as thought-stopping can be used to replace depreciating self-talk with affirmations or positive statements. Negative thoughts can be interrupted by mentally saying, "Stop," or by snapping an elastic band on the wrist as a reminder to divert the self-talk (Martin and Pear, 1992; Young, 1998).

Defense Mechanisms. Sigmund Freud first described defense mechanisms in 1894, and over a period of 40 years he identified most of the ones we still use today (Vaillant, 1988). A **defense mechanism** is a mental process or reaction that shields a person from undesirable or unacceptable thoughts, feelings, or conclusions that, if accepted, would create anxiety or damage one's self-esteem. Significantly, defense mechanisms usually involve some distortion of reality and are unconscious (Corsini, 1984). All people, including social workers, use defense mechanisms to protect themselves. Simply put, defense mechanisms help us guard our feelings and self-esteem. Most people use one or more methods to defend themselves from perceived threats. Simple defenses include blaming others or making excuses for one's own failures. Social workers might take credit for counseling successes but blame failure on their clients. Common defense mechanisms used by social workers include:

- *Denial:* People refuse to acknowledge the existence of feelings or problems. When social workers use denial, they fail to consider that their actions might be the reason for their clients' inappropriate behavior.
- *Displacement:* People relate with the feelings that they should express toward others; for example, social workers who deal with their own work stress by behaving aggressively with clients.
- *Rationalization:* People develop excuses or explanations to protect their self-image; for example, social workers who justify their inability to confront clients by concluding that it is best to offer only positive feedback.

- *Suppression:* People avert stressful thoughts by not thinking about them; for example, social workers who refuse to consider that personal biases might be affecting their decisions.
- *Regression:* People deal with conflict or stress by returning to behavior from an earlier stage of their lives; for example, social workers who deal with aggressive clients by becoming overly compliant or by trying to please.

Social workers should be alert to circumstances when they use defense mechanisms. Facing this reality requires courage and taking risks, for to give up one's defenses means sacrificing safety. Feedback from others can be threatening because it challenges people to let down their defenses by addressing aspects of their situations that they might prefer to avoid.

When social workers understand themselves, they recognize when their defenses are up and can take steps to change their reactions and behavior. They know when and where they are vulnerable, then they use this knowledge to cue or trigger nondefensive alternatives. For example, when clients are angry or hostile, social workers can discipline themselves to take time to empathize and encourage clients to ventilate, rather than respond more impulsively by fighting back.

Personal Needs. Social workers have the same basic needs as everyone else, including the need to be loved, respected, and valued by others. This is natural, but they must understand how their personal needs can adversely affect counseling outcomes. Lack of self-awareness regarding personal needs can lead to unconscious structuring of the session to meet their needs instead of the clients' (Brammer, 1985; D'Augelli, D'Augelli, and Danish, 1981; Kell and Mueller, 1966). "Sometimes helpers want to help themselves with their own problems through assisting others, or satisfaction is acquired through the power and influence over others afforded by the helping relationship" (Brammer, 1985:25).

Corey and Corey warn that lack of self-awareness can impede helpers from keeping their clients' remarks in proper perspective: "As a beginning helper you are especially vulnerable to believing everything positive that your clients tell you about yourself. Thus, if clients tell you how sexually attractive you are, how understanding you are, and how different from anyone else they have met, it may be very difficult for you to resist believing what they tell you" (1989:192). Therefore, even positive feedback from clients must be interpreted cautiously. Clients may try to placate social workers or use ingratiating tactics to manipulate, or it may be their way of relating to authority.

A range of counselor needs may interfere with counseling, including the need to be liked; achieve status or prestige, control, and perfection; and cultivate social relationships. Table 2.5 summarizes the major warning signs and risks of these needs.

Need to Be Liked. In the next chapter we will explore the importance of a warm and trusting counseling relationship. To a great extent, counseling depends on establishing and maintaining a safe environment, one in which clients feel safe enough to take risks. Obviously, this is easier if clients like their counselors, but counselors need to remember that having clients like them is not the primary goal of counseling. The aim of counseling is to support client change or problem management. This means that counselors have to be assertive enough to risk making reasonable demands on their clients, which, in turn, may

TABLE 2.5   Managing Personal Needs in Counseling

Personal Need	Warning Signs and Risks
Need to be liked and to be helpful	• Withholding potentially helpful but critical feedback • Inappropriately avoiding controversy or conflict • Trying to ingratiate (e.g., excessively praising, telling clients what they want to hear) • Acting with rescuing behavior • Expecting or reaching for compliments from clients
Need for status, prestige	• Trying to impress with "exotic"' techniques or brilliant interpretations • Taking credit for client success • Name dropping • Bragging about successes
Need for control	• Advice giving • Interfering with client self-determination (e.g., unnecessarily using authority, manipulating, dominating) • Imposing personal values • Stereotyping clients as needy and inadequate (which creates a role for someone to be "helpful")
Perfectionism	• Focusing on mistakes • Pushing clients toward unrealistic goals • Responding with self-depreciation to mistakes (e.g., "I'm a failure")
Need for social relationships	• Becoming overinvolved with clients (e.g., meeting clients socially, continuing counseling relationships beyond the normal point of closure) • Indiscriminate self-disclosure

generate tension and anxiety. Otherwise, clients can easily stay locked into established but unhealthy patterns. The need to be liked becomes problematic when it becomes more important than achieving the goals of counseling. One beginning social worker wrote in his journal: "When a client says something negative or behaves in a self-destructive way, I realize I hold back. I don't say anything because I want to be liked. I want the client to like me, not see me as an authority figure. I'd rather be seen as a pal or a friend." This journal entry highlights the dangers and signals an important insight that will help this worker question some of his assumptions about counseling. He is developing insight about how his behavior may be sabotaging client progress.

Need for Status or Prestige.   Social workers who have an excessive need to impress others, perhaps because of insecurity, may become technique-centered instead of client-centered. With this switch in priorities, the needs of the client may be overlooked as the counselor acts to impress clients or others. The priority of counseling should be to bolster the self-esteem of clients.

Need for Control. Codes of ethics recognize that clients are vulnerable to exploitation. Consequently, substantial attention is given to prohibiting behaviors that will result in undue control of clients. The principle of self-determination (introduced earlier in this chapter) is a basic value that upholds the right of clients to make independent decisions. Social workers interfere with this right when they attempt to take over clients' problems and orchestrate their solutions.

In some settings, such as government agencies, social workers may have the legal mandate to impose their services. This situation requires them to be especially vigilant. As Brammer and MacDonald observe, helpers in these settings "must be wary of identifying too closely with the power of the agency under the guise of carrying out the agency's mission. Often the helpee becomes lost in such settings, and the helping services tend to support the power of the organization. The result may be an exaggerated emphasis on adjustment or pacification rather than on actualization and liberation" (1999:40).

Perfectionism. Perfectionism, an unrealistic pursuit of excellence, can negatively affect counseling. Social workers who are perfectionists may be unable to realistically appraise their work, and they may have an unjustified tendency to blame themselves for client failures. Sometimes, counselors who are perfectionists push clients toward unrealistic goals or challenge them to move at too fast a pace.

Unmet Social Needs. Social workers with unmet social needs risk overinvolvement with clients. If they do not have outlets in their own lives for social interaction, they may misuse the counseling relationship for that purpose.

Effect on Clients

Social workers need to take time to discover how clients are reacting to them. Personal needs and defense mechanisms may lead them to wrongly assume that problems in the counseling relationship arise from their clients' inadequacies or failings. Although effective workers have confidence in their own abilities, they know and accept that occasionally they may say or do the wrong thing. They need to be mature and open enough to evaluate their work and to take responsibility for their errors and insensitivities. Open-minded social workers consider the possibility that clients may be angry for good reason, perhaps because of oppressive agency routines.

Social workers who lack self-awareness may fail to understand or accept the needs of their clients, and they are more likely to take their clients' behavior too personally. As Wells and Masch remark, "Clients who should be open, confiding, and grateful for assistance often aren't—and often with good reason. The untrained worker, however, remains unaware of the reasons and ultimately feels like a failure, very angry, or even ill-used and burned-out" (1991:19). Ultimately, social workers need to be self-aware enough to know which client reactions are reactions to their behavior or personalities and which client reactions are the result of other variables beyond their control.

Self-aware social workers know their skill strengths and limitations. This self-awareness enables them to consciously avoid overusing particular skills simply because they are strengths, and it helps them to know when it is appropriate to refer clients to other counselors. It also helps them to set goals for professional skill development. Knowing the limits of one's ability is a measure of competence.

Work and personal stress may negatively affect a social worker's capacity to relate effectively to clients. Social workers must be aware of situations that are stressful and understand how they react to them. Self-aware social workers avoid or reduce stressors, and they develop personal wellness plans for coping with the inevitable demands of the job.

Personal and Cultural Values

Social worker self-knowledge of personal values and preferences is indispensable for effective counseling. Values constitute a frame of reference for understanding and assessing clients and for making decisions and choices.

Self-awareness of personal values is an important element of competence. All social workers have personal values, and it is crucial that they understand what these values are in order to avoid imposing them on clients. Self-awareness of personal values is a first step for social workers to manage the bias that comes from interpreting clients' behavior from their own perspectives or cultures rather than from the clients'.

Cultural self-awareness refers to knowledge of the customs, traditions, role expectations, and values of one's culture of origin. Language is a particularly important variable. The word *authority* will have very different meaning for individuals who come from totalitarian countries than for those who come from democracies. Cultural self-awareness prepares social workers to recognize and value the diversity of other cultures. Such awareness needs to be accompanied by a belief that one's own ethnic group is only one of many and that there are other appropriate beliefs and behaviors.

It is inevitable that the personal values of social workers will influence how they assess clients, the techniques and procedures they use, and the goals that they deem reasonable, including which topics will get more or less attention. Moreover, certain topics are more value charged (e.g., abortion, assisted suicide, sexual orientation, religion, abuse), and the beliefs of social workers may bias their work in these areas. For example, social workers who find that they never discuss sexuality in their counseling work need to find out why. Are they avoiding this topic because of personal inhibitions? Are they unconsciously judging the sexual behavior of their clients?

One way for social workers to address this problem is to disclose their values to their clients. However, they should do this in such a way that clients do not feel pressured to adopt similar values. Clients should feel free to maintain their own values without fear that they are in some way disappointing their workers.

A social worker's value system is an important variable that influences the methods and outcomes of counseling. In general, social workers are most effective when their values reflect an optimistic and nonjudgmental view of people. Intellectually and emotionally, they accept and treasure the widest possible variations in lifestyle. They believe in the inherent strength and capacity of people and in their intrinsic right to freedom of choice. Table 2.6 on page 62 examines some of the values that might impede or enhance social

TABLE 2.6   Values, Beliefs, and Attitudes That Help and Hinder Social
Workers' Effectiveness

Values That Hinder	Values That Help
To accept help from others is a sign of weakness.	To accept help is a sign of strength.
Some people are just not deserving of our respect or caring.	Everyone has intrinsic worth and the capacity to be productive.
People are inherently evil. Unless you are careful, they will take advantage of you.	People are essentially good.
I know what is best for my clients.	People are capable of finding their own answers and making decisions.
It is essential that my clients like me.	The purpose of counseling is to help clients exercise choice, not to make them like me.
I've been there myself, so I know what my clients are feeling.	I can't know what my clients are feeling until I take the time to let them teach me.
People are incapable of changing.	People can and do change.
My religion/culture/viewpoint is the best.	I can accept a wide variety of cultures, religions, and viewpoints.
In this world, it's survival of the fittest.	We depend on one another and we have a responsibility to help others.
Counselors have a right to impose service when it is in their clients' best interest.	Clients have a right to refuse service.

workers' effectiveness. When social workers have values that hinder, they are more likely to find themselves behaving contrary to the ethics of the field, such as by acting in ways that inhibit self-determination or by failing to respect the dignity of their clients. Conversely, when they have values that enhance their ability, they are more naturally inclined to support the ethics of the profession, and they are more likely to behave in ways that empower.

Summary

Professional codes of ethics define the acceptable limits of behavior for professionals. These codes recognize the potential vulnerability of clients and seek to protect them from misuse of position and power by professionals. Every counseling profession has its own code of ethics, but certain core principles are common: they put the needs of clients first, and they strictly prohibit sexual and exploitive relationships.

Ethics are the principles and rules of acceptable conduct. Ethical principles are derived from values, or what individuals and groups consider appropriate or worthwhile. The values of the social work profession are rooted in a few basic principles: belief in the dignity and worth of people, respect for diversity, and respect for the client's right to self-determination. The principle of self-determination values the right of clients to have control and autonomy over matters that affect their lives. The needs of clients are foremost.

Confidentiality is an integral part of ethical practice. Confidentiality can be absolute, meaning that information is not shared with anyone, or it can be relative and shared for legal and operational reasons. Most client communication is subject to relative confidentiality, as legal constraints may require reporting. As well, the internal operation of the agency necessitates some sharing of information.

An ethical dilemma exists when a choice must be made between competing values. Five principles can be considered when resolving ethical dilemmas: autonomy, beneficence, nonmaleficence, justice, and fidelity. Ethical decision making involves weighing the five principles and deciding which ought to have priority in a given situation.

Although it is recognized that social workers' values will influence their work, they need to be objective and to understand their clients without allowing their personal views, feelings, or preferences to contaminate their counseling role. Objectivity is the capacity to understand situations and people without bias or distortion. Social workers can lose their objectivity by making assumptions, overidentifying with clients, and becoming overly involved with their clients.

Social workers need to work at an optimum level for each client regardless of their own feelings or reactions. They need to work within the limits of their competence by using techniques and strategies that they are qualified to deliver and that have a reasonable chance of success.

Self-awareness is essential in order for social workers to work with objectivity. Self-aware social workers know themselves—their feelings, thoughts, behavior, personal needs, and areas of vulnerability. They understand how they affect clients, and they know the limits of their competence. They can answer the question "Who am I?"

EXERCISES

 1. Can we promise our clients absolute confidentiality? Why or why not?

2. What are some advantages and disadvantages to allowing clients access to files?

 3. Under what conditions would you make exceptions to the principle of self-determination?

4. Consider the following questions of ethical decision making. Imagine that you are the counselor in each of the following situations. What would be your response? What additional information would you want to have before deciding on a course of action? What values and ethical principles would you consider in making your decision?

   a. An elderly, frail woman suffering from inoperable cancer decides to kill herself.

   b. A client decides to give his life's savings to his church.

    c. A client boasts that if his girlfriend tries to leave him he will kill her.

    d. A client from a counseling relationship that terminated six months ago phones to ask you for a date. (Imagine that you are not in a current relationship.)

    e. Your client leaves your office in anger, determined to "teach my wife a lesson for the way she treated me."

    f. Knowing that you are in the market for a new car, your client, a used-car salesperson, offers to help you buy a car for wholesale price.

    g. A client inquires about your sexual orientation.

    h. Your client asks for your E-mail address so that he can keep in touch.

    i. Your client, a bisexual male, has tested HIV positive but informs you that he does not wish to tell his wife. He says that he will practice safe sex. (Variation: Imagine that you receive a call from the client's wife. She says she is concerned about her husband and asks whether you think he might be gay.)

    j. Your colleagues begin to talk about a client. You are with them at a local restaurant.

    k. One of your colleagues tells you that she has just returned from a one-day workshop on hypnosis. She says that she can hardly wait to try it on some clients.

    l. You encounter one of your colleagues having lunch with a client. You notice that they are drinking a bottle of wine.

    m. You have an erotic dream about one of your clients.

    n. While you are counseling a student (in your role as school counselor), he discloses that he is selling marijuana to classmates. (Would your answer be different if you were a counselor in a community agency unconnected to the school?)

    o. You are a social worker working with a young, gay client. He has been socially isolated and is slow to trust anyone, but over time you have managed to form a strong working relationship. Imagine that he approaches you with a request that you walk with him in the annual gay pride parade. What variables would you consider in making your decision? What are the implications of going with him? What are the implications of not going?

    p. Your client is down to her last two dollars. She offers to buy your coffee. Do you accept? What are the implications of your decision?

    q. Your car is broken and requires an expensive repair. Your client has been struggling to set up a mobile repair service, but business has been slow. He offers to fix your car for a discounted price. Do you accept? Why or why not?

5. Consider the following case study. A good friend invites you to a small dinner party. When you arrive you are introduced to the other guests, including a woman client. You have been seeing her and her husband for the past year for marital counseling. You note that her companion for the evening is not her husband. From observing their behavior, there is no doubt that this is a romantic relationship. She has never mentioned this relationship in the past.

    a. What would you do for the rest of the evening?

    b. Do you have an obligation to disclose this relationship to the woman's husband?

    c. If she asks you to keep your knowledge of this relationship from her husband, could you could continue to see them for marital counseling?

6. Assess the extent to which you believe that each of the following counselor behaviors might be acceptable. Use the following rating scale:

5 = always
4 = often
3 = sometimes
2 = seldom
1 = never

Be prepared to defend your answer. How might your answer vary depending on the circumstances?

___ seeing a client after having had one alcoholic drink

___ accepting an invitation for dinner at a client's home

___ hugging a client

___ inviting a former client to a party at your home

___ dating a former client

___ having sex with a client

___ driving your client home

___ discussing your client with a supervisor

___ assisting a client to end his or her life

___ accepting a client's decision to commit suicide

___ allowing your teenager to baby-sit for your client

___ buying a car from your client

___ lending money to a client

___ reporting your client to the police (after the client tells you that he or she committed a crime)

___ reporting suspected child abuse by your client

___ sharing personal experiences, feelings, problems, and so on, with your client

___ getting angry with your client

___ discussing a client with your family or friends (without mentioning names)

___ giving a present to a client or receiving a present from a client

___ sharing information about clients with other professionals

___ warning a person that your client has threatened to harm him- or herself

___ telling a client's partner that he or she is HIV positive

___ advising a client to leave an abusive marriage

___ crying in the presence of a client

___ counseling a friend or neighbor at your agency

(Adapted from Shebib, 1997.)

7. Give examples of appropriate physical contact between social workers and clients. Be prepared to justify your answer.

8. The case recording below is excerpted from a case record completed by a social work student. Use the ACA and NASW codes to evaluate the appropriateness of the language used.

I visited the Smith home to investigate allegations of child neglect. I was met at the door by Mrs. Smith, a single parent. I was surprised by her size; she was morbidly obese and smelled as if she hadn't showered in weeks. Rolls of fat hung out of Mrs. Smith's shirt, and portions of her legs were covered with dirt. Mrs Smith's slovenly appearance suggests she is unable to care for herself, much less her children (Reamer, 1998:93).

9. Explore the issues involved in discussing clients with friends and relatives. Is it acceptable to discuss clients if you change their names and other identifying data? Defend your answer.

10. Should some clients be forced to attend counseling?

11. Do you think black humor is ethical? Defend your answer.

12. What strong beliefs do members of your cultural/ethnic group hold?

13. Use the questions and situations below to examine your values related to sexual orientation issues.

   a. If your client were gay or lesbian, how might it influence the way you work with him or her?

   b. What would you do if a friend told you an antihomosexual joke or story? What if the person telling the joke were a client or a colleague?

   c. Do you have gay or lesbian friends?

   d. Do you think homosexuality is an illness?

   e. Your daughter discloses that she is lesbian. Predict how you might feel, think, and behave.

   f. Your best friend confides that he feels he is the wrong gender.

   g. What are your views on same-sex marriage?

14. Write an essay answering the question "Who am I?"

15. Explore your views regarding the following value-charged issues:

   a. Are people basically good or bad?

   b. Should people have the right to take their own lives?

   c. What religion(s) are acceptable?

   d. Should immigrants be required to speak the language of their new homeland?

16. The following questions will help you to examine your values and beliefs. Work in a small group to explore and debate your answers. Use this process as a tool to reevaluate your position on matters you deem important.

   a. What are the characteristics of the client you would most want to work with? (Be specific regarding as many variables as possible, such as age, gender, personality, culture, and religion.) Why would you choose these characteristics?

   b. What are the characteristics of the client you would least want to work with (e.g., age, gender, personality, culture, religion)?

   c. What topics or issues are likely to evoke strong personal reactions from you?

   d. What does authority mean to you? How do you behave and feel when you are relating to people in authority?

   e. In your opinion, what is the meaning of life?

   f. Where do you draw your strength?

   g. When you die, what do you most want to be remembered for?

17. Examine your reasons for wanting to become a counselor. What needs do you expect to meet through your work? In what ways might your personal needs be an impediment?

18. What are your five most important values?

19. Work in a small group to explore your spiritual values through the following questions.

    a. Are religions basically good or bad?

    b. Are some religions better than others?

    c. Should cults be illegal?

    d. What does spirituality mean to you?

    e. Should spiritual issues be introduced by counselors?

    f. When is it appropriate to discuss religion with clients?

    g. What are the implications of your religious views when working with someone with a similar perspective and when working with someone with a radically different view?

20. Explore your personal strengths and limitations. Use the following topics to structure your assessment:

- capacity to be assertive (as opposed to shyness or aggressiveness)
- degree of self-confidence
- comfort dealing with a wide range of emotions
- need to control or be in charge
- capacity to relate to diverse populations (age, gender, culture, religion, etc.)
- ability to give and receive feedback (positive and critical)
- need to be helpful
- anxieties and fears
- competence in initiating relationships (beginnings)
- ability to deal with conflict
- self-awareness regarding how others see you
- overall awareness of personal strengths and limitations
- values and attitudes that will help or hinder your work as a counselor
- capacity and willingness to change

Based on your answers, identify what you consider to be your five major strengths and your five major limitations.

21. Evaluate your capacity for handling feedback from others. Are you generally open and nondefensive when others critically evaluate your behavior or performance? Do you tend to avoid asking for feedback, or do you actively solicit it? Interview friends and colleagues to see if their opinions of how you respond to feedback agree with your self-evaluation.

22. Are you excessively dependent on your clients? Rate how accurately each statement below describes you using the following scale:

4 = always
3 = frequently

2 = sometimes
1 = rarely
0 = never

___ **a.** I often feel responsible for the feelings, thoughts, and behavior of my clients.

___ **b.** I get angry when my help is rejected.

___ **c.** I feel worthless and/or depressed when clients don't change.

___ **d.** I feel compelled to help people solve problems by offering unwanted advice.

___ **e.** I want to take care of my clients and protect them from painful feelings.

___ **f.** When clients don't like me, I feel rejected or inadequate.

___ **g.** I do things to make my clients like me, even if what I do is not helpful.

___ **h.** I avoid confronting or challenging clients.

___ **i.** I tell clients what they want to hear.

___ **j.** I feel most safe when I'm giving to others.

___ **k.** When clients fail, I take it personally.

___ **l.** I spend an excessive amount of time trying to prove to myself and my clients that I'm good enough.

___ **m.** I tend to be very controlling with clients.

___ **n.** I tolerate abuse from clients to ensure they keep liking me.

___ **o.** I feel responsible for solving my clients' problems.

Interpretation: Carefully review any statements that you scored 4 or 3. Determine whether there are any patterns in your behavior and in the beliefs that you hold. Are you able to identify particular ways that you are dependent on your clients? What self-defeating thoughts are associated with each? Use your awareness of problem areas to develop a program of self-change by following this process:

- Think about where you are vulnerable.

- Set some change goals.

- Develop a concrete action plan to achieve your goals.

- Develop a plan to learn about the cultures in your community.

- Develop a plan to increase your understanding of world religions.

23. Imagine that you are a client. What might your counselor need to know about you (e.g., values, needs, preferences) in order to work effectively with you?

24. How do you deal with the demands of an increasingly diverse society?

25. Take an inventory of your friendship circle. To what extent do your friends come from the same cultural and values base as your own? Predict what might happen if you broadened your circle to include more diversity.

ENDNOTE

1. See Shulz (2000:12–13) for a detailed example using the six-step model.

3 Relationship

The Foundation for Change

Preview

After reading this chapter you should be able to:

- define the characteristics of a counseling relationship
- list the essential relationship-building objectives of each of the four phases of counseling
- explain the importance of the core conditions of warmth, empathy, and genuineness
- describe the core conditions
- describe the counseling contract
- demonstrate the ability to negotiate a counseling contract
- define *immediacy*
- use basic immediacy skills
- explain how transference and countertransference influence counseling relationships
- describe the importance of empowering clients
- explain the importance of relationship endings

What Is a Counseling Relationship?

A **counseling relationship** is a time-limited period of consultation between a social worker and one or more clients in order to assist the client in achieving a defined goal. Developing and sustaining an effective counseling relationship is widely accepted as critical to success in counseling (Kadushin, 1990; Rogers, 1980; Shilling, 1984; Shulman, 1992; Young, 1998). In fact, the relationship itself is often viewed as having primary importance (Kadushin, 1990). Capuzzi and Gross conclude that "specific procedures and techniques are much less important than the alliance between counselor and client" (1997:65). Almost 40 years ago, Carl Rogers (1961) emphasized that a counselor's attitudes and feelings are more important than technique and noted that the client's perception of the counselor's attitudes is what is most crucial.

Young echoes these sentiments: "Without a strong therapeutic alliance, the goals of therapy cannot be reached" (1998:155). Moreover, the quality of the counseling relationship is a major determinant of whether the client will continue with counseling (Brammer and Shostrom, 1982).

Rogers, in his counseling classic, *Client-Centered Therapy* (1951), described the experience of a client who successfully completed counseling following an unsuccessful experience with another counselor. The client was asked by the second counselor why he had been able to work through his problems on his second attempt. The client responded, "You did about the same things he did, but you seemed really interested in me" (Rogers, 1951:69).

Counseling relationships are not always comfortable. In fact, as Keith-Lucas proposes, "The attempt to keep the relationship on a pleasant level is the greatest source of ineffectual helping known" (1972:18). The helping relationship provides the necessary security for clients to disclose their feelings and ideas. As trust develops in relationships, so does the capacity of clients to become increasingly open to revealing themselves. Drawing from the strength of their relationships with counselors, clients may risk new ways of thinking and behaving, and in this way the relationship becomes the medium for change. In positive counseling relationships, clients perceive their counselors as allies. Clients become increasingly willing to disclose because they do not fear that they will be rejected, judged, or coerced to change in ways that they find unacceptable. In its purest form, the counseling relationship becomes a collaborative endeavor.

Counseling relationships have some of the same components of intimacy, caring, and support that characterize deep personal relationships. High-level communication skills are as important to friendships as they are to counseling. In fact, many of the skills of counseling are also the skills of effective everyday communication. Friendships grow out of mutual attraction and common interest, whereas counseling relationships focus on helping clients achieve goals such as resolving crises, making decisions, and learning new skills. Counseling relationships are structured for the primary purpose of reaching these goals, and, once the clients have achieved them, the counseling relationships are terminated.

Personal relationships can be terminated for personal reasons. However, social workers are expected to persist in their efforts on behalf of clients even when they are frustrated by lack of progress or client resistance. Counseling may be ended when there is little likelihood of reaching its goals, but not simply because the social worker prefers other clients. One measure of professionalism is the capacity of the practitioner to sustain commitment, patience, and caring despite frustrating obstacles.

Creating a Counseling Relationship

Rogers (1961) asserted the importance of seeing others as "becoming." This notion underscores a fundamental belief in the capacity of people to change. Clients are not bound by their past, and social workers should not use diagnosis and classification as tools for depersonalizing clients and treating them as objects. In counseling, clients need to be seen for their potential, strength, inner power, and capacity to change. Rogers's philosophy continues to have an enormous impact on counseling thought and procedures. His convictions suggest a number of questions for social workers to ponder regarding their attitudes and behavior in helping relationships:

- *How can I act so that clients will perceive me as trustworthy?* This means their helpers do what they say they will do and act in a way that is consistent with how they feel. It requires them to communicate without ambiguity and contradiction.

- *Can I permit myself to experience positive attitudes of warmth, caring, liking, interest, and respect toward clients?*

- *Can I be strong enough as a person to be separate from my clients?* This requires a high level of maturity, self-awareness, and courage. Rogers summarizes this challenge:

  Am I strong enough in my own separateness that I will not be downcast by his depression, frightened by his fear, nor engulfed by his dependency? Is my inner self hardy enough to realize that I am not destroyed by his anger, taken over by his need for dependence, nor enslaved by his love, but that I exist separate from him with feelings and rights of my own (1961:52)?

- *Am I secure enough to permit clients their separateness?* Clients are not under social workers' control, nor are they to be molded as models of what social workers feel they should be.

- *Can I let myself fully empathize with my clients' feelings and world perspectives without evaluating or judging?*

The Phases of Counseling

Each of the four phases of counseling—preliminary, beginning, action, and ending—has associated relationship tasks and challenges (Shebib, 1997). In all phases, social workers need to develop effective skills and attitudes for engaging and retaining clients, including the following: sincerity, perceptiveness, honesty, respect for diversity, capacity to initiate conversations, ability to be a good listener, comfort with discussing feelings, empathy, ability to communicate confidence without conceit, and warmth.

Preliminary Phase.   The goal of the preliminary phase is to create the necessary physical and psychological conditions for the relationship to begin. The counseling environment (e.g., agency setting, office layout, reception procedures) can have a dramatic impact on the client's mood and expectations even before the interview begins (Kadushin, 1990; Shebib, 1997). Preliminary phase work attempts to create first impressions that say to clients, "You will be respected here. You are important. This is a place where you will be supported."

Beginning Phase.   The relationship goal in the beginning phase is to develop rapport, trust, and a working contract, or agreement, regarding the purpose of the work and the roles of the participants. The relationship at this phase must provide enough safety for clients that they will engage and continue with counseling. Social workers create this environment of safety by communicating that they do not judge the client and that change can occur. The relationship enables clients to feel sufficiently free to take on the first risks of counseling—sharing their feelings and concerns.

Action Phase.   In the action phase, the relationship continues to develop and strengthen, and new counseling risks are taken as clients find the courage and strength to change their ways of thinking, feeling, and behaving. During this phase, relationship work may need to focus on addressing communication problems, including, at times, tension or conflict.

Ending Phase.   Termination of the counseling relationship comes when counseling has served its purpose and clients have reached their goals. Termination focuses on reviewing the work accomplished, helping clients consolidate learning, and saying goodbye.

Core Conditions

Building on the work of Carl Rogers, Truax and Carkhuff (1967) defined three aspects of attitude as prerequisites to forming and maintaining effective helping relationships: warmth, empathy, and genuineness. Knowledge and skill are critical to success in counseling, but it is important to remember that clients will "not pay attention to how much the worker knows until they know how much he or she cares" (Sheafor, Horejsi, and Horejsi, 1991:83). Although social workers can use certain behaviors and skills to demonstrate core conditions, the conditions must represent their authentic values and attitudes. When they exhibit these **core conditions,** the potential for positive relationships with clients is increased. However, there is no guarantee that clients will interpret warmth, genuineness, and empathy (or any communication) in the way that they were intended. Prior experiences and expectations, as well as cultural and individual differences, can easily lead to discrepancies in how communication is perceived. Social workers can expect to be rejected as least some of the time despite their best efforts. Empathy may be perceived by a client as an intrusive attempt to "get into my head" and caring as manipulation. Secure social workers accept this reality, knowing that considerable resistance may be encountered as they work to develop the helping relationship.

Warmth.   Rogers (1961) urged professionals to shun any tendency to keep clients at a distance by treating them as objects with detailed diagnostic labels. Instead, he argued that they need to learn that it is safe to express their warmth and to let clients know that they care. Warmth, although a difficult concept to define, is an expression of nonpossessive caring. As Mehr interprets it:

> People who lack warmth are described as cold, uncaring, or uninvolved. Thus, warmth implies involvement. The expression of warmth requires a non-judgmental attitude and an avoidance of blaming. Warmth involves acceptance of the equal worth of others. . . . Nonpossessive warmth entails a feeling of caring and concern without placing conditions on the relationship (1998:182).

Warmth is a precursor to trust. It attracts clients to take risks because it signals the goodwill and motivation of their helpers. In the beginning, clients often come to counseling reluctantly, perhaps driven by external pressure or by the weight of their problems. The first task of treatment, then, is to find a way of communicating cues to the social worker's attitude so the client will engage with the work and return for subsequent visits. Warmth seems to say, "I'm approachable, you don't need to be afraid of me. I won't take advantage of your vulnerability. I'm a kind person." As a result, warmth is particularly important during the formative or beginning stage of the relationship. Warmth is also crucial for supporting clients during a crisis, and it is a necessary partner to caring confrontation. Clients will be more receptive to receiving feedback when they are persuaded that it originates from a caring attitude.

Although the nature of warmth can be defined behaviorally to some extent, it must arise from genuine feelings of caring for the client. Otherwise, the social worker's actions will appear lacking in genuineness. Warmth is demonstrated by smiling appropriately and by showing sincere interest in the comfort of the client. Social workers show warmth when they communicate nonverbally that they are totally focused on their clients. Simple courtesies, such as eliminating distractions from the interview, asking clients if they are physically comfortable, offering them a beverage, and making eye contact, convey warmth. Well-timed humor can also add a warm touch to the interview.

Brammer and MacDonald suggest flexibility in the amount of expressed warmth and caring depending on the comfort level of clients. From their research, they conclude:

> From a multicultural perspective, overt expression of emotion must be used sensitively. Asian American helpees might be quite uncomfortable receiving strongly emotional care, especially early in the relationship. In the Hispanic American culture, overt warmth might be more acceptable between female helpers and helpees, but not so for males (1999:32).

Being warm doesn't preclude dealing with difficult topics nor does it imply that a great deal of the interview needs to be spent making small talk, as one might do during a social visit.

Sometimes in busy social service agencies caseloads become unmanageable and the pace of the work is frantic. Constant crises and unrelenting paperwork can exhaust even the most energetic and caring workers, who may begin to lose the "spark" they had when they first entered the field. Unless controlled, the office routine can begin to feel more like an assembly line than a counseling service, as clients become numbers and the work becomes increasingly task oriented. How does one continue to feel and express warmth under such conditions? The answer must be discovered individually, but we can learn something from the observations of one worker, a senior caseworker with over twenty-five years' experience.

> What works for me is to remind myself that no matter how overwhelmed I feel, it's worse for my clients. Often, they're broke, in crisis and not sure whether they want to live or die. They don't need me to be part of the problem. What doesn't work for me is to get caught up in coffee room negativism. You know what it's like—the ones who never have anything good to say and always expect things to get worse. It also helps if I take a few moments, sometimes precious seconds, between interviews to meditate. When I meet my client, I try to spend some time just being friendly.

Empathy. Empathy describes the capacity to understand the feelings and views of another person. Empathic attitudes and skills can generate powerful bonds of trust and rapport. With empathic skill, social workers are able to communicate understanding and acceptance to their clients. An empathic attitude is characterized by one's willingness to learn about the world of another and begins with suspending judgment. To be nonjudgmental requires considerable discipline in controlling personal biases, assumptions, and reactions that might contaminate understanding. "Without judging (or perhaps even liking) a client, the worker tries to understand the person's problem, accepting feelings without necessarily condoning his or her acts" (Schram and Mandell, 1997:123).

Social workers need to be able to enter the emotional world of their clients without fear of becoming trapped in their pain. Social workers who are secure with themselves and their feelings have the capacity to enter their clients' worlds without fear of losing their own identity. Brill notes that when a counselor communicates acceptance, the client has "freedom to be oneself—to express one's fears, angers, joy, rage, to grow, develop, and change—without concern that doing so will jeopardize the relationship" (1998:97).

Chapter 6 explores the skills of communicating empathy, but a preview of the components of this important skill is provided here. Empathic skill has two components. First, social workers must be able to perceive their clients' feelings and perspectives. This requires them to have abundant self-awareness and emotional maturity so that they do not contaminate their clients' experience with their own. As Garvin and Seabury observe, "The concept of empathy relates to the act of experiencing something in a manner similar to another person while still retaining a sense of who one is and what one's separate responses may be" (1984:110).

The second component of empathy is to make an empathic response. This involves putting in words the feelings that the client has expressed. This task can be particularly difficult, because clients often communicate their feelings in abstract, ambiguous, or nonverbal ways. Empathic responses require a vocabulary of words and phrases that can be used to precisely define feelings. At a basic level, empathic responses acknowledge obvious and clearly expressed feelings. At a more advanced or inferred level, empathic responses are framed from hints and nonverbal cues.

Genuineness.   Being genuine means one is authentic and real in a relationship. Social workers who are genuine show high consistency between what they think and do, and between what they feel and express. Rogers (1961) used the term *congruent* to describe this quality and emphasized the importance of self-awareness to unambiguous communication. They need to be aware of how they are feeling and how they are transmitting their feelings in order to avoid giving contradictory messages.

Social workers who are genuine are highly trustworthy. They don't lie to clients. They are willing to provide feedback that is timely and helpful. They show respect for clients by being open and honest while maintaining warmth and empathy in the relationship. They do not work from hidden agendas, nor do they put on "masks" or play roles to hide their true feelings. As well, genuine counselors are reliable. They do what they say they are going to do. Mehr offers this perspective on arriving at genuineness or congruence: "Awareness is the first step toward achieving congruence between internal experiences and outward behavior. Genuineness also, however, requires the maturity and skills to be able to express these feelings in the context of a warm and empathic relationship" (1998:183).

Benjamin (1981) emphasizes the importance of being human in the interview and discarding false facades or professional equipment that might create distance and barriers in the relationship. "If the interviewer is remote and cold, can the interviewee be expected to come close and be warm? When the interviewer is cautious and wary, can the interviewee be unguarded? Will the latter be free to express openly his thoughts and feelings to someone barricaded behind a wall of professionalism? . . . We must be sincere, genuine, congruent—not act so, but be so" (53–54).

CONVERSATION 3.1
Genuineness

STUDENT: How far should I go with genuineness? What if I'm angry with my client? Should I say so? Or suppose I find my client disgusting. Should I express that too?

TEACHER: You've identified an important dilemma. On the one hand, the need for genuineness suggests that we should be open and honest with our clients. We shouldn't put on false fronts, lie to clients, or fake our feelings. At the same time, ethical principles clearly prohibit us from doing harm. Being genuine doesn't entitle counselors to "dump" on their clients. Genuine social workers are truthful, but they are also timely. They share personal perceptions and feelings in an assertive way in order to meet their clients' needs. They might express their anger, but they do so without intending to punish, ridicule, or trap their clients. As for feeling disgust toward a client, I can't see how sharing that information would serve any purpose. On the other hand, it may be useful to the client if you explored the specific behaviors or attitudes that gave rise to those feelings. With sensitive feedback, your client can have the benefit of learning about his or her impact on others. One final point: Strong reactions toward our clients may hint at our own vulnerabilities. If you find a client disgusting, I'd want to ask you, 'Where does that feeling come from? Are you sure it is related only to the client?'

STUDENT: Maybe the client "pushes my buttons" the same way my father did.

TEACHER: Exactly.

The Contract

A **contract** is a negotiated agreement between the social worker and the client regarding important variables that will define the work. Because clients and counselors often have different ideas about the objectives and methods of counseling, it is important for them to reach understanding regarding the nature of the work (Gladding, 1996). Such understanding results in a contract that "helps clarify the counselor–client relationship and give it direction; protect the rights, roles, and obligations of both counselors and clients; and ensure the success of counseling" (Gladding, 1996:117).

The contract is like a route map that provides general directions on how to get from A to B. It confirms that all parties are working toward the same ends. When social workers and their clients are working toward agreed-on objectives, it is much more likely that clients will "own" the work, rather than see it as something that has been imposed on them. Contracting reduces suspicions that social workers may have hidden agendas.

A counseling contract predicts an end point to the relationship. Defining tasks and goals makes it clear when the relationship should be ended. In this way, the counseling relationship is clearly distinguished from a friendship, which may last for a lifetime.

Shulman's (1992) research confirmed the importance of contracting to counseling success. In particular, his findings supported the relevance of helping clients participate in setting the contract. Egan underscores the empowering nature of contracting. He describes the contract as a kind of charter that can "give clients a flavor of the mechanics of the helping process, diminish initial client anxiety and reluctance, provide a sense of direction, and enhance clients' freedom of choice" (1998:56).

Contracts may be formal and signed by both the counselor and the client, but more frequently they are informal and ratified with verbal agreement or a handshake. The simplest form of contract concerns agreement on the purpose of the interview or counseling relationship. The essential elements of the contract include:

1. definition of the objective or purpose of the counseling relationship

If there is no agreement on the purpose of counseling, the work is apt to be directionless. Without agreed-on purpose, social workers tend to make assumptions about the needs and wants of their clients. The problem with assumptions is that they are so frequently wrong. The multiple purposes of counseling can include helping clients with problem solving, decision making, and managing feelings; providing support; giving information; and fostering skill acquisition.

2. discussion of the roles and expectations of the participants

Social workers should know something about what clients want from them. Do clients expect them to provide advice on how to manage their problems? Do they want to be challenged with new information and new perspectives? Are they looking for someone who is warm, gentle, and supportive or someone who will just listen? Similarly, social workers need to tell clients about any expectations they have of them. Role discussion may also address issues such as how the participants might address conflict and how they can provide feedback to each other.

3. discussion of the methods and routines of counseling

Social workers do not need to work from a secret script with mysterious techniques that they hide from clients. They should develop their ability to describe their work in simple, nonjargonistic language. In this way, clients can know something about what is happening as well as what remains to be done.

4. practical details

These include issues such as the time and place of meetings and any fees for service. Ethical issues, including the limitations of confidentiality, are also part of the contract.

Home builders usually prewire new homes so that future installation of services such as cable television will be easy. In the same way, relationships can be "prewired" to make resolution of communication difficulties easier. Contracting strategies, such as discussing in advance how conflict will be addressed and working to develop and refine open communication, are the tools for prewiring relationships. If conflicts occur, a mechanism is already in place for resolving them.

Social workers and other professionals generally initiate contracting on the purpose of counseling early in the first interview. However, rigid adherence to a negotiated contract is hazardous. Counseling contracts need to be periodically revisited and updated as necessary. Clients may develop new insights that change their priorities. Increased trust may enable clients to address more difficult topics and feelings that they were unwilling to consider at the beginning of the relationship. As well, new problems and issues may emerge as a result of changing circumstances.

Contracting on the Roles and Purpose of Counseling

Every social service agency has a purpose that defines and limits its service. Specialty agencies such as employment counseling centers may focus on career testing and job search skills, while a transition home may provide crisis counseling and shelter. A community center might provide a broad range of counseling, education, and group support services.

Professionals define and limit their role based on their position in the agency and their training. An intake worker, for example, may be restricted to initial screening and assessments, while a community outreach worker might specialize in reaching clients who do not voluntarily seek service.

Clients have specific wants and needs that may or may not mesh with the mandate of the agency or its workers. Abraham Maslow's (1954) famous hierarchy of needs can be a useful way of understanding client priorities. Maslow suggested that people normally seek to fulfill their basic needs before pursuing higher order needs. He arranged his hierarchy in the following order:

1. physiological or basic survival needs (air, water, and food)
2. safety needs (personal security, stability, protection, and freedom from fear)
3. belonging/love needs (relationships)
4. self-esteem needs (sense of worth and importance)
5. self-actualization needs (achieving one's full potential)

Maslow's theory can be a useful reference for social workers. As one social worker put it, "You can't counsel a client who hasn't eaten." In simplest terms, helpers need to begin by ascertaining where clients are in terms of unmet needs. As basic and higher order needs are met, the goals of counseling need to be adjusted accordingly.

Contracting explores three variables: agency, helper/counselor, and client. Contracting is viable when the client's needs match the agency's mandate and the helper's competence. When the service the client needs is beyond the mandate of the agency or the competence of the helper, referral to another counselor or agency is appropriate.

The contracting process aspires to establish a relationship of equality between clients and social workers, while recognizing each person's role. Zastrow's observation about social workers is relevant to understanding role:

> The expertise of the social worker does not lie in knowing or recommending what is best for the client. Rather, the expertise lies in assisting clients to define their problems, to develop and examine the alternatives for resolving the problems, to maximize the client's capacities and opportunities to make decisions for themselves, and to help clients to implement the decisions they make (1990:62).

Clients may be aware of their pain and recognize and accept the need for change and help, but they may have no idea what form this help might take. In such situations, social workers need to be able to help them understand the potential assistance that counseling can provide.

Some clients have unrealistic expectations of their social workers or the process. They may believe that social workers will tell them what to do and solve all their problems. Or they may have no faith in the process whatsoever. As Wicks and Parsons describe it, when people enter counseling, they often anticipate "either a miracle or complete failure" (1984:175). Contracting is a significant opportunity for demystifying the process and for challenging unreasonable positive or negative expectations. The following example is taken from the midpoint of a second interview. It illustrates how the social worker gently encourages the client to reexamine some self-imposed restrictions on the relationship.

> **CLIENT:**   *Let's keep my feelings out of this. I simply want to look at ways to improve my relationship with my son. If you could teach me some techniques, I'd be most grateful.*
>
> **SOCIAL WORKER:**   *Of course you're entitled to privacy on issues or feelings that you don't want to share with me. At the same time, I wonder if you might be too hasty in restricting what we can discuss.*
>
> **CLIENT:**   *I don't get it. What do you mean?*
>
> **SOCIAL WORKER:**   *Well, you've been through a lot. With your son's arrest and his disappearance for over a month, I'd be surprised if you weren't feeling stress.*
>
> **CLIENT:**   *Who wouldn't?*
>
> **SOCIAL WORKER:**   *That's exactly my point. When I don't talk about feelings that are bothering me, I have to keep them inside or pretend they're not there. I've found that doesn't work. Sooner or later, I have to face my feelings.*
>
> **CLIENT:**   *I'm just afraid that if I start crying, I won't be able to stop.*
>
> **SOCIAL WORKER:**   *That tells me that the pain must be very deep. (silence as the client tears up)*
>
> **SOCIAL WORKER:**   *I won't push you, but I hope our relationship can become a safe place for you. It's okay with me if you cry.*

Many clients are slow to develop trust, perhaps for good reason. They may have lifelong experiences of betrayal or abuse by people they trusted. Why should it be any different with a counselor? As a result, it is understandable that they approach counseling with a degree of mistrust. Wicks and Parsons provide a compelling observation: "Though there may seem to be a great distance between counselors and their clients during the beginning phase of counseling, they should not be discouraged because at that point their clients may be closer to them than anyone else" (1984:168). In fact, social workers can foster relationship development if they try to match their responses to their clients (Huber and Backlund, 1991). For example:

> **CLIENT:** *I really don't see the point in being here. My situation is hopeless. I've been to other counselors and nothing worked. I'm only here because my wife insisted. She thought you might be able to help.*
>
> **SOCIAL WORKER (CHOICE 1):** *You certainly do sound discouraged. But I think you should give counseling a chance. Maybe by talking about your problems we can discover some solutions you've overlooked.*
>
> **SOCIAL WORKER (CHOICE 2):** *Given your past experiences, I can see why you're pessimistic. You're wise to be skeptical until you find out if you can trust me. In the end, the results will be the most important thing.*

In this example, Choice 1 is well meaning but ill timed. Responses such as this may "impede the client's cooperation . . . especially if the client has already been discouraged by previous counselors who began treatment on a positive, optimistic note, only to end counseling efforts with no improvement" (Huber and Backlund, 1991:24). Choice 2, however, is not condescending and does not provide false hope.

Shulman (1992) emphasizes the need for workers to provide clear, nonjargonistic statements that describe the range of services available. This is particularly important in settings where the social worker may be the one who initiates first contact. When the purpose of the meeting is explicit, clients do not have to worry about workers' hidden agendas, and they are in a more informed position to take advantage of assistance. In the example below, a school counselor is attempting to engage with an eleven-year-old boy who has transferred to the school in the middle of the academic year. He has been referred by his teacher, who is concerned that he seems depressed and alone.

> **SOCIAL WORKER:** *My name is Mr. Smith. I'm here because your teacher thought I might be able to help you with some of the problems you're having at school. I know that it can be tough to be the new kid. Sometimes it's just not much fun. Maybe we could meet and see if we can figure out a way to make things better. What do you think?*

Interview 3.1 illustrates part of the contracting process. The excerpt is taken from about the 15-minute mark of a first session with a parent of a teen who is abusing drugs. Sometimes, contracting can start very early in the interview. At other times, as in this example, it is helpful to give clients some space to describe their feelings and problems before proceeding to contracting.

Immediacy

Immediacy is a tool for exploring, evaluating, and deepening relationships. The goal of immediacy is to strengthen the counseling relationship. Egan (1990; 1998) describes two major types of immediacy: relationship immediacy and here-and-now immediacy.

INTERVIEW 3.1
Contracting

Dialogue	Analysis
SOCIAL WORKER: This might be a good time to pause and talk about how we might work together Then we'll both have a shared sense of direction.	A simple, nonjargonistic statement initiates the contracting process. The importance of contracting is identified.
CLIENT: Yes, I was wondering where we go from here.	
SOCIAL WORKER: Perhaps you have some ideas on what you'd like to achieve. I'd like to hear them; then, if you wish, I can add some of my own.	By seeking input, the social worker communicates respect for the client's needs and signals that the counselor is not going to take control and make all the decisions. This helps to empower the client and minimize any tendency for the client to become overly dependent.
CLIENT: As I told you, my big goal is to keep my son alive. I don't want to receive a call from the hospital saying he has overdosed.	
SOCIAL WORKER: Whether your son uses drugs is not under your control. But we could talk about some of the ways you could deal with his behavior, like how to handle it when he breaks curfew or what to do when you think he's high.	The social worker attempts to gently contain the work within areas that the client can control, namely her behavior.
CLIENT: That would be great! Those are two of my biggest problems.	The client's reaction confirms understanding and provides agreement on one target for work.
SOCIAL WORKER: Obviously this is a time of stress for you. One of the ways I may be able to work with you is to help you deal with your feelings. Sometimes you might feel overwhelmed by everything that's happening, and I'd be happy just to listen or to help you sort out your feelings.	Social workers can use statements of purpose to suggest additional ideas to help clients make the best use of the services available. In this statement, the social worker attempts to introduce feelings as one of the areas on which counseling might focus.
CLIENT: You have no idea how tough this has been for me as a single parent. My father was addicted to alcohol, and my son brings back all those memories.	The client's willingness to begin to share some of her feelings signals to the social worker that she has accepted the offer to explore feelings.
SOCIAL WORKER: So, you're no stranger to the pain that is caused by addiction.	Empathy is the preferred response to strong feelings.
(five minutes later)	
SOCIAL WORKER: What do you need and want from our relationship?	This work sets the stage for feedback. It gives the counselor a clear picture of the client's preferred style. Knowing this, the worker can tailor any feedback to fit the client's expectations. Notice that the social worker makes no assumptions of meaning and asks the client to define the vague term *honest*.
CLIENT: I want you to be honest with me.	
SOCIAL WORKER: What do you mean?	
CLIENT: Don't try to spare my feelings. If you think I'm wrong, say so. Don't sugarcoat the truth.	
SOCIAL WORKER: So, if I have some ideas about how you might do things differently or another way of looking at things, I'll just tell you.	Later, if the social worker wishes to challenge the client, he or she can use an introductory statement such as the following to remind

CLIENT: Exactly.

SOCIAL WORKER: Can I expect the same from you?

CLIENT (HESITATES): I guess so.

SOCIAL WORKER: You seem unsure. Would it be tough to confront me if you thought I were wrong?

CLIENT: I'm the kind of person who likes to keep those kinds of things inside.

SOCIAL WORKER: Sometimes it makes sense to hold back. But it's better to have choices. I'd like to convince you to risk telling the truth to me. Then you can decide if that works better, at least in dealing with me.

(a few minutes later)

CLIENT: About a year ago, I went to a family counselor for help. That was a disaster.

SOCIAL WORKER: You might be worried that this will turn out the same way.

CLIENT: Yes.

SOCIAL WORKER: Now I'm worried too. (counselor and client laugh) Tell me what went wrong; then we can talk about how we can avoid the same problems here. Just tell me what happened, but don't tell me who your counselor was.

CLIENT: Well, for one thing, he never gave me any information. If I asked for a brochure or something on heroin, he'd always say sure, then he'd forget.

(a few minutes later)

SOCIAL WORKER: Do you have any questions?

CLIENT: Who gets to see my file?

the client of the contract: "Remember when we agreed that if I had some ideas that were different from yours, I should be honest?" Because there has been prior agreement, the client is more likely to support the process and to be open to feedback or challenges. Some clients have trouble dealing with people in authority. Others are simply shy and have habitual patterns of taking a passive approach to relationship problems. The counseling relationship can be an opportunity to experiment with new ways of relating. When social workers create conditions of safety for risk taking, clients can learn skills that they can transfer to other relationships.

The purpose of this process is not to engage the client in a gossip session about the mistakes of colleagues. Candid discussions about what was effective and ineffective provide important information on the client's expectations and fears for the current relationship. This gives the social worker a chance to customize counseling to meet the needs and wants of the client. Reviewing the client's counseling history may enable both the client and the social worker to learn and build on the mistakes of the past. Of course, this discussion must be conducted in a professional manner that does not involve maligning colleagues.

A little humor adds warmth to the relationship.

Discussion regarding the limits of confidentiality and any other ethical concerns that the client has can now be addressed.

Relationship Immediacy

Relationship immediacy refers to the process of evaluating the general working climate of the counselor–client relationship. The focus is not on a particular incident but on the way the relationship has developed and how it is helping or standing in the way of progress. "The relationship is evaluated or reviewed, and relationship strengths and weaknesses are examined by exploring the respective feelings, hopes, and frustrations of the parties involved" (Shebib, 1997:114).

Relationship immediacy might be used effectively when feelings such as anger, resentment, or resistance to the work seem to be adversely affecting the relationship.

Similarly, positive feelings of liking or attraction might also need to be addressed if these feelings are clouding objectivity or progress. The example below illustrates how a social worker might initiate relationship immediacy.

> **SOCIAL WORKER:**   *I want to put aside what we've been talking about and take a look at what's happening between us. I think we have great rapport, and we both seem relaxed when we're together. But I believe I've become reluctant to be totally honest. Maybe it's because I don't want the relationship to become unpleasant. If I'm not mistaken, you seem to hold back too.*

Remember that the counseling contract should be reviewed on a regular basis. Exploration of problems may promote insight, and this may lead to changed expectations and revised goals. As the counseling relationship matures, the roles of social workers and their clients must also evolve.

Here-and-Now Immediacy

Here-and-now immediacy focuses on interactions as they occur within the interview. With here-and-now immediacy, social workers reveal their current feelings and perspectives. Here-and-now immediacy addresses and deals with relationship issues such as tension, lack of trust, and lack of direction in the session (Egan, 1998; Young 1998).

All relationships, including the counseling relationship, are occasionally tested with minor or serious personality conflicts and communication breakdowns. Describing the counseling relationship, Compton and Galaway conclude that "it is not necessarily pleasant or friendly; sometimes the problem is worked out in reaction and anger, in conflict as well as in collaboration or bargaining" (1984:226). Handled wisely, these conflicts have the potential to deepen rather than impair relationships.

Here-and-now immediacy is a tool for preventing communication breakdowns. By addressing relationship difficulties as they arise, more serious problems are prevented from developing from the build-up of unresolved feelings. This does not imply that every relationship issue must be explored. Here-and-now immediacy should address significant feelings and issues that affect the relationship as they occur, but it is important for professionals to be sensitive to timing and pacing. Generally, here-and-now immediacy should not be introduced at the end of a session, when there is no time for resolution, or before sufficient trust has developed in the relationship. However, immediacy has the potential to build trust.

Social workers can ensure the appropriateness of using here-and-now immediacy by asking: Would immediacy be useful for the client? Does the client have the capacity (personal strength and resources) to profit from immediacy at this time? Immediacy is a way to get closer to clients. In the following example, the social worker uses here-and-now immediacy to identify a sharp change in the mood of the interview.

Example 1

> **SOCIAL WORKER:**   *You seem to have become somewhat quiet. When I ask a question, you give me one- or two-word answers. Usually, you're quite expressive. Is something wrong?*

> CLIENT: *Now that you mention it, yes. I'm just not sure how much I'm willing to trust you. At first it was okay, but now you seem intent on pushing me to deal with things I'd rather keep private.*
>
> SOCIAL WORKER: *Perhaps I'm moving too fast or bringing up issues we haven't agreed to talk about.*
>
> CLIENT: *Mostly, you don't take no for an answer. When I say I don't want to talk about something, I mean it.*
>
> SOCIAL WORKER: *Like earlier today when I kept coming back to how you felt when you broke up with your wife.*
>
> CLIENT: *That's a perfect example.*
>
> SOCIAL WORKER: *I guess I was pushy. I knew you would rather avoid the topic. At the same time, I could see that there was so much pain involved that I thought it might be useful to talk about your feelings.*
>
> CLIENT: *You're probably right. I should face it, but I'm afraid.*

When responding with immediacy, it is important to use **I-statements** to underscore responsibility and ownership of feelings. In general, the emphasis should be on statements such as "I'm uncomfortable," not "You make me feel uncomfortable."

Example 2

> SOCIAL WORKER: *Let's stop for a moment. I'm feeling confused, and I'm not sure where we're headed. What's happening for you?*
>
> CLIENT: *We do seem to be headed in circles. I'm lost, too.*
>
> SOCIAL WORKER: *All right, let's talk about how we can get back on track.*

In Interview 3.2, the social worker uses immediacy to address concerns that his client has become dependent. Initially, the client is reluctant to discuss this issue, but the worker's persistence sets the stage for the client to emerge with some important feedback. Changes in the relationship can then be negotiated. Moreover, the process models communication and relationship problem-solving skills that are transferable to other situations.

Transference

Transference is a concept first introduced by Freud to describe the tendency of clients to communicate with their counselors in the same way that they communicated with significant people in the past. Transference can include reactions of both attraction and aversion. When transference is strong, clients have intense feelings and reactions that are unconnected to experiences with their counselors. Transference is likely present when there are strong feelings of liking or disliking another person on the basis of first impressions (Young, 1998). For example, a client might relate to the authority of a social worker with the same withdrawal and inner anger that characterized earlier relationships with family. In addition, as Egan notes, "Some of the difficulties clients have in their day-to-day relationships are also reflected in their relationships to helpers. For instance, if they are compliant

INTERVIEW 3.2
Immediacy

Dialogue	Analysis
SOCIAL WORKER: I'd like to suggest that we take a few minutes to talk about you and me. I think it might be useful to look at what's working and what's not working.	The social worker signals an interest in looking at the relationship and provides a brief rationale (relationship immediacy).
CLIENT: I think it's been great. You always seem to know what to say. I don't know if I could cope if it weren't for you.	Many clients are uncomfortable with immediacy discussions, perhaps because of past failures. The client's praise of the social worker may be justified, or it may be an attempt to avoid the issue.
SOCIAL WORKER: Thanks. To be honest, I have mixed reactions to what you're saying. It's nice to be appreciated, but I'm also concerned. I wonder if, by relying on me so much, it's becoming harder for you to do it on your own.	The social worker discloses feelings (here-and-now immediacy).
CLIENT: I can't do it on my own.	
SOCIAL WORKER: Okay, so you need help. Being able to seek and accept help is a sign of strength. My concern is that I may be doing things for you that you need to do youself.	Without attempting to argue with the client, the the social worker gently persists in encouraging the client to look at the issue. The client is able to identify an important parallel to her relationship with her father (transference).
CLIENT: Now you sound like my father. He's always saying that I should stand on my own two feet more and not rely on him so much. But every time I try to be independent, he interferes.	
SOCIAL WORKER: Does that happen between you and me?	
CLIENT (HESITATES): A little.	
SOCIAL WORKER: Can you elaborate?	The social worker uses a simple probe to make sure that he understands. An empathic response recognizes the client's **ambivalence,** or mixed feelings. Asking for an example is important to confirm that both worker and client have the same reference point.
CLIENT: Don't get me wrong, I really want your help, but sometimes it seems like you've already decided what I should do. I figure that you probably know what is best, so I just go along with your plan.	
SOCIAL WORKER: It sounds as though you have mixed feelings. On the one hand, you value my help, but at the same time I also sense some reluctance. I wonder if part of you knows it isn't good for you if you don't have the freedom to make your own decisions.	
CLIENT: That's right.	
SOCIAL WORKER: Can you think of a recent example? I want to make sure I understand.	
CLIENT: Earlier today, when I mentioned that I wanted to go back to school, you were really supportive, and I appreciated that, but it seemed	

like you were bulldozing me to take art. I like to paint, but it's a hobby, not something I want to pursue as a career.

SOCIAL WORKER: That's a good point. Thanks for the feedback. Let's talk about how we can change our relationship to avoid similar problems. I'll try to be more sensitive to interfering. I'll need your help. If you think I'm pushing, will you tell me?

CLIENT: I promise to do that.

Immediacy enables the social worker and the client to negotiate changes in their relationship.

---

outside, they are often compliant in the helping process. If they become aggressive and angry with authority figures outside, they often do the same with helpers" (1998:180).

Below are some examples of relationships in which client transference is apparent:

- Kevin desperately wants to be liked. He gives his counselor unsolicited praise and gifts. Increasingly, he begins to act and talk like his counselor.
- Claire suffered abuse from her father and both of her brothers. In the first session with a male counselor, she immediately begins to cry, despite the fact that she felt optimistic and self-confident before she entered his office.
- Amar has a strong need for approval. He withholds information that he thinks might provoke the counselor's disagreement.
- Jaimie, a six-year-old who has been abused, behaves in a sexually provocative way.
- Toby, age eighteen, has had a very strained relationship with his father. His counselor notes how easily he becomes angry during the interview at the slightest provocation.

With transference, unresolved issues result in distortions in the way that others are perceived. Consequently, successful examination and resolution of counselor–client relationship difficulties helps clients develop communication and problem resolution skills that will be useful to them in their daily lives. It is important that social workers distinguish client reactions and feelings that arise from the current relationship from those that arise from transference. Social workers should not be too quick to rationalize clients' feelings and behaviors as transference. Their clients' responses may be valid reactions to what has transpired in the counseling session.

Countertransference

Countertransference is the tendency of counselors to inappropriately transfer feelings and behaviors to clients. Young views countertransference as an ethical issue that should be addressed by supervision so counselors can get help to "monitor the tendency to be too helpful, and to deal with feelings of sexual attraction as well as anger, fear, and insecurity" (1998:169). Corey and Corey warn of the dangers of countertransference: "The emotionally intense relationships that develop with your clients can be expected to bring your unresolved conflicts to the surface. Because countertransference may be a form of identification with your client, you can easily get lost in the client's world, and thus your value as a helper becomes limited" (1989:94).

Countertransference issues are emotional reactions to clients, whereby counselors come to see clients as projects, sexual objects, friends, or even extensions of themselves (Young, 1998:169). Below are some signs that countertransference is happening or that a risk for countertransference is present for counselors:

CONVERSATION 3.2
Self-Disclosure

STUDENT: I think that many helpers misunderstand self-disclosure. Some of my colleagues make a point of telling their clients about their past, whereas others share little or nothing about their private lives.

TEACHER: Helper self-disclosure can be an important part of effective counseling. The problem is knowing what to share, how much to share, and when to share it.

STUDENT: I agree. I think some disclosure conveys that the helper is warm and human, and it helps clients overcome the common mistaken belief that they are the only ones with problems.

TEACHER: Self-disclosure models appropriate sharing of feelings and gives clients the courage to open up. Some clients may feel reassured knowing that their counselors have faced similar problems, but, unless it's handled carefully, clients may see their workers as needy.

STUDENT: Back to your earlier statement. What do you share? How much? When?

TEACHER: The answers will vary depending on the client and the situation. In general, a moderate level of self-disclosure is appropriate (Cormier and Cormier, 1985), but some situations may warrant a great deal of self-disclosure, and some none at all. Depending on the situation, too much self-disclosure may be as bad as too little.

STUDENT: As I see it, the most important principle is that self-disclosure should be an option, not a compulsion. Effective helpers need to be able to self-disclose, but they also should be able to constrain themselves from always disclosing. If the session is moving smoothly without self-disclosure, then it's probably unnecessary. Self-disclosure must strengthen the relationship or otherwise contribute to the work. The primary goal is to meet the client's needs.

TEACHER: For me, the most important principle is to avoid letting counselor self-disclosure shift the focus of the interview from clients to counselors. That leads to role reversal, with clients counseling counselors. As I said earlier, too much self-disclosure leads clients to see helpers as incapable and to lose confidence in the process and the capacity of their counselors to help. The counseling relationship is not mutual, with each person taking turns sharing a problem.

STUDENT: What's often forgotten is the fact that self-disclosure involves more than sharing details of your past or your personal problems. Sharing your feelings with clients about the relationship or the work is also self-disclosure and a key element of the skill of immediacy. Rogers (1961; 1980), a central figure in counseling and the founder of client-centered (person-centered) therapy, emphasized the importance of being transparent and real in the relationship by sharing moment-to-moment feelings that are relevant to the relationship. After all, if we can't be open about our feelings, how can we expect clients to be?

- having intense feelings (e.g., irritation, anger, boredom, sexual attraction) for clients you hardly know
- feeling attraction or repulsion
- being reluctant to confront or tending to avoid sensitive issues or feelings
- continually running overtime with certain clients and wishing that others would not show up for scheduled appointments
- acting with rescuing behavior, such as by wanting to lend money, adopt abused children, or protect clients
- being reminded by clients of other people you know
- dealing with clients who have problems or personal histories similar to yours
- employing unnecessary or excessive self-disclosure
- feeling reluctant to end the counseling relationship

Dependent Relationships

A **dependent relationship** arises when clients become overly reliant on their counselors for decision making. Common indicators that a dependent relationship exists include excessive permission seeking, frequent phone calls or office visits for information, and an inability to make simple decisions or take action without consulting the counselor. A dependent relationship undermines the principle of self-determination by shifting power away from clients and preventing them from developing independence.

Reactions to Power and Authority

Transference happens to some degree in all relationships, but it is much more likely to occur in relationships in which authority is present. However, to some extent all counseling relationships involve power and authority. Social workers and other professionals may have roles of authority when clients have clear social control issues. Probation and parole officers may have formal power, or they may work with clients as part of a court order. Counselors may have power because clients perceive them as having superior or expert knowledge. Some workers, such as those in welfare settings, have control over services and benefits that clients are seeking. Clients also may react to other variables, such as age, socioeconomic status, position, gender, marital status, appearance, size, intelligence, and social demeanor.

Need for Empowerment

Often, clients come to counseling with low self-esteem and confidence. Seligman's (1975) concept of **learned helplessness** is a useful perspective for understanding. He suggests that individuals can become demoralized through failure to the point that they give up trying to alter their circumstances, even in situations in which change is possible. People with learned helplessness can be difficult and frustrating to work with because "to initiate changes, you must envision that your actions are possible and your effort will make a difference. You must believe that you are capable of taking action and garnering resources to augment your own" (DuBois and Miley, 1996:24). People who have learned helplessness do not believe that their efforts will make a difference.

If clients are locked into seeing themselves as victims, they are likely to resist change, or they may enter into dependency relationships in which they relinquish power and control to others, including their counselors. In working with clients who show signs of learned helplessness, it is crucial that counselors remember that "helplessness is a perception and not an accurate description of an individual" (Arnhold and Razak, 1991:102). The reality is that "many who are afflicted with crippling low self-esteem are in fact quite capable in some respects—the problem is that they think and feel otherwise about themselves" (Arnhold and Razak, 1991:102).

Social workers need to be self-aware so that they can take steps to manage their own unmet needs that might impede their capacity to be helpful. For example, if they have a high need for control, they can potentially take power from clients, who, for their part, may freely give it away. The concept of **empowerment** gives priority to assisting clients to maintain or assume control over their lives. Empowerment is concerned with giving clients access to resources and with enabling clients to achieve a sense of control over matters that affect their lives. As clients become empowered, there is an increase in their self-respect, confidence, knowledge, and skills.

Strategies for Empowering Clients.   Social workers who are committed to empowering their clients must start with a basic belief that their clients are capable of managing their own lives. They must relinquish the mistaken notion that clients depend on them for advice, decision making, and problem solving. Clients are empowered when they participate in decisions about counseling goals and procedures.

An empowerment attitude gives priority to clients' capacities and strengths. Thus, social workers should search for and recognize their clients' strengths and resources. Questions and statements can be used to shift the focus of the interview in this direction, such as "What's working well for you?" "Let's talk about how you were able to cope with this problem for so long." "When you were able to manage, what were you doing that helped you succeed?" "Why don't we take an inventory of your strengths?" Sometimes social workers can offer other perspectives that empower. For example, responding to a woman who has struggled for six months to find work and get off welfare, a workers might say, "I'm impressed with your ability to hang in there. Many people would have given up." Ignoring or questioning self-deprecating remarks that reinforce low self-esteem is another choice for focusing on strength.

The principle of self-determination introduced in Chapter 2 promotes empowerment by helping clients recognize choices and by encouraging them to make independent decisions. To avoid promoting unhealthy client dependency, social workers should not do for clients what clients can and should do for themselves. Furthermore, when clients are successful as a result of their actions, their confidence and self-esteem will increase. Social workers should acknowledge and give clients credit for their success.

Strengths Approach.   Clients are often besieged by debilitating problems and surrounded by chaos in their lives. Social workers cannot ignore real problems, but in the process they should not focus all their attention on problem situations and what is dysfunctional in their clients' lives. Social workers should adopt a strengths approach to clients in order to acquire a balanced perspective. The strengths approach assumes the inherent capacity of people. Individuals and communities are seen to have assets and resources that can be mobilized for problem solving. Sheafor, Horejsi, and Horejsi (2000), Saleeby (1997), Cowger (1994) and others have discussed techniques and guidelines for maintaining a focus on client strengths. Building on their work, the following suggestions are offered:

1. Trust that clients have the capability to change, and that they can learn to cope with their problems and challenges. Every experienced social worker and counselor can relate amazing stories of people who have recovered from adversity and overwhelming odds.
2. Stay interested in strengths. Acknowledge clients' skills, resourcefulness, motivation, and virtues. When social workers value their clients' strengths, clients learn to value themselves. Social workers and clients can become energized by discovering overlooked abilities, knowledge, and experience.
3. Ask questions or make statements that uncover strengths such as: Think of a time when you were able to handle problem such as this. What skills and resources enabled you to cope? What are the things in your life that you feel good about? What's working well for you? What would your friends say are your best qualities?
4. Negotiate a partnership with clients in which they share responsibility for identifying priorities, goals, and preferred ways of proceeding. Accept that they are the "experts" on their own lives, and with encouragement they can make decisions on what will and will not work. Social workers need to be flexible and accept that every intervention plan will be individualized to the unique needs and attributes of each client. What works with one client may be counterproductive with another.
5. Avoid diagnostic labels as a way of describing clients. Labels tend to ignore strengths by focusing on pathology and deficits.
6. Focus on problem solving and goal setting rather than on discussions of blame or on finding the root causes of current behavior or problems. There may be cathartic benefit to discussing history, but once this purpose is achieved the focus of the work should shift to present and future events. Setting goals energizes clients to action and it mobilizes their resources and motivation for change.
7. Consider that families, neighborhoods, and communities have formal and informal resources that are potential sources of help and strength for clients. Challenge clients to identify and discover these resources. Ask questions such as: Who do you trust? Who supports you when you need help? Use community directories to pinpoint agencies, services, and self-help groups that could be supportive.

Ending the Counseling Relationship

Counseling relationships vary in length from a single interview or a short encounter to many years. Some are superficial, with minimal emotional investment by the participants, while others result in considerable intimacy and emotional involvement, but all relationships, regardless of their length, have the potential to be intimate. The counseling relationship is not designed to be permanent, but, owing to its intimacy, the ending of the relationship may trigger powerful feelings and behaviors in both clients and counselors. For some clients, intense satisfaction and feelings of accomplishment punctuate their success, but others may feel abandoned and deserted. The ending may remind them of the pain and sadness of other endings, and they may need help dealing with their loss and grief (Shebib, 1997; Shulman, 1992). Hess and McCartt Hess note that the end of the helping relationship brings attention to the fact that "the impending separation is a violation of the wish intrinsic in most meaningful attachments that the relationship would remain permanently active" (1984:561).

The initial reaction of both clients and helpers to a pending termination of an intimate counseling relationship is often denial (Hess and McCartt Hess, 1984; Shulman, 1992). Social workers need to be sensitive to signals that clients are having trouble with endings. Some clients who have shown progress might regress to previous ways of coping, or they may present new and complex concerns that seem to say, "I'm not ready for this to end."

Other clients might express their pain about the ending by expressing unfounded anger and resentment (in effect, avoiding the pain of the ending or denying the importance of the relationship). Still others fail to show up for the final meeting as another way to avoid dealing with the pain of the ending.

Social workers who have invested heavily in the relationship will also have to deal with their own feelings about the ending. This may result in a variety of denial reactions such as:

- denial of the ending by allowing or encouraging clients to remain in counseling longer than necessary. The counseling relationship is not designed to be lifelong. The counseling contract should include defining an end point to the relationship. As well, individual interviews should be structured within a time frame. With a time frame, "both worker and client tend to mobilize their efforts more effectively to accomplish the tasks of the contract within the time designated" (Kadushin, 1983:239). Then the relationship ends.
- denial of the ending by making false or unrealistic concessions or promises, for example, by promising to visit or correspond with clients
- denial of feelings by behaving apathetically or avoiding discussion of feelings about the ending
- denial of feelings by abruptly ending without warning

Dealing with Endings

One way to assist clients in dealing with endings, including denial responses, is to teach them about "the predictable reactions to loss and to aid them in identifying those reactions when either directly or indirectly expressed" (Hess and McCartt Hess, 1984:561). The ending phase, when handled effectively, offers rich potential for work. Surprisingly, many books on counseling do not examine the therapeutic possibilities of the ending phase. With trust firmly established in the relationship and the urgency of the end approaching, clients may broach significant themes and topics (Shulman, 1992). Shulman describes the phenomenon of doorknob communication, whereby clients bring up important issues at the end of the interview/relationship when there is little or no time to address them. Clients are typically ambivalent about dealing with the issues, but their need to address them finally overcomes their need to avoid them.

A second strategy is for social workers to honestly express their feelings about the termination of the relationship. This models appropriate sharing for clients, and it stimulates them to risk sharing their reactions and feelings. Of course, this discussion requires them to be open to strong feelings, such as sadness and anger. Shulman (1992) underscores the importance of workers sharing their own feelings, but he acknowledges that this is a difficult skill to develop. In part, this arises from the fact that workers may be struggling with their own sense of loss as they prepare to end their relationship with a valued client. Continued self-examination can help them develop self-awareness about their own behaviors and feelings regarding endings and separations.

Interview 3.3 illustrates how the ending process can be used to address feelings. The client is a young adolescent about to be discharged from a residential treatment center. For the last six weeks, he and his social worker have been actively planning for his return home. The client has been looking forward to more freedom and release from the rules and restrictions of the center. As part of his prerelease planning, he has spent two weekends with his family.

Summary

The counseling relationship is negotiated in order to assist clients to achieve defined goals. Developing and sustaining an effective counseling relationship is widely accepted as critical to success in counseling. It is characterized by some of the same elements of a deep friendship, but it differs in important ways, such as its time-limited nature and its emphasis on goal achievement.

Over the four phases of counseling—preliminary, beginning, action, and ending—the counseling relationship needs to be developed, sustained, and then ended. Throughout all phases, counselor warmth, empathy, and genuineness are essential.

The counseling contract is an important tool that enables social workers and their clients to agree on their respective roles and the purpose of the counseling relationship. The contract is negotiated early in the relationship, but periodic revision is necessary because of changing client needs and priorities. Counseling relationships are formed for one or more broad purposes, such as to offer support, assist with problem solving, help clients learn skills, or help them deal with painful feelings.

Immediacy is a tool for exploring, evaluating, and deepening relationships. Relationship immediacy refers to the process of evaluating the general working climate of the counselor–client relationship. Here-and-now immediacy focuses interactions as they occur within the interview.

Self-disclosure has an important place in counseling, but social workers must use it intelligently to ensure that it meets the needs of their clients and that it does not move the focus of the interview away from their clients.

Transference is the tendency of clients to communicate with their helpers in the same way that they communicated with significant people in their past. Countertransference is the tendency of helpers to inappropriately transfer feelings and behaviors to clients. It is important that counselors are able to distinguish between client reactions and feelings that arise from the current relationship and those that arise from transference. All counseling

INTERVIEW 3.3

Endings

Dialogue	Analysis
SOCIAL WORKER: If I'm not mistaken, you look a little glum today.	The social worker risks empathy by picking up on nonverbal cues from the client. The worker suspects that the client's anger may be connected to the ending of the relationship.
CLIENT: Can't you ever let anything pass? Why don't you just get off my back?	
SOCIAL WORKER: Tomorrow, you will be leaving the center to return home. Maybe we could talk about that. I'm wondering how you feel about it. I wouldn't be surprised if you had mixed feelings, being happy to be leaving, but also sad to be leaving your friends here.	The client's first reaction is to deny his feelings by discounting the value and importance of the relationship.
CLIENT: It's no big deal, but why should you care?	
SOCIAL WORKER: I feel sad knowng you're leaving. We've become very close and I'll miss our time together.	By sharing her own feelings, the social worker communicates her willingness to deal with emotions. This acts as a model for the client. Of course, any feelings the worker shares must be genuine.
CLIENT: It's been all right. I guess you're okay.	
SOCIAL WORKER: Thanks, and you're okay with me too. (ten seconds of silence) How do you feel about us not seeing each other anymore?	Although his anger softens, he is still reluctant to acknowledge his feelings. The worker persists.
CLIENT: I wish it wasn't happening. I don't know if I'm ready to go.	Although the client has trouble labeling his feelings, he begins to open up. The social worker uses empathy to acknowledge the feelings suggested by the client's remark.
SOCIAL WORKER: It's very scary thinking about leaving.	
CLIENT: I want to go home, but my mother and I always seem to end up fighting. You and I can talk and not fight. Why can't it be that way with my mother?	The client risks talking about his feelings about going home. The social worker tries to get the client to accept credit for success in the counseling relationship. She challenges him to consider how he can transfer some of his behavior in their relationship to his relationship with his mother.
SOCIAL WORKER: Maybe you have more control than you think. What do you do differently with me than with your mother?	

relationships involve power and authority; thus, clients are particularly vulnerable to transference reactions.

Persons with learned helplessness believe that change is not possible through their own efforts. Counselors need to look for ways to empower such individuals so that they can assume control over their lives. One way to do this is to adopt a strengths approach that assumes that people, individuals, and communities have assets and resources that can be mobilized for problem solving.

The inevitable ending of the counseling relationship may trigger powerful feelings in both clients and counselors. The ending phase, when handled effectively, offers rich potential for work.

EXERCISES

1. What were (or are) the attributes of your most positive relationship with another person? The most negative? How can you use this information to be a more effective counselor?

2. Interview friends and colleagues on the topics of warmth, empathy, and genuineness. Ask them to describe how they know when someone exhibits these inner qualities.

3. Talk to people who are happy in their work. Ask them to describe how they sustain their energy and enthusiasm.

4. Pay attention to the people you see and meet over the next week. Who evokes strong emotional reactions? Who seems most similar to your parents or other authority figures? Now examine your feelings and try to identify transference reactions—feelings that you carry over from prior relationships and that are not based on objective reactions to the current relationship.

5. Orchestrate an immediacy encounter. Contract with a colleague with whom you have a working relationship to spend one hour evaluating and strengthening your relationship. Use the following open-ended statements to develop themes for your discussion, but be sure to explore your ideas and responses:

   - The thing I value most in this relationship is . . .
   - The one thing that is missing in our relationship is . . .
   - When I first met you, my reaction was . . .
   - You are most like . . .
   - When I think about sharing feelings with you . . .
   - In order for us to become closer, I would have to . . .
   - What I want most from you is . . .
   - When I think of the future of our relationship, I . . .

   Periodically, share how you are feeling using a statement such as "Right now I am feeling. . . ." You are free to add other significant themes in your relationship that are not suggested in the above list. When you are finished, discuss what changes you would like to make in your relationship.

6. Imagine that you wished to use immediacy in each of the following situations. Develop an introductory response to begin the encounter.

   a. You are dealing with a client who hints that he or she is sexually attracted to you.

   b. You are counseling a client who has become demanding.

   c. You are feeling confused and you are not sure what to do next in the interview.

   d. Your client continually questions your training.

7. Do you agree with the observation made by Keith-Lucas (1972:18) that "the attempt to keep the relationship on a pleasant level is the greatest source of ineffectual helping known"? Examine your own needs with respect to keeping the counseling relationship warm and pleasant. How far

would you go to ensure this as an outcome? Under what conditions might you need to sacrifice pleasantness?

8. Imagine that you are the designated counselor in each of the following situations and that you are about to see each client for the first time. What barriers might you anticipate in developing a relationship with each client? Develop a relationship-building strategy.

    a. Hospital setting: A man, age 64, has just learned that he has terminal lung cancer. The ward nurses tell you that he is angry with his doctor and that he blames him for not making an earlier diagnosis.

    b. A young woman (age 21) has just been released from prison and is about to see you, her probation officer. Reports from the prison note that she has considerable difficulty dealing with people in authority.

    c. Employment counseling setting: A middle-aged man with 25 years' experience and four university degrees has been laid off after 15 years with the same company. As you walk to your office, he remarks, "I don't see the point of this. I think this is a big waste of time, but the company is paying for it, so I might as well get all I can."

    d. School counseling office: A teenager is referred by her teacher, who suspects that she might be using drugs.

    e. Crisis line: A man, age 33, is threatening suicide.

    f. Health clinic, working with a physician colleague: A woman is HIV positive. Your task is to tell her about her HIV-positive diagnosis.

    g. Home visit: You are a social worker interviewing parents to investigate anonymous allegations that their children are suffering physical abuse.

    h. Mediation center: You are working with a couple that has sought mediation assistance to work out custody and visiting rights.

    i. Community counseling agency: The client, age 35, has a long history at the agency. Other counselors have noted that the client has a tendency to become dependent and makes daily phone calls for advice.

    j. Transition home: A woman is returning to the house for the third time after being severely abused by her husband. On previous occasions she has vowed never to go back to her husband, but each time she has reconciled.

    k. A mental health counseling center: A man is seeking assistance for depression. He has considerable difficulty relating to women.

9. What are the issues (pros and cons) involved in counseling friends?

10. This exercise is designed to expand your self-awareness regarding issues that might affect your counseling relationships. Complete each sentence quickly, without attempting to edit your thoughts.

    - The one thing I have to have from other people is . . .
    - What's missing in my personal life is . . .
    - Something that people do that bothers me is . . .
    - The one type of person I'd hate to work with is . . .
    - Relationships would be better if . . .
    - What I like most about people is . . .
    - What I dislike most about people is . . .

11. Most of us tend to repeat established patterns when we begin new relationships. Interview others who have observed you during your "beginnings." Explore questions such as the following:

   - What first impressions are you likely to leave with others?
   - How do their perceptions compare with your intentions or inner feelings?

   Now consider the following questions:

   - What are your typical beginning feelings, thoughts, and behaviors?
   - How are beginnings the same or different for you when you are relating to different individuals or groups, for example, clients, colleagues, or supervisors?
   - What works for you?
   - What doesn't?

12. Based on your observations and insights from the previous question, begin the process of developing a range of different skills and strategies for beginning relationships. This will help you avoid becoming locked into established patterns. Define personal goals for development, related to how you handle beginnings. As part of this, detail three different beginning styles you wish to add to your skill repertoire. Describe when and how you will experiment with these three approaches. What problems do you anticipate might interfere with achievement of these goals?

13. Think about significant relationships in your life that have ended because of separation, death, or other reasons. How did you respond emotionally and behaviorally to these endings? In retrospect, are there things you wish you had said or not said? What remains unresolved in these relationships? (Suggestion: If this exercise evokes strong emotions, you may find it useful to debrief with a friend or colleague.)

14. In your answer to the previous question, what behavioral patterns are evident? What are the implications of your insights for your work as a counselor?

15. Rate the extent to which you think it would be appropriate for you to disclose the information listed below. Use the following scale:

   5 = always appropriate
   4 = usually appropriate
   3 = sometimes appropriate
   2 = usually not appropriate
   1 = never appropriate

Be prepared to defend your answers with examples.

   ____ **a.** details of your education and training

   ____ **b.** your philosophy of counseling

   ____ **c.** information about your age, marital status, and number of children

   ____ **d.** your sexual orientation

   ____ **e.** particulars about your life, such as personal problems that you have faced

   ____ **f.** details about your everyday life, such as your hobbies, reading preferences, and vacation plans

   ____ **g.** intimate details about your personal life, such as marital problems and recovery from addictions

   ____ **h.** feelings such as anger, boredom, confusion, or sexual attraction that are influencing the interview

To what extent were your answers influenced by your comfort level with each of the categories?

16. Under what conditions do you think it would be wise for a social worker to avoid self-disclosure?

17. Evaluate your general comfort with self-disclosure. What areas of your life are you reluctant or unwilling to talk about? To what extent would your friends and colleagues describe you as open or closed? Do you tend to be guarded about sharing information, or do you generally disclose a great deal to others? How does your comfort with disclosure vary depending on whom you are talking with (e.g., family, friends, authority figures, clients, colleagues, strangers)?

18. What are the implications of your answers to the previous question for your work as a counselor?

19. Evaluate the potential appropriateness of each of the following counselor self-disclosures (the counselor is speaking to a client).

    a. Your situation reminds me of my own problems. Maybe we can pool our energies and find a solution that works for both of us.

    b. I'm sorry to say that it's none of your business whether I have children.

    c. When my husband abused me for the first time, I knew the marriage was over and I left.

    d. (addictions treatment center, meeting a client for the first time) Hi, I'm John and I'm a recovering alcoholic, so I know what you're going through.

    e. I'm feeling confused. I think we need to stop for a minute and decide where we're going.

    f. Your problems are really getting to me. They remind me so much of my own struggles. They bring back all my pain.

    g. You have the most beautiful eyes.

    h. I like what you're wearing today. It's really sexy.

    i. Generally, I like to try to establish open communication in my relationships, so I push myself to be open with my feelings even when it's difficult.

    j. Your attitude really makes me want to just give up on you.

    k. This has been a bad day for me. There have been some cutbacks at the agency and I'm worried about losing my job, so if I seem a little preoccupied today I hope you'll understand.

    l. What a weekend! We partied all night. I could hardly make it to work today.

20. Describe how counselor self-disclosure might be appropriate in response to each of the following client statements or questions. Suggest a response.

    a. Have you ever felt so angry that you wanted to kill someone?

    b. My mother never gives me the support I need.

    c. I began using drugs when I was eleven.

    d. Are you gay?

    e. I'm terrified about going back to school. I don't think I can handle it. It's been so many years since I wrote an essay or read a book.

    f. My teenage son is driving me crazy.

    g. I think this counseling session is a waste of time.

    h. I really like you.

    i. I don't think anyone has ever been as depressed as I am.

4 Listening

The Basis for Understanding

Preview

After reading this chapter you should be able to:

- explain the importance of listening
- define the components of effective listening
- list common obstacles to listening
- describe techniques for overcoming listening obstacles
- explain the importance of active listening
- describe the components of attending
- demonstrate attending skills
- list and explain the multiple meanings of silence in counseling
- identify a range of choices for dealing with silence
- define and describe what is meant by paraphrasing
- demonstrate paraphrasing skills
- define and describe what is meant by summarizing
- demonstrate summarizing skills

The Challenge of Listening

Listening is defined in Webster's dictionary as "hearing with thoughtful attention." A more technical definition is provided by Wolvin and Coakley, who describe listening as "the process of receiving, attending to, and assigning meaning to aural and visual stimuli" (1996:69). Listening is a complex process that involves sensory, mental, and behavioral competence. Obviously, effective listeners need to hear, but simply hearing words is insufficient for listening. Skilled listeners also must be able to perceive associated relevant and often complex nonverbal information, such as voice tone and gestures, which support, enhance, or contradict verbal messages. As a mental process, listening involves separating relevant information from irrelevant information, assigning meaning to words and experiences, remembering, and linking related data. Put simply, listening is making sense of what has been heard. Behaviorally, proficient listeners are dynamic and responsive. They ask questions to get clarification, definitions, and examples to ensure that they have enough information to hear what the sender meant them to hear. They use summaries and statements to ensure the accuracy of their observations and conclusions, such as "Do you mean. . . ?"

Listening is the cornerstone of counseling and is essential to understanding and relationship development. Often clients come to counseling with considerable experience of not being heard. They may have turned to family and friends for help but found that their concerns were discounted or were met with simplistic advice by people who were so anxious to help that they failed to listen with attention.

Effective counselors and social workers are distinguished by their capacity to listen. As a fundamental building block for the relationship, listening communicates to clients that their ideas and feelings are important. Skills such as probing and insightful empathy are incomplete unless they are balanced with competent listening. Indeed, listening must be an active partner in all other counseling skills. Listening educates social workers about the uniqueness of their clients, thus minimizing any tendency to make erroneous assumptions. Listening encourages clients to tell their stories and disclose their feelings. In the process, they may gain enormous therapeutic value from releasing pent-up emotions. When social workers listen to clients, clients become better able to listen to themselves. Systematic listening, punctuated with appropriate probes, clarification responses, and summaries, helps clients organize confusing and contradictory thoughts.

Listening is an act of acceptance and caring that says to clients, "Your feelings are precious and unique. I won't insult you by assuming that I know what you're going to say before you say it. I won't judge or ridicule what you say. I won't try to change you to fit my idea of what you should be." Listening means joining our clients in understanding their world, their perceptions, and their feelings.

Listening requires social workers to be silent, but being silent does not necessarily mean that one is listening. A silent person may hear the words and even be able to repeat verbatim what has been said, but a tape recorder or a clever parrot can do the same thing. Egan (1977) introduced the term *hollow listening* to mean listening without responding. Hollow listeners are silent or use clichés such as "I know just what you mean." Hollow listeners may be attentive to the speaker, nod their heads to signal approval, and look as though they're involved, yet there is very little intimacy to the encounter. As Egan concludes, "The ultimate proof of good listening is good responding" (1977:137).

Listening in its purest form is a search for meaning. Kadushin says:

> Listening is the dynamic process of attaching meaning to what we hear, making sense of aurally received, raw verbal-vocal symbols. It is a purposive, selective process in which sounds communicated by a speaker are screened, given attention, recognized, comprehended, and interpreted by the hearer. Listening is not the passive reception of sound, but the active processing of sounds we hear. It involves not only listening to sounds, but listening for sounds that would further our understanding (1990:244).

Therefore, listening is not a passive act. Effective listeners are busy with the task of trying to comprehend what is happening for their clients. Sometimes, social workers will be patiently quiet as they respectfully yield the right to speak to their clients. At other times, they will be vocal, with questions and directives for more detail, example, or clarification. At all times, they should carefully observe and try to understand nonverbal behavior. Daly's distinction between perceived listening and actual listening underscores the importance of active involvement in listening: "No matter how effective, skilled, or competent an individual is in listening, unless he or she is perceived as listening by the other interactants, little may be accomplished" (cited in Wolvin and Coakley, 1996:31). Active listening, a collection of skills discussed in this and subsequent chapters, is the way that social workers and other professionals show their clients that they are listening. This is possible because they are, in fact, mentally and physically committed to the task of listening.

Good listening can be physically and emotionally exhausting. Nichols noted that "listening is hard work. It is characterized by faster heart action, quicker circulation of the blood, a small rise in bodily temperature" (cited in Wolvin and Coakley, 1996:29). It requires social workers to focus all their intellectual and physical attention on clients so that they have the social workers' unwavering commitment. Listening is the client's reward for talking.

Overcoming Listening Obstacles

Close-minded listeners respect only those who agree with them. Because they already have the "right" answers, there is no need to entertain new thoughts and ideas, nor is there any reason for them to seek additional information. Open-minded listeners, on the other hand, are willing to explore new ideas and are secure enough to hear different opinions. They endeavor to receive messages and understand meaning without distortion. Open-minded listening requires the participants to shift between speaking and listening while attempting to understand. Open-minded listeners use several skills.

Being Patient. In order to make themselves understood, people need to be able to frame their ideas. Clients who lack the ability to express themselves, perhaps because they have a limited vocabulary or capacity to articulate in precise terms, use words that are vague, ambiguous, or contradictory. Others may not have sufficient awareness or insight to describe their feelings. In such circumstances, social workers can become impatient, and this becomes an obstacle to listening. They may try to hurry the process by finishing sentences for clients who are struggling to express themselves. Or they could become lazy and content to assign their own meanings to words and phrases.

Encouraging Trust. Client messages could be incomplete or missing because of trust issues. In the beginning phase, the client may be reluctant to share. This is understandable, because the counseling relationship has yet to be tested. Consequently, the client could hold back information or feelings that are ultimately vital for understanding and present "safe" issues to test the relationship or only hint at more important concerns. As counseling progresses, clients learn that they can depend on their social workers to respond with respect and understanding. Unfortunately, in some cases, they may learn that their social workers cannot be trusted with feelings.

Controlling Noise.   Once messages are sent, they must be received and interpreted accurately, hence the importance of conducting the counseling interview in an environment that is free from distraction and interruption. Professionals should, of course, never discontinue an interview to answer the phone. In addition to the dangers of inadvertently breaching confidentiality, suspending the interview to attend to other business seriously impedes relationship rapport and the flow of information. Even a ringing phone left unanswered can destroy the ambiance of the meeting. Similarly, pagers, fax machines, computer alerts (beeps and electronic voices) that signal incoming E-mail, and cell phones may interfere with listening and communication. Ideally, all such equipment should be turned off. Alternatively, professionals might consider conducting the interview in an office that has no such distractions.

Staying Focused.   Good listening is difficult work that requires effort to stay focused. Because we can think many times faster than others can talk, it's easy to allow our thoughts to wander. The trick is to keep our minds busy with listening. Active involvement in listening, through summarizing, paraphrasing, and asking questions, will help social workers stay alert and focused. Mental involvement will also help social workers concentrate and understand what's being said. For example, as they listen they can ask themselves, "What does the client mean by. . . ?" "What are the key points of what is being said?" When they do this, counselors should try to avoid becoming overly absorbed in figuring out what they are going to say next, as this will only divert their attention from listening.

Internal noise can also interfere with listening. Social workers might be preoccupied with their own needs or ideas. They could be looking forward to their vacation and imagining their break. They may be under personal stress, suffering from fatigue, or engaged with thoughts of other clients. Such interference can cause them to stop listening or to fail to engage in important aspects of the listening process. A social worker who is tired might deliberately neglect to explore or define important ideas.

Controlling Assumptions.   If social workers believe that they already know what others are going to say and are not open to new information, then listening is not possible. Social workers' apparent patient attention and silence could give the illusion that they are listening, but their assumptions and preconceptions quickly become obvious to astute clients. Typically, clients are guarded and defensive with people who have opinions different from their own. In the example below, a high-school student has just told her social worker that she has been offered a scholarship at a prestigious university.

> **STUDENT:**   *It's one of the finest universities in the area. It's really quite an honor to have been chosen from all the applicants. My father, who never had a chance to go to university, is ecstatic.*
>
> **SOCIAL WORKER (CHOICE 1):**   *Wow! That's terrific. You must be so proud of yourself. This is really an outstanding opportunity.*
>
> **SOCIAL WORKER (CHOICE 2):**   *How do you feel about it?*

Choice 1 in this example assumes feelings and meaning. As a result, further exploration is discouraged or cut off. Choice 2 is a listening response that encourages more information. It allows for the possibility that the client might say, "I'm depressed about it. I've
been going to school for twelve years and I really wanted to take a year off." Choice 2
illustrates a basic principle of effective listening: Good listeners are open to learning, and
they "go to school" with every client. This requires a willingness to give up any notion that
they know what others are about to say.

Managing Personal Reactions.   Tension and anxiety may be aroused within the social
worker, either by the content of what a client is saying or by the manner of the client.
Emotions in the client can trigger emotions in the worker, which, if unchecked, can lessen
his or her capacity to listen. For example, an angry client might stimulate fear in the counselor. The worker may become preoccupied with his or her own fear or insecurity and
begin to act defensively. As well, a depressed client can have a contagious effect and cause
the worker to become similarly despondent. Certain words or messages might act as emotional triggers for social workers and lead to faulty listening and understanding.

Many beginning workers react strongly to clients who have been abusive, and they
erect listening barriers. They get so trapped in their own need to condemn the abhorrent
behavior that they have no room left to become aware of their clients' frames of reference.
Consequently, they fail to establish any base for understanding and any credibility to promote change. Entering into the private world of clients whose behavior and attitudes differ
sharply from one's own requires emotional maturity, skill, and, often, abundant courage.
Such capacities distinguish and define competent counselors.

Sometimes workers become bored, particularly when dealing with clients who speak
in a monotone. Clients who are repetitious and long-winded can also stimulate boredom.
To stay alert during an interview, social workers must arrive alert. They should get enough
sleep and exercise and avoid heavy lunches that might lead to drowsiness. Short breaks to
take a walk, stretch, or clear the mind are important ways of sustaining energy.

When clients present difficult feelings and topics, some social workers handle their
own discomfort by becoming inappropriately quiet or silent, becoming excessively talkative, changing the subject, or offering premature advice or reassurance. Such responses
may communicate that the worker does not understand or is not listening or, in the case of
inappropriate silence, that the counselor does not care. Social workers need to become confident in their skills and abilities so that they can tolerate clients' feelings, reactions, and, at
times, verbal assaults with a minimum of defensive reactions that obscure listening and
understanding.

Knowing That Listening Does Not Mean Agreeing.   Sometimes people confuse listening with agreeing. This misconception is common and is apparent in the way people
talk. For example, a person might say, "I told him what I want. Why doesn't he change?
He doesn't listen to me." Failure to comply with one's wants and needs is used as evidence
that the other person isn't listening. Similarly, people may not listen because they are
afraid that this will be construed as consent. This belief is one of the main reasons that
many people cannot communicate effectively. If each party to an argument tenaciously
clings to his or her own beliefs without hearing the other side, then how is communication

possible? Social workers need to be cautious that they don't succumb to this trap. One new social worker remarked, "If I listen to someone who abuses children, aren't I condoning it?" Social workers need to remind themselves that listening does not mean agreeing. Weaver provides a useful perspective:

> We may listen carefully and at length to the presentation of our opponent. We may question; we may explore; we may do our best to hold our own biases in abeyance as we try to see the world through his eyes. And we may, after all this, decide that our own position is the better and cling to it still. This does not mean that we did not listen (1972:22).

Exemplary social workers become vigilant when they are dealing with clients who test their values and beliefs. They discipline themselves by taking extra precautions to ensure they are listening accurately. They try to become alert to any internal noise that might impair their capacity to hear. They know they are vulnerable, and they take preventive measures.

Being Aware of Blind Spots.   Because everyone's frame of reference is different, we can never perfectly understand how other people are experiencing their world. Our understanding is always clouded to some extent by the meanings we assign to events and by our own thoughts and feelings. Social workers also have blind spots that make it difficult for them to hear or understand their clients. In this respect, they are vulnerable when they have unrecognized or unresolved problems that are parallel to those of their clients. For example, one worker experienced unusual discomfort when trying to work with a client who was dealing with an unwanted pregnancy. Ten years before, the worker had placed her own child for adoption, but she had never addressed the guilt she felt over the decision. Whenever her client focused on her options, the social worker's own feelings made it tough for her to separate her feelings from the client's.

Table 4.1 summarizes some strategies for overcoming common listening problems. These strategies are intended as ideas, rather than as recipes for responding. Each interview situation requires individualized and creative responses.

Active Listening

Understanding is always tentative, but it is even more speculative until we provide an opportunity for clients to confirm or deny its accuracy. *Active listening* describes a cluster of skills that are used to increase the accuracy of understanding. Attending, being silent, summarizing, paraphrasing, questioning, and empathizing are the essential skills of active listening. They breathe life into listening so that it becomes a continuous process of paying attention, hearing, exploring, and deepening. Active listening involves hearing what is said, as well as what is left unsaid. Social workers need to use both their eyes and ears to ascertain meaning. Careful attention to such cues as word choice, voice tone, posture, and verbal hesitations is necessary to discover confirming or conflicting messages in the verbal and nonverbal messages. Subtle changes in voice tone or sudden shifts in the topic may signal important areas for the social worker to consider or pursue. In one case, a 28-year-

TABLE 4.1   Overcoming Listening Obstacles

Problem	Counselor Choices
The client has problems with language, e.g., misleading word choice and difficulty verbalizing ideas.	Ask questions to clarify meaning Pay careful attention to nonverbal communication for clues to meaning
Messages are incomplete, ambiguous, or unclear.	Probe for detail and examples Paraphrase to confirm understanding Ask for definition
Relationship problems/trust issues are resulting in client censorship of feelings and ideas.	Show empathy Provoke candid discussion of trust or relationship issues Go at a slower pace, reduce questions Communicate openness through nondefensive responses
There is outside interference, e.g., noise and lack of privacy.	Hold phone calls, move interviews to a private setting
There is internal interference, e.g, social worker fatigue, difficulty concentrating, boredom, hearing impairment.	Start a personal wellness plan Start time management Defer the interview Use discipline to increase concentration (e.g., mentally summarize key details) Summarize, paraphrase, empathize
The counselor has a loss of objectivity when dealing with ideas that are contrary to his or her values.	Use supervision or consultation to address personal issues that cloud objectivity Become self-disciplined to explore ideas that are different
There are cultural barriers between worker and client.	Enlist the client's help to understand cultural values and issues, then adapt the interview style to fit Use translators or refer the client to a worker of the same culture
Content is overwhelming for the social worker, e.g., when the client rambles or is long winded.	Summarize to identify themes and priorities Selectively interrupt to control the flow of the interview
The client is inappropriately silent.	Attempt to understand the meaning of silence, then respond appropriately
The client has speech problems (e.g., mumbling, stuttering, whispering).	Remember that problems may decrease as the counselor becomes more familiar with the client's style Ask the client to speak up

old woman, describing her career goals., mentioned her sister. As she did so, the worker noticed that she avoided eye contact and her voice dipped slightly. He asked how she felt about her sister. The woman began crying as she related how her sister had always been the favored one in the family and how she had felt rejected by her mother. Subsequently, this relationship became a central issue in the counseling, and the client developed insight into how she was using her career as a desperate attempt to gain her mother's acceptance.

Active listening skills can also be used to defuse critical incidents. The FBI, for example, has trained negotiators to use active listening skills to handle situations involving hostages or barricaded subjects (Noesner and Webster, 1997). They found that active listening, particularly the skills of paraphrasing, empathizing, and open-ended questioning, helps subjects (i.e., hostage takers) release frustration, despair, anger, and other powerful feelings, with the result that they return to a more normal level of arousal and rational thinking. One of the reasons active listening is so effective is that it does not threaten people with an overt attempt to change them. Active listening builds rapport because it shows that the listener is nonjudgmental and is interested in understanding. Individuals in crisis may erect heavy psychological defenses, but "because active listening poses no threat to an individual's self-image, it can help a subject become less defensive. Thus, active listening creates fertile ground for negotiation and, eventually, change" (Noesner and Webster, 1997:16). In short, active listening is critical for nonviolent crisis intervention.

Attending, use of silence, summarizing, and paraphrasing will be explored in the following sections of this chapter. Subsequent chapters will address the skills of questioning and empathy.

Attending

Attending is a term used to describe the way that workers communicate to their clients that they are ready, willing, and able to listen. When coupled with understanding and appropriate verbal responses, attending promotes exploration. As a basic active listening skill, attending conveys physical and psychological commitment to the helping interview. Attending says to clients, "I'm here for you. You have my undivided attention. I'm not afraid of your feelings and what you have to say." It conveys an overall physical and psychological openness. Wolvin and Coakley (1996) use the term *energetic attention* to underscore the importance of bringing both effort and desire to listening.

Certain core attending skills are universally applicable, and social workers can use them with confidence. First, counselors need to ensure that their feelings, attitudes, and commitment to clients are genuine. Egan describes attending as a learned set of skills; however, he cautions that counselors cannot fake it: "Your mind-set, what's in your heart, is as important as your visible presence. If you are not 'for' your client, if you resent working with a client, this will ooze out into your behavior" (1998:62). If a social worker has negative feelings about a particular client, then referral to another worker may be warranted. On the other hand, if such negative feelings permeate a counselor's attitude toward many clients, then additional remedies may be necessary, such as personal counseling, assistance to deal with burnout, consultation and supervision to manage feelings, or career change.

Second, providing space to clients so that they can speak begins the active listening process. This includes efforts by workers to control physical noise and self-discipline to curb internal distractions. Self-discipline to suspend hasty assumptions and judgments is essential. Social workers must avoid reacting with verbal or nonverbal messages that express impatience, disagreement, or judgment. As noted earlier in this chapter, this may be difficult when clients present ideas that are offensive or conflict with one's values and beliefs.

Third, social workers can show that they are attending by being on time for the interview, remembering important details, and following through with agreed-on plans. There is a certain physical and verbal presence that conveys commitment. Verbal and nonverbal behaviors such as head nods and encouraging probes convey interest. Social workers need to bring a certain warmth to the interview, which is communicated through appropriate smiling, changes in voice tone, and expressions of caring and support. An unemployed client who reports with glee to his counselor that he has found work has a right to expect more than a monotone "That's great."

There is general agreement that the following behaviors convey appropriate attending, particularly when they match the client's nonverbal behavior: keeping an open posture, maintaining eye contact, leaning forward, using responsive facial expressions, giving brief encouraging comments, and speaking in a warm and pleasant tone (Egan, 1998; Kadushin, 1990; Wolvin and Coakley, 1996). Social workers should avoid displaying a "poker face," which can easily be taken as a "don't care" attitude. Wolvin and Coakley reviewed the research and reached a number of conclusions that have implications for social workers. Some of the highlights of their findings are summarized below.

- Individuals whose shoulders and legs are turned toward rather than away from the other person are perceived to be more empathic.
- Individuals with open body positions (e.g., arms and legs uncrossed) are perceived more positively than those with closed body positions.
- Individuals who lean toward others are perceived to possess more warmth and empathy.
- Listeners who engage in head nodding provide positive reinforcement for speakers.
- The smile is the best indicator of interpersonal warmth.
- People who engage in eye contact and gazing (looking at another person) project more attentiveness, interest, warmth, empathy, intimacy, truthfulness, sincerity, and credibility than those who do not engage in eye contact.
- Individuals who are embarrassed, ashamed, sad, submissive, guilty, or deceptive tend to have less gazing behavior (1996:176–83).

As with any counseling skill or procedure, attending must be applied intelligently, with respect to diversity. Social workers should avoid rigid adherence to one style of attending. For example, the needs of a client who is embarrassed may be best served by averted or less intensive eye contact until more trust and comfort develops. As with any counseling skill, the general rule for attending is to seek to determine how attending can be communicated to this client in this situation.

Careful attention to words, phrases, and nonverbal communication opens counselors to learning. Social workers need to hear what is said, as well as what is not said. They need to reflect on how ideas are communicated, through tone of voice, posture, and other clues, and to listen carefully for confirming or conflicting messages. As well, they need to sift through what may be complex, sometimes confusing information to identify patterns, priorities, and areas of relevance. This work may involve the major senses of hearing, sight, smell, and touch. Although counseling work generally centers on hearing and sight, significant information can be gleaned from our other senses. For example, alcohol and some other drug use may be detected by smell.

When social workers are patient, they give clients space to confront painful emotions and to gather their thoughts. When workers sit still, maintain culturally appropriate eye contact, and avoid needless questions, they do much to convey to their clients their unwavering attention. These actions focus the attention of the interview completely on clients. To accomplish this, social workers must develop their ability to be comfortable with silence.

However, it is important to remember that effective listening involves more than silence. As Garrett points out, "One who frequently interrupts to say what he would have done under similar circumstances is not a good listener, but neither is he who sits quietly and says nothing" (1982:29). Knowing how and when to continue or interrupt silent moments during interviews is a core skill that will be explored in the next section of this chapter.

CONVERSATION **4.1**
Problems Listening and Responding

STUDENT: I find that I'm so busy trying to think of what to say next that I miss what the client is saying.

TEACHER: Yes, it is tough. That's a common problem, even for experienced workers. It is hard to stay focused on what's being said without some thought of what to do next. But with practice it can be done. One trick is to think about what is being said before thinking about what to say. As you reflect on what is being said, try to identify major themes and feelings. Often, your response will emerge naturally out of this effort.

Remember that listening is hard work and you need to be "in shape" for the interview. One essential component of this is to address your psychological needs by dealing with your own issues that might make it difficult to hear clients. If you have unresolved difficulties, especially if they mirror those of your client, it will be particularly difficult to listen effectively. A second component is to make sure you fully disengage from your last client before engaging with the next. Finally, make sure you understand before you move on. Summarize, paraphrase, and ask defining questions to enhance and confirm your understanding. As a rule, the more you occupy yourself with the active demands of listening, the less you will be tempted to let your thoughts wander.

Silence

We should not break silence unless we can improve on it!

—Elbourne, 1997

Drawing on my fine command of language, I said nothing.

—Benchley, cited in Kadushin, 1990:254

The Personal Meaning of Silence. The second major active listening skill is silence. One distinguishing quality of effective social workers is their mastery of language to communicate ideas and promote change. However, language fluency alone is insufficient. Social workers also need to understand the importance of silence in communication. They need to balance their verbal agility with an equally strong capacity for silence.

Individuals and cultural groups show considerable differences in their comfort with silence. In some cultures, silence is a sign of respect. For many people, silence is unnatural, and, if pauses occur in the conversation, they become anxious and fear that their clients will see them as incompetent. They often burden themselves with pressure to fill the silent void with words. A silent pause even as short as a few seconds may lead to inner panic. Almost on reflex, they act to fill silent moments with questions and interpretations.

Some people judge silence harshly. Quieter people may be seen as unmotivated, uninterested, aloof, rejecting, and ignorant. In a discussion with a group of students in a counseling class, I asked members who rated themselves as "more verbal" to talk to "less verbal" members about their typical reactions to silence. The more verbal members made statements such as "I feel judged," "I don't think you are very interested," "I am boring you," and "I wonder if you care about what we are doing?" These comments clearly indicated that they felt threatened by silence or viewed it as evidence of judgment or lack of interest.

In contrast, the members who rated themselves as quieter noted that they often did not have enough time to respond and revealed that they were fearful or felt inadequate. Sample comments from this group were: "You don't give me enough time to speak," "I'm scared to talk . . . I worry about making a fool of myself," and "By the time I think of what to say, someone else has already said it."

Many philosophers, poets, spiritual leaders, and writers have reflected on the meaning of silence. Typically, they extol its virtues and its power.

"There was silence deep as death. . . ." (Thomas Campbell)

"Silence is the perfect herald of joy." (William Shakespeare)

"Let thy speech be better than silence, or be silent." (Dionysius)

"I have often regretted my speech, never my silence." (Syrus)

"Silence is golden." (Carlyle)

"Observe silence and refrain from idle talk." (Bahá'u'lláh)

"The cruelest lies are often told in silence." (Robert Louis Stevenson)

"I'll speak to thee in silence." (William Shakespeare)

"Silence gives consent." (Oliver Goldsmith)

"There is no reply so sharp as silent contempt." (Montaigne)

"Silence is one great art of conversation." (William Hazlitt)

"The world would be happier if men had the same capacity to be silent that they have to speak." (Spinoza)

"Silence is the most perfect expression of scorn." (George Bernard Shaw)

"There is an eloquent silence; it serves sometimes to approve, sometimes to condemn; there is a mocking silence; there is a respectful silence." (La Rochefoucauld)

Silence in Counseling.   Social workers may have the same anxieties about silence as other people have. Silence may heighten their sense of inadequacy as counselors and lead to uncertainty in the interview. As a result, they may become impulsive and try to fill silences too quickly.

However, social workers who discipline themselves to allow silence in their interviews may find that their relationships take on an entirely different tone, with their clients answering their own questions and discovering their own solutions. A repertoire of skills positions counselors for dealing with silence in an interview. Social workers should develop comfort in allowing silence, as well as knowledge of when to interrupt silences appropriately. Knowing when to speak and when to allow silence requires some understanding of the various meanings of silence.

During silence, workers need to do more than just keep quiet; they need to *attend* to the silence. **Attended silence** is characterized by eye contact, physical and psychological focus on the client, and self-discipline to minimize internal and external distraction. Silence is not golden if it communicates lack of interest or preoccupation or if it says, "I'm not listening." This means refraining from fidgeting and from other digressions such as taking notes or answering the phone. At the same time, workers should not stare or turn the silence into a contest to see who is the first to break it. Workers should not automatically assume that silence is a measure of failure, nor should they think that a few moments of silence means that the work of counseling has stopped. Passive clients may be busy with thought, or they may be seeking to gain control or understanding of painful and forgotten feelings.

Every silent interlude will have a different meaning, and social workers need to be astute to discover the significance of each quiet moment and the most appropriate response. Understanding the different types of silence positions them to look for cues and makes it easier for them to consider appropriate responses. There are six common meanings to silence:

1. The client is thinking.

Although all clients need time to process information and to frame their responses, some need more time than others. Some clients talk with only a momentary pause to catch their breath, but others punctuate their speech with periods of reflection. If social workers do not allow this time for contemplation, their clients may feel disempowered or inadequate. Clients may be formulating their thoughts or feelings, only to be prematurely cut off by workers whose own anxiety with silence does not permit them to wait.

When clients need time to reflect, social workers can simply remain attentive and nonverbally show their interest and involvement through eye contact, open posture, and so on. They can also verbally indicate their willingness to listen by using simple phrases such as "I sense you need some time to think. That's okay. I'll wait" and "It's okay with me if you just need to think without speaking."

2. The client is confused and unsure of what to say or do.

Sometimes questions are unclear, the focus of the interview is ambiguous, or clients do not know what is expected of them. Clients may sit in silence, shifting uncomfortably and attempting to sort out what to do next.

When clients become quiet because they are confused, allowing the silence to continue sustains or increases the clients' anxiety. These circumstances warrant interrupting the silence to clarify meaning, direction, or expectations. Rephrasing, summarizing, paraphrasing, and even repetition can help in such situations.

SOCIAL WORKER: *Perhaps you're confused.*

(client nods)

SOCIAL WORKER (CHOICE 1): *I think I might have confused you with my last question. It didn't make sense to me either. Let me reword it.*

SOCIAL WORKER (CHOICE 2): *Let's slow down a bit. Help me to understand what's unclear or confusing.*

Clients may have difficulty expressing their ideas, or language problems may be a barrier. Sometimes patience will suffice and clients just need a little more time to find the right word or phrase. At other times social workers can tentatively suggest ideas or help clients label feelings.

Clients are more likely to be silent during the beginning phase of counseling and during first interviews. This is normal and usually indicates that clients are unsure of what to say or do. Consequently, they depend on the worker to take the lead to clarify role and direction.

3. The client is encountering painful feelings.

Interviewing and counseling can stimulate powerful feelings and memories. Professionals who can tolerate silence give space to their clients so that they can experience and deal with pain or anxiety. In some cases, clients may be ambivalent about facing their feelings. They may be afraid of their intensity, or they may be unwilling to face their feelings, at least at this time. Silence is a chance for clients to examine the merits of continuing further or retreating to safety. Usually, such moments are obvious because the discussion is intense immediately before the silence.

When clients are struggling with powerful feelings, social workers have several choices. First, there are benefits to allowing this type of silence to continue. Responding with attentive silence can be very therapeutic and supportive. It says, "I am here. I understand. I have the courage to be with you as you deal with your pain."

Second, when dealing with powerful feelings, silence needs to be supported with empathy. Otherwise, there is a danger that clients will feel ignored or misunderstood. Empathy confirms that feelings have been heard, then subsequent silence gives the client time to process. Empathy might be used to let clients know that they have been understood. As well, empathy tells clients that they have not been abandoned and that their workers are ready, willing, and able to be with them while they consider their feelings. Once the worker has expressed empathy, silence may be appropriate. In the following example, empathy frames two long silent moments.

> **SOCIAL WORKER:** *As I listen to you, I'm beginning to sense your feeling of resentment that your mother continually tries to run your life.*
>
> *(15 seconds of silence)*
>
> **CLIENT:** *(tears in her eyes) Resentment. That's only part of it. I don't think I could ever live up to her expectations.*
>
> *(social worker maintains eye contact, faces client)*
>
> *(10 seconds of silence)*
>
> **CLIENT:** *But it's going to be okay. I realize that I have my own expectations to meet. It's me I have to face in the mirror.*
>
> **SOCIAL WORKER:** *Sounds like you're beginning to accept that your mother is not going to change, and that only you have control over who you are and how you act.*

4. The client is dealing with issues of trust.

Before trust develops in the counseling relationship, clients may be hesitant to share personal information. They may communicate their reluctance through silence. This is a normal and self-protective way for people to avoid rejection and to maintain a sense of control over private matters. A different type of trust issue may arise with involuntary clients who use silence as a way to control the interview and to demonstrate hostility to the fact that they are there against their will. They use their silence to sabotage the interview. It says what the client may want to express, "I'm here, but you can't make me talk." Silence becomes a way of retaining dignity and control in a situation in which they feel disempowered.

Generally, social workers will want to gently move the interview toward more openness and intimacy. One way to proceed is to acknowledge the risk in sharing and to candidly discuss issues of trust. A comment such as the following opens the door: "I know it's not easy to share your feelings with a stranger. You don't know me yet and you can't be sure how I might respond." Another strategy is to move at the client's pace and discuss less threatening content until trust in the relationship develops.

Sometimes it is preferable to put trust issues on the table, rather than trying to proceed when there is so much obvious resistance. Leads such as the following can be used:

> **SOCIAL WORKER:** *I'd like to share a perception with you. I've noticed that, whenever I ask a question, you answer me quickly, then you become rather silent. I'm worried that there might be some problems between you and me that we should discuss. Or perhaps you see it differently. In any case, I think it would help if we could discuss it. I'm certainly willing to listen to any of your concerns or feelings.*
>
> *(client is silent)*

SOCIAL WORKER: *I'm not you, and without your help I can't understand how you feel. But I suspect you'd rather not be here. That's how I'd feel in the same circumstances.*

In the above example, the social worker's invitations do not guarantee that the client will open up to discuss feelings of being forced to attend the interview. However, such openness to discuss the issue frequently motivates clients to be candid about their concerns. In any case, clients will have heard the invitation, and it may help to build trust.

5. Silence is the client's usual way.

Some clients are quiet by nature. They are unused to giving long or spontaneous responses, and they may be more comfortable keeping their ideas to themselves. It is important that social workers do not consider clients' silence a personal failure and that they avoid the temptation to end any silence prematurely. Sometimes counselors need to modify their own expectations and ways of relating to allow for some clients' extended silences.

As we will see in the next chapter, some interview techniques are effective in drawing out quieter clients. For example, open-ended questions that cannot easily be answered with a simple yes or no may help overcome patterns of continued silence that impede the counseling work. Another technique is to discuss with clients how silence is affecting the counseling work, then to explore ways for them to become more expressive. Professionals should reflect on the fact that, whereas they have had training on the skills and process of counseling, their clients have not. Sometimes, clients don't understand what is expected of them, but, once they do, they are willing to cooperate. Clients may be inaccurately seen as resistant when they are just unsure what to say. This underscores the importance of social workers keeping clients fully informed by taking advantage of opportunities to explain their intent and procedures. Simple statements are usually sufficient:

SOCIAL WORKER: *I'm sure there's more that you can tell me. It will help me to understand better if you tell me more details and perhaps give me a few examples.*

Social workers can also adapt their methods by using strategies that require less verbal interaction. Children, for example, may respond more to play, art, music, and drama. Adolescents may be more motivated to talk if the interview is conducted in conjunction with an activity such as a walk in the park or a game of pool. Social workers are wise to remember that while they tend to be most comfortable with verbal interaction, their clients might favor other means. For example, some clients like to write in journals, which gives them a chance to think introspectively without time pressures. With these clients, workers might seek agreement to use relevant journal entries as reference for discussion. In the following case, a social worker relates how poetry was used.

The client was a 20-year-old woman who seemed, at first, reluctant to talk about her depression. Her usual responses were one-word or short answers. I remembered that she had mentioned that she liked poetry, so I asked her if she would be willing to bring some of it to our meeting. She was willing and, in fact, eager to share her work. She brought a short poem to the next session which she read to me. The poem revealed her deep depression and her preoccupation with death. Afterward, we talked about her torment at a level that would not have been otherwise possible. Each week she brought a new poem, and these poems became our starting point. As she began to feel better about herself, her poems became more buoyant and optimistic, and they became one measure of her progress.

6. The client has reached closure.

Silence happens when there is nothing more to say about a particular topic or idea. Silence is a way of saying, "I'm finished. Let's talk about something else."

When natural and appropriate closure is reached, there is a need to move on to a new subject. The silence may be broken by seeking confirmation that an end point has indeed been reached. One strategy that helps to ensure that closure will not be premature is to acknowledge the possibility of closure, as well as the possibility that the client may need time to formulate more ideas. A comment can acknowledge both alternatives:

> **SOCIAL WORKER:** *I'm thinking that we might have gone as far as we can with that idea. Or perhaps there's more you'd like to say.*

Subsequently, a transition to a new topic is appropriate, or it may be valuable to take a few moments to summarize before moving to a new area of discussion.

CONVERSATION 4.2
Learning to Deal with Silence

STUDENT: How long is a reasonable time to allow a silence to continue?

TEACHER: Without knowing the context, I cannot answer your question. Sometimes, after a few seconds of silence, it is appropriate to break in and say something, but, in other circumstances, an extended silence of several minutes is okay. Each situation must be looked at individually.

STUDENT: I agree, but my problem is that I get uncomfortable after a few seconds. I get so anxious that I usually rush to say something, even when I know I should keep quiet.

TEACHER: Try paying attention to what you are saying to yourself during silent moments. Watch for deprecating self-talk, such as "If I don't say something, the client will think I'm incompetent." Counter this by reminding yourself that silence has its place in counseling. If you interrupt too soon, you rob clients of important opportunities to reflect. Remember that comfort with silence can be learned, but, like all skills, learning requires practice. It may help to have a glass of water so that you can take a long, slow sip to prevent speaking prematurely. Deep breathing may also help. Finally, don't overcompensate. Some silences should be interrupted.

Nonverbal Cues and Silence. Sometimes, nonverbal cues can reveal the meaning of silence. Presenting the open palms of one's hands may say, "Wait; I need time." Looking away and clenching a fist may signal an angry silence. At other times, the meaning of silence is unclear. In such situations, workers may choose to let the silence continue for a while to see if its meaning becomes apparent, or they may wish to seek help from their clients to understand it. Below are some sample responses that workers can use:

- You've (We've) become very quiet. I'm wondering what that means.
- Help me understand the meaning of your silence.
- Perhaps you're hesitant to tell me, or maybe you just need some time to think.

Although there is often ambiguity to silence and it is difficult to understand its meaning with certainty, some clues can be used to interpret silence. Table 4.2 presents some of the messages of clients' silence. The table includes a range of nonverbal clues and ideas

TABLE 4.2   **Responding to Silence: Nonverbal Cues**

Intended Message	What to Watch for	Counseling Choices
"Please be patient. I need time to think."	One palm of hand raised 90 degrees, squinting, furrowed brow, eye movement, smiling (positive or pleasing thought).	Verbalize willingness to wait. Indicate attended silence with eye contact and other nonverbal expressions of support.
"Help—I'm confused and don't know what to do next."	Shoulder shrugging, raised palms, rapid eye movement.	Set the direction; clarify instructions. Rephrase the last response.
"You can't make me talk." "I don't want to be here."	Glaring, anger in voice, pursed lips, arms folded across the chest, clenched fist. Ignoring or providing inappropriately short answer, moving the chair back.	Communicate that it's okay not to talk. Empathize with resistance. Describe your feelings when forced to talk.
"I don't know whether to talk or not."	Starting to talk, abruptly stopping, shaking head, stuttering.	Empathize with ambivalence. Discuss the risks of sharing and not sharing.
"I'm scared of what you might think of me."	Physical withdrawal, averted eye contact, carefully measured words, whispering.	Reassure and convey a nonjudgmental attitude.
"I'm overwhelmed with these feelings."	Tears, covering eyes, quivering lips, flushed face, looking at the floor, trembling.	Show empathy, use attended silence, then reveal further empathy.
"This is the way I am. I don't say much."	Low voice tone, a pattern of short answers.	Accept it as a cultural/ individual norm. Gently encourage with open-ended questions. Explain the importance of sharing.
"I'm finished."	Leaning back, smiling, saying, "That's it."	Summarize. Change the topic; move on.

about how to respond to each. However, all nonverbal behavior needs to be interpreted with extreme caution. The same behavior may have multiple meanings. Crossed arms may suggest defensiveness but may also signal that the client is physically cold, or the client may be both defensive and cold. All nonverbal behavior must be interpreted by considering the individual client and the overall context in which the behavior occurs, then it must be checked out with the client to confirm accuracy.

Encouraging Silence.   Silence can serve a number of useful purposes in counseling. It provides time for experiencing feelings and time to contemplate. Insight may emerge from moments of uninterrupted thought. Therefore, it makes sense for social workers to promote periodic silence in their interviews with clients. This may be particularly useful when working with clients who are impulsive and with clients who seem reluctant to use silence. The following are examples of counseling leads:

- I think it might be useful if we each took a quiet minute or two to think about this idea.
- Let's pause for a moment.
- It's okay with me if you want to think about it for a while.
- When you're ready, we can talk about it. In the meantime, I'm comfortable if we don't say anything.
- Occasional silence is something that may occur during our time together. Sometimes one or both of us will need time to think.

Paraphrasing

Paraphrasing is a way of restating the client's words and ideas in your own words. Paraphrasing is not the same as repeating what the client says. Repetition confirms memorization, but it does not mean that the words and ideas have been understood. Paraphrasing is a way of stating thoughts from a different angle. The defining feature of an accurate paraphrase is its interchangeability with the client's ideas. In the process, paraphrasing can help clients organize disjointed thoughts.

Paraphrasing is an important active listening skill that serves two purposes. First, paraphrasing confirms that workers have been listening and have understood clients. Second, paraphrasing gives clients an opportunity to correct any inaccuracies. In the beginning phase of counseling, paraphrasing is particularly important because the social worker is just starting to understand how the client thinks and feels. Paraphrasing helps the worker "get on board." Paraphrasing, together with summarizing and empathizing, assists in developing the counseling relationship. As well, it helps clients to explore their problems in a way that is less forceful and directive than direct questioning techniques.

Paraphrasing concentrates on immediate client statements; it is presented without judgment and without an attempt to problem-solve. The important point to remember about paraphrasing is that it does not add to or alter the meaning of a client's statement. In the example below, notice how the social worker's paraphrase responses capture the essence of what the client has said.

CLIENT: *Losing my job was just the start of a bad year. I've had big marriage problems too, and now my daughter is on the street.*

SOCIAL WORKER: *You've had a number of serious things go wrong this year.*

CLIENT: *Right now the most urgent thing is to find some way to get my daughter back home. I need to know she's safe.*

SOCIAL WORKER: *So, the focus of your attention is seeing that your daughter is out of danger.*

> **CLIENT:** *I'd love to be able to leave my husband and move to a new city, but what would happen to my daughter? I can't be selfish.*
>
> **SOCIAL WORKER:** *If it were just you, you'd know what to do. But your daughter really is your priority.*
>
> **CLIENT:** *You're absolutely right. Once she's okay, then I'll take care of myself.*

Social workers can add variety to their interviews by using a range of different lead-ins for paraphrasing. Some examples are listed below:

- Put a different way, you seem to be saying . . .
- As I understand it . . .
- Is this right? You're saying . . .
- In other words . . .
- It seems like . . .
- It sounds a bit like . . .
- As I hear it . . .
- The picture I get is . . .

It is preferable for social workers to present paraphrases tentatively. This provides the opportunity for clients to correct errors, confirm accuracy, or provide more detail. A tentative paraphrase opens discussion for deeper exploration. Statements such as "Correct me if I'm wrong" and "Would it be fair to say . . ." suggest tentativeness.

Sometimes social workers move too quickly by doing two things at once. In the example below, the worker offers a potentially useful paraphrase, then abruptly switches to a question that will move the interview in a different direction.

> **SOCIAL WORKER:** *As I see it, you've reached a point in your life where you're not going to take any more abuse. What do you see as your options?*

In this example, a vocal pause or short silence might have allowed the client the chance to confirm that the paraphrase was correct. Client confirmation may come from both verbal and nonverbal channels.

Paraphrasing and Empathy. Paraphrasing differs from empathy because it concentrates on the content of messages—information, facts, details, and descriptions—whereas empathy focuses on feelings. Paraphrasing may be less threatening to clients who have trouble discussing feelings. Paraphrasing can be used as a prelude to empathy, with empathy being introduced as clients become more trusting and willing to address their feelings. Paraphrasing arises from words that the client has actually said, but empathy builds on verbal and nonverbal cues, responding to feelings that the client may never have identified. Paraphrasing is related to summarizing. Both paraphrasing and summarizing condense content, and both highlight key ideas in the client's communication.

The following example shows the difference between paraphrasing and empathy:

> **CLIENT:** *Not having a job is getting me down. I know it doesn't help to sit in front of the TV all day hoping someone will call with my dream job.*

> **SOCIAL WORKER PARAPHRASE:** *You're aware that you have to become more active in searching for a job in order to stop the downward slide.*

> **SOCIAL WORKER EMPATHY:** *You're aware that wishing for a job offer is making you depressed.*

In the paraphrase response, the worker paid attention to the key message (content) in the client's statement, then restated it in different words. In the empathy response the worker picked up on the emotional component. Social workers will find that simple paraphrases such as the one above have a powerful, positive effect. Paraphrasing helps clients realize that workers are listening and that they are interested. Subsequently, clients who feel heard and understood often release their defensiveness and fears about sharing. In turn, the process of sharing and exploring may generate new understanding or insight for clients regarding their feelings and problem situations.

CONVERSATION 4.3
Effective Paraphrasing

STUDENT: If the client has just said something, what's the point in restating it? I think that a client might find paraphrasing very irritating.

TEACHER: You're saying why anger your client by repeating what's obvious?

STUDENT: That's right.

TEACHER: Notice that I just paraphrased what you said and you seemed okay with it.

(student nods in agreement)

TEACHER: An effective paraphrase is more than just mechanical restatement or parroting of the client's words. Verbatim restatements may irritate clients because they don't add anything to the interview. A useful paraphrase considers clients' ideas from a different perspective. Paraphrases are most potent when they invite or stimulate further elaboration and discussion. Nevertheless, I think it's best to avoid excessive use of paraphrasing or any other skill. Use paraphrasing when you need to check your perceptions and when it seems important to let a client know that you understand.

Summarizing

Summarizing is an active interviewing skill that can serve a number of purposes. First, summarizing is a way of confirming understanding and checking assumptions. Because client messages may be complex, vague, and ambiguous, it is crucial that counselors validate their interpretations. When they summarize content, social workers present a snapshot of their clients' main ideas in condensed format for verification.

> **SOCIAL WORKER:** *So far you seem to be saying that you don't see any point in trying the same old strategies. Talking to her didn't seem to work. Ignoring her was even worse. Now you're not sure what else you can do. Does that seem like an accurate summary?*

Second, summarizing is a way of organizing complex data and content by tying disjointed but related ideas together. This may provide clients with a different way to look at existing problems, thus promoting insight. Such summaries can significantly reduce a client's confusion by ordering ideas in a more coherent sequence. The example below is excerpted from the midpoint of an hour-long counseling session. Prior to this point the client had been talking about a variety of ways to manage his depression.

> **SOCIAL WORKER:** *Let me see if I can sum up what we've been talking about. Essentially, as you see it, you need to work on long-term solutions, some related to improving your fitness, others targeting your social life. As well, you want to look at things you can do immediately to reduce your depression, including getting a medical examination and looking for some fun things to do. Is that a fair way to outline our discussion?*

The social worker's summary helps the client systematize his action plan. Summaries such as this help clients and workers identify priorities. By summarizing, counselors configure their clients' problems and issues in a particular way that might give precedence to certain ideas.

Third, summarizing can be helpful in working with clients who are overly verbose, are prone to introduce irrelevant material, or wander from topic to topic. Summarizing separates what is important from what is irrelevant by focusing the interview on particular themes and content.

> **SOCIAL WORKER:** *From what you've been saying, it seems that your problems at work with your supervisor are your top priority. Do you agree?*

Summarizing may focus on a short time within an interview, or it can encompass a broader period, including the whole interview or the entire helping relationship. Two types of summaries are content, or simple, summaries and theme summaries. A content summary focuses on content and is an unedited condensing of the client's words. All ideas are included. A theme summary edits unnecessary detail and attempts to identify key patterns and areas of urgency. The following examples illustrate the two types of summaries. The client, a 45-year-old male, has been describing how unhappy he has been as a welder.

> **CLIENT:** *From the first day on the job, I knew that welding wasn't for me. Even as a child, I always wanted to work with people. As a welder, I spend most of my time on my own. Last week was a good example. From Monday to Thursday, I was in the shop basement, and the only time I had any human interaction was when I went to lunch. It's not much better at home. My wife has gone back to school, so she's busy with homework every night. The kids are grown and we don't see them that often. All I seem to do is work and watch TV. With the junk on TV, that's not much of a life. The only thing worth watching is CNN.*

> **CONTENT OR SIMPLE SUMMARY:** *From the beginning, you were aware that your welding career didn't meet your long-standing need to work with people. It seems that your work, with last week as a typical example, leaves you on your own. With your wife studying and your children gone, TV offers little comfort.*

THEME SUMMARY: *You're feeling isolated. Neither your job nor your home life gives you much opportunity to fulfill your long-standing need to work with people.*

Content summaries make little or no judgment about relevance. The major goal of the content summary is to organize ideas and data. Theme summaries are more risky. They require interviewers to judge which information is relevant and which is irrelevant. In the above example, different interviewers might focus on different themes, depending on their mandate. A researcher investigating television programming would hear this client's statement differently than would a career counselor or a marriage counselor.

LIVE is an acronym that describes the four essential steps of summarizing: listen, identify, verbalize, evaluate.

Step One: Listen.   During this step the task is to listen carefully to verbal and nonverbal messages that provide clues to content and meaning. Social workers must exercise a great deal of self-discipline to avoid contaminating clients' ideas with personal bias and definition. Workers can ask questions, request examples, and probe for definitions as ways to reduce any risk of imposing their own biases and assumptions. As well, they need to control distractions, including outside noise, daydreaming, attending to other activities, or becoming preoccupied with what to say next. Active involvement in what is being said diverts counselors from any temptation to become distracted. Another technique to avoid distraction is to silently repeat or review client messages.

Listening means paying attention to the five *W*s: Who? What? Where? When? Why? and How? Sample questions to consider are: Whom are clients talking about? What are they saying? What are they feeling? What are they thinking? When does this happen? Where does it occur? Why does it happen? How are clients saying it?

Step Two: Identify.   The primary goal of this step is to make sense of all that has been said and heard. This involves distinguishing important information from irrelevant information, identifying underlying themes and patterns, and setting priorities. It means hearing what has been said in context, or avoiding a common pitfall in listening: not seeing the forest for the trees. The social worker's goal is to attach as similar meaning as possible to the meaning the client intended. At this step, workers need to remember that their perspectives are biased. What they deem significant and what their clients view as important may differ sharply. This reality underscores the importance of discussing these differences openly within the interview.

One tool that social workers can use is to listen for key words that will help them understand how clients think. Use of the words *should* and *must* may signal self-imposed unrealistic or irrational expectations. Ellis (1993a) believes that individuals may develop excessive needs for certain things, such as achievement, approval, and love. Problems develop when these needs become translated into dogmatic "musts," and "shoulds." For example, a client might say, "I have to get my master's degree in order to be happy." In other circumstances, the word *can't* might suggest feelings of inadequacy or self-esteem problems.

Step Three: Verbalize. The goal of this step is to verbalize understanding of what the client has said in a summarization response, using words and phrases that the client can understand. Understanding is always tentative, at least until clients have an opportunity to confirm or challenge counselors' perceptions, so this step is crucial to test the accuracy of comprehension. The move to a summarizing statement can be flagged by leads such as:

- To summarize what you have been saying . . .
- If I may offer a summary . . .
- To be sure I understand . . .
- Let's summarize.
- Summing up . . .
- Let's pause for a moment to recap.

Step Four: Evaluate. After summarizing for clients, the next step is to watch and listen carefully for signs that the summary is correct. Accurate summaries are confirmed nonverbally by the client's head nods, smiles, and relaxed posture, and verbally with short statements, such as "that's right" and "exactly." Disagreement may be direct ("No, that's not right"), or it may be nonverbal as clients move back, hesitate, or look away. Subtle clues that understanding is incomplete or inaccurate are lukewarm responses, such as "kind of," and paralinguistic cues, such as speech that is drawn out, even though the words may appear to confirm understanding. Social workers can use questions and statements to invite confirmation. This reinforces the notion that the client's right to be heard accurately will be respected, and it empowers clients to take an active role in evaluation. Such leads include:

- Does my summary capture the important points?
- I'm wondering if you agree with my summary?
- Is that accurate?
- How does that sound to you?
- Have I missed anything important?
- What have I missed?
- How would you summarize what we have talked about?

Selective Perception. **Selective perception** is a term used to describe the natural tendency to avoid being overwhelmed by information by screening out material that is irrelevant. In counseling, the obvious problem is that what clients consider relevant may differ from what workers consider relevant. What a person deems important is likely to be influenced by one's frame of reference, which is uniquely defined through elements such as past experiences, personal values, current mood, interests, concerns, fears, prejudices, health, culture, and context. For example, a tow-truck driver looks very different when you're stuck on a dark and stormy night than when you're being towed for illegal parking. The word *mother* may call up images of love and support or memories of abuse and pain. The notion of selective perception was illustrated in a popular anecdote about a social worker who was surprised to discover how many of his clients developed sexual problems after he took a course on sexual counseling. Johnson underscores the dangers of selective perception: "There is evidence that you will be more sensitive to perceiving messages that are consistent with your opinions and attitudes. You will tend to misperceive or fail to perceive messages that are opposite to your opinions, beliefs, and attitudes" (1997:129).

Social workers need to be alert to the dangers of selective perception in their own thinking and responses. They must be vigilant to make sure they understand how and when their interpretations are influenced by prior learning, values, and current expectations. They need to be careful that they don't impose their own sense of what's important.

Of necessity, social workers must ignore some parts of a client's communication and selectively attend to others. Typically, it is not possible to respond to everything. Consider how many ways a social worker might respond to the following statement:

> **CLIENT:**   *You could say my life is complicated. Six months ago I started a new job and it's terrific. I'm making more money than ever. But I don't have much time to enjoy it, given that I'm working six days a week. Maybe I should just force myself to take a vacation. With my wife working too, I think its been hard on the kids. My youngest daughter's not doing too well in school, and she seems very depressed. Most nights, she just goes to her room right after supper and shuts the door. Maybe it's just a stage and she's like all teenagers. Now I've just heard that my father can't live on his own anymore. I don't know whether to take him in with us, arrange home care, or place him in a senior center.*

In this example, there are many areas of potential importance (financial management, work pressures, stress, daughter, caring for parents). Let's took at some possible responses:

> **SOCIAL WORKER (CHOICE 1):**   *Sounds like the most urgent need is to deal with your dad. Why don't we spend some time looking at the options?*
>
> **SOCIAL WORKER (CHOICE 2):**   *Sounds like you've got a lot on your plate. How do you manage your work stress? How do you support your daughter? What can you do with your father? Have I missed anything? (client says no) What's most important to you?*

Choice 1 illustrates the danger of selective perception. The social worker assumes that caring for the father is the most urgent concern. In contrast, Choice 2 avoids this pitfall. The worker uses summarizing skills to identify major themes, then checks for accuracy, then encourages the client to set priorities.

Clients are also prone to selective perception, which may impair their ability to see all parts of a problem or available solutions that are within their grasp. Summarizing can be used to bring these overlooked aspects to the foreground.

> **SOCIAL WORKER:**   *You've told me many times that you don't see any way out of your situation. At the same time you've mentioned a couple of strategies that have worked for you in similar conditions.*

INTERVIEW **4.1**
Listening, Silence, and Summarizing Skills

The following interview excerpt illustrates some of the important concepts from this chapter. This is the second interview with a client who is seeking help with anger management. The excerpt begins about five minutes into the interview.

Dialogue	Analysis
SOCIAL WORKER: Maybe we could take a minute to review the key points we discussed last week.	This opening comment sets the stage for a review of the last interview. This is important for reestablishing the contract. It confirms that issues that were important during the last session still remain priorities.
(three seconds of silence; client smiles and nods her head)	After offering a summary, it is important to confirm its accuracy. In this case, the worker uses the brief silence to confirm the client's (nonverbal) agreement.
SOCIAL WORKER: I remember two points. First, you indicated that you wanted to find out what your triggers are—the things that lead you to lose control. Second, you wanted to explore some ideas for staying in control. Have I missed anything?	This theme summary focuses on what the social worker considers to have been the priority of the last session. Checking for client agreement is an important adjunct.
CLIENT: Yes, that about sums it up. But I don't want to become a pushover.	The client confirms partial accuracy, then adds a point that the social worker's summary has missed. This should alert the social worker to the client's priorities.
SOCIAL WORKER: So anger management, but not at the expense of giving up your rights.	A succinct paraphrase acknowledges the client's priority.
(ten seconds of silence)	Initially there is not enough information for the worker to understand the meaning of the client's silence. It might be tempting to move on with further questions, but the worker suspects that the silence is significant. A gentle statement invites the client to give meaning to her silence. Nonverbal cues (looking away, tears) suggest that the client is encountering strong feelngs. The worker now focuses on feelings.
SOCIAL WORKER: You've become very quiet. I'm struggling to understand what that means.	
(ten seconds of silence; client look at at the floor, tears in her eyes)	
SOCIAL WORKER: Perhaps this is painful for you to think about.	
CLIENT: In every relationship I've ever had, I end up being the underdog. I do everything to please my partner, but nothing for me. I always give in, but inside, it's a different story. I'm full of rage and resentment.	The client's comments suggest that she is willing to take a trust risk. This is a critical moment in the interview. The client will be watching carefully for signs of rejection.
SOCIAL WORKER: Tell me more. (leans toward client, maintains eye contact)	This directive encourages the client to go on with her story. It confirms direction and is

(continued)

INTERVIEW 4.1 Continued

short enough not to interfere with the momentum that the client has established. Attending behavior shows that the worker is interested and open to hearing the client's ideas and feelings.

CLIENT: That's the essence of the problem. I let things build up inside, then I explode. Once, I was even fired when I blew up at my boss.

The client continues to risk. This signals that trust is growing, but the connection may still be very fragile. As we will see in Chapter 6, it is now important for the social worker to make an empathic connection with the client's feelings.

SOCIAL WORKER: So your anger is a bit like a time bomb, ticking away until you explode.

Here the social worker paraphrases using a simile that is consistent with the client's phrasing.

CLIENT: Exactly. (short silence)

This silence may be a simple pause that allows the client to decide what to talk about next.

CLIENT: But, as I think about it, it's not just my anger. I guess what I'm really afraid of is never having things go my way.

The client does not accept the worker's paraphrase as accurate. Secure workers need not fear such mistakes or corrections. The client's willingness to correct the worker indicates her trust.

SOCIAL WORKER: As I hear it, you seem to need to have more control over your life.

CLIENT: No, that's not it. It's not control so much as validation.

Summary

Listening is the basis for understanding and a prerequisite for relationship development. It requires considerable effort and patience to understand the messages of others as they were intended. Active listening involves the skills of summarizing, paraphrasing, questioning, and empathizing as tools to explore and deepen understanding. Verbal and nonverbal attending behaviors demonstrate to clients that social workers are willing and able to listen. Communication entails shifts between speaking and listening, while attempting to understand. A wide range of problems, such as cultural and language barriers, difficulty in framing ideas, outside noise, ambiguity, loss of objectivity, and speech problems, can interfere with the listening process. Competent social workers are sensitive to these problems and take steps to overcome them.

Active listening skills are tools for increasing understanding, communicating interest to clients, and letting clients know that they have been heard. Active listening involves social workers in an ongoing process of paying attention, listening, exploring, and deepening.

Attending is the way that counselors communicate that they are physically and psychologically committed to the helping relationship. Attending begins with a positive attitude and a genuine desire to get involved. This attitude is confirmed with behaviors such as making eye contact, assuming an open posture, and leaning toward others.

Effective social workers need to develop the capacity for tolerating silence, as well as the wisdom to know when to interrupt silence during interviews. An important part of this skill is understanding the different types of silence. Nonverbal cues are important indicators of the meaning of silence. In addition, workers can seek help from their clients to understand silence. Because silence can serve useful purposes in counseling, workers may wish to encourage periodic silent moments of reflection.

Paraphrasing is a way of restating someone's words and ideas in your own words. Paraphrasing is important in counseling because it confirms to clients that workers have heard and understood them. Social workers need to paraphrase without judging. Summarizing helps clients to organize complex thoughts and is used to focus on relevant themes and content. The acronym LIVE can be used to describe the process of summarizing: listen, identify, verbalize, and evaluate.

EXERCISES

1. List words, phrases, and situations that you think might be your emotional triggers.

2. Over the next week or so, pay attention to the vocal pauses and silences that you and others use in everyday and professional communication. What indicators suggest comfort with silence? Discomfort?

3. Deliberately alter your response time to experiment with using silence.

4. Ask a colleague to observe your use of silence during an interview. The following checklist may be used to stimulate discussion.

	Yes	No
The interviewer allowed the client time to think and respond.	___	___
The interviewer seemed comfortable with silence.	___	___
The interviewer attended to the silence.	___	___
The interviewer interrupted silences appropriately.	___	___

5. Explain how silence can be used effectively in counseling.

6. During interviews with some colleagues or clients, find opportune moments to call for brief periods of reflective silence, then continue the interview. Discuss with your colleague/client what the impact of the silence was on the interview.

7. Videotape an interview or ask a colleague to observe your work. Evaluate your attending behavior. Use the following checklist to evaluate attending behavior.

Checklist for Attending	Yes	No
Did the interviewer . . .		
Use nonverbal behavior that suggested comfort with and acceptance of the client's ideas?	——	——
Manage outside distractions and fidgeting?	——	——
Use questions and responses that showed openness to learning?	——	——
Give the client time to express ideas without inappropriate interruption?	——	——
Manage personal assumptions and attitudes that detracted from the counselor's ability to be present for the client?	——	——

8. Work with a colleague to explore the effects of poor listening. As an exercise, deliberately (but subtly) violate the principles of effective listening and attending. For example, interrupt inappropriately, ask unrelated questions, switch topics prematurely, and avoid eye contact and other indicators of interest. When you are finished, discuss the experience. Discuss how it feels not to have others listen to you.

9. Paraphrase each of the following clients' statements.

   - At a party the other night, I finally met someone with whom I can carry on an intelligent conversation. He seemed interested too, but he didn't ask for my phone number.

   - It's a dilemma! I don't know whether to finish the school year or drop out and get a handle on some of my debts.

   - My supervisor wants to see me today. I know she wants to talk to me because I've been late for work over the last few weeks.

   - Sure I get depressed. Who doesn't?

   - First my car broke down, then the fridge. Now it's the plumbing. I should marry someone who is good at fixing things.

   - I think that with AIDS and all the other diseases you can catch we should all take precautions. You never know who might be infected.

   - Well, to put it bluntly, I think my partner has a lover. But I could forgive that. I just want our relationship to be the way it was when we first met.

   - I've tried everything. I have a great résumé. I've called everyone I know. I look for a job five to six hours a day. Still, I can't find work.

   - Lately, I've been thinking that there has to be more to life than work and play. I'm not even sure if I believe in God, but I need to find some meaning for my life.

   - I just lost it. My anger built up and I hit her. She got so upset she packed up and left with the kids. I've never done anything like that in my whole life. I realize that I didn't solve anything by losing my temper. Now I may have ruined my marriage and turned my kids against me.

   - I guess I'm going to have to find some way of dealing with my drinking problem. The other day I was so sick from drinking that I couldn't even get out of bed. I just can't let booze continue to jeopardize my work and my family.

10. Conduct an interview with a colleague on any topic of interest. As interviewer, your job is to practice paraphrasing. After each client statement, paraphrase what you think your colleague said, then watch for verbal and nonverbal indicators that your paraphrase was correct.

11. Practice summarizing skills:

   a. Conduct a five- or ten-minute interview with a colleague on any topic of interest. As interviewer, your job is to practice content summarizing skills. Periodically, try to summarize information in the interview. Make sure you understand accurately before moving on. At the conclusion of the interview, offer a complete summary of the whole session. Check with your partner to see if you understood.

   b. Continue the interview, but now practice theme summarizing skills. Periodically, try to summarize important themes in the interview. Make sure you understand accurately before moving on. At the conclusion of the interview, offer a complete summary of the whole session. Use the following checklist to evaluate the work.

Checklist for Summarizing	Yes	No
Did the Interviewer . . .		
Listen patiently before responding?	___	___
Identify recurrent themes?	___	___
Look for issues and concerns that represent the client's most urgent priorities?	___	___
Respond with short summary statements?	___	___
Give verbal or nonverbal invitations to the client to confirm the accuracy of the summary?	___	___
Summarize without judgment, advice, or attempts to problem-solve?	___	___
Use language that was consistent with the client's frame of reference and culture?	___	___

At the conclusion of both interviews switch roles; then discuss the experience.

5 Interviewing Skills

The Search for Meaning

Preview

After reading this chapter you should be able to:

- describe the importance of asking questions
- identify and describe common questioning errors
- explain why clients might not answer questions
- define open, closed, and indirect questions
- describe the advantages and disadvantages of open, closed, and indirect questions
- demonstrate the capacity to formulate open, closed, and indirect questions
- explain the importance of concreteness in counseling
- demonstrate the ability to probe for appropriate concreteness
- identify key questions for every interview
- recognize the five different types of interview transitions

Questioning

Asking questions is an important part of active listening and serves multiple purposes. No single approach to questioning works best with every client. Social workers must consider numerous factors, such as the goals for the session, the context in which questions are asked, and the individual needs of clients, and adapt their questioning techniques accordingly. Therefore, the best social workers have a repertoire of techniques from which to select. They use questions to engage clients in higher-order thinking, kindle their curiosity, and prompt them to consider new possibilities.

Questions are important tools for gathering data. Social workers listen in order to understand, but they cannot understand if they do not have sufficient information. Questions can be used to seek relevant details, definitions, and examples. By asking questions, they lessen the probability that they will make assumptions. Questions are important adjuncts to empathy because they allow workers to explore, clarify, and define emotions.

Asking the right question often has more impact on the client and the process of change than having the correct answer (Miller, 1992).

Questions focus the work of the interview on particular topics and themes. Every interview has a purpose, and this purpose determines the nature and type of questions that will be used, but the overall purpose of counseling is to empower clients to discover choices for solving problems that interfere with their lives. A series of questions can systematically lead clients through problem exploration, goal setting, and problem solving. Asking a thought-provoking question stimulates clients to begin a reflective process that can promote insight. Asking the right questions can promote awareness by leading clients to examine issues, ideas, and feelings that they might have otherwise overlooked. By sequencing questions, social workers can teach clients logical ways of analyzing and responding to problems. Effective questioning can also help clients to make connections and uncover patterns in their thinking and problem solving.

Structured interviews follow a defined sequence of predetermined questions. Every person is asked the same question in exactly the same manner. Interviews that require social workers to complete forms to establish clients' eligibility or to make assessments are examples of structured interviews. The distinguishing feature of structured interviews is their specific and standard questions. In structured interviews, there is little or no freedom of choice regarding the focus and pace of the interview.

Unstructured interviews permit interviewers and clients freedom to go in any direction without predetermined control or set questions. The distinguishing feature of unstructured interviews is their emphasis on flexible worker–client contracts. In these types of interviews, a more conversational tone is apparent and there is less rigidity concerning when and how questions are asked.

Errors in Asking Questions

Asking questions is a skill. Faulty questioning may bias answers, antagonize clients, or keep the interview at a superficial level. Insensitive questions can disregard client feelings or leave them feeling judged or abandoned. Poorly timed questions may rush the interview or frighten clients with demands for disclosure before trust has been established.

Jargon.   Common sense tells us that in order for questions to be effective they must be presented so that they are clear and understandable—in other words, so they are consistent with the language or culture of the client. Social workers, like other professionals, have their own words and language to describe their activities. Furthermore, each field of practice and each setting has abbreviations, distinctive words, and phrases that are commonly understood by the people who work there. This jargon allows for streamlined communication and helps to define activities and routines precisely. Unfortunately, jargon is often used inappropriately with clients who do not understand it, as in the following example:

> **SOCIAL WORKER:**   *I'm assuming that this is the first time that you've gone through the intake process. After we complete your app., I can refer you to an appropriate community resource.*

A new client may have no idea what is meant by the terms *intake process* and *community resource* or the abbreviation *app.* Too embarrassed to ask, these clients may be left feeling demoralized, stupid, and incapable. Nonassertive clients frequently respond to jargon by acquiescing or pretending that they understand. Their answers may create the illusion that they understand, while, in fact, they have no idea what has been said. One woman phoned an immigrant services center in a state of panic. She had been to the local welfare office and signed a form but had no idea what she had endorsed. Now she feared that she had made some mistake, because her monthly welfare check was $100 less than the previous month's.

Leading Questions.   How you word a question may dramatically affect the answer. Asking your spiritual leader, "Is it all right to smoke while praying?" may get a very different answer than asking, "Is it all right to pray while smoking?" (Sudman and Bradburn, 1983:1).

Leading questions manipulate clients to choose what appears to be the preferred answer; for example, "Don't you believe it's time you took care of yourself instead of putting your husband first?" and "You like school, don't you?" bias the answers. Clients who have a high need to be liked by their workers and clients who tend to be compliant are especially vulnerable to leading questions. These clients are less likely to be assertive by disagreeing with their workers.

Social workers may use leading questions to camouflage their own ideas. For example, the counselor who asks, "Do you think you should be doing that?" is probably saying, "I don't think you should be doing that." Leading questions tend to corner clients, as in the following interview excerpt, in which a social worker talks to a man about his mother.

> **SOCIAL WORKER:**   *Given what you've been saying, it's time for action. Wouldn't you agree that allowing your mother to live alone at home is not in anyone's best interest?*
>
> **CLIENT:**   *I suppose you're right.*
>
> **SOCIAL WORKER:**   *Would you prefer to put her in a seniors' home?*
>
> **CLIENT:**   *I really don't want to put her in a home. That wouldn't be right.*
>
> **SOCIAL WORKER:**   *Don't you think this might be easier on your family than taking on the enormous problems involved in moving her in with you?*
>
> **CLIENT:**   *(hesitates) I suppose you're right. But . . .*
>
> **SOCIAL WORKER:**   *(interrupts) I have a list of possible placements. Do you want to make some calls now?*

It's easy to see how the worker's agenda in the above encounter discounted the views and needs of the client. By selectively emphasizing one alternative, the worker allowed the client little freedom of choice. Consider how the outcome might have been different had the counselor used the lead below.

> **SOCIAL WORKER:**   *Given what you've been saying, it's time for action. What do you see as your options?*

Such a lead would have allowed the client to identify alternatives such as arranging for in-home care for his mother or inviting her to live with him. The social worker's favored alternative is not put on the discussion table to contaminate the discussion.

Excessive Questioning. Although questions are an indispensable part of most interviews, excessive questioning can leave clients feeling interrogated and bombarded. As a response to intense questioning, some clients fail to return for a second interview. Others become increasingly defensive and terse with their responses, particularly if they are unsure of the purpose of the questions. Excessive questioning can overwhelm clients, leaving them frustrated, confused, and exhausted.

Benjamin offers this warning about conducting the counseling interview by relying on questions: "By initiating the question-answer pattern we are telling the interviewee as plainly as if we put it into words that we are the authority, the expert, and that only we know what is important and relevant . . ." (1981:72). He suggests that the client may submit to the "humiliation" of questions "only because he expects you to come up with a solution to his problem or because he feels that this is the only way you have of helping him" (72). Martin (1983) warns that counselors need to be careful not to behave as if they are conducting an investigation, by asking lots of questions. He suggests that this behavior locks clients and counselors into set roles. Relying on questions results in the interview digressing to "a question-and-answer interrogation in which the client waits for the counselor to come up with the next topic" (George and Cristiani, 1986:147). Consequently, "it is not reasonable of the therapist to expect to ask a lot of questions and then have the client suddenly start self-exploration" (Martin, 1983:81).

Some clients simply do not respond well to questions. For example, involuntary clients may experience questions as an invasion of their privacy. As well, clients from some cultures may react unfavorably to questions. In such circumstances, reliance on questions will frustrate the goals of the interview. Workers may find that, rather than getting more information, they are obtaining less, so they should be alert to signs that their clients are reacting poorly to questions. For example, their clients' answers may become more brief, signaling their intention to be less cooperative. Clients also may communicate their displeasure nonverbally by shifting uncomfortably, grimacing, or averting eye contact. Some clients may refuse to answer by becoming silent, but others may be more outspoken with their disapproval, saying, "I don't see the point of all these questions." If workers continue with questions when it is clear that their clients are rejecting this approach, serious damage to the counseling relationship may result.

Questions put workers in control. To some extent, workers need to have control of the interview in order to establish its focus and structure. However, clients may be left feeling that they have lost control. As Leeds argues, "Because the other person is compelled to answer, the power goes to the person asking the question. Just watch the power shift when someone asks, 'Where are you going?' and you answer, 'Why do you ask?'" (1993:58).

Consequently, it is important that social workers are able to modify their approaches to reduce or eliminate questions. Sometimes, for example, an empathic response can achieve the same purpose as a question:

CLIENT: *I just don't know what I'm going to do. Since she left, I've felt lost and unsure of what I should do with my life.*

SOCIAL WORKER (CHOICE 1):   *What are some possibilities?*

SOCIAL WORKER (CHOICE 2):   *Sounds like you feel all alone and uncertain of what to do next.*

Choice 1 seeks more information from the client about what alternatives he sees for himself. This question helps move the interview toward problem solving and decision making. With Choice 2, the social worker acknowledges the client's feelings, as well as his indecision. With both choices, the client is likely to respond by listing his options. However, the social worker's empathy in Choice 2 is more likely to be experienced by the client as sensitive and supportive.

Social workers may have to ask a lot of questions—for example, to determine eligibility for service or to complete an intake (first) interview. One way that social workers can lessen the impact of excessive questions is to have periodic pauses to check how their clients are doing. For example, they might say, "I'm asking a lot of questions. How are you doing? I know it can be a bit overwhelming." Such comments convey respect and concern. Consequently, they tend to motivate and energize clients.

Not asking questions can be as serious a problem as asking too many questions. As a result, it is important for social workers to remember to balance questions with responses that confirm understanding (summaries) and empathic responses that affirm sensitivity to feelings. Benjamin's terse observation is worth remembering: "We ask too many questions, often meaningless ones. We ask questions that confuse the interviewee, that interrupt him. We ask questions the interviewee cannot possibly answer. We even ask questions we don't want the answers to, and, consequently, we do not hear the answers when forthcoming" (1981:71).

Multiple Questions.   Multiple questions are two or more questions asked at the same time. If the questions are complementary, they are not problematic. A second question may be asked simultaneously that embellishes or clarifies the first. For example:

SOCIAL WORKER: *How did you feel about it? How did you feel when he rejected you?*

In this example the second question does not detract from or contradict the first. Of course, the second question alone would have sufficed. In contrast, the example below illustrates how multiple questions can be confusing:

SOCIAL WORKER: *How did you feel about it? Did you see any other way of handling the situation?*

In this example, both questions are potentially useful, but not when they are asked simultaneously. The client has to decide which question to answer. Each will take the interview in a different direction. At their worst, multiple questions can bombard and assault clients with complex and conflicting demands. Imagine if you were the client in the following interview:

> **SOCIAL WORKER:**   *So, is there anything you can do? Do you think you might have told her how you felt? Or maybe you see it differently. How long do you think you can continue to hang on?*

The social worker may be well meaning, but responses such as this complicate matters and may add to the client's confusion. Generally, workers need to curb any impulse to ask more than one question at a time. When they ask a question, they should wait for the answer before proceeding to another question or topic.

Irrelevant and Poorly Timed Questions.

One way that counseling interviews are distinguished from everyday conversations is that interviews have a definite purpose or intent. When workers know the purpose of the interview, they are able to frame questions that support that purpose. Conversely, workers who are unsure of the purpose are more likely to ask random questions.

Social workers should have a purpose when they ask questions. Moreover, they should be prepared to share this purpose with their clients. They might offer a brief explanation, for example, "It would help me to understand your situation better if I asked you some questions. This will give me an idea of how you see things." Preambles such as this inform the client of the social worker's motives and procedures. When clients know what is happening, they are less likely to be defensive and more likely to support the process.

Sometimes social workers ask excellent questions but ask them at the wrong time, which leads to inappropriate topic change. A common error of this type occurs when workers ask content questions after clients have expressed their feelings. For example:

> **CLIENT:**   *I was furious with her. I never imagined that my best friend would be having an affair with my husband. We've been married for ten years, and I thought I could trust him. I feel like a complete fool.*
>
> **SOCIAL WORKER:**   *How did you find out they were seeing each other?*

In the example above, the social worker's question is valid, but it is timed insensitively. Because the client has just risked expressing strong feelings, the worker should consider empathy as the preferred response. The next chapter addresses this critical skill.

A second common error occurs when social workers shift the topic without exploring beyond a superficial level. This can happen for several reasons. First, workers may be unskilled at using probes. Second, they may be overly cautious about probing, perhaps fearing that they will be invading their clients' privacy. Third, they may be fixated on problem solving, as in the example below:

> **CLIENT:**   *We fight all the time.*
>
> **SOCIAL WORKER:**   *How do you think you might cut down on the fighting?*

In this example, the social worker jumps to problem solving far too quickly. Once a client introduces a topic, the next step should be to focus on the issue. The social worker can use a series of questions to acquire and deepen understanding. For example, it is essential that the worker learn what the client means by *fight*. Do they yell and scream? Do they refuse to talk to each other? Perhaps there is physical conflict.

Why *Questions*.   *Why* questions should be used cautiously; as a rule, they are more threatening for clients. *Why* questions tend to ask for justification, and their tone often suggests judgment, disapproval, or embedded advice. The question "Why don't you leave him?" may put a client on the defensive with the implied message "You should leave." *Why* questions ask people to explain and justify their behavior. Frequently, this requires a degree of insight that they simply do not have. In response, clients may make up answers or feel exposed and stupid for being unable to answer the question.

Benjamin echoes these sentiments, arguing that, even when judgment is not intended by the interviewer, "that is generally how the word will be understood" (1981:86). As a result, "whenever the interviewee hears the word 'why,' he may feel the need to defend himself, to withdraw and avoid the situation, or to attack" (86). Furthermore, clients may perceive *why* questions as advice, as in the following excerpt:

> **CLIENT:** *I can't relate to my father anymore. He can't see that I need my independence.*
>
> **SOCIAL WORKER:** *Why don't you just move out and be on your own?*
>
> **CLIENT:** *Impossible. I've got two more years of college and I can't afford it.*
>
> **SOCIAL WORKER:** *Why not just tell him how you feel?*

Kadushin (1990) suggests asking *what* instead of *why* questions. For example, "What prevents you from sharing your feelings?" is more helpful than "Why don't you share your feelings?" The first question seems to accept that there are explanations and reasons for the client's behavior, whereas the second question seems to demand justification.

When Clients Do Not Answer Questions

Sometimes clients do not answer questions, or their answers may be superficial. To decide how to proceed in such cases, social workers need to consider some of the reasons why clients might be reluctant to respond.

Not Understanding Questions.   Clients may not understand questions because they have not heard them. Clients may be hard of hearing or deaf, or workers may be speaking too softly. As well, clients may not have been listening. Workers may be using words, phrases, metaphors, and expressions that are not part of their clients' repertoire. Effective workers adapt their idiomatic language and voice volume to meet their clients' needs and expectations. They avoid using technical terms and jargon. Workers become models for their clients, and one of the interesting and positive outcomes of counseling is that clients may learn how to listen. When workers demonstrate effective listening and responding skills, clients tend to imitate them. Alternatively, workers can teach clients some tools for listening. For example, to encourage clients to summarize, leads such as this can be used: "Please tell me in your own words what your understanding of our agreement is. I want to make sure we both have the same understanding."

Not Understanding the Purpose. Clients have a right to know about the interview process and the motivation for particular questions. Moreover, they are more apt to respond when they feel included and informed. At any point in the interview, workers should be prepared to state, "The reason I am asking this question is. . . ." Of course, if workers don't have a valid reason for asking particular questions, they ought not to ask them. Questions are crucial for accomplishing the goals of counseling, but they must be used cautiously. Garrett suggests the following general rule: "Question for only two purposes—to obtain specifically needed information and to direct the client's conversation from fruitless to fruitful channels" (1982:33).

Not Knowing the Answers. Some questions are difficult for clients to answer. The questions may call for insight and explanations that are beyond the clients' current level of understanding. Sometimes, clients are unable to articulate their ideas and inner feelings. Learning disabilities also are a factor for some clients.

Believing That Their Answers Are Private. Clients may say, "That's not an issue I care to explore." They may change the topic abruptly, or they may respond with silence. Some clients resist questions, perhaps because of experiences of being embarrassed, interrogated, or put on the spot. Moreover, cultural norms may discourage questions of any type, or they may restrict the areas in which questioning is appropriate. In some cases, clients withhold answers because they fear that their answers will not be understood or that they will be judged. At other times, they are simply not ready or able to address the issues the questions raise.

Social workers can use a number of strategies to overcome this problem. First, they should evaluate whether they have given their clients enough time to answer. Some clients are slower to respond, and social workers may misinterpret their silence as reluctance to speak.

Second, social workers might tactfully ask clients what prevented them from answering. Sometimes, trust issues impede candor. Candid discussion of barriers to trust usually increases trust, provided that workers are nondefensive. By remaining nondefensive, they demonstrate their capacity to be open and nonjudgmental. They show their ability to handle tough issues without retaliating. As well, when questions target sensitive or private information, social workers can express empathy regarding how hard it might be to share such personal material.

Third, when clients do not answer questions, social workers can respect their wishes not to explore the particular area and shift the discussion to less threatening content. In addition, they can stop asking questions. If workers continue to ask questions even though clients refuse or dismiss them, unfortunate consequences will likely arise. Clients may become increasingly frustrated, or they may feel inadequate because they have been unable to successfully meet their worker's directives. They may become increasingly angry and resistant.

Questions and Cross-Cultural Communication

Social workers and other professionals need to be careful that their counseling and questioning methods are not culturally biased. For example, people may have profound differences in how they react to questions. In a book on effective cross-cultural interviewing, McDonald makes this important observation:

> In mainstream society, a person being interviewed will barely wait before responding to a question. Aboriginal people, however, may pause before answering a question. Culturally, the pause may be related to thinking about the answer, considering whether the answer may affect the relationship between the interviewee and the interviewer, or wondering whether the question even requires an answer at all, especially if the answer appears obvious. The question of "small" talk which is so prevalent is also related to this point. Traditionally, native people do not engage in this kind of exchange. They may be judged as shy, reticent, or uncooperative by an interviewer when, in fact, the behavior may actually indicate they feel that there is nothing worthwhile to say, so there is simply no reason to comment (1993:19).

When attempting to relate effectively to members of various cultures, social workers need to avoid stereotyping and overgeneralizing. Within a culture, an individual may subscribe to all, some, or none of the cultural norms. Table 5.1 summarizes considerations for using questions appropriately.

TABLE 5.1 Guidelines for Questioning

Don't	Do
Bombard clients with questions	Balance and add variety to the interview with a range of other skills
Ask more than one question at a time	
	Pause after each question to give clients time to answer
Use leading questions to control clients and their answers	
	Remember that summary and empathy responses are important to confirm understanding
Use *why* questions, as they usually imply blame or convey judgment	
	Ask questions one at a time
Ask questions unless you have a reason for knowing or a right to have the answer	Respect cultural norms and individual styles that may make certain questions inappropriate
	Ask questions for a specific purpose

Types of Questions

Interview vitality is heightened and more effective use of time is possible when social workers use a variety of ways of asking questions. The effectiveness of any questioning technique depends on a number of factors, including timing, the nature of the relationship, the purpose of the interview, and the mood of the participants. Questions that are surprisingly useful with one client may generate hostility in another. Perhaps the most important point to keep in mind is that there is an art to asking questions that precludes any attempt to structure questioning in the same way for each client.

Closed Questions. **Closed questions** can be easily answered yes or no. Closed questions enable interviewers to confirm facts and obtain specific information. Because closed questions do not invite detailed responses, they can effectively bring closure to an interview or slow the pace of clients who are overly verbose. On the other hand, closed questions should be avoided with clients who tend to be succinct. For example, clients can easily dismiss the question "Do you have anything you want to talk about today?" with the

TABLE 5.2   Types of Questions

Type	Description	Advantage	Disadvantage	Examples
Closed questions	Questions that can be answered yes or no	Provide specific information Confirm facts, conclusions, or agreements Slow the pace of the interview by limiting focus Are easy for clients to answer	Restrict answers When repetitive can lead clients to feel interrogated	Will you be going to the parents' group tonight? Did you say everything that you wanted to say?
Open questions	Questions that promote a more expansive answer	Allow for an unrestricted range of responses Empower clients by giving them increased control of answers	Client answers may be more time consuming Are more challenging for clients to answer	What are your plans for this evening? How are you feeling?
Indirect questions	Statements that act as questions	Are less threatening than traditional questions	Client may choose not to respond	I am interested in knowing if you have plans for the evening.

answer "No." Typically, closed questions begin with words such as *can, did, are, have, is, will, would,* and *do,* as in the examples below:

- Can you tell me what you've done about it?
- Did you have an opportunity to call the school?
- Are you feeling depressed?
- Have you thought about taking your own life?
- Is my understanding correct?
- Do you agree that the most important problem right now is. . . ?

Although clients may answer each of the above questions with yes or no, they may also choose to provide a more expansive answer to a closed question. When workers want a definite yes or no answer to an important question, then a closed question is preferable. In the example below, the client hints that suicide might be an issue. This possibility is too significant to be ignored, so the worker uses a closed question to see if this is a risk.

> **CLIENT:**   *Lately, I've been so down, I wonder what's the point of going on.*
>
> **SOCIAL WORKER:**   *Have you been thinking about killing yourself?*

Sometimes, organizations require an intake interview that requires a great deal of information. A series of closed questions is an efficient way to gather some data quickly. Unfortunately, too many closed questions may irritate clients and leave them feeling interrogated and restricted. To minimize these effects, social workers should blend closed questions with various interview strategies, in particular, other active listening skills. Garrett suggests that, "when considerable information is desired, it is often best obtained by encouraging the client to talk freely" (1982:22). This perspective is echoed by Kadushin (1990), who contends that clients are grateful when they are given freedom to explain themselves in their own way.

Open Questions.   The distinguishing feature of **open questions** is the fact that they are difficult to answer with a simple yes or no. In general, open questions are preferable to closed questions. They provide a great deal of freedom for clients to answer the questions in the way they choose, with as much or as little depth as they wish. Open questions may be used to begin an interview, for example, "What brings you here today?" They may be used to explore thoughts, feelings, or behavior: "What were you thinking?" "How did you feel?" "How did you respond?"

The vast majority of open questions are "five W" questions, which ask who, what, where, when, and why, and how questions, such as those listed below:

- Who knows about your situation besides your wife?
- What have you been able to do to cope with this problem?
- Where do you see this relationship going?
- When did this begin?
- Why do you think it has been difficult for you to cope? (As noted earlier, *why* questions should be used cautiously.)

- How do you see it?
- At what point do you think you might be ready to make a decision?

With some clients, both open and closed questions have the same result. With these clients the closed question "Did you have any feelings about what happened?" and the open alternative "How did you feel?" will generate the same response. Social workers should avoid using the closed alternative with less verbal clients. If workers want an expansive answer, they should avoid using closed questions, particularly when dealing with clients who tend to provide single-word or short answers to questions. For example, instead of asking, "Did you come here for help with your résumé?" social workers might ask questions that convey a greater expectation for detail, such as "What were your reasons for coming in today?"

Closed questions are leading when they suggest the right or expected answer to the client. In the example below, a single mother describes her situation:

> **CLIENT:** *I often think that my kids don't give me enough respect. Just once, I'd like them to ask me how my day went. When I'm tired, they could help out more.*
>
> **SOCIAL WORKER:** *Do you feel angry?*
>
> **CLIENT:** *Sure I do. Who wouldn't?*

In this example, the client hints at strong but undefined feelings. Even though the client affirms anger, this may not be her main feeling. The client may indeed be angry, but other feelings may be dominant. However, for some clients it's easier to go in the direction suggested by the question by exploring anger than it is to shift the answer. A less biased question might be "How do you feel about this?"

Kadushin suggests that open-ended questions can be intimidating for inexperienced clients who are unsure of their expected role: "For such an interviewee, open-ended questions give him little structure, little guidance about what he is supposed to talk about and how he is supposed to talk about it" (1990:185). Straightforward discussion with such clients about expectations can be a useful way to reduce embarrassment.

Indirect Questions. **Indirect questions,** or embedded questions, are statements that act as questions. Indirect questions are a softer way of seeking information. Their wording tends to be less intimidating than more direct open and closed questions. Indirect questions are effective for breaking up the monotony and threat of constant questioning, particularly when they are combined with other skills, especially empathy. The following are some examples of indirect questions:

- I wonder whether you believe that it is possible.
- Perhaps you're feeling confused over her response.
- I'm curious about your opinion.
- Given what you've said, I would not be surprised if you decided to accept the offer.
- I have no idea what you might be thinking.
- I would not be surprised to find that you have strong feelings on the matter.

- You may have already reached a conclusion.
- Your views on this are very important to me.

CONVERSATION **5.1**
Alternatives to Questions

STUDENT: Sometimes, it feels like all I do in the interview is ask questions. I can't help but think that if I were the client I'd be really irritated. I don't want to leave clients feeling interrogated, but questions seem to be the only way to get the information I need. Do you agree?

TEACHER: You're right. There is a real danger that clients will become defensive if they feel cross-examined. By paying attention to the needs, feelings, and responses of individual clients you will be able to see if you are alienating them with too much questioning. Sometimes counseling works best if you avoid or minimize questions. For example, clients who have not yet developed trust in their workers may respond better in interviews when questions are minimized.

Another drawback to asking too many questions is that too much responsibility for the direction and content of the interview can be left on your shoulders. This can be disempowering for clients and can lead them to become overly dependent.

STUDENT: But are there ways to explore and get information without asking questions?

TEACHER: Yes, there are a number of skill alternatives to questions for gathering information and making assessments. Techniques such as showing empathy, summarizing, using silence, and self-disclosing may, in some situations, be more effective ways of getting details, facts, and examples.

Empathy, for example, is a powerful counseling tool that tells clients that we understand or are trying to appreciate their feelings and perspectives. Empathic responses and summaries create an essential base of trust by showing that you are nonjudgmental and capable of listening and understanding. In response, clients often become more courageous and motivated to share and explore. Appropriate use of silence creates space for clients to speak. Questions are important for effective interviewing, but you should try to add variety to your interviews by using a range of skills.

Concreteness

Concreteness concerns the extent to which messages convey clear and specific meanings. When communication is concrete, all participants share understanding of words, phrases, ideas, feelings, and behaviors. When communication lacks concreteness, understanding is incomplete and subject to error and distortion. "Concreteness is a way to ensure that general and common experiences and feelings such as depression, anxiety, anger, and so on are defined idiosyncratically for each client" (Cormier and Cormier, 1985:48).

Social workers probe for concreteness not only to promote precision, but also to funnel the discussion and deepen the focus of inquiry. The importance of concreteness is underscored by George and Cristiani, who assert, "This dimension, perhaps more than empathy, genuineness and positive regard, moves the client through the helping process by encouraging the client to explore the problematic areas of his life and his relationship to others" (1986:128).

Table 5.3 rates concreteness on a scale of one to three. Probes for increased concreteness should be considered at levels one and two. Table 5.4 analyzes examples of client responses that lack concreteness and suggests leads for promoting concreteness.

Unclear or Ambiguous Messages. Concreteness is necessary because messages are often unclear or ambiguous. Communication involves alternating roles of sender and receiver. Senders must frame their ideas and feelings in words and gestures that can be understood. Receivers, in turn, must accurately decode these ideas and feelings. Shared understanding between two people is possible only when each participant understands a message in the way that the sender intended. This is an exceedingly complex task, with considerable potential for distortion. Probes for concreteness can reduce or eliminate distortion.

People may lack the vocabulary and self-awareness to express their ideas precisely, and their messages may be incomplete, superficial, or ambiguous. A client might say, "I feel strongly about it." However, the same statement also provides the social worker with an opportunity to help the client become more specific. Let's look at the choices:

CLIENT: *I feel strongly about it.*

SOCIAL WORKER (CHOICE 1): *I'm not surprised. From what you've been saying, who wouldn't feel that way?*

SOCIAL WORKER (CHOICE 2): *Perhaps you could be more specific. What exactly are your feelings?*

TABLE 5.3 Levels of Concreteness

Level	Description	Examples of Client Statements
one	Minimal or no detail and examples to convey meaning Nothing is said about a particular topic area	There are some things I could comment on. I know exactly how you feel.
two	Meaning is suggested, but content is vague, ambiguous, or inadequate	I have the usual share of problems with my kids. I have strong feelings about my relationship with him. We'll have to get together soon.
three	Language is precise and there is shared understanding of ideas	My eldest child has been absent from school for two of the last three weeks. I feel disappointed and rejected when my husband forgets my birthday.

TABLE 5.4 Promoting Concreteness

Client Response	Analysis	Response Choices
I have strong feelings about abortion.	The client does not provide enough information for the interviewer to understand the precise emotional reaction or point of view.	Describe those feelings. Tell me about those feelings.
I feel angry.	Further inquiry is necessary to prevent any natural tendency for the worker to attribute personal meaning to the word *angry*.	Angry? What does angry mean to you?
I hope you understand what it's like to be a single mother on welfare.	Personal experience or work with other clients could leave the worker open to making assumptions.	Everyone's experience is different. I need to hear what it's like for you.
There are several things missing in our relationship. My family is weird. I've learned a great deal.	Detail is lacking.	What's missing? In what ways are they weird? What are some things you have learned?
I'm fed up.	The target is missing (i.e., whom or what the person is angry with).	What are you fed up with? Whom are you fed up with?
She's really quite old.	The speaker's perspective is unclear.	How old is she?
I wish he'd show some respect.	The desired behavioral response is not detailed.	If he showed respect, what specifically would he be doing?
Everyone has a right to their views.	The client's views are not personalized.	What are your views?
Sometimes, I feel like giving up.	*Sometimes* is a vague modifier. Giving up is not defined.	When you say "sometimes," how often do you mean?

In Choice 1, the social worker is supportive but does not probe to find out how the client is feeling. This client hints at feelings but conveys sparse information about their precise nature and intensity. Unless the worker probes further, as in Choice 2, assumptions and misunderstanding are the likely outcomes.

Information Gaps and Missing Data. Probes for concreteness should be considered when defining details are missing and when there are missing details or gaps in information that interfere with understanding. Such probes are used to obtain examples, quantify data, or check the client's frame of reference.

Although people may have links and similarities in their experiences and common human needs, everyone is unique. All people have a different frame of reference based on their learning and experience. Consider the images that a word such as *anger* might evoke for different people. One person might vividly recall an abusive childhood, in which anger always led to someone getting hurt. Another might visualize screaming and hurtful words, while someone else thinks of withdrawing and saying nothing. What is "old?" To a twelve-year-old, thirty might seem like old age, but to a man in his late eighties, seventy is young. Intended humor may be perceived as such, or it may be seen as provocative, insulting, or sexist by different receivers of the message.

There is a natural tendency for each of us to make assumptions based on prior learning and experience. Someone tells us they are happy, and we ascribe our own meaning to the feeling. We hear about events or problems that we have faced ourselves, then we draw on our reactions and feelings as a base for empathy. Someone asks if we know how they feel, and we answer "Yes," without further inquiry or clarification. Although personal experience can be an enormous advantage for appreciating the problems and feelings of others, communication breakdowns are risked if we neglect to openly explore our assumptions for accuracy.

Using Simple Encouragers and Directives. The simplest way to probe for more information is to use short phrases and gestures that encourage clients to continue with their stories. Nonverbal gestures, such as head nodding, sustained eye contact, and attended silence, convey such support and interest. Short statements and directives, such as "Tell me more," "Yes, go on," "What else?" "Please expand on that," and "Un huh, hmm," can be used to sustain client sharing without interrupting the flow of the interview. A short example will illustrate.

> **CLIENT:**   *I guess I'm pretty angry.*
>
> **SOCIAL WORKER:**   *Meaning?*
>
> **CLIENT:**   *Our relationship is on the rocks.*
>
> **SOCIAL WORKER:**   *Tell me more.*
>
> **CLIENT:**   *My brother always puts me down. It's got to the point where I don't want to be around him.*
>
> *(social worker nods, attended silence)*
>
> **CLIENT:**   *We used to be so close. We were inseparable. In the last year, it's become so competitive.*

Using Questions. Questions are the primary tool for seeking information. Intelligent questioning can be used to get examples, define terms, or probe for detail. When social workers think that information is incomplete or superficial, they can use questions to clarify and embellish understanding. The interview excerpt below demonstrates this process.

> SOCIAL WORKER: *I want to make sure I understand. What do you mean when you say "competitive"?*
>
> CLIENT: *It's something ugly. Not just wanting to win, but needing to win. It's as if everything rides on winning.*
>
> SOCIAL WORKER: *Is that true for both of you?*
>
> CLIENT: *At first it was just him. Now I'm just as bad.*
>
> SOCIAL WORKER: *What's a typical example?*

Social workers can use series of questions to explore beyond a superficial level. This procedure encourages clients to elaborate on vague statements and to provide more details and supporting examples. The following excerpt illustrates:

> CLIENT: *I know there are many times when I let my feelings get the better of me.*
>
> SOCIAL WORKER: *What kinds of feelings?*
>
> CLIENT: *Sometimes I let my anger build to the point where I'm ready to explode.*
>
> SOCIAL WORKER: *"Ready to explode"—what does that mean?*
>
> CLIENT: *I would never become physical and hurt someone. I'm just afraid of getting really mean and saying hurtful things.*
>
> SOCIAL WORKER: *Has that happened?*
>
> CLIENT: *Yes. (hesitates) A lot.*
>
> SOCIAL WORKER: *Can you think of a good example?*
>
> CLIENT: *My mother. She's always trying to control my life. Most of the time I just try to ignore her constant nagging. But lately it seems that every second day she phones with advice. I don't want it and I don't need it. Yesterday, I blew up at her.*
>
> SOCIAL WORKER: *What did you do or say?*
>
> CLIENT: *I told her in no uncertain terms to butt out of my life. She started to cry, then I felt guilty.*

Opening Up Sensitive Areas for Discussion.   One characteristic that distinguishes exemplary professional interviewers and social workers is their capacity to be comfortable with any topic. Skilled workers take the initiative to open sensitive areas up for discussion. Often, clients hint at a concern, which provides workers with a natural opportunity to probe for more detail and to open up the discussion to a greater level of intimacy.

> CLIENT: *(avoiding eye contact) It's not easy to open up to a stranger.*
>
> SOCIAL WORKER: *It is tough. You might wonder how I'm going to react or whether I will hold what you say against you.*
>
> CLIENT: *It's just so embarrassing.*

SOCIAL WORKER: *One way to overcome that is to take a chance on me. I'm open to anything you have to say. I find that, when I avoid talking about a tough area, it becomes even more difficult to deal with later.*

CLIENT: *Lately, I can't sleep at night because I'm wondering if I might be gay.*

Probes for concreteness are invitations to clients to trust their workers by revealing thoughts that they might prefer to keep hidden. Embarrassment, fear, uncertainty, taboos about accepting help, and simple mistrust of the interview process, including suspicion about the motives of the interviewer, present natural barriers to sharing information. Shulman (1984) suggests that the same societal taboos that inhibit open discussion in sensitive areas also affect helping relationships. Among the taboos that Shulman identifies are reluctance to talk about sex, money, dependency, and authority. For some people, taking help from someone else suggests dependency, which may result in feelings of inadequacy. "To feel dependent is equated with feeling weak. The image of a 'real man' is of one who is independent, able to stand on his own feet, and competent to deal with life's problems by himself" (86).

Clients often view social workers and interviewers as authority figures, and they tend to relate to them based on their prior experiences and images of people in power. In particular, people in authority "have power to hurt us, and therefore, we will, at best, hint at our feelings and reactions" (Shulman, 1984:86). To Shulman's list of common taboo areas could be added discussions of death, spiritual issues, and health, as well as others that vary between people and between cultures.

Probes for concreteness propel the interview from a superficial level of discussion to an intimate level that requires a deeper investment from everyone involved in the interview. In Chapter 1 the illusion of work concept was introduced as a kind of implicit partnership between workers and clients. In this implicit arrangement, clients are permitted to avoid the pain and struggle that are often associated with growth, while workers can avoid the risk that purposeful challenge entails.

> We have all developed the capacity to engage in conversations which are empty and which have no meaning. It is easy to see how this ability to talk a great deal without saying much can be integrated into the helping interaction. . . . Workers have reported helping relationships with clients that have spanned months, even years, in which the worker always knew, deep down inside, that it was all illusion (Shulman 1992:145).

Appropriate probes for concreteness are one way to avoid this illusion of work. Skilled workers are continually working toward understanding the perspectives and feelings of their clients. Effective interviewers and social workers are learners, and they recognize that the best teachers are their clients. This means having the courage and assertiveness to ask difficult questions about private matters. At the same time, it means behaving responsibly by treating client responses with care. To be ethical, social workers must question wisely, exploring only those matters that are relevant to the work and within their competence. Asking clients for more concreteness requires that workers are willing to invest time and energy to listen, probing responsibly only in those areas where there is legitimate work to be accomplished.

Some thoughts may be private, and lack of relationship trust may preclude full disclosure. For example, people fearing judgment or ridicule may tell others what they think they want to hear or what they believe will result in acceptance. Individuals also may distort or exaggerate messages because of past experiences. Social workers need to know when to back off. As Garrett notes, "It is, of course, possible to probe too far. Some sleeping dogs should be left undisturbed, particularly when the interviewer is not equipped to deal with them should they be aroused. Even a skilled interviewer should use a great deal of discretion and wisdom in going beneath the surface" (1982:25).

In relationships, everyone must decide how much, when, and with whom they are willing to reveal personal thoughts and feelings. Restraint and self-censorship of some ideas and feelings are normal and necessary. Everyone differs in the degree to which they are comfortable with disclosing intimate thoughts and feelings. Some people prefer to remain private, sharing little or nothing. Others open up very slowly and only with people whom they deeply trust. Cultural norms may also influence what individuals are willing to share. Social workers need to be alert to signs of client resistance, such as when they ask to change the subject or when their nonverbal cues signal reluctance to continue. Then they can work with the client to make an intelligent decision on whether to continue, as in the following example:

SOCIAL WORKER: *How did you feel when your father said that?*

CLIENT: *(shifts uncomfortably, averts eye contact) I don't know if I'm ready to discuss it.*

SOCIAL WORKER (CHOICE 1):   *Okay. Let's talk about something else.*

SOCIAL WORKER (CHOICE 2):   *This is a difficult area for you, and you have mixed feelings about continuing.*

In Choice 1, the social worker moves quickly to change the subject. This will lessen the client's anxiety, but it also robs the client of the opportunity to deal with a difficult, yet potentially important, topic. In Choice 2, the worker is more patient and attempts to empathize with the client's ambivalence toward continuing. In response, the client may say, "You're right, it is tough. But I can handle it." Or the client might say, "I'd rather we talked about something else." With Choice 2, the worker has respected the client's right to self-determination.

CONVERSATION **5.2**
Increasing Your Ability to Be Concrete

STUDENT: Do you need a large vocabulary to help clients express themselves concretely?

TEACHER: It helps, but it's probably more important that you use the vocabulary you already have. Be curious. Ask questions. Express interest in hearing more. Seek definition of unfamiliar words or familiar words that are open to misinterpretation. Listen. These are the essential steps to concrete understanding.

Social workers need to have the time to deal with the results of any probe for concreteness. Concreteness opens new avenues of inquiry, stimulates feelings, and invites clients to share at a deeper level. Consequently, the end of the interview is a poor time to begin probing. It may seem obvious, but an important principle is that interviewers should be purposeful and their questions and responses must be pertinent.

Making Choices. A theme throughout this book is that effective counselors have a broad range of alternatives for responding. When they have choices, counselors are not locked into repetitive patterns, and interviews are more interesting and vibrant for both clients and counselors. The following example demonstrates some of the many ways that a counselor might answer a client:

> CLIENT: *I suppose I should have expected it. My girlfriend said she needed time to think, to "reevaluate our relationship," as she put it. It was tough, but I gave her some time alone.*
>
> SOCIAL WORKER (CHOICE 1): *How did you feel about what was happening? [an open question that focuses the discussion on the client's feelings]*
>
> SOCIAL WORKER (CHOICE 2): *What was your plan? [an open question concentrating on the client's behavior and thoughts]*
>
> SOCIAL WORKER (CHOICE 3): *Tell me what you planned to do (felt) (thought) (wanted to do). [directives]*
>
> SOCIAL WORKER (CHOICE 4): *Sounds like this was a painful time for you. [empathic response directed to the clients feelings]*
>
> SOCIAL WORKER (CHOICE 5): *I'd be interested in knowing how you handled it. [indirect question]*
>
> SOCIAL WORKER (CHOICE 6): *(silence) [silence used to give the client an opportunity to continue sharing]*
>
> SOCIAL WORKER (CHOICE 7): *It was hard, but you were able to give her time to reassess your relationship. [paraphrase]*

Key Questions for Every Interview

Some interviews are highly structured with a series of questions to answer, such as a survey or a standardized assessment tool. Others are much less predictable, and the discussion may take unexpected detours. Whatever the nature of the interview, social workers can use the following six key questions and their variations as reference points for most interviews:

- What brings you here today?
- What are your expectations of me?
- What do I need to know about your situation?
- What do you mean by. . . ?

- What did we accomplish?
- What have we missed?

It is important to remember that these questions are starting points. Additional follow-up interviewing and counseling skills are probably required before the targeted topic area can be considered complete.

1. What brings you here today?

One distinguishing feature of the counseling interview is that the relationship is purposeful. Consequently, it is essential that the goal of the interview is defined. Only then can social workers structure the work to achieve this agreed-on purpose. The question "What brings you here today?" begins the process of establishing a reason and direction for the interview. Of course, this direction may change as the interview progresses. Clients may develop more trust in their workers and decide to share more risky information or feelings. As well, exploration within the interview may result in increased client insight that moves the work in different directions. Therefore, it is important that social workers are alert to shifts in focus and are willing to negotiate changes in the contract when appropriate.

Shulman (1992) emphasizes the importance of discovering client priorities. He supports the assumption that clients will be committed only to those areas that they see as important. "The worker's task is not to decide what the client should be working on. Instead, using sessional contracting skills, the worker attempts to discover what the client is working on" (113). Although this approach is useful, it should not prevent social workers from encouraging clients to work on other issues, such as with parents who are abusing their children but who do not see their discipline methods as problematic.

It is always preferable to have a repertoire of ideas for accomplishing the same task. This permits flexibility and contributes to keeping the interview interesting and individualized. Listed below are some alternative ways of asking the question "What brings you here today?"

- How would you like to spend our time together? (Because this type of open question gives maximum control to clients, it is useful for working with reluctant clients.)
- Perhaps you might bring me up-to-date on what has happened since we last met.
- Do you have feelings and concerns from our last session that you want to address?
- What do you think would be a good starting point?
- There are a number of things we could do. For example . . .
- What would you like to talk about?

2. What are your expectations of me?

This question is important for clarifying roles. Clients may come to counseling with clear ideas of what they want, or they may be aware only of their pain and be hopeful that some help will be forthcoming. In any case, it is important that both clients and social workers understand their respective roles in the process. This agreement is, of course, always open to modification.

3. What do I need to know about your situation?

At the beginning of an interview or when a new topic is introduced, an open-ended question such as "What do I need to know about your situation?" empowers clients to identify areas of immediate concern or indicate willingness to explore. This question communicates to clients that their social workers will respect their needs and wants. The question demonstrates to clients that counselors will not make assumptions and that they are willing to listen and learn. It seems to say, "I will treat you as a person, not as a number or a category." Clients may not put forward (at least initially) their most urgent need. They may start with a safe topic to test the waters for understanding and acceptance. Once they feel more trust, they may present more serious matters.

Sample variations of this question are "What are the important things I need to understand about you and your problem?" and "Can you tell me the key points we need to explore?" Questions designed to learn about a client's situation generally target three important areas:

1. how the client feels about the problem—**affective area**
2. how the client thinks about the problem—**cognitive area**
3. what the client is doing about the problem—**behavioral area**

Affective Area.　Sometimes solutions to problems are obvious to clients, and they do not need help with decision making or problem solving, but still they lack the capacity to cope with their dilemmas. This inability to cope may result in painful, perhaps debilitating, feelings that are hindering their power to problem-solve. How clients feel is, therefore, very important to the work of counseling. In fact, emotions are frequently the center of counseling work. In many circumstances, management of emotions is a prerequisite to problem solving. The question "How do you feel?" is one way to introduce feelings and to encourage clients to explore the emotional components of their problems.

Social workers who are task oriented, with a focus on problem solving, may move the counseling interview prematurely to problem solving or, worse still, ignore feelings that are at the heart of their client's struggle. While questions can encourage expressions of emotions, the active listening skill of empathy is the foundation for working with feelings. (Empathy will be the central theme of Chapter 6.)

Cognitive Area.　How people think about their difficulties is often more important than the problem itself. An event that may be no big deal to one client may represent a life-threatening crisis to another. **Self-talk** refers to the mental messages we give to ourselves. Golden and Lesh (1997) use the acronym **MOANS** for five words that often signal negative self-talk: *must, ought, always, never*, and *should*.

- I must succeed or I am worthless.
- I ought to be able to do it.
- I always screw up.
- I will never be able to get a job.
- I should feel differently.
- Everything must be perfect.

In contrast, positive self-talk builds confidence and is self-empowering. It moves people away from a victim mentality of feeling powerless. It enables individuals to deal with crisis realistically, without self-imposed rigid and punishing demands.

By seeking to understand how clients think about problems, social workers can get valuable clues regarding important issues, such as self-esteem, motivation, and irrational thinking. Subsequently, they can directly challenge clients' negative self-talk.

Sometimes, quick and dramatic counseling interventions can be achieved when social workers challenge the rationality of the worrier. By offering facts, challenging assumptions, and inviting clients to consider the real probabilities of dreaded events, workers introduce much-needed critical thinking that may interrupt the worry cycle (Shebib, 1997:81). Questions that can prompt exploration of the cognitive area include:

- What do you say to yourself about this problem?
- What does your "inner voice" say?
- What messages do you give yourself that are self-defeating?
- What are you telling yourself?

Behavioral Area.   Although it is important not to move too quickly to work on problem solving, an important part of work in the beginning phase involves interviewing clients to understand what they are doing and not doing about their problems. Such information is important for assessment. It tells workers whether their clients are active in seeking and working on solutions or whether they have become withdrawn and have given up. Some questions for exploring the behavioral area are the following:

- What have you been doing?
- What do you do just before the problem occurs?
- How do you respond?
- What did you do?
- What did you say?
- Has the way you have been handling your problem changed?
- What are some of the ways you have been coping with this issue?

4. What do you mean?

This is a central question during all phases of the interview. It ensures clarity of expression, encourages detail and example, and prevents workers from making erroneous assumptions about meaning. It moves the interview from superficial understanding to specific or concrete exploration.

5. What was accomplished?

This question makes evaluation part of the work, thus enabling workers and their clients to review progress and identify accomplishments. Evaluation reviews the counseling relationship and assists with making changes to the contract. Evaluative questions include:

- How has our work met your expectations?
- Looking back on our session, what were the things that you found helpful? Unhelpful?

- How would you like things to be the same or different next time we meet?
- What remains to be done?
- How would you evaluate the work?

CONVERSATION **5.3**
Working with Children

STUDENT: Do you need to modify basic counseling and interviewing skills when working with children?

TEACHER: Yes, you have to modify your approach when working with children, but this is also true for every client. Having said that, there are some basic principles for working with children. First, you have to speak in words appropriate to the child's age and developmental level. A young child, for example, may not understand the concept of time. When my kids were young, a half-hour was "one Mr. Roger's show" and three days were "three sleeps." Second, play and art are often better ways to engage children than interviewing. Children often act out their problems during play. Third, children may not respond well to questioning, particularly to *why* questions. Listening, empathy, and gentle encouragement to talk are more effective. Fourth, you need to recognize that children have unique ways of expressing their feelings. As Erdman and Lampe observe, "Pouting, crying, remaining silent, laughing, fidgeting, and fighting are some of the natural means children use to express their needs and feelings, and counselors need to recognize these as such" (1996:375).

6. What have we missed?

At the end of an interview (or as a significant topic draws to a close) the question "What have we missed?" often yields surprisingly rich information. This question provides an opportunity for clients to talk about issues and feelings that might have been missed. When clients are ambivalent about sharing some details, this question may tip the scales in favor of sharing. It empowers clients by giving them control of content and a final chance to make sure their needs are on the table for discussion. Some variations of this question are:

- What else do we need to talk about?
- What's left to explore?
- Have we covered all that is important?
- What questions haven't I asked?

In the following example, the social worker prompts the client to examine the session:

SOCIAL WORKER: *Our time is almost up, and I want to make sure I haven't over-looked anything that is important to you. What have we missed?*

CLIENT: *Well, we haven't even begun to talk about how my divorce has changed my kids. In many ways, they have been the real victims.*

SOCIAL WORKER: *I agree with you. It's very important that we don't overlook them. Does it make sense to you to make that discussion part of our next meeting? I want to make sure there is enough time.*

CLIENT: *Yes, that makes sense.*

SOCIAL WORKER: *Then let's make that number one on our list for next time.*

There are some risks to opening up new areas at the end of an interview, particularly if the topic involves strong emotions for the client. In the above example, the social worker suspected that this was a topic that needed a lot of time, so she suggested deferral to the next session. In such circumstances, the social worker might have been tempted to ask further questions or to empathize, but these responses might have prolonged the interview beyond the time available. It is important to end the interview without leaving the client in a state of distress.

Interview Transitions

An **interview transition** occurs when the topic of conversation shifts from one subject to another. Such shifts may occur spontaneously in the course of the interview, or they may be orchestrated in order to further the objectives of the interview. The need for a transition arises in the following situations:

1. the discussion of a particular issue is finished and it is time to move on
2. the discussion triggers ideas in another area or links to earlier areas of discussion
3. the subject being discussed is too threatening or painful and a topic change is needed to reduce tension
4. the subject has limited relevance or has lost its relevance to the goals of the interview
5. a change from one phase of the interview to another is necessary (Shebib, 1997:156).

There are five types of transitions: natural, strategic, control, phase, and connect, or linking (Shebib, 1997:156).

Natural Transitions

Natural transitions arise as the discussion flows seamlessly from one topic to another, with clear links between the two topics. The most common natural transition occurs when clients mention new themes as part of the interview and workers use this information to jump to the new topic.

CLIENT: *As I talk about my dissatisfaction with my job I realize that the same could also be said about my marriage.*

SOCIAL WORKER: *Perhaps we could address that now. Tell me what's happening in your marriage.*

Clients are unlikely to resist natural transitions because the interview moves clearly in the direction they have suggested. The topic change is not abrupt, and transition responses indicate that social workers have heard what their clients have just stated.

Strategic Transitions

Strategic transitions arise when workers make choices among topic alternatives. Imagine that a client makes a statement such as the following:

> CLIENT: *This has been the worst year on record for me. My finances were a disaster anyway, and now that I've lost my job, I think I'll go under. Needless to say, this hasn't been good for my marriage. I can see how hard it is on my kids. My eldest daughter seems to avoid me entirely, and I'm sure my son is on drugs. What's the point in living?*

How might the worker respond? Would he or she select finances as a priority for follow-up? Or, would he or she go with one of the other problems: marriage, relationships with children, drug abuse, or unemployment? Should he or she focus on problems or feelings or both? How a worker responds is a strategic decision that affects the direction of the interview.

Control Transitions

Workers have a responsibility to orchestrate the flow of the interview. They use control transitions to manage the direction of the interview in a variety of circumstances.

Redirecting the flow of an interview is warranted when the discussion topic is irrelevant or when it prevents dialogue on more important issues. Preventing premature subject changes is crucial for ensuring concreteness or full exploration of content and feelings. Moving too quickly from topic to topic may render the interview superficial (Shebib, 1997).

Control transitions are used not to dominate clients, but to exercise one's professional duty to ensure that the interview time is productive. In practice, workers and their clients should share control, with workers giving clients as much power as possible to set the course of counseling, based on their needs. Commenting on the role of counselors, Kadushin notes that "skillful control of the interview involves giving direction without restriction; it implies stimulation and guidance without bias or pressure" (1990:356). He lists the following elements of the interview that are open to control:

1. topics to be discussed
2. sequence in which topics are discussed
3. focus within each topic
4. level of emotionality
5. person initiating the transition from one topic to another (356).

Social workers are responsible for negotiating (contracting) with clients on the goals of counseling. Subsequently, they have an obligation to monitor and control the flow of work to support the achievement of these goals. In practice, this means making sure that there are not premature shifts in focus and that topics are fully explored and addressed. The example below illustrates a control transition.

> **SOCIAL WORKER:**   *I think we might be moving too quickly here. We haven't had a chance to talk about your feelings. I wonder if you'd agree that we should do that before we move on to a different topic. It might help us both to understand why its been so difficult for you to make a decision.*

In this example, the social worker gives a brief reason for slowing down the interview and focusing on feelings. Clients who understand what is happening are much more likely to support the process.

Clients may suddenly change the subject of the interview. There may be a variety of reasons for this sudden topic shift. For example, it might indicate that they were revealing too much or that the material was too painful or personal to discuss. Consequently, social workers need to use control transitions wisely and be mindful of the underlying feelings that client-initiated shifts signal. One way for workers to deal with a topic shift is to openly acknowledge the shift, then gently explore its meaning.

> **SOCIAL WORKER:**   *Am I right in thinking that you seemed uncomfortable talking about your relationship with your father?*
>
> **CLIENT:**   *It's not something I want to get into right now.*
>
> **SOCIAL WORKER:**   *That's okay. I won't force you. On the other hand, you might decide later that you're ready.*

Social workers can use summaries as a way to introduce control transitions. As the example below illustrates, summarizing makes the topic switch seem less abrupt. This is important because abrupt transitions, such as the one below, may appear harsh to clients and accentuate their feelings of being cross-examined.

> **SOCIAL WORKER:**   *So, as I understand it, drug abuse has had a significant impact on your work. Your boss has reached a point where he will support you, but only if you enter rehab. Let's shift our focus for a minute and talk about problems with your family.*

Using directives is another way of controlling the flow of an interview. Directives are short statements that provide direction to clients. Directives such as "Describe your feelings," "List your main reasons," "Give an example," "Tell me what you did," "Share your thoughts," "Tell me more," "Expand on that," "Don't move too quickly," and "Put it in your own words" are used to control the pace of the interview and to get more information. Because overuse of directives may leave clients feeling controlled, they should be used sparingly.

Phase Transitions

In simplified terms, the work of counseling can be organized into clusters of activity. In the beginning phase, for example, problem exploration is paramount. However, at some point it becomes clear that sufficient time has been spent on problem exploration, and it is time to move on. Phase transitions bridge the work of one phase to another, as illustrated by the following example:

> **SOCIAL WORKER:** *I wonder if we've reached a point where it makes sense to begin talking about the changes you want to make. We could begin to discuss some of your goals, then think about how to achieve them.*

In the example below, the social worker uses a phase transition to end the interview and to establish a link to the next session.

> **SOCIAL WORKER:** *I'm impressed with your insights about how you tend to put yourself down. It seems to me that the next logical step might be to explore how to combat this tendency. If you agree, we can start with that next time.*

Generally, interviewers should proceed at a pace that their clients can manage. This does not mean that clients must always be 100 percent comfortable with the intensity of the interview. Indeed, the work of interviewing and counseling can be demanding, and exploring difficult topics can be exhausting. Here are some general guidelines for pacing:

- Move more slowly in new relationships and first encounters.
- Expect differences between clients.
- Don't expect to maintain the same intensity or an ever-increasing intensity throughout the interview—periodic "rest" periods with nonthreatening or less demanding topics can energize clients.
- End interviews with less demanding questions and responses.

Social workers need to carefully manage interview transitions between one topic and another. As well, they should avoid rigid agendas, such as might be followed in a formal meeting, and, instead, allow some freedom of movement between topics. However, social workers also need to be careful not to sprint from one topic to another without adequate exploration or completion.

Connect (Linking) Transitions

Connect transitions are used to join or blend ideas. Interviews often have recurrent themes. For example, a client may make continual subtle references to a need to have everything just right. The social worker might use a connect transition to bring this theme to the foreground:

> **SOCIAL WORKER:** *In all your examples, you talk about how you make sure that you pay attention to every little detail. Then you seem to beat yourself up if everything isn't perfect.*

Connect transitions can have a powerful effect on clients by stimulating them to think about issues in new ways. Clients who have felt stuck and hopeless may find new energy. By connecting apparently discrete events, connect transitions allow problems to be understood from new perspectives, pressures to be seen to emanate from different sources, and new actions to be taken to lessen the pressures (Middleman and Wood, 1990:80).

C O N V E R S A T I O N   5.4
Note Taking

STUDENT: What are your thoughts on taking notes during an interview?

TEACHER: You first.

STUDENT: I have mixed feelings. On the one hand, I don't want to forget anything, but it seems so cold and clinical to be writing when clients are talking. It seems to take away from the intimacy of the relationship.

TEACHER: Suppose you were the client and I were taking notes.

STUDENT: I'd wonder about what you were writing about me. I'd be really scared that someone else might see the notes. I'd probably be really careful about what I said.

TEACHER: What if I told you that you could see the notes?

STUDENT: That would help. Then I'd be able to correct any mistakes. I'd really want to know who would have access to the file.

TEACHER: All clients have a right to that information. They may not ask, but, as a rule, you should tell them. You raised a good point earlier about how note taking can detract from rapport in the interview. I agree. I think it's particularly important to put the pen down when clients are talking about feelings or other private matters. On the other hand, most clients expect that you'll write down information such as phone numbers and addresses.

STUDENT: I'd prefer not to take notes at all.

TEACHER: That would be ideal. Of course, that's not always possible. There may be forms or computerized questionnaires to complete that can't be delayed until after the interview. Or you may have clients waiting, so there will be no time after the interview.

Summary

Asking questions is an art. Faulty questioning may bias answers, antagonize clients, or keep the interview at a superficial level. Questions can systematically lead clients through problem solving, or they can help clients examine areas that they might otherwise overlook. It is important to balance questions with responses that confirm understanding (summaries) and empathic responses that confirm sensitivity to feelings. The best workers have a repertoire of techniques from which to select.

Structured interviews follow a defined sequence of predetermined questions. Unstructured interviews permit interviewers and clients freedom to go in any direction without any predetermined control.

INTERVIEW **5.1**
Interviewing Skills

The following excerpt illustrates some of the important concepts from this chapter. This is the first interview with the client. The social worker works in a community service center that offers a variety of programs.

Dialogue	Analysis
(During the first five minutes of the interview the worker and the client engage in small talk.)	Interview openings establish first impressions. A few minutes spent on small talk can help clients relax. Workers should not consider this time wasted.
SOCIAL WORKER: Perhaps you can tell me what brings you here today. You did not tell me much on the phone, but I had the impression that you felt some urgency.	A simple phase transition begins the process of establishing the purpose of the interview. By making a link to the intake phone call, the social worker demonstrates that the client's sense of emergency was heard. This lets the client know that the worker is sensitive to feelings.
CLIENT: I've been on welfare for six months and I just can't make ends meet.	
SOCIAL WORKER: Sounds rough. Tell me more.	A supportive and sympathetic reaction communicates warmth and concern. The social worker uses a directive to seek more concreteness.
CLIENT: It's not just the money—it's what it's doing to my kids.	
SOCIAL WORKER: What do you mean?	It would be easy to assume what the client is talking about. Instead, the counselor probes for definition.
CLIENT: My oldest is 18. He doesn't seem to have any motivation. Sometimes he says he can hardly wait until he's 19 so he can go on welfare too.	
SOCIAL WORKER: I wonder if it seems to you that being on welfare somehow connects with your son's attitude.	The worker uses an indirect question to ask for clarification.
CLIENT: Sure it does. It's all he's known for the last five years.	
SOCIAL WORKER: I need your help to understand what you were hoping would happen when you came here today.	The worker's statement initiates the working contract.
(The client explains that she would like some help to get into retraining.)	
(20 minutes later)	
CLIENT: I'm willing to work anywhere, but eventually I want to find something that fits.	
SOCIAL WORKER: Fits?	The worker's response accents a key word. This is yet another way to seek more concrete

(continued)

INTERVIEW 3.1 Continued

CLIENT: I'd really like to work with people.

SOCIAL WORKER: I noticed earlier that as you described your volunteer work with kids, you seemed really happy.

CLIENT: I'd love to do it full time, but there's no way.

SOCIAL WORKER: What prevents you?

CLIENT: I need to earn a living. Volunteers don't get paid. To get hired full time, I'd need to get a diploma.

SOCIAL WORKER: Sounds like you've already looked into it. Have you thought about going back to school?

CLIENT: Yes. Like I said earlier, I'm determined to get out of this rut. I suppose I should do something about it.

information. Accenting encourages clients to say more.

A linking transition connects two parts of the interview.

The worker uses an open question to probe for concreteness. This will help the worker understand the real or imagined barriers that this client foresees.

The counselor uses a closed question to check if the client is prepared to go to school. Because the client has introduced the idea, the worker's question is not leading. In other circumstances, such questions might need to be avoided or approached cautiously.

Faulty, insensitive, and poorly timed questioning may bias clients' answers, antagonize them, or keep the interview at a superficial level. Common errors include using jargon, asking leading questions, excessively questioning, asking multiple questions, asking irrelevant or poorly timed questions, and asking *why* questions.

Clients may not answer questions for a variety of reasons. For example, they may not understand the questions or their purpose, they may not know the answers, or they may believe their answers are private. As well, cultural norms influence how people react to questions.

Closed questions can be easily answered yes or no. Open questions are difficult to answer with a simple yes or no. The vast majority of open questions will be "five *W*" and *how* questions. Indirect questions are statements that function as questions.

Concreteness concerns the extent to which words, phrases, and behaviors convey clear and specific meaning. When communication is concrete, all participants share understanding of language, ideas, and feelings. Probes for concreteness propel the interview from a superficial level of discussion to an intimate level that requires a deeper investment from everyone involved in the interview. A number of strategies are important for promoting concreteness, including recognizing the need for concreteness, demonstrating comfort and willingness to communicate at a deeper level, knowing when to pursue concreteness, using simple encouragers, and probing for detail with questions and directives.

The following key questions can be used as a rough template for interviews:

- What brings you here today?
- What are your expectations of me?

- What do I need to know about your situation?
- What do you mean by. . . ?
- What did we accomplish?
- What have we missed?

Interview transitions occur when the topic of the interview shifts from one subject to another. Such shifts may occur spontaneously in the course of the interview, or social workers may orchestrate them in order to further the objectives of the interview. There are five different types of transitions: natural, strategic, control, phase, and connect, or linking.

EXERCISES

1. Classify each of the following questions as open, closed, or indirect.

   a. How do you feel about your brother?

   b. I'm puzzled over your reaction.

   c. Do you have time to see me next week?

   d. I'd like to know something about your strategy.

2. Reword the following closed questions as (a) open questions and (b) indirect questions.

   a. Are you enrolled in the secretarial program?

   b. Were you referred by the principal?

   c. Are you feeling sad?

   d. Do you want to talk about your feelings?

   e. Did you tell her how you felt?

3. Conduct an interview with a colleague. Use questions inappropriately (e.g., ask irrelevant questions, change the topic frequently, bombard with questions, and ask leading questions). After the interview is completed, discuss how it felt to be in both the interviewer and the client role.

4. Conduct a ten-minute focused interview with a colleague. Your task is to explore one topic in as much depth as possible. However, in this interview you are not allowed to ask questions. Try to use a range of skills. (Note to the client: Try not to be overly cooperative.) After the interview is over, discuss the experience.

5. As a conditioning exercise for interviewing quiet clients, conduct an interview with a colleague. Set up the interview so that your colleague does not respond verbally. Use a variety of techniques other than questions.

6. Imagine that you are responding in each situation below. Suggest follow-up responses that are open questions, closed questions, indirect or embedded questions, and directives.

   a. SOCIAL WORKER: What are your feelings about your work?

      CLIENT: I have mixed feelings.

   b. SOCIAL WORKER: What do you see as the next step?

      CLIENT: The next step is to solve the problem.

   c. SOCIAL WORKER: How long have you felt this way?

CLIENT: A long time.

d. SOCIAL WORKER: What is your sense of what she means?

CLIENT: I know exactly what she means.

e. CLIENT: You have no idea how I feel.

f. CLIENT: I'm really angry with you.

g. CLIENT: There are some significant things happening in my life right now.

h. CLIENT: I'm not sure I can handle this problem. I need help.

7. Each of the following client statements has one or more problems with concreteness. First, identify the concreteness problem. Second, suggest a possible counselor response to promote concreteness.

   a. I still have feelings for her.

   b. I've given it a lot of thought.

   c. I hardly sleep at night.

   d. I've tried to control my kids, but nothing seems to work.

   e. She's an elderly person.

   f. I feel bad.

8. Each of the following worker statements contains phrases or jargon that may be unfamiliar to clients. Reword each, using everyday language.

   a. It seems as though your son has a lot of interpersonal difficulty, and it is generating acting-out behavior.

   b. Cognitively, he seems well within the mean.

   c. It appears to me that you are feeling ambivalent.

   d. After intake, it seems appropriate to make a referral to one of our community resources.

9. Work in a small group to brainstorm jargon that social workers and other professionals use. Next, reword these terms and phrases so that they are easily understandable.

10. Pick an issue that you have very strong feelings about (e.g., abortion, capital punishment, increases in tuition fees). Conduct a five- to ten-minute interview with a colleague to explore his or her views on the same topic. However, do not reveal any of your feelings or thoughts on the topic. After the interview is over, discuss the experience.

11. Watch a talk show. See if you can identify the interviewing skills that are used. Look for evidence of improper interviewing technique.

12. Conduct an extended interview with a colleague (in the client's role). Use the following questions to guide your interview:

What brings you here today?

What are your expectations of me?

What do I need to know about your situation? (explore feelings, thoughts, and behavior)

What do you mean by. . . ?

What did we accomplish?

What have we missed?

13. Videotape an extended interview. Classify each response that you make (in the counselor's role) in terms of type—open question, closed question, summary, and so on. Identify patterns. Are there skills that are overused or underused?

14. *Interview Aerobics*

Prepare flash cards with the names of various skills on each card (e.g., open question, closed question, paraphrase, summary, empathy, indirect question, directive, silence, wild card [any skill], self-disclosure, contracting).

Note: The exercises below are designed to help you develop a range of skills. The more comfortable you are with a wide array of responses, the more you will be able to respond based on the needs of the client and the situation.

Exercise 1: Shuffle the cards. The interviewer should listen carefully to what the client says, then select the first card in the stack and follow the directions on that card. For example, if the next card reads "closed question," the interviewer must ask a closed question, even if that might not be the best response.

Exercise 2: Work with a partner. One acts as interviewee and chooses an appropriate skill card for you to use.

Exercise 3: Conduct an interview using the cards in any order that you choose. Continue interviewing until all of the cards are used. Cards may be used more than one time.

Exercise 4: Conduct an interview using the cards in any order that you wish. However, you can use each card only once.

Exercise 5: Develop your own strategy for using the cards.

(Adapted from Shebib, 1997:161.)

6 The Pursuit of Empathic Understanding

Preview

After reading this chapter you should be able to

- explain the importance of emotions
- name the basic families of emotions
- describe how clients' emotions can be recognized from nonverbal behavior
- define what is meant by empathy
- define the three types of empathy: basic, inferred, and invitational
- explain when not to use empathy
- identify what to avoid when responding with empathy
- demonstrate the basic ability to formulate empathic responses
- explain the importance of "tough empathy"

Emotions

> *Emotions play a central role in the significant events of our lives. Although they have many characteristics, some behavioral and others physiological, emotions are above all psychological. We feel proud when our loved ones do something worthy. When demeaned, we become angry or ashamed. We experience joy at the birth of our children, anxiety when threatened, and grief at the death of a loved one.*
>
> —Lazarus, 1991:3

Because the human experience is so closely connected with emotions (feelings), any study of counseling and interviewing must give priority to exploring and understanding client emotions. However, there is no consensus on the definition of *emotion,* the number of emotions that exist, whether some emotions are more basic than others, the commonality of emotions between cultures, and whether different emotions have different physiological attributes (LeDoux, 1995).

Emotions are defined by Barker as a "state of mind usually accompanied by concurrent physiological and behavioral changes and based on the perception of some internal or external object" (1995:110). Emotional responses trigger our bodies to respond in unique physiological ways. Historically, these responses helped humans respond in very different ways, including:

- Anger—The hands swell with blood, making it easier to use weapons or strike back; increased heart rate and adrenaline serve to increase energy and power.
- Fear—Blood flow to the legs increases, making it easier to escape; the body may freeze for a moment, giving time to gauge whether hiding is a better response.
- Happiness—Brain activity inhibits negative thoughts and fosters increased energy.
- Love—General bodily responses promote well-being and a general state of calm and contentment.
- Surprise—Raising the eyebrows expands the field of vision, thus making it easier to figure out what is going on and to plan the best action.
- Sadness—A general drop in energy and enthusiasm creates an opportunity to mourn (Goleman, 1995).

Social workers work with clients' emotions in a number of ways. The counseling relationship provides safety for clients to explore and understand their feelings. Friends and family may be well-meaning but poorly equipped to deal with complex emotions. They may be prone to simplistic advice giving, or they may try to change the subject when painful feelings are revealed. Social workers, on the other hand, are able to deal with feelings. They don't tell clients how they should feel, nor do they insult or frustrate clients with quick-fix solutions. They allow clients to express emotions without needing to censor what they reveal.

The overall goal is to help clients gain **emotional literacy,** "the ability to experience all of one's emotions with appropriate intensity and to understand what is causing these feelings" (Parrott, 1997:260). In a similar vein, Goleman (1995) suggests that the ability to recognize feelings as they happen is the cornerstone of emotional intelligence and that people who are more in touch with their feelings are better able to navigate their lives and are more competent decision makers.

Weisinger (1998) argues that understanding emotions comes from appreciating the interactions of three components—thoughts, physiological changes, and behavior. Johnson provides a perspective:

> Feelings are internal physiological reactions to your experiences. You may begin to tremble, sweat, or have a surge of energy. Your heart may beat faster. Tears may come. Although feelings are internal reactions, they do have outward signs. Sadness is inside you, but you cry or frown on the outside. Anger is inside you. But you may stare and shout at the person you are angry with. Feelings are always internal states, but you use overt behaviors to communicate your feelings to other people (1997:134).

Black gives another perspective in attempting to capture the nature of joy:

> Joy may be looked on as anxiety's opposite. It, too, is a composite of feelings: delight, fulfilment, and refreshment, along with the warm glow that comes with an increased heart rate, deeper breathing, and a general relaxation of muscular tension. When we are in the

midst of an experience as pleasantly exhilarating as joy, we are likely to identify it in an inner conversation with ourselves as a wonderful feeling (1983:3–5).

Social workers can help clients consider how their emotions might be interfering with decision making or everyday life. Decision making, for example, may be difficult when the clients' emotions pull them in different directions. Of course, feelings such as sadness, anger, grief, and disappointment are part of everyone's life. In fact, feelings such as grief are healing responses, and they are not usually pathological or in need of treatment.

Diversity and Emotions

As one might expect, there are wide variations in the extent to which various cultures and individuals express emotions. While underscoring the importance of exceptions, Dodd offers the following generalizations:

> Asian cultures generally practice reserve and emotional restraint. The idea of extreme emotion, such as loud sobs during a funeral or boisterous laughter on festive occasions, would be considered too emotional. To a lesser extent, some Scandinavian cultures appear publicly reserved. Britons and Germans appear more reserved than Italians, Greeks and Czechs (1995:121).

Ivey, Ivey, and Simek-Downing offer this interesting perspective: "There may be four participants in the interview: the counselor/therapist and his or her cultural/historical background and the client and his or her cultural/historical background" (1987:94). Their observation highlights the importance of exploring the four major participants in the interview, with the goal of understanding how the history and culture of both client and worker might influence interactions and perception.

Classifying and Understanding Emotions

Table 6.1 categorizes emotions. Similar attempts may be found in Carkhuff (1981), and Cormier and Cormier (1985), and Young (1998). Social workers need to respond to the range of subtle feelings that clients express and in language that clients can understand. This table should be interpreted with caution, as word choice alone is an insufficient indicator of emotional intensity. A client who says, "I'd kill for a chocolate ice cream" is clearly exaggerating. Another might minimize a problem, saying, "It doesn't bother me," but context and other cues might reveal evidence of profound pain.

Although there are hundreds of words for emotions in the English language, most fall into one of ten categories or families of emotions, as in Table 6.1. As with any classification system, the categories are arbitrary tools designed to organize our thinking. One might argue for more or fewer categories. Closely related feelings (e.g., anger, outrage, and annoyance) can be considered as one category. Specific words for emotions within the categories are used to more precisely define emotional states and to provide some information about the intensity or strength of the emotion.

Sometimes people confuse feelings and thoughts. For example, the statement "I feel that this is the best alternative" expresses a point of view (thought), but it does not convey

TABLE 6.1   Feeling Words

Feelings	Intensity		
	Low Level	**Medium Level**	**High Level**
Anger	annoyed, irritated, miffed, offended, resentful, provoked, displeased, aggravated, put off, ticked, upset, disturbed	angry, mad, hostile, hateful, disgusted, inflamed, in a tiff, fed up, sore, agitated	outraged, furious, vengeful, repulsed, boiling, in a rage
Fear	alarmed, nervous, anxious, tense, uneasy, timid, bothered, apprehensive, intimidated, butterflies	frightened, scared, worried, distressed, fearful, jumpy	shocked, horrified, panicked, terrified, mortified, terrorized, cold sweat
Strength	adequate, up to the challenge, able to cope, stable	confident, capable, adept, healthy, qualified, whole, energized, dynamic, tough, strong, brave, determined, secure	invulnerable, in control, bold, potent, courageous, unbeatable
Weakness	delicate, insecure, timid, shy, small, fragile, tired, weary	weak, vulnerable, falling apart, burnt out, cowardly, helpless, useless, sick, incompetent, inadequate, unprotected, frail	defenseless, impotent, worthless, no good, powerless, exhausted, lifeless, useless
Joy	satisfied, glad, good, pleased, comfortable	happy, contented, joyful, loved, excited, optimistic, cheerful	euphoric, ecstatic, thrilled, delighted, passionate, elated, marvelous, full of life, terrific, overjoyed
Sadness	disappointed, hurt, troubled, downcast, upset, bothered	unhappy, glum, sad, depressed, melancholy, blue, lonely, dismal, pessimistic	agonized, dejected, despairing, despondent, hopeless, miserable
Confusion	distracted, muddled, uncertain, doubtful, hesitant, mixed up, unsure, indecisive	confused, baffled, perplexed, puzzled, ambivalent, stumped, jumbled, disjointed, frustrated	(in a state of) pandemonium or chaos, mystified, swamped
Shame	embarrassed, humbled, regretful	belittled, discredited, guilty, shamed, remorseful, ashamed	disgraced, scandalized, humiliated, mortified
Surprise	startled, puzzled	surprised, stunned, shocked	astonished, astounded, flabbergasted, amazed, overwhelmed, awed
Love	attracted, friendly	close, intimate, warm, tender, cherished, smitten with, doting on	loved, adored, raptured, crazy about, wild about, flip over, idolize, worship

any information about the emotions involved. On the other hand, the statement "I feel confident that this is the best alternative" does express an emotion. One might think that this distinction is insignificant, but the importance of emotional clarity becomes evident if the example statement becomes "I feel outraged that this is the best alternative." To describe their emotions, clients may use specific feeling words, which they may further define with modifiers such as *very*. As well, clients may communicate their emotions through metaphors and nonverbal channels of communication.

Word Modifiers.   Word modifiers (e.g., *very, extremely, somewhat, mostly, little*) may change the level of emotion expressed. We can expect some difference in emotional level between people who describe themselves as somewhat happy and others who say they are incredibly happy.

Metaphors.   Metaphors are a way of describing something by using a symbol in a direct comparison. A client who says he is going around in circles is using a metaphor to describe his feelings of confusion.

Here are some metaphors with the possible feeling that each suggests:

- tied up in knots (stressed)
- about to blow up, bent out of shape (furious)
- in a pressure cooker (stressed)
- on a sinking ship (hopeless)
- tearing my hair out (overstressed or frustrated)
- in a sticky situation (vulnerable)
- between a rock and a hard place (helpless)
- butterflies in my stomach (fear or excitement)
- on top of the world (happy/ecstatic)

Nonverbal Behavior.   Most people are familiar with the physiological reactions that occur in a moment of great fear. Our bodies, powered by increased adrenal secretion, respond automatically with elevated heart rate, rapid breathing, dry mouth, and other symptoms. Many of these reactions are clearly visible to any observer, even before any verbal declaration of fear. Nonverbal behavior is usually outside our conscious control and is less likely to be censored. Consequently, social workers can often trust nonverbal communication as a more reliable indicator of feelings than the verbal channel. With respect to nonverbal communication, the visual channel is the most significant. For example, research has shown that often more than 55 percent of the meaning of a message is conveyed nonverbally, accentuating the importance of understanding nonverbal communication (Wolvin and Coakley, 1996). A person's emotions may be conveyed much more accurately by body posture and eyes than by words. Furthermore, social workers who are able to respond to nonverbal as well as verbal messages "project an unusual warmth, sensitivity, and perceptiveness that enhances the intimacy of the relationship" (George and Cristiani, 1986:145).

Social workers can learn a great deal about their clients' feelings from carefully observing their manner and the way they present their ideas. Nonverbal cues act to confirm, contradict, or even substitute for verbal expressions of emotions. For example, a client might say, "I'm ecstatic," but saying it in a sarcastic manner conveys the opposite. Another common example occurs when people say, "I'm interested in what you have to say," but at the same time they continue with another activity. Below are additional examples:

Confirmation:

  a. client says, "I'm happy," accompanied by a smile
  b. client expresses anger by shaking a fist

Contradiction:

  a. client says "Yes," while shaking head
  b. client says, "I'm not angry," while shouting or avoiding eye contact
  c. client says, "It's not a big deal," while crying

Substitution:

  a. client cries, looks away, moves chair back, glares, frowns, shifts uncomfortably
  b. client uses gestures such as pointing

Social workers need to interpret nonverbal behavior cautiously. Typically, nonverbal behavior can have many meanings that vary according to a multitude of factors, such as culture, context, and individual comfort level. People from some cultures, for example, interact at very close personal distance, but others experience the same personal distance as intrusive or even aggressive. Some people consider direct eye contact rude, while others view avoidance of eye contact as cold or as evidence that people are trying to hide something. In fact, for some cultural groups, lack of eye contact is considered a sign of respect and courtesy (Corey and Corey, 1989:84).

Body Language. *Kinesics* is the study of body language, including such variables as posture, facial expressions, gestures, and eye motion. Sometimes body language is easily interpreted, such as when people use gestures that have direct verbal equivalents. For example, people might point to indicate direction or use their fingers and hands to signify size or numbers. At other times, body language is ambiguous and more difficult to interpret, particularly when people communicate contradictory messages. For example, a person might be listening intently and making appropriate eye contact, but this is accompanied by fidgeting and rapid finger tapping, which seems to say, "I'm bored." Johnson offers a perspective on this difficulty:

> For one thing, the same feeling can be expressed nonverbally in several different ways. Anger, for example, can be expressed by jumping up and down or by a frozen stillness. Happiness can be expressed through laughter or tears. Any single nonverbal message, furthermore, can arise from a variety of feelings. A blush may show embarrassment, pleasure, nervousness, or even anger. Crying can be caused by sadness, happiness, excitement, grief, pain, or confusion (1997:173).

Even a simple smile may have multiple meanings: (1) it may show warmth, pleasure, or amusement; (2) it may be an attempt to appease or humor someone in order to reduce threat or obtain approval; (3) it may reveal nervousness; or (4) it may simply be a habit with no particular meaning (Wolvin and Coakley, 1996:180). Consequently, social workers should look for multiple indicators of meaning rather than for a single signal.

Voice.   Social workers can learn a great deal from their clients from their voice tone, volume, and pitch. These variables can reveal if clients are depressed, euphoric, angry, or sad. For example, Kadushin (1990) concluded that anger tends to be expressed with speech that is more rapid and loud, whereas sadness is characterized by more pauses and slowness of speech. Silence is an important component of nonverbal communication (see Chapter 4). Social workers need to be able to read nonverbal cues to decide how, when, and if they should interrupt a silent moment.

Spatial Distance.   *Proxemics* is a term used to describe how people use space and distance. Hall's model (1959) is widely used to describe the four main distances:

1. Intimate distance is a zone of up to .5 m (2 feet) reserved for private exchanges of intimate thoughts and feelings.
2. Personal distance is a zone of about .5 to 1 m (2 to 4 feet) that is used for less intense exchanges with friends and family.
3. Social distance is a zone of approximately 1 to 3.5 m (4 to 12 feet) used for more impersonal meetings and social contact.
4. Public distance beyond 3.5 m (12 feet) is used for casual exchanges such as giving a speech or lecture.

How an individual uses space is influenced by many variables, including gender, age, culture, physical characteristics, status, various personality traits, and the nature of the relationship. For example, people tend to want more space as they become older (Wolvin and Coakley, 1996:186). Social workers should adapt their seating to meet the needs of individual clients and situations and remember that angry clients may need more personal distance. In such situations, workers also need more space for safety reasons. Social workers should also be mindful of spatial shifts during the interview. Often these changes are subtle, such as when a client shifts his or her chair back, as if to say, "I'm not comfortable with what we're talking about." Similarly, as clients lean in and move toward them, counselors can conclude that intimacy and trust are increasing. If a client seems to be physically and psychologically withdrawing, this may be the wrong time to confront or to introduce more sensitive topics.

Social workers need to be aware of their own nonverbal behavior and how it might influence their clients in subtle ways. They easily communicate their displeasure by frowning, turning away from clients, or increasing the physical distance between them. Alternatively, they disclose that they like clients by smiling, using a pleasant voice tone, increasing eye contact, and leaning toward clients (Mehrabian, 1981:162).

Individual Definition

Each feeling can be experienced as positive or negative at varying levels of intensity, but this subjective determination is individually defined. Anxiety for some people can be debilitating, seriously affecting the quality of their lives. However, the same emotion for an athlete may arouse a competitive spirit and the individual might thrive on its physiological consequences.

Circumstances and context may not be good predictors of feelings. One person might be anxious about public speaking but find the experience exhilarating, while another person is terrified by the prospect. One individual might enjoy parties and be stimulated by the chance to meet new people, but a second person looks for any excuse to avoid the panic brought on by crowded social events. Consequently, when not obvious, social workers should ask clients what particular meaning they give to any emotional experience. In the following example, the worker makes assumptions, then, sensitive to the client's nonverbal message, works to correct the error.

> **CLIENT:** *My mother is coming to visit me next week.*
>
> **SOCIAL WORKER:** *Oh, that's nice. It's always great when you have a chance to see your folks.*
>
> **CLIENT:** *(hesitating) I guess so.*
>
> **SOCIAL WORKER:** *(picking up on the client's hesitation) How do you feel about her visit?*
>
> **CLIENT:** *I dread it. My mother always wants to tell me how to run my life.*

In the above example, another valid choice would be for the social worker to admit the error. This would model openness to the client and it serves to reinforce the reality that the social worker is not perfect. Subsequently, it may be easier for the client to be open about his or her mistakes.

> **CLIENT:** *(hesitating) I guess so.*
>
> **SOCIAL WORKER:** *Perhaps I was too hasty in assuming you would be happy that she was coming. I should have waited until you told me how you felt.*
>
> **CLIENT:** *I dread it. My mother always wants to tell me how to run my life.*

Individuals are often governed by cultural norms, and there are wide variances in the extent and manner to which they express emotions. Some value emotional expression, whereas others favor emotional restraint. Social workers need to be careful to avoid using their own measuring criteria when attempting to understand the emotions of others. If they expect that people in crisis will be verbal and declare their pain, then they might miss the fact that the quiet child is much more in need than the one who is acting out.

Mixed Feelings

Problems and experiences are often defined and frequently complicated by multiple and seemingly contradictory feelings from two or more emotional families. A great deal of stress and confusion can arise from the pushes and pulls of competing feelings that, if unmanaged, can control a client's life. The terms *ambivalence* and *of two minds* are often used. Ambivalence is normal, and it can be a valuable help to decision making.

TABLE 6.2   Common Mixed Feelings

happy/scared	This often arises in conjunction with a lifestyle change (e.g., getting married, returning to school, starting a new job, sending children to day care, experiencing "empty nest" when children leave home).
happy/sad	Some transitional life events, such as leaving one job for another or seeing a child off to college (kindergarten, etc.), elicit these feelings. A sense of loss as well as gain is often present.
depressed/fed up	These feelings may suggest that the person has "bottomed out." Significantly, being fed up may be used as a strong motivator for change (e.g., deciding to change a self-destructive drug habit).
angry/afraid	Fear is often the most significant emotion, but anger is more commonly expressed (e.g., a parent facing a teenager who is two hours late for curfew).
hopeful/despairing	Many clients fluctuate between believing that change is possible and life will get better and that nothing will improve and further effort is futile. Developing and sustaining motivation is particularly crucial in such situations (e.g., a person coping with a life-threatening illness).
attracted/repulsed	Many people who are considering changes in their lives experience these feelings. Part of them wants things to be different, and part wants the security of their present situation, however distressful (e.g., a person contemplating leaving an abusive relationship).
love/hate	This usually arises in the face of contradictory evidence (e.g., a friend whose behavior is erratic—sometimes loving, sometimes abusive).

EXAMPLE: *A woman describes the joy she felt when her son left home to begin training as a counselor, but as she talks her eyes well up with tears. Clearly, she is experiencing a strong sense of loss, despite the fact that words speak to her pride and happiness. More accurately, both feelings exist simultaneously.*

People also have feelings about the emotions they experience. Sometimes they are very aware of these mixed feelings, sometimes not. Try this simple experiment. Close your eyes and recall a recent strong emotion, such as anger or joy. Take a moment to get in touch with your feelings. Now try to complete this sentence, "I feel _____ about feeling (your recent strong emotion)." Many readers will find that this simple exercise leads to a deeper understanding of their emotions. Some may find guilt behind their joy. Others, fear behind their anger.

Mixed feelings are often associated with anxiety and stress, especially when the feelings require opposing responses. If a person is both attracted to and repelled by a particular choice, anxiety is likely to continue until he or she resolves the dilemma.

Mental Health Issues

Affect is a term used to describe how people express emotions such as sadness, excitement, and anger. Culture and context help to define what is considered within the "normal range." Affect is communicated through voice tone and quality, posture, facial expressions, and other nonverbal cues. Terms used to describe affect include:

- *Blunted:* Emotional expression is less than one might expect.
- *Flat:* There is an absence or near absence of any signs of emotional expression.
- *Inappropriate:* The person's manner and mood contradict what one might expect. For example, a client might laugh while describing the death of his mother.
- *Labile:* There is abnormal variability in affect, with repeated, rapid, and abrupt shifts in affective expression.
- *Restricted or constricted:* There is a mild reduction in the range and intensity of emotional expression (for more information see American Psychiatric Association, 1994:763).

Psychologists and other mental health professionals use the term **affective disorder** or **mood disorder** to describe a variety of disturbances in mood. The most common mood disorders are depression and mania. Clients with depression are likely to experience many of the following symptoms: a depressed mood; inability to experience pleasure; loss of energy and interest in life and work; changes in appetite; sleep disturbances (especially insomnia); decrease in sexual energy; feelings of worthlessness, helplessness, guilt, anxiety, or pessimism; and thoughts of death or suicide. Clients with mania are likely to experience many of the following: abnormally elevated mood; irritability; hostility; grandiosity; overactivity; flight of ideas; decreased need for sleep; and involvement in buying sprees and other indicators of poor judgment (American Psychiatric Association, 1994; Nicholi, 1988:315). Referral to a physician should be considered as an adjunct to counseling (see Chapter 8 for more in-depth discussion).

Empathy

The Nature of Empathy

In everyday terms, *empathy* means seeing the world through someone else's eyes. For purposes of counseling, *empathy* is defined as "the process of accurately understanding the emotional perspective of another person and the communication of this understanding" (Shebib, 1997:177). This definition underscores the twin components of empathy: understanding and communication. A social worker who is perceptive and adept at understanding the client's major feelings but cannot communicate that understanding is a limited helper (Gladding, 1996:130). The primary target of empathy is to reply to feelings, but in the process counselors typically capture elements of their clients' thoughts and situations. Responses that deal primarily with clients' thoughts may be more appropriately described as reflective responses (Garvin and Seabury, 1984).

Empathy is a central condition for all helping relationships, regardless of the counseling or therapeutic model adopted (Walrond-Skinner, 1986:113). Empathy is a fundamental building block for the helping relationship, and empathy is clearly connected to positive outcomes in counseling (Rogers, 1980). Appropriate empathy communicates understanding, builds trust, and assists in establishing the social worker's credibility. It is widely ranked as among the highest qualities that a counselor can possess (Egan, 1998; Shulman, 1992; Walrond-Skinner, 1986). Shulman's (1992) research, for example, concluded that empathy contributes substantially to overcoming the challenges of developing a counseling relationship. As well, his research confirmed that empathy is a powerful helping tool.

When social workers are empathic, they are less likely to oversimplify complex problems. Because they understand more, they are less prone to insult their clients with well-meaning but unusable advice. Egan puts it bluntly when he says that empathy restrains the counselor: "Empathy keeps helpers from doing useless things such as asking too many questions and giving premature and inept advice. Empathy puts the ball back into the client's court and thus in its own way encourages the client to act" (1990:135). Social workers need to remember that clients have real and rational reasons for feeling as they do.

Social workers who accept the feelings of their clients help clients accept themselves and their feelings. As Parrott observes, "Empathy communicates to clients that they are worth understanding, that their inner hopes and private fears have value" (1997:196). Rogers notes, "True empathy is always free of any evaluative or diagnostic quality. The recipient perceives this with some surprise: 'If I am not being judged, perhaps I am not so evil or abnormal as I have thought. Perhaps I don't have to judge myself so harshly.' Thus, the possibility of self-acceptance is gradually increased" (1980:154).

Rogers suggests that empathy is more than just a skill—it is a way of being with another person. As he succinctly puts it, "The ideal therapist is, first of all, empathic" (1980:146). Empathy is essential for understanding, and some clients "cannot even begin to think about changing their painful situations until they are satisfied that the essence of their pain has been communicated" (Middleman and Wood, 1990:59).

Empathy assists clients in identifying and labeling feelings, which allows clients to then deal with the feelings. Moreover, with strong and supportive workers, clients can find the courage to deal with feelings that may have been too painful or overwhelming to address on their own. In this sense, empathy contributes to therapeutic change.

Empathy is not just for social workers and other counselors. Empathy is a skill that clients can use to improve their relationships with others. Often clients adopt the communication patterns of helpers, so they should be sensitive to what they model. Empathy models a healthy way of relating to others.

In order to effectively empathize, social workers need to be able to demonstrate comfort with a wide range of feelings, without needing to avoid pain or grief. Just as doctors and nurses need to be able to deal with catastrophic injury without losing control or running away, counselors must develop their capacity to work with intense feelings without needing to change the subject, intellectualize, or offer quick fixes. Sometimes, professionals misinterpret this capacity as meaning that they need to be emotionally detached and coldly indifferent. In fact, empathic workers are deeply involved with their clients. They put aside or suspend their own reactions to their clients' feelings and adopt an accepting and nonjudgmental attitude. Hancock describes the importance of **controlled emotional**

involvement, which she defines as "the empathic sensitivity of the worker to the client's feelings, disciplined by self-awareness, such that the worker's feelings do not inappropriately affect his or her understanding and purposeful response" (1997:131).

Rogers emphasizes the need to "sense the client's private world as if it were your own, but without ever losing the 'as if' quality. . . . To sense the client's anger, fear, or confusion as if it were your own, yet without your own anger, fear, or confusion getting bound up in it" (1961:284). Rogers also provides this important observation about empathy:

> You lay aside your own views and values in order to enter another's world without prejudice. In some sense it means that you lay aside your self; this can only be done by persons who are secure enough in themselves that they know they will not get lost in what may turn out to be the strange or bizarre world of the other, and that they can comfortably return to their own world when they wish (1980:143).

CONVERSATION **6.1**
Increasing Empathic Vocabulary

STUDENT: I would really like to increase my empathy skills, but my vocabulary is so limited. I seem to know only a few feeling words, such as *happy, sad,* and *angry.* How can I increase my feeling word choice?

TEACHER: It's not necessary to have an encyclopedic vocabulary, but you should have enough word choice to capture a broad range of feelings. Study Table 6.1 for new feeling words, then take advantage of every opportunity to practice empathy and try these words. Remember that feelings are often mixed. Read books and watch TV with a special ear for discerning how people are feeling. One of the best ways is to ask others how they feel, then to listen carefully to their words. This will help sensitize you to the unique vocabulary that each individual has adopted.

Types of Empathy

Three types of empathy are basic, inferred, and invitational. In basic empathy, a social worker mirrors what the client has explicitly said, whereas a worker uses inferred empathy to reach empathic understanding from less obvious clues. Invitational empathy involves strategies to encourage clients to talk about their feelings.

Basic Empathy. **Basic empathy** requires social workers to accurately perceive their clients' feelings and concerns and to communicate that understanding. It may include labeling feelings or summarizing expressed feelings. Frequently, clients want to talk about feelings, particularly those closely related to their problem situations. When clients take the initiative to introduce feelings, it is relatively easy and nonthreatening for workers to respond with basic empathy. Basic empathy simply says, "I have heard how you feel and I accept your feelings without judgment." With basic empathy, no attempt is made to interpret, judge, or promote greater awareness or insight beyond that which the client has already articulated.

Despite its apparent simplicity, basic empathy can be a powerful helping tool. When people express feelings in everyday communication, they may be blocked or discouraged when others react by judging, ignoring, or giving advice. For example, one common but extremely unhelpful response is "You shouldn't feel that way." In contrast, basic empathy creates a climate in which clients do not have to defend or hide their feelings. Basic empathy responses are, for many people, an unusual and satisfying experience. As one client described it, "For the first time, I felt safe. Someone had finally listened and heard me." Hancock states that "empathy helps to establish an atmosphere that gives each client a secure feeling that this is a place where 'it's safe to be me, this me, here and now'" (1997:167).

Workers who punctuate their work with frequent empathy are more likely to build rapport and evoke further information from clients (Egan, 1998). Simple logic suggests that when people believe that they are accepted and understood, they are more likely to feel secure and less likely to raise defenses. As a result, clients are more inclined to share and explore at a deeper level of intimacy than they would under more threatening conditions. The example below illustrates basic empathy:

CLIENT: *I was ready to kill her. How could she embarrass me in front of all those people?*

SOCIAL WORKER: *So you are angry that she didn't have enough sense to keep quiet.*

CLIENT: *Angry, but also hurt. After all, she was supposed to be my best friend. How could she double-cross me?*

SOCIAL WORKER: *Sounds like you felt betrayed.*

Empathic responses need to be presented with an air of tentativeness in order to give clients an opportunity to offer corrections. A simple pause or a question such as "Have I got it right?" can be used to achieve this end.

Inferred Empathy.   **Inferred empathy,** sometimes called *advanced accurate empathy* (Egan, 1998), includes attempts to identify clients' feelings based on nonverbal cues, themes, and hints. Inferred empathy is a powerful counseling skill that enables clients to deal with feelings at a deeper level than they may have been able to express.

Some clients say that their trust level increased because their counselors identified their feelings: "My worker seemed to know how I felt without me saying so. Finally, I felt understood." Inferred empathy may be particularly useful when working with clients who lack feeling vocabulary and clients who are unaccustomed to expressing feelings. Inferred empathy seems to say, "I have the courage and the ability to hear your feelings."

CLIENT: *It was a tough situation. Here I was in front of all those people with my private life laid bare.*

SOCIAL WORKER: *From the tears in your eyes, I suspect this was a painful and embarrassing moment for you.*

In the above example, the client seems willing to explore her experience, yet she stops short of verbally identifying her feelings. The social worker takes a mild empathic risk and considers context and nonverbal cues to infer empathy. Inferred empathy should always be presented tentatively to allow room for correction and further exploration.

With inferred empathy, some speculation based on the evidence of feelings is necessary. Consequently, there is more risk involved than with basic empathy. There are two significant risks. First, because the database for inferred empathy is more ambiguous, more errors are likely. Hence, social workers should be especially tentative with inferred empathy. As well, they should avoid becoming overly speculative to the point where they are simply guessing at their clients' feelings. Second, inferred empathy may be met with resistance from clients who are unwilling or unable to acknowledge their feelings. Inferred empathy picks up on subtle cues, and clients may be surprised to hear that their feelings have been communicated. They may react with anger and resentment that their feelings have been uncovered. Some clients are afraid of the intensity of their feelings, whereas others have strong needs for privacy. Thus, inferred empathy must be timed appropriately. The counseling relationship should have a reasonable level of trust, and there should be sufficient time left in the interview to process any reactions. Otherwise, it is best to defer inferred empathic responses.

Clients provide clues to their feelings in a number of ways. Clients might be embarrassed about sharing their feelings or reluctant to ask for help, so they talk about a "friend who has a problem." Understanding nonverbal behavior is crucial. Astute social workers learn a great deal about their clients' feelings by carefully observing changes in voice tone, sudden shifts in posture, nervous behavior, tears, grimaces, clenched fists, finger tapping, and smiling. As well, certain behaviors could suggest feelings. For example, a boy who runs away from a group home just before a visit from his mother may be saying something about his fear and anger. A client who arrives late, refuses to take his coat off, and sits with arms folded across his chest might be saying, "I don't want to be here."

Another way that many clients share feelings is through analogies. For example, a client who compares his life to a speeding train may be expressing his fears of being out of control. Some clients hint at their feelings by asking questions such as "Do you worry about your kids when they are out late at night?" Clients who minimize problems, as in "I have a bit of a problem. Do you have a minute?" or "This is probably not important," may be signaling that they have significant issues and feelings that they need to discuss.

Tuning in, or **preparatory empathy** (Shulman, 1992), is a useful way to prepare for inferred empathy. Preparatory empathy is a preliminary phase skill that involves trying to anticipate the feelings and concerns that clients might bring up in the interview. Such advance tuning in is useful because clients often do not directly reveal their feelings. Tuning in helps workers anticipate feelings and consider how clients might communicate indirectly. Shulman gives an example of the potential value of tuning in by describing a common situation involving a new, 22-year-old worker meeting with a 38-year-old mother of seven children. The mother asked the worker, "Do you have any children?" The worker responded defensively by listing her training in child psychology. Shulman suggests that the worker missed the implicit feelings expressed by the mother—the fear that the worker will not understand her. Had she used the tuning-in skill, the worker might have been able to consider in advance the range of feelings that a mother of seven kids might have when meeting with a young worker who has no children. With such advance preparation, the worker might have been more sensitive to the mother's real question, perhaps responding, "No, I don't have any children. Are you wondering if I'm going to be able to understand what it's like for you having to raise so many? I'm concerned about that as well. If I'm going to help you, I'm going to have to understand, and you are going to have to help me to understand" (Shulman, 1992:58). This response might have set the stage for a discussion of the mother's feelings about workers and given the worker a chance to share her own feelings.

CONVERSATION **6.2**
When Not to Use Empathy

STUDENT: I don't think empathy is always such a good thing. I watched one taped interview of Carl Rogers and two other therapists interviewing the same client. If I had been Rogers's client, I would have been irritated. He seemed to continually regurgitate what the client had just said.

TEACHER: You've raised a good point. Too much empathy, particularly when you get stuck at a basic level, might leave you and your client going in circles. It's also true that, if you move too fast with empathy, your clients can feel threatened and put up their defenses. This is particularly true with clients who have strong needs for privacy. They may view your empathic statements as unwanted intrusions into their feelings. Empathy invites greater relationship intimacy, and some clients are not ready for the risks that this entails. Having said that, I think it's important to remember that Rogers's client evaluated his method positively. This reminds us that clients respond differently to the same technique.

Other clients who may not be ready for empathy are those who are so caught up in their own talking that they do not even hear empathic statements. As Shea (1988) suggests, attempts to empathize with this group may actually be counterproductive because empathy interferes with what they want most— an audience to listen.

STUDENT: I think one way to handle that is to test your client's capacity for empathy with a few basic empathic statements. If they are not well received, you can back off by switching to less demanding content or more basic empathy.

TEACHER: I agree, back off, but not forever! As trust develops the client may welcome that same empathic response that he or she first rejected. To continue the list of times when empathy may not be a good idea, I'd add the following:

- when your clients reject empathy
- when it's clearly time to move on to problem solving or another activity
- when empathy is continuously misinterpreted by clients, for example as controlling

We should always remember that counseling techniques will not work the same with all clients. Cultural norms and expectations, for example, may affect how empathy is received.

Invitational Empathy.   **Invitational empathy** encourages clients to explore emotions. Social workers can draw on their knowledge of human growth and development, such as how people tend to deal with particular life events and crises. Some clients are reluctant to share their feelings for fear of judgment, or they may believe that they shouldn't feel a particular way. Others may think they are the "only one" or that they are "crazy," "evil," or "abnormal." For example, it is common to feel some relief, even happiness (as well as grief) when a loved one who has been struggling with a painful illness dies, but a client may feel guilty for feeling this way. Invitational empathy normalizes the experience, making it easier for the client to talk about it and to accept it: "It's normal at a time like this to struggle with mixed feelings—grief, pain, comfort, and perhaps joy that her suffering is at an end."

Invitational empathy also says to the client that the social worker is ready and able to talk about difficult feelings. By identifying and labeling feelings, the worker is saying, "It's okay to feel this way." In the following example, the worker uses invitational empathy to "give permission" to a client, who might otherwise suppress or ignore his pain, to experience and verbalize his emotions.

> **CLIENT:** *I guess it's no big deal. So what if they know the scoop on my marital problems.*
>
> **SOCIAL WORKER:** *A lot of people in the same situation might feel embarrassed and perhaps disappointed or angry that a friend could be so indiscreet about something said in confidence.*

In the following example, the counselor uses nonverbal cues as a basis for invitational empathy to encourage the client to explore a difficult topic.

> **SOCIAL WORKER:** *Would you mind if I shared an observation with you? I may be wrong, so I'd like your opinion.*
>
> **CLIENT:** *Sure, go ahead. Say it.*
>
> **SOCIAL WORKER:** *I notice that, whenever mention of your father comes up, you seem keen to change the topic.*
>
> *(long silence, client stares at the floor)*
>
> **SOCIAL WORKER:** *Some memories are painful—maybe even too painful to talk about.*
>
> **CLIENT:** *(softly, tears in his eyes) It's just that his death was so unexpected. We had a fight that morning, and I didn't even get a chance to say goodbye.*

Invitational empathy begins with questions and responses targeted to encourage clients to express feelings. Choosing a strategy to encourage the expression of feelings is influenced by the usual variables, including the amount of trust in the relationship, time constraints, culture, and the counselor's role. Timing, for example, is one of the most important variables. Because the exploration of feelings can be time-consuming, it is important for counselors to make sure that they have enough time to complete the process. Intelligent use of silence is another important variable. Clients may need their workers to patiently listen and restrain themselves from filling every silent moment with words.

One way to bridge the interview into a discussion of feelings is to use invitational statements, such as "I do not know how you feel, but if you are feeling pain or loneliness, I am ready to listen." Comments such as "I need your help in understanding your feelings" can also move the interview into the affective, or feeling, area.

Frequently, natural opportunities are provided when clients share a bit about how they are feeling. Then the social worker can use questions to encourage further sharing. Open questions such as the following promote clients to share feelings: "How are you feeling?" "What feelings best describe how you reacted?" Closed questions such as the following target specific information about feelings: "Did you feel angry?" "Is this something you feel strongly about?"

Helping clients understand the importance of addressing feelings is an important step that keeps clients involved in decision making (contracting). When social workers inform clients and solicit their support for the process, clients' motivation is higher. Here are some sample leads:

- I think it might help if we shift our focus and talk a bit about how you feel. This might help us both to understand why your decision is so difficult.
- We haven't yet talked about your feelings. In my experience, feelings often present one of the biggest barriers.
- Until feelings are understood and accepted, they can distort our thinking and even reduce the amount of control we have over our behavior. So, you might find it useful if we spend some time exploring how you feel.

Directives such as the following can be also used to move the interview into the feeling area: "Tell me how you feel." "Let's switch our focus and talk about your feelings." Directives are one way to manage the flow and focus of the interview. With some clients, worker self-disclosure, if used sparingly, is a powerful tool as well. "I don't know how it is for you, but I know that for many months after my marriage ended, I was in a state of shock."

Another interview tool is the use of sentence completion statements. Sentence completion statements give workers a way to focus feelings on a particular area, and they give freedom to clients to control the answer. For example, they can make statements such as the following and ask clients to complete them:

- When I think about all my problems, I feel . . .
- If I could use one feeling to describe my situation it would be . . .
- When I first came for counseling I felt . . .
- The feelings that I most need to deal with are . . .

Invitational empathy should respect clients' rights to privacy. Compton and Galaway point out:

It is questionable whether any client wants to be fully and totally known. There is something very frightening about someone's knowing everything about us as an individual for in knowledge lies control; so in the ordinary course of living people reveal their intimate selves only to those they trust. Without the pain of the problem and the hope that the worker can offer some help toward coping with it, few clients would be willing to share themselves with an unknown other person (1984:238).

TABLE 6.3   Types of Empathy

Type	Description	Major Use	Comments
Basic	Response to clearly articulated feelings	To encourage continued expression of feelings To confirm capacity to hear feelings	Basic empathy contributes to the development of trust. It signals to clients that workers are willing and able to deal with feelings.
Inferred	Response to nonverbal cues and other indicators of feelings	To move feelings into the verbal channel of communication	Inferred empathy may generate more anxiety in some clients as feelings that they avoided, suppressed, or wanted to keep hidden are made visible. Inferred empathy may promote client insight.
Invitational	Encouragement of clients to talk about feelings	To stimulate discussion of feelings To normalize feelings	Invitational empathy is useful for working with clients who are reluctant or unable to articulate feelings. Timing is critical, and workers should present invitational empathy in a gentle and tentative manner.

Four Generalizations about Empathy

Generalization One.   When clients share feelings, empathy is often the preferred response. The **principle of positive reinforcement** states that "if in a given situation, somebody does something that is followed immediately by a positive reinforcer, then that person is more likely to do the same thing again" (Martin and Pear, 1992:26). Clients take an interpersonal risk when they share their feelings. Empathy serves to acknowledge this risk by conveying recognition and acceptance of the clients' feelings. In this way, it reinforces the wisdom of the risk and motivates clients to continue sharing feelings. On the other hand, when clients share feelings and they are not rewarded (reinforced) with empathy, they tend to keep their feelings more private. This underscores the importance of expressing empathy early in the relationship.

Generalization Two.   Usually, social workers should risk expressing empathy early in the relationship. Early empathy establishes for the client that the counseling relationship is a safe place to express feelings. To become comfortable with empathy, workers need to overcome their own fears about bringing emotions into the foreground. Shulman (1992) suggests that many workers fear that, by encouraging clients to express emotions, they might trigger extreme reactions, particularly suicide. As a counterargument he proposes that "the greater danger is not in the facing of feelings but in denying them. The only thing worse than living with strong emotions is the feeling that one is alone and that no one can understand" (1992:128). By helping clients express and get in touch with their feelings, social workers can help them decrease the negative power that these feelings may have over them.

In the early part of a relationship or interview, workers may not have enough information to offer empathic understanding, but, given its central importance, they should give priority to acquiring, maintaining, and deepening it throughout the helping relationship. Therefore, they should be alert to empathic opportunities. One obvious opportunity arises whenever clients verbalize feelings. In such moments, workers can use basic empathy to confirm understanding. Sometimes clients reveal feelings nonverbally, and social workers can use inferred empathy. When clients have not shared feelings, workers can adopt invitational empathy to encourage them to share their emotions.

Generalization Three.   Social workers should express empathy tentatively. They need to refrain from using empathy as a weapon by insisting that their clients must feel a particular way. They should look for indicators that clients have accepted their empathy and that it is accurate. Clients provide confirmation through head nods, smiles, reduction in anxiety, and verbal confirmation, for example, "That's right" or "You seem to know exactly how I'm feeling even before I tell you." Clients also implicitly confirm willingness to accept empathy when they continue to share feelings at a deeper level. Sometimes clients correct workers. This is an important and positive outcome of empathic risk. It enables workers to adjust and refine their understanding and helps them reach a point of shared meaning with their clients. Thus, empathy should be seen as an active process of developing understanding.

Generalization Four.   Empathy requires flexibility in its use, including the ability to refrain from using it. Empathy is an important and powerful skill, but social workers need to use it intelligently. When clients are willing to address feelings, empathic responses are effective. With some clients, empathic statements result in the opposite of what was intended. Instead of deepening trust and encouraging clients to open up, empathy arouses defenses. This may happen when empathy suggests feelings that clients would prefer not to address, or it may arise when clients experience empathy as invading their personal space. When clients resist empathy by withdrawing or becoming defensive, it might be better to discontinue using it for a while.

Situational differences influence how the work of empathy unfolds. Some clients are very verbal and open with their feelings and respond positively to empathy. Others need gentle encouragement to talk about feelings, and they open up discussion of feelings gradually and in a very controlled manner. Social workers will find that they encounter less resistance when they match their clients' pace.

Empathic Response Leads

Using a range of different responses adds interest and variety to the interview, but using the same words and phrases can irritate clients and reduce the energy and vitality of the interview. Having a range of leads for empathic response prevents the interview from sounding artificial. The following list provides some variations

- So, you feel . . .
- My sense is that you might be feeling . . .
- From your point of view . . .
- As you see it . . .
- I wonder if what you're saying is . . .
- Perhaps you feel . . .
- I gather that . . .
- It seems to you that . . .
- What I understand from what you have said is . . .
- It sounds like . . .
- You appear to be feeling . . .

This list could easily be expanded, and counselors should adapt it to fit the style and the language of their clients. (For additional ideas see Martin, 1983:42; Shebib, 1997:191.)

Why Achieving Empathic Understanding Is So Difficult

Empathic errors are less likely when workers are similar to their clients (in age, gender, race, etc.) and when they have had similar problems and experiences, provided they do not use their own experiences and background as a script for how the client must feel. Social workers need to remember the importance of allowing for individual differences. It is critical that they remember that they can never fully understand how other people feel. Through empathy, they can get a better sense of their clients' feelings, but this understanding will never be perfect. The challenge is to "see beyond conventional facades, refrain from imposing personal interpretations and judgments, and be willing to risk understanding another person's private logic and feelings, which in superficial daily contacts the counselor might see as weak, foolish, or undesirable" (Hammond, Hepworth, and Smith, 1977:3).

Empathy is perhaps the most difficult counseling skill to master. As Egan notes, "Although many people 'feel' empathy for others, the truth is that few know how to put it into words" (1998:83). Empathy demands a lot of social workers. They must manage their own emotional and judgmental reactions. They have to find meaning and discover feelings from their clients' verbal and nonverbal communication. This can be exceptionally demanding, because clients may keep feelings hidden, suppress feelings, or lack understanding or awareness of their emotions. As well, relationship issues, including lack of trust, embarrassment, and fear of being judged, can inhibit clients from disclosing. For example, there may be societal, cultural, or personal norms that prohibit sharing of feelings. Or clients may not have the ability (language) to adequately communicate their emotions.

Further complicating the empathic process is the need for social workers to respond right away. In an interview, there is no time for workers to use a thesaurus or dictionary to find the right words and there is no opportunity to consult others, rehearse their empathy, or ponder the feeling state of their clients. Empathic risk means daring to share perceived understanding with clients using concrete words and phrases. Table 6.4 lists some procedural reference points for responding empathetically.

Responses to Avoid

When attempting to express empathy, social workers need to avoid certain responses. In particular, they need to be aware of the effect of cutoffs, empty responses, and sympathy.

Cutoffs.   Cutoffs are phrases that inhibit the further expression of feeling. Workers who make statements such as "Don't feel" and "You should feel" are demonstrating a low level of understanding and acceptance of how their clients feel. Although such statements may have some limited supportive value, they generally force clients to defend their feelings. Similarly, when workers ask clients questions such as "Why do you feel. . . ?" a judgmental tone is present that can leave clients feeling defensive (see Chapter 5).

Another response that may inhibit clients is silence. When clients risk sharing feelings, some response (empathy) is appropriate. When workers fail to acknowledge feelings, they may be saying, "This is not important" or "I'm not capable of dealing with your emotions." In response, clients might feel abandoned, embarrassed, or judged.

Social workers also cut clients off when they change the subject and when they offer advice. A subject change has a clear message, "Let's not talk about that," and advice trivializes feelings.

Empty Responses.   Empty responses are devoid of content. Phrases such as "I hear what you are saying" and "I understand what you mean" convey no real confirmation that the social worker has understood. Another empty response is parroting, or repeating, what the client has said. Egan describes parroting as "a parody of empathy" (1998:96). In contrast, empathy communicates the worker's effort to go beyond merely hearing the words by un-

---

TABLE 6.4   The Empathic Communication Process

- Listen for or probe for feelings
- Observe nonverbal indicators of emotion
- Consider context—problem, phase, setting, relationship
- Identify general category of feeling (e.g., anger, sadness, etc.) including mixed or ambivalent feelings
- Identify level or intensity of emotion (i.e., low, medium, high)
- Choose an appropriate specific feeling word, phrase, or metaphor
- Formulate a tentative empathic response
- Wait for or encourage the client to confirm or correct your empathic perception
- Based on client response, correct or offer a deeper empathic response

derstanding the client's feelings and perspectives. Using empathy, the worker rephrases the client's statements and assigns labels to feelings that the client expressed but did not name.

Clichés and platitudes such as "Everybody has to have a little pain in their life" patronize and reject clients' feelings. As Egan puts it, clichéd responses say, "You don't really have a problem at all, at least not a serious one" (1998:96).

Sympathy.   Sympathy refers to concern for other people's problems and emotions and is related to our own emotional and behavioral reactions. Sympathy is our reaction, and though it is intimately connected to another's feelings, it is not the same as empathy. Empathy is a process whereby we come to understand another's feelings. When successful, empathy is objective, and the social worker achieves understanding from the client's frame of reference.

Social workers are human and it is normal for them to have emotional responses when listening to their clients. In fact, their reactions are the basis for compassion, an indispensable component of a caring counseling relationship. Clearly, there are moments when it is appropriate to express sympathy. This lets clients know that workers support them and are moved by their pain. At the same time, it is essential for social workers to develop the ability to separate their emotional reactions (sympathy and compassion) from those of their clients. Social workers also need to ensure that their sympathy does not detract from the client's feelings by interfering with their need to express feelings, tell their stories, and face the reality of their problems.

> **CLIENT:** *I'm really worried about telling my dad that I've dropped out of college. Even when I was a little girl my father kept saying, "You've got to get an education or you'll never get anywhere in life."*
>
> **SOCIAL WORKER (CHOICE 1—SYMPATHETIC REACTION):** *I don't think it was very fair for him to have laid such a heavy burden on you. It always makes me kind of angry when I hear about parents pushing their kids.*
>
> **SOCIAL WORKER (CHOICE 2—EMPATHETIC REACTION):** *So, you fear that you've let your father down.*

In the above example, Choice 1 is a misguided attempt to offer support. Judgmental in tone, it shifts the focus from the client's feelings to those of the social worker. Choice 2 expresses basic empathy, setting the stage for further exploration.

Empathy Reminders.   When you express empathy, acknowledge the feelings that have been expressed (verbally and/or nonverbally). You could include a brief *because* clause that summarizes content. In most situations, you will want to stop there. This gives your clients a chance to process what they have heard and to offer corrections. Alternatively, when clients experience empathy they may be motivated to share at a deeper level. Consequently, *avoid* combining empathy with subject changes and other cutoff responses, content questions, sympathy, or any other response that diverts attention away from empathy. Some examples of appropriate and inappropriate empathic responses are:

CLIENT: *Sometimes when he speaks to me that way, I just want to go hide in a corner.*

COUNSELOR 1 (APPROPRIATE EMPATHY):   *It sounds like maybe you're feeling embarrassed.*

COUNSELOR 2 (INAPPROPRIATE EMPATHY—SUBJECT SHIFT):   *It sounds like maybe you're feeling embarrassed. Would you like to talk about ways of overcoming it?*

COUNSELOR 3 (SYMPATHY CONFUSED WITH EMPATHY):   *I feel sorry for you that he treats you that way.*

COUNSELOR 4 (NONEMPATHY):   *There's no reason why you should have to put up with such treatment.*

COUNSELOR 5 (NONEMPATHY—FAILURE TO IDENTIFY FEELINGS):   *You're feeling like he should stop doing that.*

Tough Empathy

It's not hard to feel caring and compassion for most people in pain—the aging client who loses his job, the young mother who has had a second miscarriage, and the single parent who is trying to raise children on a limited income. However, some clients challenge workers' tolerance. Even the most accepting workers occasionally find it difficult to lay aside personal reaction, suspend judgment, and respond with empathy to clients such as the following:

- Bob, an angry 20-year-old who savagely attacked an elderly woman
- Pernell, a father who argues for the morality of sex with his children
- Eileen, an HIV-positive prostitute who asserts her right to have unprotected sex with her customers
- Ruby, a woman who rejects and attacks efforts to help

Social workers working with clients such as these are likely to experience strong emotional reactions, and they may find it difficult to put aside their personal feelings in order to feel and express empathy. Often these are clients who appear to lack empathy and feelings for others in their lives. In fact, "the blotting out of empathy as these people inflict damage on victims is almost always part of an emotional cycle that precipitates their cruel acts" (Goleman, 1995:106).

Why then should social workers respond with empathy to such people? First, empathy is a way for them to understand how their clients think and feel. Second, as noted earlier, empathy is instrumental in forming the helping relationship, the prerequisite condition for the contract between client and worker. One outcome of empathy is that clients come to feel valued and understood. As a result of the empathic relationship, clients begin to reveal more, make discoveries about themselves, and alter their perspectives about themselves and others. With clients who lack empathy for others, empathy teaches them that they cannot block out feelings and that their victims do hurt.

INTERVIEW 6.1

Poor Substitutes for Empathy

The following excerpt illustrates some of the inappropriate responses that workers sometimes use instead of empathy. Ignoring feelings and offering empty responses, simplistic advice, and sympathy are some responses below that are inadequate substitutes for empathy.

Dialogue	Analysis
CLIENT (SOFTLY, WITH TEARS IN HER EYES): I just haven't been the same since he left. I still look out the door and expect him to come home. **SOCIAL WORKER:** How old was he when he ran away?	Inappropriate topic shift. The client is clearly experiencing some pain, perhaps grief, and she trusts the social worker enough to share these feelings. Generally, when clients share feelings, particularly feelings that are strong, empathy is the preferred response.
CLIENT: He was just 16. I still thought of him as my baby. Now I go to sleep at night wondering whether he's dead or alive.	The social worker's response shifts the focus away from feelings to content. This may subtly signal to the client that the social worker is uncomfortable with feelings. Continual shifts such as this will "train" the client not to share feelings.
SOCIAL WORKER: You thought of him as your baby. Now you go to sleep at night wondering whether he's dead or alive.	Parroting: Repetition at this point serves no purpose. Sometimes key words or phrases can be emphasized as a way to focus attention, but this type of parroting is inappropriate here.
(silence) **SOCIAL WORKER:** I understand how you feel. **CLIENT (BURIES HER FACE IN HER HANDS):** Sometimes I just don't know whether I can go on living. If something doesn't happen soon, then . . . *(counselor interrupts)*	Superficial response: The social worker tries to be supportive, but the response is empty. Until the worker risks empathy with specific feeling words and phrases, the client cannot know whether she has, in fact, been heard.
SOCIAL WORKER: You have to think of your husband and your other children. **CLIENT:** Yes, I know, but do you have any idea what I'm going through, how tough it is just to get out of bed in the morning?	Rescuing, ignoring feelings: It seems obvious that this social worker is unable to deal with the powerful feelings that the client presents. After an ill-timed interruption, the worker offers a misguided and simplistic solution, while ignoring the emotions the client expressed.
SOCIAL WORKER: My guess is that you feel very angry at the world, maybe even some guilt that you are somehow responsible for your son's running away. **CLIENT:** No! I don't feel guilty. I was always a good mother. I think if my son were here, he'd say that too. When he became addicted to drugs, it was more than either of us knew how to handle.	Inaccurate empathy: The social worker attempts invitational empathy. Unfortunately, there is insufficient evidence to support the worker's conclusion that the client feels angry or guilty. The worker may be right, but, as suggested, it is merely a guess, a poor substitute for empathy. Moreover, the worker is not attending to the feelings that the client has already expressed.

(continued)

INTERVIEW 6.1 Continued

SOCIAL WORKER: I hear what you are saying.
CLIENT: So what am I supposed to do? I feel so empty and useless.
SOCIAL WORKER: It's a very bad feeling.

(brief silence)

SOCIAL WORKER: You shouldn't feel that way. One day your son might walk in the door. You have to go on living.
CLIENT: I suppose you're right. Thanks for listening. It felt good to get it off my chest.
SOCIAL WORKER: I'm glad I was able to help.

Superficial response: This response has the same problems as her earlier one, "I understand how you feel."

Inaccurate empathy, lack of specificity: The worker attempts empathy but misses the intensity of the client's feelings. Then, the worker quickly shifts the focus without giving the client time to respond.

One important requirement is to accept clients' feelings without judgment and without trying to tell them how they should feel.

Sometimes clients benefit from the interview, even when the worker's responses are as poor as those depicted in this encounter. Simply telling one's story and verbalizing feelings can help people deal with pain or problems. However, it is much more likely that this client is ready to dismiss the worker. The worker may be just as relieved that the interview is over.

In situations in which it is difficult for them to respond with empathy, social workers may need to work on their own issues. For example, they can ask themselves, "What is it about this particular client that makes it difficult for me to be empathic?" "Does this client remind me of someone else (e.g., parent, former partner)?" "To what extent do I have unresolved feelings and issues that this client triggers?" Another strategy is to spend time getting to know the client. Usually, familiarity increases empathy.

Carl, an employment counselor, carefully read Antonio's file. Antonio was a 19-year-old, unemployed male. From all indications, Antonio was not very interested in finding a job. His mother complained that he usually slept until noon and that he rarely even read the newspaper want ads. Antonio arrived for his appointment twenty minutes late and gave out a clear message that he didn't want to be there. "How long will this take?" he asked sternly.

Carl's natural reaction was anger and disgust at Antonio's attitude. He wondered to himself why he should spend time with this client, who was clearly unmotivated. Putting his personal feelings aside, Carl decided to respond with empathy, and he gently replied, "My hunch is that you don't see much point in being here. Maybe you're even a little angry at being forced to come." Antonio, a bit surprised at Carl's perceptiveness, told him how much he resented everyone trying to run his life.

Gradually, Antonio began to let down his defenses and a very different picture emerged. Antonio talked about the rejection he felt from countless employers who turned him away. Soon, it was clear to Carl that Antonio was deeply depressed. He slept late because he couldn't sleep at night. He had stopped looking for work because it was the only way he knew to deal with the pain.

Sometimes social workers fear expressing empathy because they mistakenly believe that empathy will endorse their clients' beliefs or lifestyles. They need to remind themselves that being empathic does not mean that they have to agree with their clients' feelings or perspectives. Empathy simply attempts to say, "I understand how you feel and how you see things." In fact, clients must feel understood before they will respond to any efforts to promote change. Empathy is one of the ways that social workers establish credibility and win the trust of their clients. When a trusting relationship exists, clients may be willing to consider other perspectives and look at the consequences of their choices.

Social workers may find wisdom in Nicholi's observation that "whether the patient is young or old, neatly groomed or disheveled, outgoing or withdrawn, articulate or inarticulate, highly integrated or totally disintegrated, of high or low socioeconomic status, the skilled clinician realizes that the patient, as a fellow human being, is considerably more like himself than he is different" (1988:8).

Summary

Owing to the central role that emotions play in our lives, it is essential that social workers give priority to exploring and understanding clients' feelings. Emotions are characterized by physiological as well as psychological and behavioral reactions. Ten families of emotions—anger, fear, strength, weakness, joy, sadness, confusion, shame, surprise, and love—provide a starting point for organizing thinking about emotions. To describe their emotions, clients may use specific feeling words, which they may further define with modifiers. As well, clients may communicate their emotions through metaphors and nonverbal channels of communication.

Body language, or kinesics, involves observing variables such as posture, facial expressions, gestures, and eye motion. Sometimes body language is easily interpreted, but at other times it is ambiguous and, thus, needs to be interpreted with caution.

Voice tone, volume, and pitch can help social workers identify emotions. Voice variables can reveal if clients are depressed, euphoric, angry, or sad.

Proxemics is a term used to describe how people use space and distance. Social workers should adapt their seating to meet the needs of individual clients. They should observe spatial shifts during the interview.

Feelings can be experienced as positive or negative, but this subjective determination is individually defined. An emotion may be debilitating for some but exhilarating for others. Circumstances and context may not be good predictors of feelings.

Mixed feelings, including contradictory emotions, are common. A great deal of stress and confusion can arise from the pushes and pulls of competing feelings, which, if unmanaged, can control a client's life.

INTERVIEW 6.2
Effective Use of Empathy

Dialogue

CLIENT: For as long as I can remember, I've been drinking on a daily basis. It's no big deal.

SOCIAL WORKER (SOFTLY, WHILE MAINTAINING EYE CONTACT): Drinking has been part of your life and you don't see a problem with it.

(client nods)

SOCIAL WORKER: You mentioned that your family gives you a hard time about drinking. How do you feel about that?

CLIENT: Yeah. I work hard all day. If I want to have a drink, no one has a right to tell me to stop. Drinking helps me to relax.

SOCIAL WORKER: Sounds as though you resent it when others interfere with something that gives you pleasure.

CLIENT (LOUDLY): They should back off and mind their own business. I don't tell them how to live.

SOCIAL WORKER: It's more than just resentment. Perhaps you're angry that they don't respect your right to live your life as you see fit.

CLIENT: I guess I shouldn't be so ticked off. After all, my father was an alcoholic, and I know firsthand what it's like to live with a drunk.

SOCIAL WORKER: To some extent your feelings are mixed—you feel anger because you think they should mind their own business, but you also see where they are coming from, and you are sympathetic to their fears.

CLIENT: Well, to be perfectly honest, it's not just their fear. I don't want to drink myself to death like my father did.

SOCIAL WORKER: You've done some thinking about how you'd like your life to be different. When your wife confronts you, it really touches a nerve, and you're reminded of fears you'd rather not have.

CLIENT: No way I'm going to let that happen to me.

Analysis

The worker tries to proceed cautiously with basic paraphrasing. Mirroring the client's thoughts conveys that he has been heard. Suspending verbal and nonverbal judgment helps to develop trust.

The worker uses an open question to encourage the client to talk about his feelings. Such statements also say to the client that the worker is willing to listen.

The worker uses inferred empathy. Although the client does not directly label his feelings, from the words, context, and nonverbal messages, the worker speculates that resentment might be the predominant feeling.

The client's response suggests that he is responsive to the worker's empathy. He signals this by continuing to share at a deeper level. This is a significant event in the interview, which should give the worker confidence to continue to risk empathy.

Here, again, the worker infers anger from the client's nonverbal expression. By labeling the anger, the worker gives the client "permission" to discuss his anger.

Because the worker accepts his anger, the client may feel that he has to defend it less.

The worker picks up and identifies the client's mixed feelings. Mixed feelings can often be a source of anxiety for clients, particularly if they pull their emotions in different directions.

This client was initially guarded and defensive, quick to defend his right to drink. As he finds acceptance from the worker, he begins to let his guard down. In some interviews, such as this one, trust can develop quickly, but, more often, the worker requires extended patience.

The worker responds with inferred empathy.

The worker uses a basic empathic response. A

SOCIAL WORKER: You're determined to control your drinking.

CLIENT: I'm not going to be like my father.

SOCIAL WORKER: Correct me if I'm off base, but as you talk, I wonder if a part of you is afraid that your drinking could get out of hand.

return to basic empathy gives the client some space. Workers should avoid constant pressure on clients to move to a higher level of intimacy. The worker needs to move deeper, but caution is critical to avoid moving too quickly.

The worker uses both confrontation and invitational empathy in this statement. Presenting the ideas in a tentative manner softens the confrontation.

Empathy is a core skill for all helping relationships. Empathy helps to build the helping relationship, assists clients in identifying and labeling feelings, models a healthy way of relating to others, and helps clients to accept their own feelings. Although social workers can never know exactly how their clients feel, empathy enables them to move closer to understanding how they think and feel.

Three types of empathy are basic, inferred, and invitational. Basic empathy mirrors what the client has explicitly said, while inferred empathy attempts to reach empathic understanding from less obvious clues. Invitational empathy involves strategies to encourage clients to talk about their feelings.

Tuning in, or preparatory empathy, is a way for social workers to prepare for inferred empathy. Preparatory empathy involves trying to estimate the feelings and concerns that clients may bring to the interview.

A variety of strategies can be used to encourage clients to express feelings, including invitational statements, questions targeted to feelings, explaining the importance of addressing feelings, providing directives, self-disclosing, and using sentence completion statements.

Four generalizations about empathy are: (1) When clients share feelings, empathy is often the preferred response, (2) social workers should risk expressing empathy early in the relationship, (3) social workers should express empathy tentatively, and (4) empathy requires flexibility in its use, including the ability to refrain from using it.

EXERCISES

1. Begin a log to track your feelings. At periodic intervals (e.g., every hour), record words and phrases that best describe how you are feeling at that moment. Try to be as precise as possible, using terms that capture the essence and intensity of how you feel. Maintain your log for at least one week.

   a. What patterns or cycles are apparent? Are there times of the day or week when you are more likely to feel particular emotions?

   b. How were your emotions linked to events or people?

   c. How could you have altered your emotions, for example, to increase pleasurable feelings and decrease negative feelings?

    d. What have you learned about yourself from this exercise that will assist you in your work as a counselor?

2. Recall the ten families of emotions: anger, fear, strength, weakness, joy, sadness, confusion, shame, surprise, and love. Rate your ability to express each on a scale of 1 to 5.

5 = strong ability to express the emotions within the category
1 = unable to express the emotions within the category

    a. What are the emotions that you have more difficulty expressing? Are there feelings you would never express?

    b. How do your ability and willingness to share emotions vary depending on the person you are with?

3. Would you find it easier to tell your friends (your parents, family, etc.) that you love them or that you are angry with them?

4. What did you learn about expressing emotions when you were growing up? Discuss and compare your experiences with a colleague.

5. Describe in detail how you feel, think, and act when you experience specific emotions. For example, you might write, "When I feel scared I want to escape. My breathing is shallow. I tend to look away. I become quiet. I think I might vomit." To increase your awareness, imagine a situation in which you are experiencing a particular emotion. Alternatively, when you experience an emotion, focus intensely on the experience and record your observations.

6. Share the details of an intense emotional experience with a partner. What was easy and difficult about sharing your feelings? What responses from your partner were helpful? Unhelpful?

7. For each of the following situations, predict and describe the emotions that the individual might experience. Remember that there may be many possibilities and that some experiences (although apparently negative) may result in positive emotions. What nonverbal cues might you observe in each case?

    a. man whose wife of sixty years has just died

    b. a young teenager on a first date

    c. a middle-aged man fired from his job

    d. a student denied admission to a training program

    e. a mother discovering her teenage daughter using drugs

    f. a student about to take an exam

    g. a teacher on the first day of class

    h. a person who witnessed the terrorist attack on New York City

    i. a prisoner about to be sentenced

    j. a 16-year-old with sexual identity problems

    k. a job applicant

    l. a job interviewer

    m. an angry client

    n. a client seeing a counselor for the first time

    o. a client seeing a counselor for the last time

    p. a patient in a hospital waiting for major surgery

    q. a child entering a foster home

    r. a man who has just abused his wife

    s. a person dealing with depression

    t. a parent dealing with a child who has ADD (attention deficit disorder)

    u. a couple on the day of their marriage

    v. a couple on the day their divorce becomes final

    w. a serial killer

    x. a compulsive gambler

    y. a 12-year-old boy coming to a new school

    z. an 11-year-old girl who has been sexually abused by her father

8. Identify feeling words and phrases that best describe how each of the following clients may be feeling:

    a. "Everyone in my life keeps putting me down. Even my own children constantly criticize me."

    b. *(shaking)* "Fifteen hard years with the same company and what do they do? They dump me with three weeks' notice."

    c. *(a 6-year-old boy, crying)* "No one wants to play with me."

    d. "When I saw the airplanes crash into the World Trade Center I just couldn't stop crying."

    e. *(an ex-offender to parole officer)* "Have you ever been to jail?"

    f. *(a 16-year-old boy)* "I'd rather live on the street than go to another foster home. Five foster homes in five years. I've had enough!"

    g. "I didn't expect to live long enough to see the millennium."

9. Assume that the clients below are speaking to you and that an empathic response is appropriate.

    a. *(client, looking at the floor)* "It's not just my job that 1 hate. I've lost a sense of purpose to my life. I live alone, and I have no special relationships. Most days I wonder why I should bother."

    b. *(client, smiling)* "For the first time, things are really starting to come together for me. My kids are all doing well in school, my marital problems are on the upswing, and I finally put some money aside for a rainy day."

    c. *(parent to a teacher)* "I don't know what to do. I know you said I should try to help my son with his homework and show some interest in his work. But he comes home from school and goes straight to his room. When I ask about his homework, he always says that there wasn't any. When I offer to help, he makes it clear he'd rather do it on his own."

    d. *(teenager, crying)* "I'm pregnant. This will kill my dad, but first he'll kill me."

    e. "Everyone always says how together I am. But I don't feel together. Sometimes I get so wound up that I think I'm going to burst."

    f. *(man, 57, talking about his family problems)* "I have to make every decision. I can never count on my wife or kids for help."

    g. *(parent to a teacher)* "My son does not have ADD. I don't care what you say. I'm not going to put him on drugs."

10. In each of the following client statements more than one feeling is expressed. Identify feeling words and phrases that best describe the mixed feelings. Next, formulate an empathic response.

a. "Thanks for seeing me today. It really felt good to get things off my chest. No one has ever listened to me the way you did. I hope you don't think I'm crazy or stupid. . . .

b. *(eyes welling up with tears)* "It's over. I don't care to be with him any more."

c. *(shouting)* "I am calm."

d. "To tell you the truth, I'd like to just march right in, look him in the eye, and tell him exactly where to go. I don't know what to do."

e. "Finding out that my former girlfriend had my baby was totally shocking. After we broke up, she didn't even tell me she was pregnant. I'd love to be a father, but I don't want a relationship with her. Maybe it would be best if I just forgot the whole thing. But I want to do what's right."

f. "Living on your own is the pits. Now I don't even know where my next meal is coming from. I used to love being married. I felt like life really had meaning. But at least now I don't have to worry about being beat up by my husband every time he gets drunk. It's just so difficult. Maybe I should give him another chance."

11. The statements below may evoke strong personal reactions. Assume that the person is speaking to you and that you are responding with empathy, even though empathy may not be the preferred response.

a. "This country was much better when it was white and Christian. With such high unemployment, don't you think it's time to stop letting every damn immigrant into the country? No wonder I can't get a job."

b. "I'm not ashamed to admit it. Once in a while I hit my wife. It's no big deal."

c. "I don't care what you say. I won't give up on you until you become a Christian."

d. *(teacher)* "Your paper is really substandard. You haven't followed any of the directions. I'm really frustrated that you just don't seem ready to do the work that is necessary to be successful in this course. I'm so fed up. I don't see any way that you can pass this course."

e. *(employer)* "This is really hard for me to do. I've tried everything possible to cut costs, but unfortunately I'm going to have to make some major changes. I just don't know what else I can do. I have to lay you off."

f. *(applicant for welfare)* "Don't you even think about turning me down. I'm not leaving this office without a check."

g. *(student to teacher)* "I suppose this course is going to be like all the others. Lots of reading, a bunch of papers. I only hope there's some relevance to it all."

h. *(client, 35-year-old)* "I had no idea she was only fifteen. She was the one who wanted to have sex. From the look in her eyes I could tell she was begging for it. It's really unfair that I'm now charged with rape. Besides, fifteen is old enough for someone to make up their own mind."

i. "This counseling isn't very helpful. So why don't we just forget it and do what both of us really want? How about it, sweetheart? Let's go out for dinner."

j. "I really don't worry too much about AIDS. What can I do about it? if I'm meant to get it, then I'll get it. So what? We all have to die sometime."

k. "I'm not stupid. I know that he shouldn't hit me. But I guess I deserved it, the way I put him down. I should learn to keep my mouth shut. When I see him, I'll apologize."

l. *(client to physician, eyes brightening)* "So, I'm HIV positive. That's great. Now I can get a higher welfare rate and all those extra benefits."

m. *(client, with angry tone)* "No one is willing to talk to me about the fact that I might be dying. I can accept it, but every time I ask the big question people change the topic."

12. In question 11 above, what do you think are the advantages of responding with empathy?

13. Videotape a television program. While taping it, turn off the sound. Pay attention to the nonverbal communication of the actors. Watch the tape, this time with the sound turned on. How successful were you in correctly reading the nonverbal cues?

14. Interview people from different cultures, preferably people who have been in this country for only a short time. What are the differences between their use of nonverbal communication (e.g., eye contact, spatial distance, touching) and yours?

15. Conduct practice interviews with a colleague to experiment with spatial distance. Deliberately increase or decrease the distance between the two of you to learn about the effect of space. At what point did your space become violated? How did physical distance affect the quality of your verbal exchange?

16. The following is the typescript of a portion of a worker's interview. The setting is a social service agency and the worker is an employment counselor.

    Consider the following questions:

    a. How appropriate are the number, type, and timing of the worker's questions?

    b. Was there evidence of abrupt changes of subject?

    c. Were important clues to the client's feelings or concerns addressed?

    d. What attitude does the worker convey to the client?

    SOCIAL WORKER: Hello. Are you Leah? I'm Mr. Short. Won't you come into my office? (brief small talk in office)

    SOCIAL WORKER: So, what is your problem? How can I help you?

    CLIENT: Well, I don't really know where to begin. Right now my life is a mess. I've gotten along well so far, but lately . . . well, I'm just not coping very well. (client pauses, wipes tears with a Kleenex)

    SOCIAL WORKER: Okay, calm down. Try not to cry. Have you been to this agency before? By the way, how old are you?

    CLIENT: No, this is the first time. I wonder if anyone will ever give me a chance. Sometimes I feel, Why not give up? I feel so scared all the time. Don't get me wrong—I really want to work, to be independent, to buy my kids all the things I haven't been able to afford. I just don't know if I can do it. I haven't worked in ten years. Plus, there's the problem of daycare . . . the things you read . . . it's hard to know whom to trust. Things just seemed so much easier when my husband was alive.

    SOCIAL WORKER: You say you haven't worked in ten years. What was the last job you held? What did you do? What are your job skills?

    CLIENT: Mostly, I've worked as a secretary. It was okay, but I don't want to do that anymore. I really don't have a clue what I'd like.

    SOCIAL WORKER: So, you know you want to get out of clerical work, but you're unsure what else you might do or like.

    CLIENT: Yes, exactly.

    SOCIAL WORKER: Have you considered social services? There are lots of good programs that you could complete in a short time.

    CLIENT: No, I don't think I'd like that.

SOCIAL WORKER: How can you be sure until you give it a try? Sometimes volunteer work is a really good way to find out if you like it.

CLIENT (HESITATES):   Well . . . I guess so.

SOCIAL WORKER: Actually, I was in the same boat as you. Then I volunteered. Next thing I knew I was back in school. Now I'm working full time and loving it. I have a friend who works at the volunteer bureau. Why don't I give her a call and set up an appointment for you?

CLIENT (HESITATES):   Okay . . . thanks.

SOCIAL WORKER: No problem. I was glad to be of help. I'll phone her, then I'll give you a call. It'll probably be next week or so.

17.   The purpose of this exercise is develop your ability to "track" the flow of an interview including identifying the use of particular interviewing and counseling skills. Work with student colleagues. One student will be the counselor, another the client, with one or more observers. Videotape a fifteen-minute segment of a counseling interview and/or use a verbatim transcript of the session to assist your review. Classify each counselor response (e.g., open question, closed question, silence, empathy, self-disclosure or mixed response). Use the following table to compile interview statistics. Place a check in the box each time a particular skill is used. Notice that the table is organized to divide the interview into time segments.

	0–5 minutes	6–10 minutes	11–15 minutes
Open question			
Closed question			
Indirect question			
Silence			
Empathy			
Self-disclosure			
Directive			
Summary			
Paraphrase			
Other (specify)			

Some questions to consider:

- Did the counselor use a variety of different responses?
- To what extent did the counselor vary his or her approach as the session progressed?
- What interview transitions were apparent? Were they appropriate? Consider, for example, whether the transition occurred prematurely, before concrete understanding or exploration was completed.
- What skills were overused or underused?
- Which responses were productive? Which responses were counterproductive?

7 Empowerment

The Purpose of Counseling

Preview

After reading this chapter you should be able to:

- describe the elements of empowering clients
- identify the categories of motivational problems
- describe strategies for overcoming motivational problems
- explain the use of confrontation
- know the principles of effective confrontation
- detect when to avoid confrontation
- identify different types of thinking errors
- be aware of strategies for confronting thinking errors
- define reframing
- demonstrate the ability to assist clients by reframing
- explain the importance of goal setting
- list criteria for effective goals
- demonstrate the ability to use problem statements as the basis for goal setting
- demonstrate the ability to help clients set goals
- identify the steps of action planning and implementation

Empowerment and Change

In Chapter 3, the concept of empowerment was introduced and defined as the process of helping clients discover personal strengths and capacities so that they are able to take control of their lives. The foundation for empowerment in counseling is the belief that clients are capable and have a right to manage their own lives. An empowerment attitude focuses on the capacities and strengths of clients. Empowerment values and methods require workers to forego any need to control clients by taking on an "expert" role that puts clients in positions of dependency. Giving priority to empowerment constrains social workers from hiding behind professional jargon. Social workers should demystify the counseling process by discussing their methods and assumptions with clients.

Self-determination, an important component of client empowerment, is promoted by helping clients recognize choices and by encouraging them to make independent decisions. Social workers should not do for clients what they can and should do for themselves. When empowerment is the priority, clients become the experts.

McWhirter asserts that the potentially empowering aspects of counseling include "an underlying belief in basic human potential and in clients' ability to cope with their life problems, a collaborative definition of the problem and therapeutic goals, skill enhancement and development, recognition and analysis of systemic power dynamics and an emphasis on group and community identity" (1991:226).

Often clients come from disadvantaged and marginalized groups, in which they have significant feelings of powerlessness. McWhirter defines the term *powerless* as "being unable to direct the course of one's life due to societal conditions and power dynamics, lack of skills, or lack of faith that one can change one's life" (1991:224). Sometimes powerlessness arises from negative self-evaluation and low self-esteem. Sometimes the systems that are set up to assist clients are themselves oppressive and contribute to powerlessness. Carniol, in describing the welfare system, observes, "As for the clients, evidence shows that they often find themselves blamed for the problems they face. They find they don't get the help they need or they don't get nearly enough to make a difference—or they get 'cut off'" (1995:3).

Similarly, racism and other prejudices may deny clients access to jobs and resources such as adequate housing. A full discussion of these realities is beyond the scope of this book, but they serve as a reminder to social workers and other professionals that they have some responsibility to advocate for progressive changes within the systems that serve clients. As well, their work should involve them in advocating for clients by assisting them in accessing services and resources that will help them meet their needs. Shulman (1992) stresses the need for workers to have faith in the capacity of systems to change. Moreover, he argues that professionals have a responsibility not just to work with the problems of individuals, but also to promote social change. His view is echoed by Carniol, who ends his book with this challenge: "Social justice demands a transformation of power, including a basic redistribution of wealth—so that the practice of democracy comes within the reach of everyone, rather than being manipulated by those who now dominate the heights of our political and social structures" (1995:153).

This perspective draws professionals into broader activities, including working to identify and remove gaps and barriers to service and encouraging more humane and accessible policies and services. In addition, as McWhirter argues, empowerment requires that clients "gain some degree of critical awareness of systemic power dynamics" (1991:225). One way workers can achieve this end is to provide clients with information on groups and organizations whose efforts are directed toward changing problematic elements of the system.

The beginning phase offers many clients a unique opportunity to explore their situation and their feelings. Active listening skills help clients bring long-forgotten or misunderstood feelings to the surface. Ventilation of feelings can energize clients, and it can lead to spontaneous insight into new ways of handling problems that seemed insurmountable. For some clients, the work of counseling is finished at this phase.

Other clients need additional assistance as they work to change established patterns. This may involve workers in one or more of five empowering activities:

1. *Motivating.* Clients may have made conscious decisions to change and their motivation may be high, but they often have mixed feelings about replacing established behavior with new ways of behaving. Sometimes change involves a "selling" job. Clients need to convince themselves that the benefits of change outweigh the risks, and they need to develop attitudes and beliefs about their capacity for change. Social workers can try to motivate clients to take the risk of developing and executing action plans based on measurable and achievable goals. Ultimately, the principle of self-determination requires that clients make the decision to change, but adherence to this principle does not preclude workers from involving clients in critical thinking about their behavior and the wisdom of change.

2. *Confronting.* Confronting, one of the challenging skills introduced in Chapter 1, is a tool for providing new information to clients so that they critically evaluate their behavior and ideas. Confrontation can be provocative because it challenges clients' perceptions and assumptions. It brings to the foreground issues that clients might ignore, deny, or rationalize. Confrontation may push clients to take responsibility for their actions, or it may cause them to face the painful reality of the effect of the behavior on themselves and others.

3. *Helping clients think differently.* Sometimes clients remain stuck because they cling to established but ineffective ways of thinking. Social workers can use a range of techniques for helping clients think differently. Reframing, for example, helps clients become unstuck from the limits of their current thinking by providing alternative explanations for events.

4. *Goal setting.* Goals provide specific targets for clients to work toward. Having clear goals is essential for developing action plans or strategies to reach these targets. Goal setting is used as a first step in helping clients to plan a systematic change in their lives.

5. *Action planning.* Action planning involves setting up strategies for achieving goals. Typically, this involves helping clients identify, evaluate, and select alternatives, then helping them execute systematic action plans. As a result, clients expand their repertoire of coping skills. For example, they develop new or expanded capacities to manage feelings and to make intelligent decisions, or they learn to be assertive and able to utilize community and societal resources.

The balance of this chapter discusses the skills of motivating, confronting, helping clients to think differently, goal setting, and action planning.

Motivating Clients

Motivational Problems

Motivation in counseling refers to the extent to which clients are willing to involve themselves in the change process. Johnson identifies three factors that are important for motivation: "the push of discomfort, the pull of hope that something can be done to relieve the problem or accomplish a task, and internal pressures and drives toward reaching a goal" (1992:113). Thus, a person must not only want to change, but also must have some belief in his or her capacity to change.

The concept of secondary gain is a useful way of understanding why some people resist change despite the obvious pain or losses involved in maintaining their current situation. Secondary gain refers to the benefits that people derive from their problems. These benefits may include "increased personal attention, disability compensation, and decreased responsibility, as well as more subtle gratifications such as satisfying the need for self-punishment or the vengeful punishment of others who are forced to take responsibility" (Nicholi, 1988:13).

Change is stressful because it requires giving up established patterns of behavior or thinking, and clients will differ in the extent to which they have the skill or energy to take the associated risks. The essential elements of high motivation are:

1. willingness to engage in the work of counseling
2. commitment to devote energy and resources to the change process
3. capacity to sustain effort over time and in the face of obstacles
4. sufficient self-esteem to sustain the courage to change (Shebib, 1997:252)

Social workers can assess clients based on these four elements and then design appropriate strategies to meet each client's particular need. These four elements suggest two major motivational tasks for counselors: engaging clients to commit to change and supporting and energizing clients as they deal with the stresses of obstacles to change.

CONVERSATION **7.1**
Working with "Lazy" Clients

STUDENT: The clients I have the most trouble with are the lazy ones—like the ones who won't even get out of bed in the morning to go looking for a job or the clients who never follow through on commitments.

TEACHER: Sure, these clients can be exceptionally difficult and frustrating to work with. Sometimes it's hard to do, but we should discipline ourselves to be nonjudgmental regarding motivation. Although it might be tempting to label some clients as lazy, we should remember that they may have given up for good reason. Perhaps society has not provided the resources or support they need for change. Clients may have given up in order to protect themselves from the further damage to their self-esteem that would come from repeated failure. In this way, their behavior may be seen as adaptive. It's normal for people to lose patience with them and give up, but it's important to remember that that's precisely what they did to themselves—give up. That's one of the reasons they need counseling.

One way to further organize thinking about motivating clients is to classify motivational problems. Five categories are identified, but individual clients may have characteristics from more than one category. There are five categories: clients in denial, involuntary clients, burnt-out clients, ambivalent clients, and energized clients.

Clients in Denial.   Some clients do not perceive themselves as having a problem, despite the fact that their behavior is problematic for them or others in their lives. Predictably, their motivation is low unless feedback, confrontation, or personal crisis can be used to overcome their denial and increase their awareness of the need for change. These clients are not thinking about change.

> **EXAMPLE:** *Andy's drinking is clearly a problem, but even though he lost his last job owing to chronic absenteeism caused by his drinking, he continues to assert that he is a social drinker.*

For these clients, workers need to direct their attention toward getting their clients to look at their situation and its consequences. Workers can provide information, offer feedback, or encourage reflection with questions such as "Is what you're doing now working to meet your needs?" Workers should proceed slowly when confronting denial, and they should remember that denial may be a defense mechanism that enables people to cope, perhaps by shielding them from feelings of hopelessness (George, in McNeece and DiNitto, 1998).

Involuntary Clients.   Some clients are involuntary and resent being forced into counseling. These clients may resist change because they are in denial and do not see the need for change or because their feelings about being forced into counseling have aroused their defenses.

> **EXAMPLE 1:** *Rupert was referred by his employer because of his continual difficulty in getting along with coworkers. He claims that others in his work team have difficulty dealing with his assertive manner. He comes to see the counselor, but it is quickly evident that his main motivation is to preserve his job.*
>
> **EXAMPLE 2:** *As a condition of probation, Harold was required by the judge to see a counselor for help with his anger.*

However, not all involuntary clients are unmotivated. Some would not have entered counseling on their own, but once coerced they accept and even welcome the opportunity.

> **EXAMPLE:** *Chris begins withdrawing large amounts of cash from his life savings. An alert bank teller who has known Chris for some time is concerned about what appears to be a sudden change in his behavior. She phones his son, who confronts Chris. When confronted, Chris says that he hears voices that are directing him. His son urges him to seek help, but he refuses. Reluctantly, his son consults with the family doctor, who arranges for Chris to be admitted to a hospital for assessment. Almost immediately, Chris responds and thanks his son for his intervention.*

Burnt-out Clients.   Another group of clients may be "burnt-out" from previous unsuccessful attempts at change. They may lack self-esteem and believe that they do not have the skill, capacity, or energy to change.

EXAMPLE: *Peter (55) has been unemployed for almost two years, but he has not looked for a job for months. He says, "There's no work out there. Besides, who is going to hire a man of my age?"*

Seligman's (1975) concept of learned helplessness is a useful perspective for understanding these clients. People with learned helplessness come to believe that their actions do not matter. They believe that they have no control over their lives and that what happens to them is more likely because of chance. Hence, they are unlikely to extend any effort to change. Their beliefs are reflected in statements such as the following:

- "You have to be at the right place at the right time to succeed."
- "If I'm successful, it's because the task was easy."
- "It doesn't matter if I work hard."
- "To get ahead, you have to know the right people."
- "There's nothing I can do about it."

These clients may have made many unsuccessful efforts to solve their problems or cope with their situation. They are often in a state of crisis, with considerable associated stress. Although they desire change, they doubt it will happen, and they believe that if change is to occur, it will be beyond their control.

Ambivalent Clients.   A common motivational challenge for workers is dealing with clients who are ambivalent about change. These clients may vacillate between wanting to alter their lives and resisting any shifts in their behavior or lifestyle.

EXAMPLE: *Agnes has been in an abusive relationship for years. She wishes that she could leave and start over. In fact, she has left her husband twice in the past, but each time she returned within a few weeks.*

Energized Clients.   For some clients, dissatisfaction with their current lifestyle or personal crisis precipitates a need for change, and they voluntarily seek counseling for assistance. These clients come to counseling energized and committed to the change process. Their motivation is high, and they readily engage as willing participants in counseling. Although these clients are highly motivated, their motivation may be fragile if they are not helped to deal with obstacles and setbacks that might arise as they develop and carry out action plans. They also may need help to sustain any changes they make.

EXAMPLE: *Iris, a young single parent, is excited about the possibility of returning to school. She sees a school counselor for assistance with enrollment in the high school's special program for teen moms. She has not yet considered issues such as day care.*

Table 7.1 provides some strategies for dealing with a range of motivational challenges. Counselors need to appropriately adapt these strategies to individual clients.

TABLE 7.1   Motivational Strategies

Motivational Problem	Counseling Goal	Strategy Choices
Denial: clients who do not believe that they have a problem	Increase awareness of the need for change	Provide or encourage clients to seek information about their behavior and its effect on others Provide feedback confrontation Use family and friends to influence clients to change Use authority Help clients become aware of "attractive" alternatives Use films, brochures, books, self-assessment questionnaires as tools to increase clients' insight
Involuntary: clients who resent being forced into counseling	Empower client, reduce hostility and resistance	Explore feelings and concerns openly Show empathy Self-disclose your own responses to being forced against your wish Empower clients (e.g., give them choices, involve them in decision making and goal setting) Encourage client-initiated goals (i.e., try to find an issue, however small, that interests the client)
Burnt-out: clients who have given up owing to failure or frustration, and clients who do not believe in their ability to change	Rekindle hope and optimism; improve self-esteem regarding capacity to change	Explore to assess why previous action plans failed (emphasize failure of plans, not failure of clients) Search for elements of success in previous actions Help clients understand and manage self-defeating inner talk Set small but achievable goals and develop detailed action plans Give positive reinforcement for any effort at change Reframe past failures as learning experiences Use support groups Convey hope
Ambivalent: clients who are ambivalent about changing	Resolve ambivalence in favor of change	Demonstrate empathy toward mixed feelings and pressures Avoid arguing in favor of change (this

(continued)

TABLE 7.1   Continued

Motivational Problem	Counseling Goal	Strategy Choices
		leaves the client free to argue against change) Assist clients to identify obstacles and barriers to change and help them develop ways to overcome these barriers
Energized: motivated clients who are actively seeking to change	Maintain the momentum of change	Provide positive reinforcement and encouragement Help with systematic planning and goal setting Help clients identify and deal with potential obstacles

Confronting Clients

For many people, confrontation suggests conflict and hostility, but in counseling, effective confrontation is not considered a hostile act. Confrontation is a way of directing clients' attention to aspects of their personality or behavior that they might otherwise overlook. It is a tool to move clients to a higher level of understanding of themselves and others. Caring confrontation can deepen the level of trust in the counseling relationship. It is a major skill for helping clients develop fresh perspectives on themselves and their behavior. Gilliland and James (1998) contend that caring confrontation is a way of valuing or respecting the client. They conclude that "confronting client excuses, explanations, or rationalizations is necessary to facilitate client movement toward responsible behavior" (283). Egan (1998) describes confrontation as a way to encourage clients toward more effective living.

In general, confrontation may be useful for addressing incongruities between what clients believe and the way they act; self-defeating ways of thinking and behaving; behavior that is harmful to self or others; blind spots; blaming behavior; communication problems; and strengths.

Types of Confrontation

Two types of confrontation are feedback confrontation and confrontation of incongruities. **Feedback confrontation** is used to provide new information to clients about who they are, including how they are perceived by others and the effects of their behavior on others. Feedback confrontation can be used to help clients become aware of the consequences of their decisions and actions. Feedback confrontation is not reserved for negative or critical feedback—it can also be used to identify strengths.

In some cases, clients have blind spots regarding the harmful effect of their behavior on themselves and others. They continue to behave in ways that are hurtful, yet they lack insight into how they are affecting others. Because they are unaware and fail to see their behavior as problematic, they have no motivation to change. Feedback confrontation is designed to help clients examine the consequences of their actions. Some examples of clients' blind spots are:

- Jerry thinks of himself as humorous, but he is unaware that his jokes are offensive and sexist.
- Nathan has bad breath and body odor.
- Parvinder is unaware of how his aggressive behavior pushes others away.
- Estelle has been in a series of relationships in which she has been battered. She does not understand how this has affected her children.

Despite its potential to be a powerful helping tool, feedback is often misused. Some workers avoid it, perhaps because they fear that they might alienate their clients or arouse their anger. At other times, counselors feel the need to keep the helping relationship pleasant, so they distort or lie to clients to sustain their approval.

In fact, there are risks to confrontation, and some clients do react poorly. They may respond with hostility and attempt to question the integrity or credibility of the worker. Such a hostile reaction may be a type of denial, indicating that the client is simply not ready to acknowledge the validity of the confrontation. Hostile reactions are more likely when feedback or confrontation is unsolicited, but they may occur even when clients appear to be seeking information or feedback, usually out of a need for approval or support for the status quo. Workers also need to consider that harsh client reactions may arise for legitimate reasons. Sometimes feedback is confusing, or the manner and tone of the worker are abrupt. Mature workers are open to the possibility that they may have erred.

Confrontation of incongruities is directed at inconsistencies and mixed messages, for example:

- discrepancy between a client's verbal and nonverbal messages

    CLIENT: *(crying) It's really nothing. I'm not bothered.*

- discrepancy between a client's values or beliefs and behavior

    CLIENT: *There's nothing more important to me than my kids. I know I haven't spent much time with them. It's just so hard to say no to my buddies when they ask me to help.*

- discrepancy between what a client says and what he or she does; for example, a client commits to look for work, yet consistently has an excuse for not acting on agreed-on plans

In confronting discrepancies, it is important that social workers remain calm and nonjudgmental while presenting clients with specific facts. Ivey offers these confrontation leads as suggestions: "The model sentence, 'On the one hand . . . , and on the other hand . . . ,' provides a standard and useful format for actual confrontation. Variations include 'You say . . . but you do . . . ,' 'I see . . . at one time, and at another time, I see . . . ,' and 'Your words say . . . , but your actions say . . .' " (1982:196).

Principles for Effective Confrontation

Confrontation is an option, not a requirement. When deciding to confront, social workers should consider a number of variables, including relevance, client receptivity, contracting, specificity, and the use of other skills in combination.

Relevance.   Confrontation should serve the goals of counseling by leading the client to improved ways of behaving, thinking, and feeling. Relevant confrontation meets the needs of the client. It is inappropriate for a worker to use confrontation as a means to vent frustration or anger. When confrontation arises for this reason, the worker may frame it as being "in the client's best interests," but, in reality, it is the need of the worker that is being met. Workers may rationalize that they are confronting clients in order to help them when, in fact, they are confronting in order to punish them (Egan, 1998).

When workers have feelings related to the relationship or the work, it is better if they deal with them directly by using *I*-statements rather than by trying to mask their feelings as helpful feedback (Gordon, 1971; Martin, 1983). *I*-statements are assertions about personal feelings or reactions that do not blame or judge others. Instead of saying "You don't care," an *I*-message would be "I feel hurt and angry when you don't answer my letters." *I*-statements are much less likely to cause resistance.

Client Receptivity.   Confrontation must be timed appropriately to minimize defensive reactions. Workers can use confrontation when clients are ready and willing to take advantage of feedback or if there is a reasonable possibility that feedback can motivate them to change. Workers need to pay attention to timing and ensure that there is a well-developed counseling relationship to support confrontation. As a general rule, it is preferable to avoid strong confrontation in the beginning phase of counseling. Clients are more receptive and likely to accept feedback as credible when there is a relationship of trust. Otherwise clients may feel insulted and misunderstood. They may never return.

Confrontation should be timed closely to relevant behavior, events, or circumstances. If a worker uses confrontation to challenge a client's defensive behavior, it is more appropriate immediately after a client is defensive rather than a week later. However, there should be enough time left in the interview to adequately handle the confrontation.

Contracting.   Social workers can use the contracting process to increase clients' acceptance of confrontation. The following excerpt provides an example of this technique:

> **SOCIAL WORKER:**   *One of the ways I might be able to help is by sharing some of my impressions about what you're doing, or even about our relationship. What do you think?*
>
> **CLIENT:**   *Sure. I'd appreciate that.*

>**SOCIAL WORKER:** *Well, let's look ahead. Suppose I wanted to give you some feed-back about something I thought you were doing wrong that you were not aware of. What would be the best way for me to approach you?*
>
>**CLIENT:** *I don't like to be overwhelmed. And I like the good mixed with the bad.*

In the above example, the social worker and the client are working toward agreement about how and when feedback might be given. Such contracting enables the worker to "customize" feedback to meet the needs and expectations of the client. Subsequently, when the worker offers feedback, it is much less likely to meet with resistance because it is given in a way that is most acceptable to the client. Contracting is a way of asking for the client's permission to confront or give feedback. As with all skills of counseling, social workers must develop versatility so that they can confront or give feedback in a variety of ways. Some clients like blunt feedback; others prefer it "sandwiched" between positive statements.

Specificity.   Effective confrontation needs to be specific without attacking the personality of the client.

>**COUNSELOR (CHOICE 1—INEFFECTIVE CONFRONTATION):** *You don't seem at all interested in what's happening here. If you're too lazy to care about our work, why don't you just quit?*
>
>**COUNSELOR (CHOICE 2—MORE EFFECTIVE CONFRONTATION):** *When you don't show up for appointments, I wonder whether you're as committed to your goals as you say you are.*
>
>**COUNSELOR (CHOICE 3—MOST EFFECTIVE CONFRONTATION):** *I think your best work has happened on those days when you came on time and when you took the effort to focus. My sense is that if you could make every appointment you'd get a lot more out of our time together.*

In Choice 1, the worker's words attack the client. The worker judges the client's behavior but provides no concrete or usable information. In Choice 2, the worker is more effective because the confrontation is linked to specific client behavior. Choice 3 focuses on strengths. The principle here is that people are motivated more by positive feedback than by negative feedback (Hamachek, 1982). Moreover, by focusing on strengths, clients can be clearer about what they can do that will be more effective.

Combining with Other Skills.   As a rule, confrontation should be used in combination with other counseling skills, particularly empathy and support. Confrontation may involve feedback that is unsettling for clients, and empathy helps workers remain sensitive to the impact of confrontation. Social workers should confront clients, but not without offering them assistance to develop new methods. Confrontation should be measured to avoid overwhelming clients with more than they can handle. Ideally, confrontation should not undermine the self-esteem of clients. Egan offers this valuable suggestion: "Confront only if you want to grow closer to the person you're confronting" (1977: 220). Similar sentiments are reflected by Corey and Corey, who offer this advice to counselors: "Challenge clients only if you feel an investment in them and if you have the time and effort to continue building the relationship with them" (1989:54).

Clients may respond defensively to feedback, but after reflection they may be more accepting. Alternatively, they may appear to be accepting but later become resentful. Thus, it is important to check with clients how they feel about the feedback or confrontation. Social workers should monitor immediate reactions. As well, they should check back with the client during the next session to identify delayed reactions and to pick up on any feelings that might impair the relationship. The example below illustrates the process:

> **SOCIAL WORKER:** *I'm wondering how you felt about our last meeting. Remember, I shared with you some of my opinions about what you are doing that seems to distance you from your family.*
>
> **CLIENT:** *I almost didn't come today.*
>
> *(silence)*
>
> **SOCIAL WORKER:** *Because?*
>
> **CLIENT:** *I was embarrassed by what you thought of me.*
>
> **SOCIAL WORKER:** *You thought that I might think less of you.*
>
> **CLIENT:** *Yes.*
>
> **SOCIAL WORKER:** *Would you like to find out for sure what I think?*
>
> **CLIENT:** *Okay.*

This worker's strategy sets the stage to help the client correct any distortions, and it is crucial for dealing with the aftermath of confrontation. It also reinforces that any feelings about what happens in the counseling relationship can be dealt with openly.

Self-Awareness and Confrontation

Some workers are reluctant to confront. As Egan (1998) concludes, this is a potentially healthy position that can help them guard against overusing this skill or using it in a way that is destructive to clients. However, effective workers need to have the ability and willingness to confront when necessary. Self-awareness regarding one's beliefs, fears, and expectations regarding confrontation is crucial to using this skill appropriately.

Sometimes, beginning professionals (and some experienced ones, too) are reluctant to confront. Here are some of their candid thoughts:

- "I was brought up to believe that if you don't have something good to say, then don't say anything at all."
- "If I confront, I might damage the relationship. I don't want to upset my clients."
- "I don't want to hurt my clients."
- "My clients might retaliate."

Most of the above beliefs arise from an erroneous understanding of confrontation as a "no holds barred" assault on clients. Such confrontation strategies should, of course, be avoided. On the other hand, refraining from confronting clients under any circumstance is an evasion of responsibility that cuts clients off from the potential benefits of new information and feedback. Competent workers do not withhold potentially useful feedback.

When to Avoid Confrontation

Confrontation should never be used as an outlet for a worker's anger or frustration. When workers are not in control of their own feelings, clients are more likely to view them as aggressive and to feel their confrontation is unsupportive. The counseling relationship is formed to meet the needs of clients, and responsible workers will forego their own needs to this end. They should be self-aware to know their reasons for wanting to confront.

Confrontation requires that workers are willing to invest time to help their clients understand any feedback. As well, they must be available to help clients deal with any feelings that may result from the confrontation. Consequently, the end of a counseling interview is generally a poor time to confront.

Workers should consider their clients' ability to handle confrontation. When clients are already overwhelmed with feelings, confrontation may add to their stress but contribute little to their ability to cope. Some clients, such as those who are highly defensive and guarded, may respond poorly to confrontation. In such situations, workers may find it wise to delay or avoid confrontation entirely.

Although confrontation has potential for motivating clients to change and can assist clients in developing insight, misuse of confrontation can be destructive. As a rule, workers should use it sparingly and should be prepared to offer support and caring to ensure that confrontation does not overwhelm or devastate their clients.

Helping Clients Think Differently

> *The fact that a client firmly defends a life style that he knows is unworkable is proof that he is in need of great assistance and support.*
>
> —Wicks and Parsons, 1984:171

Thinking Errors

Sometimes clients have difficulty breaking out of established patterns because of the way they think about issues or problems (DeBono, 1984). Five types of **thinking errors** are distortion, incomplete analysis, egocentricity, rigidity, and self-defeating thought. Of course, there may be overlap between the five categories. The five types of thinking errors that result in faulty logic are discussed below.

Distortion.   This type of thinking error arises from misinterpretations, faulty assumptions, or cultural biases. If a client from a culture in which direct eye contact is discouraged works with a social worker who interprets direct eye contact as a sign of warmth, there is a risk that the client will come to erroneous conclusions about the worker. He or she may determine that the workers is intrusive or disrespectful.

Incomplete Analysis.   This error comes from failure to look at all aspects of a problem or situation. For example, prison inmates may overestimate their ability to cope with life outside jail. Their thinking may become clouded by unrealistic optimism that they will be able to avoid getting caught, or, if they are apprehended, by rationalization that they will beat the charges. In addition, they may neglect to consider the long-term consequences of their criminal behavior, a pattern of thinking that is characteristic of lifestyle of habitual criminals. Walters reached this conclusion: "Until high rate offenders realize the self-destructive nature of their super-optimism, they will continue to resist change because they are operating on the mistaken belief that they can get away with just about any crime" (1991:36). Walters attributes lazy thinking as the root of the offenders' problems. Even those with the best of intentions may find themselves in trouble because they failed to think about long-term outcomes.

Egocentricity or Lack of Empathy.   Egocentricity thinking errors come from a failure or inability to consider other people's ideas or to look at how one's behavior affects others. Clients may adopt an arrogant position of self-righteousness, being confident that their ideas and conclusions are sound. Egocentric thinkers are likely to be seen by others as aggressive and insensitive, interested in meeting only their own needs. Egocentric thinkers are not only poor thinkers, they are also poor listeners. Typically, they believe that the purpose of thinking, listening, and responding is to prove themselves right. De Bono contends that self-protection is a major impediment to thinking: "The main restriction on thinking is ego defence, which is responsible for most of the practical faults of thinking" (1985:29).

Rigidity.   This common thinking problem is characterized by failure to be open to new ideas and by "black-and-white" thinking. De Bono made this important observation: "Unfortunately, Western thinking, with its argument habits, prefers to give a conclusion first and then to bring in the facts to support that conclusion" (1985:35). Rigid thinkers act as if to say, "We'll keep talking until you agree with me."

Self-Defeating Thought.   Albert Ellis has written a great deal about irrational thinking and its impact on emotions and behavior (1962; 1984; 1993a; 1993b). Ellis argues that people's belief systems influence how they respond to and understand problems and events. When their beliefs are irrational and characterized by an unrealistic "should," they are likely to experience emotional anxiety or disturbance. This thinking is often accompanied by self-deprecating internal dialogue: "I'm no good. . . . Everyone must think I'm an idiot," and "No one likes me." Ellis concludes that irrational beliefs fall into three general categories with associated rigid demands or "shoulds":

1. "I (ego) absolutely must perform well and win significant others' approval or else I am an inadequate, worthless person."

TABLE 7.2 Helping Clients Change Thinking Patterns

Problem	Example	Counseling Choices
Distortion	A client assumes that quiet members in her social circle are "aloof and stuck-up."	Provide alternative explanations (e.g., cultural norms). Encourage clients to check the validity of assumptions (e.g., by talking with others about the meaning of their behavior).
Incomplete analysis	A man decides to quit drinking but neglects to consider the obstacles that he must overcome. A young man decides to quit school so he can get a job and buy a new car.	Ask questions targeted to the overlooked area. Provide or encourage clients to find new information. Confront gaps in reasoning. Encourage clients to consult others. Challenge clients to consider the long-term implications of their actions.
Egocentricity or lack of empathy	A juvenile offender has no remorse and does not consider how his crimes adversely affect people. A client does not realize that his humor is sexist and offensive to others.	Teach empathy skills. Role play (i.e., ask clients to assume others' roles). Self-disclose personal feelings. Offer feedback or encourage clients to seek feedback from others.
Rigidity	An aggressive male believes that the only alternative to his present style is to say nothing. A client is prejudiced.	Stimulate new ideas through education and information. Use brainstorming to generate alternative ideas. Identify a range of alternatives. Suggest another frame of reference (reframing). Confront blind spots. Ask clients to assume the role of devil's advocate in order to self-critique their ideas. Assist clients in identifying and critically evaluating assumptions.
Self-defeating thought	A client demands perfection. A client constantly tells herself that she is inadequate.	Encourage clients to become aware of self-defeating thought. Teach techniques such as "thought stopping" to overcome self-defeating inner dialogue.

2. "You (other people) must under all conditions and at all times be nice and fair to me or else you are a rotten, horrible person!"

3. "Conditions under which I live absolutely must be comfortable, safe, and advantageous or else the world is a rotten place, I can't stand it, and life is hardly worth living" (1993a:7).

Wicks and Parsons offer a similar perspective when they suggest that many clients are discouraged because they set unattainable goals: "These goals are often based on irrational, simplistic views: (1) if a person acts properly, everyone will like him; and (2) either a person is totally competent or he is completely inadequate" (1984:170).

To counteract **self-defeating thought,** people need to change their way of thinking and correct irrational beliefs.

One of the important goals of counseling is to help clients correct faulty reasoning by encouraging them to consider things differently. Table 7.2 (page 207) lists possible strategies for dealing with common thinking errors.

TABLE 7.3   Reframing

Client's Perspective or Statement	Counselor's Reframed Idea
This counseling is a waste of time.	Sounds like you've done some thinking about how our work could be more relevant to you.
I don't fit in. I come from a different culture and my ideas and values must seem strange.	Of course, some people have not had experience with your culture and they may be frightened. Perhaps you could look at this in a different way. Your experiences might also be fascinating for people who have not lived outside the country. They might welcome your fresh ideas.
I'm very shy. When I first join a group, I usually don't say anything.	You like to be patient until you have a sense of what's happening. People who are impulsive are working to develop this skill. You also seem to want to develop alternatives, such as being more expressive in the beginning.
For the first time in 20 years, I'm without a job.	Obviously, this is devastating. At the same time, I wonder if this might also be an opportunity for you to try something different.
Whenever I'm late for curfew, my mother waits up for me and immediately starts screaming at me.	I'm curious about why she might do this. Perhaps she has trouble telling you how scared she is that something may have happened to you. It might seem strange, but her anger could be her way of saying how much she loves you.

Reframing

Reframing is a counseling skill that helps clients shift or modify their thinking. Reframing attempts to help clients look at things differently by suggesting alternative interpretations or new meanings. It empowers clients by focusing on solutions and redefining negatives as opportunities or challenges. Cormier and Cormier (1985) emphasize that reframed ideas should be positive; for example, client stubbornness might be reframed as independence, or greediness as ambitiousness. Table 7.3 lists some examples of reframing.

In each of the examples in Table 7.3, other counseling responses may need to be used before presenting reframed ideas. For example, exploration is important in order to fully understand the client's current perspective. As well, empathy is crucial; otherwise, clients may conclude that their feelings are discounted or trivialized.

Reframing should not be confused with issuing platitudes, such as "It's always darkest just before dawn" or other such statements, which are typically not very supportive or helpful. An example of a well-meaning but misguided reframe that people are apt to give in times of grief over the loss of a child is "You're young—you can have more children." "Because strong emotions of sadness and loss are present, most people cannot accept a reframing that does not take into account the most salient feature of their experience—the grief itself" (Young, 1998:282). Reframing does not trivialize complex problems with pat answers; rather, it offers a reasonable and usable alternative frame of reference.

Clark (1998) offers guidelines for the use of reframing in group counseling, but the principles apply equally well to individual counseling. His guidelines are summarized as follows:

1. Use reframing to help clients break out of thinking that is self-defeating, constricted, or at an impasse.
2. Make sure that clients are not so emotionally distracted that they are unable to hear or process the reframed idea.
3. Offer a reframed idea in a tentative way that invites consideration.
4. Ensure that reframed ideas are plausible.
5. Allow clients sufficient time to consider a reframed idea. Clients with firmly entrenched perspectives may not immediately accept logical and sound reframes, but with gentle persuasion and patience, they may begin to accept new ideas.

Even though it may be obvious that a client's thinking is distorted, it may be wise to hold back on reframing until the client's problem is fully explored. Moreover, as suggested above, it is important that the client's feelings be acknowledged through empathy. Exploration and empathy ensure that the worker understands the client's feelings and situation, and they provide a basis for the client to consider reframed ideas as reasonable or worthy of consideration. If counselors push clients too quickly, clients may feel devalued and misunderstood and, in response, may resist new ideas. Empathy helps workers to establish and maintain credibility with their clients.

Workers can use directives to invite clients to use different language (Young, 1998). For example, when clients avoid responsibility for their actions with statements such as "I can't get organized," workers can challenge them by proposing that they rephrase with statements such as "I won't let myself get organized." A client might say, "She makes me

INTERVIEW 7.1
Reframing Techniques

The following interview excerpt illustrates how reframing might be used in a counseling session. The social worker has been working with a community college student to help her deal with some of her fears about public speaking. Note: Reframing is only one of the ways that the worker might help the client deal with the situation. For example, relaxation techniques may help decrease the client's anxiety.

Dialogue	Analysis
CLIENT: Next week I have to make my class presentation. I'm so nervous and it's still a week away. What am I going to be like on the day of my talk? **SOCIAL WORKER:** You're wondering, "What if I'm so rattled I can't handle it at all?" **CLIENT:** Exactly.	In all phases of counseling, empathy is an important response. More than any other skill, it tells clients that they have been heard and that their feelings have been understood.
SOCIAL WORKER: Let's try something different for a minute. What if it were possible to look at your fears differently? **CLIENT:** What do you mean? **SOCIAL WORKER:** I think it's natural when we have a problem to dwell on all its unpleasant aspects. I know that I tend to do that unless I discipline myself not to. For example, when you think of how nervous you are, you think of all the negatives, such as that you might make a fool of yourself or your mind might go blank while you're talking. **CLIENT (LAUGHS):** Or that I might throw up in front of everyone. **SOCIAL WORKER:** Okay, those are real fears. But by considering only your fears, you become fixated on the negatives and you may be overlooking some important positives. If you can look at it differently, you might discover a whole new way of dealing with your class presentation.	The social worker introduces the technique of reframing with a brief rationale. Later in the interview, the worker or the client may wish to discuss the rationale in more detail. The worker's short self-disclosure communicates understanding and a nonjudgmental attitude.
SOCIAL WORKER: Want to try it? (the client nods) Okay, try to identify some positive aspects of your fear. **CLIENT:** Well, I guess I'm not the only one who is scared of public speaking. **SOCIAL WORKER:** So, you know that there will be other people in the class who understand and will be cheering for you to succeed. **CLIENT:** I never thought of that before. Here's another idea: Because I'm so nervous, I'm going to make sure that I'm super prepared.	As a rule, it's more empowering for clients to generate their own suggestions before workers introduce their ideas and suggestions. In this way clients become self-confronting and are more likely to come up with ideas that they will accept as credible.

SOCIAL WORKER: Great. Do you think it might be possible to look at your fears differently? Consider that it's normal to be nervous. Or go a step further. Look at it positively. Maybe there's a part of it that's exciting—kind of like going to a scary movie.

CLIENT: I did come back to school because I hated my boring job. One thing for sure, I'm not bored.

SOCIAL WORKER: So the more you scare yourself, the more you get your money's worth. (the counselor and client laugh)

SOCIAL WORKER: Try this over the next few days. Every time you start to think negatively about your presentation, I want you to deliberately interrupt your thinking to focus on some of the positives.

CLIENT: Okay. Do you think that will help?

SOCIAL WORKER: Absolutely. (explains the theory behind thought stopping) But it takes practice, and you have to discipline yourself not to give up.

The social worker offers the client a reframed way of looking at nervousness. The client's response suggests that this notion is plausible.

Spontaneous humor adds color and vitality to counseling relationship.

The social worker introduces thought stopping—a technique to help clients control self-defeating thinking (Cormier and Cormier, 1985; Gilliland and James, 1998). The basic assumption is that, if self-defeating thoughts are interrupted, they will eventually be replaced by more empowering, positive perspectives.

feel hopeless." In response, the worker can propose that the client rephrase the statement by stating, "I have decided to feel helpless." The latter response underscores the client's control over personal feelings. As part of this work, workers can empower their clients by explaining that clients have ownership over their feelings and no one can make them feel a certain way. After offering a reframe, workers should check for the client's questions and reactions to it. Then, if the reframed idea is accepted, they can encourage further exploration and problem solving based on the new perspective.

Reframing can energize clients. When clients are locked into one way of thinking about their problems, their solutions are limited. When they consider new perspectives, problems that seemed insurmountable might now have new answers. Moreover, reframing can serve to redirect client anxiety away from self-blame to other rational explanations that are less self-punishing. In these ways, effective reframing empowers clients to action, problem resolution, and management of debilitating feelings.

Goal Setting

> *Obstacles are those frightful things you see when you take your eyes off your goals.*
>
> —Anonymous

The Importance of Setting Goals

Goal setting is a counseling process that helps clients define in precise, measurable terms what they hope to achieve from counseling. Two types of goals are outcome goals and process, or task, goals (Jacobs, Masson, and Harvill, 1998; Shebib, 1997). **Outcome goals** relate to what the client hopes to achieve from counseling. These goals have to do with changes in the client's life, such as getting a job, improving communication with a spouse, dealing with painful feelings, or managing self-defeating thoughts. **Process goals** concern the procedures of counseling, including such variables as the frequency of meetings and the nature of the counseling relationship. Process goals include the tasks clients and workers undertake in order to reach the outcome goal. Clearly, the purpose of counseling is to assist clients to reach appropriate outcome goals. Process goals are set as the means to this end. In practice, there may be some overlap between process and outcome goals. For example, a process goal might be to develop trust in the counseling relationship. Success in achieving this process goal might assist the client in achieving an outcome goal targeting improved communication with family and friends.

There is wide support in the counseling literature for the importance of setting goals (Egan, 1998; Young, 1998). Goal setting serves many important purposes, including giving direction, defining roles, motivating, and measuring progress.

Giving Direction.   Goals help to give direction and purpose to the work of counseling. Clearly defined goals serve as beacons that guide and structure the client's actions. Goals help workers and clients make decisions regarding the topics and activities that are relevant to counseling. When clients are clear about their goals, they can begin to structure their thinking and action toward their attainment. Setting goals helps clients make reasoned choices about what they want to do with their lives. Goal setting helps clients prioritize these choices.

Defining Roles.   Goals provide a basis for defining roles. When goals are clear, workers know which skills and techniques are appropriate, and clients know what is expected of them. Moreover, when workers know the goal of the work, they can make intelligent decisions regarding whether they have the skills, capacity, and time to work with the client. If not, they may make a referral.

Motivating.   Goals motivate clients. Setting and reaching goals is therapeutic. Setting goals energizes clients and helps them develop optimism that change is possible. Simply having goals can build self-confidence. Goal achievement confirms personal capacity and further promotes action. Writing down goals may add an extra measure of motivation.

Measuring Progress.   Goals help provide benchmarks of progress, including definition of when the counseling relationship should end—i.e., when the goals have been reached or their pursuit is no longer viable.

Developing Effective Goal Statements

Sometimes clients are able to clearly articulate what they hope to achieve as a result of counseling. Other times they have difficulty expressing their goals. Through systematic interviewing, workers can help these clients define and target their goals. In addition, workers can use their knowledge base to develop simple checklists of potential goals, customized to the common needs and problems of particular client groups. However, goals should be concrete, measurable, challenging but realistic, and "owned" by the client.

Effective Goals Are Concrete.   One defining feature of a counseling relationship is that it is goal directed, but clients may begin counseling with vague and undefined goals, such as:

- "I want to feel better."
- "My husband and I need to get along better."
- "I need to make something of my life."

These goals are useful starting points, but they are useless until they are shaped into terms that are clear and concrete. In the beginning phase, the focus of counseling is to explore problems and feelings. Successful work at the beginning phase should lead to the development of goals that define and structure subsequent work. In the action phase, an important component of this work is helping clients to develop their goals as specific and measurable targets. This step is a prerequisite for action planning—the development of strategies and programs to achieve goals. Vague goals result in vague and ill-defined action plans, but explicit goals lead to precise action plans.

In Chapter 5 tools for increasing concreteness were introduced. Concreteness is the remedy for vagueness. Concreteness can add precision to unclear and ambiguous goals. For example, when clients are describing their goals, workers can use simple encouragers such as "Tell me more" and "Yes, go on" to get a general overview of what clients hope to achieve. This is the first step in shaping workable goals. The next step is to use questions to identify goals, define terms, probe for detail, and develop examples. This step helps to cast the emerging goals in precise language and to move from good intentions and broad aims to specific goals (Egan, 1998). Listed below are some examples of probes and directives that might be used to start the process:

- What is your goal?
- When you say you'd like to feel better, what exactly do you mean?
- Describe how your life would be different if you were able to reach your goal. Try to be as detailed as possible.
- If your problem were to be solved, what would need to be different in your life?
- What do you think would be the best resolution to your problem?
- What are some examples of what you would like to achieve?
- As a result of counseling, what feelings do you want to increase or decrease?
- What do you want to be able to do that you can't do now?
- If I could watch you being successful, what would I see?

Some clients are reluctant or unable to identify goals, and they may respond with a dead-end statement such as "I don't know" when they are asked for their goals. Some responses that might be used to break this impasse include the following: "Guess." "What might your best friend (mother, father, teacher, etc.) suggest as your goal?" "What would you like to achieve, but don't think is possible?" A good general technique is to encourage clients to visualize themselves reaching their goals.

When clients say, "I don't know," their responses may indicate friction in the counseling relationship, and this answer may be a way of sabotaging the work. In such cases, goal setting might be premature, and the focus of the interview may need to shift to relationship problem solving (immediacy). When clients say, "I don't know," they also might be saying, "I can't do it" or "I'm afraid." In such situations, suggesting a very small goal may be a starting point, for example, "If you could make just one tiny change in your life, what would it be?"

The **miracle question** (de Shazer, 1985) is widely used in brief or single-session counseling as a way to help clients who have difficulty coming up with defined goals. A typical miracle question might be formulated as follows: "Suppose that tonight while you're sleeping a miracle happens and your problem is solved. When you wake up, what will be different about your life?" Variations of this question may need to be developed to accommodate different clients. For example, some clients may object to the religious overtones in the question, and a more neutral phrase, such as *something remarkable,* could be used.

Effective Goals Can Be Measured.   Goals need to be able to be measured in some way. When goals are measurable, clients will be able to evaluate progress, and they will know precisely when they have reached their goals. Clear goals sustain clients' enthusiasm and motivation. Vague and unmeasurable goals, on the other hand, can result in apathy and vague action plans. Goals can be defined in terms of changes (increases or decreases) in behaviors, thoughts, or feelings. Example (skill): "My goal is to express my opinion or ask a question once per class." Example (thoughts): "My goal is to manage self-deprecating thought patterns by substituting positive affirmations." Example (feelings): "My goal is to reduce anxiety."

Whenever possible, goals should be framed in quantifiable language with questions such as "How often?" "How many times?" and "How much?" For example, a goal may be to target weight reduction of 20 lbs. Goals should have some realistic schedule or target date. Workers should help clients determine when they are going to start working toward their goals and when they expect to reach them. For example, "Target weight reduction of 20 lbs. in 10 weeks." "Make five calls per day to potential employers."

Effective Goals Are Challenging But Realistic.   Goals have to be something that clients can reasonably expect to achieve, even though it may require effort and commitment. Workers need to consider variables such as the client's interest in achieving the goals, the client's skills and abilities, and the resources (including the worker) that are available to help in reaching the goals. In addition, it is important to help clients set goals that will be significant to managing or changing their problem situation.

Some clients may be reluctant to set challenging goals or even to set goals at all. This could arise for a number of reasons, including:

- poor self-esteem
- fear of failure
- lack of awareness of capacity for change

- fear of change and reluctance to give up established patterns
- lack of resources to support pursuit of the goal (Shebib, 1997:210)

Addressing these issues is a prerequisite to goal setting. In addition, for complex problems and situations in which the client's capacity or self-esteem is low, setting short-term goals or subgoals is particularly useful. Short-term goals represent small, attainable steps toward long-term goals. Their achievement is important for building optimism and helping clients overcome a sense of inadequacy (Pincus and Minahan, 1973).

During the beginning phase of counseling, workers may develop ideas or views on what might be appropriate goals for their clients. Workers should share these ideas, not as prescriptions, but as starting points for negotiation regarding what needs to be done.

> Evelyn was referred to a social worker for help in coping with Trevor, her 18-year-old stepson, who was involved in petty crime. Evelyn's immediate goal was to encourage Trevor to move out of the house, and she hoped that the social workers might help her do this. During the interview, it became apparent to the worker that Evelyn needed help developing parenting skills for dealing with Trevor and her two other teenage stepsons. Without dismissing Evelyn's objective, the social worker suggested that this be part of their agenda.

Effective Goals Are "Owned" by Clients. Clients need to see goals as relevant to their needs and consistent with their values. When clients are involved in the process of deciding what their goals are, they are more likely to be motivated to work toward achieving them. When clients are forced to come to counseling by a third party, they may not feel committed to any of the goals of counseling; thus, the chances of success are diminished greatly unless some mutually acceptable working agreement can be reached.

Understanding a client's values is an important part of goal setting. Some clients are motivated by spiritual values, some by material gain, and others by family values. Some clients focus on immediate gratification, while others have objectives that are long-term.

> Ming left his family in China to come to North America. He has seen his wife only once in the last five years when he returned to his country for a short visit. He maintains regular contact with her and their six-year-old son. He sends much of his monthly pay home to support his wife and extended family. Although he hopes that one day his family will be able to join him, he has accepted that his purpose is to position future generations of his family for a better life.

Clients sometimes set goals that require others to change, such as "I want my husband to stop treating me so badly." Workers need to encourage clients to form goals based on what is under their control, namely their own feelings, behavior, and thoughts.

Client complaints and problem statements can usually be reframed as positively worded goal statements. Here are some examples:

Example 1

CLIENT: *Everyone always takes advantage of me.*

SOCIAL WORKER: *Sounds as though you'd like to learn to stand up for yourself.*

Example 2

CLIENT: *I'm tired of not working.*

SOCIAL WORKER: *Put simply, your goal is to get a job.*

Example 3

CLIENT: *My life is a mess.*

SOCIAL WORKER: *You would like to find a way to get your life in order.*

The above responses change the focus of the interview from problems to goals. Of course, the worker and client will have to work together to shape these vague goals into more explicit terms.

The overall goal of any counseling relationship is change, but, depending on the needs of individual clients, the targets for change might focus on behavior, feelings, thoughts, skills, relationship enhancement, or other areas of the client's life. Table 7.4 (page 220) provides examples of vague goals and specific goals.

Action Planning

Counseling is a developmental process. In the beginning phase, the focus is on establishing a strong working relationship based on a contract that describes the work to be done and the respective roles of both the counselor and the client. The beginning phase is also concerned with problem identification and exploration. This work provides the foundation for clients and workers to define goals. Attention to detail in the beginning phase helps to prevent the problems that come from premature action. Problem exploration leads to goal setting, which, in turn, forms the foundation for action planning.

Problem Exploration ⟶ **Goals** ⟶ **Action Planning**

Goals represent the outcomes that clients are working toward. Having clear goals is a prerequisite to defining action programs for reaching these goals. Some clients, once they have their goals in mind, do not need further counseling assistance. The overall process of developing goals, including the important work of exploring their problems in the begin- ning phase, is sufficient to meet their needs. Other clients may need additional coaching and support to develop and implement systematic action plans. Otherwise, goals can be quickly abandoned like well-intended but ill-conceived New Year's resolutions.

Action planning and implementation consist of a series of steps leading to the client's goal (or subgoal). Put simply, action planning involves developing strategies to help clients get where they want to go. This involves four steps: (1) identify alternatives for action, (2) choose an action strategy, (3) develop and implement plans, and (4) evaluate outcomes.

INTERVIEW 7.2
Goal Setting

The following interview excerpt illustrates goal-setting techniques. Prior to this point, exploration and active listening have enabled the counselor to develop a solid base of understanding. With this work apparently finished, it seems timely to move on to goal setting.

Dialogue	Analysis
SOCIAL WORKER: You've talked about how unhappy you've been and how it's, as you put it, "now or never." That suggests to me that you're ready to make some changes.	The worker recognizes the client's positive motivation for change and uses it to make a transition to goal setting. Problem statements can often be reframed to make goal statements.
CLIENT: Yeah, I'd like to get out of the rut that I've been in for too long.	The client makes a general statement confirming motivation for change. This undeveloped goal is a useful starting point, but it it not yet an operational goal.
SOCIAL WORKER: I think it might be helpful at this point to figure out what you want to achieve, what you'd like to change. This would give you something to work toward. What do you think?	The worker seeks to contract with the client to work on goal setting, and uses the criteria for effective goals as a reference point. As the interview progresses, other questions will be asked that help frame the goal. There is no secret agenda to this, and the worker might decide to review the process with the client. The final open question reaches for client input and agreement.
CLIENT: Sounds good. I think it's time to do something. For one thing, I really haven't invested too much in my marriage. I have to change my priorities.	The client begins to identify an area for change.
SOCIAL WORKER: What do you mean, change your priorities?	The worker requests more definition (goal specificity). This ensures that no assumptions are made.
CLIENT: If possible, I've got to stop spending so much time at work. By the time I get home, I'm so tired that I have no energy or motivation to be involved with my family.	Often, as here, client goals are stated in the negative, i.e., in terms of what the client would like to stop doing.
SOCIAL WORKER: Okay, I think I get a sense that what you'd like is to be more committed to your family. In order to do that, you'd have to cut back on work.	The worker attempts to help the client put an emerging goal statement in behavioral terms by reframing the idea.
CLIENT: Exactly.	
SOCIAL WORKER: Just so we can be clear, can you try to be more specific? Suppose you're successful. What will be different from the way things are now?	This request for more specificity encourages the client to reframe the goals in positive terms by stating what will be done differently.

(continued)

I N T E R V I E W   7.2   Continued

CLIENT: I don't understand. What do you mean?

The client is confused, but the relationship is strong enough that the client is able to ask for help.

SOCIAL WORKER: Well, maybe you can't plan it out exactly, but what do you see happening in terms of the amount of time you'd like to spend with your family? Try to be specific so you'll have something to aim for.

The worker clarifies the question. This helps to educate the client regarding some of the criteria for goal setting.

CLIENT (LAUGHS):   Oh, I see. You want to nail me down and close the deal. You should be a salesperson. Well, I think it's important that I free up the weekends and at least two nights a week. Sunday should be strictly family, a time to do something with the kids.

A clear goal statement has emerged, but the work is not yet finished.

SOCIAL WORKER: From your excited tone, I get the sense that you'd feel really good if you could do that.

Empathy lets the client know that the worker has recognized the client's feelings and their importance.

CLIENT: In my heart, it's what I've always wanted.

The client confirms acceptance of the worker's empathy.

SOCIAL WORKER: A while back, you used the words "if possible" when you talked about cutting back on work. What problems do you anticipate?

An important part of goal setting is to assist the client to look at potential problems, including the relative advantages and disadvantages of goal attainment.

CLIENT: I'd like to try for a management position at the company. But everyone's so competitive. I've got to put in the hours if I'm going to keep my sales above the others. And high sales is the first thing they look for when it's time for promotion.

Having identified this potential barrier, the client can address it, for example, by considering ways to overcome it, or make a decision about whether the costs involved are too high.

SOCIAL WORKER: You're torn. To compete you've got to put in the hours. But if you do that it takes away from your time and energy with the family. That's a lot of stress.

The worker recognizes the client's ambivalence.

CLIENT: Now that you point it out, it seems obvious. I've been under stress for so long, I don't even think about it any more. It's clear to me now that the price of success is just too much.

Solutions to problems, however obvious, are often not acted on because of such ambivalence.

SOCIAL WORKER: Meaning that if you have to sacrifice time with your family in order to get ahead, you're not interested. (client nods) Sounds like you've made a decision. But let me play devil's advocate. Suppose you cut back on your job and lost a promotion. How would you feel about that?

The worker's empathy provides a basis for insight.

Such responses ensure that the client will not gloss over or minimize difficulties. The worker prevents the client from acting impulsively. By anticipating risks, the client is challenged to decide whether the costs are acceptable.

CLIENT: It would be hard on me. But I think not nearly so hard as what's happening now. At

The client confirms a decision. If the worker is satisfied that the client has taken a serious heart, I'm really a family man. I'm certain of it. Family has to be number one. My career is important to me, but it's my second priority.

SOCIAL WORKER: Let's go back to your goal. What other problems do you anticipate?

(20 seconds of silence)

CLIENT: Here's one. My family is so used to getting along without me, they've developed lives of their own. I guess I can't expect them to drop everything for me.

SOCIAL WORKER: So, how can you deal with that reality?

CLIENT: That's easy. I guess I'll just have to negotiate with the family on how much time we'll spend together.

SOCIAL WORKER: One thought occurs to me. How will your boss react if you suddenly start spending less time on the job? Do you think that's something to consider?

(Adapted with permission from Shebib, 1997.)

look at all reasonable risks, it's time to move on.

The worker challenges the client to look ahead to see if there are other risks. Similar responses are called for until all difficulties are explored.

The worker must be patient and give the client enough time to complete the thought process.

This type of response ensures that the client sets goals and embarks on action plans with a clear sense of direction and planning. Problems may be prevented or anticipated, and the client is far less likely to face a crisis that leads to abandonment of otherwise healthy objectives.

It is appropriate for the worker to tentatively introduce some of her own ideas, leaving a lot of room for the client to respond. As a rule, workers should let the client have the first opportunity.

Step One: Identify Alternatives

The first task in selecting a plan is to list the range of alternatives for achieving goals. This step serves two purposes. First, it holds clients back from impulsive action based on the first alternative available, which may simply be a repeat of previous unsuccessful attempts at change. Second, it helps to ensure that clients have choices based on a full range of possibilities. When there is choice, clients can make more rational decisions.

Both workers and clients may contribute ideas about possible plans. As well, consultation with others and brainstorming can generate ideas. Some basic rules for effective brainstorming are listed below (Cragan and Wright, 1991; Egan, 1998; Shebib, 1997; Young, 1998).

1. Do not evaluate or criticize ideas. Adherence to this principle ensures that self-censorship does not result. Clients might hold back potentially valuable and usable suggestions because they fear that they will be criticized or embarrassed.
2. Generate as many ideas as possible. Encourage wild and creative suggestions. At this stage any alternative, however bizarre, is acceptable. Social workers can use leads such as these to encourage clients to generate ideas: "Let your imagination run wild and see how many different ideas you can come up with that will help you

TABLE 7.4 Sample Goals

Target Area	Vague Goal	Specific Goal Statements
Behavior	To do better in my courses	To improve my grade-point average from C to B– by the end of the semester
Feelings	To feel better	To overcome depression so I am able to enjoy life. That would include mixing socially with people and having a sense that life is worth living. I'll be more able to accept my problems without withdrawing or drowning in self-pity.
Thoughts	To stop putting myself down	To look at mistakes as normal and as learning opportunities. When I'm successful, I'll take credit. Overall, I'll be able to say to myself that I'm capable.
Skills	To get organized	To develop skill at organizing my time and setting priorities. I need to set up a schedule so I can plan at least a month in advance.
Relationship	To be able to communicate better with my husband	To reduce the number of fights that we have by not being so explosive. Instead of yelling, I need to remain calm. Instead of not listening, I need to check with him to make sure I understand what he wants, too.
Health and fitness	To get in shape	To lose 5 lbs over the next two months. To increase my weekly running from 5 to 10 miles
Spiritual	To be closer to God	To attend religious services regularly—at least once a week. To make prayer a daily part of my life. To read something spiritual at least once a day. To walk in the forest three times a week

achieve your goals." "Don't worry for now about whether it's a good idea or a bad one." Sometimes social workers can prompt clients to be creative by generating a few "wild" ideas of their own.

3. Emphasize quantity—more is better.
4. Look for ways to combine or "piggyback" ideas. Sometimes apparently ridiculous proposals can be modified to work. Or they can be combined with other ideas to

come up with new alternatives. Some key questions for stimulating further alternatives include "How can we join suggestions?" "In what ways can we sort or rearrange these ideas?"

Case Study (Lisa)

Lisa, age 33, and her worker come up with a list of possibilities for Lisa to deal with her shyness and her need to meet more people. Some of the ideas they generated are listed below:

- join a singles club
- take an acting class
- learn to sing
- put an ad in the personals column
- become a volunteer
- use counseling to role-play problem situations in order to develop assertiveness
- forget the goal and become a nun
- use counseling to deal with self-deprecating inner talk
- try hypnosis
- join a social group at a place of worship
- participate in an assertiveness training group

Step Two: Choose an Action Strategy

Once a creative list of alternative action strategies is identified, the next task is to assist clients in evaluating alternatives and making choices. At this point, the worker's role is to ensure that clients are able to make informed choices. This involves helping clients to intelligently consider each alternative with respect to a number of criteria. An obvious first criterion is that the alternative for meeting the client's goal is potentially effective. It must be sufficient to make a difference and relevant to the problem being addressed. A second criterion is that alternatives are within the capacity of the client. Otherwise, failure is inevitable. A third criterion is that alternatives are consistent with the values and beliefs of the client. A fourth is that alternatives are reviewed in terms of their potential cost. Cost might be measured by time, money, and energy expended in finding resources to execute the alternative. As well, alternatives might result in other losses for the client. For example, suppose a client wishes to end a pattern of alcohol abuse, but the person's friends are drinking buddies. If quitting drinking involves developing new activities, the potential loss of friends and social structure must be considered as a negative consequence that will have an impact on the client. Understanding and exploring this loss is important, for unless clients are aware of and prepared for these contingencies, they may be unable to sustain any efforts at changing.

Step Three: Develop and Implement Plans

Developing and implementing plans involves four substeps: (1) sequencing plans, (2) developing **contingency plans,** (3) putting plans into action, and (4) evaluating.

Effective plans are maps that detail the sequence of events leading to the final goal. Social workers should avoid tailor-made plans in favor of customized strategies that are designed in collaboration with individual clients. Some of the important questions that need to be answered include the following:

- What specific strategies will be used?
- In what order will the strategies be used?
- What resources or support will be needed at each step?
- What are the risks and potential obstacles?

Effective plans anticipate the potential obstacles that clients might encounter along the route. Once clients know and accept the possible barriers that could interfere with their plans, they can develop contingency plans to deal with these barriers. This preventive work helps to prevent clients from giving up when things don't go smoothly.

Case Study (Lisa, Continued)

Lisa decided that joining a singles group would be a great way for her to meet people, but she admitted that she would probably back out before going to the first meeting. With her counselor's help, she came up with two ideas for managing this problem. She recruited a friend to go with her to the group, and she phoned the group leader to volunteer to bring refreshments. Lisa knew that she wouldn't back down if it meant that others would be affected by her actions.

Lisa said that what bothered her most was first meeting someone. She told her counselor, "I feel so awkward. I just don't know what to say." Her counselor helped Lisa accept that feeling awkward is normal under such circumstances. The worker self-disclosed some of her own anxieties and suggested that they could role-play some ideas for handling these tough moments.

During the implementation phase, social workers need to support and encourage clients as they deal with the stress of change. One way they can help is to remind clients that anxiety, awkwardness, and periodic slumps are normal when change is occurring. Workers can look for ways to reframe failure or setbacks as learning opportunities. Wilson's comments might be offered to clients:

Although you may fail to reach the goal, there are benefits of having worked toward it. One benefit is the practical education of making the effort. Another is the opportunity to practice specific skills. A third is the recognition that meeting some goals and failing to meet others is part of the ebb and flow of life. Recognize that you probably will not achieve significant goals without some failures. Failing provides unique learning opportunities that ultimately contribute to your personal growth (1994:18).

Empathy is particularly important at this time as a way of supporting clients in dealing with feelings that accompany change. During implementation, workers should also encourage clients to use family, friends, and support groups to assist them.

Step Four: Evaluate Outcomes

Effective plans include continual evaluation as part of the implementation phase. Evaluation recognizes and confirms success and is a powerful motivator. However, evaluation may uncover problems that need to be addressed. For example, it may become apparent that the goals are too unrealistic. If they are too challenging and unreachable, workers can help clients define smaller goals. When goals prove to be too easy, they can be modified to provide more challenge. Regular review of progress ensures that goals and action strategies remain relevant and realistic.

When evaluation reveals that the plan is unlikely to be successful, efforts can be redirected toward redesigning the plan or selecting a different strategy for action. In some cases, the client may need help that is beyond the capacity of the worker; in this case, referral to another counselor or service is appropriate.

CONVERSATION **7.2**
I've Tried Everything

STUDENT: I get stuck when a client says, "'I've tried everything and nothing seems to work."

TEACHER: You feel stuck, which is precisely how the client feels. Clients often bring out in counselors the same feelings that they are experiencing. This reality can be a useful tool for empathy. When clients say they've tried everything, it's important not to get into a "yes, but" game, whereby counselors generate ideas and clients dismiss them with a "yes, but" response.

STUDENT: So, what are my choices?

TEACHER: I'd be interested in exploring what the client did. Did he or she try long enough? At the right time? In the right way? Sometimes problems get worse before they get better, and clients may give up too soon. A mother might try ignoring her child when he has a tantrum. She tells you ignoring doesn't work, but she may have abandoned this tactic after a few minutes when it appeared that the intensity of her child's tantrum was increasing. In this situation, you could help her anticipate this obstacle so that she would not be demoralized when it occurred. Or maybe she was giving her child lots of nonverbal attention, not realizing how this was reinforcing the tantrum.

STUDENT: I can think of another example. One of the members of my work group was having trouble with her supervisor. She told us that there is no point in talking to him because he doesn't listen anyway. But from the way she described how she talked to him, I wouldn't listen either. She was vicious and cruel.

TEACHER: So, if she were your client, she would need some help developing awareness about how she affects others.

Summary

The foundation for empowerment in counseling is the belief that clients are capable and have a right to manage their own lives. In order to empower clients, social workers need to forego controlling them, demystify the counseling process, promote client self-determination, advocate for progressive changes in the system, and assist clients to change established patterns of thinking and acting that are interfering with their lives. Social workers can help clients change established patterns through five major activities: motivating, confronting, helping clients think differently, goal setting, and action planning.

Motivating involves engaging clients in a change process, as well as supporting and energizing them as they deal with the rigors of change. Workers may face a range of motivational challenges, and they can employ different strategies to address each of them. Five categories of motivational problems are clients in denial, involuntary clients, burnt-out clients, ambivalent clients, and energized clients.

Effective confrontation is not a hostile act. It is a way to move clients to a different level of understanding, behaving, or feeling. Confrontation can address incongruities between what clients believe and the way they act; self-defeating ways of thinking and behaving; behavior that is harmful to self or others; blind spots; blaming behavior; communication problems; and strengths. Confrontation should be relevant to the goals of counseling and timed appropriately to minimize defensive reactions.

Clients may have trouble breaking out of established patterns because of the way they think about problems. Thinking errors include distortion, incomplete analysis, egocentricity or lack of empathy, rigidity, and self-defeating thought. An important goal of counseling is to help clients discontinue faulty reasoning. Reframing is a tool for helping clients look at problems from another perspective. Reframing empowers clients by focusing on solutions and redefining negatives as opportunities or challenges.

Goal setting serves many important purposes, including giving direction, defining roles, motivating, and measuring progress. Effective goals need to be concrete, measurable, challenging but realistic, and owned by clients. Effective goals can be developed from problem statements.

Action planning consists of a series of steps leading to the client's goal or subgoal. Selecting a plan involves systematic identification and evaluation of the possibilities for action, then choosing one or more alternative action plans. Developing and implementing plans involves four substeps: sequencing plans, developing contingency plans, putting plans into action, and evaluating.

EXERCISES

1. What style do you prefer others to use when they give you feedback? Compare your preference with those of your colleagues.

2. Consider the various ways in which your colleagues prefer to receive feedback. Which ways would you have most trouble with?

3. What are the essential differences between a counseling confrontation and an attack?

4. Identify the person(s) from whom you would be most receptive to receiving feedback and those from whom you would be least receptive. Give your reasons why.

5. Self-evaluate your personal comfort when confronting others.

   a. What people would you have difficulty confronting?

   b. Do you avoid confronting?

    c. Think of times when it was reasonable to confront, but you didn't. What prevented you from confronting?

    d. Finish the following sentence: When I confront, I feel . . .

6. Write a short concept paper that describes what you believe are the elements of effective confrontation.

7. Hamachek says, "Do not confront another person if you do not wish to increase your involvement with that individual" (1982:230). Develop a rationale that supports this statement.

8. Work with a colleague to role-play an appropriate counseling confrontation for each of the following situations.

    a. a client who has hygiene problems

    b. a colleague who has, in your opinion, behaved in an unprofessional manner

    c. a client who consistently arrives late for appointments

9. Identify an area in your own life that you are willing to accept feedback about (e.g., the first impressions you leave with others, your style of communication, the way others see you). Spend about twenty minutes with a friend or colleague exploring their opinions about the identified area.

    a. What were your feelings during the encounter? Did they change?

    b. What did your colleague say or do that made it easier to accept the feedback? What made it more difficult?

    c. What did you learn about giving or receiving feedback that will be useful to you in your work as a counselor?

10. Evaluate the effectiveness of each of the confrontations below. Suggest improvements.

    a. Try to do better next time.

    b. You're an idiot.

    c. You're saying that you're okay, yet you're crying.

    d. Grow up and act your age.

    e. As long as you continue to act like a doormat, you're going to get abused. If you're serious about protecting yourself, leave him.

11. Suggest reframed responses for each of the following client statements.

    a. I can't do it.

    b. *(a student counselor)* I feel so unnatural and phony expressing empathy all the time.

    c. I really want my kids to avoid making the same mistakes I did. I don't know why they don't listen to me.

    d. If he really loved me, he'd send me flowers.

    e. My life is a mess.

    f. I'm tired of being depressed all the time.

12. Name at least ten different ways to motivate clients.

13. Evaluate how effectively the following statements meet the criteria for effective goals:

    a. to be a better person

    b. for my boss to stop hassling me

    c. to drink less

    d. to be able to disagree with someone without dismissing them or their ideas

    e. to improve my fitness by next year to the point where I can run 1 mile in 20 minutes

14. Practice brainstorming techniques. Identify thirty different action strategies for a client who wishes to quit drinking.

15. Use the concepts from this chapter to practice goal setting and action planning. Pick one or more target areas (behavior, feelings, thoughts, skills, or relationship).

8 Difficult Situations

Preview

After reading this chapter you should be able to:

- understand the different forms of client resistance
- explain reasons for resistance
- describe techniques for dealing with resistance
- explain the importance of worker self-awareness when dealing with clients who are resistant
- define intimidating and violent behavior
- identify key variables for predicting which clients might become violent
- understand violence in relation to mental illness
- list key questions for assessing the potential for violence
- describe techniques for preventing violence
- identify and describe the four phases of violence
- describe strategies for intervening at each phase of violence
- explain the importance of debriefing critical incidents
- identify debriefing techniques

Resistance

Resistance is a defensive reaction of clients that interferes with or delays the process of counseling. Simply put, "resistance is the client's opposition to change in the counseling process" (Otani, 1989:458). It is a term first introduced by Freud, who described its ever present influence on the therapeutic process: "Every step of the treatment is accompanied by resistance; every single thought, every mental act of the patient's, must pay toll to the resistance and represents a compromise between the forces urging towards cure and those gathered to oppose it" (cited in Rosenthal, 1987:3). Resistance is essentially a defensive reaction designed to protect clients from the stress of change. It serves to maintain the status quo against the threat that typically accompanies any change process.

Sometimes clients are resistant because they have been forced to come for counseling. They do not see the need for change and they resent being coerced. At other times, clients come voluntarily for counseling and they appear motivated to change, but they resist it because of prior bad experiences with counselors or because they fear the unknown risks and pain of changing. In this sense, resistance is a way of maintaining the status quo and the relative stability (however painful) of the current situation. In fact, resistance can be viecwed as a natural and protective reaction to change. As Young observed, "When the helper begins to disrupt long-held and cherished beliefs about the world, the client tries to protect his or her core beliefs from sweeping changes that may bring chaos" (1998:251).

Harris and Watkins echo Young's sentiments, arguing that resistance to change indicates a degree of stability that would be upset if people changed randomly. They conclude that "resistance has positive value and a counselor should expect to find some good reasons why clients don't change—at least from their point of view" (1987:17).

Sometimes clients become increasingly resistant as counseling progresses. This may signal that the process is moving too quickly or that there is unresolved conflict in the counselor–client relationship. Resistance may also arise at critical moments in counseling, such as when counselors challenge long-established behavior or attempt to encourage discussion or goal setting in areas that clients would like to avoid.

Forms of Resistance

Resistance may show itself in a variety of ways, ranging from overt hostility to passivity that impedes the work. Among the range of client behaviors and signs that may suggest resistance are the following (Corey and Corey, 1989; Gladding, 1996; Otani, 1989; Shulman, 1992; Young, 1998):

1. failure to comply with the basic procedures of counseling, including keeping appointments, being on time, and paying fees
2. statements (direct or subtle) that indicate resistance, e.g., "This is a waste of time," "You can't make me cooperate," "That's none of your business," and "I don't want to be here."
3. passivity (e.g., silence, withholding information, persistent short responses such as "I don't know," extreme self-censorship of ideas and feelings). Such passivity may indicate that the client does not want to be there, or it may mean that the demands of the interview are excessive. For example, the feelings and content of the interview may be more than the client is willing or able to face.
4. diversion (e.g., changing subject, using excessive humor, making small talk, introducing irrelevant material, being overly talkative, intellectualizing). This type of resistance is a way of avoiding difficult, threatening, or incriminating content.
5. uncooperative behavior (e.g., failure to follow through with plans or homework, false promises)
6. subtle undermining (e.g., acting seductively, attempting to redefine the counseling relationship as a friendship, excessively praising, being sarcastic)
7. creating the illusion of work, described by Shulman (1992) as engaging in conversations that appear important but that, in reality, are empty and have no real meaning. Interviews may be filled with apparent cooperation and verbosity, but the work does not empower clients or enable them to change.

8. nonverbal cues suggesting a passive/aggressive response, such as not making eye contact, folding arms, sitting on the edge of the seat, using an angry tone of voice, clenching fists, raising eyebrows, frowning, and sighing

9. limiting the setting (e.g., restricting discussion on certain topics by insisting that the topics are irrelevant)

Otani (1989) cautions against using a single incident as evidence of resistance. A client may become silent when a new topic is introduced. This silence may or may not be resistance, but if the client becomes silent again when the same topic is introduced, then resistance is likely.

Sometimes clients expect workers to be cold and indifferent. This expectation may be based on past experience with helping professionals or other persons in authority. If their prior encounters were unsatisfying, then it is understandable for clients to be cautious in similar situations and to believe that the same outcome is likely. Consequently, these clients will be quick to pick up on anything that might support that belief. Indeed, they view caring as manipulative and empathy as intrusive. Workers who understand the importance of such prior expectations are less likely to be taken aback by clients who reject or who are suspicious of their caring actions. As Irving Layton, a Canadian poet, commented, "The virtues of those we dislike irritate us more than their vices."

Dealing with Resistance

Some resistance is normal and perhaps desirable, so workers do not always have to treat resistance as problematic. In fact, most clients are resistant to some extent (Cormier and Cormier, 1985; Haley, 1987). Sheafor, Horejsi, and Horejsi note that it is common for clients to be somewhat defensive, particularly in the beginning phase: "The need to make even small changes generates some degree of discomfort in all people. Change can be particularly threatening to clients with well-established, or rather rigid beliefs, attitudes, and behavioral patterns. Fear is at the heart of such resistance" (1991:172). Skilled helpers recognize resistance, but they are not threatened by it; instead, they consider it a clue that their clients' defenses are engaged. By understanding the nature of the resistance, workers can open a pathway to greater understanding of their clients.

In the beginning phase of counseling, before trust and a working contract are negotiated, many clients tend to hold back. At this stage, their workers are strangers, and it would be unwise for clients to open up too quickly without knowing how precious personal information might be treated.

Clients who are open and candid about their resistance may present less of a challenge than those who mask their resistance with silence or feigned cooperation. When resistance is clearly labeled by clients, frank discussion seems to follow, but when clients mask their uncooperativeness, they can deny resistance when workers introduce the subject. Before workers assume that their clients are resistant, they should eliminate other factors. For example, clients who appear resistant may not understand the expectations or the process of counseling; thus, they remain cautious and guarded. Workers should remember that whereas they have considerable training in how to counsel, their clients have not had training in how to be a client. Unless the process is clarified, clients may remain frightened or confused. Workers need to be explicit regarding their expectations. They should not assume that what is obvious to them will also be obvious to their clients.

Resistance may arise for a number of reasons. These may be categorized in five major groups: (1) relationship, (2) motivational, (3) attitudinal, (4) fearful, and (5) involuntary. Client resistance may be unconscious and unintended, or it may be a deliberate act of sabotage or avoidance.

Relationship Resistance.   This type of resistance is linked to variables in the counseling relationship. Clients may be resistant because of transference reactions or simply because they feel they are not a good match with their workers. Sometimes clients are influenced by past experiences with counselors. For example, if they perceived their former counselors as rude or untrustworthy, clients might understandably be guarded and defensive with any new worker. This is a way to protect themselves from further rudeness, inconsistency, or breach of trust. Therefore, it is useful for workers to inquire about any past experiences that clients have had with other counselors. This helps to bring feelings and issues into the open, including any preconceptions or fears about the current relationship. When workers do this they should provide a brief explanation to let their clients know they are not prying for gossip. The example below demonstrates.

> **SOCIAL WORKER:** *Have you had any other experiences with counseling in the past?*
>
> **CLIENT:** *Yes, my husband and I went for marital counseling about two years ago.*
>
> **SOCIAL WORKER:** *What did you like and dislike about that experience? I'm asking because I think it will help me to understand a bit about your expectations. I'd like to learn what worked for you and what didn't.*

Resistance may also develop as a result of conflict in the current relationship. Counseling relationships, like all relationships, are subject to periodic stress and conflict. Helpers can make mistakes and say the wrong thing, and they can offend their clients. Clients who are vulnerable may be overly sensitive, or they might misinterpret messages and feel angered. This is an inevitable reality of the chemistry of human encounters. What distinguishes effective workers is their ability to be sensitive to clues that all is not well in their relationships. Workers are alert for verbal and nonverbal shifts in the tone of the interview that might signal that there is friction. Effective workers are further distinguished by their willingness and capacity to address these issues in a caring and nondefensive manner. By doing so, they not only prevent further resistance, they also build trust and understanding with their clients.

Motivational Resistance.   This type of resistance results from some of the motivational problems discussed in Chapter 7. Clients who are in denial do not accept that they have a problem, even though there might be considerable evidence that their behavior is problematic for them and others. If this is the source of resistance, one option is to provide accurate information to clients about the effects or consequences of their behavior. With clients who deny they have an addiction problem, providing information (questionnaires, handouts, date and time of an open AA meeting, etc.) may persuade them to reassess their situation.

Some clients hold to their current mode of thinking, feeling, and acting because they lack the energy necessary for change or they are pessimistic that change is possible. Whatever the reason, these clients resist counseling because to do so appears easier and safer than embracing change. Workers might deal with this resistance by communicating optimism and by helping clients set small but achievable goals. By supporting and reinforcing small successes, workers contribute to the empowerment of their clients. In the process, it is important that workers express empathy regarding the challenges and fears associated with any change. Clients need to understand that they will not be humiliated or overwhelmed by the demands of counseling or change.

In Chapter 7, the concept of secondary gain was introduced as a way of understanding why people resist change. As Bezanson, DeCoff, and Stewart explain: "For some clients, the risks involved in bringing up reluctance and moving toward change are simply too great and the rewards of remaining with the status quo too powerful to be abandoned. The responsibility of counsellors is to attempt to find the resources to motivate the client to assume responsibility and accomplish the desired counselling targets" (1985:104).

Attitudinal Resistance.   Some clients are resistant because they believe that taking help is a sign of weakness. They may believe, as well, that counseling will undermine their personal autonomy. One way for workers to address this resistance is to look for appropriate opportunities to reframe counseling as a sign of strength, rather than feebleness. Workers can deal with fears about loss of independence by making sure that clients are active and informed partners in the work of counseling.

Sometimes workers can modify hostile intentions through goal setting. The following interview excerpt provides a brief illustration:

SOCIAL WORKER: *What do you hope to achieve?*

CLIENT: *Nothing.*

SOCIAL WORKER: *What's behind that answer?*

CLIENT: *I just think that counseling is a waste of time. What good does it do to talk about problems anyway?*

SOCIAL WORKER: *You also seem to be saying that, if counseling could in some way help you with your problems, you'd be more satisfied.*

CLIENT: *I guess so.*

Another technique described by Cormier and Cormier (1985) is to avoid direct challenges of resistance by matching the resistance statement. This strategy shows clients that their concerns have been heard and accepted. This approach is illustrated below.

CLIENT: *I just think that counseling is a waste of time. What good does it do to talk about problems anyway?*

SOCIAL WORKER: *Given your pessimism, it seems to me that you're wise to be cautious about what we might accomplish here.*

By responding in this way, the worker relieves the client of the burden of trying to convince the worker of the validity of his position. The client may begin. to see the worker more as an ally. The wisdom of not attacking clients' beliefs and values directly is nicely illustrated by the following story:

> A holy man and an atheist met one day. The atheist challenged the holy man to debate, exclaiming, "I don't believe in God!" The holy man replied, "Tell me about the God you don't believe in." The atheist talked at length about the absurd wars that had been fought in the name of God. He attacked the "hypocrites" who espoused their religious values and beliefs but behaved quite the opposite. The holy man listened patiently until the atheist had said his piece. Only then did he respond: "You and I have a lot in common. I don't believe in that God either."

At the same time, workers need to accept some truth in criticisms, such as "Counseling isn't going to put food on my table." Harris and Watkins offer this perspective:

> Counseling cannot solve problems like discrimination and the economic punishment that goes with it. Counseling can help people choose how they want to respond to discrimination and how to take advantage of what economic resources may be available. But people who feel victimized by society see their problems as caused by circumstances outside themselves. Thus counseling, which seeks personal change, is viewed as valueless because it is society that needs changing (1987:46).

Fearful Resistance.   For most people, it is difficult to change from established routines and ways of coping. They communicate fears regarding the imagined consequences of change through resistance. Some clients have trouble with intimacy, and counseling may be seen as an unwanted intrusion that threatens their need to maintain personal distance and privacy. Depending on the situation, a variety of counseling initiatives might prove useful, including candid discussion with clients about their fears and the real risks of change. Here, again, working on small but achievable goals will be less threatening (see Chapter 7). As well, it is crucial that workers support and empathize with their clients' fears. Clients need to hear that they will not be pushed beyond their capacity. Sometimes limited worker self-disclosure can be a useful way of normalizing fears about change.

Johnson and Yanka suggest that "resistance is the opposite of motivation and is sometimes a sign that other influences on a person are stronger than the need for change" (2001:83). For example, cultural and familial values or responsibilities may prevent clients from seeking or taking help. It is important that workers understand how clients may perceive them, for example:

> Clients and others typically do not understand the limits of the social worker's span of control and ascribe more authority to the worker than is legally allowed. Clients may believe that the worker can withhold an income maintenance check if they do not do what they think the worker wants them to do. Such situations can become complex when the client acts according to what she believes the worker wants rather than what the worker has said (Johnson and Yanka, 2001:84).

When clients credit workers with more power than they have, they might withhold information, avoid meetings or otherwise resist counseling. Frank discussion of roles, responsibilities. and the limits of power may assist in clients' fears. In cross-cultural situations, workers can try to modify their approach to be more congruent with their clients' culture, or they can use or partner with indigenous workers.

Involuntary Resistance.   This type of resistance stems clients' resentment at being forced to come for counseling and their inability to see a need for change. These clients may see themselves as fighting the "system," and they view the worker as a representative of the system (Harris and Watkins, 1987). Involuntary clients typically receive services from large bureaucratic organizations, but the structure and procedures of these agencies can work against clients. Johnson offers this viewpoint: "The complexity of rules and regulations and the inability of an organization to individualize for clients often gets in the way of the worker providing the service needed by the client. The worker may have feelings of powerlessness and may not feel appreciated by the agency. This can lead to frustrations that get in the way of responding to the client appropriately" (1992:137).

With involuntary clients, it is important to restore their sense of control and right to self-determination. These clients need to be able to answer the question "What can counseling do for me?" They need to see goals and outcomes that they desire as opposed to those that feel imposed. Workers need to be patient with unwilling clients by remaining nonjudgmental and caring. They can decrease resistance by demonstrating their ability to talk calmly with their clients about their reasons for not wanting to be there, and they should be especially diligent about informing unwilling clients about their rights, including the limits of confidentiality. Clear, succinct statements about these issues will help to reduce their suspicions.

Table 8.1 provides some strategies for dealing with each type of resistance. Two points need to be emphasized. First, clients may show more than one type of resistance, and, second, techniques always have to be adapted and modified to meet the needs, culture, and language of each client and situation. Workers need to exercise choice. Creativity and flexibility are essential for handling resistance. Sometimes this can mean dealing with resistance directly by inviting clients to talk about their feelings. At other times, workers may prefer to avoid direct challenges to resistance. For example, a worker who observes that a client becomes hostile when a certain topic comes up could shift the focus to a less threatening topic until more trust is developed.

Leads for Dealing with Resistance.   Immediacy was introduced in Chapter 3 as the process of exploring, deepening, and evaluating counseling relationships. When the work of counseling is blocked by resistance, immediacy provides a way to deal directly with clients' concerns regarding the counseling process or the relationship itself. As a general rule, if resistance is increasing, it is wise to deal directly with it; otherwise, the client may never return. The following leads illustrate the potential variety of responses that can be used to move the interview toward a discussion of resistance.

- How do you feel about being here?
- Do you resent being forced to see me?
- If I felt forced to come, I think I'd feel quite angry.
- I'm wondering what's happening between us. Are you feeling angry toward me?
- Let's see if we can agree on what we want to accomplish.

TABLE 8.1   Strategies for Dealing with Resistance

Origin of Resistance	Description	Strategy Choices
Relationship	There is unresolved conflict in the helping relationship, or clients are defensive because of prior bad experiences with counseling.	Problem-solve relationship difficulties. Discuss prior experiences with counseling, then use this information to work out contracts that clients can support (but do this in a way that does not undermine the integrity of other workers). Refer to other counselors. Respond nondefensively and do not personalize.
Motivational	Clients lack motivation to change either because they see no problem or because they do not believe that change is possible.	Use confrontation to help clients become aware of problems. Use authority. Deal with learned helplessness (see Chapter 7). Communicate optimism about clients' skills and abilities. Acknowledge and reinforce all efforts and progress.
Attitudinal	Personal or cultural values define taking help as a sign of weakness.	Encourage clients to voice concerns regarding counseling. Adjust counseling methods to be culturally sensitive. Persuade clients that taking help is a sign of strength. Use strategies that fully empower and involve clients in making decisions.
Fearful	Clients are afraid of the risks and potential pain of changing.	Encourage clients to share fears, then use empathy to acknowledge feelings. Prompt candid discussion of the risks of change. Support and encourage the client. Gear pacing toward small, achievable goals. Help clients identify and deal with self-defeating inner dialogue. Target work in less threatening areas until confidence increases.
Involuntary	Clients do not want to be in counseling but have been	Encourage clients to share feelings, then empathize.

TABLE 8.1   **Continued**

Origin of Resistance	Description	Strategy Choices
	forced by a third party (e.g., courts, school counselor).	Negotiate a contract to add voluntary objectives to those that are involuntary. In general, look for opportunities to give clients control, choices, and power. Help clients answer the question "What's in it for me?" Redirect the work to less threatening areas.

- If I'm not mistaken, every time I mention your father you change the subject. Is that a topic you would rather avoid?
- How committed are you to making changes?
- Do you believe it's possible for you to change?
- What does it mean to you to be seeing a counselor?
- Are you worried that I will try to force you to do something you don't want to do?

Counselor Self-Awareness and Management of Self

Client resistance can be unsettling and demoralizing for helpers. Social workers who have a high need to be liked by their clients may interpret resistance as personal rejection. Resistant clients can test almost every worker's ability to be nonjudgmental. Therefore, it is important that they find ways to depersonalize the situation. Otherwise, they run the risk of further worsening the situation by rejecting the client or retaliating in subtle ways. Frequently, workers respond with their own insecurities and defenses. In turn, clients may view their worker's annoyance as proof that the situation is hopeless. In worst-case scenarios, workers turn against their clients and blame them for their problems. Ultimately, they look for ways to refer them in order to get rid of them. Such referrals are a way of "dumping" the client, rather than an attempt to help them meet their real needs through connection with alternative resources.

Social workers need to be able to objectively evaluate their own conduct and take their fair share of responsibility for resistance. When workers have high self-awareness of their actions, they are able to monitor themselves and change their behavior to be more effective. Weisinger underscores the importance of counselor self-awareness when dealing with difficult clients: "By being aware, for example, that your voice is getting louder and you are becoming increasingly angry at a client who is making yet another unreasonable demand—and recognizing, of course, how important your client is to your ongoing employment—you might lower your voice, defuse your anger, and respond to your client respectfully" (1998:xx).

INTERVIEW **8.1**
Dealing with Resistance

The following interview excerpt shows some ways for dealing with client resistance. The client is a young male, age 19, who has been referred to a social worker (addiction counselor) as a condition of his probation. This excerpt is from the first interview, and it begins about 15 minutes into the interview. It is clear from the client's nonverbal behavior that he doesn't want to be there (e.g., he has not removed his coat, he gives single-word or short answers to questions, and his voice tone is hostile).

Dialogue	Analysis
CLIENT: How long is this going to take? I'm really not in the mood to be cross-examined.	The worker chooses to address the client's resistance directly. The is the first interview and some softening of the client's hostility might be expected over time, but the degree of resistance seems pronounced enough that it should be dealt with directly. In her response, the worker also attempts to remind the client that he does have a choice about whether to stay or go. However, this is a bit risky, because the client may decide to walk out.
SOCIAL WORKER: Of course, you're free to leave at any point. But before you do, why don't we take a moment to talk straight. I know that you were forced to come here by your probation officer. I'm wondering how you feel about that.	
CLIENT (SARCASTICALLY): It's no big deal. I can handle it.	Frequently, clients deny that they are resistant. This can be exceptionally hard to deal with, because such clients evade taking responsibility for their behavior.
SOCIAL WORKER: We do agree on one thing. You don't want to be cross-examined and I don't intend to try. You don't have to tell me about anything you don't want to talk about.	The worker tries to find a point of agreement, but her response is greeted by more anger. At this point, it is important that the worker not give up. Even though the client's response is less than ideal, he has heard what the worker said.
CLIENT: Let's get one thing clear. I don't need your permission to do anything.	
SOCIAL WORKER: Agreed. But since you've decided to stay, let's talk. If you're feeling angry because your probation officer thinks you need counseling, I can understand. I sure don't like it when I'm forced to do something against my will.	The worker tries to ally herself with the client by using self-disclosure to encourage him to talk about his resistance. She emphasizes that the client has made choices. Sometimes it is less threatening for clients when workers avoid questions. The client's earlier statement that he "doesn't want to be cross-examined" is a good indication that questions would be inappropriate in this interview.
CLIENT: It's not you. I just don't see the point. There's nothing wrong with me. I don't understand why I have to come here.	
SOCIAL WORKER: Sounds like you really want to stand up and say, "This is my life. Butt out."	The worker's persistence works, as the client begins to open up. At this point, it is important for the worker to avoid becoming defensive. If she starts to "sell" her client on the merits of counseling, she may lose him.

CLIENT: Yeah. What gives them the right to say I'm crazy?

SOCIAL WORKER: And now that you're here, you might be worried that I'll do the same thing. That I'll try to get into your head, tell you what to do.

CLIENT: Of course. Isn't that how it works? I've been to counseling before.(laughs) You guys aren't happy unless you're mucking someone up.

SOCIAL WORKER (LAUGHS):   Well, we have to shrink our quota of heads.

CLIENT (LAUGHS):   My head is staying just where it is.

SOCIAL WORKER: I'm impressed that you're able to say what you want.

CLIENT: I don't believe in playing games.

SOCIAL WORKER: Me neither. So, let's talk about what's going to happen here. Let's try to work out something that works for both of us.

Cautiously, the client begins to share his feelings, including his reservations about what will happen in the relationship.

A little humor from the worker helps build rapport, while showing empathy with the client's feeling. The worker has the ablitiy to talk about the issues without becoming defensive. When using humor, timing is crucial. What works well in one situation might result in disaster in another.

The worker does not attempt to break down her client's defenses, which are an important part of the way this client has coped.

There is much work to be done to establish a solid working relationship with this client. Resistance may be a reality throughout the life of the counseling relationship. However, an important beginning has been established.

Bezanson, DeCoff, and Stewart link counseling's effectiveness to the ability of workers to handle reluctant or resistant clients: "Reluctant behaviours are the responsibility of the client; feelings of anger or anxiety with reluctant behaviours are the responsibility of the counsellor" (1985:78).

Colleagues and supervisors should be used for support when dealing with highly resistant clients, who can tax the patience of even the most dedicated worker. Collegial support can help workers unwind from tough sessions. Colleagues can help workers process their reactions and regain or test objectivity, and they can be a source of fresh ideas for reaching difficult clients.

Culture and Resistance

Sue and Sue (1990; cited in Diller, 1999) present a case study that portrays how cross-cultural miscommunication can easily be misinterpreted as client resistance. The client was a 13-year-old girl who was referred to a school counselor for allegedly selling drugs. The school counselor consulted for help in dealing with the parents, whom she described as "uncaring, uncooperative and attempting to avoid responsibility for their daughter's delinquency."

Describing the case, the counselor said that she called the parents, a Hispanic family living in San Jose, California, and talked with Mrs. Martinez. She said she asked Mrs.

Martinez to come in as soon as possible to see what could be done to resolve the situation. The counselor said Mrs. Martinez hesitated and excused herself from the phone when pressed. The counselor said she overheard whispering, then Mr. Martinez came on the line. He also avoided and made excuses, saying he had to work and could not come in for the meeting. The counselor emphasized the importance of the meeting for his daughter's welfare and suggested that missing work for a few hours was not important, given the gravity of the situation. The father proposed an evening meeting, but the counselor rejected this because school policy prohibited evening meetings. Finally, the father agreed, and a meeting was set up for the next day. Mr. and Mrs. Martinez and a brother-in-law (the girl's godfather) showed up. The counselor reported that she was upset that the brother-in-law

---

CONVERSATION 8.1
Saying No

STUDENT: What are some ways to say "no" to clients? I really hate it when I have to deny them what they want or need.

TEACHER: That's my reaction, too. None of us in the helping professions wants to be seen as harsh or uncaring. Saying "no" may evoke feelings of guilt in us, as well as strong negative reactions from our clients. We really need to be able address our own emotions as well as the clients'.

STUDENT: Suppose it's a reality of the business. Sometimes we have to make tough decisions such as, "Who gets the training money?" and "Who qualifies for assistance?" In the residential part of the program where I work, we often have to say "no" when the kids want exceptions to the rules. No problem when you're able to give clients what they want. But what about when you have to turn down requests?

TEACHER: Even when you are saying "no" it's important that clients know you care. You need to listen and be available to respond with empathy and compassion. Find a way to show you understand, even if you are not able to give your clients what they want. Or, see if there is a way to compromise to help your client save face. What do you think?

STUDENT: I've learned a couple of things: Be direct, clear, and brief. Don't waffle, hint, or avoid the "bottom line." With kids, I've found that, even when they test the limits, they may need and even welcome limits when they are imposed. It increases their sense of safety and control when they learn the boundaries of acceptable behavior.

TEACHER: I agree. I think it's important that you don't make a hasty retreat. Expect that anger, defensiveness, and counterattack are the ways that some clients respond to frustration. In extreme situations, you need to protect yourself. Anticipate potentially violent situations and take defensive action. Be sure to debrief with a colleague or supervisor after difficult encounters. If necessary, take a break to ensure that your reactions do not contaminate your ability to deal with your next client objectively. Finally, remind yourself that no matter how your client reacts, you must remain professional.

STUDENT: When someone says "no" to me, I find it a lot easier to accept if I know why. So, I try to explain my rationale, or the policy. Then, I invite questions.

TEACHER: If you can, help your clients identify other ways to meet their needs.

was present, and she explained that this would unduly complicate the session. She stressed that she wanted to see only the family. The counselor said the meeting went badly, and the parents were evasive and not forthcoming with their answers.

Diller, analyzing the counselor's conclusions, describes the encounter as a clear case of misunderstanding cultural differences. He cites a number of erroneous assumptions. For example, "The counselor appears unaware that in a traditional Mexican family, the wife would not make a decision without first consulting her husband" (57). The counselor assumes that Mr. Martinez is unwilling to take off work because he is apathetic about his daughter. "Like any middle-class professional, she assumes he can make himself available during the day and even presumes to moralize at him, something he is probably not used to from a woman, about several hours of work being more important than his daughter" (57). As well, the counselor hides behind school policy to excuse herself from accommodating an evening meeting. Finally, the counselor has a narrow definition of family and has no appreciation of the appropriateness of the brother-in-law's presence. In Hispanic culture, godfathers are responsible for the spiritual welfare of their godchildren. In the eyes of this family, the girl was experiencing a serious spiritual crisis.

This case serves as a reminder to workers to be mindful of imposing their cultural values and expectations on clients. The Martinez family was clearly victimized by a culturebound system that was unresponsive to their needs and wants. The very system that was designed to help them became oppressive. Its representative, the school counselor, reached inaccurate and insulting conclusions because she was unable to view the Martinez family from their own frame of reference.

Potentially Dangerous Clients

The deadliest form of violence is poverty.

—Gandhi

Many workers are employed by agencies in which their work may include some elements of social control (e.g., probation, involuntary clients, establishing eligibility). The nature of this work may leave them increasingly vulnerable to violence (Newhill, 1995). For example, a worker's denial of a client's request for financial assistance may evoke retaliation.

Hospital emergency rooms are particularly dangerous places for social workers, counselors, and other health-care professionals (Lanza et al., 1996). In one case, a 27-year-old social worker was shot, without provocation, while interviewing a client in a psychiatric emergency room, and, in another case, a social worker was stabbed to death by her client in her office (Newhill, 1995).

Although some statistical studies suggest that societal violence may be decreasing at a modest rate, anecdotal and some empirical evidence suggest that most of those who work in the counseling field admit that issues of personal safety are an increasing concern (Newhill, 1995). A study at one private psychiatric hospital found that the frequency of violence by male patients was 50 percent higher than a decade ago and that violence by female patients was 150 percent higher than a decade ago (Tardiff et al., 1997). Newhill's review of the literature supported the conclusion that violence against social workers is increasing. In part, this is because "social workers handle front-line situations that previous generations of workers did not encounter (for example, increased violence attributed to female, elderly, and deinstitutionalized clients and new intervention roles in domestic violence situations, police-social worker teams, custody and divorce mediation, and emergency room work)" (1995:632).

Sometimes workers fear their clients because their behavior is threatening or they have a history of violent behavior. At other times, workers' fears are based on intuition or hunches, the internal response to subtle signals that all is not well. In fact, some clients provide abundant reasons for fear, either because of intimidating behavior or overtly violent acts.

Intimidating behavior includes name-calling; obscene or sexually harassing language and gestures; shouting; threatening displays of power such as fist shaking; invasion of personal space; stalking; and verbal threats. Clients also behave in an intimidating manner when they won't take no for an answer or when they refuse to leave the office. As well, clients may attack workers with personal insults, or they may intimidate them with threats to call the newspaper or civil rights groups. In general, intimidating behavior should be controlled or managed in order to prevent escalation to violence. The following case examples of threatening behavior are all based on real incidents:

- A new client to a welfare office says, "If I don't get some help, you'll be sorry."
- A man in his late twenties stares obstinately at an intake worker.
- An angry parent tells a child protection worker that, if his child is not returned, the worker will know what it's like to lose someone you love.
- A teenager in a group home refuses to comply with house rules. He tells his child-care counselor, "I've had enough. Things are going to change around here."
- A parole officer meets a new parolee for the first time. He is pleasant and cooperative, but the parole officer can't ignore the fact that this man has a long history of assault charges and is known to have a short fuse.
- A mental health counselor deals with her client, a young male with a history of self-destructive behavior. It is obvious that he is not taking his medication, and he seems unusually agitated.
- A ten-year-old child who witnessed abuse at home grabs a pair of scissors and lunges toward the school counselor.

Violent behavior means hitting, pushing, biting, slapping, kicking, throwing objects, and using weapons such as guns, knives, or syringes. It also refers to kidnapping and stalking.

- A social worker in a hospital emergency ward is threatened with a syringe by an angry HIV-positive patient.
- An angry client picks up a chair and hurls it at the counselor.
- A client, disgruntled with the worker's refusal to provide him with money, spits in the worker's face.

It is important that workers do not become hypervigilant and conduct their work in constant fear. Such a stance makes it difficult for them to separate actual hazards from situations that present no real risk. Unwarranted fear of clients leads to uninformed responses. Though very real dangers exist in the workplace, by and large it is a place of safety. The challenge is to be able to answer some basic questions:

- Which clients are likely to become violent? What are the indicators of potential violence?
- Under what conditions should a client's anger be cause for concern?
- What are the skills and behaviors that can be used to de-escalate dangerous situations?

Predicting Violence

Violence rarely arises from a single cause (Roth, 1987). A complex array of psychological, social, biological, and physiological factors must be considered when assessing potential for violence. Although certain variables may be isolated as more likely risk factors, risk assessment is difficult. Every person has a unique history and circumstances, so it is difficult to predict who will become violent. There is no foolproof way to predict with certainty who is likely to become violent.

Violence may be perceived as a desperate act by an angry client to regain control and power. Multiple stressors, such as poverty, the loss or absence of supportive relationships, and substance abuse may magnify a client's vulnerability. These clients may be under considerable stress and near the breaking point. Social workers may be in positions of authority and may have to deny clients access to goods or services. Clients may perceive such denials as further threats to their fragile power, and the risk of violence may escalate. Kaplan and Wheeler suggest that "this denial may be seen not only as a personal rejection but also as a denial of his or her power as a person. This may trigger an uncontrollable need for self-assertion" (1983:343). Attacking others works as a psychological defense against feelings of shame and humiliation.

Key variables that have been found to have some validity for predicting violence include (1) past and current behavior, (2) substance abuse, (3) age and gender, and (4) personality.

Past and Current Behavior.   The best predictor of future violence is a history of violence, and the more recent and severe the violent behavior, the greater the risk. Kelleher's conclusion that a history of violent behavior should always be given serious consideration is echoed consistently in the research on violence: "Although the argument can be made that historical evidence of violence is not a guaranty of future violent behavior, an understanding of any form of violent criminal activity clearly supports the contention that a history of violence is often a predictor of future violence" (1997:13).

Workers should be particularly interested in noting how a client has handled difficulties and frustrations in the past. Some clients who were victims of abuse as children grow up without a capacity for warmth and empathy for others, which can make them particularly oblivious to the suffering of others (Roth, 1987; Weaver, 1982). In extreme cases, violence may even bring these clients pleasure or sexual gratification. Workers should assess the level of remorse that clients show for past acts of violence. Clearly, workers should be most concerned about clients who show no regret. On the other hand, clients who have learned other ways of managing their anger now have more choices and are less likely to act out physically. In this respect, it might be revealing for workers to explore how their clients are managing stress outside the counseling relationship. For example, do they show evidence of a lack of concern for the safety of others? Are there indicators of inappropriate or uncontrolled anger? Are they typically extremely defensive, irritable, or self-centered? To what extent are they prone to impulsive behavior? Impulsive clients might assure workers that they have no intent to harm anyone but ten minutes later attack another client in the waiting room. As Newhill suggests, this type of client has no control over immediate urges, and if the worker points out that his or her behavior may harm others, the client will not disagree, "but neither will he or she constructively integrate what is said" (1992:74).

Clients who have a specific plan of violent action and the means to carry it out represent an immediate risk of violent behavior. Workers need to consider their professional obligations and legal requirements to warn any intended victim by examining their codes of ethics, as well as relevant legislation or legal precedent.

Substance Abuse.   Common sense and empirical research suggest that intoxicated and agitated clients should be approached cautiously. Reviewing the role of drugs in violence, Roth (1987:13–14) concludes:

- Hallucinogens such as LSD and PCP, glue sniffing, amphetamines, and barbiturates have been associated with aggressive and homicidal behaviour.
- Narcotics tend to suppress violence, but individuals might become violent in order to get these drugs.
- Alcohol has a disinhibiting effect on behaviour and is implicated as the most frequent drug linked to violence.

Newhill reviewed the available research and recorded that certain drugs subdue aggression, whereas others escalate it. "Anticholinergics, antipsychotics, antidepressants, sedative hypnotics, and analgesics tend to suppress aggression. Amphetamines and withdrawal from drugs such as morphine or alcohol induce aggression" (1992:70).

Many studies link substance abuse to violent behavior (Swanson et al., 1997; Tardiff et al., 1997). Moreover, people who abuse drugs are at an increased risk of victimization. The link between drug abuse and violent behavior may arise, at least in part, from the fact that alcohol and other drugs are more likely to be abused in a dangerous place.

Age and Gender.   The vast majority of people who are violent and who have been arrested for violent behavior are male. The highest risk for violence is found in people from 15 to 39 years of age; in this age group, the rate of violént acts is three times that of the general population (Roth, 1987; Weaver, 1982).

Personality.   Roth (1987) says that it is important to consider clients' self-esteem to assess their capacity for introspection and their tolerance for ambiguity. Some clients deal with their sense of personal fragility by lashing out at others, and they are hypervigilant in protecting themselves from perceived threats from others.

De Becker cautions that some people assume the worst possible motives and character and that they write their own scripts: "The Scriptwriter is the type of person who asks you a question, answers it himself, then walks away angry at what you said. . . . The things that go wrong are the work of others who will try to blame him. People are out to get him, period" (1997:148–49).

These clients believe that you are uncaring and out to get them. Whatever workers do and however caring their actions, these clients will react based on their expectations. They may try to control the relationship through manipulation and intimidation. This behavior should be interpreted as a warning signal only. These clients may not escalate to violence.

Violence and Mental Illness

The question of whether people with mental illnesses are more dangerous than the general public continues to be the subject of research, debate, and controversy. A study conducted by Davis (1991) concludes that the answers to whether mentally ill people are more dangerous is uncertain. Although his review of the literature found a higher arrest rate for people with mental disorders, he notes that "a small criminal subset, perhaps wrongly diverted into the mental health system, may account for most of the offenses in the dangerousness studies" (177). Moreover, when "this subset is considered separately, most offenses by the rest of the mentally ill population are petty" (177) and arise from similar factors to those with the general public.

Newspaper headlines underscore the dangers that persons with mental illnesses present to their communities:

- "Paranoid Woman Involved in Standoff"
- "Policeman Killed by Ex-Mental Hospital Patient"
- "Schizophrenic Man Kills Wife, Then Turns Gun on Himself"
- "Voices Told Me to Kill My Child"

Not surprisingly, many people believe that there is a strong link between mental illness and violence, but advocate groups argue that the media, through selective and exaggerated reporting, have stimulated the development of false assumptions about the dangers of people with mental illnesses.

In recent decades, deinstitutionalization of psychiatric patients has resulted in unprecedented numbers of people with mental illnesses in the community. Clients with a history of severe mental illness and violence who stop taking their medications can be very dangerous, particularly if they have command hallucinations (voices and images directing them to be violent).

Harris and Rice reviewed risk appraisal work on the prediction of violence and conclude that "the factors most highly and consistently related to risk of violent behavior are historical and include age, sex, past antisocial and violent conduct, psychopathy, aggressive childhood behavior, and substance abuse. Major mental disorder and psychiatric disturbance are poor predictors of violence" (1997:1168).

Another study (Swanson et al., 1997) confirms the links between violent behavior and substance abuse, particularly when there has been absence of recent contact with mental health service providers. A recent study concluded that predictions of violence based on a history of violence were more accurate than clinical predictions based on diagnosis (Gardner et al., 1996).

A comprehensive follow-up study of patients discharged from psychiatric hospitals concluded that former patients who do not abuse drugs are no more violent than a random population sample (Bower, 1998). Pastor concluded that unrealistic and delusional thinking tends to increase the likelihood that violence will result. He also noted: "Manic symptoms, such as irritability, increased energy or activity, psychomotor agitation and grandiosity, also increases the risk of violent behavior. A belief that 'others' are responsible for the person's misfortune increases the likelihood of striking out against those persons" (1995:1173). Organic brain disease and head trauma may reduce a client's impulse control and cause him or her to act in ways that are dangerous to self and others. Organic disease or injury should be suspected when clients show disturbance in attention, orientation, and short-term memory (Dubovsky and Weissberg, 1986:258).

Assessing Potential for Violence

Although long-term prediction of violence is difficult, workers should be able to make reasonable short-term forecasts based on consideration and assessment of the following questions and issues:

1. Does the client have a history of violent behavior and/or an arrest record for violent crime? The worker should review agency file records and other anecdotal evidence for information.
2. To what extent does the client appear dangerous, as evidenced by marked or escalating agitation or threatening behavior? The worker should consider verbal threats as well as nonverbal expressions of aggression.
3. If the client is threatening violence, are the threats concrete and specific? Does the client have a plan? Does the client have the means to carry out the stated plan? Does the client have a weapon or access to one, especially a gun?
4. Is the client under duress from one or more stressors, such as poverty, unemployment, or loss of social support? Has there been a recent precipitating event that represents the last straw for the client?
5. What agency factors might be exacerbating the situation (e.g., missed or delayed appointments, denial of benefits)?
6. What worker variables might be heightening the client's anger? Is the counselor acting in ways that the client might see as provocative? For example, is the worker defensive or judgmental toward the client?
7. What high-risk symptoms are present? For example, is the client experiencing command hallucinations? Is the client prone to impulsivity? Is the client near panic? Is the client narcissistic or self-centered and prone to blame others for his or her misfortune? Is the client hypersensitive to any criticism or hint of rejection?
8. Is there evidence of substance abuse?

9. Has the client failed to take psychiatric medication? Has the client cut off or failed to keep scheduled contact with a psychiatric caregiver?
10. Does the client believe that he or she is able to control his or her behavior? Is the client socially isolated?

These questions are references for the purpose of assessment only. The presence of any of the factors does not mean that the client will necessarily become violent. However, when there are numerous strong clues that suggest violence, workers should proceed cautiously and look for ways to reduce risk factors to establish safety.

Preventing Violence

Many clients come to counseling in a state of crisis, with low tolerance for added stress. Consequently, it is important that agency policies and routines do not compound the risk. Congested and noisy waiting rooms, unexplained delays for appointments, insensitive receptionists, and indifference to the clients' right to privacy can exacerbate frustration. Nevertheless, even when these factors are controlled, workers may have to deny assistance. Their clients may perceive themselves as "losers" and look for ways to save face, including resistance, with statements such as "I don't have to put up with this treatment."

Agency Safety Precautions. In settings where there is significant risk for violence, procedures should be developed for dealing with potentially violent clients. In fact, employers usually have a legal responsibility to provide a safe working environment. Minimum safety precautions might include the following:

Policy. Agencies should develop policies and procedures for dealing with potentially violent situations. The agencies should review these policies regularly and incorporate them as part of in-service training for new staff. Policies should address issues such as the procedures for home visits, giving clients home phone numbers, using last names, and interviewing after hours. Generally, workers should not make home visits alone if there is a possibility for violence. Many workers who work with potentially dangerous clients use unlisted phone numbers as a way to ensure privacy and safety. In extreme situations, such as dangerous child-abuse investigations, social workers who have a legislated mandate to investigate allegations of abuse may need to be protected by police. Generally, workers should avoid making unescorted visits to high-crime areas.

Staff Training. Training should address tactics for dealing with difficult clients, including those who are involuntary, angry, or acting out. Front office and reception staff should also be trained so that they can relate to clients in ways that do not escalate the clients' frustration or anger. Periodic team simulations will ensure that everyone is familiar with their roles and responsibilities. This prevents members of the team from becoming confused during a critical incident. Simulations also help staff to build confidence in themselves and trust that their colleagues are ready and available to assist.

Interviewing Procedures. Workers who are interviewing difficult or dangerous clients should work in offices where access to immediate help can be provided. A silent system for alerting others that a dangerous situation is developing should be implemented (e.g., panic button, encrypted phone message). Leaving the door open during the interview can allow other staff to monitor any increasing danger, but this practice may violate the client's confidentiality. Workers should make sure that clients have a clear path to the doorway so they can leave abruptly if they choose.

Files on clients with a history of violence should clearly document details of any past violent behavior or threats. For some clients with a high propensity toward violence, a team approach may be desirable, with two or more persons being present during the interview. In such cases, it is usually preferable if only one person does the interviewing. This can lessen any feelings the client might have of being ganged up on. Too many people may heighten the client's anxiety. Backup help can be stationed out of sight but on quick standby for dangerous situations.

Office Design.   Office furnishings should be carefully chosen to minimize risk. For example, shatterproof glass can be used, and items that are potential weapons, such as scissors, should be removed. Soft lighting and calming colors may have some modest effect on mood. As noted earlier, workers and clients should have an unobstructed path to the exit. The agency itself should have good external lighting. During high-risk hours, such as late at night or early in the morning, access doors should be locked, and workers should not have to walk alone to dark parking lots.

Crisis Intervention.   A written script for staff who must call police or emergency backup intervention will ensure that relevant information is presented quickly and clearly. In a panic situation, people may forget basic information, such as emergency phone numbers. After a violent or hostile act, it is important to have a mechanism for debriefing. This enables the worker to restore a sense of equilibrium. It is important to remember that a critical incident may also affect staff who were not directly involved, including clerical, janitorial, and kitchen personnel. They, too, may suffer trauma; therefore, they should be involved in the debriefing.

The Phases of Violence

The National Crisis Prevention Institute (1986) has identified four **phases of violence** that describe how crises escalate to violence. Each phase is characterized by particular indicators and demands specific responses. In applying this or any other model, it is important to remember that individual incidents may not conform to the model. The four phases are (1) anxiety, (2) defensiveness, (3) acting out, and (4) tension reduction.

Anxiety Phase.   In the anxiety phase there is a marked change in the client's behavior. This phase represents an early warning that the client is becoming agitated. The individual may show increased signs of anxiety, including verbal challenges such as refusal to follow directions or questioning of authority. Statements such as "You can't tell me what to do," accompanied by finger pointing, may suggest escalating anger. Shea (1988) cautions that other signs of escalation, such as pacing, intense staring, and refusing to sit down, should be noted. At this point, the client may respond to gentle directives and invitations, such as "Let's talk and see if we can work things out" and "I'm willing to listen." This phase offers workers the best opportunity to intervene early to prevent anger from intensifying into acting-out behavior.

Usually, clients enter the anxiety phase because of stress, which can come from multiple sources, including jobs, relationships, health, and finances. Stressful events are defined by clients; thus, workers cannot measure stress just by knowing the facts about a situation. What one client might see as an opportunity another might experience as a threat. Kelleher describes the triggering event as an incident that pushes the potentially violent person toward violence: "It is the proverbial 'straw that broke the camel's back' and, like the straw, may often be perceived by others with far less significance than it's perceived by the perpetrator" (1997:11). Before clients see workers, they may already be feeling help-less and abandoned. Any worker behavior that the client views as provocative or rejecting may further propel the client toward violence.

Individuals who are predisposed to violence respond to stress with increasing anger and anxiety. A person's emotional reaction can also influence whether he or she might become violent. Labig observes:

> Emotional reactions that make it more likely that a person will become violent in reaction to a stressful situation are anger, hatred, blame, and terror. People who typically react emo-tionally in these ways are at higher risk of escalating into violence. Emotional reactions can also intervene to inhibit an individual's behavior. Empathy and guilt make it less likely that a person will strike out (1995:24–25).

Dealing with Threats.   Gavin de Becker, an expert on predicting violent behavior, offers this strategy for dealing with threats

> When any type of threat includes indirect or veiled references to things they might do, such as "You'll be sorry," or "Don't mess with me," it is best to ask directly, "What do you mean by that?" Ask exactly what the person is threatening to do. His elaboration will al-most always be weaker than his implied threat. If, on the other hand, his explanation of the comment is actually an explicit threat, better to learn it now than to be uncertain later (1997:117).

Workers need to take action when clients exhibit changes in their normal behavior. This action could include referral for psychiatric assessment and reevaluation of medica-tion. Immediate crisis intervention might result in moving the client out of the environment where others might be injured, for example, a crowded waiting room. As well, long-term counseling might focus on anger management or relaxation training. The immediate goal is crisis management, but the long-term goal is crisis prevention.

Workers should be attuned to their own fears and anxieties. Appropriate anxiety is a clue that the situation is escalating and that remedial action is necessary. De Becker (1997) argues that people have a basic intuition that tells them when all is not well, but that they often disregard the red flags of danger. It is only in the aftermath that they reflect and realize that they had sufficient information to make better choices but that they ignored it.

Defensiveness Phase.   This is a late warning phase with clear indicators that the person is about to lose control. The client may become more challenging and belligerent by mak-ing direct threats and provocations. The client has become irrational, and clear warning indicators may be present, including clenching or raising of fists, grasping objects to use as weapons, and showing signs of movement toward attack (e.g., grasping the arms of the chair, denoting that they are about to rise and advance) (Shea, 1988:172).

At this point, it is crucial that workers refrain from reciprocating with the same aggressive behavior that the client is using. This requires some discipline, as the worker's natural reaction might be to respond in kind, which only serves to escalate or precipitate violence. Decreased eye contact might be appropriate with some clients. As well, workers are wise to increase the physical distance between them and their clients, because potentially violent persons may have an increased need for space. Physical contact, however well intentioned, should be avoided. Sometimes workers try to calm clients by touching their shoulders, but this is ill advised, as clients may interpret it as aggression.

During this phase, workers need to be self-disciplined and remain calm. This calmness should be reflected in their voice and manner and in slow, nonjargonistic language. Workers who speak calmly and avoid any loud or authoritarian tone may have a contagious effect on their anxious clients. On the other hand, workers who match their clients' defensiveness and anger exacerbate the situation and increase the possibility of violent retaliation.

Defusing Explosive Situations.   When dealing with clients who are hostile and on the verge of losing control, it is essential that workers maintain their own equilibrium and remain in control. They need to resist any tendency to be baited by clients into angry confrontation or retaliation, which only escalates the crisis. Moreover, if clients perceive that their workers are not in control, they may become more irrational.

Basic communication and counseling skills are excellent tools for both preventing violence and for dealing with clients who are on the verge of losing control. In particular, active listening skills communicate that workers are willing to listen to and learn about clients' wants and needs. Workers should remember the importance of modeling. When workers stay calm, clients are more likely to emulate their composure. Helpers should try to speak calmly and avoid any mannerisms that clients might interpret as threatening (e.g., touching a client, making sudden movements, or invading a client's personal space). "Encourage the client to sit and to be comfortable. Listen, empathize, paraphrase, and summarize while avoiding defensiveness. With clients who are exhibiting early warning signs such as a noticeable escalation of anxiety, supportive and empathic responses are best, whereas an authoritarian (rigid) stance may leave the client feeling pressured or trapped" (Shebib, 1997:246).

However, some clients may misinterpret empathy as an unwanted intrusion on personal privacy and react defensively. Workers should be alert to clients' reactions to certain topics or questions. This will help them make intelligent decisions about when it is appropriate to challenge or confront and when they should back off because the subject is clearly agitating their clients to a dangerous level. They should be careful that they don't overreact and should avoid interview topics that could be controversial.

Promoting Compromise.   Clients often feel disempowered and disadvantaged. When workers promote compromise, they restore some balance of power in the relationship and show their willingness to reach a solution. When workers argue with, threaten, or ignore the needs of their clients, the clients may become increasingly belligerent. As Dubovsky and Weissberg conclude, the client "protects himself from feeling powerless, inadequate and frightened by attempting to demonstrate how powerful and frightening he can be" (1986:262).

Workers need to help clients find a way to save face and retain their dignity. While they have the responsibility to set appropriate limits, they must not argue with, ridicule, challenge, threaten, or unfairly criticize clients. The language used by the worker can help to establish an atmosphere of compromise and mutual problem solving, for example, "Let's work together to find a solution we can both live with" and "I really do want to find a solution."

> CLIENT: *(yelling loudly) I'm sick and tired of getting the runaround.*
>
> SOCIAL WORKER: *(calmly) Your anger makes it clear to me how strongly you feel about this. I can see that this is an important issue for you. But we will work better if you stay calm and don't threaten. Let's see if there's another way to approach it.*
>
> CLIENT: *(pacing and yelling) Are you going to help me or not?*
>
> SOCIAL WORKER: *(calmly) I'm willing to work at this problem to solve it.*
>
> *(client sits, stares intently)*
>
> SOCIAL WORKER: *I understand that you think that this is the best solution. I also appreciate your reasoning. But there are two of us here. We need to find a solution that both of us can be satisfied with.*
>
> CLIENT: *(loud, but not yelling) I'm trying to be reasonable.*
>
> SOCIAL WORKER: *Okay, I'm listening. I'd like to hear your ideas on how to . . .*

Hocker and Wilmot identify five principles for establishing effective collaboration: (1) join with the other, (2) control the process, not the people, (3) use productive communication, (4) be firm in your goals, flexible in your means, and (5) remain optimistic about finding solutions to your conflict (1995:212). They suggest a variety of means for operationalizing the principles, such as using *we* language that affirms common interests, actively listening even when you disagree, and persuading rather than coercing. As well, they emphasize the importance of separating the issues from the relationship and dealing with the important items one at a time. Such a collaborative approach requires that workers remain positive, creative, and constructive. The general goal must be "We, working together, can solve this problem that is confronting us" (Hocker and Wilmot, 1995:205). Dubovsky and Weissberg (1986) underscore the importance of promoting collaboration. They contend that the client "protects himself from feeling powerless, inadequate and frightened by attempting to demonstrate how powerful and frightening he can be. His threatening behavior increases if he feels he is not being taken seriously" (262).

Labig (1995) says that some people can react with intense emotion because of the emotional tone with which they are addressed. Similarly, intimidating body language such as crossed arms, staring, or a fighting stance can have the same effect.

A loud, intense, and menacing voice can create an instantaneous emotional response in certain people. This is all it takes to push some people into retaliatory action. . . . Generally, the more emotionally calm and safe an individual feels, the less likely he is to become violent. The more frightening and threatening he finds his environment, the more likely he is to respond with violence (Labig, 1995:25).

Setting Limits.   In the defensive phase, clients may still respond to appropriate limits. Limits let clients know what will and what will not be tolerated, but workers need to apply certain principles in setting limits. They should be specific and tell clients which behavior is inappropriate. Clients may not be aware of what is acceptable. Moreover, they may not know how their behavior is affecting others. Limits should include enforceable consequences, and workers should state the consequences of noncompliance.

Clients, particularly those in institutional settings, may rely on staff to assist them with controls and limits. However, "if staff become overly anxious while managing a violent patient, the potentiality for that patient's violence increases" (Roth, 1987:246). Thus, it is important for workers to understand how their own behavior may escalate a client's potential for violence. Furthermore, they need to learn how to monitor their own feelings, when to ask for help, and when to terminate an interaction because they are not in control (Roth, 1987).

Acting-out Phase.   At this stage, the client has lost control and has become assaultive. Protection of self and others is the primary goal. ideally, agency procedures are operative, and workers who are dealing with such situations will receive immediate assistance from the staff team. Police intervention and restraint of the acting-out client may also be required. When dealing with acting-out clients, a team approach with a well-organized and trained staff is the preferred way to address the crisis. A team approach provides increased safety for everyone, including the client. A well-trained team may subdue violent clients before they injure themselves or others, but staff should be trained in techniques for physical restraint and control (for a brief description of physical control techniques see Roth, 1987:254). The team members provide support and can act as witnesses if litigation should arise as a result of the incident.

Police Intervention.   Workers should not hesitate to call the police if a client becomes too threatening or aggressive. No one is expected to risk his or her life or endure physical assault as part of the job. Sometimes clients are unwilling or unable to constrain their hostility, and police or psychiatric restraint is essential for managing the crisis. Police intervention is particularly crucial when dealing with clients who have weapons. Workers should not try to prevent a client who is determined to leave by blocking the exit. Moreover, workers who are assaulted by clients should consider filing criminal charges. This establishes the importance of clients' taking responsibility for their actions.

Tension Reduction Phase.   The tension reduction, or recovery, phase is characterized by a gradual reduction in aggressive behavior and a return to more rational behavior. The client may still be driven by adrenaline for up to ninety minutes (Kaplan and Wheeler, 1983), so it is important that workers proceed cautiously to avoid reactivating aggressive acting out.

Follow-up Counseling Interventions.   Clients can be counseled to become alert to their own warning signs, such as "tenseness, sweating palms, a tightening of the stomach, pressure in the chest and a surge to the head" (Morrissey, 1998:6). Once clients are aware of their own triggers, they can be counseled on appropriate diversionary tactics, such as employing relaxation techniques, taking time out, and using **assertiveness** or other behavioral response alternatives. Morrissey describes a technique that a worker used with a client who was on the verge of violence. The worker reassured the client "that he was there to help him and commended the client for coming to see him rather than acting on his feelings of rage. He also asked the client what was keeping him in control thus far and used that as proof to reinforce the fact that he could indeed control himself" (1998:6).

At the end of the tension reduction phase and after the client has returned to normal, the client may be mentally and physically exhausted and show signs of remorse and shame. Consequently, counseling can be directed toward helping the client use the experience as a learning opportunity, for example, to develop alternative responses for future similar stresses. Interview 8.2 provides an example.

Because of their communication skills training, counselors are well prepared to teach their clients techniques for resolving conflict and crises nonviolently. The skills of counseling are also, to some extent, the skills of effective everyday communication. Communication skill training equips clients with more choices for asserting their rights and respecting others. Assertiveness training can help clients express feelings in a nonaggressive manner. When clients are able to respond assertively, they establish an atmosphere of cooperation and conflict can be peacefully resolved. Often conflict is difficult for clients to settle because they are unable to see the perspectives or feelings of others in the conflict. Clients who learn empathy and other active listening skills are better able to compromise because they are less likely to judge their own behavior as absolutely right and that of others as absolutely wrong.

Sometimes, long before violence erupts, workers may intuitively feel that the situation is worsening. This feeling may be based on unconscious reactions to subtle cues and indicators. Both workers and clients might find it useful to try to concretely identify these clues. Doing so will assist clients in becoming sensitive to those initial psychological responses that signal the imminent onset of the anxiety phase. Clients who become adept at recognizing early warning indicators are in a much better position to take early warning action, such as withdrawing from an explosive situation or switching to healthier problem-solving strategies.

Critical Incident Debriefing

Workers who have been assaulted or threatened with assault may be traumatized and experience symptoms such as recurrent images or thoughts of the event, distressing dreams, flashbacks, and intense stress when returning to the scene of the incident. There may be a marked decline in their ability to handle routine work tasks, and they may feel detached and isolated from colleagues. They may develop sleep difficulties and have difficulty concentrating. Frequently, they return to work in a state of hypervigilance, constantly expecting further trauma. Often they describe themselves as "numb" and unable to enjoy activities that usually gave them pleasure. When symptoms such as these are present, counselors should consider obtaining medical assessment and/or professional counseling.

Even when workers are not injured, the threat of violence can be just as traumatic. Typical responses may include helplessness and thoughts of leaving the profession. These

TABLE 8.2 The Phases of Violence

Phase	Strategy Choices
Preventive	Recognize risk factors. Structure the agency to reduce client stress and danger to personnel. Set up emergency response protocols. Practice crisis responses with simulations. Take steps to protect identified intended victims.
Anxiety phase	Promote clients' involvement in decision making to give them a sense of empowerment and control. Attend to changes in the clients' behavior. Take gut instincts and threats seriously. Use empathy and reassurance to acknowledge and attend to the clients' needs.
Defensiveness phase	Set clear, reasonable, and enforceable limits. Respect clients' need for increased space. Remain calm and avoid sudden movement. Avoid using an authoritarian tone. Respond assertively. Use basic counseling skills. Search for compromises and "win–win" solutions.
Acting out phase	Call the police (do not try to disarm clients who have weapons and do not risk personal safety unless unavoidable). Try to ensure the safety of everyone, including bystanders, other staff, and the client. Use a team approach, including, if necessary and appropriate, physical restraint. Refer clients to a hospital for assessment and/or medication.
Tension reduction phase	Try to reestablish verbal communication. Support the client's return to a state of calm. Reestablish communication. Elicit available family support.
Follow-up	Involve clients in long-term counseling. Help clients learn nonviolent solutions to problems. Implement consequences, if any. Conduct individual and team debriefing. When clients have plans to harm a specific victim, warn the victim and/or notify the police. Review procedures for handling disruptive clients.

INTERVIEW **8.2**
Follow-up to a Violent Incident

In the following example, the social worker, a group-home worker, is reviewing an incident with her client. The incident occurred two hours earlier and was precipitated when the worker denied the client, a 16-year-old male, permission to meet with some of his friends later that night. The client smashed an ashtray on the floor and stormed out of the office while screaming obscenities.

Dialogue	Analysis
SOCIAL WORKER: Let's talk about what happened. **CLIENT:** I guess I got a bit carried away. **SOCIAL WORKER:** I was scared. **CLIENT:** I'm sorry. I won't let it happen again.	Whenever possible, it's important that clients be invited to review prior incidents. By telling the client how she felt, the worker may be giving the client new information that will increase the client's capacity for empathy. Often, violent or acting-out clients are so preoccupied with their own needs and fears that they don't realize the impact they have on others.
SOCIAL WORKER: I accept your apology.	This helps the client to retain some dignity. Notice that the worker's acceptance of her client's apology does not condone his behavior, as would a statement such as "It's okay. Don't worry about it. No real harm was done."
SOCIAL WORKER: It might be helpful for both of us to go over what happened to see how it might have been prevented. **CLIENT:** I was still upset from seeing my mother. When you said no, it was just too much.	One goal of counseling is to help clients recognize their own early warning indicators that they are in danger of losing control.
SOCIAL WORKER: It's never been easy for you to talk to your mom. You always seem to come back really wound up.	Empathy confirms that feelings have been heard and understood.
CLIENT: Yeah, those are the days that people should stay out of my face.	The client rationalizes his behavior, putting the responsibility on others.
SOCIAL WORKER: Good point. Sounds like you know that you need some time alone when you're stressed.	Without directly challenging the rationalization, the worker shifts the focus back on the client.
CLIENT: You got it.	
SOCIAL WORKER: As we talk, I'm wondering what prevented you from taking that time. If you'd taken the time to cool off before approaching me, things would have been a lot different. **CLIENT:** Sure, I know I have to learn to control my temper, but once I get going I just can't seem to stop myself.	Feedback confrontation challenges the client to consider some new alternatives.

(continued)

INTERVIEW 8.2 Continued

SOCIAL WORKER: Put another way, your hope is to find a way to deal with your feelings so that you don't get angry and hurt someone.

CLIENT: I don't know if that's possible.

SOCIAL WORKER: You've already shown me that you have some skill at doing this. You threw the ashtray and you said some awful things, but afterward you left the room without doing any more damage. This tells me that you have the ability to bring things under control. You need to find a way to do this a little earlier.

The counselor takes advantage of an opportunity to reframe the client's problem statement into a goal.

Acknowledgment of the client's restraint, however late he was in using it, provides a base for further development. By doing so, the counselor reinforces nonaggressive behavioral alternatives.

---

feelings may develop immediately or emerge after a delay of months or even years. Consequently, it is important to debrief critical incidents in order to lessen the shock, reduce isolation, and restore personal control. Team debriefing should take place as soon as possible after the incident. As well, some affected staff may require private debriefing. It is important that everyone, not just the professional staff, be included as a member of the team. Support and other front office staff, for example, are often intimately involved in a crisis.

Debriefing should be conducted by an objective third party in a safe setting, and it should be held as soon as possible after the critical incident, usually within 24 to 72 hours in order to minimize the effects of any trauma that victims or witnesses may be experiencing. This is important in order to promote a return to the normal routine of the agency. A typical debriefing session is like a counseling interview. The debriefing should reinforce team interdependence. Sometimes counselors are reluctant to ask colleagues for assistance, believing that asking for help is a sign of incompetence. One goal of a debriefing is to develop a staff culture in which asking for help is a sign of strength, rather than weakness. A critical incident debriefing generally has the following elements:

1. All team members are invited to share feelings and reactions about the current or prior incidents. Active listening can be used to promote this process. This will help individuals who were threatened or assaulted to "normalize" their own reactions. Counselors should require little persuasion of the benefits of talking about one's feelings. They might be reminded that sharing feelings is something they routinely ask of their clients. Helping team members manage feelings is the major objective of the debriefing. At this time, it is important to identify the potential physical and emotional reactions that staff may experience. As well, information regarding services such as employee assistance programs (EAPs) that are available to staff who need additional help to manage their emotions should be detailed.

2. The team conducts a postmortem on the violent event. A thorough analysis of what transpired is used to review and reinforce procedures for dealing with violent clients.

An important question for the team to consider is: "What, if anything, could we have done to prevent this incident?" For example, the team can explore whether any early warning indicators of pending violence were overlooked. They can investigate whether there were things that individuals or the agency did or did not do that contributed to the client's behavior.

3. The team debriefing is an important "teachable moment," when staff are highly motivated toward skill development. It is a chance to explore alternative responses that might have been utilized at all stages of the critical incident. Role plays and simulations can be used to practice alternative responses. This step helps empower individuals and the team by moving them away from any tendency to feel helpless.

Summary

Resistance is a defensive reaction by clients that interferes with or delays the process of counseling. Client resistance to counseling is common. It may be evident in a variety of ways, such as failure to cooperate with the basic routine of counseling, subtle or direct attacks, passivity, and nonverbal cues. Resistance arises for a number of reasons that may be categorized under five major groupings: (1) relationship, (2) motivational, (3) attitudinal, (4) fearful, and (5) involuntary. Workers can use a range of techniques for dealing with each of the five types. Client resistance may be unconscious, or it may be a deliberate act of sabotage or avoidance. Because client resistance can be unsettling for workers, it is important that they objectively evaluate their own feelings and behavior when dealing with it. They need to be sensitive to the possibility that cross-cultural miscommunication can be mistaken for resistance.

Intimidating behavior includes such things as name-calling, using obscene language, shouting, threatening through displays of power such as fist shaking, invading personal space, stalking, and issuing verbal threats. Violent behavior means hitting, pushing, biting, slapping, kicking, throwing objects, and using weapons such as guns, knives, or syringes.

Clients may become violent for a number of reasons. Although it is difficult to predict with certainty which clients will become violent, some risk factors may be isolated. The best predictor of violent behavior is a history of violence. Substance abuse is also a common variable. Other factors that workers should consider when assessing risk are age, gender, and personality characteristics.

To prevent or minimize violent incidents, counseling agencies should develop policies and routines that address this issue. Simulations can be used to practice responses to potentially dangerous situations.

The four phases of violence are anxiety, defensiveness, acting-out, and tension reduction. In the anxiety phase there is marked change in the client's usual behavior, with signs of increasing agitation. To prevent anxiety from escalating, workers should attempt to establish a climate of cooperation and mutual problem solving. In the defensiveness phase, anxiety has increased to the point that the client is in danger of losing control. At this point, clients may still respond to appropriate limits. In the acting-out phase, the client becomes assaultive, and emergency intervention is crucial. Because the client has lost control and has become assaultive, protection of self and others is the primary goal. During the tension reduction phase, the client's aggressive energy gradually recedes, and the client returns to more rational behavior.

It is important to debrief critical incidents in order to lessen shock, reduce isolation, and restore personal control. Team debriefing should take place as soon as possible after the incident. It should provide an opportunity for people to talk about their feelings. As well, the debriefing can be used to review what went wrong. Role plays and simulations can be used to practice alternative responses. Overall, the debriefing is designed to empower individuals and the team and to move them away from any tendency to feel helpless.

EXERCISES

1. Review your experiences dealing with persons who are angry, resistant, or potentially violent. What aspects of your experience will help you deal effectively with difficult situations? What aspects will impede your ability?

2. Interview counselors from different settings regarding their experiences with violent or potentially violent clients. Discuss strategies that they have found effective.

3. Work in a small group. Assume that you are members of an inner-city needle exchange center. Develop detailed policies and procedures for dealing with violent and potentially violent clients.

4. Suppose you review the file on your next client and discover that he was loud and abusive with his previous worker. What are some possible explanations for this client's behavior? Suggest some strategies for working with this client.

5. Work in a small group to explore the potential benefits and risks of each of the following actions:

    a. having an unlisted phone number

    b. making home visits alone

    c. making home visits only when accompanied by a colleague

    d. conducting joint interviews for potentially hostile clients

    e. using only your first name with clients

    f. knowing that a client has a history of violence

    g. interviewing a client with a police officer present

    h. refusing to see a client with a history of violence

    i. striking a client in order to defend yourself

    j. calling the police

    k. warning an intended victim

    l. seeing a client who has been drinking

6. What is your natural reaction when someone's anger starts to escalate? Do you tend to fight back, or do you withdraw?

7. Research legal and ethical codes in order to explore your responsibility to notify intended victims of violence. Talk to counselors and agencies in the field to get their opinions on this issue.

9 Variations with Selected Target Groups

Preview

After reading this chapter you should be able to:

- demonstrate knowledge of the impact of job loss
- identify the four major activity target areas for employment counseling
- describe techniques for networking and accessing the hidden job market
- distinguish between traditional and nontraditional job search methods
- explain the use of electronic resources in an employment search
- explain the structure and use of *DSM-IV*
- describe the characteristics of and treatment for major mental disorders, including schizophrenia, mood disorders, anxiety disorders, and eating disorders
- identify suicide warning signs
- identify strategies for dealing with clients who are suicidal
- identify issues and strategies for counseling clients who are HIV positive and clients who have AIDS
- explain the practice of brief counseling
- describe techniques of brief counseling

Employment Counseling

Unemployment can have a devastating impact on individuals and families. Aside from the obvious loss of income from not having a job, there may be significant consequences to job loss (see Bolles, 1997; Kirsh, 1983; Steinweg, 1990; Sunley and Sheek, 1986). For example, unemployment can lead to increased stress; health and mental health problems, including depression; increased suicide rate; premature death; and increased hospitalization (Kirsh, 1983). Holmes and Werbel (1992) reviewed the research on the physical and mental health effects of job loss and found that job loss leads to higher incidence of coronary disease, hypertension, ulcers, headaches, depression, anxiety, and hostility, as well as increased family conflict and higher illness rates among children whose parents are unemployed.

For many people, a job or career is a pivotal part of their identity. A protracted period of unemployment can result in a loss of self-esteem and personality. Persons who are unemployed lose the routine of their daily lives, the structure of the workday, their sense of purpose, and the social contact with friends and colleagues at the workplace. As one unemployed journalist describes the experience, "I feel like I no longer have a life . . . I'm a participant in a script that someone else has taken over" (Burman, 1988:5).

The financial impact of job loss can be devastating. Day-to-day survival can be tenuous at best as individuals and families struggle to survive on savings or meager social assistance benefits. Financial problems become a crisis when unanticipated expenses such as car repairs, school fees, or medical bills appear. Job loss can easily result in the loss of savings, one's home, and the ability to maintain one's lifestyle, including social and recreational life. As Burman describes it, "It means not being able to reciprocate a dinner invitation, not seeing one's way clear to join a friend for lunch or a movie, and not being able to afford the price of a favourite recreation. As the weeks and months of unemployment pass, one's social orbit shrinks, placing a heavy emotional load on family relationships" (1988:xii).

Challenges and Goals for Counselors

David Steinweg reviewed the research on counseling people who are unemployed and concludes that "recent research suggests that interventions focusing primarily on alleviating the negative consequences of job joss (e.g., financial pressures and subsequent job rejections) are not sufficient to help unemployed workers sustain a successful job search" (1990:40). He suggests that helpers need to broaden their activities to include other counseling goals and activities.

Because sustained unemployment can be damaging to clients' self-worth and esteem, it is important for workers to encourage clients to maintain as much as possible their daily routine. In addition, whenever possible, clients should continue activities and commitments, such as parenting and volunteering, that enhance self-esteem.

Clients are often unemployed for reasons beyond their control, such as high unemployment rates, organizational downsizing, and economic downturns. Workers can help clients normalize the experience of job loss by helping them feel less isolated. They can help clients change their thinking about job loss by encouraging them not to blame themselves.

In general, employment counseling is concerned with four major activity target areas: (1) job loss counseling, (2) career counseling, (3) job search skills, and (4) life skills counseling (see Table 9.1). An assessment interview will help workers determine if a client needs assistance with one or more of the four areas.

Job Loss Counseling

Job loss counseling aims to help clients regain equilibrium after being laid off and deal with the psychological stress that typically accompanies job loss and unemployment. As well, workers can help clients adjust to living on reduced or low incomes. They can help them access services that might help alleviate financial stress (e.g., welfare, employment insurance, loan negotiation, use of community resources such as subsidized daycare).

Self-esteem counseling is essential because it affects how job seekers market themselves. Sometimes clients develop learned helplessness as a result of repeated failure in

TABLE 9.1   Employment Counseling

Activity Area	Counseling Targets
Job loss counseling	Improving self-esteem Managing stress Managing physical needs
Career counseling	Researching careers Testing interests Testing aptitudes Researching employers
Job search skills	Overcoming barriers (e.g., age, a criminal record, racism, sexism) Writing résumés Identifying leads Networking Conducting informational interviews Getting interviews Preparing for interviews Using interview follow-up techniques Using electronic resources
Life skills counseling	Teaching work and life skills Helping with job survival

their job search. Arnhold and Razak (1991) suggest a number of strategies for helping unemployed clients overcome learned helplessness.

1. Short-circuit self-depreciation by ignoring such remarks, challenging the basis for the remarks, and inviting clients to rationally consider changing the basis for their beliefs. Workers might use reframing and other techniques for changing thinking (see Chapter 7).
2. Reassure clients that "perfection is neither attainable nor expected" (103).
3. Reinforce current or past successes. "Positive comments on a neat desk, a new outfit, reliable punctuality, and other small past and present triumphs can be to the helplessness-oriented individual what a meal is to a starving person" (103).
4. Encourage action. In this respect, setting small but achievable goals can help clients break out of pessimism.

When dealing with clients who feel and act helpless it is important for workers to remember Arnhold and Razak's observation that "helplessness is a perception and not an accurate description of an individual. Many who are afflicted with crippling low self-esteem are in fact quite capable in some respects—the problem is that they think and feel otherwise about themselves" (102).

Amundson (1996) suggests a series of strategies to help clients change their perspectives. These strategies include helping clients make positive affirmations, normalizing the experience of unemployment (i.e., assuring them that their feelings and reactions are normal), and encouraging them to avoid blaming themselves for unemployment. As well, workers can encourage clients to identify and use transferable skills (skills from other jobs, activities, hobbies, and experiences) in the job search. Amundson proposes challenging negative thinking patterns by having clients change "I can't" statements to "I won't" declarations. By changing the wording, clients can consider the power that they have to change any thinking or behavior that might be acting as a barrier to action. Amundson also suggests giving clients specific activities that interrupt established but ineffective patterns of activity. For example, workers could ask clients to research employers, develop contact lists, and make phone calls. "By actively engaging in meaningful activity, with support, clients will gain confidence and will have a greater likelihood of persisting with career exploration and job search" (Amundson, 1996:160).

Career Counseling

Career counseling is appropriate for clients who do not have a clear perspective on either their interests or their abilities. The results of interest and aptitude testing are a starting point for consideration and further exploration. Professionals should never use them as prescriptions for dictating what clients must or should do. With clear career possibilities identified, clients can then use a variety of resources to find out about the occupations that match their unique interests, values, and personal styles. This process should result in the establishment of a career goal.

Job Search Skills

Counseling in job search skills includes tasks such as researching employers and careers, preparing for job interviews, handling difficult interview questions, and following up phone calls or employment interviews. For example, workers can help clients anticipate interview questions, then role-play answers. Videotapes can be used to help clients review their manner and the quality of their answers.

Job search skills training focuses on nontraditional job search methods, such as networking and using the hidden job market (see Table 9.2). Small groups for support and role playing may support this process.

Most uninformed job seekers rely on newspaper and other advertisements or employment agencies to find job vacancies. However, most jobs are never advertised. Only 15 to 20 percent of all jobs are filled through job ads (Angel and Harney, 1997; Farr, 1996). The remaining 80 to 85 percent of vacancies are part of what is known as the **hidden job market**.

Networking is the primary tool used to access the hidden job market. It involves using contacts such as friends, family, neighbors, and others who might provide information or access to others with information about job opportunities. Workers can assist clients by asking them to brainstorm the names of absolutely everyone they know or have known.

TABLE 9.2   Traditional versus Modern Job Search Methods

Traditional Search Method	Modern Strategies
Mail the same résumé widely to employers	Tailor multiple résumés to individual employers
Be ready to take any job	Link job and career objective to targeted employer or industry
Learn about the job after you are hired	Conduct prior research to learn about the organization Prepare for the job interview by anticipating and rehearsing questions
Emphasize specific skills and experiences	Emphasize transferable skills Use work skills derived from other areas (e.g., volunteer work, hobbies)
Gear job search to available vacancies	Gear job search to aptitude and interests and not to one type of job
Respond to job ads—"door to door" contact (dropping in on all employers in a defined geographic area to ask about job openings)	Use multiple approaches to job search including: • networking • phone contact • use of Internet • direct contact with targeted employers • use of the hidden job market • follow-up of contacts • call back
Effort is part-time and sporadic	Effort is full-time

Clients network by contacting these people to let them know that they are looking for a job. An important part of networking is asking contacts for the names of other people who might have jobs or information about potential openings. In this way, the network contact list grows dramatically, and clients gain access to people that they would not otherwise have known about.

Life Skills Counseling

Life skills counseling may be appropriate for clients who lack basic abilities in such areas as managing finances, maintaining proper hygiene, getting to work on time, and getting along with supervisors and coworkers. For clients in this category, this work is essential in order for them to become job ready. Some clients will need continued support and assistance in the workplace.

Job Clubs

Steinweg's (1990) work confirms the importance of group support as a way to reduce isolation and to buffer the adverse impact of unemployment. One of the most popular forms of group support is the **job club** method developed by Azrin and Besalel (1980). The job club method is based on the notion that looking for work is in itself a full-time job that is best done with a group of people. The job club leader provides support, job search skills training, and materials and supplies for completing a successful job hunt. Job clubs provide participants with access to phones, computers, photocopying, stationery, daily newspapers, and other sources of job leads. Secretarial assistance for producing effective résumés is provided as well. In recent years, Internet access allows participants to use on-line resources for leads and information. An important part of the job club is the buddy system. Every job club participant has another member in the group who provides support and assistance.

The job club has a single goal: to help members obtain a job. Job club leaders remain unwavering in their optimism that everyone is employable and that there are job opportunities even during times of recession or depression. Job clubs typically have eight to twelve members who meet for a period of two to three weeks. Job club counselors use behavioral methods and standardized routines to teach participants job-finding methods. The "brief talk" rule requires trainers to speak very briefly about a technique or procedure, usually for a maximum of one or two minutes. Participants then immediately practice the skill. Every session has specific learning objectives. By taking part in a job club, participants have an opportunity to acquire the skills of an effective job search, including how to network with family, friends, acquaintances, and others for job leads, how to develop an effective résumé, how to make phone calls to secure interviews, and how to handle interview questions. Azrin and Besalel offer this summary of the job club method:

> The general counseling style in the Job Club method is one of continuous encouragement and praise while still being very structured and task oriented. The counselor is constantly complimenting and encouraging the job seekers, speaking to each of them very frequently and yet briefly. . . . The counselor promotes mutual assistance among group members. He has a single overriding objective of helping each job seeker to obtain a good job and he devotes every moment of the meeting to instructing and encouraging the members in the specific activities that will help them obtain that objective (1980:12).

Electronic Resources

In recent years, electronic technology has necessitated that clients become familiar with new strategies for managing their job and career searches. Fax machines, electronic databanks, software that guides users through résumé construction, and the Internet will likely continue to dramatically change the nature of the job search. The Internet, for example, offers unprecedented opportunities for clients to communicate with employers and other job seekers. As well, clients can visit company home pages for background information on the business, or they can search the Internet for detailed data on industry trends. The Internet has many resources for career information, self-assessment, job search tips, job bulletin boards, and government grants. The vast majority of colleges and universities now have Web sites where clients can get information on training programs and educational opportunities. The Internet can also help clients who may be considering moving by giving them geographic, economic, and demographic data. Chat rooms and other discussion groups can provide support, information, and sometimes network contacts. However, Bratina and Bratina caution, "Information found on the Internet is not necessarily accurate. Counselors should encourage job seekers to give Internet sources the same critical review they would give to other sources" (1998:21).

Many companies are now inviting applicants to submit electronic résumés via the Internet. Electronic résumés are somewhat different from traditional paper résumés. Action verbs such as *planned, directed,* and *organized* are best for paper résumés, but nouns such as *bachelor's degree, teller, top 10 percent of class,* and *WordPerfect* are best for electronic versions because computers sort and screen electronic résumés based on nouns such as these (Bratina and Bratina, 1998).

Employment Counseling and Immigrant Clients

Westwood and Ishiyama have called attention to the unique employment counseling needs of culturally diverse clients. They note that clients from immigrant minority groups often face unique problems related to "language, racial prejudice, lack of knowledge of the world of work, limited contacts or networks, lack of cultural knowledge of job finding and interviewing techniques, plus the additional stress due to the cultural adjustment to a new society" (1991:130). In dealing with these clients, workers need to be particularly sensitive to the cultural attitudes and norms. For example, Asian immigrant clients consider their career search in "light of the financial burden that may fall to them by virtue of their place in the family" (140). Thus, workers need to take family into account more than they might when dealing with clients from other cultures. Westwood and Ishiyama offer this caution for employment counselors working with immigrants:

> Client resistance and distrust in the counseling process may be set in motion by cross-cultural insensitivities, such as the counselor's disregarding the client's age and social status and calling him or her by the first name, using excessive informality and friendliness, probing into private feelings, demanding high levels of self-disclosure and expressiveness, and giving advice (137).

Counseling People with Mental Disorders

Historically, treatment of people with mental disorders was barbaric and included such practices as exorcising, burning "witches," bloodletting, whipping, starving, imprisoning, or housing in overcrowded "snake-pits," or insane asylums. During the twentieth century, especially in the last fifty years, mental disorders have gradually been recognized as a health problem, and more humanitarian practices have been developed to replace procedures based on superstition, fear, and ignorance.

Over the past forty years there has been a major shift in the delivery of mental health services from long-term treatment in hospitals to treatment of patients in the community.

Today, the population of mental hospitals is only about one fifth of what it was thirty years ago (Skidmore, Thackeray, and Farley, 1991). The development and refinement of a range of psychotropic drugs has been the driving force behind deinstitutionalization because these drugs enable patients to control hallucinations and behavior that might otherwise preclude them from living in the community. However, this move toward community treatment has often been poorly funded, and new problems for those with mental disorders have resulted, particularly homelessness and its associated problems. Skidmore, Thackeray, and Farley estimate that as many as one third of all homeless Americans are mentally ill. Cleghorn and Lee (1991) note that various studies have shown that in Canada and the United States:

- One out of every five people will develop a mental disorder during his or her lifetime.
- One in eight persons will be hospitalized.
- Psychiatric problems are the second leading cause of hospital admissions among those 20 to 44 years old.
- Suicide is the second leading cause of death of persons aged 15 to 39.

According to the National (USA) Institute of Mental Health (NIMH, 1998) the most severe mental disorders (schizophrenia, bipolar disorder, major depression, panic disorder, and obsessive-compulsive disorder) affect some five million American adults, and one in ten Americans experiences some disability from a diagnosable mental disorder in the course of any given year.

Psychiatric assessment and diagnosis typically involve an in-depth interview, including a thorough history of the person's situation. As well, physical examinations, including brain scans, electroencephalograms (EEGs), and lab tests, may be used to rule out organic illness (brain tumors, AIDS, drug reactions, etc.). Psychological tests may be used to assess thinking, personality, and other variables. The purpose of psychiatric diagnosis is not to label clients, but to match diagnosis to treatment decisions based on the best scientific evidence regarding which treatments are likely to be most effective with each disorder (Reid, 1989).

It is beyond the scope of this book to fully explore mental disorders. However, it is important to note that the concept is influenced by cultural and societal values. For example, at various times in history, homosexuality has been considered both an aberration and a gift. It is no longer considered a mental disorder.

It is important to remember that there may be vast differences between individuals with the same mental disorder. Psychological, social, and biological variables influence how illness manifests in each person. In addition, people with mental disorders may have concurrent problems, such as poverty, substance abuse, and social/relationship difficulties. **Dual diagnosis** is a term used to describe a person who has both a substance abuse addiction and a psychiatric disorder.

DSM-IV-TR

DSM-IV-TR is the Diagnostic and Statistical Manual of Mental Disorders published by the American Psychiatric Association. it is important to note that *DSM-IV-TR* was not developed as a way to classify people. It is used by psychologists, psychiatrists, and other psychotherapists to classify and diagnose mental disorders. Consequently, social workers should follow the lead of the *DSM-IV-TR* text, which "avoids the use of such expressions as 'a schizophrenic' or 'an alcoholic' and instead uses the more accurate, but admittedly more cumbersome, 'an individual with Schizophrenia' or 'an individual with Alcohol Dependence'" (American Psychiatric Association, 2000:xxxi).

DSM-IV-TR organizes mental disorders into sixteen major groups or classes. Each diagnostic class is further subdivided into specific disorders. A cursory overview of the sixteen groups follows:

1. disorders usually first diagnosed in infancy, childhood, or adolescence (e.g., mental retardation, learning disorders, autism, conduct disorders, Tourette's syndrome). Disorders in this category have their onset during childhood or adolescence, but they may not be diagnosed until adulthood.
2. delirium, dementia, and amnesiac and other cognitive disorders (e.g., dementia owing to HIV, Huntington's, Alzheimer's, or Parkinson's disease). The significant feature of disorders in this section is a disturbance in memory or thinking.
3. mental disorders resulting from a general medical condition. Here, the distinguishing feature is the judgment that the mental disorder is the direct result of a medical condition.
4. substance-related disorders (e.g., alcoholism and other addictions)
5. schizophrenia and other psychotic disorders. Disorders in this section are typically accompanied by psychotic symptoms such as hallucinations and delusions.
6. mood disorders (e.g., depression, bipolar disorder). The predominant feature is a disturbance in mood or feeling.
7. anxiety disorders (e.g., panic attacks, agoraphobia, post-traumatic stress disorder, phobias, obsessive-compulsive disorder). The predominant feature of anxiety disorders is much greater than usual anxiety or tension.
8. somatoform disorders (e.g., hypochondria or the fear that one has a serious disease). Here, the common feature is the presence of physical symptoms that suggest a medical problem, but there is no medical condition that is diagnosable.
9. factitious disorders (e.g., Munchausen syndrome). These disorders are characterized by the fact that the patient intentionally fakes symptoms in order to assume the role of patient.
10. dissociative disorders (amnesia, depersonalization disorder). Disorders in this category are characterized by significant changes in the consciousness, memory, or identity of the person.
11. sexual and gender identity disorders (e.g., pedophilia, sexual sadism). These disorders concern disturbances in sexual desire and functioning.
12. eating disorders (e.g., anorexia nervosa, bulimia nervosa). These disorders are noted by severe disturbance in eating behavior.
13. sleep disorders (e.g., insomnia, narcolepsy). Sleep disorders are characterized by abnormalities in the amount, quality, or timing of sleep.
14. impulse control disorders not elsewhere classified (e.g., pathological gambling, pyromania, kleptomania). The essential feature of impulse control disorders is the inability to resist impulses or temptations.

15. adjustment disorders. These disorders arise from stressful events, such as the end of a relationship or loss of job.
16. personality disorders (e.g., paranoid personality disorder, obsessive-compulsive personality disorder). A personality disorder "is an enduring pattern of inner experience and behavior that deviates markedly from the expectations of the individual's culture, is pervasive and inflexible, has an onset in adolescence or early adulthood, is stable over time, and leads to distress or impairment" (American Psychiatric Association, 2000:685).

DSM-IV-TR strives to look at patients as more than just diagnostic labels. The manual recognizes that individuals are complex and that medical conditions, social circumstances, and other factors affect how people function. To facilitate a more comprehensive assessment, *DSM-IV-TR* uses a five-level multiaxial system.

Axis I: Clinical Disorders. This axis is used to report the specific mental disorder that is being diagnosed. Two exceptions are personality disorders and mental retardation, which are reported on Axis II.

Axis II: Personality Disorders, Mental Retardation. Personality disorders and mental retardation are reported on this axis.

Axis III: General Medical Conditions. This axis is used for reporting relevant medical conditions that affect a current or past mental disorder (Axis I or Axis II). For example, hypothyroidism can cause depression; thus, the individual would be coded on Axis I with a mood disorder due to hypothyroidism and also on Axis III as hypothyroidism (American Psychiatric Association, 2000:29).

Axis IV: Psychosocial and Environmental Problems. This important axis is used for reporting significant stressors that might be contributing to the mental disorders. *DSM-IV-TR* groups stressors into nine categories: (1) problems with primary support groups, (2) problems related to the social environment, (3) educational problems, (4) occupational problems, (5) housing problems, (6) economic problems, (7) problems with access to health-care services, (8) problems related to interaction with the legal system/crime, and (9) other psychosocial and environmental problems.

Axis V: Global Assessment of Functioning. This axis is used to report an individual's highest level of functioning. This axis may be used to track progress, and it may have some predictive value because people usually return to their previous highest level of adaptive functioning after an episode of illness (Klerman, 1988). The Global Assessment of Functioning (GAF) scale is used to judge a person's level of functioning. This scale is based on a continuum from 0 to 100, in which 100 represents a superior level of adaptation (American Psychiatric Association, 2000:34).

***Appropriate Uses of* DSM-IV-TR.**   Social workers should use the *DSM-IV-TR* classification system as a diagnostic tool only if they have appropriate specialized clinical training. The overview in this chapter is a brief introduction to the basic structure of the manual. Typically, individuals who use *DSM-IV-TR* in their counseling practice are licensed psychiatrists or those with graduate degrees in counseling or psychology and courses and supervised field practice in using it. Untrained practitioners should not attempt to make psychiatric diagnoses.

However, workers may find that the manual is valuable for understanding the essential definitions and features of mental disorders that their clients may be dealing with. *DSM-IV-TR* contains valuable information regarding variations in culture, age, and gender with respect to particular mental disorders. The manual also provides workers with reference material on the prevalence of mental disorders, including lifetime risk, the typical patterns of disorders, and data on the frequency of specified disorders among biological family members.

DSM-IV-TR and Social Work

Social workers should have a working knowledge of mental disorders and how they are classified. *DSM-IV-TR* is an important reference point for social workers who work in mental health settings who consult it on a regular basis. However, it often does not meet the needs of most social workers outside of mental health. Social work is concerned primarily with individuals in social contexts with an emphasis on helping them to deal with relationship problems, crisis events, difficulties related to inadequate resources, and problems dealing with organizations such as schools or government welfare offices. *DSM-IV-TR,* however useful as a tool for intellectually understanding mental disorders, is a model based on pathology and deficits. It does not address or prioritize human empowerment, which is a central objective of social work. Contemporary social workers adopt a strengths approach to problem solving that assumes the power of individuals to overcome adversity. Using a strengths approach, social workers endeavor to find and respect the successes, assets, and resources of people including those resources available within their culture such as sweat lodges and other healing rituals. As Compton and Gallaway express it:

> The emphasis is on knowing them in a more holistic way: acknowledging their hopes and dreams, their needs, their resources and the resources around them, their capacities, and their gifts. The strengths perspective invites a more affirming interaction with individuals and families; as a profession, you engage them conversationally as collaborators and peers, recognizing that they and you are both experts and have a mutual interest in improving their quality of life (1999:17).

Selected Major Mental Disorders

This section explores some of the most common mental disorders that counselors are likely to encounter, including schizophrenia, mood disorders, anxiety disorders, and eating disorders. This section provides a very brief synopsis. It is expected that professionals who work with people who have mental disorders will have had appropriate academic courses in the subject area, as well as supervised field practice.

Schizophrenia.   **Schizophrenia** is a chronic (continuing) mental disorder affecting about 1 percent of the population (NIMH, 1998). In rare cases children can develop schizophrenia, but it usually starts in the late teens or early twenties for men, and in the twenties and early thirties for women. The children of a parent who has schizophrenia are ten times more likely to develop it than children of a parent who does not have it (NIMH, 1998). Most people with schizophrenia suffer from it throughout their lives, and an estimated 1 of every 10 people with the illness dies by suicide (NIMH, 1998). Schizophrenia is believed to affect about 1 percent of the general population, with annual health-care costs in the United States exceeding $30 billion. In the United States, about 25 percent of all persons in hospital on any given day have schizophrenia (Cleghorn and Lee, 1991; Dubovsky and Weissberg, 1986).

Contrary to popular opinion, people with schizophrenia do not have split personalities, like Dr. Jekyll and Mr. Hyde. Furthermore, although it was once accepted as truth by some, parents do not cause schizophrenia. The current perspective on the disorder is that it is caused by an imbalance of the complex, interrelated chemical systems of the brain (NIMH, 1998), but there may be no single cause. The symptoms of schizophrenia vary between individuals, sometimes dramatically. The following symptoms are common: hallucinations, delusions, disordered thinking, and social isolation.

Hallucinations.   There may be wide variation in the symptoms of persons with schizophrenia. Most sufferers, however, experience **hallucinations,** usually auditory but sometimes visual or olfactory (related to smell). These hallucinations may be voices that tell clients what to do (**command hallucinations**), or they may be visions of things that do not exist.

Hallucinations can affect any of a person's senses, causing them to hear, see, taste, touch, or smell what others do not. Auditory hallucinations are the most frequent type of hallucination and are most common for people with schizophrenia. Visual hallucinations are much less common, and they are more likely to occur as a result of acute infectious disease. Olfactory hallucinations may occur because of schizophrenia and organic lesions of the brain. Tactile hallucinations (touch) may occur as a reaction to drugs. Kinesthetic hallucinations may occur after the loss of a limb ("phantom limb") and owing to schizophrenia. Withdrawal from drugs may cause vivid hallucinations, such as the sensation that insects are crawling under the skin (delirium tremens common with alcohol withdrawal) (Nicholi, 1988). In fact, the symptoms of alcohol withdrawal may be clinically indistinguishable from schizophrenia (Reid, 1989). With auditory hallucinations, clients may hear voices that command or compliment them, but with disorders such as schizophrenia, the voices are usually hostile (Shea, 1988). These voices may be so real that clients believe that they have had broadcasting devices planted in their bodies. For example, one client was convinced that her dentist had secretly implanted receivers in her fillings. It is so real to the person that he or she cannot dismiss it as imagination.

It is important to know that a wide range of factors can cause hallucinations, including psychosis, high fever, mind-altering drugs (marijuana, psilocybin, LSD, and opium), medications, withdrawal from depressant drugs such as alcohol, brain disease and injury, epilepsy, sensory deprivation or sensory overload, oxygen deprivation, hyperventilation, hypoglycemia, extreme pain, extended fasting, dehydration, and social isolation (Beyerstein, 1998; Nicholi, 1988). Hallucinations can also occur in persons who have impaired vision but no mental disorder.

Delusions. Persons with schizophrenia may experience **delusions,** or distorted beliefs involving bizarre thought patterns. Delusions of persecution, typical in paranoid schizophrenia, may lead people to believe they are being cheated, controlled, or poisoned. Other common delusions include religious delusions (belief that one is a manifestation of God), delusions of grandeur (bizarre beliefs about one's abilities), delusions of being controlled (e.g., belief that one is being directed by radio messages), **thought broadcasting** (belief that one's thinking can be heard by others), and **thought insertion** (belief that thoughts are being inserted into one's brain by others) (Nicholi, 1988).

One client, a young university student, gives us a sense of what the world of a person with schizophrenia is like:

> I want to sue my dentist. Over the past year he has been installing radio transmitters in my fillings. Now he uses them to control me. At first he was nice, then he raped me while he worked on my teeth. Sometimes he makes me sleep with complete strangers. If I don't get them removed soon, I might be forced to do something awful. . . . There are others. I talked to a woman on the phone the other day. Her dentist did the same thing. We need to go underground where we can be safe from the enemy.

Disordered Thinking. Another common feature of schizophrenia is disordered thinking. Individuals may be unable to think logically, or they may jump from one idea to another without any apparent logical connection. Thinking may be so disorganized and fragmented that it is totally confusing to others.

Social Isolation. Persons with schizophrenia are often socially isolated and withdrawn. They may be emotionally numb, have poor communication skills, and show decreased motivation and ability to care for themselves.

Treatment of Schizophrenia. **Antipsychotic medications** are used to decrease the symptoms of the disorder—hallucinations, agitation, confusion, distortions, and delusions. These medications must be prescribed by a medical doctor, frequently a psychiatrist. Counseling is an important adjunct to antipsychotic medication. Workers typically target their activities toward helping clients deal with the social aspects of the disease. As well, they can be instrumental in encouraging clients to seek psychiatric attention when necessary, and they can support psychiatric initiatives by encouraging clients to continue with any prescribed medication. This is crucial, because about 50 percent of people with schizophrenia are noncompliant in taking their medication (Dubovsky and Weissberg, 1986).

Mood Disorders. The two most severe mood disorders (also known as affective disorders) are major **depression** and **bipolar disorder,** or manic-depressive illness.

Depression. About one in four women and one in ten men in North America will experience major depression during their lifetimes, but almost 90 percent of people who develop depression can be treated (Cleghorn and Lee, 1991:55). Although everyone has bad days, the depressed feelings that accompany them usually pass quickly. A clinical diagnosis of depression is made when a person's depressed mood becomes pervasive over time and

CONVERSATION 9.1
When Clients Are Hallucinating

STUDENT: What should I do when clients begin hallucinating?

TEACHER: Let's talk about what not to do. First, you need to resist the temptation to argue with clients about the reality of their hallucinations. Although some clients are aware of when they are hallucinating and have learned to live with it, others are convinced of their authenticity and dismiss arguments to the contrary. Their experience is very real and has to be accepted as such.

Second, you should avoid patronizing or humoring clients about their hallucinations, as this behavior may promote further hallucinating.

STUDENT: Okay, but what can I do?

TEACHER: Hallucinations are generally treated with antipsychotic medications. Consequently, referral to a physician or psychiatrist is essential to make sure that clients have been assessed for an appropriate medication to control their hallucinations. Subsequently, it is important to ensure that clients are taking their medication and that their dosage is appropriate.

One way that you can respond without arguing is to simply state that you do not sense what your client is sensing. You can combine this statement with empathic statements that acknowledge the feelings that clients may be experiencing as a result of their hallucinations.

You also can help clients deal with any stressors that may be increasing the frequency of hallucinations. For example, if being in large crowds or missing sleep brings on hallucinations, clients can take steps to minimize these precursors. It may be helpful to work with clients to help them learn skills for controlling their hallucinations. For example, they can discipline themselves to direct their thoughts and activities elsewhere. One researcher found that silence, isolation, and attention to oneself tend to promote hallucinations, but distraction, exploratory activity, movement, and external stimulation tend to impede hallucinations (Silva and Lopez de Silva, 1976). So, simply diverting clients' attention can be a useful strategy.

STUDENT: I learned something from one of my clients that I found helpful and profound. I remember him saying to me, "I have a mental disorder, but don't forget, I have the same needs and fears as everyone else." I was reminded that he and I were more alike than unlike each other.

interferes with the person's ability to cope with or enjoy life. In this way, depression is differentiated from the normal mood swings that everyone experiences. Depression is almost certainly more widespread than statistics suggest because it often goes untreated. In fact, it is sometimes referred to as the "common cold of mental illness." The signs of depression, sometimes described as clinical depression or major depression to separate it from ordinary sadness, can be organized into four major categories with specific symptoms.

Mood Disturbances
- constant sad, anxious, or empty mood
- feelings of hopelessness or pessimism
- feelings of guilt, worthlessness, or helplessness

Changes in Behavior
- diminished interest or pleasure in daily activities, including sex
- fatigue and decreased energy
- withdrawal from others

Alterations in Thinking
- difficulty thinking, concentrating, remembering
- inability to make decisions
- recurrent thoughts of death or suicide

Physical Complaints
- restlessness or irritability
- fatigue or loss of energy
- sleep disturbances, including insomnia
- loss or gain of appetite and weight
- chronic pain or other persistent bodily symptoms that are not caused by physical disease
- suicide attempts

(American Medical Association, 1998, American Psychiatric Association, 1994; Cleghorn and Lee, 1991; NIMH, 1998)

Scott Simmie, a journalist, describes how his depression included obsession with thoughts of suicide:

> I spent weeks in bed, unable to find a reason to get up. Sleep was my drug—the only, albeit temporary, way to escape what had befallen me. When awake I brooded, almost obsessively, on death. Pictured myself rigging pulleys so I could hang myself in the condo. . . . Most mornings, the first thought that entered my head was to put a gun to it. Bang. Problem solved (Simmie and Nunes, 2001:27).

Depression is believed to caused from a complex combination of three primary variables: biological, genetic (inherited), and emotional and/or environmental (American Medical Association, 1998). Biological origins are associated with brain chemistry and hormonal activity. Research has demonstrated that some families are more likely to have members who suffer depression. Although no specific gene has been linked to depression, there appears to be ample evidence that heredity leads to an increased vulnerability to depression. Emotional and environmental causes might include stressors such as death of a loved one, job loss, or the breakup of a relationship. As well, depression might be the result of a sleep disturbances, illness, or drug reaction. Depression that originates from physical illness usually abates once the physical illness is treated. Depression is symptomatic of a medical condition in about 10 to 15 percent of all cases. Known physical causes of depression include thyroid disease, adrenal gland disorders, hyperparathyroidism, diabetes, infectious diseases such as viral hepatitis, cancer, autoimmune disorders, vitamin and mineral deficiencies (American Medical Association, 1998; O'Conner, 1997). Thus, clients who are dealing with depression should be referred for a medical checkup as an adjunct to counseling.

Current thinking suggests that it is the combination of factors that results in depression. For example, if people with a predisposition to depression experience stressful life crises, they may develop depression. Subsequently, their first depressive episode may stimulate changes in brain chemistry leaving them more vulnerable to further episodes when even small stressful events can trigger depression (American Medical Association, 1998).

Social workers can assist people who are depressed in a number of ways:

- helping them recognize and identify the symptoms of depression
- referring for appropriate medical examination and treatment, which might include medication or hospitalization
- helping them to develop coping strategies for dealing with stress
- loss or grief counseling
- assessing and managing suicide risk
- helping them to develop cognitive/behavioral strategies for overcoming low self-esteem and other self-defeating thought patterns that often accompany depression
- supporting and understanding emotions
- family counseling to interrupt communication patterns that contribute to or escalate depression

Bipolar Disorder.   With bipolar illness, depression alternates with manic episodes. During manic periods people typically experience heightened energy, a euphoric mood, and a greatly increased sense of confidence, sometimes to the point of grandiosity. They may have sharpened and unusually creative thinking, along with a much decreased need for sleep. Or they may experience a flight of ideas (thoughts without logical connection). Although they may engage in increased goal-directed activities at work or school, they often engage in them without regard to the consequences, thus leading to irrational behavior, such as uncontrolled buying sprees, sexual indiscretion, and foolish business investments (American Psychiatric Association, 2000; NIMH, 1998; Nicholi, 1988).

Scott Simmie's recollection of his mind-set when he was in the midst of the manic phase illustrates the irrationality of this state:

> Despite everything I'd been through, I was still convinced that I was in perfect health, that the real problem was the failure of others to recognize that something extraordinary and wonderful had happened to me. That I had been spiritually reborn. That my limitless potential had finally been freed (Simmie and Nunes, 2001:25).

Thus, it is very difficult, but not impossible, to persuade people to accept treatment, including hospitalization, during the manic phase of the illness. Supportive counselors, family, and friends may convince them to seek treatment, but, in some cases, particularly when their behavior becomes self-destructive or dangerous, involuntary hospitalization may be necessary.

Bipolar disorder usually begins in adolescence or early adulthood and continues throughout life. It is often not recognized as an illness, and people who have it may suffer needlessly for years or even decades. There is evidence that bipolar disorder is inherited (NIMH, 1998). Persons with untreated bipolar illness may experience devastating complications, including marital breakup, job loss, financial ruin, substance abuse, and suicide. However, almost everyone with bipolar illness can be helped through the use of medications such as lithium, which has demonstrated effectiveness in controlling both depression and mania. Bipolar disorder cannot be cured, but for most people treatment can keep the disease under control.

Anxiety Disorders. **Anxiety disorders** are characterized by higher than normal levels of fear, worry, tension, or anxiety about daily events. High anxiety may be present without apparent reason. Four serious anxiety disorders are obsessive-compulsive disorder (OCD), phobias, panic disorder, and post-traumatic stress disorder (PTSD).

Obsessive-Compulsive Disorder (OCD). An **obsessive-compulsive disorder** involves recurrent, unwanted thoughts and conscious, ritualized, seemingly purposeless acts such as counting the number of tiles on the ceiling or needing to wash one's hands repetitively. Behavioral techniques and medication have proved effective in treating this disorder.

Phobia. A **phobia** is an irrational fear about particular events or objects. Phobias result in overwhelming anxiety in response to situations of little or no danger. Most people have phobias of one sort or another, such as fear of flying, heights, public speaking, or snakes. For the most part, people deal with their phobias through avoidance, which decreases the anxiety associated with the fear. Unfortunately, avoidance increases the fear of the particular object or situation. Treatment of phobias is necessary when they interfere with a person's capacity to lead a normal life. For example, agoraphobia (fear of open or public spaces) prevents people from leaving the safety of their homes. Treatment in such cases is essential to help clients overcome what would otherwise be severely restricted lives.

Specialized behavioral techniques such as flooding, systematic desensitization, relaxation training, and pharmacologic (drug) treatment may be necessary to relieve anxiety disorders.

With systematic desensitization, persons with a phobia are first taught how to manage anxiety through relaxation. With the help of the counselor, they construct a hierarchy of anxiety-provoking events associated with the phobia. Finally, they learn how to control their anxiety with progressively more difficult exposures to the anxiety-producing object or event.

Panic Disorder. A **panic disorder** involves sudden attacks of terror and irrational fear, accompanied by an overwhelming sense of impending doom. During a panic attack a person may experience symptoms such as an accelerated heart rate, sweating, shaking, shortness of breath, chest pain, and nausea, as well as a fear of dying or losing control (American Psychiatric Association, 2000). Medication and psychotherapy have proved effective in treating this disorder.

Post-traumatic Stress Disorder (PTSD). **PTSD** symptoms develop following traumatic events such as rape, assault, natural disasters (earthquakes, floods, etc.), war, torture, or automobile accident. Symptoms may occur immediately after the event, or they may be delayed by months or years (Nicholi, 1988). Recollections of the event result in disabling symptoms, such as: emotional numbness; sleep disturbance (nightmares, difficulty sleeping); reliving the event; intense anxiety at exposure to cues that remind the person of the trauma; avoidance of activities, people, or conversations that arouse recall of the trauma; hypervigilance; and outbursts of anger (American Psychiatric Association, 2000; Nicholi, 1988). PTSD symptoms often dissipate within six months, but for others the symptoms may last years. Relaxation training and counseling are effective tools for treating this disorder.

Eating Disorders.   The two most common eating disorders, anorexia nervosa and bulimia, are most likely to affect adolescent and young adult women, with about 90 percent of all those afflicted coming from this group (Cleghorn and Lee, 1991; NIMH, 1998; Nicholi, 1988). Approximately 1 percent of adolescent girls develop anorexia nervosa (NIMH, 1998) and as many as 10 percent develop bulimic disorder (Nicholi, 1988). Eventually, half of those with anorexia will develop bulimia (NIMH, 1998). Eating disorders are difficult to treat because many people refuse to admit that they have a problem and resist treatment. Counselors and family need to persuade those affected to seek treatment, but this is hard because people with these disorders may argue that their only problem is the "nagging" people in their lives. Because of the life-threatening nature of eating disorders, involuntary treatment or forced hospitalization may be necessary, particularly when there has been excessive and rapid weight loss, serious metabolic disturbances, and serious depression with a risk of suicide.

Social and Cultural Variables.   For most of recorded history, plumpness in women was deemed desirable and fashionable. During the last fifty years, particularly in Western cultures, women have been bombarded with media messages that promote slimness as the route to a successful and happy life. Societal emphasis on dieting, combined with the unrealistic body image of supermodels, contributes to an obsessive preoccupation with body image and dieting (Abraham and Llewellyn-Jones, 1997). One study found that the top wish of a group of girls aged eleven to seventeen was "to be thinner," while another survey discovered that girls were more afraid of becoming fat than they were of cancer, nuclear war, or losing their parents (Berg, 1997:13). Mothers and fathers who are overly concerned or critical about their daughters' weight and physical attractiveness may put the girls at increased risk of developing an eating disorder. People pursuing professions or activities that emphasize thinness, such as modeling, dancing, or gymnastics, are more susceptible to the problem (Nicholi, 1988; NIMH, 1998).

Anorexia Nervosa.   **Anorexia nervosa** occurs when people reject maintaining minimally healthy body weight. Driven by low self-esteem and an intense fear of gaining weight, people with anorexia use techniques such as purging (e.g., fasting, vomiting, taking laxatives) and excessive exercise to reduce body weight. Even though they may diet to the point of starvation and they look emaciated, they will still insist that they are too fat. Anorexia nervosa can be life threatening, and as many as 10 to 15 percent of sufferers die of the effects of prolonged starvation (Cleghorn and Lee, 1991; NIMH, 1998).

The symptoms of anorexia may include excessive weight loss, belief that the body is fat and continuation of dieting despite a lower than normal body weight, cessation of menstruation, obsession with food, eating in secret, obsessive exercise, and depression. People with anorexia are often perfectionists with superior athletic ability. There is some evidence to suggest that people with anorexia starve themselves in order to gain a sense of control in some area of their lives (NIMH, 1998).

The treatment of eating disorders requires a team approach consisting of physicians, counselors, nutritionists, and family therapists. Group therapy may be a helpful adjunct to individual counseling to reduce isolation. Reframing and other methods for helping clients change the distorted and rigid thinking patterns associated with eating disorders may be extremely helpful (see Chapter 7). As well, antidepressant medications such as fluoxetine (Prozac) and imipramine may be used.

Bulimia.   **Bulimia** occurs when people adopt a pattern of excessive overeating followed by vomiting or other purging behaviors to control their weight. Individuals with bulimia usually binge and purge in secret. Typically, persons with bulimia feel isolated, and they deal with their problems through overeating, then, feeling guilty and disgusted, they purge. Because they may have normal or even above normal body weight, they often hide their problem from others for years. By the time they finally seek treatment (sometimes not until their thirties or forties), their eating disorder is firmly entrenched and difficult to treat.

The symptoms of bulimia may include: cessation of menstruation; obsession with food; eating in secret; obsessive exercise; serious depression; bingeing, vomiting, and other purging activities (often with the use of drugs); and disappearance in the bathroom for long periods to induce vomiting. From excessive vomiting, the outer layer of the teeth can be worn down, scarring may be present on the backs of hands (from pushing fingers down the throat to induce vomiting), the esophagus may become inflamed, and glands near the cheeks can become swollen (NIMH, 1998). Persons with bulimia are at increased risk for substance abuse and suicidal behavior.

Treating Mental Disorders

Ideally, persons with mental disorders should be dealt with through a team approach that includes psychiatrists, psychiatric social workers, social service workers, counselors, oc-cupational counselors, nurses, and volunteers. As a team, they share common objectives:

1. motivating clients to seek and remain in treatment and, in severe cases, arranging for involuntary treatment
2. supporting clients to remain in the community (helping with housing, life skills training, employment, and career counseling)
3. helping hospitalized clients return to community living as soon as possible
4. assisting clients in dealing with the challenges of medication
5. educating clients and their families about the nature of their disorder
6. assisting clients in dealing with the consequences of mental disorders
7. helping clients and their families develop and use support systems, including self-help groups and professionals

Psychiatric Medications.   The 1950s witnessed the introduction of powerful chemicals that have resulted in dramatic advances in the treatment of mental disorders. Medications have enabled the vast majority of persons with mental disorders to be treated and managed in the community as opposed to locked up in psychiatric facilities. Medications may be able to control the symptoms of mental disorders, such as hallucinations, but they do not cure the illness. They can increase the effectiveness of counseling by increasing the capacity of the clients to hear and respond. Many people need to take medication to control their illness for the rest of their lives. There may be wide variations in people's reaction to medication (e.g., some respond better to one than another, some need bigger doses, some experience side effects and others do not). Medications may result in unwanted side effects, such as tardive dyskinesia (a serious side effect of antipsychotic medication characterized by uncontrollable movement), drowsiness, weakness, tremors, slurred speech, sleep disturbances, and headaches. Some clients may stop taking medication in order to avoid these side effects.

Antipsychotic (or neuroleptic) medications such as loxapine, haloperidol, clozapine, and risperidone, are used to treat illnesses such as schizophrenia. Antipsychotic medications may be taken daily, but some medications are available through injection (once or twice a month). Injections are particularly useful for ensuring that clients take the medication. **Antimanic medications** such as lithium are used to control the manic symptoms of bipolar disorder. **Antidepressant medications** such as Prozac, Paxil, and Zolof are used to help people deal with serious depression. **Antianxiety medications** such as valium and librium are used to control serious and persistent anxiety, phobias, and panic attacks.

Suicide Counseling

In Canada and the United States, the annual death rate from suicide is about 15 per 100,000 population, but because it is likely that a large number of suicides go unreported, the actual rate is almost certainly higher than that reported by official statistics (Cleghorn and Lee, 1991).

The American Association of Suicidology (1998) describes suicide as a permanent solution to a impermanent problem. They emphasize that suicidal crises are almost always impermanent and that often they are associated with problems that can be treated. Suicide intervention represents a unique challenge for social workers and other professionals. They must assess the immediate risk and intervene to prevent their clients from completing the suicide. This challenges them to rapidly establish a supportive relationship. Active listening skills are crucial, for unless suicidal clients can be convinced that the worker is genuinely interested in their welfare, the client may cut off communication.

Warning Signs and Risk Assessment

There is no absolute way of predicting that a person will attempt suicide, but there are some important warning signs to consider. Suicide risk assessments should include careful observation and interviewing in the following key areas: threats of suicide, history of attempts, methodology, stressors, personality factors, alcoholism, social supports, and gender and demographic variables (American Association of Suicidology, 1998; Harvard

Medical School, 1996; Othmer and Othmer, 1989; San Francisco Suicide Prevention Institute, 1998).

Threats of Suicide.   Clients who talk about suicide or who appear preoccupied with death and dying are often at risk. Research has shown that 8 out of 10 suicidal persons give some sign of their intentions. Sometimes the clues are clear, such as when clients directly threaten to take their lives. At other times, their suicidal objectives are hinted at, such as when they start giving away their possessions, making final arrangements (e.g., expressing wishes for their funeral, writing a will), and involving themselves in increased risk-taking behavior. Threats of suicide and other warning signs may represent a cry for help, an expression of frustration, a desire to induce guilt in others, or an effort to get rid of depressed feelings (Othmer and Othmer, 1989). Whatever the reason for the clients' suicide threats or attempts, social workers should take them seriously.

History of Suicide Attempts.   About 30 to 40 percent of suicides have made a previous attempt, and about 10 percent of those who attempt suicide succeed within ten years. Eight times as many people make suicide attempts as those who complete suicide (Cleghorn and Lee, 1991). However, it is likely that the number of completed suicides is underreported, as some cases of what appear to be accidental deaths are, in fact, suicides.

Methodology.   As a rule, clients who have a specific plan for taking their lives are at greater risk than those who do not have such a plan. Moreover, the more developed the plan and the greater the potential lethality of the proposed method, the greater the risk. For example, "hanging, shooting and jumping from high places are serious, mostly successful suicide methods" (Othmer and Othmer, 1989:267).

Stressors.   Clients who are currently coping with significant stress are at greater risk. Such stressors can be broadly defined and may include such events as a recent loss (e.g., death, divorce, and loss of job, money, status, self-confidence, self-esteem, religious faith). As well, recent medical illness may be a factor. Many clients who commit suicide have seen a doctor shortly before their death (Hirschfeld and Russell, 1997).

Personality Changes.   Workers should explore whether there have been recent and drastic changes in their clients' usual manner. Changes such as social withdrawal, sudden changes in their moods, loss of interest in activities that previously gave them pleasure (sex, work, friends, family, job, hobbies), increased substance abuse, changes in sleep patterns, and loss of interest in personal appearance ought to be closely assessed. As well, workers should look for signs of depression, apathy, anxiety, and general pessimism about the future. Not all suicidal people are depressed, nor are all depressed people suicidal. Some people contemplating suicide may seem at peace, even euphoric. However, depression should always signal to workers that they should assess suicide risk.

Suicide and Alcoholism.   Research has shown that persons who are addicted to alcohol have an increased risk of suicide compared with the general population. Roy's (1993) review found that the lifetime risk of suicide among alcoholics is 2.2 to 3.4 percent in English-speaking countries and at least double the general population, but an astounding 60 to 120 times higher than that of the general population without psychiatric illness. Furthermore, he reported that about 20 percent of suicide victims are alcoholic.

Gender and Demographic Differences

Women attempt suicide three or four times as often as men, but men tend to use more lethal methods and account for 75 percent of all completed suicides. The ratio of attempts to suicides is about 10 to 1 (Harvard Medical School, 1996). One study (cited in Cleghorn and Lee, 1991:204) identified high-risk groups as those with a mental disorder, young people, seniors, Aboriginal people, and those in prison. They also reported that males aged 15 to 24 are at the highest risk among the young group and that these young men often choose violent means to end their lives.

A study by Devons (1996) revealed that the suicide rate for elderly people was the highest of all age groups, perhaps as high as double the rate in the general population. She suggests that the profound losses associated with aging leave elderly persons vulnerable, but early identification of depression can lead to appropriate treatment intervention.

Drugs such as antipsychotic medication, sleeping pills, antidepressants, and analgesics such as aspirin are all potential overdose drugs, especially when taken in combination with other drugs. Roberts reports that, as a rule, a lethal dose is 10 times the normal dose, but in combination with alcohol, as little as half the normal dose can result in death (1991:58).

Counseling Intervention

Suicide prevention and crisis intervention require that social workers be aware of the dangerous myths about suicide, including the following (Devons, 1996):

Myth 1: Suicide occurs without warning signs.
Myth 2: People who talk about suicide aren't serious about killing themselves.
Myth 3: Bringing up the topic gives people the idea.
Myth 4: People who attempt suicide are just trying to get attention.
Myth 5: The best response to a threat is to say, "Go ahead."

Assess the Risk.   Although no professional can determine with certainty whether a client will try to commit suicide, knowledge of and exploration of risk factors is essential in order to intervene intelligently. As described earlier in this section, some of the key risk factors that workers should consider include past attempts, current mental and physical status, the presence of a viable plan, the means to kill oneself, talk about suicide, personal losses, efforts to put one's affairs in order, and substance abuse. Workers need to explore these variables in a calm, nonjudgmental manner, without moralizing, and offer support and empathy throughout the process.

To assess the potential lethality of a plan, workers should investigate factors such as the following: lethal potential of the method (e.g., time between attempt and likely death), the extent to which the person has access to the means (e.g., presence of a gun or sleeping pills), and possibility of discovery and access to rescue.

Ask about Suicide Intent.   Social workers need to overcome any reluctance to ask clients if they have considered suicide as a solution to their problems. Roberts (1991) reports that there is clinical and empirical evidence to strongly support the value of direct inquiry. Asking about suicide will not plant the idea in the client's mind. In fact, bringing the issue into the open can relieve clients of the stress of trying to hide their intent, whereas avoiding the topic increases feelings of isolation and hopelessness in the suicidal person. As Roberts concludes, "Critically, direct inquiry gives the potentially suicidal individual permission to discuss feelings that may have seemed virtually undiscussable. Direct inquiry can bring great relief to the client—at last the inner battle of life or death can be openly discussed and explored in a safe, supportive, and accepting climate" (59).

A veiled or vague comment about suicide should always be taken seriously. When clients make statements such as "Sometimes life doesn't seem worth it," a follow-up question such as "Have you thought about killing yourself?" should be used to put the issue on the discussion table.

Implement Crisis Intervention.   Social workers and other professionals have a responsibility to prevent suicide once the client makes this intent known. The immediate goal is crisis intervention to thwart clients from taking their lives. A number of strategies can be considered, including the following:

1. removing the means of suicide from the client (e.g., flushing pills down the toilet, confiscating guns). This prevents clients from acting impulsively.
2. negotiating a "no-suicide" contract. This involves an agreement that the client will not hurt him- or herself until the next contact with the worker, when a new contract may be negotiated. This plan might need to be very concrete and detailed, outlining exactly what the client will be doing, hour by hour, until the next contact with the counselor.
3. emergency hospitalization. All jurisdictions have mental health legislation that defines when clients can be hospitalized. Typically, imminent risk for suicide is a compelling reason for involuntary hospitalization. Authorization from one or more physicians is usually required.
4. future linkage. This involves setting up short- and long-term goals that give the client something to anticipate. Through this process the client is diverted from the present crisis to thinking about an improved future.
5. decreasing isolation and withdrawal. For many clients, talking about their problems with a counselor is sufficient to reverse the drive to suicide. In addition, counselors should make every effort to recruit capable family members or friends to be with the client through the crisis phase. For their support to be helpful, the client must perceive these people as credible and supportive.
6. decreasing anxiety and sleep loss. Medication and/or hospitalization may be necessary if the risk of suicide is high or if supportive family and friends are not available.
7. treatment of coexisting problems, including addictions and mental disorders

8. management of problems such as poverty, unemployment, and uncontrolled pain
9. initiatives to increase self-esteem

Counseling HIV-Positive Clients and Clients with AIDS

All ethics worthy of that name are based on life, and seek to reinforce and strengthen it. What interests me is not whether there is life after death, but that there should be life before it. And that life should be a good life, not one of mere survival or constant fear of death.

Ana Luisa Ligouri at the 12th World AIDS Conference in Geneva, July 1998, quoting the Spanish philosopher Fernando Sabater

HIV is an acronym for Human Immunodeficiency Virus. This virus attacks the immune system, weakening its ability to fight off infections. People may have the virus and not be aware of it, and they may have no symptoms for as long as five to fifteen years. HIV is spread when HIV-infected blood, semen, or vaginal fluids get into the body of another person. Sharing dirty needles (through drug taking, tattooing, body piercing, etc.) and unprotected sex (anal, vaginal, and oral) are considered high-risk behaviors. HIV cannot be transmitted by hugging or kissing, nor can it be transmitted through the air by coughing or sneezing. It cannot be transmitted through water, food, or insect bites.

AIDS is the acronym for Acquired Immune Deficiency Syndrome caused by HIV infection, resulting in a number of different illnesses and opportunistic infections, such as Kaposi's sarcoma (cancer), thrush, and many others. In the last twenty years more than 40 million people have tested HIV positive, and almost 12 million people have died. In 1997, it was estimated that 16,000 people a day acquired HIV.

AIDS has left at least 8 million orphans (Mann and Tarantola, 1998). Since the discovery of AIDS in 1981, remarkable progress in its treatment has been realized in the Western world. Aggressive treatment routines using antiretroviral therapies (HIV is a retrovirus) have resulted in a decline in the number of AIDS-related deaths in the industrialized nations, but a cure and a vaccine for the disease are not expected in the immediate future. In poorer nations, particularly those in Africa, where they are ill equipped to handle the massive costs of treatment, the ravage of AIDS continues unabated.

Prevention

Prevention of HIV infection is the best way of controlling the AIDS epidemic. Social workers can play a significant role in educating target populations to prevent new HIV infections by encouraging such practices as safer sex, particularly the use of condoms, and the use of clean needles for injection drug users.

Some clients are reluctant to be tested. In part, this may arise from their mistaken belief that there is nothing they can do about positive results. They may fear (often justifiably) that an HIV-positive diagnosis may lead others to devalue and oppress them. Fears about homophobia may lead individuals to isolate themselves from services that could provide information. Educating clients and the public about new treatments and the importance of early intervention may help to overcome their aversion to being tested.

In some jurisdictions HIV-positive test results must be reported. As a result, people may resist testing because they fear systematic discrimination. When anonymous testing is available, it encourages people to take the test.

Rapid testing with results available in as little as fifteen minutes is useful for testing people who are highly anxious. These tests have high reliability, but they are always confirmed with other measurements such as a Western Bloc test.

The primary preventive goal for professionals is to educate clients to abandon high-risk behaviors such as unprotected sex and needle sharing. This goal may involve initiatives to help clients deal with barriers to making changes (e.g., reluctance of partners to use condoms, fatalistic attitudes). A second counseling goal is to help clients resolve reluctance or ambivalence about taking an HIV test by exploring the advantages of testing. For example, workers might reframe the test as an opportunity to achieve peace of mind if it shows the client has no HIV infection. They can also inform clients that an HIV-positive diagnosis puts them in a better position to take advantage of new treatments and allows them to direct their focus to nutrition and wellness in order to try to keep their immune systems strong.

Counseling Clients Who Are HIV Positive

Awaiting test results is an anxious time for most clients. Workers can effectively use this period to help clients explore the meaning they attribute to the results. In the process, they need to support clients' feelings and fears.

Most clients who test negative experience relief At this time, workers may take advantage of the opportunity to educate these clients about appropriate preventive routines.

Workers should also be prepared for the reality that some gay male clients feel ambivalent about negative results. "Some gay male clients may feel disappointed when anticipating or when informed that they are not HIV positive. Though the gay community has done much to provide a supportive environment for people living with HIV positive, many gay men who are HIV negative feel isolated, without support, and without a place to belong" (Kain, 1996:6).

Kain suggests that preresult counseling should address these feelings directly in order to reverse the possibility that HIV-negative men might practice unsafe sex in order to join the supported ranks of the infected. As well, this group may think that their concerns (e.g., guilt at having survived, dealing with the grief of losing friends who have died from AIDS) may be considered by others to be insignificant when compared with the problems of people who are infected.

Clients' reactions to testing positive may vary. Some clients are totally shocked, whereas others see the results as confirmation of what they already knew; some see the diagnosis as a death sentence, but others experience denial and act as though the results mean nothing (Kain, 1996). Clients who receive the results as death sentences need immediate help to deal with the psychological shock of receiving the diagnosis. At this point, workers should encourage them to explore and cope with complex feelings, which might include guilt, anger, fear, despair, and thoughts of suicide. Subsequently, support and education about the realities of the disease can help them reach a more rational understanding about their future.

A particularly difficult situation arises when counseling HIV-positive men who have engaged in high-risk homosexual activity while remaining in heterosexual relationships. They need considerable support and counseling to deal with both the trauma of their diagnosis and the unique challenge of telling their partners.

Kain reminds counselors that denial is a psychological defense that protects people from feelings that are too overwhelming, and he suggests that "unless the consequences of denying testing positive is harmful to clients, there is no reason for us to rush the process" (1996:15).

In the 1980s counseling focused on assisting clients in dealing with the shock of their diagnosis and their impending death. Now that an HIV-positive diagnosis no longer means imminent death (at least in the industrialized world), counseling goals have shifted to helping people live with the disease.

The principal focus of counseling people with HIV is to provide support for them to adopt healthy practices, including aggressive treatment that bolsters their immune systems. A second major goal is to promote lifestyle practices that prevent the spread of infection. More specific counseling activities and goals for working with clients who are HIV positive may include the following:

- providing empathy and support to help clients deal with their fears and anxieties while awaiting test results
- helping clients deal with the feelings associated with a positive test and living with the disease
- helping clients deal with the complex challenges of disclosure (to family, friends, sexual partners)
- assisting clients in dealing with issues of discrimination
- supporting clients to make lifestyle adjustments and to prevent spread of the infection, including adopting safe sex practices
- helping clients deal with the challenges of dating and maintaining relationships
- educating clients about preventive treatment, personal health, nutrition, and wellness issues
- working with families to help them understand how to create a safe and supportive environment for people who are HIV positive
- helping clients meet basic needs (living arrangements, finances, medical, transportation)
- helping clients with sexual identity confusion issues
- supporting couples when one partner is HIV positive and one is negative
- linking clients to appropriate support groups and community services

Counseling Clients with AIDS

An AIDS diagnosis may bring to the foreground a range of reactions, including depression, despair, and preoccupation with end-of-life issues, such as matters of spirituality and suicide. An AIDS diagnosis means that people have to deal with dying young, as well as with partner and family issues. Many clients are members of communities that have experienced multiple losses, and this needs to be addressed in counseling. People with AIDS must deal directly with discrimination arising from such issues as physical stigma (fear of contagion) and the moralistic judgment of their behavior and lifestyle. Anecdotal evidence from front-line workers is accumulating that some clients react positively to an AIDS diagnosis when it means that they will have access to medical and social assistance benefits that have previously been denied to them.

Social workers and other professionals working with people with AIDS need to make sure that they don't neglect their own needs for emotional support, and they need to find ways to sustain their energy and prevent burnout. Those who work in hospice settings may have to deal with multiple deaths each week. They need to be aware of their own grief at the loss of their clients, and they must find ways to process this grief. Support and consultation with colleagues is essential for dealing with the feelings and stress of counseling people with AIDS.

Spirituality. Frequently, clients living with HIV-positive diagnosis and AIDS raise spiritual questions regarding the meaning of life and life after death. Clients' spiritual values and beliefs are legitimate considerations in the counseling process (Kelly, 1995), and effective counselors must be open and nonjudgmental when dealing with spirituality. It requires that they understand the different ways that individual clients might define and approach religion and spirituality. Kain underscores the importance of spirituality in counseling persons with HIV:

> We need to remember that many people living with HIV disease may feel alienated from all sources of spiritual guidance; the counseling session may be the only place where they feel comfortable enough to risk elaborating on issues of faith. At times we may be surprised to find that when we provide clients with the room to pursue spiritual matters accelerated psychological growth often occurs (1996:117).

Counseling is not an opportunity for workers to convert clients to their religious beliefs. Instead, they must be open to the wide range of paths that individuals may choose for spirituality. This may be an appropriate time to refer them to an appropriate minister, rabbi, priest, and so on.

The most important counseling goal is to help clients sustain health. For example, helpers can work with clients to ensure that they have access to the latest information regarding the disease and its treatment. This may mean referral to appropriate physicians who specialize in the area. Or it may mean helping clients use databases of information so that they make intelligent choices about their physical and psychological health and wellness. Other appropriate counseling activities and goals for working with clients with AIDS include the following:

- helping clients meet basic needs (living arrangements, finances, medical, transportation)
- assisting clients in dealing with the feelings associated with this disease, such as fear of death, depression, and fear of being abandoned

- grief counseling to help clients cope with the decline and loss of significant others who have AIDS
- helping clients find meaning and purpose to their lives, including how they wish to live out their remaining time
- helping clients deal with issues of discrimination
- assisting clients in connecting with appropriate supportive groups and services
- helping clients make decisions about end-of-life issues (e.g., increasing dependency on others, hospice care, wills, pain control, suicide)
- helping caregivers (i.e., partners, family, friends) deal with their emotional and physical stress
- supporting clients who are dying (e.g., helping with funeral arrangements, saying goodbye to significant others, exploring the process and meaning of death)
- referring clients to appropriate religious organizations for spiritual support

Brief Counseling

Be kind whenever possible. It is always possible.

—Dalai Lama

Brief counseling is an approach to counseling characterized by a focus on resources and solutions rather than problems. The purpose of brief counseling is "to provide people with a pleasant experience that turns problems into challenges, fosters optimism, enhances collaboration, inspires creativity, and, above all, helps them to retain their dignity" (Furman and Ahola, 1994:65).

How Brief Counseling Helps

Often counseling relationships are brief, sometimes limited to a few sessions, a single session, or even a brief encounter. Michael Hoyt (1994) reviewed the literature and found that single-session therapy is often the norm and that a significant number of clients and counselors found it desirable and useful. In three systematic studies of the effectiveness of single-session therapy (SST), more than 50 percent of clients showed improvement (1994:41).

Many people solve psychological problems without professional consultation. For others, the "light touch" of a single visit may be enough, providing experience, skills, and encouragement to help them continue in their life journey (Hoyt, 1994:153).

An important assumption is that a change in some part of a client's life will affect other aspects of his or her life, including relationships with significant others. Brief counseling that helps a client achieve some success (e.g., insight, reduction of painful feelings, new skills), however small, can have a dramatic long-term impact if it switches the client to a position of optimism from a point of despair, and a ripple effect occurs. "When clients alter their behaviors ever so slightly, it causes a chain reaction in response to the initial change. Those affected by the change find themselves adjusting their responses, which in turn elicits further changes in clients" (Sklare, 1997:11).

When clients come voluntarily for counseling, they may have already established a certain momentum for change. In fact, some clients realize progress while waiting for their first scheduled appointment.

De Shazer (1985) argues that it is not necessary to spend time searching for the root causes of a problem, nor is it necessary to have elaborate knowledge about the problem. In brief counseling, the goal is to help clients do something different to improve their situation, rather than repeating the same ineffectual solutions.

Brief counseling may help in many ways. Because of its emphasis on action and change, it helps clients to become "unstuck" from ineffectual ways of thinking, feeling, and acting. Clients can be encouraged to reframe by focusing their attention on what's working, thus interrupting their preoccupation with problems and failure. This focus may generate or renew the clients' optimism that change is possible. Brief counseling, even a single session, can be therapeutic for clients if they are able to unload pent-up feelings. A caring and empathic counselor can encourage such ventilation and reassure clients that their reactions and feelings are normal. This can significantly reduce any feelings of isolation by disputing the belief that many clients hold: "I'm the only one who feels this way."

Brief counseling can also provide important information to clients. For example, they can be referred to appropriate alternative services. Or they can be given information that might help them deal with their situation. Finally, brief counseling can be used to demystify the counseling process and to help clients understand what they might reasonably accomplish in counseling. In this way, brief counseling may be useful for motivating reluctant clients to engage with or to continue with counseling.

Brief or single-session therapy is not appropriate for all clients. It is less likely to be effective with client groups such as the following: clients who need inpatient psychiatric care, including those who are suicidal; clients with schizophrenia, bipolar disorder, or drug addiction; clients who need help in dealing with the effects of childhood abuse; and clients with chronic eating disorders (Hoyt, 1994).

Selected Brief Counseling Techniques

Helping Clients Get on Track.   Social workers and other professionals need to shift their own thinking away from believing that they have to stay with clients until the clients' problems are solved and their lives are in order. For example, they might assist clients to organize their thinking about grieving, but the process of grieving is normal and might last a long time, and workers do not have to be present for the whole of that grieving process (Walter and Peller, 1994). Counseling ends with the client still grieving but with a much greater sense of control and of being on track. If clients have a plan in mind for dealing with their problems, they have the capacity to put that plan into action, and they are implementing that process, workers should consider getting out of their way.

Looking for Exceptions.   Huber and Backlund (1991) propose working with the exceptions to the times when clients are having difficulty. They contend that, regardless of the severity of their clients' problems, there are moments when clients are managing their troubles. Moments such as when anxious persons feel calm, acting-out children listen to their parents, and angry people are peaceful can be studied to discover potentially successful answers to chronic problems. Huber and Backlund believe that clients become fixated on their problems and on what doesn't work. By doing so, they often fail to notice those times when their problems have abated. In fact, they often continue to repeat or exaggerate "solutions" that have already proved unworkable. Using this approach, workers ask clients to focus on those moments, however rare, when they are coping successfully.

> So when clients are asked, 'What is different about those occasions when your child obeys you or at least responds more receptively to your requests?' or 'What is different about those times that you're not angry or only minimally upset?' the counselor is requesting that clients report on experiences to which they have paid almost no attention. . . . As a consequence, they have given little or no credence to the more successful manner in which they were resolving what at other times they experience as a persistent difficulty (66).

Working with exceptions provides a dramatic and quick way to motivate and energize clients to think about solutions rather than problems. In the following brief excerpt, the social worker uses the technique of working with exceptions to assist a client who is having trouble dealing with her teenage son.

> **SOCIAL WORKER:** *From what you've been saying, it's a rare moment when you and your son can sit together and talk calmly.*
>
> **CLIENT:** *Maybe once or twice in the last year.*
>
> **SOCIAL WORKER:** *Let's look at those two times. I'm really curious about what was different about them that enabled you to talk without fighting. Pick one time that worked best.*
>
> **CLIENT:** *That's easy. My son was excited because he was going to a rock concert and he was in a really good mood. I felt more relaxed, too. He just seemed more approachable that day.*
>
> **SOCIAL WORKER:** *Have you considered that part of your success might have to do with your mood? Perhaps your son was more approachable because you were more relaxed.*
>
> **CLIENT:** *Interesting point.*
>
> **SOCIAL WORKER:** *Let's explore that a bit further. Because you were more relaxed, what else was different about the way you handled this encounter?*
>
> **CLIENT:** *I didn't feel stressed so I think I was more open to listen to him.*
>
> **SOCIAL WORKER:** *What were you doing differently?*
>
> **CLIENT:** *I let him talk without jumping in to argue.*

The social worker's goal in the above interview is to find what works, then to encourage the client to apply successful solutions more frequently. The process is as follows:

1. Identify exceptions to those times when the client is having difficulty.
2. Explore what was different about those times, including what (specifically) the client was doing differently.

3. Identify elements (e.g., behavior, setting, timing) that contributed to a successful solution.
4. Help the client increase the frequency of the success elements when dealing with the problem situation.

Clients are often more experienced using ineffectual strategies to deal with their problems. Despite the fact that these strategies do not work, clients may compulsively repeat them to the point where they give up and conclude that their problems are hopeless. Consequently, workers need to encourage clients to apply the elements of success. Techniques such as a behavioral rehearsal (role play) that focuses on systematic exploration of the elements of success can be used. They need to encourage clients to pay attention to what they are doing when they are managing their problem, as in the following case:

> Rodney came to counseling asking for help to quit what he described as "compulsive marijuana use." He was concerned that he might slip into heavy drug use. The counselor asked him to observe what he was doing when he was not using marijuana and what he did to overcome his urge to use. This technique empowered Rodney by helping him become aware of successful strategies he was already using. Subsequently, he was encouraged to increase the frequency of these successful behaviors.

Using Solution Talk.   Furman and Ahola (1994) introduced the idea of "solution talk" as a way to evoke a solution-oriented focus to the counseling interview. The goal is to create a climate of discovery and action. For example, in order to get clients to notice their skills and capacities, workers can use statements and questions such as the following:

- You have dealt with this problem for a long time. Many people would not have survived. How did you manage to keep going? What strengths were you able to draw on?
- When you've successfully coped, how did you do it?

In addition, workers need to be alert for opportunities to reinforce clients' strengths. Personal qualities, actions that underscore their determination, attitudes, positive decisions, accomplishments, effort toward change, courage in the face of adversity, and so forth, can all be used to bolster clients' sense of capacity and self-esteem.

Clients may already have a rich understanding of their problems and the ways in which they might be solved. Social workers need to tap their clients' expertise about possible answers to their problems. The central assumption here is that clients have the capacity to resolve their distress.

- What solutions have you already tried?
- What would your best friend advise you to do?
- Suppose one day you received an invitation to give a lecture to professionals ab ut the kind of problem you have had to live with. What would you tell them? (F and Ahola, 1994:51)
- In order to solve your problem, what will you have to do?

Creative solution finding can be stimulated with statements and questions such as these:

- Let's try to identify something different for you to do to solve your problem.
- Let's brainstorm ideas. Don't censor anything. The wilder the idea, the better.

Reframing was introduced in Chapter 7 as a way to help clients modify their thinking. Reframing suggests another way of looking at problems, which, in turn, generates new ways of looking at solutions. The miracle question (Hoyt, 1994; Sklare, 1997) can also be used to direct clients to thinking about solutions:

If a miracle occurred and your problem were solved, what would be different in your life? How could you make the miracle happen? What would you have to do differently?

A variation is to use the miracle question to probe for examples of success and exceptions to clients' problems:

Tell me about the times when part of this miracle has already happened, even just a little bit (Sklare, 1997:68).

The Change Continuum

The basic idea behind this technique is to assist clients to become motivated in the direction of positive change. A central assumption is that it is not necessary for the counselor to be present for the whole change process. The counselor's role is to promote/assist with small changes in the direction of larger goals.

Step One: Draw a continuum such as the one illustrated below. The continuum will be used to assist clients to represent where they are, what direction they are heading, and where they would like to be.

As bad as
it could be
(Negative)

As good as
it could get
(Positive)

Step Two: Ask clients to put forth indicators that represent both ends of the continuum. Below is an example.

As bad as
it could be
(Negative)

As good as
it could get
(Positive)

- using hard narcotics
- prostitution
- HIV positive
- criminal activity

- job
- drug free
- place of
  my own

Step Three: Use questions such as the following to promote discussion and exploration.

- At this time in your life, where are you on the continuum?
- Where would you like to be?
- What direction are you heading?
- What might cause or help you to change directions?
- What would be an indicator that you are moving in the right direction?

Step Four: Suggest to clients that the direction they are heading is more important than where they are on the continuum. Your role may be limited to assisting them to change direction. Help clients identify incremental steps toward their final goal. Remember: "less frequent" and "less severe" can also signal progress.

Summary

Job loss or unemployment can have a significant impact on a person's well-being. Issues of self-esteem and identity and financial consequences can lead to increased stress and mental health problems. Employment counselors deliver service in four major areas: (1) job loss counseling, (2) career counseling, (3) job search skills, and (4) life skills counseling.

Modern job search methods differ significantly from traditional strategies. Modern strategies focus on a targeted approach to particular careers and employers with customized résumés and use of the hidden job market through networking. Electronic technology has necessitated that clients become increasingly familiar with new strategies for managing their job and career search.

The job club method is a group approach that provides support, job search skills training, and materials and supplies necessary to complete a successful job hunt. Job clubs provide participants with phones, computers, photocopying, stationery, and daily newspapers and other sources of job leads.

The last forty years have witnessed dramatic shifts in the delivery of services to people with mental disorders. Deinstitutionalization, propelled by the introduction of new medications, has enabled the majority of people with mental disorders to live in the community.

DSM-IV-TR is the *Diagnostic and Statistical Manual of Mental Disorders* published by the American Psychiatric Association. It is used by psychologists, psychiatrists, and other psychotherapists to classify and diagnose mental disorders. A multiaxial system is a comprehensive evaluation that includes not only mental disorders, but also medical conditions, psychosocial and environmental problems, and an assessment of a client's overall level of functioning.

Schizophrenia is a serious mental illness that results in a range of symptoms, including hallucinations, delusions, disordered thinking, and social isolation. There may be wide variations in the symptoms people experience.

The two most severe mood, or affective, disorders are major depression and bipolar illness. Major depression affects as many as one in four women and one in ten men in

North America. The defining symptoms of depression include feelings of hopelessness and difficulty sleeping, thinking, or concentrating, and they may include thoughts of suicide.

Anxiety disorders are characterized by greater than normal levels of fear, worry, tension, or anxiety about daily events, or there may be high anxiety without apparent reason. Four serious anxiety disorders are obsessive-compulsive disorder (OCD), phobias, panic disorder, and post-traumatic stress disorder (PTSD).

The two most common eating disorders, anorexia nervosa and bulimia, are most likely to affect adolescent and young adult women. Eating disorders can be life threatening, and involuntary hospitalization is necessary in some cases.

There is no certain way to predict that a person may attempt or complete suicide, but certain warning signs and risk factors can be considered. The principal risk factors include past attempts, current mental and physical status, the presence of a viable plan and the means to kill oneself, talk about suicide, personal losses, efforts to put one's affairs in order, and substance abuse.

Social workers and other professionals have important educational roles to play in preventing the spread of HIV infection. They can help by promoting practices such as safer sex, particularly the use of condoms, and the use of clean needles for injection drug users. The principal focus of counseling people with HIV is to provide support for them to adopt healthy practices, including aggressive medical treatment that bolsters their immune systems. When working with people with AIDS, workers may address a wide range of areas, including helping clients deal with depression and the possibility of premature death.

Often counseling relationships are limited to a few sessions or even a single session. Nevertheless, these brief encounters have the potential to be helpful for clients. Brief counseling works on the assumption that a change in some part of a client's life will affect other aspects of his or her life, including relationships with significant others. One major technique of brief counseling is working with the exceptions to the times when clients are having difficulty. Workers can help clients study moments such as when anxious people feel calm to discover potentially successful answers to chronic problems. A second major technique is to focus the work of counseling on solutions to problems.

EXERCISES

1. If you were responsible for defining mental illness, how would you define it?

2. How do you think the following affect families and society?

   a. mental illness

   b. learning that a family or community member is HIV positive

   c. learning that a family or community member has AIDS

   d. losing a job

   e. eating disorders

3. For what reasons might a person stop taking psychiatric medication?

4. Browse through the magazine section at a local newsstand. How many publications can you identify in which a feature story related to dieting is highlighted on the cover? How many of these articles include discussion about realistic dieting, body image, and weight?

5. Examine your own attitudes and beliefs about mental illness. How have your values been shaped by personal experience? By the media?

6. Imagine that you tested positive for HIV. What feelings and challenges might you face in dealing with your situation?

7. Do you believe that it is ethically acceptable for counselors to openly explore with their clients without judgment their clients' desire to kill themselves? Should they be required to prevent clients in advanced stages of AIDS from killing themselves?

8. Review your personal experiences with death and dying. How might these experiences help or hinder your work if you were counseling clients with AIDS?

9. How might you respond to a client who says, "I'm not going to get AIDS. I'm not gay."

10. Your client is HIV positive but continues to engage in unsafe practices. Explore your ethical, moral, and legal responsibilities, for example, the dilemma of whether to reveal the client's HIV status to a known sexual partner. What if this client is a prostitute?

11. Work with a partner. Use selected brief counseling techniques from this chapter to help him or her deal with a problem area.

10 Cultural Diversity

The Future of Counseling

Preview

After reading this chapter you should be able to:

- describe the diverse nature of society
- describe how social workers can avoid stereotyping
- define *worldview* and its importance to counseling
- explain why realities such as oppression and racism impact counseling
- explain the key elements of cross-cultural understanding
- identify the unique issues that social workers might encounter in multicultural counseling
- identify strategies and guidelines for multicultural counseling
- describe the importance of spirituality and multicultural counseling
- identify multicultural competencies

Context for Counseling Culturally Diverse Clients[1]

"No matter how similar we are, there will be differences."
"No matter how different we are, there will be similarities."

(Pedersen, 2001:18)

Demographics

Typical counseling caseloads in North America are characterized by diversity in terms of culture, age, race, gender, and sexual orientation. It is a virtual certainty that social workers will work with clients who have different cultural backgrounds than their own. The U.S. Census 2000 showed that the United States population had exceeded 275 million. Racially, the United States remains predominately Caucasian (not Hispanic), with about 71 percent of the population in this racial category. Hispanics or Latinos, who may be of any race, comprised 12.5 percent of the population. The non-Caucasian U.S. population includes 12 percent African American, 1 percent American Indian and Alaska Native, and 4 percent

Asian (U.S. Census Bureau, 2001). The United States has citizens from every country and linguistic group but, generally, the major multicultural groups that social workers will be working with will be Hispanics, African Americans, American Indians, and Asians. Within each major group are many separate groups. For example, Asians include Chinese, Japanese, Koreans, and others. Hispanics include Mexicans and Cubans.

The U.S. Census 2000 also reported that, among the population five years and over, almost 18 percent spoke a language other than English at home and 7.6 percent said that they spoke English less than "very well." Spanish is the second most spoken language in the United States. The 1996 Canadian Census revealed the rich ethnic mix of the Canadian population. Among Canada's 28 million people (estimated by Statistics Canada at 31 million as of July 2000), more than 4.5 million speak a mother tongue other than English or French, Canada's two official languages. Significantly, about 20 percent of Canada's people were born in another country and immigrated to Canada.

While culture is defined by many variables including religion, dress, customs, and food, language is a major defining variable. The world's complex cultural mosaic is dramatically illustrated by the fact that there are over 2,700 languages and over 7,000 dialects spoken in the world. Africa has over 1,000 different language groups. Although English is the dominant language of the United States, it is only the third most widely spoken language in the world as more people speak Mandarin and Spanish than they do English (Factmonster, 2001).

Comparisons of Canadian internal approaches to ethnic relations with the United States often suggest that the U.S. "melting pot" contrasts with the Canadian "cultural mosaic." The assumption is that the United States promotes integration of cultures whereas Canadians encourage preservation of ethnic culture. However, studies have shown that the differences between the two countries are not as distinct as the two models suggest (Isajiw, 1999). In fact, the United States more closely resembles the Canadian mosaic metaphor than the melting pot. In both countries, the tendency is for ethnic groups to retain their distinct individual identity (Isajiw, 1999). Of course, each culture contributes to the national identity and it is, in turn, subject to its influence. One clear example is the extent that the Chinese New Year is celebrated by the non-Asian population.

Even though the United States is a country of immigrants, there remains the potential for tension. Isajiw's (1999) observation is relevant to the United States.

> Yet, the mood in the country appears to be an uneasy balance between an understanding and acceptance of the immigrants and feelings of suspicion and even moderate hostility towards them and towards minority ethnic groups in general. A factor in this mood is a degree of racist feeling against the predominately non-white immigrants (p. 93).

As well, economic stressors, including company downsizing and consequent unemployment, can result in the scapegoating of immigrants and minorities who are unfairly blamed for societal problems.

Stereotypes

Social workers are expected by their codes of ethics to appreciate and respect the uniqueness and individuality of each client and to avoid stereotyping groups and cultures.

Stereotyping may be defined as holding firm judgments about people based on preconceptions. They are illustrated by such statements as "Jews are miserly" and "Indians can't hold their liquor." Abundant evidence of stereotypes can be found in ethnic jokes that typecast and smear various ethnic groups.

Avoid Stereotyping.   It is critical that social workers realize and accept that people from different cultures have different standards of behavior, and that they will often respond or interpret actions in widely divergent ways. Social workers can study particular cultures and they may reach conclusions that support certain broad generalizations about that culture, but this is no guarantee that any one member of that culture will adhere to the defining norms of their subgroup. Consequently, social workers should make no assumptions. In fact, clients are simultaneously under the influence of many cultural groups, each of which may exert powerful, but contradictory, leverage.

> Baljit, a twenty-year-old East Indian woman is a first-generation American. Her parents immigrated from India shortly before her birth. They retain many of the values of their traditional culture including the expectation that Baljit will have an arranged marriage. Baljit respects her parents, but this conflicts with her growing desire to choose her own marriage partner. She also wants to honor her spiritual traditions. Baljit is active in the Indian community, but she also has many Caucasian friends.

Thus, a client like Baljit may "belong to multiple groups, all of which influence the client's perceptions, beliefs, feelings, thoughts, and behavior. The social worker must be aware of these influences and of their unique blending or fusion in the client if counseling is to be successful" (Patterson, 1996:230). In general, one's personal culture is influenced by many factors including family of origin, social circle, community, and education. As well, it may change over time and be influenced by catastrophic events such as illness and war, or by economic realities such as poverty.

Although individuals within cultural or other groups tend to share certain values and customs, individual differences may prevail and any one person within the group may or may not conform to the cultural norms. There may also be wide diversity within the same group. For example, there are many Native American[2] groups including (to name only a few) Algonquin, Blackfoot, Cree, Cherokee, Mohawk, Haida, Navajo, and Ojibway. In addition, many Native Americans have mixed ethnicity resulting from intermarriage with other races.

In working with any culturally different client, it is important to assess the extent to which they have moved away from their own ethnic group values to adopt the dominant cultural values. Generally, first-generation immigrants conform closely to their cultural origins, but subsequent generations become more assimilated. This may lead to stress in families as children tend to integrate more quickly than their parents who wish to retain "old country" traditions.

Exploring and understanding the culture, language, and history of the populations social workers work with is an important step in preventing stereotyping. To some extent, books and films can provide this knowledge base, but direct contact and experience with different cultures is a better way to learn. Social workers can gain this experience in a number of ways, such as by visiting ethnic districts, attending cultural festivals, and cultivating friendships with diverse people. However, it is important to remember that the cultural values that characterize a particular culture are not necessarily held by a member of that culture. Within any culture there can be a wide range of individual differences. Even members of an individual family may exhibit wide variations in their cultural identity.

Cross-Cultural Understanding

> *Culture provides a unique perspective, in which two persons can disagree without one being right and the other being wrong when their arguments are based on culturally different assumptions.*

(Pedersen, 1994:19)

Worldview

Worldview is the window through which clients see the world. Worldview is described by Dodd (1995) as:

> a belief system about the nature of the universe, its perceived effect on human behavior, and one's place in the universe. Worldview is a fundamental core set of assumptions explaining cultural forces, the nature of humankind, the nature of good and evil, luck, fate, spirits, the power of significant others, the role of time, and the nature of our physical and natural resources (p. 105).

Because the worldviews of social workers and their clients may involve different belief systems based on different assumptions and explanations, misunderstanding can easily occur. Social workers may, for example, encounter clients whose essential worldview is fatalistic, i.e., they believe that they have little control over what happens to them and that luck is the primary factor governing their fate. Hindus, for example, believe that it is futile to try and change things—fate is the key factor that decides our outcomes (Kottler, 2001). This has profound implications for counseling, and it may serve to explain (at least partially) why such clients may persist with passivity and pessimism.

Native People view mental and physical health in a unique way. "Illness, both mental and physical, are thought to result from disharmony of the individual, family, or tribe from the ways of nature and the natural order. Healing can only occur when harmony is restored" (Diller, 1999:61). Traditional healing practices are directed at restoring this harmony. Jack Lawson, a Native addictions counselor, summarized his approach in an interview:

> We sit in a talking circle, but it is the issues we talk about that are important. The issues have to do with Native culture, identity, how they see themselves as Native People, the effects of stereotyping, justified anger, positive identity development, and ceremony. And we use ritual objects and ceremonies as part of the process: eagle feathers and pipes, smudging, sweat lodges, and so on, introducing our culture into the treatment process and acknowledging what they are going through ritually and with ceremonies. Such a process

fits naturally with our cultural understanding of health and sickness. We also discuss the effects of oppression, while at the same time addressing the issues around denial, relapse prevention planning, and recovery maintenance (Diller, 1999:171).

Poonwassie and Charter (2001) have attempted to describe the clash of worldviews that occurred when European Christians encountered Aboriginal peoples. They suggest that the European's believed that:

> they were meant to dominate the Earth and its creatures. The Aboriginal peoples believed that they were the least important creatures of the universe and that they were dependent upon the four elements (fire, water, earth and air) and all of creation for survival (p. 65).

Culture is not an adjunct to counseling; it provides the essential context for understanding and responding to clients. It is not "something to be gotten over or gotten around in order to get on with the real business" (Ruskin & Beiser, 1998:438). Social workers need to understand how cultural origin influences their clients' behavior and worldview. Similarly, they need to be aware of how their own cultural past influences their assumptions and responses. Moreover, social workers need to remember that they are members of a professional community that adheres to a specific social/political ideology, and they hold to a belief system that may be at odds with that of their clients. This awareness is a prerequisite for developing consciousness to ensure that they don't impose their worldview on their clients. By doing so, they can avoid some of the problems described by Evans et al. (1979), who reported that:

> Workshops on listening skills conducted in Alaska and the Canadian Northwest Territories have floundered on the critical issue of cultural differences. Eye contact among some Eskimos and Inuit is considered inappropriate and distracting. In the US, patterns of eye contact among Blacks sometimes differ from those of Whites. Individuals in the Middle East stand closer together when they talk than people in the United States and Canada; therefore, interviewing at what is considered normal distance in America would be uncomfortable for individuals from Egypt or Lebanon. The direct approach of staying on one topic and focusing on problems may be inappropriate for some Asian populations who may prefer more indirect, subtle approaches (p. 12).

Ross (1992) suggests we should expect differences that will lead to different interpretations of our words and actions. He proposes that:

> whenever we find ourselves beginning to draw negative conclusions from what the other has said or done, we must take the time to step back and ask whether those words and acts might be open to different interpretations, whether that other person's actions may have a different meaning from within his cultural conventions (p. 5).

Ethnic Minorities

Experience with Counseling.   Capuzzi and Gross (2001) report that research has demonstrated that ethnic minority clients tend to seek help from mainstream counseling agencies only in emergency situations. As well, they noted that they are typically not satisfied with the outcomes of counseling and they "may distrust the counseling experience which may be viewed as intrusive, objectifying, and dehumanizing" (p. 417). "Overlooking client strengths, misreading nonverbal communication, and misunderstanding family dynamics are among the most common errors made in cross-cultural helping. Behaviors motivated by religion and spirituality, family obligation, and sex roles are often misunderstood" (Sheafor, Horejsi, and Horejsi, 2000:169).

Reviewing some of the literature, Ruskin and Beiser (1998) concluded that Asians were more likely to avoid seeking mental health services because of the fear of the possible stigma. They were less likely to accept referrals for assistance and they typically terminate service more prematurely than Caucasians. This is not surprising given Ivey's (1995) observation that "traditional counseling and therapy theory are White, male, Eurocentric, and middle-class in origin and practice" (p. 55). One study reached this conclusion:

> Ethnic groups in Canada avoid the mental health system because they feel that barriers impeding access to appropriate services are often insurmountable. They also feel that, even if they sometimes succeed in overcoming barriers, the treatment they receive is inappropriate or ineffective. . . . Large cultural groups who have been in Canada for generations also feel disenfranchised from care (Canadian Task Force, 1988:37).

Various ethnic groups may differ in their expectations regarding counseling. While Western-trained social workers may favor more passive approaches that empower clients to develop solutions to problems, others may expect that the helper will be more active and give them directive answers.

Barriers.   Turner and Turner (2000) identify two barriers that prevent culturally sensitive practice from being the norm:

1. ignorance regarding the "underlying philosophy, structural, and technological alternations" that are necessary
2. inability or reluctance to develop agency services from a "one-size-fits-all" approach to one founded on respect for multicultural diversity.

Smith and Morrissette (2001) conducted a study of the experiences of Caucasian counselors who work with Native clients. Some of their key observations and conclusions are summarized below:

- Honoring difference, maintaining flexibility, and creative approaches are critical to effective counseling. A central part of this is willingness of counselors to understand Native experiences and culture in terms of their traumatic historical context.
- Counseling relationships may need to include extended families, elders, and traditional healers. Counselors need to believe in the community's capacity to solve its own problems.
- Willingness to learn from clients, elders, and Native coworkers was important to relationship development and success in counseling. Counselors must be willing to

relinquish the expert role and adopt "A willingness to have one's knowledge challenged, to work with uncertainty, and [to] seek guidance from the Native community . . ." (p. 80).

- Counselors need to respect and be open to the power of Native spirituality. They need to be willing to become involved in community events, which may test and redefine contemporary professional boundaries.

These conclusions are echoed by Choney, Berryhill-Paapke, and Robbins (1995), who also remind counselors to consider such variables as "differences in communication styles, gender role definitions, medicine, and social support networks including family relationships" (p. 87).

Recent Immigrants and Refugees.   There are unique challenges for social workers who work with recent immigrants, particularly those who do not speak English. These challenges are magnified when clients are refugees, who may be poorly prepared for life in their host country.

> Not only is their arrival usually preceded by an arduous, often dangerous journey, their flight was usually precipitated by social, ethno-racial, religious, or political strife—even war. Many refugees have been the victims of, or witnessed, torture and other atrocities (Turner and Turner, 2001:171).

Social workers who cannot draw on their own experiences for understanding need to be willing to actively learn from these clients about the enormous trauma and suffering they have experienced. Such empathic interest will help them to avoid duplicating the experience of many survivors of concentration camps who were prevented from getting treatment and assistance "because the examining psychiatrists were unable to comprehend the enormity of their suffering" (Ruskin & Beiser, 1998:428).

> Parivash fled from her home in the Middle East after a long period of religious persecution. Her father and her brother were both executed for refusing to deny their faith, although she claims the official explanation cited various fictitious crimes against the state. As a teenager she was imprisoned and was subjected to torture, but without explanation she was released from jail. At this time, her eldest brother remains imprisoned, with his fate unknown. Newly arrived in the United States, Parivash has only marginal English, but strong determination to make a new life. Her spiritual commitment remains central to her worldview.

Sociopolitical Realities

Typically, when dealing with ethnic minority clients, there are sociopolitical realities that cannot be ignored. Often, these are rooted in history and are associated with racism. This is particularly relevant when working with Native clients whose cultures, including their languages, spirituality, customs, leadership, and social structure, were eroded through colonization and systematic undermining by government policies and legislation (Backhouse,

1999; Poonwassie and Charter, 2001; Sue & Sue, 1999). Their history includes much pain because they were displaced from their land. For some, their children were removed to abusive residential schools where they were forbidden to practice their culture or speak their language. In the boarding schools, the goal was to make the children forget their Indian culture and adopt Caucasian and Christian values. Government policies were based on the assumption that Native Peoples were primitive and that they needed to adopt the culture of the European settlers. A review of history demonstrates clearly that governments systematically attacked the tribal systems and this has resulted in a loss of identity and marginalization of Indian peoples. The gay community is another example of a group that has endured oppression and continued hate crimes including harassment, assault, and murder. For some Jews, mass extermination happened within their lifetime, and many others have direct family connections to the Holocaust.

African American history included experiences with slavery and oppression, and racism, which continues to this day in the United States. Commenting on the disparities that separates African Americans from the dominant Caucasian group in the United States, Diller (1999) observed:

> The long list of statistical inequities—from average salaries to unemployment, from incarceration figures to education levels, from teenage pregnancies to poverty statistics—is staggering. African Americans have in turn been the "point men" for the struggle that has been waged against the inequality and social injustice that continues to exist in this country (pp. 174–175).

Ethnic minority groups are often living in poverty. For some, such as Hispanics, because many of them hold jobs that do not give them access to health care, they are more likely to have higher rates of diabetes, hypertension, measles, tuberculosis, alcoholism, AIDS, and violent deaths (Hepworth, Rooney, and Larsen, 1997).

Social workers should not be surprised to find that their culturally different clients present with suspicion and caution, expecting that counseling will be yet another experience in which overt or subtle evidence of bias will come to the foreground. Sue and Sue (1999) argue that counselors need to remember that "many problems encountered by minority clients reside externally to them (bias, discrimination, prejudice, etc.) and they should not be faulted for the obstacles they encounter. To do so is to engage in victim blaming" (p. 29). Summarizing their perspective on culturally different clients, they suggest that "Suspicion, apprehension, verbal constriction, unnatural reactions, open resentment and hostility, and passive or cool behaviour may all be expressed" (p. 39). They conclude that culturally effective counseling requires professionals to have the capacity to understand these behaviors nonjudgmentally, avoid personalizing them, and that they be able to resolve questions of their credibility.

Social workers should acknowledge racial differences early in the relationship. Davis and Proctor (1989) argue that:

> Acknowledgment by the worker of a worker–client dissimilarity will convey to the client the worker's sensitivity and awareness of the potential significance of race to the helping relationship. It will also convey to the client that the worker probably has the ability to handle the client's feelings regarding race (p. 120).

They suggest questions such as "How do you think my being white and you being nonwhite might affect our working together?" be used, along with statements that voice openness to discuss issues related to culture. When social workers and clients are from different cultures, frank discussion of their differences is an opportunity to "put on the table" variables related to dissimilar values and perspectives that might otherwise adversely impact the work. Although this is an important process with all clients, it should be a priority whenever there are sharp differences between social workers and clients. This will assist counselors to understand their clients' worldviews, including their priorities for decision making.

> **SOCIAL WORKER:** *Clearly, you and I are very different. I wonder if it might help me to spend a bit of time talking to you about your culture and your take on things.*
>
> **CLIENT:** *Lots of people in this country think it's rather odd that my wife's mother and father live with us. But they just don't understand.*
>
> **SOCIAL WORKER:** *What don't they understand?*
>
> **CLIENT:** *Here, kids grow up and, once they reach nineteen or twenty, they can't wait to get away from home to establish their independence. In our culture, we want to be with our families as much as possible. Living with our parents is natural and expected. We don't see it as a burden. It's a great blessing that we can be together.*

Social workers who endeavor to learn about cultural history and differences will, inevitably, hear about experiences of oppression and discrimination. These experiences are the common bond that links all marginalized groups.

Diversity and Individual Differences

It is now commonly accepted that social workers are increasingly called on to serve clients from diverse cultures. Speight et al. (1991) caution workers against seeing multicultural counseling as something different from "regular" counseling. They warn against using a "multicultural 'cookbook' with each group receiving a 'recipe' that includes a checklist of the group's characteristics and some instructions regarding how the counseling should proceed" (p. 30). Such an approach may result in stereotypes and in a failure to recognize individual differences. Respect for diversity challenges social workers to modify their approaches to fit the needs and expectations of their clients. Social workers need to become alert to any conflicts between how they see and do things and the different worldview that drives their client's perception and handling of the same situation. Two key questions need to be considered:

- To what extent does the client hold cultural values and traditions consistent with his or her own culture of origin?
- What cultural values and traditions are unique to this individual, i.e., different from his or her own culture of origin?

Social workers do not have to struggle to answer these questions on their own. As emphasized earlier, clients can be used as consultants. Given encouragement, they can be rich sources of information and understanding. Additionally, the process of inquiry serves to deepen the development of the basic foundation of counseling, namely the social worker–client relationship. In fact, this approach empowers clients, and it should be followed with all clients, not just those who are culturally different.

Key Elements of Cross-Cultural Understanding

A multicultural orientation to counseling begins with a quest for understanding our own worldview, then continues with curiosity and willingness to discover the unique and personal worldview of the client. Although different priorities may emerge for each client, the following broad areas should be considered:

1. individual identity and role within family and community
2. verbal and emotional expressiveness
3. relationship expectations
4. style of communication
5. language
6. personal priorities, values, and beliefs
7. time orientation

Individual, Family, and Community

When working with clients of different cultures, it is important to determine where the client's identity emphasis lies: within the individual or within the family/community (Hackney and Cormier, 2001). North Americans place high value on individuals becoming independent from their family, but in many cultures separation from family is not sought or desired. In North America, rugged individualism tends to be prized, but among many Asian and Hispanic groups greater priority is given to family and community (Sue and Sue, 1990). "Individual identity is always subsumed under the mantle of family" (Ruskin and Beiser, 1998:427). Consequently, social workers need to consider whether clients would expect that extended family or even members of their community should be included in counseling. For example, many African, Asian, Middle Eastern and Native people expect that their families will be involved (Ruskin and Beiser, 1998).

Culturally sensitive social workers need to be aware of the influence of extended family in decision making. Consider, for example, the potential dilemmas regarding confidentiality with the client who comes from a family in which the family leader, not the client, is responsible for decisions regarding counseling. There may be sharply different role and relationship expectations between cultures. Culture-bound social workers, who define a healthy male–female relationship as one based on equal division of household responsibilities, will find themselves in difficulty if they try to impose their assumptions on a family that holds a more traditional gender division of roles and power.

Although all cultures tend to have at least some respect for its elders, some cultures place very high value on them. Many Africans, especially younger ones, defer decision making until they consult with older family members, and in Asian cultures elders may be valued more than one's children (Dodd, 1995). The North American tendency to stress individuality and personal decision making might be regarded as disrespectful to parents in many African, Middle Eastern, and Asian cultures. In these cultures, "to honor one's parents throughout life is considered one of the highest virtues" (Dodd, 1995:117). Obligation to one's family or even to the community may take precedence over self, and failure to fulfill one's obligation may bring shame and embarrassment to the family.

Social workers should consider family and community helping networks that exist within their clients' cultural community. The Filipino community, for example, has a strong sense of loyalty and capacity to offer support that extends beyond the nuclear family (Hepworth, Rooney, and Larsen, 1997). Such natural helping opportunities should be utilized as adjuncts or alternatives to professional counseling. For many African Americans, the church is central to family, and they may expect that the minister would be included in the counseling sessions (Paniagua, 1998). However, involving others should be with the permission of the client, except under unusual circumstances such as when the client is incapacitated or incapable of making an informed choice.

Some people, for example, Natives and Middle Easterners, may include the deceased as part of their natural helping network. Many Iranians believe that deceased relatives can appear in their dreams to offer guidance and support. Morrisseau (1998), from the Ontario Couchiching First Nation, eloquently describes his belief:

> Since all life is based on a circle, and a circle has no beginning and no end, life cannot end in death but rather takes on a different form and meaning. When we understand 'all our relations,' we will know our ancestors are just as much a part of us today as when they were physically walking Mother Earth. In this sense, we are never alone. Our relations are still present to help us (p. 90).

The 1978 Iranian revolution resulted in large numbers of Iranians, mostly Muslims and Baha'is, coming to the West. Shahmirzadi (1983) noted that Iranians are highly family-oriented and workers can expect that elder relatives may accompany them to counseling. As well, Iranians will tend to be formal, particularly when dealing with people in authority, so last names should be used until familiarity is established.

Verbal and Emotional Expressiveness

An important consideration is the client's beliefs regarding emotional expression and disclosure of personal information. The Western approach to counseling "involves heavy dependence on verbal expressiveness, emotional disclosure, and examination of behavior patterns" (Hackney and Cormier, 2001:121). This may be in stark contrast to other cultures, notably Asian and Hispanic, in which emotional control is favored. Also, what is acceptable in one culture may be offensive in another. For example, what is considered assertive behavior in North America might be seen as arrogance in other parts of the world, and what North Americans interpret as shyness might be defined as respectful behavior elsewhere.

Many social workers place heavy emphasis on exploration of problems and feelings as a means to assist clients to develop insight and understanding. This course of action may conflict with the approach favored by some cultures, namely to ignore feelings by concentrating on activity. This issue is highlighted by Sue and Sue (1990), who offer this observation:

> Rather than introspection and self-analysis, which many Third World people may find un-appealing, the concrete tangible approach of behavioral counseling is extremely attractive. The Rogerian condition of paraphrasing, reflecting feelings, and summarizing can be in-compatible with cultural patterns. Blacks, for example, may find the patient, waiting and reflective type of a nondirective technique to be antagonistic to their values (pp. 163–164).

Similarly, Sue and Sue (1999) observe that, because many Asians have difficulty expressing their feelings openly to strangers, worker attempts to empathize and interpret feelings many result in shaming the client. Consequently, they propose more indirect or subtle responses: "In many traditional Asian groups, subtlety is a highly prized art, and the traditional Asian client may feel much more comfortable when dealing with feelings in an indirect manner" (p. 45). Whereas Western counseling methods tend to emphasize open expression and exploration of feelings as a method to develop insight and manage pain, many cultural groups do not favor this approach. Native People, for example, may feel threatened by demands for personal disclosure, particularly from non-native workers (Diller, 1999). Sue and Sue (1990) observe that many Asians believe that "the reason why one experiences anger or depression is precisely that one is thinking about it too much! . . . 'Think about the family and not about yourself' is advice given to many Asians as a way of dealing with negative affective elements" (p. 65). Consequently, social workers should consider that keeping one's emotions private is, for some cultures, an indicator of maturity. This will assist social workers to avoid negatively labeling such clients as resistant, unco-operative, or depressed. However, this does not rule out open discussion between social workers and clients about the merits of dealing with repressed or painful feelings.

Versatile social workers will be able to shift from introspective approaches that em-phasize insight and exploration of feelings when this meets the needs of culturally different clients. For example, action-based strategies that focus on developing skills or accessing resources may be more culturally appropriate. This shift has equal validity when working with clients with limited economic means whose primary need may relate to getting a job, finding housing, or feeding their families.

Alexander and Sussman (1995) suggest creative approaches to multicultural coun-seling that draw on the minority client's everyday life experiences. Culturally relevant mu-sic, for example, might be used in waiting rooms as a way of welcoming clients. Similarly, agency and office architecture and art should be culturally inviting.

Relationship Expectations

Clients from some cultural groups may have expectations that test the North American guidelines for social workers. Ruskin and Beiser (1998) provide examples related to the field of psychiatry that parallel the challenges faced by social workers.

> In many cultures, people expect to express positive feelings by giving a gift. Should a therapist accept patients' gifts? Is this an aspect of transference that must always be

interpreted? Is a gift a bribe? Giving a gift to a therapist may be a culturally appropriate expression of gratitude and respect. Depriving the patient of this culturally sanctioned process may invoke feelings of hurt pride, shame, or anger that interfere with the therapy. Inviting the psychiatrist to family ceremonies and special occasions may at first seem inappropriate, but is not at all unusual. In such instances, the therapist may be well advised to consult with other therapists or culturally literate colleagues before making a decision (p. 437).

In another case study, Joyce, a young social worker, recalled how she became anxious when her client, a Jamaican single parent, told her that she wished to give her a gift to thank her for her help. Joyce did not want to insult the woman by refusing the gift, but she was acutely aware that her client was poor and could barely afford to feed her family. Moreover, she was concerned that she not violate professional ethics. Fortunately, her dilemma was resolved by her client who presented her with a grapefruit tied with a red ribbon. For Joyce's client, the grapefruit had great symbolic value.

Another area in which social workers need to carefully navigate concerns physical contact and culture. Cultural groups differ on the extent that touch is expected or tolerated, with further issues related to gender a complicating factor. The National Association of Social Workers code outlines the responsibility of social workers to set "culturally sensitive boundaries" (Standard 1.10) regarding physical contact, but no specific guidance beyond this directive is offered.

There are cross-cultural variations on how people greet each other and the spatial distance that is maintained during conversation or greeting. Whereas a handshake is common in North America, others may bow, hug, nod, or kiss on introduction, and this may vary depending on setting, degree of intimacy, or nature of the relationship. Vietnamese men do not shake hands with women or their elders, nor do two Vietnamese women shake hands (Dodd, 1995). Another variation concerns how people greet each other. Some clients are comfortable with first names only, but others are more formal and prefer to use titles. Some cultures expect one to greet the head of a family or elders first (Dodd, 1995). Iranians, who favor formality, may stand up when others enter or leave the room and same-sex members stand closer than in North America, but opposite sex members are likely to be further away (Shahmirzadi, 1983).

Relationships between various cultures may have historic roots of friction and oppression. Social workers may expect that the feelings that minority group clients have toward the dominant culture will influence the counseling relationship, particularly when social workers are perceived to be representatives of the controlling culture. In some cases, feelings such as anger and suspicion will be overtly expressed, but they may also be unexpressed, and revealed only through subtle or indirect ways. Clients who are overly compliant or ingratiating may, in fact, be masking their anger or hiding the fact that they feel inadequate in a relationship of unequal power. In any case, clients will carefully observe how social workers process and deal with their feelings, with the future of the relationship, and/or whether they will return for a second session, hinging on their social workers' capacity to address such feelings nondefensively.

Many clients, such as Iranians, have limited experience with counseling (Shahmirzadi, 1983). Consequently, it is important that roles and procedures be defined clearly, a step that is, of course, important for all counseling relationships, regardless of experience with the process.

Style of Communication

Some clients are expressive and keen to talk about their experiences and feelings, whereas others are more reserved and carefully guard their privacy. Some clients like to get to the point and task quickly, but others prefer to informally build up to it. Clients may also differ sharply in their nonverbal communication style, including how comfortable they are with eye contact, their need for physical space and distance, their comfort with touch, their concept of time, and how they use silence. Some clients find that a conversational distance of 3 to 5 feet is comfortable, whereas others find the same distance intrusive. For example, many people from the Middle East stand close enough to breathe on others. "In fact, the breath is like one's spirit and life itself, so sharing your breath in close conversation is like sharing your spirit" (Dodd, 1995:166).

Generally Native People tend to speak softer, have less eye contact (indirect gaze), and their responses tend to have more delays (silence) (Sue and Sue, 1999). A similar style is evident among Asians, who also maintain a low-key approach and are more likely to defer to persons in authority. McDonald (1993) offers this simple, but impressive suggestion: "Interviewers must also be careful to remember that a response is not necessarily over when the speaker pauses. There may be more. Give time for full expression" (p. 19).

In the dominant Caucasian community, eye contact is experienced as a sign of listening and showing respect. Conversely, lack of eye contact may be seen as evasive and inattentive. In other cultures, however, casting one's eyes downward is the sign of respect. For Navajo and many other Native People, direct eye contact communicates harsh disapproval (Dodd, 1995). Ross (1992) relates some important principles he learned from a Native mentor and elder from Northern Ontario, Charlie Fisher, who commented on communication errors Ross made in speaking to an elder of the local Native community:

- Verbal expressions of praise and gratitude are embarrassing and impolite, especially in the presence of others. The proper course is to quietly ask the person to continue making his contribution next time around.
- Looking someone in the eye, at least among older people in the community, was a rude thing to do. It sends a signal that you consider that person in some fashion inferior. The proper way to send a signal of respect was to look down or to the side, with only occasional glances up to indicate attention (p. 3).

Ross also notes that Mr. Fisher reassured him that his errors probably did not offend the elder who "knew, after all, that a great many white men simply hadn't learned how to behave in a civilized manner" (p. 4).

McDonald (1993) offers a number of pointers for working with Native people, summarized below:

1. In contrast to mainstream society, where responses are quick, Native People may pause before offering a response.

2. Native People tend not to engage in "small talk." As a result, they may be misjudged as "shy, reticent, or uncooperative by an interviewer when, in fact, the behaviour may actually indicate they feel that there is nothing worthwhile to say, so there is no reason to comment" (p. 19).

3. Native People may appear stoic or unconcerned because of a belief that it is improper to share personal feelings or information with a stranger.

4. Expect short and direct answers to questions. As well, there may be a cultural tendency not to "volunteer" information.

5. Lack of eye contact from Native People may mean respect for the person.

Poonwassie and Charter (2001) and others stress the importance of accepting Native practices as valid and preferred alternatives:

> In order to facilitate community empowerment, all those who collaborate with Aboriginal communities in healing initiatives must understand and accept that Aboriginal peoples have practiced viable healing methods based on their worldview throughout their history, and these methods must be recognized and accepted as equal to Euroamerican therapeutic approaches (p. 70).

Language

Social workers need to listen carefully to the vocabulary and idioms that their clients use to express ideas and feelings. The more that social workers can match their clients' style, the greater their rapport with them will be. When social workers use jargon or unfamiliar words, clients may feign understanding, or the experience may leave them feeling vulnerable and disempowered. Of course, social workers also need to avoid talking down to clients.

Words may have different meanings or connotations for different cultures. The word *school* may evoke terror from some Native People who associate the term with the abuses of residential schools. Social workers should also consider the degree of formality that may be expected by clients. Addressing clients as Mr. or Mrs. may be much more appropriate than using first names. Indiscriminate use of first names may be seen by some clients as overly familiar and insulting.

Culturally different clients are often particularly attuned to nonverbal communication (Sue and Sue, 1999), and they will respond very quickly to subtle indicators of worker bias. In counseling, they may test social workers with questions about their racial views and attitudes to measure how much they can be trusted. Social workers' nonverbal responses to such inquires will often reveal more about their real views than their words.

Racial Labels. It is important for social workers to use appropriate terms when referring to their clients. African Americans have historically been called Colored, Negro, black, and, more recently, African American. Reviewing the literature, Paniagua (1998) concluded that the term *African American* is more acceptable because it does not emphasize skin color, but includes reference to cultural heritage and the African connection. Because some clients may have different preferences, preferring to be called black, for example, it is prudent for social workers to ask clients what they favor.

Personal Priorities, Values, Beliefs

Everyone is differently motivated. Some people are career oriented, and others are driven by spiritual beliefs. Social workers may find themselves working with clients whose views and attitudes on such major issues as gender equality, spirituality, and sexuality differ sharply from their own. When social workers understand their clients' priorities, they are in a much better position to support decision making and problem solving that is consistent with their clients' beliefs. Social workers need to be self-aware and to have self-discipline in keeping their personal views and values from becoming a burden to their clients. If social workers cannot work with reasonable objectivity, referral may be necessary.

For some clients, ideas and values that define personal and familial responsibilities and priorities are deeply rooted and defined in the traditions of their culture. There may be little room for individual initiative and independent decision making that is separate from considerations of family and one's position in the hierarchy of the family. For these clients, family and community are their sources of help and this reality has enormous implications for counselors. To proceed without understanding, involving, or considering central family figures predestines counseling initiatives to failure.

European and North American notions of healthy adaptation include a focus on "self-reliance, autonomy, self-actualization, self-assertion, insight, and resistance to stress" (Diller, 1999:61). In contrast, Asians have different value priorities that include "interdependence, inner enlightenment, negation of self, transcendence of conflict, and passive acceptance of reality" (Diller, 1999:61). Thus, individualism and personal assertion are not as important for Asians as they tend to be for the dominant cultures of the United States. In order to process information correctly and make accurate assessments, workers, "need to determine what is relevant behavior within the client's current cultural context that may be quite different from that of the dominant group" (Arthur & Stewart, 2001:8). For example, they need to know when the value of family or tribal responsibility supersedes personal need. Thus, all behavior must be interpreted based on its learned and cultural origins.

Pedersen (2001) offers an amusing, but profound, comment on the natural tendency to assume that others see the world the same as ourselves: "We have been taught to 'do unto others as you have them do unto you' whether they want it done unto them or not!" (p. 21).

A client's personal values can be identified through interviewing or simple tests and questionnaires. Lock (1996), for example, utilizes an inventory that assists people to rank order twenty-one different values (e.g., need for achievement, creativity, power, wealth, etc.) based on their relative priority.

Beliefs about How People Should Act.   This includes clients' beliefs about receiving help from social workers. Do they believe that taking help is a sign of weakness? Do they think that families should be able to solve their own problems without outside intervention? Asians, for example, may believe that problems must be shared only within the family (Paniagua, 1998). Understanding this reality will help social workers understand why Asians may appear guarded during counseling interviews. Who do they believe should initiate conversations? What are their expectations of the role of the worker? What expectations do they have of people in authority? How do they feel men and women should relate to each other?

Clients from some cultures will tend to defer to authority and wait for their workers to take the lead in the interview, rarely volunteering information or taking the initiative. They may be reluctant to challenge the authority of their workers or even to admit that they do not understand. Asians, for example, strive to be polite by responding affirmatively to all questions (Paniagua, 1998). Consequently, social workers need to be particularly alert to nonverbal indicators of disagreement.

Time Orientation

There are interesting and important differences between cultures on how they view time. The dominant Canadian society tends toward preoccupation with time, with people's lives divided and regulated by appointments and time constraints. The common saying, "Time is money," describes the drive toward getting ahead and making progress. Other societies may be less future oriented and more focused on the present or past. Consider, for example, the importance that Asians and First Nation peoples place on one's ancestors and elders for defining their lives. Native Peoples are more grounded in the present and "artificial division of time, as in making schedules, is disruptive to the natural pattern" (Sue and Sue, 1999:110). Similarly, Ahia (1997) suggests that Africans are primarily concerned with the past and the present and that "social events, as opposed to fixed calendars or mechanical devices, control responses to time" (p. 75).

Counseling Immigrants and Multicultural Clients

Multiculturalism has been described as a "fourth force" in counseling, supplementing psychodynamic (emphasis on thoughts and feelings), behavioral, and humanist counseling ideologies (Pedersen and Locke, 1996). Diversification of society has made it imperative that social workers develop new attitudes and skills in order to deliver effective service to their multicultural clientele, particularly because research has shown that "many traditional counseling approaches are not effective (and in some cases are even harmful) when used among culturally and racially diverse client populations" (D'Andrea, 1996:56).

Each client has unique values and beliefs and each may belong to many different cultures at the same time. Because within-group cultural differences may actually exceed between-group differences, "all counseling, and, in fact, all communications, are inherently and unavoidably multicultural" (Pedersen, 2001:18). However, this should not lead social workers to "color blindness," or unwillingness to acknowledge the very real differences that exist when their clients belong to minority groups, particularly visible minorities subject to racism or discrimination.

Immigrants face a wide range of practical problems that may result in their coming or being referred for counseling. Examples of the issues that social workers might expect to emerge when working with immigrants include:

1. *Language.* Clearly, one of the most challenging problems for immigrants is to acquire sufficient knowledge of the country's language so that they can participate in the society. Inability to speak the language significantly limits an immigrant's ability to access community resources and can lead to social isolation.
2. *Unemployment.* For many immigrants, their move results in loss of status as credentials acquired in their home country may not be accepted. For some, the problems are insurmountable and they never return to their former occupations.
3. *Poverty.*
4. *Discrimination.* Discrimination can frustrate an immigrant's ability to find employment and housing. Moreover, the experience of discrimination can evoke feelings of bitterness or hostility and affect their psychological well-being.
5. *Culture shock.* This phenomenon, which may be experienced in varying degrees, can include such feelings as bewilderment, increased self-consciousness, embarrassment, shame, and loss of self-esteem.
6. *Parent–child relationship problems.* As a rule, children learn the host language quicker than their parents and they make a quicker adaptation. Parents may adapt by over-reliance on their children for translation or interacting with their new country. Fears for their children may lead them to become overprotective, which can lead to parent–child conflicts or acting out behavior in teenage years.
7. *Male–female role adjustment issues.* Clients may come from cultures in which male dominance is accepted and embedded in the routines and beliefs of their society.

Table 10.1 summarizes major guidelines for working with multicultural clients.

Learning from Clients

Given the range of diverse clients that social workers work with, it is not realistic to expect that social workers can know about the cultural values and customs of all groups. Consequently, social workers need to use each client as a source of information by asking clients to teach them about their beliefs. Smith and Morrisette (2001) stress the importance of social workers avoiding the "expert role" when working with Native peoples by becoming students of the client's culture. Simple questions such as, "What do you think I need to know about your culture and values in order for me to understand your situation?" can start the process. Such inquiries not only educate and empower social workers with relevant material, but they also communicate to clients that they will not be stereotyped.

Every client represents diversity with his or her own cultural mix. In this respect, Kadushin's (1983) comments on cultural attitudes are particularly relevant:

> What may ultimately be more important than knowledge is an attitude. The interviewer needs to feel with conviction that her culture, way of life, values, etc., are only one way of doing things; that there are equally valid ways, not better or worse, but different. Cultural differences are easily transmuted into cultural deficiencies. There needs to be an openness and receptivity toward such differences and a willingness to be taught by the client about such differences . . . Because the interviewer is less likely to have had the experience which permits empathic understanding of the racially different interviewee, she needs to be more ready to listen, less ready to come to conclusions, more open to guidance and corrections of her presuppositions by the interviewee (p. 304).

TABLE 10.1   Guidelines for Multicultural Work

1. Openly acknowledge and discuss differences in race, gender, sexual orientation, and so forth.
2. Avoid stereotyping by exploring individual differences. Encourage clients to teach you about their values, beliefs, and customs. Physical appearance does not necessarily mean that a person speaks the language or adheres to the values or customs of the culture he or she belongs to. Relate to the client as an individual.
3. Remember that spiritual and religious values are important components of multicultural understanding.
4. Increase multicultural awareness through personal study, professional development, and personal involvement (e.g., cultivate multicultural friendships, attend multicultural events).
5. Seek to understand how historical events such as the Vietnam war, slavery, residential schools, and internment of the Japanese influence current beliefs and behavior.
6. Explore how system problems such as poverty, unemployment, agency policy/procedure, and systemic prejudice affect your client. Whenever possible, advocate for appropriate systemic change. For example, examine how agency structure or policy may be skewed to serve dominant groups while excluding minorities.
7. Remain nondefensive when dealing with clients who have experienced discrimination. Expect that they may be distrustful, sometimes hostile, towards professionals who represent what they perceive as the oppressive power of the dominant group.
8. Be alert to how language, including nonverbal variables, can have different meanings for people.
9. Adapt counseling strategies and goals to meet the needs of individual clients instead of expecting clients to fit into your style and expectations. Consider cultural context when working with all clients, especially ethnic minority clients.
10. Pay particular attention to family, community, or tribal expectations and roles. (Who makes important decisions? Who should be invited to counseling meetings?)
11. Make self-awareness a priority. Understand and appreciate how your culture, attitude, beliefs, customs, experience, and religion influence what you say and do in counseling.
12. Seek and use natural helping networks including family and community resources. For example, encourage Native American clients to access and use traditional healing practices (as appropriate).
13. Basic needs (food, shelter, employment) may need to be discussed first.
14. When dealing with clients for whom English is a second or subsequent language, speak slower (not louder). Sometimes single words or phrases are easier for them to understand than complete sentences.
15. If you are using a translator, look at your client, not the translator.

Respecting Traditional Healing Practices

For some clients, traditional healing practices rooted in their own culture are preferred and more effective ways for them to address issues. For Native People, various practices and ceremonies are used in which the "underlying goal of these ceremonies is almost always to offer thanks for, create, and maintain a strong sense of connection through harmony and balance of mind, body, and spirit with the natural environment" (Garrett, Garrett, and Brotherton, 2001:18). Examples of the various ceremonies include sweat lodges, vision quests, and powwows. They are used in a number of ways such as "honoring or healing a connection with oneself, between oneself and others (relationships; i.e., family, friends, and community), between oneself and the natural environment, or between oneself and the spirit world" (p. 19). In the tradition of Native people, life is embraced through the senses, which includes the awareness of *medicine*, which might include physical remedies (herbs and spices) but also extends beyond:

> Medicine is in every tree, plant, rock, animal, and person. It is in the light, the soil, the water, and the wind. Medicine is something that happened 10 years ago that still makes you smile when you think about it. Medicine is that old friend who calls you up out of the blue because he or she was thinking about you. There is medicine in watching a small child play. Medicine is the reassuring smile of an elder. There is medicine in every event, memory, place, person and movement. There is even medicine in empty space if you know how to use it. And there can be powerful medicine in painful or hurtful experiences as well (Garrett et al., 2001:22).

Elders and are being reaffirmed as central figures as many Native People are once again adopting traditional holistic healing approaches, which might include:

- medicine wheels
- storytelling
- teaching and sharing circles
- various ceremonies (e.g., sundances, medicine lodges, fasts, sweats, pipe ceremonies, moon ceremonies, give-aways, and potlaches)
- use of traditional role models such as elders, healers, medicine people, traditional teachers, or healthy community members (Poonwassie and Charter, 2001).

Spirituality and Counseling

Social workers may hesitate or be uncomfortable about making spirituality a component of counseling. Fear of imposing one's values and beliefs, general discomfort with discussing religious issues, and lack of knowledge or skill in addressing religious issues, all may lead social workers to unnecessarily avoid making spiritual beliefs a target for counseling discussion. Many counseling texts fail to address or even mention this important dimension. One major counseling textbook of more than 600 pages is totally silent on the issue. When spirituality is addressed, typically the discussion is confined to ethical issues, usually confined to discussion of the professional requirement that practitioners respect and accept diversity. However, spiritual and/or religious dimensions, often intimately entwined with culture, are beginning to receive increased attention in the literature and professional organizations. For example, the Association for Spiritual, Ethical, and Religious Values in Counseling has been formed under the auspices of the American Counseling Association.

The majority of people are likely to report some religious affiliation or conviction. Moreover, for some individuals and many cultural subgroups their religious organization plays a central role in their social lives and it may be seen as a major source of support. Indeed, all cultures have important religious perspectives that must be understood as part of the process of understanding clients and their worldviews. Consequently, social workers should not refrain from work in this important area, particularly *when it meets the needs and expectations of their clients.*

Social workers may work in a religious setting where their work is clearly framed within the teaching of their particular faith. Such religious counseling is guided by the values and beliefs of the sponsoring religion. Spiritual counseling, on the other hand, involves framing counseling within the client's spiritual values and beliefs. Social workers who practice spiritual counseling understand their own religious position, but their counseling work is based on their client's spiritual convictions. This requires that social workers are comfortable with religious diversity, and that they have sufficient awareness and control so that their personal views are not imposed on their clients. Examples of spiritual issues that might be discussed in counseling include:

- emotional struggles to reconcile emerging personal beliefs that are in conflict with one's religious background (e.g., a client "losing his or her faith")
- feelings, such as guilt, that emerge from lifestyle choices that are in conflict with one's religious values (e.g., a client contemplating an abortion, conflicted because of her spiritual teaching that forbid abortions)
- exploring client feelings such as anger toward God (e.g., a client whose child has died provides an opportunity to assist the client to consider loss and grief in light of his or her own spiritual/religious beliefs)
- familial conflict (e.g., common-law unions in violation of religious laws, intermarriage)
- family discord related to one's level of involvement (e.g., children who lose interest in attending religious services)
- meaning of life (e.g., exploring experiences that clients describe as spiritual or religious in order to discern the meaning of these experiences for them)
- death and dying (e.g., position regarding an afterlife, meaning of tests and difficulties)
- establishing life plan or problem solving that is consistent with spiritual values (e.g., dealing with a marriage breakdown when religious teachings abhor divorce)

Frequently, cultural identity is meshed with religious identity. To understand culture, social workers must understand religion and spirituality. Religion influences the way that people think; it shapes their values and it sways their behavior. Ethnic customs, calendar observances, music, and art may all be rooted in religious beliefs and practices. For many cultural minorities (and some from the dominant culture), their lives center around their religious institution. For example, Sue and Sue (1999) highlight the central importance and influence of the Catholic church in the lives of Hispanic groups.

Ethnic minority clients may be more inclined to seek help from elders and religious leaders from within their own community. Clients with a strong religious connection will respond best to counseling initiatives that take into account their spiritual community, values, and practices. This might include helping them to access and consider relevant sacred writings as well as helping them to use the resources and practices of their faith, including prayer and meditation. Conversely, social workers who are not informed, or do not consider spiritual issues when they are important for their clients, will have difficulty establishing credibility in the counseling relationship. Not surprisingly, research has demonstrated that highly religious clients do better in counseling and they are less likely to drop out prematurely when they are matched with workers who have similar religious values (Kelly, 1995). Members of the Baha'i faith, who tend to come from a variety of ethnic origins, generally strive to obtain counseling services from professionals who are versed in their faith. Cultural understanding, while important, is secondary to spiritual connection.

John Turner, a psychologist in Oakland, California, in an interview described the importance of spirituality in the African American community:

> There is also a belief in the African American community that many problems can be handled spiritually and/or religiously. If you go to church, live a "good" Christian life, and turn your life over to God, then issues of substance abuse, marital disharmony, difficulties in child-rearing, depression, and alienation, will go away or at least be handled in the context of the church. For many African Americans, church is where their mental health needs are met (Diller, 1999:180).

Social workers who are versed in the spiritual teachings of their clients' belief systems should discuss with them the extent that they wish counseling to be framed within tenets of their faith. Social workers who are not versed in the spiritual teachings of their clients can establish credibility by demonstrating that they are open to spiritual elements as they are experienced by their clients. Subsequently, they can best assist clients by helping them to articulate and/or sort out spiritual/religious issues. Kelly (1995) offers this perspective:

> A counselor who understands and respects the client's religious dimension is prepared to enter that part of the client's world. At this point the counselor does not need an expert knowledge of the client's particular spiritual or religious belief but rather an alert sensitivity to this dimension of the client's life. By responding with respectful understanding to the spiritual/religious aspect of the client's problem, the counselor in effect is journeying with the client, ready to learn from the client and to help the client clarify how his or her spirituality or religiousness may be understood and folded into fresh perspectives and new decisions for positive growth and change (p. 117).

Empathic responses are powerful ways to respect clients and to communicate understanding of clients' feelings. An illustrative counseling response to a client struggling with spiritual issues might be: "Seems like you're feeling a bit lost or disconnected. This frightens you and you're looking for a way to find spiritual peace."

In the same way that there are wide variations within cultures, it is important to remember that there may be variations within religions. For some, religion and spirituality are central to their lives and all of their decisions and choices in life are considered in the context of their spiritual commitment. Others may identify with a particular religious belief, but their involvement and the extent that religion influences their actions may be marginal. Moreover, complexity is increased because individuals may give a different interpretation to their religious teachings. Clients may self-identify as spiritually oriented, but they may not be affiliated with any organized religion, or they may be members of a particular faith but report that spirituality is not central to their lives.

Social workers need to acquire a broad knowledge of the world's major religions. This is a formidable but important task, considering the wide array of beliefs and traditions that exist. They will certainly encounter clients from the following groups: Christianity, Judaism, Islam, Hinduism, Buddhism, and Baha'i. Although basic knowledge can be obtained from books, this should be supplemented with appropriate field exploration. Many faiths permit visitors at religious ceremonies and sponsor public information events. Understanding something about the faith of their clients will give social workers an edge for hearing and understanding concerns and conflicts.

Cross-Cultural Competency

In recent years, there has been a shift toward a broader definition of culture and multicultural competence to include factors such as sexual orientation, physical disability, and socioeconomic status (Fuertes, Bartolomeo, and Nichols, 2001). The term *diversity* refers to the wide range of variations in terms of lifestyle, culture, behavior, sexual orientation, age, ability, religion, and so on. Johnson offers a useful perspective on diversity:

> The human diversity approach considers human behavior from the stance of cultural relativity. It sees normal behavior as an irrelevant concept and behavior as functional or dysfunctional relative to the social situation in which a person is functioning. What may be functional in one situation may be dysfunctional in another. Deviations of developmental patterns found in different cultures should not be considered as necessarily abnormal (1992:7).

Respect and acceptance of diversity compels social workers to be sensitive and aware of their own cultures as well as those of their clients. Competent social workers don't just tolerate diversity; rather, they welcome and value individual and cultural differences. Cross-cultural counseling competence requires social workers to adjust their approaches to understand and respond effectively to clients with a different worldview. In order to achieve knowledge about the factors that shape their client's worldviews:

> Counselors need to possess knowledge about the history, values, and socialization practices of cultural groups . . . how their heritages, including the socio-political issues facing these groups may have influenced their personal and social development. . . . Cultural knowledge includes information about the client's cultural roots, values, perceived problems and preferred interventions, as well as any significant within–group diversity, including differing levels of socioeconomic status, acculturation and racial-identity commitment (Arthur and Stewart, 2001:7).

Sue, Arredondo, and McDavis (1992) have proposed a series of multicultural counseling competencies as the basis of counselors' education, training, and practice. These competencies and standards have gained wide acceptance in the counseling field and have been adopted within the American Counseling Association. They are organized into three clusters: counselor awareness of own values and biases, counselor awareness of clients' worldview, and culturally appropriate intervention strategies, which, in turn, are detailed

CONVERSATION 10.1
Praying with Clients

STUDENT: What should you do if a client asks you to pray with him or her?

SOCIAL WORKER: It's unlikely that you'd ever get such a request in a secular or nonreligious setting. However, in religious settings, or when clients seek help from workers affiliated with an organized religion, prayers might be used at the beginning and the end of a session. For clients this helps to establish the spiritual nature of this particular counseling work. Clients who come for religious counseling will not be surprised that this is part of the process; indeed, they might expect such a spiritual frame. In a secular setting, most workers and agencies would agree that it is usually inappropriate to pray with clients. They might witness a client who wishes to pray, but not participate actively.

STUDENT: In fact, it did happen to me. I have a field placement at a hospital where I was assisting a Catholic woman. Her husband was terminally ill and she asked if I would join the family as they celebrated last rites with their priest. I accepted, but I wonder if perhaps I broke any ethical or professional rules.

SOCIAL WORKER: From the circumstances you describe, I don't believe that anyone could reasonably accuse you of unprofessional conduct. In a situation such as this, I think you need to ask two important questions. First, did you interfere with your client's right to self-determination? The request was initiated by your client and, given the context, your response seems supportive and appropriate. What's important is that you did not impose your religious views on her. Second, did you violate the legitimate boundaries of your role? It doesn't appear that you compromised your role with her by entering into a dual relationship. This would occur if you started to meet her outside of your professional mandate, for instance, if you agreed to accompany her to church on a regular basis. Or, if you invited her to attend one of your religious ceremonies. In fact, you may have enhanced your capacity to work with her in that you gained further insight into her spiritual values and beliefs. A colleague of mine works with people who are terminally ill. He says that his clients who are near death will occasionally ask him to be present while they perform a spiritual ritual or prayer. He says he's willing to be present and supportive, but that he does not participate. To me that seems to be the key. Kelly (1995) argues that, when a worker and a client have the same religious values, the worker may accept an invitation to participate in a prayer, but he advises extreme caution.

STUDENT: Suppose clients ask what religion you are. Or, if they ask you to teach them something about your religion. What then?

SOCIAL WORKER: Our role in situations such as this is to help clients make informed choices based on independent investigations. You might answer the question about your religion directly, then ask what prompted the question. If appropriate to your role and mandate, you could assist them to explore spiritual questions, but this must be done from a position of neutrality, without any attempt to persuade clients toward your personal belief system. This would clearly interfere with their rights to self-determination. As for teaching them your religion, I wouldn't go there. Instead, refer clients to religious specialists to help them meet their spiritual and prayer needs.

STUDENT: When prayer and spirituality are important for clients, I think it's okay to assist to set goals and action plans that will help them fulfill this need.

SOCIAL WORKER: Sure, and this might include encouraging them to use prayer if they believe that this is an important part of their life.

STUDENT: I also think that it's okay to pray for your clients. A significant part of the population believes that others will benefit from our prayers. So, why should we deny our clients this benefit?

in terms of the counselor's attitudes and beliefs, knowledge, and skills. These competencies are reproduced in Table 10.2.

Awareness of Self

Counselors who presume that they are free of racism seriously underestimate the impact of their own socialization.

(Pedersen, 1994:58)

Culturally competent social workers are committed to understanding their own ethnic and value base. They consider how factors such as their own race, culture, sexual orientation, and religion shape their worldview and impact their work with clients who are different from them. They strive to develop and demonstrate understanding and comfort with diversity.

Social workers must constantly question the relevance of their behavior, values, and assumptions for particular clients and cultures. **Ethnocentrism** is the inclination to judge others negatively in relation to one's own cultural values and norms. Social workers who work from an ethnocentric perspective may be predisposed to discount the importance of cultural traditions and beliefs. Worse still, they may see cultural traits as something to be treated or changed because they use their traditions, standards, and majority norms as a measure of normal behavior. Respect for individual and cultural diversity implies more than just tolerance: It requires social workers to accept that other cultures and lifestyles are equally valid, albeit different. This is an ethical responsibility for professional social workers.

Typically, social workers are well-meaning individuals who see themselves as moral and accepting. Thus, as Sue and Sue (1999) suggest, it may be very difficult for them to understand how their actions may be hurtful to their minority clients. As examples:

- stereotyping, for example, accepting the commonly held, but erroneous belief that Native people can't hold their liquor
- adhering to counseling strategies that are culture-bound, for example, by not adapting to the approach favored by many people of color, namely that "the helper is more active, self-disclosing and not adverse to giving advice and suggestions where appropriate" (Sue and Sue, 1999:29).
- believing that one's own cultural heritage and way of doing things is superior. Unchecked, this can lead to oppression.

The Importance of Personal Involvement

Books, films, courses, and seminars can be invaluable sources of information for social workers in their quest for deepening cultural understanding. These tools can greatly deepen social workers' intellectual knowledge and awareness about cultural customs and variations. They are important for stimulating thought and broadening knowledge about diversity. However, social workers also need to embrace experiential learning. Multicultural events, travel, visits to various churches, synagogues, and other places of worship,

TABLE 10.2   Cross-Cultural Competencies

I. Counselor Awareness of Own Cultural Values and Biases

   A. Beliefs and Attitudes

      1. Culturally skilled counselors have moved from being culturally unaware to being aware and sensitive to their own cultural heritage and to valuing and respecting differences.

      2. Culturally skilled counselors are aware of how their own cultural background and experiences, attitudes, values, and biases influence psychological processes.

      3. Culturally skilled counselors recognize the limits of their competencies and expertise.

      4. Culturally skilled counselors are comfortable with differences that exist between themselves and clients in terms of race, ethnicity, culture, and beliefs.

   B. Knowledge

      1. Culturally skilled counselors have specific knowledge about their own racial and cultural heritage and how it personally and professionally affects their definitions and biases regarding normality–abnormality and the process of counseling.

      2. Culturally skilled counselors possess knowledge and understanding about how oppression, racism, discrimination, and stereotyping affect them personally and in their work. This allows them to acknowledge their own racist attitudes, beliefs, and feelings. Although this standard applies to all groups, for Caucasian counselors it may mean that they understand how they may have directly or indirectly benefited from individual, institutional, and cultural racism (Caucasian identity development models).

      3. Culturally skilled counselors possess knowledge about their social impact on others. They are knowledgeable about communication style differences, how their style may clash or facilitate the counseling process with minority clients, and how to anticipate the impact it may have on others.

   C. Skills

      1. Culturally skilled counselors seek out educational, consultative, and training experiences to enrich their understanding and effectiveness in working with culturally different populations. Being able to recognize the limits of their competencies, they (a) seek consultation, (b) seek further training or education, (c) refer out to more qualified individuals or resources, or (d) engage in a combination of these.

      2. Culturally skilled counselors are constantly seeking to understand themselves as racial and cultural beings and are actively seeking a nonracist identity.

II. Counselor Awareness of Client's Worldview

   A. Attitudes and Beliefs

      1. Culturally skilled counselors are aware of their negative emotional reactions toward other racial and ethnic groups that may prove detrimental to their clients in counseling. They are willing to contrast their own beliefs and attitudes with those of their culturally different clients in a nonjudgmental fashion.

      2. Culturally skilled counselors are aware of their stereotypes and preconceived notions that they may hold toward other racial and ethnic minority groups.

   B. Knowledge

      1. Culturally skilled counselors possess specific knowledge and information about the particular group that they are working with. They are aware of the life experiences, cultural heritage, and historical background of their culturally different clients. This

(continued)

TABLE 10.2   Continued

particular competency is strongly linked to the "minority identity development models" available in the literature.

2. Culturally skilled counselors understand how race, culture, ethnicity, and so forth may affect personality formation, vocational choices, manifestation of psychological disorders, help-seeking behavior, and the appropriateness or inappropriateness of counseling approaches.

3. Culturally skilled counselors understand and have knowledge about sociopolitical influences that impinge on the life of racial and ethnic minorities. Immigration issues, poverty, racism, stereotyping, and powerlessness all leave major scars that may influence the counseling process.

C. Skills

1. Culturally skilled counselors should familiarize themselves with relevant research and the latest findings regarding mental health and mental disorders of various ethnic and racial groups. They should actively seek out educational experiences that foster their knowledge, understanding, and cross-cultural skills.

2. Culturally skilled counselors become actively involved with minority individuals outside the counseling setting (community events, social and political functions, celebrations, friendships, neighborhood groups, and so forth) so that their perspective of minorities is more than an academic or helping exercise.

III. Culturally Appropriate Intervention Strategies

A. Attitudes and Beliefs

1. Culturally skilled counselors respect clients' religious and/or spiritual beliefs and values, including attributions and taboos, because they affect worldview, psychosocial functioning, and expressions of distress.

2. Culturally skilled counselors respect indigenous helping practices and respect minority community intrinsic help-giving networks.

3. Culturally skilled counselors value bilingualism and do not view another language as an impediment to counseling (monolingualism may be the culprit).

B. Knowledge

1. Culturally skilled counselors have a clear and explicit knowledge and understanding of the generic characteristics of counseling and therapy (culture-bound, class-bound, and monolingual) and how they may clash with the cultural values of various minority groups.

2. Culturally skilled counselors are aware of institutional barriers that prevent minorities from using mental health services.

3. Culturally skilled counselors have knowledge of the potential bias in assessment instruments and use procedures and interpret findings keeping in mind the cultural and linguistic characteristics of the clients.

4. Culturally skilled counselors have knowledge of minority family structures, hierarchies, values, and beliefs. They are knowledgeable about the community characteristics and the resources in the community as well as the family.

5. Culturally skilled counselors should be aware of relevant discriminatory practices at the social and community level that may be affecting the psychological welfare of the population being served.

C. Skills

1. Culturally skilled counselors are able to engage in a variety of verbal and nonverbal helping responses. They are able to send and receive both verbal and nonverbal messages accurately and appropriately. They are not tied down to only one method

TABLE 10.2   Continued

or approach to helping but recognize that helping styles and approaches may be culture-bound. When they sense that their helping style is limited and potentially inappropriate, they can anticipate and ameliorate its negative impact.

2. Culturally skilled counselors are able to exercise institutional intervention skills on behalf of their clients. They can help clients determine whether a "problem" stems from racism or bias in others (the concept of healthy paranoia) so that clients do not inappropriately blame themselves.

3. Culturally skilled counselors are not averse to seeking consultation with traditional healers and religious and spiritual leaders and practitioners in the treatment of culturally different clients when appropriate.

4. Culturally skilled counselors take responsibility for interacting in the language requested by the client and, if not feasible, make appropriate referral. A serious problem arises when the linguistic skills of the counselor do not match the language of the client. This being the case, counselors should (a) seek a translator with cultural knowledge and appropriate professional background or (b) refer the client to a knowledgeable and competent bilingual counselor.

5. Culturally skilled counselors have training and expertise in the use of traditional assessment and testing instruments. They not only understand the technical aspects of the instruments but are also aware of the cultural limitations. This allows them to use test instruments for the welfare of the diverse clients.

6. Culturally skilled counselors should attend to as well as work to eliminate biases, prejudices, and discriminatory practices. They should be cognizant of sociopolitical contexts in conducting evaluations and providing interventions, and should develop sensitivity to issues of oppression, sexism, and racism.

7. Culturally skilled counselors take responsibility for educating their clients to the processes of psychological intervention, such as goals, expectations, legal rights, and the counselor's orientation.

(Sue, Arredondo, and McDavis, 1992:484–86. Reprinted with permission of the American Counseling Association.)

will expose social workers to the subtleties of culture including the wide variations in style and practice that exist within various groups. Multi-faith calendars can be used as a starting point to learn about the religious holidays and festivals that different people celebrate. Cultivating multicultural friendships and involvement in multicultural organizations will help social workers broaden their worldview, increase their tolerance, and help them learn about the many different ways to make sense of the world.

Cross-cultural experiential learning exposes social workers to the reality that there may be many different ways to view and solve the same problem. Achieving cross-cultural competence will be difficult, perhaps unobtainable, if social workers remain personally isolated within their own cultural community of friends and family.

> Contact with different cultures provides opportunities to rehearse adaptive functioning skills that will help us survive in the diversified global village of the future. By learning to work with those different from ourselves we already know we can develop the facility for working with future cultures that we do not yet know (Pedersen, 2001:20).

Reminder.   The importance of avoiding stereotypes needs to be emphasized. Individuals of any culture may or may not hold to the values and customs of their group. Some adhere completely, while others may be assimilated into the mainstream society. As well, physical appearance does not mean that the person speaks the language or adheres to the culture that they appear to represent.

Summary

The diversity of the population has made it essential that social workers develop their understanding and capacity for working with different cultures. Stereotyping means holding firm judgments about people based on preconceptions. Individuals may adhere strongly to the values and customs of the culture to which they belong, or their worldview may differ sharply. Social workers must avoid assumptions while accepting that people from different cultures have different standards of behavior. However, because it is not realistic to expect to know about all cultures, social workers need encourage clients to provide information about their cultures.

Worldview is the window through which clients see the world, including their core beliefs and assumptions. Social workers need to understand how cultural origin influences their clients' worldview. Similarly, they need to be aware of how their own cultural past influences their assumptions and responses.

Research has shown that ethnic minority clients avoid seeking counseling, and, when they do, they are typically not satisfied with the outcomes. Moreover, they may have different expectations than Western clients.

Social workers need to be sensitive to the needs and problems faced by refugees who may have faced considerable hardship in their move to North America. Other clients need to be understood in the context of their history, which might have included oppression and racism.

The elements of cross-cultural understanding include: individual identity and role within family and community, verbal and emotional expressiveness, relationship expectations, style of communication, use of language, personal priorities, values, beliefs, and time orientation.

Cross-cultural counseling might address such issues as: language, unemployment, poverty, discrimination, culture shock, parent–child relationship problems, and male–female role issues.

Successful cross-cultural work is more likely when social workers honor differences, include extended families and elders in the process, demonstrate their openness to learn from Native People, and respect Native spirituality. As well, they need to consider differences in communication styles and gender roles. Understanding and respecting the value of traditional healing practices is essential.

Frequently, cultural identity is meshed with religious identity. To understand culture, social workers must understand religion and spirituality.

Culturally competent social workers try to understand their own ethnic and value base, including how factors such as their own race, culture, sexual orientation, and religion shape their worldview. They need to deepen their understanding of different cultures. Although books, films, courses, and seminars can be sources of information about cultures, social workers also need to embrace experiential learning.

EXERCISES

1. In what ways do diversity issues such as ethnicity, gender, and sexual orientation affect social workers' effectiveness?

2. Develop a personal plan for increasing your multicultural sensitivity. Include strategies for experiential learning, e.g., increasing your circle of multicultural friends, involvement in multicultural events, etc.

3. What is your emotional reaction when you counsel someone from a different culture?

4. Research how mental illness may be interpreted by different cultures.

5. Describe how social workers can be sensitive to cultural norms while honoring individual differences.

6. What are some of the barriers that clients from ethnic minorities face when seeking counseling services?

7. Explore the religions of the world. Most religious groups will welcome you as a visitor to their services, so supplement what you read in books with field trips. Acquire a multi-faith calendar as a first step in learning about the religious schedule and traditions of different groups.

8. How can social workers assist clients to explore spiritual and religious issues without imposing their own religious values?

9. Do you think it's appropriate for social workers to privately pray for their clients?

10. Use library databases or on-line databases to research the demographic characteristics of your community. Identify the place of birth and mother tongue of the immigrant community. Explore statistics related to Aboriginal groups in your area. What are the implications of your data for social workers who hope to practice in your locality?

11. Invite a Native American individual to share with you some of his or her experiences in a residential school. Remember that this is a very sensitive topic, so be prepared to be empathic in response to powerful feelings that might be revealed.

12. What unique problems might arise when social workers and clients are from the same culture?

13. How might different time orientations affect counseling?

14. Think about specific customs and beliefs that you might encounter when you work with different cultures. In what areas do you have difficulty working with objectivity, for example, arranged marriages, male family dominance, and female castration?

15. Interview several people who are culturally different to learn about their worldview.

16. Try to analyze the worldview of selected TV characters. For instance, what is the worldview of Tony Soprano of *The Sopranos*? Archie Bunker?

17. In what ways is your worldview the same as or different from your parents? Your colleagues? Your teacher?

18. Pedersen (1994) says, "Counselors who presume that they are free of racism seriously underestimate the impact of their own socialization" (p. 58). Do you agree or disagree with this statement?

ENDNOTES

1. Current and detailed statistical information is available at the U.S. Census Bureau Web site: <http://www.census.gov> Canadian statistical information can be accessed at Statistics Canada's Web site: <http://www.statcan.ca/start.html>
2. In Canada, many Indians prefer the term *First Nation People.*

APPENDIX 1

Code of Ethics of the National Association of Social Workers

Approved by the 1996 NASW Delegate Assembly and revised by the 1999 NASW Delegate Assembly.

TABLE OF CONTENTS

Preamble

Purpose of the NASW Code of Ethics

Ethical Principles

Ethical Standards

1. Social Workers' Ethical Responsibilities to Clients

1.01	Commitment to Clients
1.02	Self-Determination
1.03	Informed Consent
1.04	Competence
1.05	Cultural Competence and Social Diversity
1.06	Conflicts of Interest
1.07	Privacy and Confidentiality
1.08	Access to Records
1.09	Sexual Relationships
1.10	Physical Contact
1.11	Sexual Harassment
1.12	Derogatory Language
1.13	Payment for Services
1.14	Clients Who Lack Decision-Making Capacity
1.15	Interruption of Services
1.16	Termination of Services

2. Social Workers' Ethical Responsibilities to Colleagues

2.01	Respect
2.02	Confidentiality
2.03	Interdisciplinary Collaboration

2.04   Disputes Involving Colleagues
2.05   Consultation
2.06   Referral for Services
2.07   Sexual Relationships
2.08   Sexual Harassment
2.09   Impairment of Colleagues
2.10   Incompetence of Colleagues
2.11   Unethical Conduct of Colleagues

3. Social Workers' Ethical Responsibilities in Practice Settings

3.01   Supervision and Consultation
3.02   Education and Training
3.03   Performance Evaluation
3.04   Client Records
3.05   Billings
3.06   Client Transfer
3.07   Administration
3.08   Continuing Education and Staff Development
3.09   Commitments to Employers
3.10   Labor–Management Disputes

4. Social Workers' Ethical Responsibilities as Professionals

4.01   Competence
4.02   Discrimination
4.03   Private Conduct
4.04   Dishonesty, Fraud, and Deception
4.05   Impairment
4.06   Misrepresentation
4.07   Solicitations
4.08   Acknowledging Credit

5. Social Workers' Ethical Responsibilities to the Social Work Profession

5.01   Integrity of the Profession
5.02   Evaluation and Research

6. Social Workers' Ethical Responsibilities to the Broader Society

6.01   Social Welfare
6.02   Public Participation
6.03   Public Emergencies
6.04   Social and Political Action

Preamble

The primary mission of the social work profession is to enhance human well-being and help meet the basic human needs of all people, with particular attention to the needs and empowerment of people who are vulnerable, oppressed, and living in poverty. A historic and defining feature of social work is the profession's focus on individual well-being in a social context and the well-being of society. Fundamental to social work is attention to the environmental forces that create, contribute to, and address problems in living.

Social workers promote social justice and social change with and on behalf of clients. "Clients" is used inclusively to refer to individuals, families, groups, organizations, and communities. Social workers are sensitive to cultural and ethnic diversity and strive to end discrimination, oppression, poverty, and other forms of social injustice. These activities may be in the form of direct practice, community organizing, supervision, consultation, administration, advocacy, social and political action, policy development and implementation, education, and research and evaluation. Social workers seek to enhance the capacity of people to address their own needs. Social workers also seek to promote the responsiveness of organizations, communities, and other social institutions to individuals' needs and social problems.

The mission of the social work profession is rooted in a set of core values. These core values, embraced by social workers throughout the profession's history, are the foundation of social work's unique purpose and perspective:

- service
- social justice
- dignity and worth of the person
- importance of human relationships
- integrity
- competence

This constellation of core values reflects what is unique to the social work profession. Core values, and the principles that flow from them, must be balanced within the context and complexity of the human experience.

Purpose of the NASW Code of Ethics

Professional ethics are at the core of social work. The profession has an obligation to articulate its basic values, ethical principles, and ethical standards. The *NASW Code of Ethics* sets forth these values, principles, and standards to guide social workers' conduct. The *Code* is relevant to all social workers and social work students, regardless of their professional functions, the settings in which they work, or the populations they serve.

The *NASW Code of Ethics* serves six purposes:

1. The *Code* identifies core values on which social work's mission is based.
2. The *Code* summarizes broad ethical principles that reflect the profession's core values and establishes a set of specific ethical standards that should be used to guide social work practice.

3. The *Code* is designed to help social workers identify relevant considerations when professional obligations conflict or ethical uncertainties arise.
4. The *Code* provides ethical standards to which the general public can hold the social work profession accountable.
5. The *Code* socializes practitioners new to the field to social work's mission, values, ethical principles, and ethical standards.
6. The *Code* articulates standards that the social work profession itself can use to assess whether social workers have engaged in unethical conduct. NASW has formal procedures to adjudicate ethics complaints filed against its members.[1] In subscribing to this *Code,* social workers are required to cooperate in its implementation, participate in NASW adjudication proceedings, and abide by any NASW disciplinary rulings or sanctions based on it.

The *Code* offers a set of values, principles, and standards to guide decision making and conduct when ethical issues arise. It does not provide a set of rules that prescribe how social workers should act in all situations. Specific applications of the *Code* must take into account the context in which it is being considered and the possibility of conflicts among the *Code*'s values, principles, and standards. Ethical responsibilities flow from all human relationships, from the personal and familial to the social and professional.

Further, the *NASW Code of Ethics* does not specify which values, principles, and standards are most important and ought to outweigh others in instances when they conflict. Reasonable differences of opinion can and do exist among social workers with respect to the ways in which values, ethical principles, and ethical standards should be rank ordered when they conflict. Ethical decision making in a given situation must apply the informed judgment of the individual social worker and should also consider how the issues would be judged in a peer review process where the ethical standards of the profession would be applied.

Ethical decision making is a process. There are many instances in social work where simple answers are not available to resolve complex ethical issues. Social workers should take into consideration all the values, principles, and standards in this *Code* that are relevant to any situation in which ethical judgment is warranted. Social workers' decisions and actions should be consistent with the spirit as well as the letter of this *Code*.

In addition to this *Code,* there are many other sources of information about ethical thinking that may be useful. Social workers should consider ethical theory and principles generally, social work theory and research, laws, regulations, agency policies, and other relevant codes of ethics, recognizing that among codes of ethics social workers should consider the *NASW Code of Ethics* as their primary source. Social workers also should be aware of the impact on ethical decision making of their clients' and their own personal values and cultural and religious beliefs and practices. They should be aware of any conflicts between personal and professional values and deal with them responsibly. For additional guidance social workers should consult the relevant literature on professional ethics and ethical decision making and seek appropriate consultation when faced with

---

[1]For information on NASW adjudication procedures, see *NASW Procedures for the Adjudication of Grievances.*

ethical dilemmas. This may involve consultation with an agency-based or social work organization's ethics committee, a regulatory body, knowledgeable colleagues, supervisors, or legal counsel.

Instances may arise when social workers' ethical obligations conflict with agency policies or relevant laws or regulations. When such conflicts occur, social workers must make a responsible effort to resolve the conflict in a manner that is consistent with the values, principles, and standards expressed in this *Code*. If a reasonable resolution of the conflict does not appear possible, social workers should seek proper consultation before making a decision.

The *NASW Code of Ethics* is to be used by NASW and by individuals, agencies, organizations, and bodies (such as licensing and regulatory boards, professional liability insurance providers, courts of law, agency boards of directors, government agencies, and other professional groups) that choose to adopt it or use it as a frame of reference. Violation of standards in this *Code* does not automatically imply legal liability or violation of the law. Such determination can only be made in the context of legal and judicial proceedings. Alleged violations of the *Code* would be subject to a peer review process. Such processes are generally separate from legal or administrative procedures and insulated from legal review or proceedings to allow the profession to counsel and discipline its own members.

A code of ethics cannot guarantee ethical behavior. Moreover, a code of ethics cannot resolve all ethical issues or disputes or capture the richness and complexity involved in striving to make responsible choices within a moral community. Rather, a code of ethics sets forth values, ethical principles, and ethical standards to which professionals aspire and by which their actions can be judged. Social workers' ethical behavior should result from their personal commitment to engage in ethical practice. The *NASW Code of Ethics* reflects the commitment of all social workers to uphold the profession's values and to act ethically. Principles and standards must be applied by individuals of good character who discern moral questions and, in good faith, seek to make reliable ethical judgments.

Ethical Principles

The following broad ethical principles are based on social work's core values of service, social justice, dignity and worth of the person, importance of human relationships, integrity, and competence. These principles set forth ideals to which all social workers should aspire.

Value: *Service*
Ethical Principle: *Social workers' primary goal is to help people in need and to address social problems.*

Social workers elevate service to others above self-interest. Social workers draw on their knowledge, values, and skills to help people in need and to address social problems. Social workers are encouraged to volunteer some portion of their professional skills with no expectation of significant financial return (pro bono service).

Value: *Social Justice*
Ethical Principle: *Social workers challenge social injustice.*

Social workers pursue social change, particularly with and on behalf of vulnerable and oppressed individuals and groups of people. Social workers' social change efforts are focused primarily on issues of poverty, unemployment, discrimination, and other forms of social injustice. These activities seek to promote sensitivity to and knowledge about oppression and cultural and ethnic diversity. Social workers strive to ensure access to needed information, services, and resources; equality of opportunity; and meaningful participation in decision making for all people.

Value: *Dignity and Worth of the Person*
Ethical Principle: *Social workers respect the inherent dignity and worth of the person.*

Social workers treat each person in a caring and respectful fashion, mindful of individual differences and cultural and ethnic diversity. Social workers promote clients' socially responsible self-determination. Social workers seek to enhance clients' capacity and opportunity to change and to address their own needs. Social workers are cognizant of their dual responsibility to clients and to the broader society. They seek to resolve conflicts between clients' interests and the broader society's interests in a socially responsible manner consistent with the values, ethical principles, and ethical standards of the profession.

Value: *Importance of Human Relationships*
Ethical Principle: *Social workers recognize the central importance of human relationships.*

Social workers understand that relationships between and among people are an important vehicle for change. Social workers engage people as partners in the helping process. Social workers seek to strengthen relationships among people in a purposeful effort to promote, restore, maintain, and enhance the well-being of individuals, families, social groups, organizations, and communities.

Value: *Integrity*
Ethical Principle: *Social workers behave in a trustworthy manner.*

Social workers are continually aware of the profession's mission, values, ethical principles, and ethical standards and practice in a manner consistent with them. Social workers act honestly and responsibly and promote ethical practices on the part of the organizations with which they are affiliated.

Value: *Competence*
Ethical Principle: *Social workers practice within their areas of competence and develop and enhance their professional expertise.*

Social workers continually strive to increase their professional knowledge and skills and to apply them in practice. Social workers should aspire to contribute to the knowledge base of the profession.

Ethical Standards

The following ethical standards are relevant to the professional activities of all social workers. These standards concern (1) social workers' ethical responsibilities to clients, (2) social workers' ethical responsibilities to colleagues, (3) social workers' ethical responsibilities in practice settings, (4) social workers' ethical responsibilities as professionals, (5) social workers' ethical responsibilities to the social work profession, and (6) social workers' ethical responsibilities to the broader society.

Some of the standards that follow are enforceable guidelines for professional conduct, and some are aspirational. The extent to which each standard is enforceable is a matter of professional judgment to be exercised by those responsible for reviewing alleged violations of ethical standards.

1. Social Workers' Ethical Responsibilities to Clients

1.01 Commitment to Clients

Social workers' primary responsibility is to promote the well-being of clients. In general, clients' interests are primary. However, social workers' responsibility to the larger society or specific legal obligations may on limited occasions supersede the loyalty owed clients, and clients should be so advised. (Examples include when a social worker is required by law to report that a client has abused a child or has threatened to harm self or others.)

1.02 Self-Determination

Social workers respect and promote the right of clients to self-determination and assist clients in their efforts to identify and clarify their goals. Social workers may limit clients' right to self-determination when, in the social workers' professional judgment, clients' actions or potential actions pose a serious, foreseeable, and imminent risk to themselves or others.

1.03 Informed Consent

(a) Social workers should provide services to clients only in the context of a professional relationship based, when appropriate, on valid informed consent. Social workers should use clear and understandable language to inform clients of the purpose of the services, risks related to the services, limits to services because of the requirements of a third-party payer, relevant costs, reasonable alternatives, clients' right to refuse or withdraw consent, and the time frame covered by the consent. Social workers should provide clients with an opportunity to ask questions.

(b) In instances when clients are not literate or have difficulty understanding the primary language used in the practice setting, social workers should take steps to ensure clients' comprehension. This may include providing clients with a detailed verbal explanation or arranging for a qualified interpreter or translator whenever possible.

(c) In instances when clients lack the capacity to provide informed consent, social workers should protect clients' interests by seeking permission from an appropriate third party, informing clients consistent with the clients' level of understanding. In such instances social workers should seek to ensure that the third party acts in a manner consistent with clients' wishes and interests. Social workers should take reasonable steps to enhance such clients' ability to give informed consent.

(d) In instances when clients are receiving services involuntarily, social workers should provide information about the nature and extent of services and about the extent of clients' right to refuse service.

(e) Social workers who provide services via electronic media (such as computer, telephone, radio, and television) should inform recipients of the limitations and risks associated with such services.

(f) Social workers should obtain clients' informed consent before audiotaping or videotaping clients or permitting observation of services to clients by a third party.

1.04 Competence

(a) Social workers should provide services and represent themselves as competent only within the boundaries of their education, training, license, certification, consultation received, supervised experience, or other relevant professional experience.

(b) Social workers should provide services in substantive areas or use intervention techniques or approaches that are new to them only after engaging in appropriate study, training, consultation, and supervision from people who are competent in those interventions or techniques.

(c) When generally recognized standards do not exist with respect to an emerging area of practice, social workers should exercise careful judgment and take responsible steps (including appropriate education, research, training, consultation, and supervision) to ensure the competence of their work and to protect clients from harm.

1.05 Cultural Competence and Social Diversity

(a) Social workers should understand culture and its function in human behavior and society, recognizing the strengths that exist in all cultures.

(b) Social workers should have a knowledge base of their clients' cultures and be able to demonstrate competence in the provision of services that are sensitive to clients' cultures and to differences among people and cultural groups.

(c) Social workers should obtain education about and seek to understand the nature of social diversity and oppression with respect to race, ethnicity, national origin, color, sex, sexual orientation, age, marital status, political belief, religion, and mental or physical disability.

1.06 Conflicts of Interest

(a) Social workers should be alert to and avoid conflicts of interest that interfere with the exercise of professional discretion and impartial judgment. Social workers should inform clients when a real or potential conflict of interest arises and take reasonable steps to resolve the issue in a manner that makes the clients' interests primary and protects clients' interests to the greatest extent possible. In some cases, protecting clients' interests may require termination of the professional relationship with proper referral of the client.

(b) Social workers should not take unfair advantage of any professional relationship or exploit others to further their personal, religious, political, or business interests.

(c) Social workers should not engage in dual or multiple relationships with clients or former clients in which there is a risk of exploitation or potential harm to the client. In instances when dual or multiple relationships are unavoidable, social workers should take steps to protect clients and are responsible for setting clear, appropriate, and culturally sensitive boundaries. (Dual or multiple relationships occur when social workers relate to clients in more than one relationship, whether professional, social, or business. Dual or multiple relationships can occur simultaneously or consecutively.)

(d) When social workers provide services to two or more people who have a relationship with each other (for example, couples, family members), social workers should clarify with all parties which individuals will be considered clients and the nature of social workers' professional obligations to the various individuals who are receiving services. Social workers who anticipate a conflict of interest among the individuals receiving services or who anticipate having to perform in potentially conflicting roles (for example, when a social worker is asked to testify in a child custody dispute or divorce proceedings involving clients) should clarify their role with the parties involved and take appropriate action to minimize any conflict of interest.

1.07 Privacy and Confidentiality

(a) Social workers should respect clients' right to privacy. Social workers should not solicit private information from clients unless it is essential to providing services or conducting social work evaluation or research. Once private information is shared, standards of confidentiality apply.

(b) Social workers may disclose confidential information when appropriate with valid consent from a client or a person legally authorized to consent on behalf of a client.

(c) Social workers should protect the confidentiality of all information obtained in the course of professional service, except for compelling professional reasons. The general expectation that social workers will keep information confidential does not apply when disclosure is necessary to prevent serious, foreseeable, and imminent harm to a client or other identifiable person. In all instances, social workers should disclose the least amount of confidential information necessary to achieve the desired purpose; only information that is directly relevant to the purpose for which the disclosure is made should be revealed.

(d) Social workers should inform clients, to the extent possible, about the disclosure of confidential information and the potential consequences, when feasible before the disclosure is made. This applies whether social workers disclose confidential information on the basis of a legal requirement or client consent.

(e) Social workers should discuss with clients and other interested parties the nature of confidentiality and limitations of clients' right to confidentiality. Social workers should review with clients circumstances where confidential information may be requested and where disclosure of confidential information may be legally required. This discussion should occur as soon as possible in the social worker–client relationship and as needed throughout the course of the relationship.

(f) When social workers provide counseling services to families, couples, or groups, social workers should seek agreement among the parties involved concerning each individual's right to confidentiality and obligation to preserve the confidentiality of information shared by others. Social workers should inform participants in family, couples, or group counseling that social workers cannot guarantee that all participants will honor such agreements.

(g) Social workers should inform clients involved in family, couples, marital, or group counseling of the social worker's, employer's, and agency's policy concerning the social worker's disclosure of confidential information among the parties involved in the counseling.

(h) Social workers should not disclose confidential information to third-party payers unless clients have authorized such disclosure.

(i) Social workers should not discuss confidential information in any setting unless privacy can be ensured. Social workers should not discuss confidential information in public or semipublic areas such as hallways, waiting rooms, elevators, and restaurants.

(j) Social workers should protect the confidentiality of clients during legal proceedings to the extent permitted by law. When a court of law or other legally authorized body orders social workers to disclose confidential or privileged information without a client's consent and such disclosure could cause harm to the client, social workers should request that the court withdraw the order or limit the order as narrowly as possible or maintain the records under seal, unavailable for public inspection.

(k) Social workers should protect the confidentiality of clients when responding to requests from members of the media.

(l) Social workers should protect the confidentiality of clients' written and electronic records and other sensitive information. Social workers should take reasonable steps to ensure that clients' records are stored in a secure location and that clients' records are not available to others who are not authorized to have access.

(m) Social workers should take precautions to ensure and maintain the confidentiality of information transmitted to other parties through the use of computers, electronic mail, facsimile machines, telephones and telephone answering machines, and other electronic or computer technology. Disclosure of identifying information should be avoided whenever possible.

(n) Social workers should transfer or dispose of clients' records in a manner that protects clients' confidentiality and is consistent with state statutes governing records and social work licensure.

(o) Social workers should take reasonable precautions to protect client confidentiality in the event of the social worker's termination of practice, incapacitation, or death.

(p) Social workers should not disclose identifying information when discussing clients for teaching or training purposes unless the client has consented to disclosure of confidential information.

(q) Social workers should not disclose identifying information when discussing clients with consultants unless the client has consented to disclosure of confidential information or there is a compelling need for such disclosure.

(r) Social workers should protect the confidentiality of deceased clients consistent with the preceding standards.

1.08 Access to Records

(a) Social workers should provide clients with reasonable access to records concerning the clients. Social workers who are concerned that clients' access to their records could cause serious misunderstanding or harm to the client should provide assistance in interpreting the records and consultation with the client regarding the records. Social workers should limit clients' access to their records, or portions of their records, only in exceptional circumstances when there is compelling evidence that such access would cause serious harm to the client. Both clients' requests and the rationale for withholding some or all of the record should be documented in clients' files.

(b) When providing clients with access to their records, social workers should take steps to protect the confidentiality of other individuals identified or discussed in such records.

1.09 Sexual Relationships

(a) Social workers should under no circumstances engage in sexual activities or sexual contact with current clients, whether such contact is consensual or forced.

(b) Social workers should not engage in sexual activities or sexual contact with clients' relatives or other individuals with whom clients maintain a close personal relationship when there is a risk of exploitation or potential harm to the client. Sexual activity or sexual contact with clients' relatives or other individuals with whom clients maintain a personal relationship has the potential to be harmful to the client and may make it difficult for the social worker and client to maintain appropriate professional boundaries. Social workers—not their clients, their clients' relatives, or other individuals with whom the client maintains a personal relationship—assume the full burden for setting clear, appropriate, and culturally sensitive boundaries.

(c) Social workers should not engage in sexual activities or sexual contact with former clients because of the potential for harm to the client. If social workers engage in conduct contrary to this prohibition or claim that an exception to this prohibition is warranted because of extraordinary circumstances, it is social workers—not their clients—who assume the full burden of demonstrating that the former client has not been exploited, coerced, or manipulated, intentionally or unintentionally.

(d) Social workers should not provide clinical services to individuals with whom they have had a prior sexual relationship. Providing clinical services to a former sexual partner has the potential to be harmful to the individual and is likely to make it difficult for the social worker and individual to maintain appropriate professional boundaries.

1.10 Physical Contact

Social workers should not engage in physical contact with clients when there is a possibility of psychological harm to the client as a result of the contact (such as cradling or caressing clients). Social workers who engage in appropriate physical contact with clients are responsible for setting clear, appropriate, and culturally sensitive boundaries that govern such physical contact.

1.11 Sexual Harassment

Social workers should not sexually harass clients. Sexual harassment includes sexual advances, sexual solicitation, requests for sexual favors, and other verbal or physical conduct of a sexual nature.

1.12 Derogatory Language

Social workers should not use derogatory language in their written or verbal communications to or about clients. Social workers should use accurate and respectful language in all communications to and about clients.

1.13 Payment for Services

(a) When setting fees, social workers should ensure that the fees are fair, reasonable, and commensurate with the services performed. Consideration should be given to clients' ability to pay.

(b) Social workers should avoid accepting goods or services from clients as payment for professional services. Bartering arrangements, particularly involving services, create the potential for conflicts of interest, exploitation, and inappropriate boundaries in social workers' relationships with clients. Social workers should explore and may participate in bartering only in very limited circumstances when it can be demonstrated that such arrangements are an accepted practice among professionals in the local community, considered to be essential for the provision of services, negotiated without coercion, and entered into at the client's initiative and with the client's informed consent. Social workers who accept goods or services from clients as payment for professional services assume the full burden of demonstrating that this arrangement will not be detrimental to the client or the professional relationship.

(c) Social workers should not solicit a private fee or other remuneration for providing services to clients who are entitled to such available services through the social workers' employer or agency.

1.14 Clients Who Lack Decision-Making Capacity

When social workers act on behalf of clients who lack the capacity to make informed decisions, social workers should take reasonable steps to safeguard the interests and rights of those clients.

1.15 Interruption of Services

Social workers should make reasonable efforts to ensure continuity of services in the event that services are interrupted by factors such as unavailability, relocation, illness, disability, or death.

1.16 Termination of Services

(a) Social workers should terminate services to clients and professional relationships with them when such services and relationships are no longer required or no longer serve the clients' needs or interests.

(b) Social workers should take reasonable steps to avoid abandoning clients who are still in need of services. Social workers should withdraw services precipitously only under unusual circumstances, giving careful consideration to all factors in the situation and taking care to minimize possible adverse effects. Social workers should assist in making appropriate arrangements for continuation of services when necessary.

(c) Social workers in fee-for-service settings may terminate services to clients who are not paying an overdue balance if the financial contractual arrangements have been made clear to the client, if the client does not pose an imminent danger to self or others, and if the clinical and other consequences of the current nonpayment have been addressed and discussed with the client.

(d) Social workers should not terminate services to pursue a social, financial, or sexual relationship with a client.

(e) Social workers who anticipate the termination or interruption of services to clients should notify clients promptly and seek the transfer, referral, or continuation of services in relation to the clients' needs and preferences.

(f) Social workers who are leaving an employment setting should inform clients of appropriate options for the continuation of services and of the benefits and risks of the options.

2. Social Workers' Ethical Responsibilities to Colleagues

2.01 Respect

(a) Social workers should treat colleagues with respect and should represent accurately and fairly the qualifications, views, and obligations of colleagues.

(b) Social workers should avoid unwarranted negative criticism of colleagues in communications with clients or with other professionals. Unwarranted negative criticism may include demeaning comments that refer to colleagues' level of competence or to individuals' attributes such as race, ethnicity, national origin, color, sex, sexual orientation, age, marital status, political belief, religion, and mental or physical disability.

(c) Social workers should cooperate with social work colleagues and with colleagues of other professions when such cooperation serves the well-being of clients.

2.02 Confidentiality

Social workers should respect confidential information shared by colleagues in the course of their professional relationships and transactions. Social workers should ensure that such colleagues understand social workers' obligation to respect confidentiality and any exceptions related to it.

2.03 Interdisciplinary Collaboration

(a) Social workers who are members of an interdisciplinary team should participate in and contribute to decisions that affect the well-being of clients by drawing on the perspectives, values, and experiences of the social work profession. Professional and ethical obligations of the interdisciplinary team as a whole and of its individual members should be clearly established.

(b) Social workers for whom a team decision raises ethical concerns should attempt to resolve the disagreement through appropriate channels. If the disagreement cannot be resolved, social workers should pursue other avenues to address their concerns consistent with client well-being.

2.04 Disputes Involving Colleagues

(a) Social workers should not take advantage of a dispute between a colleague and an employer to obtain a position or otherwise advance the social workers' own interests.

(b) Social workers should not exploit clients in disputes with colleagues or engage clients in any inappropriate discussion of conflicts between social workers and their colleagues.

2.05 Consultation

(a) Social workers should seek the advice and counsel of colleagues whenever such consultation is in the best interests of clients.

(b) Social workers should keep themselves informed about colleagues' areas of expertise and competencies. Social workers should seek consultation only from colleagues who have demonstrated knowledge, expertise, and competence related to the subject of the consultation.

(c) When consulting with colleagues about clients, social workers should disclose the least amount of information necessary to achieve the purposes of the consultation.

2.06 Referral for Services

(a) Social workers should refer clients to other professionals when the other professionals' specialized knowledge or expertise is needed to serve clients fully or when social workers believe that they are not being effective or making reasonable progress with clients and that additional service is required.

(b) Social workers who refer clients to other professionals should take appropriate steps to facilitate an orderly transfer of responsibility. Social workers who refer clients to other professionals should disclose, with clients' consent, all pertinent information to the new service providers.

(c) Social workers are prohibited from giving or receiving payment for a referral when no professional service is provided by the referring social worker.

2.07 Sexual Relationships

(a) Social workers who function as supervisors or educators should not engage in sexual activities or contact with supervisees, students, trainees, or other colleagues over whom they exercise professional authority.

(b) Social workers should avoid engaging in sexual relationships with colleagues when there is potential for a conflict of interest. Social workers who become involved in, or anticipate becoming involved in, a sexual relationship with a colleague have a duty to transfer professional responsibilities, when necessary, to avoid a conflict of interest.

2.08 Sexual Harassment

Social workers should not sexually harass supervisees, students, trainees, or colleagues. Sexual harassment includes sexual advances, sexual solicitation, requests for sexual favors, and other verbal or physical conduct of a sexual nature.

2.09 Impairment of Colleagues

(a) Social workers who have direct knowledge of a social work colleague's impairment that is due to personal problems, psychosocial distress, substance abuse, or mental health difficulties and that interferes with practice effectiveness should consult with that colleague when feasible and assist the colleague in taking remedial action.

(b) Social workers who believe that a social work colleague's impairment interferes with practice effectiveness and that the colleague has not taken adequate steps to address the impairment should take action through appropriate channels established by employers, agencies, NASW, licensing and regulatory bodies, and other professional organizations.

2.10 Incompetence of Colleagues

(a) Social workers who have direct knowledge of a social work colleague's incompetence should consult with that colleague when feasible and assist the colleague in taking remedial action.

(b) Social workers who believe that a social work colleague is incompetent and has not taken adequate steps to address the incompetence should take action through appropriate channels established by employers, agencies, NASW, licensing and regulatory bodies, and other professional organizations.

2.11 Unethical Conduct of Colleagues

(a) Social workers should take adequate measures to discourage, prevent, expose, and correct the unethical conduct of colleagues.

(b) Social workers should be knowledgeable about established policies and procedures for handling concerns about colleagues' unethical behavior. Social workers should be familiar with national, state, and local procedures for handling ethics complaints. These include policies and procedures created by NASW, licensing and regulatory bodies, employers, agencies, and other professional organizations.

(c) Social workers who believe that a colleague has acted unethically should seek resolution by discussing their concerns with the colleague when feasible and when such discussion is likely to be productive.

(d) When necessary, social workers who believe that a colleague has acted unethically should take action through appropriate formal channels (such as contacting a state licensing board or regulatory body, an NASW committee on inquiry, or other professional ethics committees).

(e) Social workers should defend and assist colleagues who are unjustly charged with unethical conduct.

3. Social Workers' Ethical Responsibilities in Practice Settings

3.01 Supervision and Consultation

(a) Social workers who provide supervision or consultation should have the necessary knowledge and skill to supervise or consult appropriately and should do so only within their areas of knowledge and competence.

(b) Social workers who provide supervision or consultation are responsible for setting clear, appropriate, and culturally sensitive boundaries.

(c) Social workers should not engage in any dual or multiple relationships with supervisees in which there is a risk of exploitation of or potential harm to the supervisee.

(d) Social workers who provide supervision should evaluate supervisees' performance in a manner that is fair and respectful.

3.02 Education and Training

(a) Social workers who function as educators, field instructors for students, or trainers should provide instruction only within their areas of knowledge and competence and should provide instruction based on the most current information and knowledge available in the profession.

(b) Social workers who function as educators or field instructors for students should evaluate students' performance in a manner that is fair and respectful.

(c) Social workers who function as educators or field instructors for students should take reasonable steps to ensure that clients are routinely informed when services are being provided by students.

(d) Social workers who function as educators or field instructors for students should not engage in any dual or multiple relationships with students in which there is a risk of exploitation or potential harm to the student. Social work educators and field instructors are responsible for setting clear, appropriate, and culturally sensitive boundaries.

3.03 Performance Evaluation

Social workers who have responsibility for evaluating the performance of others should fulfill such responsibility in a fair and considerate manner and on the basis of clearly stated criteria.

3.04 Client Records

(a) Social workers should take reasonable steps to ensure that documentation in records is accurate and reflects the services provided.

(b) Social workers should include sufficient and timely documentation in records to facilitate the delivery of services and to ensure continuity of services provided to clients in the future.

(c) Social workers' documentation should protect clients' privacy to the extent that is possible and appropriate and should include only information that is directly relevant to the delivery of services.

(d) Social workers should store records following the termination of services to ensure reasonable future access. Records should be maintained for the number of years required by state statutes or relevant contracts.

3.05 Billing

Social workers should establish and maintain billing practices that accurately reflect the nature and extent of services provided and that identify who provided the service in the practice setting.

3.06 Client Transfer

(a) When an individual who is receiving services from another agency or colleague contacts a social worker for services, the social worker should carefully consider the client's needs before agreeing to provide services. To minimize possible confusion and conflict, social workers should discuss with potential clients the nature of the clients' current relationship with other service providers and the implications, including possible benefits or risks, of entering into a relationship with a new service provider.

(b) If a new client has been served by another agency or colleague, social workers should discuss with the client whether consultation with the previous service provider is in the client's best interest.

3.07 Administration

(a) Social work administrators should advocate within and outside their agencies for adequate resources to meet clients' needs.

(b) Social workers should advocate for resource allocation procedures that are open and fair. When not all clients' needs can be met, an allocation procedure should be developed that is nondiscriminatory and based on appropriate and consistently applied principles.

(c) Social workers who are administrators should take reasonable steps to ensure that adequate agency or organizational resources are available to provide appropriate staff supervision.

(d) Social work administrators should take reasonable steps to ensure that the working environment for which they are responsible is consistent with and encourages compliance with the *NASW Code of Ethics*. Social work administrators should take reasonable steps to eliminate any conditions in their organizations that violate, interfere with, or discourage compliance with the *Code*.

3.08 Continuing Education and Staff Development

Social work administrators and supervisors should take reasonable steps to provide or arrange for continuing education and staff development for all staff for whom they are responsible. Continuing education and staff development should address current knowledge and emerging developments related to social work practice and ethics.

3.09 Commitments to Employers

(a) Social workers generally should adhere to commitments made to employers and employing organizations.

(b) Social workers should work to improve employing agencies' policies and procedures and the efficiency and effectiveness of their services.

(c) Social workers should take reasonable steps to ensure that employers are aware of social workers' ethical obligations as set forth in the *NASW Code of Ethics* and of the implications of those obligations for social work practice.

(d) Social workers should not allow an employing organization's policies, procedures, regulations, or administrative orders to interfere with their ethical practice of social work. Social workers should take reasonable steps to ensure that their employing organizations' practices are consistent with the *NASW Code of Ethics*.

(e) Social workers should act to prevent and eliminate discrimination in the employing organization's work assignments and in its employment policies and practices.

(f) Social workers should accept employment or arrange student field placements only in organizations that exercise fair personnel practices.

(g) Social workers should be diligent stewards of the resources of their employing organizations, wisely conserving funds where appropriate and never misappropriating funds or using them for unintended purposes.

3.10 Labor–Management Disputes

(a) Social workers may engage in organized action, including the formation of and participation in labor unions, to improve services to clients and working conditions.

(b) The actions of social workers who are involved in labor–management disputes, job actions, or labor strikes should be guided by the profession's values, ethical principles, and ethical standards. Reasonable differences of opinion exist among social workers concerning their primary obligation as professionals during an actual or threatened labor strike or job action. Social workers should carefully examine relevant issues and their possible impact on clients before deciding on a course of action.

4. Social Workers' Ethical Responsibilities as Professionals

4.01 Competence

(a) Social workers should accept responsibility or employment only on the basis of existing competence or the intention to acquire the necessary competence.

(b) Social workers should strive to become and remain proficient in professional practice and the performance of professional functions. Social workers should critically examine and keep current with emerging knowledge relevant to social work. Social workers should routinely review the professional literature and participate in continuing education relevant to social work practice and social work ethics.

(c) Social workers should base practice on recognized knowledge, including empirically based knowledge, relevant to social work and social work ethics.

4.02 Discrimination

Social workers should not practice, condone, facilitate, or collaborate with any form of discrimination on the basis of race, ethnicity, national origin, color, sex, sexual orientation, age, marital status, political belief, religion, or mental or physical disability.

4.03 Private Conduct

Social workers should not permit their private conduct to interfere with their ability to fulfill their professional responsibilities.

4.04 Dishonesty, Fraud, and Deception

Social workers should not participate in, condone, or be associated with dishonesty, fraud, or deception.

4.05 Impairment

(a) Social workers should not allow their own personal problems, psychosocial distress, legal problems, substance abuse, or mental health difficulties to interfere with their professional judgment and performance or to jeopardize the best interests of people for whom they have a professional responsibility.

(b) Social workers whose personal problems, psychosocial distress, legal problems, substance abuse, or mental health difficulties interfere with their professional judgment and performance should immediately seek consultation and take appropriate remedial action by seeking professional help, making adjustments in workload, terminating practice, or taking any other steps necessary to protect clients and others.

4.06 Misrepresentation

(a) Social workers should make clear distinctions between statements made and actions engaged in as a private individual and as a representative of the social work profession, a professional social work organization, or the social worker's employing agency.

(b) Social workers who speak on behalf of professional social work organizations should accurately represent the official and authorized positions of the organizations.

(c) Social workers should ensure that their representations to clients, agencies, and the public of professional qualifications, credentials, education, competence, affiliations, services provided, or results to be achieved are accurate. Social workers should claim only those relevant professional credentials they actually possess and take steps to correct any inaccuracies or misrepresentations of their credentials by others.

4.07 Solicitations

(a) Social workers should not engage in uninvited solicitation of potential clients who, because of their circumstances, are vulnerable to undue influence, manipulation, or coercion.

(**b**) Social workers should not engage in solicitation of testimonial endorsements (including solicitation of consent to use a client's prior statement as a testimonial endorsement) from current clients or from other people who, because of their particular circumstances, are vulnerable to undue influence.

4.08 Acknowledging Credit

(**a**) Social workers should take responsibility and credit, including authorship credit, only for work they have actually performed and to which they have contributed.

(**b**) Social workers should honestly acknowledge the work of and the contributions made by others.

5. Social Workers' Ethical Responsibilities to the Social Work Profession

5.01 Integrity of the Profession

(**a**) Social workers should work toward the maintenance and promotion of high standards of practice.

(**b**) Social workers should uphold and advance the values, ethics, knowledge, and mission of the profession. Social workers should protect, enhance, and improve the integrity of the profession through appropriate study and research, active discussion, and responsible criticism of the profession.

(**c**) Social workers should contribute time and professional expertise to activities that promote respect for the value, integrity, and competence of the social work profession. These activities may include teaching, research, consultation, service, legislative testimony, presentations in the community, and participation in their professional organizations.

(**d**) Social workers should contribute to the knowledge base of social work and share with colleagues their knowledge related to practice, research, and ethics. Social workers should seek to contribute to the profession's literature and to share their knowledge at professional meetings and conferences.

(**e**) Social workers should act to prevent the unauthorized and unqualified practice of social work.

5.02 Evaluation and Research

(**a**) Social workers should monitor and evaluate policies, the implementation of programs, and practice interventions.

(**b**) Social workers should promote and facilitate evaluation and research to contribute to the development of knowledge.

(**c**) Social workers should critically examine and keep current with emerging knowledge relevant to social work and fully use evaluation and research evidence in their professional practice.

(**d**) Social workers engaged in evaluation or research should carefully consider possible consequences and should follow guidelines developed for the protection of evaluation and research participants. Appropriate institutional review boards should be consulted.

(e) Social workers engaged in evaluation or research should obtain voluntary and written informed consent from participants, when appropriate, without any implied or actual deprivation or penalty for refusal to participate; without undue inducement to participate; and with due regard for participants' well-being, privacy, and dignity. Informed consent should include information about the nature, extent, and duration of the participation requested and disclosure of the risks and benefits of participation in the research.

(f) When evaluation or research participants are incapable of giving informed consent, social workers should provide an appropriate explanation to the participants, obtain the participants' assent to the extent they are able, and obtain written consent from an appropriate proxy.

(g) Social workers should never design or conduct evaluation or research that does not use consent procedures, such as certain forms of naturalistic observation and archival research, unless rigorous and responsible review of the research has found it to be justified because of its prospective scientific, educational, or applied value and unless equally effective alternative procedures that do not involve waiver of consent are not feasible.

(h) Social workers should inform participants of their right to withdraw from evaluation and research at any time without penalty.

(i) Social workers should take appropriate steps to ensure that participants in evaluation and research have access to appropriate supportive services.

(j) Social workers engaged in evaluation or research should protect participants from unwarranted physical or mental distress, harm, danger, or deprivation.

(k) Social workers engaged in the evaluation of services should discuss collected information only for professional purposes and only with people professionally concerned with this information.

(l) Social workers engaged in evaluation or research should ensure the anonymity or confidentiality of participants and of the data obtained from them. Social workers should inform participants of any limits of confidentiality, the measures that will be taken to ensure confidentiality, and when any records containing research data will be destroyed.

(m) Social workers who report evaluation and research results should protect participants' confidentiality by omitting identifying information unless proper consent has been obtained authorizing disclosure.

(n) Social workers should report evaluation and research findings accurately. They should not fabricate or falsify results and should take steps to correct any errors later found in published data using standard publication methods.

(o) Social workers engaged in evaluation or research should be alert to and avoid conflicts of interest and dual relationships with participants, should inform participants when a real or potential conflict of interest arises, and should take steps to resolve the issue in a manner that makes participants' interests primary.

(p) Social workers should educate themselves, their students, and their colleagues about responsible research practices.

6. Social Workers' Ethical Responsibilities to the Broader Society

6.01 Social Welfare

Social workers should promote the general welfare of society, from local to global levels, and the development of people, their communities, and their environments. Social workers should advocate for living conditions conducive to the fulfillment of basic human needs and should promote social, economic, political, and cultural values and institutions that are compatible with the realization of social justice.

6.02 Public Participation

Social workers should facilitate informed participation by the public in shaping social policies and institutions.

6.03 Public Emergencies

Social workers should provide appropriate professional services in public emergencies to the greatest extent possible.

6.04 Social and Political Action

   (a) Social workers should engage in social and political action that seeks to ensure that all people have equal access to the resources, employment, services, and opportunities they require to meet their basic human needs and to develop fully. Social workers should be aware of the impact of the political arena on practice and should advocate for changes in policy and legislation to improve social conditions in order to meet basic human needs and promote social justice.

   (b) Social workers should act to expand choice and opportunity for all people, with special regard for vulnerable, disadvantaged, oppressed, and exploited people and groups.

   (c) Social workers should promote conditions that encourage respect for cultural and social diversity within the United States and globally. Social workers should promote policies and practices that demonstrate respect for difference, support the expansion of cultural knowledge and resources, advocate for programs and institutions that demonstrate cultural competence, and promote policies that safeguard the rights of and confirm equity and social justice for all people.

   (d) Social workers should act to prevent and eliminate domination of, exploitation of, and discrimination against any person, group, or class on the basis of race, ethnicity, national origin, color, sex, sexual orientation, age, marital status, political belief, religion, or mental or physical disability.

ACA Code of Ethics and Standards of Practice

Code of Ethics

Preamble

The American Counseling Association is an educational, scientific, and professional organization whose members are dedicated to the enhancement of human development throughout the life-span. Association members recognize diversity in our society and embrace a cross-cultural approach in support of the worth, dignity, potential, and uniqueness of each individual.

The specification of a code of ethics enables the association to clarify to current and future members, and to those served by members, the nature of the ethical responsibilities held in common by its members. As the code of ethics of the association, this document establishes principles that define the ethical behavior of association members. All members of the American Counseling Association are required to adhere to the Code of Ethics and the Standards of Practice. The Code of Ethics will serve as the basis for processing ethical complaints initiated against members of the association.

Section A: The Counseling Relationship
Section B: Confidentiality
Section C: Professional Responsibility
Section D: Relationships with Other Professionals
Section E: Evaluation, Assessment, and Interpretation
Section F: Teaching, Training, and Supervision
Section G: Research and Publication
Section H: Resolving Ethical Issues

Section A: The Counseling Relationship

A.1. Client Welfare
    a. **Primary Responsibility.** The primary responsibility of counselors is to respect the dignity and to promote the welfare of clients.

    b.   **Positive Growth and Development.** Counselors encourage client growth and development in ways that foster the clients' interest and welfare; counselors avoid fostering dependent counseling relationships.

    c.   **Counseling Plans.** Counselors and their clients work jointly in devising integrated, individual counseling plans that offer reasonable promise of success and are consistent with abilities and circumstances of clients. Counselors and clients regularly review counseling plans to ensure their continued viability and effectiveness, respecting clients' freedom of choice. (See A.3.b.)

    d.   **Family Involvement.** Counselors recognize that families are usually important in clients' lives and strive to enlist family understanding and involvement as a positive resource, when appropriate.

    e.   **Career and Employment Needs.** Counselors work with their clients in considering employment in jobs and circumstances that are consistent with the clients' overall abilities, vocational limitations, physical restrictions, general temperament, interest and aptitude patterns, social skills, education, general qualifications, and other relevant characteristics and needs. Counselors neither place nor participate in placing clients in positions that will result in damaging the interest and the welfare of clients, employers, or the public.

A.2. **Respecting Diversity**

    a.   **Nondiscrimination.** Counselors do not condone or engage in discrimination based on age, color, culture, disability, ethnic group, gender, race, religion, sexual orientation, marital status, or socioeconomic status. (See C.5.a., C.5.b., and D.1.i.)

    b.   **Respecting Differences.** Counselors will actively attempt to understand the diverse cultural backgrounds of the clients with whom they work. This includes, but is not limited to, learning how the counselor's own cultural/ethnic/racial identity impacts her or his values and beliefs about the counseling process. (See E.8. and F.2.i.)

A.3. **Client Rights**

    a.   **Disclosure to Clients.** When counseling is initiated, and throughout the counseling process as necessary, counselors inform clients of the purposes, goals, techniques, procedures, limitations, potential risks, and benefits of services to be performed, and other pertinent information. Counselors take steps to ensure that clients understand the implications of diagnosis, the intended use of tests and reports, fees, and billing arrangements. Clients have the right to expect confidentiality and to be provided with an explanation of its limitations, including supervision and/or treatment team professionals; to obtain clear information about their case records; to participate in the ongoing counseling plans; and to refuse any recommended services and be advised of the consequences of such refusal. (See E.5.a. and G.2.)

    b.   **Freedom of Choice.** Counselors offer clients the freedom to choose whether to enter into a counseling relationship and to determine which professional(s) will provide counseling. Restrictions that limit choices of clients are fully explained. (See A.1.c.)

c. **Inability to Give Consent.** When counseling minors or persons unable to give voluntary informed consent, counselors act in these clients' best interests. (See B.3.)

A.4. Clients Served by Others
If a client is receiving services from another mental health professional, counselors, with client consent, inform the professional persons already involved and develop clear agreements to avoid confusion and conflict for the client. (See C.6.c.)

A.5. Personal Needs and Values
a. **Personal Needs.** In the counseling relationship, counselors are aware of the intimacy and responsibilities inherent in the counseling relationship, maintain respect for clients, and avoid actions that seek to meet their personal needs at the expense of clients.
b. **Personal Values.** Counselors are aware of their own values, attitudes, beliefs, and behaviors and how these apply in a diverse society, and avoid imposing their values on clients. (See C.5.a.)

A.6. Dual Relationships
a. **Avoid When Possible.** Counselors are aware of their influential positions with respect to clients, and they avoid exploiting the trust and dependency of clients. Counselors make every effort to avoid dual relationships with clients that could impair professional judgment or increase the risk of harm to clients. (Examples of such relationships include, but are not limited to, familial, social, financial, business, or close personal relationships with clients.) When a dual relationship cannot be avoided, counselors take appropriate professional precautions such as informed consent, consultation, supervision, and documentation to ensure that judgment is not impaired and no exploitation occurs. (See F.1.b.)
b. **Superior/Subordinate Relationships.** Counselors do not accept as clients superiors or subordinates with whom they have administrative, supervisory, or evaluative relationships.

A.7. Sexual Intimacies with Clients
a. **Current Clients.** Counselors do not have any type of sexual intimacies with clients and do not counsel persons with whom they have had a sexual relationship.
b. **Former Clients.** Counselors do not engage in sexual intimacies with former clients within a minimum of 2 years after terminating the counseling relationship. Counselors who engage in such relationship after 2 years following termination have the responsibility to examine and document thoroughly that such relations did not have an exploitative nature, based on factors such as duration of counseling, amount of time since counseling, termination circumstances, client's personal history and mental status, adverse impact on the client, and actions by the counselor suggesting a plan to initiate a sexual relationship with the client after termination.

A.8. Multiple Clients

When counselors agree to provide counseling services to two or more persons who have a relationship (such as husband and wife, or parents and children), counselors clarify at the outset which person or persons are clients and the nature of the relationships they will have with each involved person. If it becomes apparent that counselors may be called upon to perform potentially conflicting roles, they clarify, adjust, or withdraw from roles appropriately. (See B.2. and B.4.d.)

A.9. Group Work

a. **Screening.** Counselors screen prospective group counseling/therapy participants. To the extent possible, counselors select members whose needs and goals are compatible with goals of the group, who will not impede the group process, and whose well-being will not be jeopardized by the group experience.

b. **Protecting Clients.** In a group setting, counselors take reasonable precautions to protect clients from physical or psychological trauma.

A.10. Fees and Bartering (See D.3.a. and D.3.b.)

a. **Advance Understanding.** Counselors clearly explain to clients, prior to entering the counseling relationship, all financial arrangements related to professional services including the use of collection agencies or legal measures for nonpayment. (A.11.c.)

b. **Establishing Fees.** In establishing fees for professional counseling services, counselors consider the financial status of clients and locality. In the event that the established fee structure is inappropriate for a client, assistance is provided in attempting to find comparable services of acceptable cost. (See A.10.d., D.3.a., and D.3.b.)

c. **Bartering Discouraged.** Counselors ordinarily refrain from accepting goods or services from clients in return for counseling services because such arrangements create inherent potential for conflicts, exploitation, and distortion of the professional relationship. Counselors may participate in bartering only if the relationship is not exploitative, if the client requests it, if a clear written contract is established, and if such arrangements are an accepted practice among professionals in the community. (See A.6.a.)

d. **Pro Bono Service.** Counselors contribute to society by devoting a portion of their professional activity to services for which there is little or no financial return (pro bono).

A.11. Termination and Referral

a. **Abandonment Prohibited.** Counselors do not abandon or neglect clients in counseling. Counselors assist in making appropriate arrangements for the continuation of treatment, when necessary, during interruptions such as vacations, and following termination.

b. **Inability to Assist Clients.** If counselors determine an inability to be of professional assistance to clients, they avoid entering or immediately terminate a counseling relationship. Counselors are knowledgeable about referral resources and suggest appropriate alternatives. If clients decline the suggested referral, counselors should discontinue the relationship.

c. **Appropriate Termination.** Counselors terminate a counseling relationship, securing client agreement when possible, when it is reasonably clear that the client is no longer benefiting, when services are no longer required, when counseling no longer serves the client's needs or interests, when clients do not pay fees charged, or when agency or institution limits do not allow provision of further counseling services. (See A.10.b. and C.2.g.)

A.12. Computer Technology

a. **Use of Computers.** When computer applications are used in counseling services, counselors ensure that (1) the client is intellectually, emotionally, and physically capable of using the computer application; (2) the computer application is appropriate for the needs of the client; (3) the client understands the purpose and operation of the computer applications; and (4) a follow-up of client use of a computer application is provided to correct possible misconceptions, discover inappropriate use, and assess subsequent needs.

b. **Explanation of Limitations.** Counselors ensure that clients are provided information as a part of the counseling relationship that adequately explains the limitations of computer technology.

c. **Access to Computer Applications.** Counselors provide for equal access to computer applications in counseling services. (See A.2.a.)

Section B: Confidentiality

B.1. Right to Privacy

a. **Respect for Privacy.** Counselors respect their clients' right to privacy and avoid illegal and unwarranted disclosures of confidential information. (See A.3.a. and B.6.a.)

b. **Client Waiver.** The right to privacy may be waived by the client or his or her legally recognized representative.

c. **Exceptions.** The general requirement that counselors keep information confidential does not apply when disclosure is required to prevent clear and imminent danger to the client or others or when legal requirements demand that confidential information be revealed. Counselors consult with other professionals when in doubt as to the validity of an exception.

d. **Contagious, Fatal Diseases.** A counselor who receives information confirming that a client has a disease commonly known to be both communicable and fatal is justified in disclosing information to an identifiable third party, who by his or her relationship with the client is at a high risk of contracting the disease. Prior to making a disclosure the counselor should ascertain that the client has not already informed the third party about his or her disease and that the client is not intending to inform the third party in the immediate future. (See B.1.c. and B.1.f.)

e. **Court-Ordered Disclosure.** When court ordered to release confidential information without a client's permission, counselors request to the court that the disclosure not be required due to potential harm to the client or counseling relationship. (See B.1.c.)

   f.   **Minimal Disclosure.** When circumstances require the disclosure of confidential information, only essential information is revealed. To the extent possible, clients are informed before confidential information is disclosed.

   g.   **Explanation of Limitations.** When counseling is initiated and throughout the counseling process as necessary, counselors inform clients of the limitations of confidentiality and identify foreseeable situations in which confidentiality must be breached. (See G.2.a.)

   h.   **Subordinates.** Counselors make every effort to ensure that privacy and confidentiality of clients are maintained by subordinates including employees, supervisers, clerical assistants, and volunteers. (See B.1.a.)

   i.   **Treatment Teams.** If client treatment will involve a continued review by a treatment team, the client will be informed of the team's existence and composition.

B.2. Groups and Families

   a.   **Group Work.** In group work, counselors clearly define confidentiality and the parameters for the specific group being entered, explain its importance, and discuss the difficulties related to confidentiality involved in group work. The fact that confidentiality cannot be guaranteed is clearly communicated to group members.

   b.   **Family Counseling.** In family counseling, information about one family member cannot be disclosed to another member without permission. Counselors protect the privacy rights of each family member. (See A.8., B.3., and B.4.d.)

B.3. Minor or Incompetent Clients

When counseling clients who are minors or individuals who are unable to give voluntary, informed consent, parents or guardians may be included in the counseling process as appropriate. Counselors act in the best interests of clients and take measures to safeguard confidentiality. (See A.3.c.)

B.4. Records

   a.   **Requirement of Records.** Counselors maintain records necessary for rendering professional services to their clients and as required by laws, regulations, or agency or institution procedures.

   b.   **Confidentiality of Records.** Counselors are responsible for securing the safety and confidentiality of any counseling records they create, maintain, transfer, or destroy whether the records are written, taped, computerized, or stored in any other medium. (See B.1.a.)

   c.   **Permission to Record or Observe.** Counselors obtain permission from clients prior to electronically recording or observing sessions. (See A.3.a.)

   d.   **Client Access.** Counselors recognize that counseling records are kept for the benefit of clients, and therefore provide access to records and copies of records when requested by competent clients, unless the records contain information that may be misleading and detrimental to the client. In situations involving multiple clients, access to records is limited to those parts of records that do not include confidential information related to another client. (See A.8., B.1.a., and B.2.b.)

e. **Disclosure or Transfer.** Counselors obtain written permission from clients to disclose or transfer records to legitimate third parties unless exceptions to confidentiality exist as listed in Section B.1. Steps are taken to ensure that receivers of counseling records are sensitive to their confidential nature.

B.5. Research and Training

a. **Data Disguise Required.** Use of data derived from counseling relationships for purposes of training, research, or publication is confined to content that is disguised to ensure the anonymity of the individuals involved. (See B.1.g. and G.3.d.)

b. **Agreement for Identification.** Identification of a client in a presentation or publication is permissible only when the client has reviewed the material and has agreed to its presentation or publication. (See G.3.d.)

B.6. Consultation

a. **Respect for Privacy.** Information obtained in a consulting relationship is discussed for professional purposes only with persons clearly concerned with the case. Written and oral reports present data germane to the purposes of the consultation, and every effort is made to protect client identity and avoid undue invasion of privacy.

b. **Cooperating Agencies.** Before sharing information, counselors make efforts to ensure that there are defined policies in other agencies serving the counselor's clients that effectively protect the confidentiality of information.

Section C: Professional Responsibility

C.1. Standards Knowledge

Counselors have a responsibility to read, understand, and follow the Code of Ethics and the Standards of Practice.

C.2. Professional Competence

a. **Boundaries of Competence.** Counselors practice only within the boundaries of their competence, based on their education, training, supervised experience, state and national professional credentials, and appropriate professional experience. Counselors will demonstrate a commitment to gain knowledge, personal awareness, sensitivity, and skills pertinent to working with a diverse client population.

b. **New Specialty Areas of Practice.** Counselors practice in specialty areas new to them only after appropriate education, training, and supervised experience. While developing skills in new specialty areas, counselors take steps to ensure the competence of their work and to protect others from possible harm.

c. **Qualified for Employment.** Counselors accept employment only for positions for which they are qualified by education, training, supervised experience, state and national professional credentials, and appropriate professional experience. Counselors hire for professional counseling positions only individuals who are qualified and competent.

d. Monitor Effectiveness. Counselors continually monitor their effectiveness as professionals and take steps to improve when necessary. Counselors in private practice take reasonable steps to seek out peer supervision to evaluate their efficacy as counselors.

e. Ethical Issues Consultation. Counselors take reasonable steps to consult with other counselors or related professionals when they have questions regarding their ethical obligations or professional practice. (See H.1.)

f. Continuing Education. Counselors recognize the need for continuing education to maintain a reasonable level of awareness of current scientific and professional information in their fields of activity. They take steps to maintain competence in the skills they use, are open to new procedures, and keep current with the diverse and/or special populations with whom they work.

g. Impairment. Counselors refrain from offering or accepting professional services when their physical, mental, or emotional problems are likely to harm a client or others. They are alert to the signs of impairment, seek assistance for problems, and, if necessary, limit, suspend, or terminate their professional responsibilities. (See A.11.c.)

C.3. Advertising and Soliciting Clients

a. Accurate Advertising. There are no restrictions on advertising by counselors except those that can be specifically justified to protect the public from deceptive practices. Counselors advertise or represent their services to the public by identifying their credentials in an accurate manner that is not false, misleading, deceptive, or fraudulent. Counselors may only advertise the highest degree earned which is in counseling or a closely related field from a college or university that was accredited when the degree was awarded by one of the regional accrediting bodies recognized by the Council on Postsecondary Accreditation.

b. Testimonials. Counselors who use testimonials do not solicit them from clients or other persons who, because of their particular circumstances, may be vulnerable to undue influence.

c. Statements by Others. Counselors make reasonable efforts to ensure that statements made by others about them or the profession of counseling are accurate.

d. Recruiting through Employment. Counselors do not use their place of employment or institutional affiliation to recruit or gain clients, supervisees, or consultees for their private practices. (See C.5.e.)

e. Products and Training Advertisements. Counselors who develop products related to their profession or conduct workshops or training events ensure that the advertisements concerning these products or events are accurate and disclose adequate information for consumers to make informed choices.

f. Promoting to Those Served. Counselors do not use counseling, teaching, training, or supervisory relationships to promote their products or training events in a manner that is deceptive or would exert undue influence on individuals who may be vulnerable. Counselors may adopt textbooks they have authored for instruction purposes.

g. **Professional Association Involvement.** Counselors actively participate in local, state, and national associations that foster the development and improvement of counseling.

C.4. Credentials

a. **Credentials Claimed.** Counselors claim or imply only professional credentials possessed and are responsible for correcting any known misrepresentations of their credentials by others. Professional credentials include graduate degrees in counseling or closely related mental health fields, accreditation of graduate programs, national voluntary certifications, government-issued certifications or licenses, ACA professional membership, or any other credential that might indicate to the public specialized knowledge or expertise in counseling.

b. **ACA Professional Membership.** ACA professional members may announce to the public their membership status. Regular members may not announce their ACA membership in a manner that might imply they are credentialed counselors.

c. **Credential Guidelines.** Counselors follow the guidelines for use of credentials that have been established by the entities that issue the credentials.

d. **Misrepresentation of Credentials.** Counselors do not attribute more to their credentials than the credentials represent, and do not imply that other counselors are not qualified because they do not possess certain credentials.

e. **Doctoral Degrees from Other Fields.** Counselors who hold a master's degree in counseling or a closely related mental health field, but hold a doctoral degree from other than counseling or a closely related field, do not use the title "Dr." in their practices and do not announce to the public in relation to their practice or status as a counselor that they hold a doctorate.

C.5. Public Responsibility

a. **Nondiscrimination.** Counselors do not discriminate against clients, students, or supervisees in a manner that has a negative impact based on their age, color, culture, disability, ethnic group, gender, race, religion, sexual orientation, or socioeconomic status, or for any other reason. (See A.2.a.)

b. **Sexual Harassment.** Counselors do not engage in sexual harassment. Sexual harassment is defined as sexual solicitation, physical advances, or verbal or nonverbal conduct that is sexual in nature, that occurs in connection with professional activities or roles, and that either (1) is unwelcome, is offensive, or creates a hostile workplace environment, and counselors know or are told this; or (2) is sufficiently severe or intense to be perceived as harassment to a reasonable person in the context. Sexual harassment can consist of a single intense or severe act or multiple persistent or pervasive acts.

c. **Reports to Third Parties.** Counselors are accurate, honest, and unbiased in reporting their professional activities and judgments to appropriate third parties including courts, health insurance companies, those who are the recipients of evaluation reports, and others. (See B.1.g.)

    d. **Media Presentations.** When counselors provide advice or comment by means of public lectures, demonstrations, radio or television programs, prerecorded tapes, printed articles, mailed material, or other media, they take reasonable precautions to ensure that (1) the statements are based on appropriate professional counseling literature and practice; (2) the statements are otherwise consistent with the Code of Ethics and the Standards of Practice; and (3) the recipients of the information are not encouraged to infer that a professional counseling relationship has been established. (See C.6.b.)

    e. **Unjustified Gains.** Counselors do not use their professional positions to seek or receive unjustified personal gains, sexual favors, unfair advantage, or unearned goods or services. (See C.3.d.)

C.6. Responsibility to Other Professionals

    a. **Different Approaches.** Counselors are respectful of approaches to professional counseling that differ from their own. Counselors know and take into account the traditions and practices of other professional groups with which they work.

    b. **Personal Public Statements.** When making personal statements in a public context, counselors clarify that they are speaking from their personal perspectives and that they are not speaking on behalf of all counselors or the profession. (See C.5.d.)

    c. **Clients Served by Others.** When counselors learn that their clients are in a professional relationship with another mental health professional, they request release from clients to inform the other professionals and strive to establish positive and collaborative professional relationships. (See A.4.)

Section D: Relationships with Other Professionals

D.1. Relationships with Employers and Employees

    a. **Role Definition.** Counselors define and describe for their employers and employees the parameters and levels of their professional roles.

    b. **Agreements.** Counselors establish working agreements with supervisors, colleagues, and subordinates regarding counseling or clinical relationships, confidentiality, adherence to professional standards, distinction between public and private material, maintenance and dissemination of recorded information, work load, and accountability. Working agreements in each instance are specified and made known to those concerned.

    c. **Negative Conditions.** Counselors alert their employers to conditions that may be potentially disruptive or damaging to the counselor's professional responsibilities or that may limit their effectiveness.

    d. **Evaluation.** Counselors submit regularly to professional review and evaluation by their supervisor or the appropriate representative of the employer.

    e. **In-Service.** Counselors are responsible for in-service development of self and staff.

    f. **Goals.** Counselors inform their staff of goals and programs.

g. **Practices.** Counselors provide personnel and agency practices that respect and enhance the rights and welfare of each employee and recipient of agency services. Counselors strive to maintain the highest levels of professional services.

h. **Personnel Selection and Assignment.** Counselors select competent staff and assign responsibilities compatible with their skills and experiences.

i. **Discrimination.** Counselors, as either employers or employees, do not engage in or condone practices that are inhumane, illegal, or unjustifiable (such as considerations based on age, color, culture, disability, ethnic group, gender, race, religion, sexual orientation, or socioeconomic status) in hiring, promotion, or training. (See A.2.a. and C.5.b.)

j. **Professional Conduct.** Counselors have a responsibility both to clients and to the agency or institution within which services are performed to maintain high standards of professional conduct.

k. **Exploitative Relationships.** Counselors do not engage in exploitative relationships with individuals over whom they have supervisory, evaluative, or instructional control or authority.

1. **Employer Policies.** The acceptance of employment in an agency or institution implies that counselors are in agreement with its general policies and principles. Counselors strive to reach agreement with employers as to acceptable standards of conduct that allow for changes in institutional policy conducive to the growth and development of clients.

D.2. Consultation (See B.6.)

a. **Consultation as an Option.** Counselors may choose to consult with any other professionally competent persons about their clients. In choosing consultants, counselors avoid placing the consultant in a conflict of interest situation that would preclude the consultant being a proper party to the counselor's efforts to help the client. Should counselors be engaged in a work setting that compromises this consultation standard, they consult with other professionals whenever possible to consider justifiable alternatives.

b. **Consultant Competency.** Counselors are reasonably certain that they have or the organization represented has the necessary competencies and resources for giving the kind of consulting services needed and that appropriate referral resources are available.

c. **Understanding with Clients.** When providing consultation, counselors attempt to develop with their clients a clear understanding of problem definition, goals for change, and predicted consequences of interventions selected.

d. **Consultant Goals.** The consulting relationship is one in which client adaptability and growth toward self-direction are consistently encouraged and cultivated. (See A.1.b.)

D.3. Fees for Referral

a. **Accepting Fees from Agency Clients.** Counselors refuse a private fee or other remuneration for rendering services to persons who are entitled to such services through the counselor's employing agency or institution. The policies of a particular agency may make explicit provisions for agency clients to receive counseling services from members of its staff in private practice. In such instances, the clients must be informed of other options open to them should they seek private counseling services. (See A.10.a., A.11.b., and C.3.d.)

b.   Referral Fees. Counselors do not accept a referral fee from other professionals.

D.4.   Subcontractor Arrangements
When counselors work as subcontractors for counseling services for a third party, they have a duty to inform clients of the limitations of confidentiality that the organization may place on counselors in providing counseling services to clients. The limits of such confidentiality ordinarily are discussed as part of the intake session. (See B.1.e. and B.1.f.)

Section E: Evaluation, Assessment, and Interpretation

E.1.   General
a.   Appraisal Techniques. The primary purpose of educational and psychological assessment is to provide measures that are objective and interpretable in either comparative or absolute terms. Counselors recognize the need to interpret the statements in this section as applying to the whole range of appraisal techniques, including test and nontest data.

b.   Client Welfare. Counselors promote the welfare and best interests of the client in the development, publication, and utilization of educational and psychological assessment techniques. They do not misuse assessment results and interpretations and take reasonable steps to prevent others from misusing the information these techniques provide. They respect the client's right to know the results, the interpretations made, and the bases for their conclusions and recommendations.

E.2.   Competence to Use and Interpret Tests
a.   Limits of Competence. Counselors recognize the limits of their competence and perform only those testing and assessment services for which they have been trained. They are familiar with reliability, validity, related standardization, error of measurement, and proper application of any technique utilized. Counselors using computer-based test interpretations are trained in the construct being measured and the specific instrument being used prior to using this type of computer application. Counselors take reasonable measures to ensure the proper use of psychological assessment techniques by persons under their supervision.

b.   Appropriate Use. Counselors are responsible for the appropriate application, scoring, interpretation, and use of assessment instruments, whether they score and interpret such tests themselves or use computerized or other services.

c.   Decisions Based on Results. Counselors responsible for decisions involving individuals or policies that are based on assessment results have a thorough understanding of educational and psychological measurement, including validation criteria, test research, and guidelines for test development and use.

    d. **Accurate Information.** Counselors provide accurate information and avoid false claims or misconceptions when making statements about assessment instruments or techniques. Special efforts are made to avoid unwarranted connotations of such terms as IQ and grade equivalent scores. (See C.5.c.)

E.3. Informed Consent

    a. **Explanation to Clients.** Prior to assessment, counselors explain the nature and purposes of assessment and the specific use of results in language the client (or other legally authorized person on behalf of the client) can understand, unless an explicit exception to this right has been agreed upon in advance. Regardless of whether scoring and interpretation are completed by counselors, by assistants, or by computer or other outside services, counselors take reasonable steps to ensure that appropriate explanations are given to the client.

    b. **Recipients of Results.** The examinee's welfare, explicit understanding, and prior agreement determine the recipients of test results. Counselors include accurate and appropriate interpretations with any release of individual or group test results. (See B.1.a. and C.5.c.)

E.4. Release of Information to Competent Professionals

    a. **Misuse of Results.** Counselors do not misuse assessment results, including test results, and interpretations, and take reasonable steps to prevent the misuse of such by others. (See C.5.c.)

    b. **Release of Raw Data.** Counselors ordinarily release data (e.g., protocols, counseling or interview notes, or questionnaires) in which the client is identified only with the consent of the client or the client's legal representative. Such data are usually released only to persons recognized by counselors as competent to interpret the data. (See B.1.a.)

E.5. Proper Diagnosis of Mental Disorders

    a. **Proper Diagnosis.** Counselors take special care to provide proper diagnosis of mental disorders. Assessment techniques (including personal interview) used to determine client care (e.g., locus of treatment, type of treatment, or recommended follow-up) are carefully selected and appropriately used. (See A.3.a. and C.5.c.)

    b. **Cultural Sensitivity.** Counselors recognize that culture affects the manner in which clients' problems are defined. Clients' socioeconomic and cultural experience is considered when diagnosing mental disorders.

E.6. Test Selection

    a. **Appropriateness of Instruments.** Counselors carefully consider the validity, reliability, psychometric limitations, and appropriateness of instruments when selecting tests for use in a given situation or with a particular client.

    b. **Culturally Diverse Populations.** Counselors are cautious when selecting tests for culturally diverse populations to avoid inappropriateness of testing that may be outside of socialized behavioral or cognitive patterns.

E.7. Conditions of Test Administration

    a. **Administration Conditions.** Counselors administer tests under the same conditions that were established in their standardization. When tests are not administered under standard conditions or when unusual behavior or irregularities occur during the testing session, those conditions are noted in interpretation, and the results may be designated as invalid or of questionable validity.

    b. **Computer Administration.** Counselors are responsible for ensuring that administration programs function properly to provide clients with accurate results when a computer or other electronic methods are used for test administration. (See A.12.b.)

    c. **Unsupervised Test Taking.** Counselors do not permit unsupervised or inadequately supervised use of tests or assessments unless the tests or assessments are designed, intended, and validated for self-administration and/or scoring.

    d. **Disclosure of Favorable Conditions.** Prior to test administration, conditions that produce most favorable test results are made known to the examinee.

E.8. Diversity in Testing

Counselors are cautious in using assessment techniques, making evaluations, and interpreting the performance of populations not represented in the norm group on which an instrument was standardized. They recognize the effects of age, color, culture, disability, ethnic group, gender, race, religion, sexual orientation, and socioeconomic status on test administration and interpretation and place test results in proper perspective with other relevant factors. (See A.2.a.)

E.9. Test Scoring and Interpretation

    a. **Reporting Reservations.** In reporting assessment results, counselors indicate any reservations that exist regarding validity or reliability because of the circumstances of the assessment or the inappropriateness of the norms for the person tested.

    b. **Research Instruments.** Counselors exercise caution when interpreting the results of research instruments possessing insufficient technical data to support respondent results. The specific purposes for the use of such instruments are stated explicitly to the examinee.

    c. **Testing Services.** Counselors who provide test scoring and test interpretation services to support the assessment process confirm the validity of such interpretations. They accurately describe the purpose, norms, validity, reliability, and applications of the procedures and any special qualifications applicable to their use. The public offering of an automated test interpretations service is considered a professional-to-professional consultation. The formal responsibility of the consultant is to the consultee, but the ultimate and overriding responsibility is to the client.

E.10. Test Security

Counselors maintain the integrity and security of tests and other assessment techniques consistent with legal and contractual obligations. Counselors do not appropriate, reproduce, or modify published tests or parts thereof without acknowledgment and permission from the publisher.

E.11. Obsolete Tests and Outdated Test Results

Counselors do not use data or test results that are obsolete or outdated for the current purpose. Counselors make every effort to prevent the misuse of obsolete measures and test data by others.

E.12. Test Construction

Counselors use established scientific procedures, relevant standards, and current professional knowledge for test design in the development, publication, and utilization of educational and psychological assessment techniques.

Section F: Teaching, Training, and Supervision

F.1. Counselor Educators and Trainers

   a. **Educators as Teachers and Practitioners.** Counselors who are responsible for developing, implementing, and supervising educational programs are skilled as teachers and practitioners. They are knowledgeable regarding the ethical, legal, and regulatory aspects of the profession, are skilled in applying that knowledge, and make students and supervisees aware of their responsibilities. Counselors conduct counselor education and training programs in an ethical manner and serve as role models for professional behavior. Counselor educators should make an effort to infuse material related to human diversity into all courses and/ or workshops that are designed to promote the development of professional counselors.

   b. **Relationship Boundaries with Students and Supervisees.** Counselors clearly define and maintain ethical, professional, and social relationship boundaries with their students and supervisees. They are aware of the differential in power that exists and the student's or supervisee's possible incomprehension of that power differential. Counselors explain to students and supervisees the potential for the relationship to become exploitive.

   c. **Sexual Relationships.** Counselors do not engage in sexual relationships with students or supervisees and do not subject them to sexual harassment. (See A.6. and C.5.b.)

   d. **Contributions to Research.** Counselors give credit to students or supervisees for their contributions to research and scholarly projects. Credit is given through coauthorship, acknowledgment, footnote statement, or other appropriate means, in accordance with such contributions. (See G.4.b. and G.4.c.)

   e. **Close Relatives.** Counselors do not accept close relatives as students or supervisees.

   f. **Supervision Preparation.** Counselors who offer clinical supervision services are adequately prepared in supervision methods and techniques. Counselors who are doctoral students serving as practicum or internship supervisors to master's level students are adequately prepared and supervised, by the training program.

   g. **Responsibility for Services to Clients.** Counselors who supervise the counseling services of others take reasonable measures to ensure that counseling services provided to clients are professional.

    h.   **Endorsement.** Counselors do not endorse students or supervisees for certification, licensure, employment, or completion of an academic or training program if they believe students or supervisees are not qualified for the endorsement. Counselors take reasonable steps to assist students or supervisees who are not qualified for endorsement to become qualified.

F.2. Counselor Education and Training Programs

    a.   **Orientation.** Prior to admission, counselors orient prospective students to the counselor education or training program's expectations, including but not limited to the following: (1) the type and level of skill acquisition required for successful completion of the training, (2) subject matter to be covered, (3) basis for evaluation, (4) training components that encourage self-growth or self-disclosure as part of the training process, (5) the type of supervision settings and requirements of the sites for required clinical field experiences, (6) student and supervisee evaluation and dismissal policies and procedures, and (7) up-to-date employment prospects for graduates.

    b.   **Integration of Study and Practice.** Counselors establish counselor education and training programs that integrate academic study and supervised practice.

    c.   **Evaluation.** Counselors clearly state to students and supervisees, in advance of training, the levels of competency expected, appraisal methods, and timing of evaluations for both didactic and experiential components. Counselors provide students and supervisees with periodic performance appraisal and evaluation feedback throughout the training program.

    d.   **Teaching Ethics.** Counselors make students and supervisees aware of the ethical responsibilities and standards of the profession and the students' and supervisees' ethical responsibilities to the profession. (See C.1. and F.3.e.)

    e.   **Peer Relationships.** When students or supervisees are assigned to lead counseling groups or provide clinical supervision for their peers, counselors take steps to ensure that students and supervisees placed in these roles do not have personal or adverse relationships with peers and that they understand they have the same ethical obligations as counselor educators, trainers, and supervisors. Counselors make every effort to ensure that the rights of peers are not compromised when students or supervisees are assigned to lead counseling groups or provide clinical supervision.

    f.   **Varied Theoretical Positions.** Counselors present varied theoretical positions so that students and supervisees may make comparisons and have opportunities to develop their own positions. Counselors provide information concerning the scientific bases of professional practice. (See C.6.a.)

    g.   **Field Placements.** Counselors develop clear policies within their training program regarding field placement and other clinical experiences. Counselors provide clearly stated roles and responsibilities for the student or supervisee, the site supervisor, and the program supervisor. They confirm that site supervisors are qualified to provide supervision and are informed of their professional and ethical responsibilities in this role.

h. **Dual Relationships as Supervisors.** Counselors avoid dual relationships such as performing the role of site supervisor and training program supervisor in the student's or supervisee's training program. Counselors do not accept any form of professional services, fees, commissions, reimbursement, or remuneration from a site for student or supervisee placement.

i. **Diversity in Programs.** Counselors are responsive to their institution's and program's recruitment and retention needs for training program administrators, faculty, and students with diverse backgrounds and special needs. (See A.2.a.)

F.3. Students and Supervisees

a. **Limitations.** Counselors, through ongoing evaluation and appraisal, are aware of the academic and personal limitations of students and supervisees that might impede performance. Counselors assist students and supervisees in securing remedial assistance when needed, and dismiss from the training program supervisees who are unable to provide competent service due to academic or personal limitations. Counselors seek professional consultation and document their decision to dismiss or refer students or supervisees for assistance. Counselors ensure that students and supervisees have recourse to address decisions made to require them to seek assistance or to dismiss them.

b. **Self-Growth Experiences.** Counselors use professional judgment when designing training experiences conducted by the counselors themselves that require student and supervisee self-growth or self-disclosure. Safeguards are provided so that students and supervisees are aware of the ramifications their self-disclosure may have on counselors whose primary role as teacher, trainer, or supervisor requires acting on ethical obligations to the profession. Evaluative components of experiential training experiences explicitly delineate predetermined academic standards that are separate and do not depend on the student's level of self-disclosure. (See A.6.)

c. **Counseling for Students and Supervisees.** If students or supervisees request counseling, supervisors or counselor educators provide them with acceptable referrals. Supervisors or counselor educators do not serve as counselor to students or supervisees over whom they hold administrative, teaching, or evaluative roles unless this is a brief role associated with a training experience. (See A.6.b.)

d. **Clients of Students and Supervisees.** Counselors make every effort to ensure that the clients at field placements are aware of the services rendered and the qualifications of the students and supervisees rendering those services. Clients receive professional disclosure information and are informed of the limits of confidentiality. Client permission is obtained in order for the students and supervisees to use any information concerning the counseling relationship in the training process. (See B.1.e.)

e. **Standards for Students and Supervisees.** Students and supervisees preparing to become counselors adhere to the Code of Ethics and the Standards of Practice. Students and supervisees have the same obligations to clients as those required of counselors. (See H.1.)

Section G: Research and Publication

G.1. Research Responsibilities

a. Use of Human Subjects. Counselors plan, design, conduct, and report research in a manner consistent with pertinent ethical principles, federal and state laws, host institutional regulations, and scientific standards governing research with human subjects. Counselors design and conduct research that reflects cultural sensitivity appropriateness.

b. Deviation from Standard Practices. Counselors seek consultation and observe stringent safeguards to protect the rights of research participants when a research problem suggests a deviation from standard acceptable practices. (See B.6.)

c. Precautions to Avoid Injury. Counselors who conduct research with human subjects are responsible for the subjects' welfare throughout the experiment and take reasonable precautions to avoid causing injurious psychological, physical, or social effects to their subjects.

d. Principal Researcher Responsibility. The ultimate responsibility for ethical research practice lies with the principal researcher. All others involved in the research activities share ethical obligations and full responsibility for their own actions.

e. Minimal Interference. Counselors take reasonable precautions to avoid causing disruptions in subjects' lives due to participation in research.

f. Diversity. Counselors are sensitive to diversity and research issues with special populations. They seek consultation when appropriate. (See A.2.a. and B.6.)

G.2. Informed Consent

a. Topics Disclosed. In obtaining informed consent for research, counselors use language that is understandable to research participants and that (1) accurately explains the purpose and procedures to be followed; (2) identifies any procedures that are experimental or relatively untried; (3) describes the attendant discomforts and risks; (4) describes the benefits or changes in individuals or organizations that might be reasonably expected; (5) discloses appropriate alternative procedures that would be advantageous for subjects; (6) offers to answer any inquiries concerning the procedures; (7) describes any limitations on confidentiality; and (8) instructs that subjects are-free to withdraw their consent and to discontinue participation in the project at any time. (See B.1.f.)

b. Deception. Counselors do not conduct research involving deception unless alternative procedures are not feasible and the prospective value of the research justifies the deception. When the methodological requirements of a study necessitate concealment or deception, the investigator is required to explain clearly the reasons for this action as soon as possible.

c. Voluntary Participation. Participation in research is typically voluntary and without any penalty for refusal to participate. Involuntary participation is appropriate only when it can be demonstrated that participation will have no harmful effects on subjects and is essential to the investigation.

d. **Confidentiality of Information.** Information obtained about research partici-pants during the course of an investigation is confidential. When the possibility exists that others may obtain access to such information, ethical research prac-tice requires that the possibility, together with the plans for protecting confiden-tiality, be explained to participants as a part of the procedure for obtaining informed consent. (See B.1.e.)

e. **Persons Incapable of Giving Informed Consent.** When a person is incapable of giving informed consent, counselors provide an appropriate explanation, ob-tain agreement for participation, and obtain appropriate consent from a legally authorized person.

f. **Commitments to Participants.** Counselors take reasonable measures to honor all commitments to research participants.

g. **Explanations after Data Collection.** After data are collected, counselors pro-vide participants with full clarification of the nature of the study to remove any misconceptions. Where scientific or human values justify delaying or withhold-ing information, counselors take reasonable measures to avoid causing harm.

h. **Agreements to Cooperate.** Counselors who agree to cooperate with another in-dividual in research or publication incur an obligation to cooperate as promised in terms of punctuality of performance and with regard to the completeness and accuracy of the information required.

i. **Informed Consent for Sponsors.** in the pursuit of research, counselors give sponsors, institutions, and publication channels the same respect and opportu-nity for giving informed consent that they accord to individual research partici-pants. Counselors are aware of their obligation to future research workers and ensure that host institutions are given feedback information and proper acknowledgment.

G.3. Reporting Results

a. **Information Affecting Outcome.** When reporting research results, counselors explicitly mention all variables and conditions known to the investigator that may have affected the outcome of a study or the interpretation of data.

b. **Accurate Results.** Counselors plan, conduct, and report research accurately and in a manner that minimizes the possibility that results will be misleading. They provide thorough discussions of the limitations of their data and alternative hy-potheses. Counselors do not engage in fraudulent research, distort data, misrep-resent data, or deliberately bias their results.

c. **Obligation to Report Unfavorable Results.** Counselors communicate to other counselors the results of any research judged to be of professional value. Results that reflect unfavorably on institutions, programs, services, prevailing opinions, or vested interests are not withheld.

d. **Identity of Subjects.** Counselors who supply data, aid in the research of another person, report research results, or make original data available take due care to disguise the identity of respective subjects in the absence of specific authoriza-tion from the subjects to do otherwise. (See B.1.g. and B.5.a.)

e. **Replication Studies.** Counselors are obligated to make available sufficient original research data to qualified professionals who may wish to replicate the study.

G.4. Publication

a. **Recognition of Others.** When conducting and reporting research, counselors are familiar with and give recognition to previous work on the topic, observe copyright laws, and give full credit to those to whom credit is due. (See F.1.d. and G.4.c.)

b. **Contributors.** Counselors give credit through joint authorship, acknowledgment, footnote statements, or other appropriate means to those who have contributed significantly to research or concept development in accordance with such contributions. The principal contributor is listed first and minor technical or professional contributions are acknowledged in notes or introductory statements.

c. **Student Research.** For an article that is substantially based on a student's dissertation or thesis, the student is listed as the principal author. (See F.1.d. and G.4.a.)

d. **Duplicate Submission.** Counselors submit manuscripts for consideration to only one journal at a time. Manuscripts that are published in whole or in substantial part in another journal or published work are not submitted for publication without acknowledgment and permission from the previous publication.

e. **Professional Review.** Counselors who review material submitted for publication, research, or other scholarly purposes respect the confidentiality and proprietary rights of those who submitted it.

Section H. Resolving Ethical Issues

H.1. Knowledge of Standards

Counselors are familiar with the Code of Ethics and the Standards of Practice and other applicable ethics codes from other professional organizations of which they are member, or from certification and licensure bodies. Lack of knowledge or misunderstanding of an ethical responsibility is not a defense against a charge of unethical conduct. (See F.3.e.)

H.2. Suspected Violations

a. **Ethical Behavior Expected.** Counselors expect professional associates to adhere to the Code of Ethics. When counselors possess reasonable cause that raises doubts as to whether a counselor is acting in an ethical manner, they take appropriate action. (See H.2.d. and H.2.e.)

b. **Consultation.** When uncertain as to whether a particular situation or course of action may be in violation of the Code of Ethics, counselors consult with other counselors who are knowledgeable about ethics, with colleagues, or with appropriate authorities.

c. **Organization Conflicts.** If the demands of an organization with which counselors are affiliated pose a conflict with the Code of Ethics, counselors specify the nature of such conflicts and express to their supervisors or other responsible officials their commitment to the Code of Ethics. When possible, counselors work toward change within the organization to allow full adherence to the Code of Ethics.

d. **Informal Resolution.** When counselors have reasonable cause to believe that another counselor is violating an ethical standard, they attempt to first resolve the issue informally with the other counselor if feasible, providing that such action does not violate confidentiality rights that may be involved.

e. **Reporting Suspected Violations.** When an informal resolution is not appropriate or feasible, counselors, upon reasonable cause, take action such as reporting the suspected ethical violation to state or national ethics committees, unless this action conflicts with confidentiality rights that cannot be resolved.

f. **Unwarranted Complaints.** Counselors do not initiate, participate in, or encourage the filing of ethics complaints that are unwarranted or intend to harm a counselor rather than to protect clients or the public.

H.3. Cooperation with Ethics Committees

Counselors assist in the process of enforcing the Code of Ethics. Counselors cooperate with investigations, proceedings, and requirements of the ACA Ethics Committee or ethics committees of other duly constituted associations or boards having jurisdiction over those charged with a violation. Counselors are familiar with the ACA Policies and Procedures and use it as a reference in assisting the enforcement of the Code of Ethics.

Standards of Practice

All members of the American Counseling Association (ACA) are required to adhere to the Standards of Practice and the Code of Ethics. The Standards of Practice represent minimal behavioral statements of the Code of Ethics. Members should refer to the applicable section of the Code of Ethics for further interpretation and amplification of the applicable Standard of Practice.

Section A: The Counseling Relationship
Section B: Confidentiality
Section C: Professional Responsibility
Section D: Relationship with Other Professionals
Section E: Evaluation, Assessment, and Interpretation
Section F: Teaching, Training, and Supervision
Section G: Research and Publication
Section H: Resolving Ethical Issues

Section A: The Counseling Relationship

Standard of Practice One (SP-1): Nondiscrimination. Counselors respect diversity and must not discriminate against clients because of age, color, culture, disability, ethnic group, gender, race, religion, sexual orientation, marital status, or socioeconomic status. (See A.2.a.)

Standard of Practice Two (SP-2): Disclosure to Clients. Counselors must adequately inform clients, preferably in writing, regarding the counseling process and counseling relationship at or before the time it begins and throughout the relationship. (See A.3.a.)

Standard of Practice Three (SP-3): Dual Relationships. Counselors must make every effort to avoid dual relationships with clients that could impair their professional judgment or increase the risk of harm to clients. When a dual relationship cannot be avoided, counselors must take appropriate steps to ensure that judgment is not impaired and that no exploitation occurs. (See A.6.a. and A.6.b.)

Standard of Practice Four (SP-4): Sexual Intimacies With Clients. Counselors must not engage in any type of sexual intimacies with current clients and must not engage in sexual intimacies with former clients within a minimum of 2 years after terminating the counseling relationship. Counselors who engage in such relationship after 2 years following termination have the responsibility to examine and document thoroughly that such relations did not have an exploitative nature.

Standard of Practice Five (SP-5): Protecting Clients During Group Work. Counselors must take steps to protect clients from physical or psychological trauma resulting from interactions during group work. (See A.9.b.)

Standard of Practice Six (SP-6): Advance Understanding of Fees. Counselors must explain to clients, prior to their entering the counseling relationship, financial arrangements related to professional services. (See A.10. a.–d. and A.11.c.)

Standard of Practice Seven (SP-7): Termination. Counselors must assist in making appropriate arrangements for the continuation of treatment of clients, when necessary, following termination of counseling relationships. (See A.11.a.)

Standard of Practice Eight (SP-8): Inability to Assist Clients. Counselors must avoid entering or immediately terminate a counseling relationship if it is determined that they are unable to be of professional assistance to a client. The counselor may assist in making an appropriate referral for the client. (See A.11.b.)

Section B: Confidentiality

Standard of Practice Nine (SP-9): Confidentiality Requirement. Counselors must keep information related to counseling services confidential unless disclosure is in the best interest of clients, is required for the welfare of others, or is required by law. When disclosure is required, only information that is essential is revealed and the client is informed of such disclosure. (See B.1.a.–f.)

Standard of Practice Ten (SP-10): Confidentiality Requirements for Subordinates. Counselors must take measures to ensure that privacy and confidentiality of clients are maintained by subordinates. (See B.1.h)

Standard of Practice Eleven (SP-11): Confidentiality in Group Work. Counselors must clearly communicate to group members that confidentiality cannot be guaranteed in group work. (See B.2.a.)

Standard of Practice Twelve (SP-12): Confidentiality in Family Counseling. Counselors must not disclose information about one family member in counseling to another family member without prior consent. (See B.2.b.)

Standard of Practice Thirteen (SP-13): Confidentiality of Records. Counselors must maintain appropriate confidentiality in creating, storing, accessing, transferring, and disposing of counseling records. (See B.4.b.)

Standard of Practice Fourteen (SP-14): Permission to Record or Observe. Counselors must obtain prior consent from clients in order to record electronically or observe sessions. (See B.4.c.)

Standard of Practice Fifteen (SP-15): Disclosure or Transfer of Records. Counselors must obtain client consent to disclose or transfer records to third parties, unless exceptions listed in SP-9 exist. (See B.4.e.)

Standard of Practice Sixteen (SP-16): Data Disguise Required. Counselors must disguise the identity of the client when using data for training, research, or publication. (See B.5.a.)

Section C: Professional Responsibility

Standard of Practice Seventeen (SP-17): Boundaries of Competence. Counselors must practice only within the boundaries of their competence. (See C.2.a.)

Standard of Practice Eighteen (SP-18): Continuing Education. Counselors must engage in continuing education to maintain their professional competence. (See C.2.f.)

Standard of Practice Nineteen (SP-19): Impairment of Professionals. Counselors must refrain from offering professional services when their personal problems or conflicts may cause harm to a client or others. (See C.2.g.)

Standard of Practice Twenty (SP-20): Accurate Advertising. Counselors must accurately represent their credentials and services when advertising. (See C.3.a.)

Standard of Practice Twenty-One (SP-21): Recruiting through Employment. Counselors must not use their place of employment or institutional affiliation to recruit clients for their private practices. (See C.3.d.)

Standard of Practice Twenty-Two (SP-22): Credentials Claimed. Counselors must claim or imply only professional credentials possessed and must correct any known misrepresentations of their credentials by others. (See C.4.a.)

Standard of Practice Twenty-Three (SP-23): Sexual Harassment. Counselors must not engage in sexual harassment. (See C.5.b.)

Standard of Practice Twenty-Four (SP-24): Unjustified Gains. Counselors must not use their professional positions to seek or receive unjustified personal gains, sexual favors, unfair advantage, or unearned goods or services. (See C.5.e.)

Standard of Practice Twenty-Five (SP-25): Clients Served by Others. With the consent of the client, counselors must inform other mental health professionals serving the same client that a counseling relationship between the counselor and client exists. (See C.6.c.)

Standard of Practice Twenty.-Six (SP-26): Negative Employment Conditions. Counselors must alert their employers to institutional policy or conditions that may be potentially disruptive or damaging to the counselor's professional responsibilities, or that may limit their effectiveness or deny clients' rights. (See D.1.c.)

Standard of Practice Twenty-Seven (SP-27): Personnel Selection and Assignment. Counselors must select competent staff and must assign responsibilities compatible with staff skills and experiences. (See D.1.h.)

Standard of Practice Twenty-Eight (SP-28): Exploitative Relationships with Subordinates. Counselors must not engage in exploitative relationships with individuals over whom they have supervisory, evaluative, or instructional control or authority. (See D.1.k.)

Section D: Relationship with Other Professionals

Standard of Practice Twenty-Nine (SP-29): Accepting Fees from Agency Clients. Counselors must not accept fees or other remuneration for consultation with persons entitled to such services through the counselor's employing agency or institution. (See D.3.a.)

Standard of Practice Thirty (SP-30): Referral Fees. Counselors must not accept referral fees. (See D.3.b.)

Section E: Evaluation, Assessment, and Interpretation

Standard of Practice Thirty-One (SP-31): Limits of Competence. Counselors must perform only testing and assessment services for which they are competent. Counselors must not allow the use of psychological assessment techniques by unqualified persons under their supervision. (See E.2.a.)

Standard of Practice Thirty-Two (SP-32): Appropriate Use of Assessment Instruments. Counselors must use assessment instruments in the manner for which they were intended. (See E.2.b.)

Standard of Practice Thirty-Three (SP-33): Assessment Explanations to Clients. Counselors must provide explanations to clients prior to assessment about the nature and purposes of assessment and the specific uses of results. (See E.3.a.)

Standard of Practice Thirty-Four (SP-34): Recipients of Test Results. Counselors must ensure that accurate and appropriate interpretations accompany any release of testing and assessment information. (See E.3.b.)

Standard of Practice Thirty-Five (SP-35): Obsolete Tests and Outdated Test Results. Counselors must not base their assessment or intervention decisions or recommendations on data or test results that are obsolete or outdated for the current purpose. (See E.11.)

Section F: Teaching, Training, and Supervision

Standard of Practice Thirty-Six (SP-36): Sexual Relationships with Students or Supervisees. Counselors must not engage in sexual relationships with their students and supervisees. (See F.1.c.)

Standard of Practice Thirty-Seven (SP-37): Credit for Contributions to Research. Counselors must give credit to students or supervisees for their contributions to research and scholarly projects. (See F.1.d.)

Standard of Practice Thirty-Eight (SP-38): Supervision Preparation. Counselors who offer clinical supervision services must be trained and prepared in supervision methods and techniques. (See F.1.f)

Standard of Practice Thirty-Nine (SP-39): Evaluation Information. Counselors must clearly state to students and supervisees in advance of training the levels of competency expected, appraisal methods, and timing of evaluations. Counselors must provide students and supervisees with periodic performance appraisal and evaluation feedback throughout the training program. (See F.2.c.)

Standard of Practice Forty (SP-40): Peer Relationships in Training. Counselors must make every effort to ensure that the rights of peers are not violated when students and supervisees are assigned to lead counseling groups or provide clinical supervision. (See F.2.e.)

Standard of Practice Forty-One (SP-41): Limitations of Students and Supervisees. Counselors must assist students and supervisees in securing remedial assistance, when needed, and must dismiss from the training program students and supervisees who are unable to provide competent service due to academic or personal limitations. (See F.3 a.)

Standard of Practice Forty-Two (SP-42): Self-Growth Experiences. Counselors who conduct experiences for students or supervisees that include self-growth or self-disclosure must inform participants of counselors' ethical obligations to the profession and must not grade participants based on their nonacademic performance. (See F.3.b.)

Standard of Practice Forty-Three (SP-43): Standards for Students and Supervisees. Students and supervisees preparing to become counselors must adhere to the Code of Ethics and the Standards of Practice of counselors. (See F.3.e.)

Section G: Research and Publication

Standard of Practice Forty-Four (SP-44): Precautions to Avoid Injury in Research. Counselors must avoid causing physical, social, or psychological harm or injury to subjects in research. (See G.1.c.)

Standard of Practice Forty-Five (SP-45): Confidentiality of Research Information. Counselors must keep confidential information obtained about research participants. (See G.2.d.)

Standard of Practice Forty-Six (SP-46): Information Affecting Research Outcome. Counselors must report all variables and conditions known to the investigator that may have affected research data or outcomes. (See G.3.a.)

Standard of Practice Forty-Seven (SP-47): Accurate Research Results. Counselors must not distort or misrepresent research data, nor fabricate or intentionally bias research results. (See G.3.b.)

Standard of Practice Forty-Eight (SP-48): Publication Contributors. Counselors must give appropriate credit to those who have contributed to research. (See G.4.a. and G.4.b.)

Section H: Resolving Ethical Issues

Standard of Practice Forty-Nine (SP-49): Ethical Behavior Expected. Counselors must take appropriate action when they possess reasonable cause that raises doubts as to whether counselors or other mental health professionals are acting in an ethical manner. (See H.2.a.)

Standard of Practice Fifty (SP-50): Unwarranted Complaints. Counselors must not initiate, participate in, or encourage the filing of ethics complaints that are unwarranted or intended to harm a mental health professional rather than to protect clients or the public. (See H.2.f.)

Standard of Practice Fifty-One (SP-51): Cooperation With Ethics Committees. Counselors must cooperate with investigations, proceedings, and requirements of the ACA Ethics Committee or ethics committees of other duly constituted associations or boards having jurisdiction over those charged with a violation. (See H.3.)

(American Counseling Association, 1997. Reprinted with permission.)

APPENDIX 3

Glossary

absolute confidentiality An assurance that client disclosures are not shared with anyone.

action planning Helping clients make changes in their lives; involves setting goals, identifying strategies for change, and developing plans for reaching goals.

active listening A term describing a cluster of skills that are used to increase the accuracy of understanding. Attending, using silence, paraphrasing, summarizing, questioning, and showing empathy are the basic skills of active listening.

affect A term that counselors use to describe how people express emotions.

affective area How clients feel.

affective disorders Disturbances in mood, including depression and mania.

AIDS An acronym for Acquired Immune Deficiency Syndrome. Caused by HIV infection, AIDS results in a number of different illnesses and opportunistic infections, such as tuberculosis, pneumonia, persistent diarrhea, fever, and skin cancer.

ambivalence Multiple, often contradictory, feelings about the same problem or experience. Ambivalence, though normal, can complicate clients' decision making and add stress to their lives.

anorexia nervosa An eating disorder that occurs when people reject maintaining a minimally healthy body weight. Driven by low self-esteem and an intense fear of gaining weight, people with anorexia use techniques such as purging (e.g., fasting, vomiting, taking laxatives) and excessive exercise to reduce body weight.

antianxiety medication Medications such as valium and librium that are used to control serious and persistent anxiety, phobia, and panic attacks.

antidepressant medication Medications such as Prozac, Paxil, and Zolof that are used to help people deal with serious depression.

antimanic medication Medications such as lithium that are used to control the manic symptoms of bipolar disorder.

antipsychotic medication Medications such as loxapine, haloperidol, clozapine, and risperidone that are used to treat illnesses such as schizophrenia.

anxiety disorders More than normal levels of fear, worry, tension, or anxiety about daily events.

assertiveness Behaving and expressing thoughts and feelings in an open and honest manner that respects the rights of others.

assumptions Distortions or false conclusions based on simplistic reasoning, incomplete information, or bias.

attended silence Counselor silence characterized by making eye contact, physically and psychologically focusing on the client, and being self-disciplined to minimize internal and external distraction.

371

attending   A term used to describe the way that counselors communicate to their clients that they are ready, willing, and able to listen. Verbal, nonverbal, and attitudinal cues are the essence of effective attending.

basic empathy   A counselor's acknowledgment of a client's clearly communicated feelings.

behavioral area   What clients are doing.

bipolar disorder   A mood disorder characterized by alternating periods of depression and abnormally heightened mood, sometimes to the point of grandiosity. Persons with bipolar disorder may behave irrationally (e.g., going on uncontrolled buying sprees, committing sexual indiscretions, and taking part in foolish business investments).

brief counseling   An approach to counseling characterized by a focus on resources and solutions rather than problems.

bulimia   An eating disorder that occurs when people adopt a pattern of excessive overeating followed by vomiting or other purging behaviors to control their weight.

burnout   A state of emotional, mental, and physical exhaustion that reduces or prevents people from performing their job.

catharsis   Verbalization of ideas, fears, past significant events, and associations, which results in a release of anxiety or tension.

challenging skills   Skills used to encourage clients to critically evaluate their behavior and ideas.

closed question   Questions that can easily be answered with a simple yes or no (e.g., "Did you go by yourself?").

cognitive area   How clients think about their situations.

command hallucination   Distorted perception of voices and images directing one to perform some action (e.g., attack or kill someone).

concreteness   A term used to describe the level of specificity. It is "a way to ensure that general and common experiences and feelings such as depression, anxiety, anger, and so on are defined idiosyncratically for each client" (Cormier and Cormier, 1985:48).

confrontation   Counseling initiatives that challenge clients to critically examine their actions and/or consider other viewpoints.

confrontation of incongruities   Used to point out inconsistencies in a client's verbal and nonverbal messages, values or beliefs, and behavior.

congruence   The capacity to be real and consistent with clients; matching behavior, feelings, and actions.

contingency plan   A preventive plan that anticipates possible barriers that clients might encounter as they carry out action plans.

contract   A negotiated agreement between counselors and clients regarding the purpose of the work, their respective roles, and the methods and routines that will be used to reach their agreed-on objectives.

controlled emotional involvement   "The empathic sensitivity of the worker to the client's feelings, disciplined by self-awareness, such that the worker's feelings do not inappropriately affect his or her understanding and purposeful response" (Hancock, 1997:131).

core conditions   Warmth, empathy, and genuineness.

counseling   A process of helping clients to learn skills, deal with feelings, and manage problems.

counseling relationship A time-limited period of consultation between a counselor and a client in order to achieve a defined goal.

countertransference Tendency of counselors to inappropriately transfer feelings and behaviors to clients.

critical incident debriefing A team meeting held to defuse the impact of violent or traumatic event such as an assault on a staff member. Debriefing assists workers to normalize and deal with the feelings that may be aroused as a result of the event. As well, debriefing is used to review and revise preventive and crisis intervention procedures.

defense mechanism A mental process or reaction that shields a person from undesirable or unacceptable thoughts, feelings, or conclusions that, if accepted, would create anxiety or challenges to one's sense of self. Common defense mechanisms include denial, displacement, rationalization, suppression, and regression.

delusion Distorted belief involving bizarre thought patterns.

dependent relationship A counseling relationship in which clients become overly reliant on their counselors for decision making. Symptoms include excessive permission seeking, frequent phone calls or office visits for information, and inability to make simple decisions or take action without consulting.

depression Pervasive deflation in mood characterized by symptoms such as sadness, hopelessness, decreased energy, and difficulty concentrating, remembering, and making decisions.

directives Short statements that provide direction to clients on topics, information, and pace (e.g., "Tell me more.").

diversity Variations in terms of lifestyle, culture, behavior, sexual orientation, age, ability, religion, and other factors.

doorknob communication A phenomenon described by Shulman (1992) whereby clients bring up important issues at the end of the interview/relationship when there is little or no time to address them.

DSM-IV-TR The *Diagnostic and Statistical Manual of Mental Disorders* published by the American Psychiatric Association. It is used by psychologists, psychiatrists, and other psychotherapists to classify and diagnose mental disorders.

dual diagnosis A person who has both a substance abuse addiction and a psychiatric disorder.

dual relationship A relationship in which there is both a counseling relationship and another type of relationship, such as friendship or sexual intimacy.

duty to warn Professional responsibility that counselors have to inform people whom they believe a client may harm.

emotion A state of mind usually accompanied by concurrent physiological and behavioral changes and based on the perception of some internal or external object.

emotional literacy The ability to experience all of one's emotions with appropriate intensity and to understand what is causing these feelings (Parrott, 1997:260).

empathy The process of accurately understanding the emotional perspective of another person and the communication of this understanding without imposing one's own feelings or reactions.

empowering skills Skills used to help clients develop confidence, self-esteem, and control over their lives.

empowerment The process of helping clients to discover personal strengths and capacities so that they are able to take control over their lives.

ethical dilemma   Situation involving competing or conflicting values or principles.

ethics   Guidelines that define the limits of permissible behavior.

ethnocentrism   The inclination to judge others negatively in relation to one's own cultural values and norms.

exploring/probing skills   Skills counselors use to gather information, clarify definition, seek example, and obtain necessary detail.

feedback confrontation   Used to provide new information to clients about who they are, including how they are perceived by others and the effects of their behavior on others.

genuineness   A measure of how authentic or real one is in a relationship.

goal setting   A counseling process that helps clients define in precise, measurable terms what they hope to achieve from the work of counseling.

hallucination   Hearing, seeing, tasting, touching, or smelling what others do not.

hidden job market   Jobs that are not advertised or made public; 80 percent or more of all jobs are filled through the hidden job market.

HIV   An acronym for Human Immunodeficiency Virus. This virus attacks the immune system, weakening its ability to fight off infections. People may be unaware that they have the virus, as they may have no symptoms for as long as five to fifteen years.

illusion of work   As defined by Shulman (1992:171), a process in which the worker and the client engage in a conversation that is empty and that has no real meaning.

immediacy   A tool for exploring, evaluating, and deepening counseling relationships.

indirect question   A statement that implies a question (e.g., "I'm curious how you responded.").

inferred empathy   A counselor's identification of a client's feelings based on nonverbal cues and indirect communication.

interviewing   Acquiring and organizing relevant information using active listening skills, including attending, silence, paraphrasing, summarizing, questioning, and empathy.

interview transition   A shift in the topic of the interview.

intimidating behavior   Behaviors such as name-calling; using obscene or sexually harassing language and gestures; shouting; and threatening through displays of power such as fist shaking, invading personal space, stalking, and issuing verbal threats. These behaviors should be restrained in order to prevent escalation to violence.

invitational empathy   A tool a counselor uses to encourage clients to explore emotions.

I-statement   Clear assertions about personal feelings or reactions that do not blame or judge others.

job club   An intensive and structured approach to job finding based on group support and structured learning activities. The sole purpose of a job club is to help participants find work.

leading question   A question that suggests a preferred answer (e.g., "Don't you think our session went really well today?").

learned helplessness   A state of mind that occurs when individuals have learned through failure that their efforts will not result in change.

listening   A process aimed at receiving and understanding messages without distortion.

LIVE   An acronym that describes the four essential steps in summarizing: listen, identify, verbalize, evaluate.

miracle question   Used in brief or single-session counseling as a way to help clients who have difficulty coming up with defined goals. The miracle question challenges clients to imagine how their lives would be different if a miracle solved their problems.

MOANS   An acronym for five words—*must, ought, always, never,* and *should*—that signals irrational or self-defeating thought.

mood disorders   *See* affective disorders.

motivation   The extent to which clients are willing to involve themselves in the change process.

networking   An integral part of job searching used to access the hidden job market. It involves using contacts, such as friends, family, and neighbors, who might provide information or access to others with information about possible job opportunities.

nonhelping behaviors   Variables that can lead to poor outcomes in counseling.

objectivity   Ability to understand feelings, thoughts, and behavior without allowing personal values, beliefs, and biases to interfere.

obsessive-compulsive disorder (OCD)   Recurrent, unwanted thoughts and conscious, ritualized, seemingly purposeless acts, such as counting the number of tiles on the ceiling or needing to wash one's hands repetitively.

open questions   Questions that promote expansive answers. These types of questions cannot be answered with a simple yes or no (e.g., "How do you feel about her?").

outcome goal   A goal related to what the client hopes to achieve from counseling.

panic disorder   Sudden attacks of terror and irrational fear, accompanied by an overwhelming sense of impending doom. During a panic attack a person may experience symptoms such as an accelerated heart rate, sweating, shaking, shortness of breath, chest pain, nausea, and fear of dying or losing control.

paraphrase   A nonjudgmental restatement of the client's words and ideas in the counselor's own words.

phases of counseling   Four sequential steps through which counseling tends to evolve: preliminary, beginning, action, ending.

phases of violence   Four-phase model (anxiety, defensiveness, acting out, and tension reduction) that describes how crises escalate to violence.

phobia   An irrational fear about particular events or objects that results in overwhelming anxiety in response to situations where there is little or no danger.

positive regard   The ability of counselors to recognize the inherent worth of people.

post-traumatic stress disorder (PTSD)   Disabling symptoms such as emotional numbness, sleep disturbance (nightmares, difficulty sleeping), or reliving the event following a traumatic event such as rape, assault, natural disaster (earthquakes, floods, etc.), war, torture, or automobile accident.

preparatory empathy   A counselor's attempt to consider (in advance of the interview) the feelings and concerns that the client may communicate indirectly.

principle of positive reinforcement   The idea that behavior tends to increase or continue when it is rewarded.

process goal   The methods and procedures that will be used in counseling to assist clients to reach their goals.

pseudocounseling   Counseling that lacks real meaning, evidenced by irrelevant exploration of issues, use of clichés and patronizing platitudes, intellectual exploration of issues, and avoidance of subjects or feelings that involve pain in favor of "safe" topics.

psychotherapy   Advanced counseling targeting severe emotional or behavioral difficulties or disorders.

questioning   An active listening skill that involves probing for information to confirm understanding and seek clarification.

reframing   Technique for helping clients to look at things differently by suggesting alternative interpretations or new meanings.

relationship-building skills   Tools for engaging clients and developing trust.

relative confidentiality   The assumption that client disclosures may be shared within the agency with supervisors or colleagues, outside the agency with client permission, or with others because of legal requirements, such as those contained within child-abuse legislation.

rescuing   Also called band-aiding, this involves a counselor's actions that prevent or protect clients from dealing with issues or feelings. Rescuing arises from the counselor's need to avoid tension and keep the session cheerful.

resistance   Defensive reaction by clients that interferes with or delays the process of counseling.

schizophrenia   A chronic mental disorder involving symptoms such as hallucinations, delusions, disordered thinking, and social isolation.

selective perception   A term used to describe the natural tendency to avoid being overwhelmed by information by screening out material that is irrelevant.

self-awareness   Process of becoming alert and knowledgeable about one's own way of thinking, acting, and feeling.

self-defeating thought   Inner dialogue of critical messages.

self-determination   The principle that promotes the rights of clients to have autonomy and freedom of choice.

self-talk   Mental messages people give to themselves (e.g., "I'm no good.").

silence   A tool used in counseling when the client is thinking, the client is confused and unsure of what to say or do, or the client has encountered painful feelings. Silence signals trust issues, is culturally defined, and indicates closure.

simple encouragers   Short phrases and gestures, such as "Tell me more," "Go on," "Uh huh," and head nods that encourage clients to continue with their stories.

skill clusters   Categories of skills based on their intended purpose or helping activity.

strengths approach   A counseling perspective that assumes the inherent capacity of people. Individuals and communities are seen to have assets and resources that can be mobilized for problem solving.

structured interview   An interview that follows a predetermined sequence of questions.

summarizing   A way of condensing content. A simple summary focuses on content and is an unedited condensing of the client's words. Theme summaries edit out unnecessary detail and attempt to identify key patterns and areas of urgency.

thinking errors   Faulty reasoning caused by distortion, incomplete analysis, egocentricity, rigidity, and self-defeating thought.

thought broadcasting   The delusional belief that one's thinking can be heard by others.

thought insertion   The delusional belief that thoughts are being inserted into one's brain by others.

transference   The tendency of clients to communicate with their counselors in the same way that they communicated to significant people in the past.

unstructured interview   An interview that does not have a preset plan that restricts direction, pace, or content.

values   What individuals and groups consider to be important or worthwhile.

ventilation   *See* catharsis.

versatility   The need for counselors to develop a broad range of skills in order to adapt their approach to fit the distinctive complexities of each individual and context.

violent behavior   Hitting, pushing, biting, slapping, kicking, throwing objects, and using weapons such as guns, knives, or syringes.

worldview   belief system about the nature of the universe, its perceived effect on human behavior, and one's place in the universe. Worldview is a fundamental core set of assumptions explaining cultural forces, the nature of humankind, the nature of good and evil, luck, fate, spirits, the power of significant others, the role of time, and the nature of our physical and natural resources (Dodd, 1995:105).

REFERENCES

Abraham, S., and D. Llewellyn-Jones. *Eating Disorders: The Facts.* 4th ed. New York: Oxford University Press, 1997.

Ahia, C.E., "A Cultural Framework for Counseling African Americans." In Lee, C.C., (ed.), *Multicultural Issues in Counseling,* 2nd Ed., Alexandra, VA: American Counseling Association, 1997.

Alexander, C.M., and L. Sussman. "Creative Approaches to Multicultural Counseling." In *Handbook of Multicultural Counseling,* by J.G. Ponterotto et al. Thousand Oaks, CA: Sage Publications, 1995.

American Association of Suicidology. [Online, cited 10 August 1998]. Available: http://www.cyberpsych.org/aas/

American Counseling Association (ACA). *Code of Ethics and Standards of Practice.* Alexandria, VA: American Counseling Association, 1995.

American Psychiatric Association. *Diagnostic and Statistical Manual of Mental Disorders,* 4th ed. Text Revision. Washington, DC: American Psychiatric Association, 2000.

Amundson, N.E. "Supporting Clients Through a Change in Perspective," *Journal of Employment Counseling* 33, no. 4 (1996):155–62.

Angel, D.L., and E.E. Harney. *No One Is Unemployable: Creative Solutions for Overcoming Barriers to Employment.* Hacienda Heights, CA: WorkNet Training Services, 1997.

Arnhold, R.M., and W.N. Razak. "Overcoming Learned Helplessness: Managerial Strategies for the 1990's," *Journal of Employment Counseling* 28 (September 1991):99–106.

Arthur, N., and J. Stewart. "Multicultural Counselling in the New Millennium: Introduction to the Special Theme Issue," *Canadian Journal of Counselling,* Vol. 35, no. 1, 2001.

Azrin, N.H., and V.A. Besalel. *Job Club Counselor's Manual: A Behavioral Approach to Vocational Counseling.* Austin, TX: Pro-Ed, 1980.

Backhouse, C. *Colour-Coded: A Legal History of Racism in Canada, 1900–1950.* Toronto, Ontario: University of Toronto Press, 1999.

Barker, R.L. *The Social Work Dictionary.* 3rd ed. Washington, DC: NASW Press, 1995.

Beckman, C.S., S.G. Turner, M. Cooper, D. Polnerow, and M. Swartz. "Sexual Contact with Clients: Assessment of Social Workers' Attitudes and Educational Preparation," *Social Work* 45, no. 3 (2000):224.

Benjamin, A. *The Helping Interview.* 3rd ed. Boston, MA: Houghton Mifflin, *1981.*

Berg, F.M. *Afraid to Eat: Children and Teens in Weight Crisis.* Hettinger, ND: Healthy Weight Journal, 1997.

Beyerstein, B.L. "Believing Is Seeing: Organic and Psychological Reasons for Hallucinations and Other Anomalous Psychiatric Symptoms." *Medscape.* [Online, cited 7 August 1998]. Available: http:Hwww.medscape.com/Medscape/MentalHealth

Bezanson, M.L., C.A. DeCoff, and N.R. Stewart. *Individual Employment Counselling: An Action Based Approach.* Toronto: University of Toronto Guidance Centre, 1985.

Black, K. *Short-Term Counseling: A Humanistic Approach for the Helping Professions.* Menlo Park, CA: Addison-Wesley, 1983.

Bolles, R.N. *The 1997 What Color Is Your Parachute: A Practical Manual for Job-Hunters and Career Changers.* Berkeley, CA: Ten Speed Press, 1997.

Bower, B. "Study Tracks Violence among Mentally Ill," *Science News,* May 1998, 309.

Brammer, L.M. *The Helping Relationship: Process and Skills.* 3rd ed. Englewood Cliffs, NJ: Prentice-Hall, 1985.

Brammer, L.M., and G. MacDonald. *The Helping Relationship: Process and* Skills. 7th ed. Boston: Allyn & Bacon, 1999.

Brammer, L.M., and E.L. Shostrom. *Therapeutic Psychology: Fundamentals of Counseling and Psychotherapy.* 4th ed. Englewood Cliffs, NJ: Prentice-Hall, 1982.

Bratina, T.G., and T.A. Bratina. "Electronic Career Search," *Journal of Employment Counseling* 35 (March 1998):17–25.

Brill, N.I. *Working with People: The Helping Process.* 6th ed. New York: Addison-Wesley, 1998.

Burman, P. *Killing Time, Losing Ground: Experiences of Unemployment.* Toronto: Thompson Educational Publishing, 1988.

Canadian Counselling Association. *Code of Ethics.* Ottawa, Ontario: Canadian Counselling Association, 1999.

Canadian Task Force on Mental Health Issues Affecting Immigrants and Refugees. "After the Door Has Been Opened: Mental Health Issues Affecting Refugees and Immigrants in Canada." *Report of the Canadian Task Force on Mental Health Issues Affecting Immigrants and Refugees.* Ottawa: Multiculturalism and Citizenship Canada, 1988.

Capuzza, D., and D.R. Gross. *Introduction to the Counseling Profession.* 2nd ed. Boston: Allyn & Bacon, 1997.

Capuzza, D., and D.R. Gross. *Introduction to the Counseling Profession.* 3rd ed. Boston: Allyn & Bacon, 2001.

Carkhuff, R.R. *The Art of Helping.* Amherst, MA: Human Resource Development Press, 1981.

Carniol, B. *Case Critical: The Dilemma of Social Work in Canada.* 3rd ed. Toronto: Between the Lines, 1995.

Choney, S.K., E. Berryhill-Paapke, and R. Robbins. "The Acculturation of American Indians, Developing Frameworks for Research and Practice." In *Cultural and Diversity Issues in Counseling,* by P.B. Pederson and D.C. Locke. Greensboro, NC: ERIC Counseling and Student Services Clearinghouse, 1996.

Clark, A.J. "Reframing: A Therapeutic Technique in Group Counseling," *Journal for Specialists in Group Work* 23, no. 1 (1998):66–73.

Cleghorn, J.M., *and* B.L. Lee. *Understanding and Treating Mental Illness: The Strengths and Limits of Modern Psychiatry.* Toronto: Hogrefe & Huber, 1991.

Compton, B., and B. Galaway. *Social Work Processes.* 3rd ed. Homewood, IL: Dorsey Press, 1984.

———. *Social Work Processes.* 6th ed. Pacific Grove, CA: Brooks/Cole, 1999.

Corey, M., and G. Corey. *Becoming a Helper.* Pacific Grove, CA: Brooks/Cole, 1989.

Cormier, W.H., and L.S. Cormier. *Interviewing Strategies for Helpers.* Monterey, CA: Brooks/Cole, 1985.

Corsini, R.J. *Encyclopedia of Psychology.* New York: John Wiley & Sons, 1984.

Cottone, R.R., and V.M. Tarvydas. *Ethical and Professional Issues in Counseling.* Englewood Cliffs, NJ: Prentice-Hall, 1998.

Cowger, C. "Assessing Client Strengths," *Social Work* 39, no. 3 (1994):262–268.

Cragan, J.F., and D.W. Wright. *Communication in Small Group Discussions: An Integrated Approach.* 3rd ed. St. Paul, MN: West Publishing, 1991.

D'Andrea, M.J. "White Racism." In *Cultural and Diversity Issues in Counseling,* by P.B. Pedersen and D.C. Locke. Greensboro, NC: ERIC Counseling and Student Services Clearinghouse, 1996.

Daniluk, J.C., and B.E. Haverkamp. "Ethical Issues in Counseling Adult Survivors of Incest," *Journal of Counseling and Development 72,* no. 1 (1993):16–22.

D'Augelli, A.R., J.F. D'Augelli, and S.J. Danish. *Helping Others.* Monterey, CA: Brooks/Cole, 1981.

Davis, L.E., and E.K. Proctor. *Race, Gender, and Class: Guidelines for Practice with Individuals, Families, and Groups.* Englewood Cliffs, NJ: Prentice Hall, 1989.

Davis, S. "An Overview: Are Mentally Ill People Really More Dangerous?" *Social Work* 36, no. 2 (1991):174–80.

De Becker, G. *The Gift of Fear: Survival Signals That Protect Us from Violence.* Boston: Little, Brown, 1997.

De Bono, E. *Six Thinking Hats.* Toronto: Key Porter, 1985.

de Shazer, S. *Keys to Solution in Brief Therapy.* New York: Norton, 1985.

Devons, C. "Suicide in the Elderly: How to Identify and Treat Patients at Risk," *Geriatrics* 51, no. 3 (1996):67–72.

Diller, J.V. *Cultural Diversity: A Primer for the Human Services.* Scarborough, ON: Brooks/Cole, 1999.

Dodd, C.H. *Dynamics of Intercultural Communication.* 4th ed. Dubuque, IA: Brown & Benchmark, 1995.

DuBois, B., and K. Miley. *Social Work: An Empowering Profession.* 2nd ed. Boston: Allyn & Bacon, 1996.

Dubovsky, S.L., and M.P. Weissberg. Clinical *Psychiatry in Primary Care.* 3rd ed. Baltimore, MD: Williams & Wilkins, 1986.

Dumont, M. *The Absurd Healer.* New York: Viking Press, 1968.

Egan, G. *You and Me: The Skills of Communicating and Relating to Others.* Belmont, CA: Brooks/Cole, 1977.

———. *The Skilled Helper.* 4th ed. Monterey, CA: Brooks/Cole, 1990.

———. *The Skilled Helper.* 6th ed. Monterey, CA: Brooks/Cole, 1998.

Elbourne, R. "Is Silence Suspicious?" [Online, cited 30 September 1997]. Available: http://home. vicnet.net.au/-gnaust/vic2/25-10.html

Ellis, A. *Reason and Emotion in Psychotherapy.* New York: Stuart, 1962.

———. *Rational-Emotive Therapy and Cognitive Behavior Therapy.* New York: Springer, 1984.

———. "Fundamentals of Rational-Emotive Therapy for the 1990s," in *Innovations in Rational-Emotive Therapy,* ed. W. Dryden and I. Hill. Newbury Park, CA: Sage, 1993a, 1–32.

———. "Reflections on Rational-Emotive Therapy," *Journal of Counseling and Clinical Psychology* 62, no. 2 (1993b):199–201.

Erdman, P., and P. Lampe. "Adapting Basic Skills to Counsel Children," *Journal of Counseling and Development* 74, no. 4 (1996):374–77.

Evans, D.R., M.T. Hearn, M.R. Uhlemann, and A.E. Ivey. *Essential Interviewing: A Programmed Approach to Effective Communication.* Monterey, CA: Brooks/Cole, 1979.

Factmonster, [online, cited August 28, 2001]. Available: http://www.factmonster.com

Farr, J. M. *The Very Quick Job Search: Get a Better Job in Half the Time.* 2nd ed. Indianapolis: JIST Works, 1996.

Fuertes, J.N., and Bartolomeo, Nichols, C. "Future Research Directions in the Study of Counselor Multicultural Competency," *Journal of Multicultural Counseling and Development,* v29, Jan 2001.

Furman, B., and T. Ahola. "Solution Talk: The Solution-Oriented Way of Talking about Problems," in *Constructive Therapies,* ed. M.F. Hoyt. New York: The Guilford Press, 1994:41–66.

Gardner, W., C. Lidz, E. Mulvey, and E. Shaw. "Clinical versus Actuarial Predictions of Violence in Patients with Mental illness," *Journal of Consulting and Clinical Psychology* 64, no. 3 (1996):602–10.

Garrett, A. *Interviewing: Its Principles and Methods.* 3rd ed., revised and enlarged by Margaret M. Mangold and Elinor P. Zaki. New York: Family Service Association of America, 1982.

Garrett, M.T., J.T. Garrett, D. Brotherton. "Inner Circle/Outer Circle: A Group Technique Based on Native American Healing Circles," *Journal for Specialists in Group Work,* Vol. 26, No 1, March 2001.

Garvin, C.D., and B.A. Seabury. *Interpersonal Practice in Social Work: Processes and Procedures.* Englewood Cliffs, NJ: Prentice-Hall, 1984.

George, R.L., and T.S. Cristiani. *Counseling Theory and Practice.* 2nd ed. Englewood Cliffs, NJ: Prentice-Hall, 1986.

Gilliland, B.E., and R.K. James. *Theories and Strategies in Counseling and Psychotherapy.* 4th ed. Boston: Allyn & Bacon, 1998.

Gladding, S.T. *Counseling: A Comprehensive Profession.* 3rd ed. Englewood Cliffs, NJ: Prentice-Hall, 1996.

Glosoff, H.L., B. Herlihy, and E.B. Spence. "Privileged Communication in the Counselor–Client Relationship," *Journal of Counseling and Development* 78, no. 4 (2000):454–462.

Golden, B.J., and K. Lesh. *Building Self-Esteem: Strategies for Success in School and Beyond.* 2nd ed. Scottsdale, AZ: Gorsuch Scarisbick, 1997.

Goleman, D. *Emotional Intelligence.* New York: Bantam Books, 1995.

Gordon, T. *Parent Effectiveness Training: The "No-Lose" Program for Raising Responsible Children.* New York: Peter Wyden, 1971.

Grinder, J., and R. Bandler. *The Structure of Magic II.* Palo Alto, CA: Science and Behavior Books, 1976.

Hackney, H.L., and L.S. Cormier. *The Professional Counselor: A Process Guide to Helping.* 4th ed. Boston, MA: Pearson Education, 2001.

Haley J. *Problem-Solving Therapy.* 2nd ed. San Francisco: Jossey-Bass, 1987.

Hall, E.T. *The Silent Language.* Greenwich, CT: Fawcett Publications, 1959.

Hamachek, D.E. *Encounters with Others: Interpersonal Relationships and You.* New York: Holt, Rinehart and Winston, 1982.

Hammond, C., D. Hepworth, and V. Smith. *Improving Therapeutic Communication.* San Francisco: Jossey-Bass, 1977.

Hancock, M.R. *Principles of Social Work Practice: A Generic Approach.* Binghamton, NY: Haworth Press, 1997.

Harris, G.A., and D. Watkins. *Counseling the Involuntary and Resistant Client.* College Park, MD: American Correctional Association, 1987.

Harris, G.T., and M.E. Rice. "Risk Appraisal and Management of Violent Behavior," *Psychiatric Services* 48, no. 9 (1997):1168–76.

Harris, H.S., and D.C. Maloney. *Human Services: Contemporary Issues and Trends.* Boston: Allyn & Bacon, 1996.

Harvard Medical School. *Harvard Mental Health Letter* 13, no. 6 (December 1996).

Hepworth, D.H., R.H. Rooney, and J. Larsen. *Direct Social Work Practice, Theory and Skills.* 5th ed. Pacific Grove, Ca: Brooks/Cole, 1997.

Hess, H., and P. McCartt Hess. "Termination in Context," in *Social Work Processes,* 3rd ed., ed. B. Compton and B. Galaway. Homewood, IL: Dorsey Press, 1984, 559–70.

Hirschfeld, R.M., and J.M. Russell. "Assessment and Treatment of Suicidal Patients," *The New England Journal of Medicine* 337, no. 13 (1997):910–16.

Hocker, J.L., and W.W. Wilmot. *Interpersonal Conflict.* 4th ed. Dubuque, IA: Wm. C. Brown Communication, 1995.

Holmes, B.H., and J.D. Werbel. "Finding Work Following Job Loss: The Role of Coping Resources," *Journal of Employment Counseling* 29, no. 1 (1992):22–29.

Hoyt, M.F. (ed). *Constructive Therapies.* New York: The Guilford Press, 1994.

Huber, C.H., and B.A. Backlund. *The Twenty Minute Counselor: Transforming Brief Conversations into Effective Helping Experiences.* New York: Continuum, 1991.

Ivey, A.E. *Intentional Interviewing and Counseling.* Monterey, CA: Brooks/Cole, 1982.

Ivey, A.E., M.B. Ivey, and L. Simek-Downing. *Counseling and Psychotherapy: Integrating Skills, Theory, and Practice.* 2nd ed. Englewood Cliffs, NJ: Prentice-Hall, 1987.

Jacobs, E., R. Masson, and R. Harvill. *Group Counseling Strategies and Skills.* Pacific Grove, CA: Brooks/Cole, 1998.

Jobes, D.A., and A.L. Berman. "Crisis Intervention and Brief Treatment for Suicidal Youth," in *Contemporary Perspectives on Crisis Intervention and Prevention,* ed. A.R. Roberts. Englewood Cliffs, NJ: Prentice-Hall, 1991, 53–69.

Johnson, D.W. *Reaching Out: Interpersonal Effectiveness and Self-Actualization.* 6th ed. Boston: Allyn & Bacon, 1997.

Johnson, L.C. *Social Work Practice: A Generalist Approach.* 4th ed. Boston: Allyn & Bacon, 1992.

Johnson, L.C., and S.J. Yanca. *Social Work Practice: A Generalist Approach,* 7th ed. Boston: Allyn & Bacon, 2001.

Kadushin, A. *The Social Work Interview.* 2nd ed. New York: Columbia University Press, 1983.

———. *The Social Work Interview: A Guide for Human Service Professionals.* 3rd ed. New York: Columbia University Press, 1990.

Kain, C.D. *Positive HIV Affirmative Counseling.* Alexandria, VA: American Counseling Association, 1996.

Kaplan, S.G., and E.G. Wheeler. "Survival Skills for Working with Potentially Violent Clients," *Social Casework* (June 1983):339–46.

Keith-Lucas, A. *The Giving and Taking of Help.* Chapel Hill: University of North Carolina Press, 1972.

Kell, B.L., and W.L. Mueller. *Impact and Change.* New York: Appleton-Century-Crofts, 1966.

Kelleher, M.D. *Profiling the Lethal Employee: Case Studies of Violence in the Workplace.* Westport, CT: Praeger, 1997.

Kelly, E.W. *Spirituality and Religion in Counseling and Psychotherapy: Diversity in Theory and Practice.* Alexandria, VA: American Counseling Association, 1995.

Kirsh, S. *Unemployment: Its Impact on Body and Soul.* Canadian Mental Health Association, 1983.

Klerman, G.L. "Classification and DSM-III-R," in *The New Harvard Guide to Psychiatry,* ed. A.M. Nicoli. Cambridge, MA: Belknap Press, 1988, 70–87.

Kottler, J., "What Matters Most," *Counseling Today,* August 2001.

Kottler, J.A. "When Clients Don't Get Better: Facing Failure as a Counselor," *American Counselor* 2, no. 4 (1993):14–19.

Labig, C.E. *Preventing Violence in the Workplace.* New York: AMACOM, 1995.

Lanza, M., H. Kayne, I. Pattison, C. Hicks, S. Islam, J. Bradshaw, and P. Robins. "The Relationship of Behavioral Cues to Assaultive Behavior," *Clinical Nursing Research 5,* no. 1 (1996):6–28.

Lazarus, A.A., and L.E. Beutler. "On Technical Eclecticism," *Journal of Counseling and Development,* 71, no. 4 (1993):381–85.

Lazarus, R., *Emotion and Adaptation.* New York: Oxford University Press, 1991.

LeDoux, J.E. "Annual 1995," *Annual Review of Psychology* 46 (1995):209–35.

Leeds, D. "The Art of Asking Questions," *Training and Development* 47, no. 1 (1993):57–62.

Liguori, A.L. Closing comments at the 12th World AIDS Conference, Geneva, Switzerland, July 1998. [Online, cited 25 July 1998]. Available: http://www.aids98.ch/archive/special/final-summarysession-trackd.html

Lock, R.D. *Taking Charge of Your Career Direction.* 3rd ed. Pacific Grove, CA: Brooks/Cole, 1996.

Mann, J.M., and D.J. Tarantola. "HIV 1998: The Global Picture," *Scientific American,* July 1998, 82–83.

Martin, D.G. *Counseling and Therapy Skills.* Belmont, CA: Brooks/Cole, 1983.

Martin, G., and J. Pear. *Behavior Modification: What It Is and How to Do It.* 4th ed. Englewood Cliffs, NJ: Prentice-Hall, 1992.

Maslow, A.H. *Motivation and Personality.* New York: Harper & Row, 1954.

McDonald, N. *Interviewing Aboriginal Peoples: A Guide to Effective Cross-Cultural Interviews.* Winnipeg: Cross-Cultural Communications International, 1993.

McNeece, C.A., and D.M. DiNitto. *Chemical Dependency: A Systems Approach.* 2nd ed. Boston: Allyn & Bacon, 1998.

McWhirter, E.H. "Empowerment in Counseling," *Journal of Counseling and Development* 69, no. 3 (1991):222–27.

Meharabian, A. *Silent Messages: Implicit Communication of Emotions and Attitudes.* 2nd ed. Belmont, CA: Wadsworth, 1981.

Mehr, J.J. *Human Services Concepts and Intervention Strategies.* 7th ed. Boston: Allyn & Bacon, 1998.

Middleman, R.R., and G.G. Wood. *Skills for Direct Practice in Social Work.* New York: Columbia University Press, 1990.

Miller, S.D. "The Symptoms of Solutions," *Journal of Strategic and Systemic Therapies* 11, no. 1 (1992):2–11.

Minuchin, S., and H. Fishman,. *Family Therapy Techniques.* Cambridge: Harvard University Press, 1981.

Morrisseau, C. *Into the Daylight: A Wholistic Approach to Healing.* Toronto, Ontario: University of Toronto Press, 1998.

Morrissey, M. "Safety Issues for Counselors Who Work with Violent Clients," *Counseling Today,* February 1998, 6.

National Association of Social Workers, *Revised Code of Ethics.* Washington, DC, 1996.

National Crisis Prevention Institute. *Nonviolent Crisis Intervention: The Preventative Techniques,* vol. 1, National Crisis Prevention Institute, 1986.

———. *Nonviolent Crisis Intervention: Therapeutic Physical Intervention,* vol. 11, National Crisis Prevention Institute, 1987.

National Institute of Mental Health (NIMH). [Online, 5 August 1998]. Available: http://www.nimh.nih.gov/home.htm

Newhill, C.E. "Assessing Danger to Others in Clinical Social Work Practice," *Social Service Review* (March 1992):65–79.

———. "Client Violence Toward Social Workers: A Practice and Policy Concern for the 1990's," *Social Work* 40, no. 5 (September 1995):631–39.

Nicholi, A.M. (ed). *The New Harvard Guide to Psychiatry.* Cambridge, MA: Belknap Press, 1988.

Noesner, G.W., and M. Webster. "Crisis Intervention: Using Active Listening Skills in Negotiations," *The FBI Law Enforcement Bulletin* 66, no. 8 (1997):13–20.

Otani, A. "Client Resistance in Counseling: Its Theoretical Rationale and Taxonomic Classification," *Journal of Counseling and Development* (1989):458–61.

Othmer, E., and S.C. Othmer. *The Clinical Interview Using DSM-III-R.* Washington, DC: American Psychiatric Press, 1989.

Paniagua, F.A., *Assessing and Treating Culturally Diverse Clients: A Practical Guide.* 2nd ed. Thousand Oaks, CA: Sage, 1998.

Parrott, L. *Counseling and Psychotherapy.* New York: McGraw-Hill, 1997.

Pastor, L.H. "Initial Assessment and Intervention Strategies to Reduce Workplace Violence," *American Family Physician* 52, no. 4 (1995):1169–75.

Patterson, C.H. "Multicultural Counseling: From Diversity to Universality," *Journal of Counseling and Development* 74, no. 3 (1996):227–31.

Pedersen, P. *A Handbook for Developing Multicultural Awareness,* 2nd ed. Alexandria, VA: American Counseling Association, 1994.

Pedersen, P.B., "Multiculturalism and the Paradigm Shift in Counselling: Controversies and Alternative Futures," *Canadian Journal of Counselling* V35, no. 1, (2001):15–25.

Pedersen, P.B., and D.C. Locke, eds. *Cultural and Diversity Issues in Counseling.* Greensboro, NC: ERIC Counseling and Student Services Clearinghouse, 1996.

Pincus, A., and A. Minahan. *Social Work Practice: Model and Method.* Itasca, IL: F.E. Peacock, 1973.

Poonwassie, A., and A. Charter. "An Aboriginal Worldview of Helping: Empowering Approaches," *Canadian Journal of Counselling* vol. 35, no. 1, 2001.

Reamer, F.G. *Ethical Standards in Social Work: A Critical Review of the NASW Code of Ethics.* Washington, DC: NASW Press, 1998.

Reid, W.H. *The Treatment of Psychiatric Disorders: Revised for the DSM-IIIR. New* York: Brunner/Mazel, 1989.

Remley Jr., T.P., B. Herlihy, and S.B. Herlihy. "The U.S. Supreme Court Decision in *Jafee v Redmond:* Implications for Counselors," *Journal of Counseling and Development* 75, no. 3 (1997):213–18.

Roberts, A.R. *Contemporary Perspectives on Crisis Intervention and Prevention.* Englewood Cliffs, NJ: Prentice-Hall, 1991.

Rogers, C.R. *Client-Centered Therapy: Its Current Practice, Implications, and Theory.* Boston: Houghton Mifflin, 1951.

———. *On Becoming a Person.* Boston: Houghton Mifflin, 1961.

———. *A Way of Being.* Boston: Houghton Mifflin, 1980.

Rosenthal, L. *Resolving Resistance in Group Psychotherapy.* Northvale, NJ: Jason Aronson, 1987.

Ross, R. *Dancing with a Ghost: Exploring Indian Reality.* Markham, ON: Octopus, 1992.

Roth, L.H. *Clinical Treatment of the Violent Person.* New York: Guilford Press, 1987.

Roy, A. "Risk Factors for Suicide Among Adult Alcoholics," *Alcohol Health and Research World* 17, no. 2 (1993):133–36.

Ruskin, R., and M. Beiser. "Cultural Issues in Psychtherapy," in *Standards and Guidelines for the Psychotherapies,* ed. P. Cameron, J. Ennis, and J. Deadman. Toronto: University of Toronto Press, 1998, pp. 422–444.

Saleeby, D., *The Strengths Perspective in Social Work Practice.* 2nd ed. New York: Longman, 1997.

San Francisco Suicide Prevention Institute. [Online, 10 August 1998]. Available: http://www.sfsuicide.org/facts.html

Schram, B., and B.R. Mandell. *An Introduction to Human Services Policy and Procedure.* 3rd ed. Boston: Allyn & Bacon, 1997.

Schram, B., and B.R. Mandell. *An Introduction to Human Services Policy and Practice.* 4th ed. Boston: Allyn & Bacon, 1997.

Seligman, M.E. *Helplessness: On Depression, Development and Death.* San Francisco: W.H. Freeman, 1975.

Shahmirzadi, A. "Counseling Iranians." *The Personnel and Guidance Journal* April, 1983.

Shea, S.C. *Psychiatric Interviewing: The Art of Understanding.* Philadelphia: W.B. Sanders, 1988.

Sheafor, B.W., C.R. Horejsi, and G.A. Horejsi. *Techniques and Guidellnes for Social Work Practice.* Boston: Allyn & Bacon, 1991.

Sheafor, B.W., C.R. Horejsi, and G.A Horejsi. *Techniques and Guidelines for Social Work Practice.* 5th ed. Boston: Allyn & Bacon, 2000.

———. *Techniques and Guidelines for Social Work Practice.* Boston: Allyn & Bacon, 2000.

Shebib, B. *Counseling Skills.* Victoria: Province of British Columbia, Ministry of Education, Skills and Training, 1997.

Shilling, L.E. *Perspectives on Counseling Theories.* Englewood Cliffs, NJ: Prentice-Hall, 1984.

Shulman, L. *Skills of Helping Individuals and Groups.* 2nd ed. Itasca, IL: F.E. Peacock, 1984.

———. *Skills of Helping Individuals and Groups.* 3rd ed. Itasca, IL: F.E. Peacock, 1992.

Shulz, W.E. *Counselling Ethics Casebook 2000.* Ottawa, Canada: Canadian Counselling Association, 2000.

Silva, Fernando, and M. Lopez de Silva. "Hallucinations and Behavior Modification," *Analisis y Modificacion de Conducta* 2, no. 2 (1976).

Skidmore, R.A., M.G. Thackeray, and O.W. Farley. *Introduction to Social Work.* 5th ed. Englewood Cliffs, NJ: Prentice-Hall, 1991.

Sklare, G.B. *Brief Counseling That Works: A Solution-Focused Approach for School Counselors.* Thousand Oaks, CA: Corwin Press, 1997.

Smith, D.B., and P.J. Morrissette. "The Experiences of White Male Counsellors Who Work with First Nations Clients," *Canadian Journal of Counselling* vol. 35, no. 1, 2001.

Specht, H., "Social Work and the Popular Psychotherapies," *Social Service Review* 64, no. 3, 1990.

Speight, S.L., L.J. Myers, C.I. Cox, and P.S. Highlen. "A Redefinition of Multicultural Counseling," *Journal of Counseling and Development* 70, no. 1 (1991):29–36.

Steinweg, D.A. "Implications of Current Research for Counseling the Unemployed," *Journal of Employment Counseling* 27, no. 1 (March 1990):37–41.

Sudman, S. and N.M. Bradburn. *Asking Questions: A Practical Guide to Questionnaire Design.* San Francisco: Jossey-Bass, 1983.

Sue, D.W., P. Arredondo, and R. McDavis. "Multicultural Counseling Competencies and Standards: A Call to the Profession," *Journal of Counseling and Development* 70, no. 4 (1992):477–86.

Sue, D.W., and D. Sue. *Counseling the Culturally Different: Theory and Practice.* 2nd ed. New York, NY: Wiley, 1990.

Sue, D.W., and D. Sue. *Counseling the Culturally Different: Theory and Practice.* 3rd ed. New York, NY: Wiley, 1999.

Sunley, R., and G.W. Sheek. *Serving the Unemployed and Their Families.* Milwaukee, WI: Family Service America, 1986.

Swanson, J., S. Estroff, M. Swartz, R. Borum, W. Lachicotte, C. Zimmer, and R. Wagner. "Violence and Severe Mental Disorder in Clinical and Community Populations: The Effects of Psychotic Symptoms, Comorbidity, and Lack of Treatment," *Psychiatry: Interpersonal and Biological Processes* 60, no. 1(1997):1–22.

Tardiff, K., P. Marzuk, A. Leon, L. Portera, and C. Weiner. "Violence by Patients Admitted to a Private Psychiatric Hospital," *American Journal of Psychiatry* 154, no. 1 (1997):88–94.

Thoreson, R.W., P. Shaughnessy, P.P. Heppner, and S.W. Cook. "Sexual Contact During and After the Professional Relationship: Attitudes and Practices of Male Counselors," *Journal of Counseling and Development* 71, no. 4 (1993):429–34.

Truax, C., and R. Carkhuff. *Toward Effective Counseling and Psychotherapy: Training and Practice.* Chicago: Aldine, 1967.

Turner, J.C., and F.J. Turner (general eds.). *Canadian Social Welfare.* 2nd ed. Don Mills, ON: Collier Macmillan Canada, 1986.

———. *Canadian Social Welfare,* 4th ed. Toronto: Pearson Education Canada, 2001.

U.S. Census Bureau [online, cited August 28, 2001]. Available: http://www.census.gov

Vaillant, G.E. "Defense Mechanisms," in *The New Harvard Guide to Psychiatry,* ed. A.M. Nicholi. Cambridge, MA: Belknap Press, 1988, 200–7.

Walrond-Skinner, A. *Dictionary of Psychotherapy.* London: Routledge & Kegan Paul, 1986.

Walter, J.L., and J.E. Peller. "'On Track' in Solution-Focused Brief Therapy," in *Constructive Therapies,* ed. M.F. Hoyt. New York: Guilford Press, 1994, 111–25.

Walters, G.D. "Identifying and Confronting Resistance in Lifestyle Criminal Offenders," in *Tough Customers: Counseling Unwilling Clients,* ed. G.A. Harris. Laurel, MD: American Correctional Association, 1991, 25–42.

Weaver, A.J. "Working with Potentially Dangerous Persons: What Clergy Need to Know," *Pastoral Psychology* 40, no. 5 (1982):313–23.

Weaver, C.H. *Human Listening: Processes and Behavior.* Indianapolis: Bobbs-Merrill, 1972.

Weisinger, H. *Emotional Intelligence at Work.* San Francisco, CA: Jossey-Bass, 1998.

Wells, C. S., and M.K. Masch. *Social Work Ethics Day to Day: Guidelines for Professional Practice.* Prospect Heights, IL: Waveland, 1991.

Westwood, M.J., and F.I. Ishiyama. "Challenges in Counseling Immigrant Clients: Understanding Intercultural Barriers to Career Adjustment," *Journal of Employment Counseling* 28, no. 4 (1991):130–43.

Wicks, R.J., and R.D. Parsons. *Counseling Strategies and Intervention Techniques for the Human Services.* New York: Longman, 1984.

Wilson, S.B. *Goal Setting.* New York: AMACOM, 1994.

Wolvin, A., and C. Coakley. *Listening,* 5th ed. Dubuque, IA: Brown & Benchmark, 1996.

Woodside, M., and T. McClam. *An Introduction to Human Services.* Belmont, CA: Brooks/Cole, 1990.

Young, M.E. *Learning the Art of Helping.* Upper Saddle River, NJ: Merrill, 1998.

Zastrow, C. *Introduction to Social Welfare: Social Problems, Services, and Current Issues.* 4th ed. Belmont, CA: Wadsworth, 1990.

INDEX

Aboriginal people (*see* Natives)
Abraham, S., 274
Acting out phase (violence), 250
Action phase, 20, 21, 29–30
  relationship and, 72
Action planning, 13, 195, 215–223
  steps
Active listening, 9–10, 27, 102–
  104, 194, 276
Advice giving, 17–18
Advocacy, xiii, 40
Affect (defined), 169
Affective area, 147
Affective disorder (*see also* Mood
  disorder), 169, 267–273
African Americans, 302, 306
Agency setting, 23
  office design, 246
  safety precautions, 245
Agoraphobia, 273
Ahia, C.E., 308
Ahola, T., 284, 287
AIDS, 280–284
  counseling, 282–284
Alcohol, 242
Alcoholism, 277–288
Alexander, C.M., 303
Ambivalence, 84, 167–168, 198
American Association of Suicidol-
  ogy, 276
American Counseling Association,
  1, 2, 311, 314
  Code of Ethics, Appendix 2, 36,
  39, 41, 51
American Medical Association,
  271–272
American Psychiatric Association,
  169, 265–266, 272–274
American Psychological Associa-
  tion, 1, 50
Amphetamines, 242
Amundson, N.E., 260
Angel, D.L., 260
Anger management, 235, 247

Anorexia Nervosa, 274–275
Antianxiety medication, 276
Antidepressant medication, 276
Antimanic medication, 276
Antipsychotic medication, 269–
  270, 278
Anxiety disorders, 273–274
Anxiety phase (violence), 246–247
Arnhold, R.M., 88, 259
Arredondo, P., 314, 319
Assertiveness, 251
Association for Spiritual, Ethical
  and Religious Values in
  Counseling, 311
Arthur, N., 307, 314
Asians, 73, 263, 302–303, 307–308
Assumptions, 49, 52, 100, 167, 207
  controlling, 100–101
Attending, 104–106
  attended silence, 108, 141
  defined, 9, 104
  energetic attention, 104
Authority, 14, 26, 87, 232
Azrin, N.H., 262

Bachhouse, C., 298–299
Backlund, B.A., 78–79, 285–286
Baha'i's, 302, 313, 314
Bahá'u'lláh, xi
Bandler, R., 7
Barker, R.L., 27, 160
Bartolomeo, N.C., 314
Beckman, C.S., 50
Beginning phase, 20–21, 26–28,
  29, 194, 215, 229
  confrontation and, 202
  relationship and, 71
  therapeutic value of, 27
Behavioral area, 147–148
Beiser, M., 296–298, 301, 303–304
Benjamin, A., 74, 129–130, 132
Berg, F.M., 274
Berryhill-Paapke, E., 298

Besalel, V.A., 262
Beutler, L.E., 6
Beyerstein, B.L., 268
Bezanson, M.L., 231, 237
Bias, 28
Bipolar disorder, 269, 272–273
Black, K., 161–162
Black humor, 45
Blind spots, 102, 207
Body language, 164, 249
Bolles, R.N., 257
Borum, R., 242, 244
Bower, B., 244
Bradburn, N.M., 128
Bradshaw, J., 239
Brief counseling, 284–289
  techniques, 285–289
Brief talk rule
Brainstorming, 207
  rules for effective, 219–221
Brammer, L.M., 58, 60, 70, 73
Bratina, T.G., 263
Bratina, T.A., 263
Brill, N.I., 13, 74
Brotherton, D., 310
Bulimia, 274–275
Burman, P., 258
Burnout
  motivating clients who are
  burnt-out, 197
  worker, 15

Canada, 292–293
Canadian Association of Social
  Workers, 1, 36
Canadian Counselling Association,
  47–48
Canadian Task Force, 297
Capuzzi, D., 69, 296–297
Carkhuff, R.R., 72, 162
Carniol, B., 194
Catharsis (*see also* Ventilation),
  27–28

Caucasians, 305
Challenging skills (*see also* Confrontation), 13, 20, 21
Change Continuum, 288–289
Charter, A., 296, 299, 306, 311
Child abuse
  need to report, 43
Children, 111, 149
Chooney, S.K., 298
Clark, A.J., 209
Cleghorn, J.M., 264, 268–269, 274, 276–278
Clients
  ambivalent, 198
  burnt-out, 197–199
  capacity for change, 70
  criminal charges against, 250
  energized, 198
  files on, 24
  involuntary, 26, 129, 197
  lack of empathy, 206
  learning from 309
  native, 297
  physical contact with, 40
  reluctance to set goals, 214–215
  resistance and, 229–235, 263
  right to be informed, 41
  sexual involvement with, 39–40, 50
  signals of change and growth, 29
  strategies for empowering, 88
  values, 215
  violent (*see* Violence)
  with strong religious values, 312
Coakley, C., 97, 99, 105, 164, 166
Cognitive area, 147–148
Compton, B., 14, 17, 38, 82, 176–267
Concreteness, 14, 138–145
  goals and, 213
  levels, 139 (table)
  promoting, 140 (table)
Confidentiality, 42–45, 140
  absolute, 42
  guidelines, 44 (table)
  guidelines for breaking, 43–44
  relative, 42
Confrontation, 200–205
  appropriate use of, 13

principles for effective, 202–204
risks, 201
self awareness and, 204–205
types of, 200–202
when to avoid, 205
Congruent, 74
Collaboration, 249
Congruence, 6, 74
Contingency plans, 221
Contract, 11, 75–79
  confrontation and, 202–203
  elements of, 76–77
  sample interview, 80–81
Controlled emotional involvement, 170
Conversations
  alternatives to questions, 138
  black humor, 45
  counseling and psychotherapy, 3
  effective paraphrasing, 116
  genuineness, 75
  I'm just a beginner, 54
  increasing empathic vocabulary, 171
  increasing your ability to be concrete, 144
  I've tried everything, 223
  learning to deal with silence, 112
  note taking, 154
  praying with clients, 315
  personal involvement with clients, 50
  problems listening and responding, 106
  rescuing and supporting, 19
  saying no, 238
  self-disclosure, 86
  should i read the file, 24
  when clients are hallucinating, 270
  when not to use empathy, 174
  why counseling works, 23
  working with children, 149
  working with "lazy" clients, 196
Cook, S.W., 40
Cooper, M., 50
Core conditions, 10, 72–75

Corey, M., 58, 85, 165, 203–204, 228
Corey, G., 58, 85, 165, 203–204, 228
Cormier, L.S., 39, 57, 86, 138, 162, 209, 229, 231
Cormier, W.H., 39, 57, 86, 138, 162, 209, 229, 231, 302
Corrections, 41
Corsini, R.J., 57
Cottone, R.R., 40, 46, 50
Counseling (*see* Counseling)
Counseling, 53
  activities and skills, 21 (table), 195
  brief (*see* Brief counseling)
  children, 111, 149
  clients with AIDS, 282–284
  contract, 75–79
  demystifying the process, 193
  employment (*see* Employment counseling)
  focus of, 2
  grief, 284
  guidelines for multicultural work, 310
  HIV positive clients, 281–282
  managing personal needs in, 59
  nature of, xiii–xiv
  "one size fits all," 19
  people with mental disorders
  phases of, xiv, 20–31, 21 (table)
  psychotherapy and, 3
  purpose of, 76
  range of activities, 2–4
  scope of, 2
  silence in, 106–112
  spirituality and, 283, 311–314
  suicide, 276–280
  way of life, xix
  working with a translator, 310
Countertransference, 85–87
Cowger, C., 12, xiii
Cox, C.I., 300
Cragan, J.F., 219
Criminal behavior, 206
Crisis intervention, 246–247
  suicide, 279
Cristiani, T.S., 129, 138, 164

Critical incident debriefing, 251–255

Cultural attitudes, 309

Cultural diversity, 292–316
beliefs about how people should act, 307–308
demographics, 292–293
personal priorities, values, beliefs, 307
style of communication, 305–306
time orientation, 308

Culture, xi–xii, 37–38, 73, 129, 144
cross-cultural communication, 134
cross-cultural competency, 314–320, 317–319 (table)
cross-cultural understanding, 295–296, 301–308 (key elements)
eating disorders and, 274
immigrants and multicultural clients, 308–309
norms, 167
resistance , 232–233, 237–239

Culture shock, 309

Cutoffs, 180

Dalai Lama, 284

D'Andrea, M.J., 308

D'Augelli, J.F., 58

D'Augelli, A.R., 58

Dangerous clients (*see* Violence)

Daniluk, J.C., 52, 53

Danish, S.J., 58

Davis, L.E., 299

Davis, S., 243

De Bono, E., 205–206

De Becker, G., 243, 247

Debriefing after a critical incident, 251–255

DeCoff, C.A., 231, 237

Defense mechanisms, 57–58

Defensiveness
phase and violence, 247–250

Deinstitutionalization, 243, 264

Delusions, 269

Denial, 57, 90, 197

Depression, 169, 269–272
symptoms, 270–271

de Shazer, S., 214, 285

Devons, C., 278

Diller, J.V., 237, 239, 295–296, 299–313

DiNitto, D.M., 197

Direct aid, 9

Directives, 11, 141, 152, 176

Discrimination, 283, 299, 309

Disordered thinking, 269–272

Displacement, 57

Distortion, 205–206

Diversity (*see also* Individual differences), 5, 37, 61, 300, 314
emotions and, 162
respect for, xvi

Dodd, C.H., 162, 295, 301, 302, 304, 305

DSM-IV-TR, 264–267
appropriate use of, 266–267
major groups of mental disorders, 265–266
multi-axial system, 266
social work and, 267

Dual diagnosis, 264

Dual relationship, 35, 39, 50

DuBois, B., 45, 87

Dubovsky, S.L., 244, 248–249, 268–269

Dumont, M, 4

Duty to warn principle, 48

Eating disorders, 274–275

Egan, G., 11, 20, 82–83, 98, 104–105, 170, 172, 179–181, 200, 202–204, 212–213, 219

Egocentricity, 206–207

Elbourne, R., 106

Elders, 311–312

Ellis, A, 57, 118, 206

Emotional intelligence, 161

Emotional literacy, 161

Emotions (*see also* Feelings), 160–169
classifying, 162–164
control and, 302–303

feeling words, 163 (table)
mixed feelings, 167, 168 (table)

Empathy, 4, 6, 10, 56, 72–74, 109, 169–187, 203, 313
as a response to silence, 109
communication process, 180 (table)
defined, 10, 169
generalizations about, 177–178
increasing vocabulary, 171
nature of, 169–171
paraphrasing and, 115–116
poor substitutes for, 183–185
preparatory, 173
response leads, 179
responses to avoid, 180–182
tough, 182–185
types of, 171–177, 177 (table)
basic, 171, 177
inferred, 171–173, 177
invitational, 171, 174–177
reminders, 181–182
why achieving empathic understanding is so difficult, 179–180
when to avoid, 174

Employee Assistance Programs (EAPs), 254

Employment counseling, 257–263, 259 (table)
career counseling, 259–260
challenges and goals, 258
electronic resources, 262–263
employment counseling and immigrant clients, 263
job clubs, 262
job loss counseling, 258–260
job search skills, 259–261
life skills counseling259, 261
traditional versus modern job search methods (table), 261

Empowering skills, 12

Empowerment, 87–88, 193–223
change and, 193–195
defined, 40

Empty responses, 180

Ending phase, 21, 30–31
relationship and, 72

Energetic attention, 104

Erdman, P., 149
Estroff, S., 242, 244
Ethical decision making, 37, 49
.(table)
Ethical dilemmas, 45–49
six-step sequence for resolving,
47
Ethics
core standards of, 37–45
defined, 8, 35
Ethnic minorities, 296–300, 313
experience with counseling,
296–297
recent immigrants and refugees,
298
sociopolitical realities, 298–300
Ethnocentrism, 316
Evaluation, 20
Evans, D.R., 296
Exploration
Exploring/probing skills, 9, 11–12
Eye contact, 105, 165, 248, 305

Factmonster, 293
Failure in counseling, 14–20
Family, 301–302, 307
Farley, O.W., 264
Farr, J.M., 260
Faulty technique, 19
FBI, 104
Feedback, xvii–xviii 56
Feelings (see also Emotions), 160–
169
feeling words, 163 (table)
mixed feelings, 167–168, 168
(table)
Files, 24, 246
Filipino community, 302
Fishman, H., xvii
Flexibility (see Versatility)
Flight of ideas, 272
Freud, S., 57, 83, 227
Fuertes, J.N., 314
Furman, B., 284, 287

Galaway, B., 14, 17, 38, 82, 176,
267
Gandhi, 239
Gardner, W., 244

Garrett, A., 106, 133, 136, 144
Garrett, J.T., 310–311
Garrett, M.T., 310–311
Garvin, C.D., 74, 169
Genuineness, 10, 74–75
George, R.L., 129, 138, 164
Gilliland, B.E., 10, 29, 200
Gladding, S.T., 75, 169, 228
Global Assessment of Functioning
Scale (GAF), 266
Goals
developing effective statements,
212–216
probes for setting, 213
sample, 220 (table)
short-term, 215
types, 212
Goal setting, 195, 211–216, 231
Golden, B.J.147
Goleman, D., 161, 182
Gordon, T., 202
Grinder, J., 7
Gross, D.R., 69, 296–297
Guess, 213

Hackney, H.L., 301, 302
Haley, J., 5, 229
Hall, E.T., 166
Hallucinations, 268
how to handle, 270
Hallucinogens, 242
Hamachek, D.E., 203, 225
Hammond, C., 179
Hancock, M.R., 170–172
Harney, E.E., 260
Harris, G.A., 232–233
Harris, G.T., 243
Harris, H.S., 55
Harvard Medical School, 276–278
Harvill, R., 212
Havenkamp, B.E., 52, 53
Heppner, P.P., 40
Hepworth, D., 48, 179, 299, 302
Herlihy, B., 42
Herlihy, S.B., 42
Hess, H., 31, 90
Hicks, C., 239
Hidden job market, 260

Highlen, P.S., 300
Hirschfeld, R.M., 277
Hispanic culture, 73, 239, 292,
299, 302, 312
HIV Positive, 280–284
counseling, 281–282
prevention, 280–281
Hocker, J.L., 249
Holmes, B.H., 257
Home visits, 245
Homophobia, 280
Horejsi, C.R., 72, 89, 229, 297
Horejsi, G.A., 72, 89, 229, 297
Hoyt, M.F., 284–285, 288
Huber, C.H., 78–79, 285–286
Humor, 12

I-statements, 83, 202
Illusion of work, 16, 228
Immediacy, 11, 79, 81–83, 233
relationship, 81–82
here and now, 82
sample interview to deal with
resistance, 236–237
Impulsive behavior, 235
Immigrants, 298
issues faced by, 308–309
Individual differences (see also
Diversity), 300–301
Information giving, 12, 17
Informed consent, 41
Internal dialogue (self–talk), 148,
208
self-defeating thought, 57, 200,
206–207, 212, 259
Internet, 262–263
Interview aerobics, 159
Interviewing, xiii–xiv, 4, 53–54,
126–156
preparation, 25
procedures with potentially
violent clients, 245–246
Interviews
sample (see sample Interviews)
structured, 127
transitions (see Transitions)
unstructured, 127
Intimidating behavior, 240
Involuntary clients, 129

motivation and, 197
resistance and, 233
Iranians, 302–304
Irrational thinking (*see* Internal dialogue)
Isajiw, W.W., 293
Ishiyama, F.I., 263
Islam, S., 239
Ivey, A.E., 162, 201–202
Ivey, M.B., 162

Job Clubs, 262
Jacobs, E., 212
James, R.K., 10, 29, 200
Jargon, 126–127, 193
Johnson, D.W., 165
Johnson, L.C., 195–232, 314
Journals use of, xxi

Kadushin, A., xiv, 7, 69, 71, 98, 105–106, 132, 136–137, 151, 166, 309
Kain, C.D., 281–283
Kaplan, S.G., 242, 250
Kayne, H., 239
Keith-Lucas, A., 70, 93
Kell, B.L., 58
Kelleher, M.D., 247
Kelly, E.W., 283, 313, 315
Kinesics, 165
Kirsh, S., 257
Klerman, G.L., 266
Kottler, J.A., 14, 295

Labig, C.E., 247, 249–250
Lachicotte, W., 242, 244
Lampe, P., 149
Language, 309
cultures and use of, 306
matching clients' styles, 6–7
Lanza, M., 239
Larsen, J., 48, 299, 302
Lazarus, A.A., 6
Lazarus, R., 160
Learned Helplessness, 87–88, 198, 234
strategies for overcoming, 259–260
Learning groups, xx–xxi

LeDoux, J.E., 160
Lee, B.L., 264, 268–269, 274, 276–288
Leeds, D., 129
Legislation
duty to report, 43
right to access, 24–25, 36
Leon, A., 239, 242
Lesh, K., 147
Lidz, C., 244
Life skills, 259, 261
Liguori, A.L., 280
Listening, 97–122
challenge of, 97–99
defined, 97
does not mean agreeing, 101–102
hollow, 98
overcoming obstacles, 103 (table), 99
problems listening and responding
LIVE (acronym), 118–119
Llewellyn-Jones, D., 274
Lock, R.D., 307
Locke, D.C., 308
Lopez, de Silva M., 270

MacDonald, G., 134, 305–306
Maloney, D.C., 55
Mandell, B.R., 74
Mania, 169
Mann, J.M., 280
Martin, G., 57, 177
Martin, D.G., 129, 179, 202
Martinez family, 237–239
Marzuk, P., 239, 242
Masch, M.K., 60
Maslow, A.H., 77
Masson, R., 212
McCartt Hess, P., 31, 90
McClam, T., 43
McDavis, R., 314, 319
McDonald, N., 60, 73
McNeece, C.A., 197
McWhirter, E.H., 194
Medication (*see* Psychiatric medication)
Meharabian, A., 166

Mehr, J.J., 51, 72, 74
Mental disorders, 263–276
as a predictor of violence, 243
treating, 275–276
Mental health, 169
Metaphors, 164
Middleman, R.R., 154, 170
Miley, K., 45, 87
Miller, S.D., 127
Minahan, A., 215
Minuchin, S., xvii
Miracle question, 214, 288
MOANS (acronym), 147
Modelling, 248
Mood disorder (*see also* Affective disorder), 169, 269–273
Morrisseau, C., 302
Morrissette, P.J., 297–298, 309
Morrissey, M., 251
Motivation, 195–200
cultural diversity and, 307
goal setting and, 212
resistance and, 230–231
strategies, 199–200 (table)
Mueller, W.L., 58
Multicultural work guidelines, 310 (table)
Mulvey, E., 244
Myers, L.J., 300

Narcotics, 242
National Association of Social Workers, 1–2, 36
Code of Ethics, Appendix 1, 5, 44, 37–43, 51–53, 304
National Crisis Prevention Institute, 246
National Institute of Mental Health (NIMH), 264, 267–268, 272, 274, 275
Native People, 294, 295–297, 302–303, 305–306, 308, 310, 311, 316
traditional healing practices, 310–311
Networking, 260
Newhill, C.E., 239, 240, 242
Nicholi, A.M., 169, 185, 268–269, 272–274

Noesner, G.W., 104
Nonverbal communication, 164–166, 305
  as an indicator of feelings, 164
  body language, 165
  proxemics, 166
  silence, 112–113, 113 (table)
  spatial distance, 166
  voice, 166
Note-taking, 154
Nunes, J., 271–272

Objectivity, 16, 49–51
  maintaining, 52 (table)
Obsessive-compulsive disorder, 273
O'Conner, R., 271
Office design, 23–24
  to minimize risk of violence, 246
Otani, A., 227–229
Othmer, E., 277
Othmer, S.C., 277
Overidentification, 52
Overinvolvement, 52

Pacing, 178
Paniagua, 302, 306, 308
Panic disorder, 273
Paraphrasing, 4, 9–10, 114–116
  empathy and, 115–116
  leads, 115
Parrott, L., 161, 170
Parsons, R.D., 78, 205, 208
Pastor, L.H., 244
Patterson, C.H., 294
Pattison, I., 239
Pear, J., 57, 177
Pedersen, P., 295, 307, 316, 319, 322
Pedersen, P.B., 292, 308
Peller, J.E., 285
Perfectionism, 60
Perls, F., 54
Personal involvement, importance of, 316, 319
Phases of counseling (see Counseling)
Phobia, 273

Pincus, A., 215
Police intervention, 250
Polnerow, D., 50
Poonwassie, A., 296, 299, 306, 311
Portera, L., 239, 242
Positive regard, 10
Positive reinforcement, 177
Post-traumatic stress disorder (PTSD), 273–274
Poverty, 309
Power (see also Authority), 14, 19, 194, 232, 304, 310
Praying with clients, 315
Preliminary phase, 20–21, 23–26
  relationship and, 71
Preparatory empathy (see also Tuning in), 26
Proctor, E.K., 299
Professional development, 15
Proxemics (see Nonverbal communication)
Prozac, 275
Pseudocounseling, 16
Psychiatric diagnosis, 264
Psychiatric medication, 275–276
Psychotherapy, 3, 53

Questions, 4, 10, 126–138
  alternatives, 138
  closed, 135–136
  cross-cultural communication, 134
  errors, 127–132
  excessive, 129–130
  guidelines, 134 (table)
  indirect, 137–138
  irrelevant, 131–132
  key questions for every interview, 145–149
  leading, 128–129
  multiple, 130–131
  open-ended, 111, 136–137, 176
  purpose, 126–127
  types, 135 (table), 135–138
  when clients do not answer, 132–134
  "why," 132

Racial labels, 306

Racism, 194, 316
Rationalization, 57
Razak, W.N., 259
Reamer, F.G., 40–43, 66
Records, client access to, 24
Referring, 9, 77
Reframing, 209–211, 288
  guidelines, 209
  reframed ideas, 208 (table)
Refugees, 298
Regression, 58
Reid, W.H., 264–268
Relationship, 20, 69–91
  contracting and, 76
  counseling, defined, 69–70
  defining, 11
  dependent, 87
  dual, 35, 39, 50
  ending, 30, 89–91
  phases of counseling and, 71–72
  "prewiring," 76
  resistance, 230
Relationship building skills, 8–9, 20
Remley, Jr., T.P. 42
Rescue fantasy, 41
Rescuing, 18–19
Resistance, 21, 26, 144, 227–239, 263
  forms of , 228–229
  leads, 233–235
  strategies for dealing with, 234–235 (table)
Respect for diversity, xvi
Restraint, 250
Rice, M.E., 243
Rigidity, 206–207
Robbins, R., 298
Roberts, A.R., 278–279
Robins, P., 239
Rogerian approach, 303
Rogers, C.R., 10, 11, 69, 70, 72, 74, 86, 170–171
Role-playing, 12, 29, 207, 255, 287
Rooney, R.H., 48, 299, 302
Rosenthal, L., 227
Ross, R., 296, 305
Roth, L.H., 241, 242, 250
Roy, A., 277

Ruskin, R., 296–298, 301, 303–304
Russell, J.M., 277

Saleeby, D., 89
Sample Interviews
  contracting, 80–81
  dealing with resistance, 236–237
  endings, 92
  effective use of empathy, 186–187
  follow-up to a violent incident, 253–254
  goal setting, 217–219
  immediacy, 84
  interviewing skills, 155–156
  listening, silence and summarizing skills, 121–122
  poor substitutes for empathy, 183–184
  reframing techniques, 210–211
San Francisco Suicide Prevention Institute, 277
Schizophrenia, 267–269
Schram, B., 74
Seabury, B.A., 74, 169
Secondary gain, 14, 196, 231
Selective perception, 119–120
Self-actualization, 71
Self-awareness, 28, 51, 54–62
  cultural, 61
  questions to ponder, 71
  with/without, 55 (table)
Self-defeating thought, 29
Self-determination, xiii, 8, 40–41, 48, 60, 194, 233
  empowerment and, 88
Self-disclosure, 11
Self-defeating thought (see Internal dialogue)
Self-esteem, 194, 203, 215, 258
Self-talk (see Internal dialogue)
Seligman, M.E., 198
Sentence completion statements, 176
Setting limits, 250
Sharmirzadi, A., 302, 304
Shaughnessy, P.
Shaw, E., 244

Shea, S.C., 174, 246, 248, 268
Sheafor, B.W., 229
Shebib, B., 10, 17, 18, 20, 22, 71, 81, 90, 148, 150, 151, 159, 169, 179, 196, 212, 219, 248
Sheek, G.W., 257
Shilling, L.E., 69
Shostrom, E.L., 70
Shulman, L., 16, 20, 25, 69, 75, 79, 90–91, 143, 146, 170, 173–174, 178, 194, 228
Shulz, W.E., 47–49
Silence, 4, 9, 107–114, 180, 305
  attended, 108
  encouraging, 114
  nonverbal cues, 113 (table)
  personal meaning, 107
Silva, F., 270
Simek-Downing, L., 162
Simmie, S., 271–272
Simple encouragers, 11, 141
Single-session therapy (see also Brief counseling), 27–28, 284
Skidmore, R.A., 264
Skills, 8
  clusters, 9 (table)
  counseling activities and, 21 (table)
Sklare, G.B., 284, 288
Smith, D.B., 297–298, 309
Smith, V., 179
Social isolation, 269
Social work
  competence, 51–53
  core values, 36
  counseling, and, 4–5
  DSM-IV-TR and, 267
  mission, 36
Social workers
  beginning and advanced, 3 (table)
  blind spots, 102
  competence limits, 2
  knowledge base, 42
  managing personal needs, 59 (table)
  managing personal reactions, 101
  need for control, 60

need for professional development, 41–41
need for status, 59
need to be liked, 58
perfectionism, 60
personal and cultural values, 61
personal problems, 16
questions to ponder, 70–71
self-awareness, xi–xiii, xvii, 54–62, 55 (table), 204, 235, 237, 307, 310, 316
Solution talk, 287
Spatial distance (see Nonverbal communication)
Speight, S.L., 4, 300
Spiritual values, 307, 310
  clients with AIDS, 283
  counseling and, 311–314
Staff training to prevent violence, 245
Statistics Canada, 293
Steinweg, D.A., 257–258, 262
Stereotypes, 293–295, 316, 320
Stewart, J., 307, 314
Stewart, N.R., 231, 237
Strengths approach, 12, 88–89, 267
strategies, 89
Students
  as clients, xvi
  as counselors, xvi–xvii
  as observers, xvii–xviii
  developing an effective learning group, xvii–xix
  keeping a journal, xix
Substance abuse, 242
Sudman, S., 128
Sue, D., 299–301, 303, 305–306, 308, 312, 316
Sue, D.W., 299, 30, 303, 305–306, 308, 312, 314, 316, 319
Suicide, 276–280
  counseling intervention, 278–280
  myths, 278
  warning signs, 276–278
Summarizing, 4, 10, 116–120
  as a way to control transitions, 152
  content, 117

theme, 117–118
Sunley, R.S., 257
Support groups (*see also* Self-help groups)
Supporting, 12
Suppression, 58
Sussman, L., 303
Sweat lodge, 310
Systematic desensitization, 273
Swanson, J., 242, 244
Swartz, M., 50, 242, 244
Sympathy, 181

Taboos, 143
Tarantola, D., 280
Tarasoff case, 43
Tardiff, K., 239, 242
Tarvydas, V.M., 40, 46, 50
Tension reduction phase (violence), 250–251
Termination, 30–31
Thackeray, M.G., 264
Thinking
  disordered, 271
  errors, 205–207
  helping clients change thinking patterns, 195, 205–211, 207 (table)
  helping clients think differently
Thoreson, R.W., 40
Thought broadcasting, 269
Thought insertion, 269
Thought-stopping, 207
Time orientation, 308
Touch, 304
Tough empathy, 182–185
Tourette's syndrome, 25
Traditional healing practices, 310–311
Transferable skills, 260–261
Transference, 83, 85

Transitions, 150–159
  connect (linking), 153–154
  control, 151
  natural, 150
  phase, 152–153
  strategic, 151
Translator, 310
Truax, C., 72
Trust, 99, 110, 133
Tuning in, (*see also* Preparatory empathy), 26, 173
Turner, F.J., 297, 298
Turner, J.C., 297, 298
Turner, S.G., 50

Unemployment, 309
U.S. Census Bureau, 293

Vaillant, G.E., 57
Values, 8
  beliefs and attitudes that help and hinder
  client, 215
  counselors'effectiveness, 62 (table)
  social work, 36–37
Ventilation (*see also* Catharsis), 194
Versatility, 303
  need for, 5–6
  variables, 7
Victim blaming, 299
Vietnamese culture, 304
Violence, 239–255
  agency safety precautions, 245–246
  assessing potential for, 244–245
  follow-up to a violent incident, 253–254 (interview)
  mental illness and, 243–244
  phases of, 252 (table), 246–255

predicting, 241–243
preventing, 245–246
defined, 240

Wagner, R., 242, 244
Walrund-Skinner, A., 170
Walter, J.L., 285
Walters, G.D., 206
Warmth, 72–73
Watkins, D., 232–233
Weaver, C.H., 102
Weaver, A.J., 242
Webster, M., 104
Weiner, C., 239, 242
Weisinger, H., 161, 235
Weissberg, M.P., 244, 249, 268–269
Wells, C.S., 60
Werbel, J.D., 257
Westwood, M.J., 263
Wheeler, E.G., 241, 250
Who Am I?, 56–60
"Why" questions, 132
Wicks, R.J., 78, 205, 208
Wilmot, W.W., 249
Wilson, S.B., 222
Wolvin, A., 97, 99, 105, 164, 166
Wood, G.G., 154, 170
Woodside, M., 43
Word modifiers, 164
Worldview, 295–296, 317
  defined, 295
Wright, D.W., 219

Yanka, S.J., 232
Young, M.E., 13, 20, 30, 57, 69, 82–83, 85, 162, 209, 212. 219, 228

Zastrow, C., 43
Zimmer, C., 242, 244